Advanced Praise for Networking Windows NT 3.51, Second Edition

In step with Microsoft Windows NT's march toward enterprise computing, the authors give network system administrators a handbook they will want both on their desks and on their bedside table as they deploy and manage business critical NT 3.5 servers and workstations. More than a technical reference, the book explains important business and operational concepts which help administrators move themselves and their systems toward enterprise service levels. For the first-time NT administrator moving from Windows for Workgroups or other network environments, detailed installation and operation instructions make success a certainty. For the experienced NT administrator, effective use of sophisticated features is described. Where NT falls short, the authors clearly say so and suggest what to do about the shortfall.

The authors' enthusiasm for their topic is infectious even when navigating through tedious details. For those seeking even greater depth, the reference and reading lists are excellent. Recognizing that the well-run network system consists of more than the operating environment, the book provides helpful design checklists, suggested operating procedures, diagnosis and repair strategies, and lists of complementary third-party products. This is a valuable and approachable resource.

David P. Rodgers
Vice President, corporate architecture
Sequent Computer Systems, Inc.

Networking Windows NT 3.51

Second Edition

John D. Ruley

David Methvin
Martin Heller
Arthur Germain III
Eric Hall

JOHN WILEY & SONS, INC.

New York • Chichester • Brisbane • Toronto • Singapore

Publisher: Katherine Schowalter
Editor: Diane D. Cerra
Managing Editor: Robert Aronds
Text Design and Composition: SunCliff Graphic Productions

Designations used by companies to distinguish their products are often claimed as trademarks. In all instances where John Wiley & Sons, Inc. is aware of a claim, the product names appear in initial capital or all capital letters. Readers, however, should contact the appropriate companies for more complete information regarding trademarks and registration.

This text is printed on acid-free paper.

This publication is designed to provide accurate and authoritative information in regard to the subject matter covered. It is sold with the understanding that the publisher is not engaged in rendering legal, accounting, or other professional service. If legal advice or other expert assistance is required, the services of a competent professional person should be sought.

Library of Congress Cataloging-in-Publication Data

Networking Windows NT 3.51 / John D. Ruley ... [et al.]. — 2nd ed.
        p.   cm.
Rev. ed. of: Networking Windows NT. c1994.
Includes index
ISBN 0-471-12705-1 (pbk. : acid-free paper)
        1. Operating systems (Computers).   2. Microsoft Windows NT.   3. Computer networks.   I. Ruley, John D., 1958–   .   II. Title: Networking Windows NT.
QA76.76.O63N473   1995
005.7'1369—dc20
                                                                                                95-16913
                                                                                                    CIP

Printed in the United States of America
10 9 8 7 6 5 4 3 2

Dedication

This book is dedicated to the authors' fathers:

David D. Dix

Arthur H. Germain, Jr.

William T. Hall

Aaron Heller

Arthur G. Methvin

Charles B. Powell

Arnold Sloman

   and

MSgt Joseph A. Ruley, USAF (deceased).

About the Authors

Arthur H. Germain III, formerly Technical Director at *WINDOWS Magazine* is now at *Communications Week*. His experience with small-, medium-, and large-scale network systems design and management made him invaluable in creating Chapters 2 and 3—and his advice was useful for the book as a whole.

Eric Hall, formerly Labs Director for *Network Computing* has gone into the commercial world—he now works for TGV Corporation. There's very little about networks that Eric doesn't know—in detail. If you want to know the details of how a particular driver architecture works, Eric can tell you at length, as he does in Appendix 2 and in parts of Chapters 6 and 7.

Dr. Martin Heller is the author of several best-selling books on Windows programming and writes the Programming Windows column for *WINDOWS Magazine*. Martin took sole responsibility for Appendix 1, which tells programmers all they need to know to write network-aware Windows NT programs.

David Methvin is the Senior Technical Editor at *WINDOWS Magazine*. Dave's been an editor at *PC Tech Journal* and at *PC Week*, and has installed several large networks as a consultant. He wrote Chapter 10, Appendix 3, and co-wrote Chapter 8.

John D. Ruley is Editor-at-Large and Windows NT columnist at *WINDOWS Magazine*. John is principle author of *Networking Windows NT*—which among other things, means that he's ultimately responsible for the technical accuracy of this book, and assumes the blame for any and all errors, omissions, and goof-ups.

Dave Dix, Jeff Sloman and Jim Powell, who helped write our first edition, weren't able to be involved in this one. We missed them.

Contents

ix

Chapter 2   Preparing to Connect   47

Chapter 7   Enterprise Connections   337

Chapter 9   Novell Connections   437

Appendix 1   Programming NT Networks   511

Foreword to the First Edition

Today's network professionals deal with change every working day. Corporate mainframe applications of the seventies are being *downsized* to local area network (LAN)-based client/server application suites, while departmental single-user PC applications of the eighties are *upsized* into multiuser online solutions. As a result, the simple local area networks of yesterday are rapidly becoming business-critical, enterprise-wide, *electronic highways*. Can this rapid evolution in information systems technology succeed? Can the distributed client/server networks of today provide the same level of reliability that yesterday's centralized mainframe systems delivered? Ultimately, will this next generation of computing systems improve our own personal productivity—and thus make a *real* contribution to your company's bottom line?

Microsoft clearly feels that the answer to all three of these questions is *yes*—and with the release of their most complex operating system to date, Windows NT, they've bet their corporate future on delivering this promise. For you and me, as networking professionals, this means we will soon be asked (or in my case, have already been asked) to take the client/server *promises* of Windows NT and create a business *reality*. That's no small challenge, considering the complexity of today's enterprise networks and the mission-critical, moment-by-moment role they play in today's corporate world.

Are you nervous? Take heart: In *Networking Windows NT* you will find something no business-critical network of today can afford to be without, a business-critical *attitude*. It's an attitude that comes from years of experience in dealing with the day-to-day issues involved in the support of business-critical information systems. With the publication of this book, John Ruley and his associates at *WINDOWS Magazine* and *Network Computing* have done something I find unique: They've truly understood what George Santayana meant in 1905, when he wrote:

> "Progress, far from consisting in change, depends on retentiveness...
> Those who cannot remember the past are condemned to repeat it."[1]

---

1. *Life of Reason*, Volume 1, Chapter 10.

This is not just another book describing the marvels contained within the first operating system that doesn't treat the network as an add-on. *Networking Windows NT* shows you how to not only make it work but *keep it working*, day-in, day-out, and month-after-month. The book covers the full spectrum of what you need to know—and do—as we move from the host-centric world of raw data to the information-centric world of distributed objects.

Networking Windows NT takes you step by step from simple NT-based LANs all the way to optimized enterprise-wide electronic networks that communicate with everyone and everything. First it covers the fundamentals of an operating system designed around the client/server model (Chapter 1, "An Operating System Designed to Connect"), then what you will need to do today (Chapter 2, "Preparing to Connect"), what you will need to do tomorrow (Chapter 3, "Administrative Connections"),and what you will need to do to link your back-end, the server, to your front-end, your clients (Chapter 4, "Using NT Networking Features").

Now the fun really begins; keeping your Windows NT network running so smoothly and flawlessly that you'll reach that loftiest goal of any networking professional, managing the network *invisibly*. Chapter 5 ("Keeping Connected") along with its associated appendix (Appendix 6: "Maintenance Theory") were my two favorite sections. Within this chapter and appendix you will learn now to *proactively* put the sophisticated administrative tools included with Windows NT to work—not only keeping your network at its peak of performance but also ensuring that you get *mission-critical* reliability. I've used this information myself at Chevron Canada's data center—and I can assure you the advice given is *well* worthwhile.

The hard lessons learned during the days of the mainframes and minicomputers are retold in the context of Windows NT. The advice is fundamental and pragmatic, something one would expect when learning about troubleshooting computer systems. Appendix 6 also explains *precisely* why following a program of preventative maintenance is so important. Yet, like the rest of the book, it has been written with a humorous style that delivers a refreshing feeling of confidence and long-term optimism. It's obvious that the authors really enjoy what they're writing about, and you will find this grain of enthusiasm throughout the book. Where else would you find the Configuration Registry included with Windows NT compared to a nuclear reactor?

As your Windows NT Advanced Server network grows it will expand beyond the comfortable confines of your data center. In Chapter 7 (*Enterprise Connections*) you'll find information on file replication, Wide Area Networking and remote network access. No doubt you will also start bumping into different operating environments such as the world of UNIX (Chapter 6, "UNIX Connections"), other network operating systems such as NetWare (Chapter 9, "Novell Connections"), and a veritable host of hosts, the legacy systems (Chapter 10, "Other Connections").

Finally, what about the future (Chapter 11, "Connecting to the Future")? Some feel we are about to enter the true second generation of information systems—an electronic environment that creates a fully distributed world of objects and (as a result) blurs the lines between information and the systems that process it. An environment that delivers something more than just raw data or static information, tomorrow's distributed systems will deliver real-time *knowledge* to the new tenants at the top of the information systems model: you and me. The final chapter of Networking Windows NT examines the precursors of this next generation of operating systems, both already in alpha form, *Chicago* (Windows 4.0) and *Cairo* (Windows NT 4.0). As we approach the twenty-first century, what you and I do today as networking professionals will be a cornerstone of this technological revolution. *We* are the *invisible facilitators of change* in today's businesses—and I honestly believe that what we do today and tomorrow can make a valuable and essential contribution to the quality of life on this planet.

It's something worth doing well.

Doug Farmer
Lead—Network Operations
Chevron Canada Ltd.
Vancouver, BC
November 1993

Preface

Advanced PCs and workstations are rarely used alone. They're nearly always *connected* to a server, a mainframe host, or other workstations. So *connecting* Windows NT systems to each other and the outside world is the theme of this book.

Networking Windows NT is organized as eleven independent chapters and six Appendices. We have attempted to make each chapter stand alone. You can feel free to browse through the book and pick an interesting topic—with confidence that it will be completely exposed in the chapter you are reading. You may find, if you start in the middle of the book, that you'll wish you'd read some of the earlier chapters first. But we will refer you in the right direction and you can always make use of the index and glossary, which we have attempted to make as comprehensive as possible.

While *Networking Windows NT* is designed for browsing, it's also possible to lay out an ordered study program that may be useful to particular individuals. Here are some suggestions:

Those unfamiliar with either Windows NT or networking, should start at the beginning and read Chapters 1 through 4. Pick one of Chapters 6, 8, 9, and 10 as appropriate—if (like most people) you're going to work in an environment that has more than just Windows NT machines. For example, if you are in a Netware environment, read Chapter 9. If you are in a TCP/IP environment, read Chapters 6 and 7, and look through Appendices 3 and 4. Once you've done that, you can look over the rest of the book for any special topic that interests you.

If you are familiar with Windows NT, but not with networks, then skim Chapter 1, skip to Chapter 3, and read Appendix 4. Again, pick from Chapters 6, 8, 9, and 10 as appropriate. If you're going to work in an enterprise environment definitely read Chapter 6—you'll want to read Chapter 7 as well. Finally, read Chapter 11, and any of the Appendix material that appears to be useful.

If you're a support professional, you'll want to read all of the above—and especially Chapters 2 and 5.

If you are familiar with networks in a Netware or TCP/IP environment, but not familiar with Windows NT, then read Chapters 1 through 4, 7, Appendix 3, pick from Chapters 6, 8, 9, and 10 as appropriate and skim Chapter 11 (or read it if you like). Again, if you're a support professional, read Chapters 2 and 5 as well.

Programmers should read Chapters 1 and 11, then Appendix 1, and refer back to appropriate chapters when you run into a concept that doesn't seem to make sense. Just go to the index, look up the first definition, turn to that page and read all about it.

Management Information Systems people and decision makers—those trying to decide where Windows NT fits into a heterogeneous network environment—should read Chapters 1–3, 6, and 7, then pick from 8–10 to match the particular system you have (you may need to read them all if you run a complex network). Then read Chapter 11 and Appendix 5. That's a pretty comprehensive set, so if you're in a hurry, a short form that may be useful is to read Chapters 1, 3, 7, and 11—referring to other information if you find it is necessary.

Getting the Most from *Networking Windows NT*

Direct your attention particularly to the "After reading this chapter you should understand: …" section at the head of each chapter. We've included this specifically to help you decide, first of all, whether a particular chapter is interesting enough to invest your time reading,—and secondly, as a help to you in getting the most out of the chapter. We encourage you to read the statement, read the chapter, go back and read the statement again, and as you go through the bullet-points, if you see something that you don't remember or don't understand, then you probably want to look through that part of the chapter again.

We've also included a "For more information:" section at the end of each chapter, with reference materials—magazine articles, books, whatever. If you find that a particular topic has not been covered sufficiently to meet your tastes, take a look through the list at the end of the chapter, and see if one of the other references doesn't cover the material you're looking for. We've included a comprehensive index and we encourage everyone to use it.

Finally, we encourage you to try things out yourself! By that we mean to apply what you've learned in a real environment. We realize that many people are likely to read this book for information without having access to a Windows NT system—that's fine. It's our fondest hope that the book will be helpful to people in exactly that situation who need to make decisions about what equipment to purchase, what version of the system to purchase, or indeed whether Windows NT fits their situation at all.

But we've also designed this book to be a useful reference to people who are doing real-world work on Windows NT networks. If you fit that description, then we cannot emphasize enough that all the fine writing we can do, all the graphs and charts we can design, all the further reference reading we recommend to you, can't do as good a job as the learning reinforcement that comes by actually getting your hands dirty and trying things out for yourself. Many people are uncomfortable experimenting with networked computers (especially servers). That's unfortunate because networked computers are not really fundamentally much more difficult to deal with than individual PCs. If you're expecting to maintain a Windows NT system and to fix it when something goes wrong, you'd better get some experience manipulating it when it is working correctly!

We can't emphasize this enough—get in there and try! That's the best possible way to learn.

The Chapters

Networking Windows NT is organized as a set of more or less independent chapters, each of which attempts to cover a particular topic in some depth.

Chapter 1, *An Operating System Designed to Connect,* is an overall introduction to Windows NT and to basic networking concepts. It includes a detailed discussion of the differences between Windows NT and Windows NT Advanced Server, as well as concepts like portability, scalability, virtual memory, and network redirection.

Chapter 2, *Preparing for Connection,* covers installation and set-up of Windows NT systems, including Windows NT Advanced Servers. It includes a discussion of how to conduct a *network needs analysis* for your organization, how to select the right hardware for your Windows NT system, and all four Windows NT installation mechanisms: diskette, CD-ROM, over-the-network, and computer profile install. Six pages of troubleshooting information guide you through solving problems as they arise.

Chapter 3, *Administrative Connections,* covers Windows NT administration issues for LANs. It includes the duties of the *network administrator*, the tools used for NT net administration (user manager, disk administrator, performance monitor, backup, event viewer, the NET command-line interface and batch files); covers user profiles and log-in scripts; and discusses in detail the differences between Windows NT *workgroups* and Windows NT Advanced Server *domains*.

Chapter 4, *User Connections,* covers the use of Windows NT's built-in networking features, including shared file access, shared printer access, shared clipboards, and use of the Windows NT network utilities. It also provides a complete introduction to the command-line NET interface that can be used to write batch files in Windows NT.

Chapter 5, *Keeping Connected,* is one of *Networking Windows NT's* strongest chapters. It provides detailed coverage on maintaining and troubleshooting

Windows NT and Advanced Server systems—including use of Performance Monitor, Event Viewer, and the Configuration Registry Editor. Fourteen pages of troubleshooting information in this chapter have page-edge tinting for quick reference. There's also coverage of the undocumented support tools and message database supplied on CD-ROM versions of Windows NT.

Chapter 6, *UNIX-style Connections*, covers TCP/IP, UNIX networking, the Internet, and the use of TCP/IP as a routable protocol for Windows NT on inter-networks and WANs. It's an essential precursor to Chapter 7. Windows NT's built-in TCP/IP utilities and TCP/IP routing capability are also discussed in detail.

Chapter 7, *Enterprise Connections*, covers enterprise-wide network issues, including Windows NT Advanced Server domain administration, wide-area networking (including both Microsoft's *Remote Access Services* and third-party alternatives), electronic mail (including detailed instructions for upgrading the *workgroup-level* version of MS-Mail bundled with Windows NT for multi-postoffice connectivity), WANs and Macintosh support.

Chapter 8, *Microsoft Connections,* covers interoperability with LAN Manager, Window for Workgroups, and other networks based on the Server Message Block (SMB) protocol used by Microsoft. Detailed instructions are included for upgrading LAN Manager networks to Window NT Advanced Server, as are instructions on interoperating in mixed LAN Manager/NT/Windows for Workgroups environments.

Chapter 9, *Novell Connections,* covers interoperation with Novell Netware, including Novell's Netware Client for Windows NT, Microsoft's NWLink protocol and NetWare-compatible Client Workstation Service (NWCS), Beame & Whiteside's Multiconnect IPX—and the "back door" NFS/FTP method of NetWare access pioneered at *WINDOWS Magazine*. This chapter shows you how to connect Windows NT systems as both *clients* and *servers* in NetWare LANs.

Chapter 10, *Other Connections*, covers using Windows NT with other networks—including IBM LAN Server and Systems Network Architecture (SNA) mainframe networks, DEC Pathworks, and Banyan VINES.

Chapter 11, *Client-Server Connections,* discusses client/server issues, including the use of Windows NT as a *network application server*—using Microsoft's SQL Server database for Windows NT as an example—as well as the distributed future of network computing and how Windows NT (and its follow-on version, code named *Cairo*) fits into it.

Appendices

Appendix 1 is a short, succinct and yet (we devoutly hope), complete introduction to the network application programming interfaces (APIs) of Windows NT. Of course, programmers cannot expect to get all the information they need from one chapter and this appendix should be used in conjunction with a good book on Windows NT programming, such as, *Advanced 32-bit Windows Programming*, by Martin Heller. However, we hope that this appendix used in conjunction with the rest of this book will serve as a good introduction and give a programmer some idea of where to begin.

Appendix 2 covers drivers, low-level protocols, and other definitional issues that cause a great deal of confusion, even among those experienced with networking.

Appendix 3 covers compatibility issues. Windows NT is capable of running the Win32 programs designed for it. But it also retains compatibility for Windows 3.0 and 3.1 programs, OS/2 1.x programs, and many DOS programs as well as POSIX programs. This appendix discusses the issues involving compatibility for each of these systems, gives some guidance on what will and will not work, and specifically in the case of DOS programs gives some guidance on how you can make adjustments to the systems so programs that otherwise would not work, will work.

Appendix 4 covers the Windows NT Resource Kit.

Appendix 5 on exotic hardware covers the new classes of systems on which Windows NT

runs. Uniquely among modern desktop operating systems Windows NT was designed to be platform independent and it is capable of exploiting very radically different processor designs. We discuss the DEC Alpha RISC CPU, the MIPS R4000/R4400 CPU, and machines constructed using symmetric multiprocessor (SMP) architectures.

Appendix 6 covers the theory behind preventative maintenance, which is the foundation for the maintenance and troubleshooting information we provide in Chapter 5.

Late-breaking developments

As with the first edition, writing a book on such a broad—and rapidly changing—topic turned out to be a real challenge. Every chapter required major updating from our first edition (which covered NT 3.1), and once again, we've found it difficult to keep our coverage ahead of the NT development team.

Those coming to this book from the first edition will find changes throughout the text—for instance, in Chapter 1, we deal with the changes to the NT product names (from Windows NT 3.1 and NT Advanced Server 3.1 to Windows NT Workstation and Server versions 3.51) and features. Chapters 2, 3, 4, and 5 update our coverage of NT installation, management and use to cover the many new features that have appeared in the last two years. Chapters 6 and 7 were substantially updated to cover major improvements in NT's UNIX-compatible TCP/IP protocol suite and the implications that has for NT as an enterprise system. Chapter 8 was updated to cover Windows 95 as a client operating system. Chapter 9—which was repeatedly changed before the first edition was published—is updated again here, covering Microsoft's CSNW, GSNW and FPNW subsystems. Chapters 10 and 11 include a substantial amount of new information in tables of NT-compatible networking products. Likewise the appendices have all been updated—and we made one drastic change: Appendices 2 and 4 from the first edition are combined here, allowing us to devote Appendix 4 to the NT Resource Kit.

With all that work, we're still struggling to keep pace with the drastic rate at which this topic changes. As we go to press, Microsoft has a new NetWare-compatible subsystem in beta-test that lets NetWare servers participate in NT domain administration. Developers have also been given access to a preview version of NT 4.0, which combines the underlying features of Windows NT with a Windows 95-style user interface; and finally, this preface is being written just one month before the public release of Windows 95, which is sure to change the way computer networks—whether or not they're NT-based—are deployed and used.

Keeping up with these developments is a full-time job; but *don't panic*! We've come up with a way to help you stay informed.

Electronic Update to *Networking Windows NT*

Since we *know* that the NT landscape will change during the life of this edition, we've decided to make information available on those changes available in electronic form. You can look for *Electronic Updates to Networking Windows NT* in the *Windows Magazine* (WinMag) file libraries on America On-Line and Compuserve. Look for the key-word "NETNT". We will update these files periodically as developments warrant—and we expect the first update to be posted by the time you read this.

Acknowledgments

Any project of this magnitude involves the assistance of many people—and this is no exception. While we can't hope to create an all-inclusive list, these are some of the main people who contributed. We hope that those who don't find their names here won't be offended too much—there were so many that it's hard to remember them all. But some we managed not to forget to include:

Mike Abrash, Sheila Ambrose, Kate Bolton, M.D., Jean Goddin, Doug Hamilton, Dave Hart, Lee Hart, Johnny Haskins, Erin Holland, Tom Johnston, Liz Misch, Mike Nash, Carole Parrot-Joppe, Matt Ragen, Ruth Rizzuto, Blanche M. Ruley, Linda Stephenson, and David Thacher. Special thanks to: Fred Langa, Editorial Director, and Jake Kirchner, Executive Editor of *WINDOWS Magazine*—who made the *WINDOWS* lab available for us to use while working on this book, and to Scott Wolf, *WINDOWS Magazine*'s publisher—who gave permission to reproduce original artwork from *WINDOWS* without charge. Many thanks also to Diane Cerra, our editor at John Wiley—and Tammy Boyd, her assistant, and to Robert Aronds, also of John Wiley, who managed the book's production. We all want to thank our families for putting up with the time we spent bringing this project together—lots of late nights in the lab instead of home. Finally, of course, we want to acknowledge Dave Cutler and the entire Windows NT development team, who gave us so much to write about!

An Operating System Designed to Connect

Windows NT Networking: A Technical Overview

After reading this chapter, you should understand the basic features of Windows NT—especially those related to networking. You should also understand the basic concepts to be used in the rest of the book, including: microkernel architecture, portability, object model, layered device drivers, installable file systems, networks, and network redirectors. Finally, you should understand the differences between the Windows NT Workstation, which is suitable for use as a network client, and the aptly named Windows NT Server.

Windows NT is uniquely well suited to a wide variety of networking applications. To understand why, we must examine a number of features of the basic operating system design. The first and most pervasive of these is Windows NT's *client/server* architecture.

Scalability and the Client/Server Architecture

"Windows NT is not a microkernel operating system... it's more accurate to call NT a client/server operating system."—David Cutler, Windows NT Professional Developer's Conference, Seattle 1995.

In the first edition of this book, we called this section "Scalability and the Microkernel Architecture." We did this because the available references made much of NT's use of a microkernel design. However, in the last year it's become clear that NT isn't really a microkernel design at all (though one low-level component retains that name), so we've changed the section head—and the text that follows—to reflect how NT was developed.

Conventional PC operating systems, such as DOS, Novell NetWare version 3.x,[1] and Microsoft's new Windows 95, are not *secure, scalable,* or *portable.* That is, they can all be hacked with more or less ease, they cannot exploit more than one central processing unit (CPU), and they cannot be executed natively on RISC processors. These limitations make such operating systems suitable only for small-scale (single-user desktop, departmental LAN) operations.

Windows NT was designed to eliminate these limits. To this end, it employs a client/server architecture in which no application program is permitted direct access to the hardware or to protected portions of the operating system. All such access is mediated by the NT *executive*—which performs the requested access on the application's behalf.

All operating systems have a *kernel*—it's the minimum set of functions that must be kept in memory. In the DOS operating system, the kernel consists largely of the basic input/output system (BIOS),[2] the basic disk operating system (BDOS),[3] and a number of essential glue functions that bring these pieces together. The other parts of DOS, which are not necessary all the time, are stored on disk and loaded into memory only when needed. As illustrated in Figure 1.1, when you type DIR on a DOS machine you're actually employing an external component: the COMMAND.COM file typically found in the root of the C drive. COMMAND.COM provides DOS with its user interface. It monitors the keyboard, looking for certain combinations of characters—of which DIR is one—interprets this as a request for a directory, and issues the necessary BIOS commands to retrieve the directory information. Another set of BIOS commands are then called to display the directory on screen, retrieving the directory information, and in turn, accessing the equivalent BDOS functions to access the disk drives and retrieve that information from the disk. Since both BIOS and BDOS functions are used by almost all DOS programs, they are kept resident in memory—and thus are part of the DOS kernel.

In Windows NT neither the equivalent of the BIOS (the Hardware Abstraction Layer or HAL), nor the equivalent of the BDOS (one of the many installable file systems) is a part of the kernel (though they do execute in kernel mode and

---

1. NetWare 4.1, just entering beta as the second edition of this book was written, is in many respects comparable to Windows NT Server.

2. We're referring here to the BIOS component of the operating system (implemented as the IO.SYS file in DOS systems)—not the ROM BIOS.

3. Actually, this is now an obsolete term—it originated with Control Program for Microcomputers (CP/M), the first OS for PCs. We find the CP/M terminology more descriptive—and DOS began as a CP/M clone, anyway.

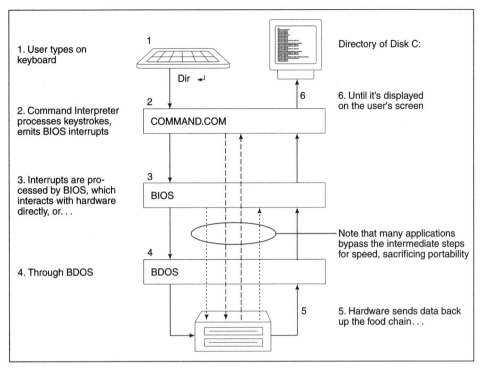

Figure 1.1 Classical OS operation.
Conventional operating system (DOS, NetWare) operation—both applications and operating system components interact directly with low-level device drivers and the hardware, limiting portability and security.

are therefore part of what is generally known as the NT *executive*). At the core of the executive lies the *microkernel,* which comprises only those services that are absolutely required to remain in memory at all times. The microkernel in Windows NT is therefore designed to be as small as possible. It functions much as a traffic light functions, directing the flow of information between various parts of the system.

When you type DIR on an NT system, your keystrokes are intercepted by CMD.EXE—which provides a text-based user interface, monitors the keystrokes, and determines what you've typed. CMD.EXE interfaces to a layer analogous to the BIOS layer; in this case, a subsection of the WIN32 Application Programming Interface (API). However, no application program in Windows NT is ever permitted to communicate directly with the HAL or any device drivers—as we noted earlier, all such interactions occur with the Windows NT executive.

The microkernel takes the requests issued by the applications program, validates those requests according to a security object model, and—if it finds the request valid—issues those requests on the applications program's behalf. The requests may pass to a transitional layer, such as some form of API. This may be implemented as a dynamic-link library, for example, so that it's loaded into the system only when it's required. The library will wish to issue commands in much the same way the BIOS issues commands to the BDOS in DOS—but, again, this is not permitted in Windows NT. Instead, requests are issued through the microkernel and—if the microkernel determines that those requests are reasonable—it issues those requests on the subsystem's behalf.

This mechanism is called a client/server approach: Any subsystem that *services* other subsystems is a server, and any program requesting those services is a client. All Windows NT functions are handled through server processes. Servers can function as clients although they do not necessarily have to. All interactions between clients and servers are controlled by the microkernel. In addition to providing the basics for the security approach that will be discussed later, this has one tremendous benefit: It makes it possible for Windows NT to employ a very small, tight microkernel. The microkernel is so small that on a multiprocessor implementation, one copy is executed on *each* CPU. This provides Windows NT with truly *symmetric* multiprocessing (each CPU can handle tasks in exactly the same manner as any other processor).

Very few operating systems behave this way, the principal ones being the Carnegie-Mellon *Mach* variant of the UNIX operating system, Sequent Computer Systems' *Dynix*, and Sun's *Solaris*. Virtually all other multiprocessor operating systems are asymmetric in some manner—each processor can do certain things, but in general only one processor can execute the operating system microkernel. By breaking down this barrier, Windows NT provides tremendous flexibility and scalability. Up to 30 processors may be employed in custom versions of Windows NT,[4] providing computing power that was, up to now, only available in mainframe-class systems. The implications for network servers are revolutionary: There is, for all intents and purposes, no upper limit on the power of a Windows NT-based network server.[5]

There is a price to pay for the scalability, security, and flexibility that the client/server architecture confers. When a DOS application calls a kernel-mode function, only one kernel-mode transition is required—all other processing occurs in the kernel until the requested information (if any) is ready to be returned to the application. In contrast, NT requires *one kernel-mode call for each*

---

4. Out of the box, Windows NT Workstation supports 1 or 2 CPUs, and Windows NT Server supports up to 4. Supporting more processors requires a customized HAL, which is provided by the hardware manufacturer. Upgrading a single-CPU system to the multi-CPU version requires the use of an NT resource kit utility—see Appendix 4.

5. Actually, there are effective limits on performance due to nonlinear scaling and system-wide bottlenecks when applications are run on a multiprocessor. See Appendix 5 for more details.

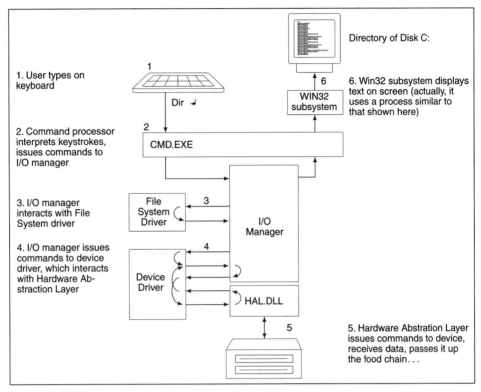

Figure 1.2 Microkernel operation.
Windows NT employs a client server architecture—applications cannot access low-level drivers or hardware services without the intervention of the operating system. Hardware dependencies are isolated in the drivers (and the Hardware Abstraction Layer), assuring portability. Security is provided when the application and operating system interact.

interaction between subsystems—as illustrated in Figure 1.2. Every time a Windows NT application calls through the API layer, there must be a transition.

To save time and speed up common operations, the Windows NT executive (the microkernel and associated subsystems) is designed to make kernel-mode access as efficient as possible—but there is some overhead involved. In practice, extensive laboratory testing at *WINDOWS Magazine* has indicated that the overhead is negligible (indeed, we were shocked to discover that NT Workstation is actually capable of outperforming Windows for Workgroups 3.11 as a 16-bit applications platform, as illustrated in Figure 1.3). It may well be that the age and complexity of other operating systems have made them so inefficient that Windows NT competes well with them. But it's also possible that some

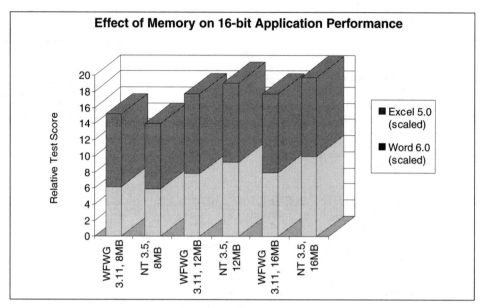

Figure 1.3 Bar chart, 16-bit app performance.

Windows NT 3.5 provides performance equal to (or better than) Windows for Workgroups 3.11 when running single 16-bit applications in the foreground.

competitor will build an operating system that provides an efficient interface between subsystems, thus bettering Windows NT's performance. Of course, one can simply execute Windows NT on an SMP system and try to make up the difference that way. But we digress....

Portable Design

Windows NT provides a second major innovation: It's designed to be independent of any particular hardware. This breaks a tradition that began with IBM's introduction of the first PC in 1981.[6] Beginning with the PC the world of desktop computing underwent a dramatic change. Prior to that time a variety of operating systems vendors had competed along with a variety of hardware systems vendors. Many desktop computers were completely proprietary, combining a unique operating system with unique hardware—but a majority of pre-PC desktop computers used one implementation or another of the CP/M operating system. CP/M could be made to work efficiently on a variety of different computers by making changes to its BIOS layer (which described the

6. In this context, we use "PC" to mean IBM-compatible Personal Computer.

behavior of the hardware to the operating system, and vice versa). Programmers, instead of writing code for specific pieces of hardware, such as the disk controller, would execute BIOS functions that would access the disk controllers for them. The advantage of this approach was that it made programs *portable*—instead of writing a whole new word processor for each CP/M computer, the programmer could write just one CP/M-compatible program, and it would run on any of them. The only disadvantage was that BIOS-based programs tended to be slower than those optimized for a particular system.

The IBM PC killed this concept stone dead. Since the PC provided a standard hardware design, programmers could bypass BIOS and access the low-level hardware directly, gaining significantly in performance. Since the hardware was standardized, programs would still run on *PC-clones* from many vendors. In effect, by providing a uniform standard for the design of desktop hardware, IBM inadvertently created the world where commodity pricing would be introduced. Cloners soon came into play, and so it's possible today to buy IBM PC-compatible computers from almost anyone, except IBM.[7]

Windows NT attempts to reverse this history by reverting to the concept of the CP/M BIOS. In Windows NT the equivalent to BIOS is the Hardware Abstraction Layer (HAL). To make Windows NT available on a particular architecture, the manufacturer must write a machine-specific HAL, provide a Microsoft-compatible C compiler, and then obtain the Windows NT sources from Microsoft and recompile them to the architecture. Most vendors will try tuning the operating system specifically for their hardware. By writing parts of the NT *microkernel* in machine language that best fit their specific architecture they can hope to achieve speed gains, but they need not do so on first release. The point is that it's relatively easy to make NT work on virtually *any* type of machine—no need to stay PC-compatible.

As I write this, Windows NT currently operates on at least four different CPU architectures: Intel *x*86, MIPS R4*x*00, Digital Alpha APX, and Motorola Power PC 60*x*. Before it became public, Windows NT also operated on the Intel i860 (this was the first architecture on which NT became operational), and versions of Windows NT are being prepared for future versions of the Sun SPARC. It undoubtedly will be made available on more architectures over time.

Why So Many Architectures?

While the Intel x86 series microprocessors have been extraordinarily successful (an installed base exceeding 100,000,000 as I write this), they do not represent the upper limit of computer performance in the 1990s. There are performance limitations in the Intel designs, because like the PCs in which they execute,

---

7. Well, AT-bus PC compatibles—which IBM stopped making in 1987.

successive generations of Intel CPUs have been forced to carry forward design limitations in order to stay compatible with their predecessors. An entirely different kind of processor design, Reduced Instruction Set Computer (RISC), has for many years been popular in high-end UNIX workstations. However, while these workstations have been theoretically capable of much higher performance than their Intel counterparts, it has not been practical to run conventional DOS- and Windows-based applications programs on them.

Making Windows NT portable to RISC systems makes it possible to bring the richness and depth of applications support we have in the DOS and Windows world onto these advanced (some would say exotic) architectures. The implication of this to a computer user, and particularly to a network user, is that for the first time there is someplace to go when the current top-of-the-line Intel CPU isn't fast enough. As of this writing the fastest Intel processor is the Pentium or P5 chip.[8] In its current top-of-the-line 120 MHz incarnation it's capable of achieving close to 240 million instructions per second of integer performance, and is a very high-performance processor by any standard. However, it's capable of only half the floating-point performance of RISC CPUs from other manufacturers. If you were running a floating-point-intensive application, such as Computer Aided Design (CAD) / Computer Aided Engineering (CAE), there was until now no place else to go: The Pentium was the fastest Intel CPU, and changing to another CPU meant changing all of your software.

With Windows NT the game has fundamentally changed. If you are unsatisfied with the performance of a Pentium-based workstation for CAD work, you can switch to one of the other architectures mentioned and possibly achieve substantially better performance.

From a networking point of view, the implication of making Windows NT portable to different architectures is astounding flexibility. NT runs on many different platforms, yet behaves nearly identically on all of them. It's possible for a Window NT network to consist of a symmetric multiprocessor functioning as a server, with an arbitrary combination of single processor or even multiple processor workstation machines, some using Intel CPUs, and some RISC. You can put together the precise hardware required to do a particular job while providing a consistent user interface, uniform networking protocols, and generally identical behavior throughout the system.

Of course, all of this flexibility comes at a price—portability has three negative implications.

First, for any architecture other than Intel x86, there is a significant performance hit when executing 16-bit legacy applications—DOS, 16-bit Windows, and OS/2 programs—which weren't developed specifically for Windows NT. These applications weren't designed to run on RISC processors, and the

---

8. April, 1995.

steps NT must take to execute them involve a substantial execution overhead (see Appendix 5 for details).

The second great limitation of portability is the need to compile applications for the specific platform on which they will be executed. Applications written directly for Windows NT, generally using the 32-bit Windows (WIN32) API, have to be *compiled* on the processor on which they will be executed. You cannot take an Intel version of a Windows NT application and expect to run it on a RISC platform, nor can you take a version of a Windows NT application developed on one RISC platform and run it on another.

Here's a specific example illustrating this second limitation: Intergraph Corporation is employing Windows NT as the operating system for its Pentium-based workstations used in Computer Aided Design and Computer Aided Engineering (CAD/CAE) applications. However, Intergraph also has an interest in the Motorola Power PC architecture. Intergraph has therefore compiled versions of their programs for both Power PC and Intel CPUs. Intergraph has not, however, compiled versions for the MIPS R4000/4400 chips and has not announced plans regarding the DEC Alpha chip. As I write this, it's possible to run Intergraph's application software on two of the currently supported Windows NT implementations. It's not possible to run those applications on the other implementations. This can be a critical problem for network administrators faced with decisions about which specific hardware to acquire. The fact that Windows NT is portable does not necessarily mean that Windows NT applications are. Worse, this situation extends to some parts of the network services— for instance, a RISC-based print server with Intel clients must provide Intel-compatible printer drivers.

The final limitation of portability is similar to the limitations of the client/server architecture defined earlier. There is an overhead associated with the fact that the Windows NT code is designed to be portable. The bulk of Windows NT is written in C—which makes it portable. Design a C compiler for a particular environment, design a HAL for that environment, recompile the Windows NT sources, and you have a version of Windows NT for the new environment. Unfortunately, C code is not optimized for a variety of performance intensive tasks. In NT 3.1, this resulted in some performance compromises which were largely eliminated by better optimization—and in some cases, rewriting critical code in assembly language—for NT versions from 3.5 on.

Object Model and the Security Subsystem

The subject of object orientation, and the broader subject of objects generally, are among the most pervasive and controversial topics in modern computer science. The idea of object orientation is to deal abstractly with data, code, and instructions as an object, without being concerned about whether the object referred to is a data file, text, a picture, a program, or whatever. The concept is not uniformly seen as effective. Fortunately, Windows NT does not claim to be an object-oriented operating system. It does however employ the concept of objects to a high degree in one subsystem—the security subsystem.

Security is an important point in Windows NT—Microsoft is positioning the security features of Windows NT as a major advantage in commercial applications, such as banking. While there is undoubtedly some truth to this, it's also interesting to speculate. Helen Custer's excellent book, *Inside Windows NT*, makes it clear that the genesis of the concept that would lead to Windows NT began in 1988. This was at the very height of the Reagan/Bush defense build-up. Could it be that Windows NT is something of a Cold War operating system? It's certain that Windows NT was designed with the needs of the United States government and the defense industry in mind, for Windows NT is unique among desktop operating systems in having been designed to be certifiable at the federal government's C2 and B security levels.[9]

To understand the implications of security requirements for an operating system, let's consider a hypothetical example. Suppose that you're an employee of the Central Intelligence Agency and are cleared for Top Secret information. You work with an employee who is cleared only for Secret information. As a Top Secret cleared employee you have the clearance necessary to see any of the documents that are used by the Secret cleared employee. The reverse, however, is not true. Suppose further that you have a need periodically to print documents. Clearly Top Secret documents cannot be printed on just any laser printer anywhere in the building. Your Top Secret documents can be printed only on a Top Secret laser printer (probably located behind armed guards, a vault door, and with whatever other security requirements the CIA may feel a need to enforce). The documents from the Secret cleared employee can be printed on your Top Secret printer (although the Secret cleared Employee may have some difficulty getting past the armed guards and through the vault door to retrieve his documents). However, should you attempt to print a Top Secret document on a printer *owned* by that Secret cleared employee, whether or not your document prints will depend upon whether the document itself is cleared Secret or Top Secret.

If you're confused upon reading these last couple of sentences, I've made my point!

The issue of security is extremely complex. To provide a truly *secure* operating system, every file and every device in the system has to have an *owner*. There is a security access level—in this case Secret or Top Secret—associated with each of those files and devices. The designers of Windows NT were very aware of this requirement and they decided that this was one place where using objects made sense.

---

9. See "Trusted Network Interpretation," a Publication of National Computer Security Conference (NCSC), tel: (202) 783-3238.

Windows NT provides an object-based security model. A security object can represent any resource in the system—files, devices, processes, programs, users, you name it—and there is a security object associated with it. A security object carries information about what the object is permitted or not permitted to do. These permissions are carried forward with the security objects associated with system resources, and a more or less sophisticated sense of inheritance will determine what is and is not permitted to be done with any such resource. Server processes that provide secure access employ a technique called *impersonation*: The process takes on the security identifier (SID) of its client, and performs operations in the client's security context. All of this is transparent to both programmers and end users, and (provided the security system is properly configured) interferes minimally with normal system operations.

The situation isn't really quite as complex as I've described, because a computer security system designed to deal with Secret and Top Secret information would have to be certifiable to the government's B security level. Windows NT is not secured at that level (because it would be all but unusable to mere civilians). In such a system all resources are totally secured by default, and it's necessary to take specific steps to apply permissions to them so that they can be used by the great masses.

Windows NT enforces a less restrictive standard called C2, which is not certifiable for the handling of Secret information. It's certifiable for the handling of Confidential information, and it's well suited to banks and other facilities requiring a degree of security without making their systems virtually unusable as a side effect. The security system is theoretically capable of being upgraded to the B standard. Moreover, the security system is implemented as a privileged subsystem (a concept that we will examine shortly), and it can be replaced by another security system if desired. As I write this, Microsoft has begun to publicly discuss their intent to replace the entire security system with the Kerberos distributed security system (implemented by the Massachusetts Institute of Technology) in future versions of Windows NT.[10]

What Does Security Mean to Me?

The implications of NT security are most significant for file servers. Windows NT's provision of a relatively sophisticated security system, including the concept of file ownership and specific access permissions granted on a per-file or per-directory basis, makes it possible to completely isolate each user's files from other users of the system. This is clearly of vital importance in a high-security environment and may be equally important to companies that carry proprietary information on their networks. The corporate nightmare in the

---

10. Code-named "Windows NT Cairo" and expected to be available in 1996… or maybe 1997.

1990s is to have accounting files hacked by a sixteen-year-old with a modem, who has recently seen the movie *War Games*. Should such a sixteen-year-old kid hack a Windows NT server, *assuming security has been properly set up*, his opportunity to do mischief will be significantly restricted. Whether the system is therefore hacker-proof is an open question (and a somewhat controversial one).

In principle, software that one human being can invent, another human being can, if sufficiently determined, sabotage. No matter how sophisticated Windows NT security may be, any Windows NT system that's physically accessible (an unauthorized person can walk up to it and access the keyboard, screen, and disk drive) is vulnerable. If you want your server to be protected, you *must* lock it up. It's also worth noting that the most sophisticated system of passwords, user accounts, and security access rights in the world is worthless if it's not used. If you create a Windows NT server and provide total access to all files for everyone in the system, then you're vulnerable—NT's sophisticated security system is meaningless because you have turned it off.

Windows NT systems also provide a powerful remote access service designed to make it possible to log into those systems remotely using a modem. While I am very impressed by Windows NT security systems, there is always a risk in connecting a system to a modem. The security procedures must be enacted with great rigor. They are vulnerable.

Finally, does the provision of such security have drawbacks? As with scalability and portability, the need for security objects to be checked as they are passed from subsystem to subsystem implies a certain amount of overhead in the system. The interesting point about this, however, is that such security capabilities have in the past been built into many kinds of software. Network databases, such as Microsoft's own SQL Server, typically incorperate private security authentication layers in their OS/2 and UNIX incarnations. Windows NT versions may dispense with that layer, improving performance and simplifying administration.[11]

Privileged Subsystems

The client/server design of Windows NT involves a certain amount of overhead. Whenever one process, such as an application program, communicates with another process, the *executive* is involved. But there are components of the system that require higher operating performance than is possible in such an arrangement. There are also components of the system requiring access to system resources not generally made available to applications programs. These

11. In practice, both Microsoft and Oracle have retained proprietary security in their NT databases for compatibility with other versions—but have provided for use of NT's built-in security as well. See Chapter 11 for details.

subsystems are referred to as *privileged subsystems*. And they run with essentially the same privileges as built-in components of the Windows NT system. Privileged subsystems are important to us, because one obvious place where the concept of a privileged subsystem applies is in the networking interface.

If Windows NT's client/server approach was carried to its limit in all components of the networking interface, one could quite reasonably expect that network performance in Windows NT would be poor by comparison with less protected operating systems. This, however, is not the case. Major components of the networking system are implemented as privileged subsystems communicating between and among themselves with privilege levels comparable with those used by the NT *executive* itself.

There is another area where privileged subsystems are employed, and it's critical in understanding NT's place in the network world on desktops. That area is in providing *programmable personalities*.

Traditionally, each operating system has had a clearly defined (and unique) user interface. For example, the CP/M operating system had a user interface characterized by a certain set of user commands, and this was paralleled by an application programming interface containing certain possibilities. The DOS operating system includes a similar but more sophisticated user interface and a similar but more sophisticated programming interface. The OS/2 operating system has a still more sophisticated user interface (major components of which are implemented graphically) and a still more sophisticated application programming interface.

This proliferation of user and programming interfaces eventually tends to become an overwhelming burden for an operating system to carry. Operating systems, such as OS/2, have had to make a terrible choice between carrying the overhead of compatibility to earlier systems (such as DOS)—or seeing their market share sharply reduced. Windows NT, by contrast, exploits the concepts of privileged subsystems and the client/server architecture to provide completely replaceable personalities. In effect, Windows NT can take on the characteristics of 16-bit Windows, DOS, 32-bit Windows, OS/2, or POSIX. From the point of view of the programmer and from the point of view of an applications program, it is *effectively the same* as 16-bit Windows, DOS, 32-bit Windows, OS/2, or POSIX. To the user it does appear a bit different.

Standard User Interface

While there was early discussion of providing interchangeable user interfaces so that those familiar with OS/2 would see an OS/2 Presentation Manager interface while those familiar with Windows would see a Windows-like user interface, Microsoft has wisely decided to standardize on a user interface governed by the 32-bit Windows (Win32) subsystem. Applications programs functioning within any of the subsystems can share this user interface, as

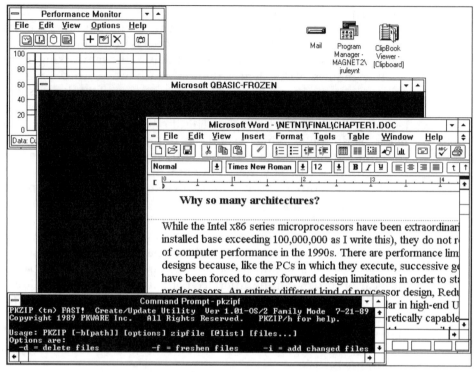

Figure 1.4 Windows NT UI with OS/2, Win16, and Win32 apps.

The Windows NT user interface provides an integrated desktop metaphor for applications designed for 32-bit Windows, 16-bit Windows, DOS, OS/2 (16-bit character mode only), and POSIX. All but the last are shown here.

illustrated in Figure 1.4. This confers tremendous advantages upon Windows NT—for both end users and system managers. It's not necessary to develop and acquire a completely new base of software when moving to a Windows NT system. Well-behaved DOS, Windows, and OS/2 1.x applications will run correctly in the Windows NT environment.[12] Well-behaved UNIX applications can be recompiled using NT's POSIX compatibility libraries, and will become native POSIX applications in the Windows NT environment.

Let's look at an example: A company that has standardized on SQL Server as its corporate database, and where employees use the DOS version of Word Perfect along with Windows Excel to get work done, should be able to move to Windows NT without changing any of its software. SQL Server is an application

---

12. See Appendix 3 for a definition of "well-behaved" in this context.

that's implemented on OS/2, UNIX, and NT. The OS/2 version of SQL Server can be executed directly under Windows NT (on Intel platforms). Windows NT also incorporates TCP/IP-compatible (UNIX-style) networking so that if a UNIX-based SQL Server implementation is employed, it can be left in place and Windows NT will use it.[13] On the other hand, if it's preferable to move directly to Windows NT, a native version of SQL Server is available.

Similarly, Word Perfect for DOS and Excel for (16-bit) Windows will execute directly under Windows NT (although it may be desirable to acquire native 32-bit versions of these applications when they become available—as they will give better performance). Should the company use a specialized application, it will probably run in one of NT's emulation subsystems (assuming the application was developed for DOS, Windows, or OS/2). If the application was developed for the UNIX environment (where portability is normally accomplished at the source-code level), then if it's a well-behaved character-mode UNIX application, it should be possible to recompile it for Windows NT's POSIX implementation. For that matter, if it's a graphics application, it could be possible to use it in conjunction with one of the third-party *X/Server* utilities for Windows NT—see Chapter 6.

Of course, there are limitations to this approach—one is reminded of the old saw "Jack of all trades, master of none." That's not true of Windows NT. It's master of one trade and that trade is 32-bit Windows. With respect to the other subsystems, it has greater or lesser limitations, depending on the particular subsystem. With respect to the DOS subsystem in particular, there is a significant problem introduced by Windows NT security architecture, which prevents low-level access to hardware. Backup applications and utility programs that expect direct access to hardware, such as the hard disk controller, will not work under Windows NT. Windows applications that take liberties with the Windows interface, employ undocumented system calls, attempt direct hardware access, or employ private device drivers (scanner applications and the like) will not work.

The OS/2 support is at the OS/2 1.3 level. This is unfortunate, as Windows NT was introduced in parallel with IBM's introduction of its second major revision of the OS/2 2.x system, and NT's built-in OS/2 support is character-mode only.[14] This is sufficient for carrying forward server-based applications, such as SQL Server. It's insufficient for carrying forward much of anything else. The POSIX implementation suffers similar limitations to the OS/2 implementation, and of course, requires that development effort in that application be recompiled. All of this is typical of the UNIX world as a whole.

---

13. See Chapter 6 for details of Windows NT's UNIX-compatible TCP/IP networking features.

14. An add-on package is available that provides an OS/2 Presentation Manager interface—see Appendix 3 for details.

So the idea that bringing Windows NT into an organization will allow the existing software base to be carried forward without *any* change is probably naive.

Having said that, Microsoft has made great strides in improving matters since NT 3.1—in Chapter 9, we'll explain how NT is able to masquerade as a native client on NetWare 3.*x* and 4.*x* LANs, and (with appropriate add-on software) can even appear to be a NetWare 3.*x* *server*. Thus, while the notion of a chameleon-like ability to change user interfaces hasn't panned out in practice, something similar has happened at the network interface level.

Access to the World Outside: I/O

No operating system exists in isolation. People buy an operating system to run application software—and they do so in the expectation that it will work with a wide range of hardware. To make this work, Windows NT provides a very rich device-independent model for I/O services. This model takes critical advantage of a concept called a *multilayered device driver*. In DOS and other conventional operating systems device drivers are generally *monolithic*—they provide a large and complex set of services that will be understood by an intermediate layer of the operating system. In DOS this intermediate layer is the Basic Disk Operating System (BDOS). The device driver then communicates directly with the hardware—so when BDOS commands are issued, the driver provides the necessary hardware interface. BDOS commands are relatively high-level functions. They do things like open a file, read a byte from a file, close a file. The physical actions needed to fill these requests are hidden (or *encapsulated*) within the driver.

This model works but it has some severe problems. Consider that there may be more than one type of file system. If the driver has been designed to respond to the Open File command it will, given a file name, go to a directory structure, find the file, and carry out the operations necessary to open it (this assumes the device driver knows the file system format to be used). Now in DOS this is no problem—there is only one file format to worry about, the File Allocation Table (FAT) format; so DOS device drivers assume that this is the format they'll see on the disk.

Windows NT, as we will see in the next section, is designed to use a variety of file system formats. So it's not safe for a device driver to make any assumptions about the underlying format. In order to get around this problem, NT uses a *multilayer* device driver approach in combination with a new operating system layer called the *I/O manager*. Application programs (and intermediate levels of the operating system) do not communicate directly with the device drivers. They communicate with the I/O manager, which in turn communicates with the device drivers on their behalf.

Let's consider how this works when an application program needs to access files on an NTFS (New Technology File System) partition. The application program issues a request to open a file. The request travels to an underlying operating system layer—perhaps the Win32 API layer. The Win32 API layer then issues an NT internal command, requesting the NT executive to open a file. The NT executive passes this request to the I/O manager, and the I/O manager communicates this request to a file system driver—specifically the NTFS file system driver. The NTFS file system driver responds by issuing the NTFS specific hardware level requests. It says "I want the information from track x sector y," which will be the location of the first tier of the directory structure; and based upon that, it issues commands to get information from other locations on the disk. I/O manager then relays these requests to a hardware device driver, which knows that it's receiving specific requests related to getting very simple information from the device. It knows nothing about the file system. Notice that this process will work exactly the same if the NTFS driver is replaced by a FAT driver or an OS/2 High Performance File System (HPFS) driver, or a UNIX file system driver, or a Macintosh file system driver, or a CD ROM driver, *or any other driver*.

Of course, there is overhead involved with the I/O manager passing requests for information back and forth. For simple devices, such as serial ports and parallel ports, Windows NT provides a single-layer device driver approach in which the I/O manager can communicate with the device driver, and the device driver will return information directly. But for more complicated devices, and particularly for hard disks, tape drives, and other devices that depend on a file system (or other logical arrangement of data), a multilayered approach is superior.

Asynchronous I/O, Synchronization, and Power-Failure Recovery

Three additional device driver features are unique to Windows NT. The first is that virtually all low level I/O operations are *asynchronous*. Rather than issue a request for information from a file and wait until the request is filled, in Windows NT, you issue the request for information to the file and then go on and do something else. When the information from the file is ready, you're notified that it's ready.

This characteristic is masked at the programmer API level, and neither programmers nor users need ever see it (programmers *do* have the option to explicitly use it through a mechansim called *overlapped I/O*). If you type DIR at an NT command prompt, it will behave in much the same way as typing DIR on a DOS system. Underneath the user interface, however, very different things are going on. Windows NT is a *preemptive multitasking system*, which may be running many tasks at the same time, so it's vital that the operating system not waste time waiting for a request to be filled if it can spend that time doing something else. The various layers in the operating system use the preemptive multitasking and multithreading characteristics of NT to enable themselves to get more work done in the same time.

Rather than waiting for a hard disk to spin up, or waiting on a request to read a directory, Windows NT continues with other tasks and deals with the directory request only when data becomes available. This feature also plays a role in NT's scalability—from our discussion of the client/server design and its application to symmetric multiprocessors, you will remember that multiple instances of the Windows NT *microkernel* execute on all CPUs simultaneously. This means it's theoretically possible for all the CPUs in a system to attempt simultaneous device driver access, causing *contention*. To avoid this problem, device drivers—like other components of the NT Executive—make use of synchronization objects (in particular, semaphores and spin locks). The precise details of how this is done are outside the scope of this chapter. Suffice it to say that while it's possible for multiple instances of a device driver or other critical code to execute on multiple processors, they are designed in such a way that only one of those drivers at a time will have access to any critical shared resource. Just as with the asynchronous I/O, this is automatic and invisible to end users.

The final unique feature of Windows NT device drivers is provision for power failure recovery. Windows NT is designed as, among other things, a platform for mission-critical applications, such as SQL Server (an Enterprise database). If a corporation has implemented its entire accounting system on SQL Server, it's absolutely critical that the system on which SQL Server is running be protected from power failure—or, should a power failure occur, it's vital that there be a graceful path to recovery. Otherwise, the entire accounting system could be corrupted—and a corrupt accounting system can cost a company millions of dollars.

Windows NT provides protection against this nightmare on several levels— the most important of which are the uninterruptible power supply service (which we will discuss later) and certain sophisticated features of the NTFS file system (ditto). There is also provision for protection from power failure *even at the device-driver level*. In a power failure, even if it is very brief, the precise operating state of hardware devices becomes unstable. A disk drive, for example, which has a memory buffer for Direct Memory Access (DMA) data transfer, may be loaded with corrupt data during a power failure. Attempting to access that data will yield garbage—or worse, if that data gets written to disk, it may damage the application requesting it.

The classic way to deal with this in an operating system is to force a *cold* (power-switch) boot, lock everything out, and restart all operations from the power-off state. That takes a long time, and itself is dangerous because there may have been I/O requests outstanding. The classic example is a power failure while writing a disk file. Typically the disk file data is lost. Windows NT attempts to protect against this by designing warm boot code into the device drivers. In other words, there is a *known good state* for device drivers short of the power-off state. In a power-failure situation the operating system will notify all device drivers that a power failure has occurred. The device drivers then set themselves to their known good states and continue with the I/O operations that were outstanding when the power failed. If this capability works—and we've seen it demonstrated—then a power glitch on a Windows NT system need have no effect other than the brief period of time that the machine was turned off. Operations pick themselves up where they were and carry on transparently.

In fairness, this capability is very new and it's tightly coupled to a number of new system components. To what degree it will work is still an open question. We've seen it demonstrated with SQL Server running on a Windows NT system on the NTFS file system. A power failure was created by physically disconnecting the system, unplugging it, while SQL Server was filling a query request. Power was restored. Windows NT system came up. SQL Server came up. The disks spun for a little while to restore themselves to their own good state, and it continued with the query. That was a *very* impressive performance. You probably shouldn't bet your company on it—but it's a reassuring capability to fall back on!

File Systems

Traditionally, operating systems are associated with a particular file structure that's used by that operating system for mass storage devices, such as hard disks. Thus, we speak of a UNIX file system (i-nodes), a DOS file system (FAT), and a Macintosh File System (resource and data forks). While there is a native NT file system (NTFS), uniquely among modern operating systems (with the possible exception of OS/2—from which some of these capabilities were inherited) Windows NT is designed to be independent of the file system on which it operates. This capability enforces some severe requirements on Windows NT's I/O system design and device drivers, as was discussed in the last section. But it provides a very high degree of flexibility in Windows NT-based applications.

By default, Windows NT supports two file systems for hard disks—the familiar File Allocation Table (FAT) system that's standard for DOS, and NTFS, which is designed to exploit Windows NT's security and fault-tolerance features. Windows NT also provides in-the-box support for OS/2's High Performance File System (HPFS)—a system with capabilities intermediate between FAT and NTFS. Windows NT also support a CD-ROM file system, eliminating the necessity for the MSCDX patch to the DOS file system that's required by all CD-ROM drives used with DOS machines. Windows NT Server also supports the Macintosh file system. Finally, *network services are treated as file systems in Windows NT*. Windows NT comes with LAN Manager-compatible network services that are, in effect, a file system extended over a network. If you add Novell NetWare support, you add NetWare network services—yet another file system that spans a network.

Windows NT is capable of running all of these file systems simultaneously. By far the most important is NTFS, which is designed as a file system for building anything from a desktop computer to a mainframe-class enterprise server. It's designed to perform well with very large disk volumes (*up to 2^{64} bytes!*), a situation that is difficult for the FAT system. All of these are features it shares with OS/2's HPFS system. But Microsoft learned some things from its experience with HPFS design and development that contributes to the NTFS design.

In contrast to HPFS, NTFS provides a unique data-logging capability that enables Windows NT to restore the state of the file system in power failure or other disk error situations, and to do so very quickly. HPFS has a similar capability, but it's implemented using an HPFS version of the DOS *chkdsk* function and in large volumes it can literally take *hours* to execute. Like HPFS, NTFS provides support for long file names.[15] You can refer to a file called "1993 Quarterly Accounts," and you can use that name for it rather than calling it something cryptic like 93QTR.ACT. However, the use of long file names creates compatibility problems for legacy applications. Windows NT eliminates this problem by providing automatic conversion of file names to standard DOS-style 8.3 names for DOS and Windows 16-bit applications. Thus, if you named your file "1993 Quarterly Accounts" while using a 32-bit Windows application, when you go back and look for the file from a 16-bit Windows application or DOS application, you will see 1993QU~1.[16]

Finally, beginning with NT version 3.51, NTFS supports *compression* as an attribute. This allows the end user or administrator to provide file compression on a per-file and per-directory basis. The compression is efficient—giving roughly a 50 percent reduction in space on most text files, 40 percent on executables—and potentially much higher compression on sparse data files, such as databases. The performance impact of compression appears to be minimal—due, no doubt, to NT's combination of dynamic disk caching (data is decompressed on entry to the cache) and asynchronous I/O (which allows compression to take place in parallel with reading the next block of data from the disk). The combination of efficient compression and a minimal perform-ance impact with an inherently reliable design is unique to NTFS—and makes it well suited to use on servers as well as desktop systems.

File System Features for Programmers

Besides supporting multiple installable file systems, Windows NT provides a couple of unique features that assure high performance. The first of these is an entirely new capability called *memory-mapped files*. Windows NT is a *virtual*

---

15. In NT version 3.5 (and later), a similar capability exists for the FAT file system as well.

16. Further details on the New Technology File System and on setting up file systems in general will be found in Chapter 2.

memory operating system—it allows for arbitrarily large memory objects to be dealt with (if the object is too large to fit in physical memory, then only part is stored in memory, while the rest resides on disk). Memory-mapped files exploit this capability by allowing a programmer to open a file of arbitrary size and treat it as a single contiguous array of memory locations. A file 100 megabytes in size can be opened and treated as an array in a system with only 12 megabytes of memory. Of course, at any one time 12 megabytes or less (probably substantially less) of file data is physically present in memory—the rest is *paged* out to the disk. When the program requests data that's not currently stored in memory, the Virtual Memory System automatically gets it from the file. But it does so very efficiently, and it completely masks this operation from the programmer.

This feature could revolutionize disk-based programs (like database applications) once programmers understand how to use it. Writing applications in which large amounts of file data are manipulated in a computer is something of an art form.[17] You must find a way to load the right data into memory at the right time and manipulate it there for speed, and then unload it and load in new data. Windows NT changes this process to one of manipulating disk-based data as you would any other array of bytes. While the entire file is never actually present in memory at any one time, Windows NT masks this behavior. The network programming implications of this and other Windows NT features is explored in Appendix 1.

Preemptive Multitasking

Computers spend much of their time doing absolutely nothing. Consider what happens when you type DIR on a DOS machine. In between your typing of the letters D, I, and R the CPU sits idle. You cannot possibly type fast enough to keep it busy. When you finish typing DIR and hit the Enter key, the CPU very quickly decides that you wanted a disk directory, issues the necessary commands, and issues instructions to the hard disk controller. It then waits while the hard disk controller gets the information, and while it waits it can accomplish no useful work.

Because of *preemptive multitasking*, this situation is very different under Windows NT. A component of the operating system called the *Task Scheduler* switches a variety of processes into or out of the CPU(s), either according to a set time schedule or based upon the existence of some high-priority event, such as an interrupt. To understand how this works in practice let's consider the very same process of typing DIR, but this time on a Windows NT machine. It's all but certain that when you type DIR that won't be the only thing you are doing with the NT machine. You will probably have a variety of other windows open,

---

17. See Appendix 1 for helpful hints on NT network programming.

and several programs running. Yet you won't have to wait any longer for the system to respond after you type DIR than you would on the DOS machine. (In fact, you may not even have to wait as long!)

The *foreground* process in Windows NT gets a substantially higher priority than background processes;[18] and *real-time* I/O (such as keyboard input) has the highest priority in the system. Therefore, whenever you hit a key the CPU will drop what it's doing to handle the keystroke, but in the intervening time between the keystrokes (when a DOS system would be idle) the Task Scheduler will switch among the other processes running in the system. Even if you're running only the window into which you're typing DIR, the Task Scheduler will still switch time between your processes and the processes of the Windows NT Executive. These include the processes that provide networking capability, and here we see one of the first and most important of Windows NT's advantages. Instead of being afterthoughts, as they are with Novell NetWare's NetX Shell and DOS, networking functions are built into Windows NT—and the preemptive multi-tasking model makes for a far more effective networking implementation.

Now, suppose you finish typing DIR and hit the Enter key. Just as in DOS, the Windows NT command interpreter determines that DIR is a command to display directory information. It then issues the necessary commands through the NT Executive to the I/O Manager, which in turn calls the installable file system for whichever file system you're using on the relevant drive. This in turn sends a series of requests for specific information to the I/O Manager, which in turn passes those requests on to a low-level hard disk driver, which in turn gets the information from the hard disk. Now this is a reasonably efficient process and happens very quickly—up to the point that the hard disk becomes involved. But the operating times of hard disks are measured in milliseconds, whereas the operating times of microprocessors occur in nanoseconds. By comparison to a modern microprocessor, a hard disk is an extraordinarily slow device.

Rather than waiting while it receives the information from the hard disk, the Task Scheduler continues to switch other processes in and out of the CPU. When the data from the hard disk becomes available, this will interrupt other processes, because I/O has a very high priority and information from the hard disk will be passed *up the food chain* to the process that requested it. This process of having I/O and other work accomplished simultaneously is called *asynchronous I/O*. Because of asynchronous I/O, preemptive multitasking systems, such as Windows NT, can be substantially faster on I/O-intensive tasks than are single-thread-of-execution systems, such as DOS. Best of all, since Windows NT's built-in disk cache manager is itself multithreaded, the benefits of asynchronous I/O are available to *all* applications that access disks—whether they are themselves mulithreaded.[19]

---

18. The process running in the topmost window on the NT machine's display.

19. Automatic disk caching does have its limitations—applications that perform continuous disk

Multithreading

What I've discussed about preemptive multitasking to this point could apply equally to a variety of other systems, particularly UNIX systems (which also run a preemptively switched, multitasking operating system kernel). Windows NT shares with OS/2 a substantial extension to this concept, called *multithreading*. A thread is a low-overhead process that can be switched by the Task Scheduler (just like any other process), but it does not carry with it the overhead of starting up, ending, and managing its own resources. It inherits these from its parent process. A single process may have many threads.

Consider a database application. If it's written in a traditional single-threaded manner, Windows NT will benefit from asynchronous I/O (through disk caching if nothing else) but the application will not. The application cannot continue to process input for a new database record until the last record has been added—it hangs up while writing to the disk (and the user's eyes glaze at the sight of that hated Windows hourglass cursor). Windows NT can use this time to get other tasks done, but that's not terribly helpful to your end user.

However, if the database application is multithreaded—as a Windows NT application should be—then you might be able to get other work done within the application while it's filling that request. Instead of hanging up, the application could accept input for the next record *at the very same time that the last record was being added* (see Figure 1.5). And, to abuse an accounting term, the extra productivity you achieve this way is "found money" that was otherwise going to waste. (You are paying for that end user's time whether or not he's waiting on his computer!)

A properly written Windows NT database will never show that hourglass cursor. Instead, Windows NT provides a combination hourglass cursor and arrow pointer. The idea being that this shows you that work is going on—but you can get other things done at the same time. Specifically, what should happen when you enter another record into the database is that one thread will start writing the last record to the disk while the thread in which you're entering the data remains active. Asynchronous I/O now applies to the human part of the I/O equation as well as to the computer's part.

Multithreading on an SMP: Parallel Processing

On multiprocessing systems, Windows NT gains an additional advantage—*each thread in a program can execute on its own CPU, speeding up the application*. As we discussed in the section on client/server design, Windows NT can simulta-

---

I/O (databases, for instance) can sometime achieve better performance if they bypass NT's cache and access the disk directly.

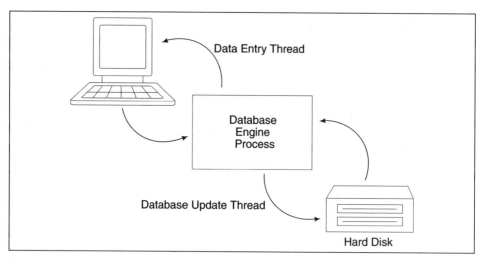

Figure 1.5 Multithread database insert.

Use of multithreading can significantly improve productivity in such applications as database inserts, because the operator need not wait for one insert to complete before beginning another.

neously execute as many copies of the microkernel as there are processors in the system. Each copy of the microkernel is in fact a thread of the Windows NT Executive—which is (obviously) multithreaded.

There are other multiprocessor operating systems—in particular, various forms of UNIX.[20] Typically, these systems employ the processors to execute separate processes or programs. Thus, for instance, a database application may be executing in one processor, and another application in another processor, and so on and on and on. Because each process can execute in its own processor, each executes faster and the system as a whole is faster. But no single process executes faster than it would if it was executing by itself.

Multithreaded processes in Windows NT can actually gain a speed benefit from executing on a multiprocessor. In the example I just gave (the database with records being entered), the thread for adding the record to the database could continue to execute not only in parallel with the execution of the thread that's taking the data from the user, but they could also execute in separate processors at the same time. Now, in fact, the advantage from multiprocessor execution of this specific example would be small. Both disk-based file I/O (the

---

20. As this second edition was written, Novell and IBM expected to introduce multiprocessor-enabled versions of NetWare and OS/2, respectively, late in 1995. Both support SMP-multithreading in somewhat the same way NT does, though since SMP capability was added on to them rather than designed in, how well they will exploit additional processors is an open question.

major limiting factor in updating the database), and human interface I/O waiting on the user to enter keystrokes, are very slow processes. There is plenty of idle time in between the user's keystrokes, and while the hard disk spins— Windows NT's asynchronous I/O capabilities can take advantage of these even on a single processor. But consider a database *search....*

As we discussed in the section on file I/O, Windows NT can provide impressive database capabilities using memory-mapped files. A programmer can, in effect, load the entire file into memory (or at least *act* as if he has loaded the entire file into memory), and then search it as he would search any memory array. In a multiprocessor implementation, one could have several threads of execution searching on that array simultaneously. If each of those threads has its own CPU, this could substantially increase the speed of the database search, as illustrated in Figure 1.6.

This approach has its limitations—specifically, in the example I've just given (a multiprocessor database search), contention will occur when two CPUs attempt to access the same memory address. If the programmer has done his job right, this will be minimized; but it can't be completely eliminated—and contention will slow down the system substantially. Similarly, multithreaded tasks that compete for single shared resources, such as the hard disk, network cards, or the video screen, are going to cause contention and performance will

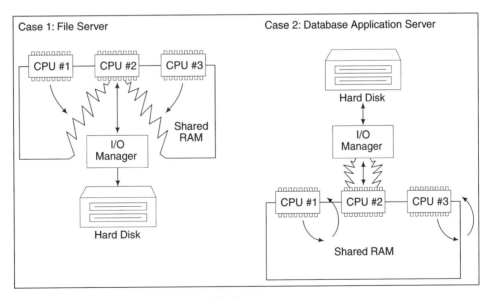

Figure 1.6 MP Contention on File Server.

By dividing a computation-intensive task, such as a database search, into multiple *threads of execution*, a Windows NT application can achieve significant performance gains when run on Symmetric Multiprocessor (SMP) hardware.

deteriorate.[21] But for a wide variety of applications—especially server applications—parallel processing is very, very important.

Consider the operation of a large server on a large network. It may be servicing requests from dozens—even hundreds—of users simultaneously. In a typical file- and print-server situation, most of what it's doing is I/O and, as in the earlier example, a single CPU machine will have no trouble keeping up with other information requests in its free time between filling I/O requests. The major problem is keeping all the requests straight (100 people can try to open files at the same time, but a single hard disk can handle only one request at a time).

The situation is different, however, if we begin to consider client/server applications—of which modern databases are a primary example. These applications tend to be compute-intensive at the server. Queries on the database are received as requests from a client computer. The actual query is conducted at the server. If five or ten people are attempting to perform database queries at the same time, you have not only an *I/O* problem (getting the data into memory from disk), but also a *compute* problem (searching the data in memory). At this point, NT's multiprocessor support becomes a tremendous advantage. By providing additional CPU resources, it can fulfill those requests. This is the key to understanding that Windows NT is more—far more—than a simple operating system for desktop computers. Windows NT is an ideal operating system for computers that until recently we would think of as being in the mainframe class.

Memory Management

In contrast to more conventional operating systems, Windows NT runs a near mainframe-class memory management subsystem that employs demand-paged virtual memory. In this scheme, programs are presented with a contiguous (flat) address space, up to 2 gigabytes in size,[22] although there will generally not be that much memory in the system. In fact, what's present in the system may not be contiguous at all.

Within the contiguous address space, memory is organized as 4-kilobyte pages.[23] Pages can be freely moved between memory and a hard disk at the command of the *memory manager subsystem*. The memory manager does this

---

21. See Appendix 5 for a more complete discussion of the contention problem on SMP systems.

22. It is technically possible for NT's memory manager to support a 64-bit address space, which would allow it to access 264 bytes. Applications would have to be rewritten to exploit such a large memory space.

23. This is true on Intel- and Mips-based systems for reasons that Helen Custer explains well in *Inside Windows NT*. Systems based on Digital's Alpha CPU use an 8KB page size, and it's possible that other processors will use different page sizes as NT becomes available on additional architectures.

through a mechanism called a *page fault.* Whenever a program attempts to access memory that's not physically present in the machine, a page fault is generated. The NT Executive then takes over and loads in the requested memory. It also unloads the least recently used memory pages from the system to make room for the memory that's being loaded in. This process is automatic and (under all but the most extreme conditions) completely transparent—and it means that programs can behave as though they have nearly unlimited memory space, when they are in fact limited to memory physically present in the machine. When Windows NT runs out of memory (programs are asking for more memory than the machine has), response slows down because the memory manager must periodically *swap* pages between memory and the hard disk.

This is particularly important in server-based applications, where as the number of users grows, eventually the physical memory in the machine is insufficient. NT's major competitor, Novell NetWare 3.*x*, does not run a virtual memory system, and (as we've personal experience—and scars to prove) when you add enough users and enough load to a system without adding memory, the system begins to crash regularly. This should not happen with the Windows NT system, because the virtual memory subsystem can take advantage of disk space (if you run out of *both* physical memory and disk space, you may very well hit a situation in which Memory Manager does run out of available memory).[24]

Besides managing virtual memory, The memory manager provides memory *protection*—preventing one application from manipulating memory within another application's address space. If memory protection was not provided, it would be possible for a rogue program to take actions that would result in other programs crashing or becoming unstable. (Sounds like a computer virus, eh?) To prevent this, the Memory Manager checks the *page boundaries* of the application's memory space. When an application attempts to address memory outside of its page boundary, a page fault will occur and the memory manager will attempt to load in the missing memory page. If it determines that the page does not belong to the application, the memory manager raises a *protection exception*—which can be caught by an exception handler in the thread requesting the page, or by a debugger. As a last resort, the Executive could shut down the offending application (making a note of this in an audit file if the system is so configured), giving the user a Dr. Watson pop-up as an error indication.

There are times when it's desirable to have two applications share memory, and thus, the memory management system has to provide a way around the memory protection. This is provided by Windows NT's *memory-mapped files*

---

24. Fortunately, NT has a graceful way to handle even this case—discussed in the section on memory management in Chapter 5.

mechanism, the same mechanism that can be used for high-speed access to disk file data (by treating the file as a memory array).

This is done by having the system allocate memory as part of a *named shared memory object*, which can be opened by name by another process, which will be given a *handle* on the object.[25] Once that handle has been made available, other applications can access it—provided they have the necessary permissions from the security object manager. Synchronization objects are provided so that even on a multiprocessor system two applications will not access the same memory location at the same time. Windows NT also provides a wide range of client/server mechanisms other than shared memory for the interaction of programs.

This brings up the final issue of memory management with Windows NT—security. Windows NT registers handles to named shared memory objects in the security object manager—which verifies whether programs requesting access to those objects have the privileges necessary to access it.

The implications of the memory management subsystem for network applications are a substantially more reliable base upon which to run applications, particularly client/server applications. The memory mapping scheme frees Windows NT from concerns about what happens when the physical memory becomes inadequate, provides an automatic mechanism for the protection of applications from interference with one another, and provides an effective mechanism for single servers to perform multiple tasks. It also provides a powerful base upon which to build sophisticated client/server applications, and it does so with great attention to security. That's a pretty effective combination.

Built-In Networking

As we've seen, every subsystem in Windows NT has been designed with connectivity and networking in mind. This is true of other operating systems as well, particularly OS/2 (in which much of the same low-level infrastructure we have discussed here is provided). But Windows NT goes a step further: It provides built-in networking features that go beyond anything packaged with any other operating system. The NEXTstep operating system comes close—but even it doesn't quite match what is provided with Windows NT.

When Windows NT 3.1 was introduced, it brought with it networking which was widely described as a "superset of Windows for Workgroups peer networking"—that is, peer-level file and printer sharing. An unlimited number of simultaneous connections was supported, irrespective of whether the base

---

25. *Handles* are identifiers that are used to manipulate objects—including files, memory locations, devices, and the like.

NT 3.1 product or the more sophisticated NT Advanced Server (NTAS) 3.1 was used (though only the latter provided the tools required to effectively manage large multiserver networks). As a result, the first edition of this book contained a long-winded discussion of when and why to use NTAS instead of NT (among other things, we recommended using NT as a file server on most smaller LANs).

Beginning with Windows NT 3.5, Microsoft changed the rules. The base product, now renamed *Windows NT Workstation*, supports a maximum of ten simultanous connections for file and printer sharing.[26] This renders it unusable as a server on all but the smallest LANs. NTAS, renamed *Windows NT Server*, continues to support an unlimited number of users—and supports basic NT-style *workgroups* as well as multiserver *domains*. As a result, we now recommend using only NT Server where a file and print server is required.

Windows NT Workstation

Adding *Workstation* to the low-end product's name marks two significant changes: the introduction of real workstation features in NT, and a much clearer distinction of what distinguishes a workstation (or advanced desktop) system from a server.

To compete with UNIX as a workstation platform, Microsoft added OpenGL graphics to Windows NT. OpenGL provides fast 3D rendering with shading, textures, and light source position handled automatically. Unlike the original NT base product, in which OpenGL support was available only as an add-on from Intergraph Corp,[27] Windows NT Workstation has OpenGL support built in at the kernel level. As a result—provided fast graphics hardware is available—it really does compete with UNIX workstations in performance, and typically does so for a much lower cost.

Moreover, as hardware accelerators for OpenGL appear (Intergraph sells several models for use with their systems, and more are coming from other manufacturers), Windows NT Workstations will provide performance equal to (or better than!) the most highly optimized UNIX workstations (for examples of NT's penetration in the heretofore UNIX-dominated Workstation realm, see Chapter 11).

---

26. The resulting *ten connection limit* has not been popular with Windows NT users—or with members of the NT development team (though statements by Dave Cutler to the effect that "There's no difference in the NT Server and Workstation Code" are a mite execessive). What NT Workstation gives up in its connection limit is more than made up for desktop users by its desktop-optimized memory tuning, and by incorporation of true workstation features, such as OpenGL 3D graphics (the latter is available on NT Server as well).

27. The company that originated the RISC-based UNIX graphical desktop workstation in 1984—and has now converted its product line to Windows NT on Intel-based systems. Intergraph sells several such systems, along with a vast range of technical workstation software and UNIX compatibility tools for NT. They're located in Huntsville AL, and can be contacted at 608-273-6585.

Aside from providing high-performance 3D graphics, Microsoft took several other steps to optimize NT Workstation as a desktop platform—in particular, NT Workstation's memory footprint was reduced significantly. Several steps that were taken to do this—such as reducing the overhead in NT's object storage, and using a different optimization when compiling the NT kernel—also benefit NT Server; but there's one obvious step that could have been taken to further shrink the operating system—removing all network server functionality from the Workstation version.

Microsoft chose not to do this. Workstations aren't servers, but they're often *used* as servers—particularly in UNIX environments, where X Windows distributed applications are run across a range of machines. After considerable debate, Microsoft decided to keep file-and-print server functionality in NT Workstation, but limited it to a maximum of ten concurrent connections.

What about people who used Windows NT 3.1 as a server in small networks? In the first edition of *Networking Windows NT* I flatly recommended that people running a simple single-server LAN buy NT 3.1 rather than NTAS, because it was cheaper and easier to install. Did the ten-connection limit leave those users out in the cold?

No. Microsoft wisely provided an alternative for users upgrading from the Windows NT 3.1 base product—those using NT mainly as a desktop environment could upgrade to NT Workstation for $99. Those using it as a server could upgrade to Windows NT Server for $149—which included licenses for 20 client connections (about which we'll learn more shortly), which brings us to the other version of Windows NT.

Windows NT Server

Just as workstations aren't optimized for file-and-printer sharing, server products aren't ideal for high-performance desktop applications. Since NT Server isn't expected to be used as a workstation, it doesn't have to make compromises—so, for instance, it doesn't automatically load DOS/Windows VDM support (as NT Workstation does in order to improve 16-bit application startup speed). NT Server also has a different lazy write algorithm on its disk cache, stores its file-and-printer sharing code in nonpageable memory, allocates more threads to system services, and provides additional performance tuning options (see Chapter 5)—all of which improve its server performance

The NT Server console can still be used as an application platform—so the option to use Windows NT as a nondedicated server on small networks is preserved—but such a system won't deliver the performance of an NT workstation.[28]

---

28. You can compensate for this to a large extent by adding additional RAM—8 to 16MB more than would otherwise be used in a server configuration will generally limit swapping and give desktop

In short, if you want to run NT as a server—get NT Server not NT Workstation.

Windows NT Server Networking

Windows NT Server provides a more sophisticated variant of the networking features that are built into Windows NT Workstation. It delivers domain-wide administration capability—important because the one great limitation of the built-in peer networking in Windows NT Workstation is that each system has to maintain its own database of user accounts. Let's say that you want to share files from your machine with one other person in your office but not with the entire office. If you want to share files with everybody in the office, it's pretty simple. You open up the File Manager, click on the directory you want to share, and you will then see a display for file permissions. You select *everyone* as having *full access*, and there you are.

The trouble with that approach is it really does mean *everyone*.[29] Everyone sitting on a Windows NT, Windows for Workgroups, or LAN Manager-compatible system connected to yours is going to see every file in the shared directory. If that directory is the accounting database, you probably did not want to select everyone and full access rights. If you want to select *limited access* rights, just to provide access to one person for example, then you must create a user account for that person on your computer. This is done using User Manager (see Chapter 4 for details). Once you've created an account for that person, you can select everyone as having *no access* rights but then override that by assigning full access rights to the boss.[30]

There are variants on the full-access and no-access privileges. You can provide *read only* access rights. This is a powerful capability that goes well beyond the security features provided with most peer-to-peer networking systems. The one problem with it is that you have to set the access rights on your computer—and I have to on my computer—and the fellow down the hall has to do it to his computer. There is no central administration and no provision for a global user account that would apply to all of the systems. That could prove to be a substantial burden if 50 different people need access to your system and all of them require separate access rights—some of the people have accounting access, and some of them do not; and some of them have access to your tape

---

performance that's almost indistinguishable from that of an NT Workstation. It's also possible to force a server to preload WOW with a registry setting—though this will be a waste of RAM unless 16-bit applications are being run. See Chapter 5 for details.

29. Provided the built-in guest account is enabled (on NT Servers it's disabled by default to prevent exactly this sort of security problem). With guest disabled, giving *everyone* full access means that all users *with valid accounts* are authorised to access the resource in question.

30. Actually, this is redundant; if you omit everyone/no access, you get the same result.

drive to perform backup operations, and others do not. The system is technically capable of supporting that many users but you as an individual Windows NT user probably are not.

By providing *domain-wide* administration, Windows NT Server gets around this problem. In an administrative domain the user has an account that applies on all servers in the domain. This is a far better approach to dealing with the kind of 50-user/50-different-access-rights scenario just described.

Windows NT Server also has more sophisticated versions of some of the basic Windows NT services. For instance, the remote access service that allows a single user to dial into to any Windows NT system is upgraded to a multiuser Remote Access Service (RAS) that allows many users to dial into a Windows NT Server domain. The Windows NT Server also provides access capabilities to Macintosh computers.

The resulting combination of features—Domain administration, Macintosh file system support, multiuser RAS—combined with the extremely powerful basic Windows NT feature set makes it possible to construct very complex (and powerful) *enterprise networks* using Windows NT (see Figure 1.7). We will now briefly examine each of these features (for more details, see Chapter 7).

Domain Administration

Windows NT Workstation *can* function as a file server—and does whenever you use the File Manager to share a directory. It can also share printers and in principle it can share other devices—so it is a server and a very powerful one. It does, however, have two serious limitations. First of all, as noted earlier, it's limited to *ten* simultaneous file and printer connections—so it's a usable server only on very small networks. Second, the user accounts created for a Windows NT Workstation extend only to that particular machine (an approach called *Workgroup Security*). Suppose you have a network with two file servers, one of which is used for accounting information and the other for sales information. Obviously, salesmen have accounts only on the sales computer, and accountants have accounts only on the accounting computer. But what about a corporate manager who has an urgent need for access to both? In a basic Windows NT Workgroup the only way to accomplish this is to give that administrator two accounts, one for each server. Now the administrator can have the same account name and password on both servers and this will make his life simpler. But life becomes complicated for a system administrator asked to maintain such a system, because anytime passwords are changed or accounts are changed he has to change the account database information individually on each server on the network.

Worse, because Windows NT Workstation is not designed to be administered remotely, the system administrator has to go to each individual server to perform these changes in the account database. This is the basic limitation of

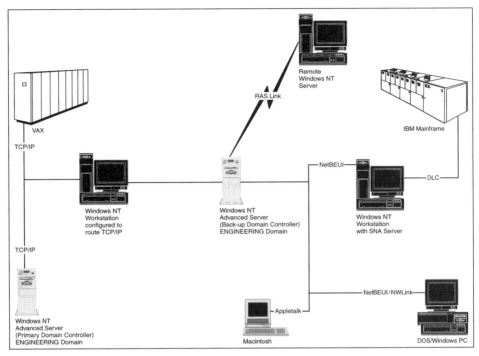

Figure 1.7 Enterprise network diagram.

Windows NT's built-in networking functions include: NetBEUI workgroup-type network-ing to local workstations and servers; routable TCP/IP networking for the enterprise; Remote Access Services (RAS) for connecting remote machines over telephone, X.25, and ISDN lines; NetWare-compatible NWLink networking for application servers; and (in the Windows NT Server) AppleTalk and Macintosh File System support. An add-on product (SNA Server for Windows NT) exploits the built-in Data Link Control (DLC) protocol to provide connectivity to IBM mainframes. Not shown are an array of built-in printer support functions that include print pooling, network printer support, and (in the Windows NT Server) PostScript printer emulation.

Windows NT Workstation-based networking. It cannot be centrally adminis-tered.

Windows NT Server changes this situation by introducing the concept of *domain-based security*. A domain is an arbitrary group of Windows NT Servers. At least one of these servers, however, will be designated as a domain controller. There may be more than one. Domain controllers maintain a central user account database that applies to all servers within the domain. The effect of this is dramatic from the point of view of a system administrator, and it is even convenient from the standpoint of end users. Each end-user needs only a single account, which can provide privileges as required to any server within the domain. Indeed, because of the unique Windows NT Server feature called *interdomain trust,* it is possible for a single user account to have privileges spanning many domains. This concept, one of the most powerful that Windows NT Server has introduced, is called a *Single Enterprise Logon,* which we will return to in Chapter 7.

Administrative User Profiles

Just having the ability to create domain-wide user accounts is a big advantage, of course. But Windows NT Server goes further by allowing administrators to define *user profiles* that span all servers on the network. The user profile determines which servers a user has access to, which workstations he may log in from, and what time(s) of day he may log in; it even allows an administrator to determine which Program Groups are displayed by Windows NT's Program Manager. This capability, used alone or in conjunction with Windows NT's powerful log-in scripts, allows tremendous administrative control, making Windows NT Server (with Domain Security enabled) your best choice for all but the most limited Windows NT installations.

Directory Replication

Another feature Windows NT Server adds is the ability to replicate directory tree structures from one server to another. This is useful on large networks to allow users to get logged in and access network-wide services without having to wait for a response from a particular server—and it can be a boon to administrators who need to provide copies of material (such as corporate standard documents) that changes regularly.

Fault Tolerance

Though modern off-the-shelf PC hardware is acceptable for a broad range of applications, including basic network servers up to the departmental level, when you consider enterprise services for mission-critical applications—situations in which file servers simply must not go down—support for fault-tolerant hardware becomes essential. Windows NT Server approaches fault tolerance by providing redundancy at the weakest points of PC hardware and software—mass data storage, generally in the hard disk. Windows NT Server achieves this redundancy through the transaction-logging features of NTFS—which assures that short of a hardware failure, the disk *structure* (but not necessarily the data) can be recovered; either alone or in conjunction with conventional redundant data storage techniques: mirrored disk partitions, disk duplexing, and RAID5 mass storage.

NTFS—A Recoverable File System

In the first place, NT provides a file system that's designed to be proof against anything short of a physical head crash. Along with its other features (per-file security, long file names, support for large media, etc.), NTFS is a *recoverable* file system. Operations on an NTFS disk are treated as transactions and are logged—redundantly—in a special log file. On bootup, the NTFS driver examines this log file, determines if any transactions are incomplete, and *rolls back* incomplete transactions from the disk.[31] This assures that after bootup, an NTFS device will always be in a known state, but it does *not* assure that the data will be written to disk—when a transaction is rolled back, any data associated with it is lost. To assure data integrity, it's necessary to use one of NT's data redundancy techniques.

Mirroring

The easiest of these concepts to understand is the concept of *partition mirroring*. In a mirrored disk environment, Windows NT Server maintains two images of the data for a particular disk. It does this on two separate disk partitions coupled to a single controller. The first drive, called the *primary partition*, receives data just as it otherwise would. The second partition, called the *mirror*, receives a backup copy of the primary's data. Windows NT Server then performs a comparison to verify that the data written to the two partitions matches. If it does, Windows NT Server assumes that the data is correct. If the data does not match, Windows NT Server can consult parity information to determine which set of data is correct. The result is a mirrored disk drive—and it is about as reliable as you can get, short of duplicating the disk controllers altogether.

Duplex Drives

This provides a level of redundancy beyond that of the mirrored disk drives and it is done in the simplest possible way. Two physical disks and two disk controllers are used. Windows NT Server writes all information twice using the two different controllers. Again, a comparison is done every time disk information is read, and this can exact a significant performance impact, as two separate disk controllers have to be accessed over and above the overhead of accessing the two drives. But it does provide an additional degree of redundancy in case of extreme failure conditions. Both drive duplexing and disk mirroring are covered in Chapter 3.

---

31. If this terminology sounds more like a database than a file system, then you're paying attention—and you'll find the much ballyhooed *Object File System (OFS)* of Windows NT "Cairo" that much easier to understand!

Stripe Sets and RAID5

Traditional methods of achieving redundancy in mass storage such as drive duplexing and disk mirroring exact a performance penalty on servers that use them. The operating system simply has to do more work, since data has to be written twice. In parallel with and to a certain extent competing with this has been a move to a new technology for creating very large disk spaces. This technology is called RAID, which stands for Redundant Array of Inexpensive Disks. The concept is very simple. Instead of buying a single 2-gigabyte disk drive, why not buy ten 200MB disk drives and drive them all in parallel? You achieve a number of advantages this way.

Small volume drives are often cheaper. While this economy can be lost when initially buying many small drives (a 2-gigabyte disk pack built on RAID principles is likely to cost more than a single 2-gigabyte disk drive), there is one overwhelming advantage—the hardware is redundant. A failure in one of the disk drives can lose, at most, one-tenth of the overall data. And the replacement cost of one small disk drive will be much less than the cost of replacing a 2-gigabyte drive. It is a very attractive proposition. It has one other great advantage—vastly increased performance.

When a RAID drive is accessed, data is *striped* across all of the disks. That is, parts of a sector are written on drive one, parts on drive two, parts on drive three, and so forth. In a RAID5 drive, data is validated by having parity information written to one of the disks. That parity information is vital, because the one great problem with a RAID drive is, What do you do when you have a disk error? Requiring data to be written simultaneously on ten disk drives means that ten times the hardware is involved, making failures ten times as likely. So, in a RAID environment, reliability and performance trade off.

RAID5 combines the advantages of performance and data redundancy. The redundancy in this case does come with a price. In a mirrored or duplexed disk drive situation, recovering from a disk failure is simple—just remove and replace the disk mirror or the duplex disk drive at fault, and copy the data from the intact partition or disk drive (simply disabling the mirroring on a mirrored partition or reverting from drive duplexing to a single drive will also let you continue to operate, but you risk losing all data because redundancy is gone). In any case, restoring data is a very quick process.

In a RAID5 drive, data restoration is a slower process because the data must be reconstructed from the parity information. However, since parity information represents total redundancy across all drives connected, short of simultaneous failure on two drives, RAID5 data is completely redundant. This combines the ultimate in protection with very high disk performance, the penalties being expensive hardware and slow restoration of redundant data in the event a write error occurs. Because of the requirement to drive many hard disks in parallel, RAID5 support is usually achieved with a high-speed SCSI disk controller and multiple SCSI hard disks. Windows NT Server can provide RAID5 support with from three to nine disk drives or partitions.

Remote Access Services

Like Macintosh file system support, Remote Access Services (RAS) is an added-cost LAN Manager feature which is a built-in feature of both Windows NT Workstation and Server. Remote Access Services amounts to a technique for providing dial-in access (through modems and phone lines or special-purpose X.25 and ISDN interfaces), which, aside from the reduced data rate, is not visibly different than logging directly into the server over a normal network connection. RAS is well suited to copying small data files, such as text files. It is ill suited to remote execution of networked programs or to transmission of a large data file, such as PostScript bitmaps or the like.

A single-user RAS implementation is provided in Windows NT Workstation, and Microsoft has similar software available for DOS and Windows clients. Windows NT Server provides a more sophisticated version, capable of supporting up to 256 remote workstations at each server.[32] Further details on Remote Access Services (and other forms of Wide Area Networking) may be found in Chapter 7.

Macintosh File System Support

As mentioned earlier, Macintosh support has been a feature available for LAN Manager since version 2.1—but it has always been an extra-cost item. Windows NT Server includes Macintosh file system support at no additional cost. That's significant because the Macintosh does represent a significant proportion of the installed base of networking personal computers, and because bridging requirements in connecting Macintosh computers into conventional networks have generally been high. Windows NT Server exploits NTFS to provide Macintoshes what amounts to a native filespace, while making that space available to DOS, Windows, OS/2, and Windows NT clients at the same time. For more details, see Chapter 7.

Other NT Server Features

Beginning with version 3.5, Microsoft enhanced NT Server to include a range of new features. Chief among these was a completely rewritten TCP/IP stack featuring Dynamic Host Configuration Protocol (DHCP), Windows Internet

---

32. In NT Server 3.5. NTAS 3.1 supported only 64 simultaneous RAS users—and RAS in 3.1 was generally much less capable.

Name Service (WINS), and UNIX-compatible line printer support (see Chapter 6 for details on TCP/IP)—followed by a range of TCP/IP-compatible Internet services in the NT 3.5 Resource Kit (see Appendix 4 for Resource Kit information). NT Server 3.5 also gained migration tools for NetWare, and a Gateway Server for NetWare service. This was followed by full NetWare 3.12-compatible server emulation, called File and Print services for NetWare (FPNW),[33] made available for NT 3.51 (see Chapter 9 for details on NetWare support).

Do You Need Windows NT Server?

Windows NT Server's many advanced features make it sound like an extremely attractive package. And indeed it is. But there is a price to be paid for all of these features—literally. As of this writing, Windows NT Workstation is *estimated retail priced* at $319.[34] That price buys one NT Workstation capable of supporting up to ten clients for file and print services. The equivalent price for NT Server—currently $700—includes no client licenses. Those are extra and start at about $30 each. This split model, in which there are two license fees—one per-server and another per-client—is a concept Microsoft refers to as an *information access* license.

Information Access Licensing

In NT 3.1, Microsoft took a very bullish positioning on licensing—it was per-server, period. NTAS 3.1 had a list price of $2,995. Users never paid that much, because Microsoft introduced it at a "promotional price" of $1,495, which never went up. As part of the promotion, they gave away the client software for free—you could download it from CompuServe or by FTP from Microsoft's FTP site. That was a great deal—especially compared with NetWare, which is traditionally licensed to a certain number of users per server.

With the introduction of Windows NT Server 3.5, Microsoft moved to an *information access license.* In this model, there are two licenses, one for the server itself—which can service an arbitrary number of clients—and another for client access to an arbitrary number of servers. For NT Server 3.5, the estimated retail prices (Microsoft no longer gives out list prices) on introduction was $700 per server, and $35 per client.

This model *seems* similar—at first glance—to the traditional up-to-a-given-number-of-clients licensing scheme used by Novell for NetWare, and by Microsoft in earlier networking products. It isn't—in that model, if you had 100

---

33. In beta as this was written—so the name may have changed by the time you read it. (Microsoft makes life exciting for authors by changing product names on a regular basis!)

34. Microsoft no longer publishes "list" prices.

users and two servers, you bought two 100-user licenses. If you added a server, you'd need to add it with another 100-client license. In the *information access* model, you buy two server licenses, and 100 client licenses. Since the client licenses authorize access to any number of servers, adding a server doesn't require adding client licenses.

This model is a bit complicated to understand at first, but is actually a bargain for many network administrators. To date, Microsoft has priced its licenses so competitively that in a worst-case scenario—where you have just one server and thousands of clients—the price is competitive with other network operating systems. In more realistic scenarios, with a lower client-to-server ratio, the information access scheme provides much lower average cost, because the server licenses are inexpensive.

The one problem with information access licensing is the necessity to have a client license, which would render NT useless as a disconnected operating system for internet use. Microsoft has recognized this, initially excepting FTP internet access from the client licensing requirements. With NT 3.51, a *concurrent connections* license option was added, in which the server may be licensed for a given maximum number of concurrent connections, with the client not requiring a license for server access. This allows you, for example, to buy a 20-user license to a given server, and make it available to hundreds of users— provided no more than 20 are logged in at any given time. The decision to use concurrent licensing as opposed to per-client information access licensing is made at the time the server is installed, and is covered in more detail in Chapter 2.

Obviously, it's a lot less expensive to use NT Workstation than NT Server—if you can. To help make the decision, here's a list of the features NT Server includes that NT Workstation lacks:

- ❑ Support for more than ten simultaneous file- and print-share connections
- ❑ Single User Accounts that Span Multiple Servers
- ❑ Administrative User Profiles
- ❑ Directory Replication
- ❑ Fault-tolerant Disk Support
- ❑ Macintosh File System Support
- ❑ Multiuser Remote Access Service
- ❑ Advanced TCP/IP Support (DHCP, WINS, etc.)
- ❑ Advanced NetWare Support (GSNW, Migration Tool, FPNW-compatible)
- ❑ Upgrade from LAN Manager 2.*x* available

If you need any of the above features, then you have no choice—Windows NT Server is your operating system. Windows NT Server is also important because of one other significant factor—it's the platform for Microsoft's *Back Office* server suite.

Microsoft Back Office

There is a larger element to all this. Microsoft is applying the NT Server information access license scheme to its entire server-based product line: SQL Server, SNA Server, Systems Management Server, and NT-based versions of MS Mail all carry information access licenses, and are available bundled in a suite called Microsoft Back Office.

Before the Back Office announcement, Microsoft had at least four different models in place for client licensing of server-based software: NTAS 3.1 was licensed per server with unlimited clients; SQL Server had a NetWare-style per-client license; SNA Server was licensed per connection, and MS-Mail had separate per-server and per-client prices (rather like the new information access model). This was something of a nightmare for both Microsoft and network managers.

Under the new policy, there's a much simpler approach: If a client needs access to file-and-print services from NT Servers, you buy the appropriate license. If the same client needs SQL Server access, that's another license, and so on. Note that these are per-client licenses, independant of which server (or how many) the client is accessing. And, as with NT Server, there aren't any hard-coded limits you have to worry about. When you add your 201st user, you need to buy your 201st client kit—not a new box of server software.

Of course, just as with NT Server, not all users are happy with information access licensing, so Microsoft has recently begun offering *concurrent connection* licensing for Back Office products. This is particularly important for products like SMS and SNA Server, in which you might well have a single server with hundreds (even thousands) of clients—if you can live with only a limited number of those clients having simultaneous access to the server, a concurrent connection license may well be cheaper.

Aside from a common licensing model, all applications in the Back Office bundle share a common Windows NT-based architecture, user interface, and administrative options.[35] The applications are available either separately or as a unified suite that includes all the component applications.

Back Office is bundled by several server manufacturers, among them AT&T GIS and Motorola, on high-end NT Server systems. Whether the economics of

---

35. The current (1995) version of MS Mail is a rather glaring exception. See Chapter 7 for details.

Table 1.1 Back Office Requirements/Pricing (as of March 1995)

Server Component	Server RAM	Server Disk	Price (per server)	Price (per client)**
NT Server 3.5	16MB	90MB	$699	$29.95
SQL Server 4.21a	16+MB	30+MB	$999	$119.00
SMS 1.0	28MB	100MB	$649	$54.95
SNA Server	20MB	11MB	$409*	$64.95
MS Mail 3.2***	n/a***	n/a***	$469*	$44.95
Complete Package	32MB	231+MB	$2,199	$239.00

*Workgroup editions of these packages are also available at lower cost. Educational discounts may also apply on some packages.

**Single-client prices. Quantity discounts also available. The same prices apply for concurrent connection licensing—see text for details.

***Pricing listed is for the obsolete OS/2-based version. No NT-based E-mail server was available from Microsoft as this was written. An NT-hosted version (MS Mail 3.5) is expected to ship in the summer of 1995.

selling several software products in a single package will prove as compelling on servers as on desktop systems remains to be seen.

System Requirements

In addition to the higher price for the Windows NT Server, you need to bear in mind that the system requirements for Windows NT Server exceed those of Windows NT Workstation. See Chapter 2 for detailed information.

NT Server Limitations

NT Server does have some limitations when operated in extremely large installations. While a limited directory replication service is built into the product, it replicates only user accounts and selected read-only data, such as log-in scripts. Scalability is currently limited to a maximum of 16 CPUs per server, and in real applications a practical limit is currently nearer 6 to 8 CPUs. There is also currently no support for clustering, and in any case, NT lacks the kind of per-user charge-back accounting and quota enforcement software that's essential in "glasshouse" operations.[36] David Cutler, the ex-Digital software architect who designed NT, has said that it won't be ready to operate as a full-scale mainframe replacement for "two years or so"; and while there are some who think otherwise (National Westminster Bank, for one, is moving to NT as a standard platform corporation-wide), we're inclined to agree with his assessment.

Other Networks

While the built-in networking features of Windows NT are quite sophisticated, they have one basic problem. They are proprietary to Microsoft and, therefore, while they will interact beautifully with other NT systems and with Windows for Workgroups systems (as well as easier Microsoft networks such as LAN Manager), they aren't designed to interoperate with Novell NetWare or other third-party networks. Microsoft has, however, provided a mechanism that makes it relatively easy to provide additional networking services in Windows NT. While Microsoft certainly would not object to dominating the PC local area networking business, they realize that they do not (nor are they likely to in the foreseeable future), so a powerful mechanism has been provided in Windows NT for after-market networking products compatible with other networking systems.

This compatibility depends, first of all, upon the layered device driver model and the treatment of networks as a file system that we described earlier, and also upon two new levels of interface that are built into Windows NT at the device driver level: The Network Device Interface Specification (NDIS), which is the way that network device drivers for Windows NT are built; and above that, the Transport Driver Interface (TDI), which provides a direct link between all redirectors or network file systems and the network transport drivers.

A network provider who wishes to provide a redirector for Windows NT needs only to write an installable file system to provide services on that network and a transport driver for the type of networking protocol that's in use (such as IPX/SPX on NetWare, NBF on NT native networks, or TCP/IP on UNIX systems).[37] There is no necessity to write drivers for the specific network cards, as NDIS can provide this. It's necessary to write only the other components. There is an option to write conventional monolithic network card drivers—and there is evidence that some network manufacturers are going to do so—in particular, Novell's NetWare Client director for NT includes Open Datalink Interface (ODI) drivers.

---

36. Third parties are working on some of these problems—see Chapter 7 for details.

37. See Appendix 2 for details on protocols and device drivers.

By doing this, Novell bypassed the various layers of the NT subsystem below the redirector. Instead of the redirector behaving like a file system, communicating with the I/O manager, then communicating with a transport driver through the transport driver interface and in turn to a network card via NDIS; in the NetWare system, the NetWare redirector communicates directly with the ODI subsystem, which communicates with an ODI driver. There are a couple of theoretical advantages to this monolithic approach. First of all, it's faster. The overhead involved in the multilayered interface used by the Windows NT native networking is eliminated. There are reports that the ODI-based Windows NT redirector is significantly faster than the built-in NT networking on the same network hardware. It's also true that this kind of approach simplifies matters for a company like Novell, which has a lot of internal expertise built up in a system like ODI and can leverage this to quickly provide services for systems such as Windows NT if they move the entire system over.

Unfortunately, this created a situation in which Windows NT users who required NetWare support would have to deal with two completely different types of network drivers. Because Novell persisted in using this nonstandard approach, Microsoft introduced its own Client Services for NetWare (CSNW) for NT Workstations, Gateway Services for NetWare (GSNW) and NetWare migration tool for NT Servers, and has File and Print services for NetWare (FPNW) in beta for NT Servers, as this is written. All are described in Chapter 9.

TCP/IP Services

In addition to the native LAN Manager-compatible networking built into Windows NT, a second kind of networking is built in: TCP/IP services of the type used by UNIX systems. Now this gets a little complicated, because one can refer to a couple of different things when one refers to TCP/IP. On one hand TCP/IP is a transport. And there is a TCP/IP transport driver which is fully compatible with the built-in networking system. If you wish, you can run TCP/IP networking instead of NetBEUI-based networking—and if you're running a large network, you'll want to. See Chapter 6 and Appendix 2 for details.

UNIX systems also use TCP/IP, but most do not use the LAN Manager Universal Naming Convention (UNC) interfaces that are used by Windows NT, nor the NetBIOS protocols on which they're based. So simply installing the TCP/IP transport to Windows NT will not immediately give you connectivity to UNIX systems. What will give you connectivity to UNIX systems are the low-level TCP/IP utilities (ping.exe, ftp.exe, etc.), which provide essentially native UNIX-style TCP/IP services. Windows NT lacks a Network File Services (NFS) file system and other facilities that would make this a complete end-to-end system (though such products are available from third parties—see Chapter 10).[38] NT Server 3.5 augmented these basic features with some exciting new ones, as already mentioned—and the NT 3.5 resource kit added a variety of internet tools, including World Wide Web, Gopher, WAIS, and DNS servers (see Chapter 6 for further details on TCP/IP support, and Appendix 4 for resource kit information).

Summing Up

The basic system features of Windows NT have been developed with connectivity in mind. From a client/server design that supports symmetric multiprocessing for very large servers to built-in networking and a file system designed to support very large volumes; virtually every element of Windows NT incorporates some feature that makes networking easier. Truly, this is an operating system *designed* to connect.

For More Information

Custer, Helen (1993), *Inside Windows NT.* Redmond WA: Microsoft Press, ISBN: 1-55615-481-X. Outstanding (and detailed) general coverage of the Windows NT architecture. Chapter 6 (on NT's networking features) is especially valuable.

Custer, Helen (1995), *Inside the Windows NT File System.* Redmond WA: Microsoft Press, ISBN: 1-55615-660-X. Thin but necessary volume that adds vital file system information to the original *Inside Windows NT.* Custer is one of the original refugees from Digital that Dave Cutler brought with him to Microsoft—and her work in documenting the system as it's being developed has been a vital factor in its success.

Microsoft Staff (1995), *Windows NT Resource Kit.* Redmond WA: Microsoft Press, ISBN: 1-55615-655-3, -654-5, -653-7, -656-1. Detailed coverage of all aspects of Windows NT operation. An essential reference for all Windows NT system administrators. Volume 2 (*Windows NT Networking Guide*) is particularly useful, containing information available nowhere else—including in this book. (Though there are *some* things better covered here!)

Zachary, G. Pascal (1994), *Showstopper!* New York: The Free Press (A division of MacMillan, Inc.), ISBN: 0-02-9535671-7. An insightful often hilarious history of NT development, written by a *Wall Street Journal* reporter. Occasionally inaccurate (one of the principle characters covered in the book calls it "about two-thirds right," but well worth reading for the flavor of how and why NT became what it is—and why its future is certain to be as unpredictable as its past.

---

38. Though this is available from third parties—see Chapter 10.

Cringely, Robert X. (1992), *Accidental Empires*. New York: Harper Business (A division of Harper Collins), ISBN: 0-88730-621-7. Biting—but generally accurate—history of the personal computer industry. The NT coverage here is limited (the book was published before NT 3.1 shipped), but the history leading up to its release—as a Windows operating system rather than an advanced version of OS/2—is excellent, as is Cringely's brilliant yet simple explanation of such esoteric topics as why computer performance changes so quickly (Moore's Law). *If you read only one of the additional books referenced in this work, read this one!*

CHAPTER 2

Preparing to Connect

Windows NT Installation

When you have finished reading this chapter, you should understand:

❑ **How to conduct a network-needs analysis**

❑ **How to select and organize components for a Windows NT network**

❑ **The Windows NT installation process**

❑ **How to install Windows NT over a network**

❑ **What the most common installation problems are, and how to work around them**

You should feel comfortable installing and configuring Windows NT Workstations and stand-alone servers. You should *not* feel *comfortable* about assuming responsibility for the planning of a network on your own—but you should understand how to go about *becoming* comfortable with your particular network needs.

Before installing Windows NT—before you even purchase the software—you must first create a plan for your network. You should think of this plan as a network blueprint which, like an architect's blueprint for a building, must contain the information necessary to create a sturdy structure for many people to use on a regular basis.

The plan will be based on the data that you provide through a network-needs analysis for your particular business. The needs analysis is really a series of questions that you answer to provide yourself with the information you'll require when you create your network plan and set up your server. A network-needs analysis checklist follows. Use this as a guide when creating your network.

Your network blueprint will provide for more than just information about the access of the users; you'll also need to include information about the type of users and the work they'll be performing, the amount of storage space they'll require, and their hours of operation. This information will help you plan for the type of hardware that you'll need, and the amount of RAM and server storage, in addition to the reliability of the equipment you'll use for your server and network.

Conducting a Network-Needs Analysis

Network-Needs Analysis Checklist

- ❑ Goal statement
- ❑ Number of initial users
- ❑ Maximum number of expected users
- ❑ Type of work to be conducted
- ❑ Application requirements
- ❑ Estimated minimum storage requirements
- ❑ Hours of operation
- ❑ Building power
- ❑ Type of office space
- ❑ Uninterruptable power supply (UPS) required
- ❑ Level of reliability required
- ❑ Level of security required

Let's begin by looking at what you intend on doing with your network and server in the first place. To start with, you should be able to define the goal of your network in a couple of sentences. Your goal doesn't need to be complex, but it should be concrete and specific. For instance, "a way for my users all over the building to store their data" is not only vague, but if it were truly all you wanted in a network, you'd be wasting a lot of time installing such a powerful network operating system as Windows NT Server, when all you really wanted was some common data storage.

Your goal statement should be more specific to your particular business requirements, such as:

Goal: A method for the twelve-person accounting department to store and share billing and payable information, including a system of electronic mail and shared printers for printing checks, invoices, and correspondence, keeping in mind the demonstrated 20 percent annual increase in staffing of this department.

This goal is concrete and finite; it defines the purpose of the network and server, and outlines the specific functions that the network must provide. It also reminds us that the department will have increased needs in the future.

While conducting your network-needs analysis, you should plan for expansion and flexibility. It's often difficult to plan for the things you are sure about, and planning for the future may seem impossible; but you do have certain facts available to assist you. For example, you can look at the historic growth rate for your department and the amount of work you will be performing. You also need to take into account the cyclical nature of the department and business. In other words, you should be aware of when your peak work cycles occur. All of this information is important when creating your plan.

From this information, you can begin to assess the requirements of your network. While you conduct your network needs analysis, it's also important to include comments from your users. If you refer again to the network-needs analysis checklist, you'll see the general nature of the questions to ask.

This is the relatively simple part of creating your plan—asking and answering questions—but people often skip this step entirely. Sometimes they forget to include those who will be using the network, or they neglect to plan for future growth. Either mistake will create a problem later when the network has been purchased and installed. Better to spend a couple of days planning now than to spend many weeks later on, debating the need to purchase more hard disk storage. Enough lecturing—don't neglect your plan.

Planning the Physical Layout

Once you have collected the information you need, you can begin to blueprint your physical network. The physical location of all the cabling and equipment necessary for your network should be drafted on a layer over the building blueprint. When planning the physical layout, be as accurate as possible so that the correct amount of cabling will be purchased and network connections will be convenient for each workstation.

Blueprinting your network in a logical order (e.g., from the server out to the desktops and peripherals) will help you take into account all needed hardware. It will also highlight any problem areas that you need to be aware of while having cabling installed.

Server Location and Power Concerns

The server needs to be located in a spot that is at once accessible to the network administrator and inaccessible to daily office traffic. A well-ventilated storage closet that can be locked would serve the purpose. If your building is not air-conditioned, you may elect to purchase and install an air-conditioner for your server closet. You need to be sure that the server receives power from a different electrical circuit than the air-conditioner.

Speaking of power, you *must* have an uninterruptible power supply (UPS) for your server. Power failures are especially common during the summer months, when severe electrical storms and heavy electrical usage for building air-conditioning combine to create an atmosphere conducive to brownouts or blackouts. An unexpected power failure can wreak disaster on an unprotected server.

UPSs vary in their power ratings and features, but all provide the same basic functionality. A UPS is a DC battery source that sits between your server (or workstation) and your building's AC power, and uses building power to sustain its charge—usually enough to keep your server running through a proper shutdown cycle. Windows NT Server's built-in UPS device management monitors the power to your server and, in case of power failure, uses the UPS battery power to automatically and gracefully shut down server operations.

The Windows NT UPS control panel option lets you configure your server to work with UPS data received via one of the serial ports. When it receives data indicating the UPS has activated, an automated shutdown procedure executes. You can specify that a custom command file run prior to shutting down the system if your server has special requirements. Chapter 3 will give you more details about the UPS services for Windows NT.

Hub Location

As you plan your network hardware, working your way out from the server, you encounter a box called a Hub or LAN Concentrator. A hub provides a method for connecting all of your workstations, servers, and peripherals.

Let's look at one type of topology: 10 Mbps Ethernet over UTP (unshielded twisted pair), or 10BaseT. 10BaseT cabling connects your desktop systems in a star configuration to a hub, which can handle as few as four and as many as 1,024 (in theory) devices. However, most stackable hubs contain 12 or 24 ports and are then connected to other hubs via 10Base2 cabling or proprietary connectors, so you can expand your network. Larger hubs employ a chasis with a single shared backplane into which multiple cards containing EtherNet ports (and other standards) are mounted. EtherNet has a practical limit of 1,024 devices, including servers, that you can connect in this fashion. Don't try to exceed it! Plan for subnets, a series of smaller networks within your LAN, connected via bridges or routers.

Typically, 10BaseT hubs are located in the telephone service closets, where the wiring can be punched down onto a block and then wired to the hub. Your hub should be mounted in a rack for stability and placed in a ventilated area.

It should also be protected by a UPS, unless it has some type of on-board power management. Again, the location of these devices should be away from high-traffic areas in a place that can be locked.

Hardware Requirements and Considerations

Chapter 1 provided an overview of the advanced features and functionality of Windows NT. Before installing Windows NT on every workstation in an enterprise, it's wise to step back and evaluate just who does and does not need NT.

Do You Really Need Windows NT on Your Workstations?

The most important consideration is the hardware you'll need to run NT. Workstations need a minimum of 12MB, and servers need a minimum of 16MB.[1] Note the word *minimum*—systems that will make heavy use of multi-tasking or act as special-purpose servers will require more (as you will see in the next section). Further, if you are running on the Intel platform, do not consider NT unless you are running on 486 machines. On older or lower-end machines with smaller amounts of memory, use Windows for Workgroups or Windows 95. However, you also need to evaluate which features you *will* use, and those you *might* use, before making your decision.

For example, if you are working in a secure environment, such as a financial institution, NT's file sharing security, file access audit trails, and C2 security features might justify a move to NT. If security is not a high priority, a suitable workstation solution may be Windows for Workgroups (or Windows 95), since such systems can easily be connected as clients to a Windows NT server.

Furthermore, not all Windows applications can run under Windows NT. Applications that directly access hardware (such as some backup programs) cannot be run in NT, because that behavior violates NT's security model.

Another consideration when making the jump to NT is the availability of drivers for your current hardware. Driver support in the initial release of NT is limited in the area of peripherals, and developers have noted that writing drivers is much more difficult under NT. Thus, you may wish to consider which drivers are available and match them to your current hardware devices to ensure that you can in fact run your applications.

Having said all that, if you've decided certain people need to run Windows NT, then here's what they'll need:

---

1. As of this writing (March 1995). However, memory requirements have come down, and we have reason to believe that future versions of NT Workstation may run in less memory. Consult Microsoft's current Windows NT Workstation Evaluation Guide for up-to-date information.

Windows NT Hardware Requirements

Here's a consolidated list of requirements and recommendations that will allow you to select and configure an appropriate computer for operation as either a Windows NT Workstation or server. The recommended configurations are based on personal experience and the information published by Microsoft. We absolutely recommend that you consult the current published Windows NT specifications for further information.

The particular system configuration that you will use will be some combination of a central processor unit, RAM (including CPU cache RAM), hard disk capacity (or other mass storage space), backup device, CD-ROM, floppy disk, network card, and printer. There are also a variety of special devices, such as modems, multiport cards, and X.25 cards, that may be appropriate in certain special circumstances.

CPU

The basic Windows NT requirement published by Microsoft is a 25MHz 386 (series B2 or greater) or better Intel-compatible CPU, or an ARCsystem-compliant RISC computer (MIPS R4000 or better).[2] The situation for RISC computers in particular is in a state of flux; as of this writing we recommend that if you're investigating purchase of a RISC system (such as one of the DEC AXP series systems), you consult with the manufacturer for current specifications. Anyway, that's what Microsoft recommends. Now let's say a few words about what *we* recommend.

To understand why we will *not* recommend that you purchase a 386 system of *any* configuration for use with Windows NT, it's necessary to explain a bit about cache memory. All advanced CPUs (Intel 486SX or better, and all RISC) employ a CPU cache. It's simply a small amount of static RAM (SRAM) which is closely coupled to the central processing unit and which can exchange data with the central processor at speeds much higher than that of the normal Dynamic Random Access Memory (DRAM) used in most microcomputers. The reason for the use of the SRAM cache is speed. In order to operate at CPU speeds, SRAM caches have to have very high memory access speeds—for instance, a 50MHz CPU will require 20-nanosecond static RAM. However, if you call around to electronics suppliers you will find that 20-nanosecond static RAM is extremely expensive. More conventional DRAM, with access speeds on the order of 70 nanoseconds, is relatively cheap. Therefore, a two-tier approach, in which a small amount of very fast memory (SRAM) is connected directly to the processor, and then that very fast cache of memory is in turn refreshed from a

---

2. Advanced Resouce Computer (ARC)—part of the Advanced Computing Environment (ACE) initiative sponsored by Microsoft, MIPS, and others.

main memory (DRAM) that runs more slowly, tends to provide the most economical system construction while retaining high performance.

The problem with this approach is that Windows NT is a multithreaded preemptive multitasking system—with *much* larger cache memory requirements than a conventional single thread operating system, such as DOS or Novell NetWare. If you remember the discussion of preemptive multitasking in Chapter 1, one concept introduced was called the *working set*. That is the sum total of system processes that have to be continuously switched in and out of memory. The working set expands as you do more with the computer. A server computer is going to have a working set that's going to include the necessary threads to maintain each of its current connections. A workstation that is undertaking a number of graphical paths simultaneously will have multiple threads continuously switched in and out of the CPU for each of the tasks that it is performing. In order for a Windows NT system to operate at full efficiency you must equip it with enough cache RAM to maintain the entire working set in memory.

Microsoft has published no specifications on this subject, but experiments conducted by *WINDOWS Magazine* indicate that providing 256K—or more—of cache RAM will provide a substantial gain in performance and a nearly linear gain as the cache size is increased.[3] The Intel 486 series processors have an 8KB on-chip cache, and the Pentium processor has a 16KB on-chip cache. Neither even begins to approach the kind of cache sizes that give a real benefit in Windows NT—they're too small by a factor of ten![4] Providing 32K of cache RAM will improve matters, 64K will improve it even more, 128K gives an enormous improvement, and providing 256KB seems to be approximately the point at which the benefit tops out. Going upward from that to 512KB or even a megabyte will still provide an incremental improvement, but the percent improvement probably will not match the additional cost, where workstations are concerned.[5]

An exception to this situation might occur in technical workstations that are principally intended for compute-intensive tasks, such as computer aided design, computer aided engineering, advanced graphics (animation and rendering), or scientific computation—tasks generally performed by RISC worksta-

---

3. See "Enterprise Windows" in the August 1994 issue.

4. Intel's as yet unreleased P6 CPU, however, has 256KB of cache *on-chip*—perhaps a reflection of Microsoft's cooperation in its design!

5. Servers can—and will—benefit from even larger caches. Compaq has a three-tier memory architecture in their latest servers, and can equip such machines with 2MB of cache. Digital is using a similar approach with their most recent AXP servers, and employing such a cache allows a 200Mhz AlphaServer 1000 to actually outperfom a 275mhz AlphaStation 400—see the Windows NT 3.5 review in *WINDOWS Magazine*'s January and February 1994 issues, and the dicussion of RAM Cache in Appendix 5 for details.

tions. In these situations, going up to 512KB or even one megabyte of cache can provide a substantial benefit and, for this reason, we recommend that all RISC workstations be equipped with at least 512KB external cache, preferably a megabyte if it's available.

Since cache is critical to system performance, and 386 processors do not include any internal cache memory (and because the processors themselves are less efficient than their 486 counterparts), *we do not recommend that anyone purchase a 386 system to run Windows NT.* If you have an installed base of 386-based systems in your organization, you can use them as Windows NT Workstations (and perhaps as print servers), but you will not see high performance. Speed will benefit if you can upgrade the system to add CPU cache. However, the nature of most 386 motherboards is such that you probably won't be able to do this—so it's probably best to think about recycling 386 systems as DOS workstations, print servers, or for other applications that don't require high performance.

Memory[6]

Windows NT is a memory hog by DOS standards. It requires a stated minimum, according to Microsoft, of 12MB RAM. However, based upon experience in this and other configurations, we recommend that *all* Windows NT Workstations have a minimum of 16MB RAM (over and above the CPU cache). The small additional cost of the RAM more than pays off in improved performance.

These requirements seem excessive to people used to DOS systems that would require a megabyte or 2 megabytes, but it's worth noting that for Windows NT, strange as it may seem, 12 or 16 megabytes is just a starting point. That's significant because, as many users are beginning to find out, 16 megabytes or more in a DOS/Windows environment may present a practical upper limit. While it's perfectly possible to expand the memory in many current systems up to 32 megabytes, there are fundamental limits in both DOS and Windows that cannot be expanded upon simply by adding more memory.

A good example is Windows 3.1 *system resources*—128K, no more, no less, of system space reserved for two system memory heaps that contain common resource information used by Windows applications. If you run many applications together and exhaust that 128K of resource space, then your system will crash. It will not matter whether the system has 16MB, 32MB, or 100MB of

6. Please note that memory requirements are changing as this is written. Windows NT 3.1 really needed a minimum of 16MB on workstations, 24MB on servers—and didn't approach optimal performance until twice as much memory was provided. NT 3.5 cut those requirements considerably (NT's internal working set was cut by 4 to 6MB). Future versions of NT may reduce these requirements further—consult Microsoft's Windows NT Workstation and Server Evaluation Guides for up-to-date information.

memory. The system *will* crash. Windows NT, on the other hand, has no fundamental upper limits.[7] Beyond the basic 16MB recommendation, various Windows NT options may require additional memory.

Print Server Memory Requirements

If a Windows NT Server will be used to provide shared print services to other Windows NT Workstations, it will need an additional 4 or more megabytes of storage space to efficiently process remote print requests. This is needed because Windows NT employs a powerful new concept in that you need not install the print device driver for a particular printer on all workstations. Instead, when a Windows NT Workstation wishes to print, it will open up a dialog with the print server and transmit the low-level graphics commands to the print server, which will then perform the print formatting itself. This is easier to administer but it does mean that the print server has to carry out a significant portion of all print operations itself. In order to avoid a significant performance hit, the additional memory is required in print servers. Based upon examination of Microsoft documentation, it would appear that 4MB of memory will be sufficient to support up to about 6 printers. If more printers are to be supported in a *print pool*, it may be necessary to add additional memory.

Windows NT Server Memory Requirements

On windows, NT Server's additional memory will be required for a variety of services. The fault-tolerance driver will require approximately 2MB additional memory (consult the Microsoft documentation or your hardware supplier for details). If, in addition to fault tolerance, you employ RAID 5 support (stripe sets with parity), then an additional 4MB of memory will be necessary to support the overhead involved with RAID 5 (three times the regular memory requirement for disk writes in order to provide space for the necessary parity computations). Employing the Windows NT Server's multiuser Remote Access Services or Macintosh file system support will also incur an additional memory requirement (again, consult the latest Microsoft documentation for minimum requirements). Our own experience with operation of Windows NT Server on 32MB RISC-based and Intel-based platforms has been completely satisfactory; we believe this will be sufficient for most small to medium network file-and-printer sharing applications. Larger networks will require more memory.

If you intend to run additional server-based applications (the various Microsoft Back Office modules, database servers, etc.), you'll need additional

---

7. The practical limit set by the 32-bit address range employed by Windows NT is 4 gigabytes—4096MB of system memory. Moreover, NT's architecture could be modified to support 64-bit addresses in future versions if necessary.

RAM. Since the published minimum for all versions of NT Server to date is 16MB, you can determine the amount of additional memory required by subtracting 16MB from the application manufacturer's recommended minimum configuration. For example, Microsoft recommends 24MB as the minimum configuration for the Systems Management Server (SMS) component of Back Office. Subtraction yields 8MB—so add 8MB to these numbers to come up with a working minimum for an NT Server running SMS.

Running *all* the components of Microsoft Back Office on a single server (not a very good idea) would require at least 32MB RAM, around 500MB of hard disk—and you'd be well advised to use a Pentium or RISC processor.

Hard Disk Space

The official Microsoft requirement for Windows NT Workstation is 75MB of hard disk space, of which at least 20MB will be used for a paging file. For NT Server, the requirement is about 20MB greater. Now you begin to reach one of the most complex parts of the overall Windows NT equation, because that paging file can grow and the efficiency of the paging file will be higher if its initial size is set near to the size it will eventually expand to. This is something that can be found only by experiment and it is discussed in more detail in Chapter 5. However, as a practical consideration, given that the operating system itself takes about 50MB of hard disk space, another 20MB is a bare minimum requirement for the paging file, and this leaves no space for applications.

We recommend a bare minimum of 100MB hard disk space for Windows NT Workstations. Note that we say *Workstations*, and it's important to be very clear about this. If you are running Windows NT stations that are connected to a network, *and* if these stations get all of their applications support over the network and store little or nothing locally, then 100MB is probably sufficient. If you wish to use any local applications, need local storage space, or wish to operate the Windows NT system as a stand-alone workstation, then we think that the disk should be at least 200MB. Server requirements, of course, are higher—and you must provide additional space for the user files, and undoubtedly (over time) for a growing paging file.

A 200MB hard disk represents a practical minimum for a small to medium size server. You should add approximately 20MB for each user who will be logged into the system, more if you make little use of server resources in your configuration. In general, if the workstations are constrained in hard disk space, then you will need more server hard disk space, or vice versa. An example of a reasonable working minimum is about 1 gigabyte (1,024MB), which, based on our experience, appears to be sufficient space for a server that will service 20 to 30 users.

Besides the basic storage space requirements, there is another consideration that should be borne in mind when selecting a hard disk for a Windows NT system: the disk controller. Windows NT's preemptive multitasking, as discussed in Chapter 1, provides for a very powerful feature to improve performance: asynchronous I/O. To recap, the central processor can initiate an I/O request—for instance, a request to read information from a disk file—and continue to work on other tasks while it waits for the hard disk controller to inform it that the request is complete. However, this applies only if a hard disk controller is used that will allow the central processor to go on and perform its work. Very inexpensive, low-end IDE and other ST-506 interface hard disk controllers don't permit this—the CPU will have to perform the actual transfer of information into the controller, and while it's doing that, it can't do anything else (such systems are particularly ill behaved when used with NTFS compression on NT 3.51 or later). Therefore, performance of both Windows NT Workstations and Servers will be significantly enhanced if you select a better type of disk controller, such as SCSI.

For servers, if either disk striping or RAID 5 (disk striping with parity) support is desired, then the only practical choice is a SCSI disk controller, as only SCSI supports chaining of more than 2 to 3 disk drives. As a practical matter, for server operations with large hard disks, we consider SCSI to be the only practical choice.[8] Choices for workstations vary, depending on the expense. For high-performance workstations, we recommend that SCSI be looked at closely, especially given Windows NT's preference for SCSI-based CD-ROMs and tape drives (discussed a little bit later in this section). In servers, best performance will be achieved using intelligent disk controllers, which can carry out operations independently of the system's CPU.[9] Investigate the Windows NT hardware compatibility list and talk to the manufacturers of the systems that you're investigating as to what specific configurations are available. You probably won't want to risk selecting a hard disk controller or *any* component not listed on the NT hardware compatibility list unless you have actually seen this component demonstrated with a non-beta driver. Otherwise, you are asking for trouble.

Bus Architectures

As you might imagine from the foregoing discussion of CPU, memory, and hard disk capacities required for Windows NT, the system bus architecture becomes extremely significant with Windows NT, especially in a high-performance

8. This was written before the advent of ESDI... and we *still* consider SCSI to be the way to go.

9. However, beware of older intelligent controllers, which employ low-speed 186 CPUs. If the disk controller is served by a 4MHz 186, you can bank on it being a bottleneck!

configuration. There are currently three popular bus architectures, each with its own advantages and disadvantages. Here's a brief discussion of each.

ISA Bus

The most popular of today's bus architectures remains the Industry Standard Architecture (ISA) bus—that is, the original IBM AT bus as updated by today's cloners. (Curiously enough, ISA is not generally available from IBM!) The ISA bus in today's incarnation is a 16-bit bus architecture generally operating at a bus data rate of 8MHz. Memory is generally not available on the bus but instead is connected locally to the CPU and will operate at significantly higher speeds, typically 25MHz. There may or may not be a local bus connection between the CPU and the video card operating at higher speeds. If this is available, this should be investigated—particularly on workstations, as it can provide a significant performance enhancement.

The major advantage of the ISA bus architecture is cost. ISA bus machines are the popular PC clones that have made modern business computers a commodity item. The major disadvantage is that ISA combines a 16-bit bus bandwidth and an 8MHz data rate—yielding a functional maximum throughput of 16MB per second. Modern CPUs operate at 32-bit data widths and hundreds of MHz—producing overall throughput on the order of 16 times the ISA bus throughput or higher! As you might imagine, this can present something of a performance bottleneck, emphatically so for high-performance servers or for diskless workstations that are transmitting most of their information over the network. No matter how fast your network interface card is, you can't access it any faster than the bus rate. Therefore, we do not recommend ISA bus for use in any but the smallest Windows NT server installations. It may make a great deal of sense in low-cost workstations, but should never be used where high performance is required.

A new development in ISA is the *Plug-and-Play* ISA specification jointly developed by Intel, Compaq, Microsoft, and others. The Plug-and-Play specification essentially provides for software control of peripheral configuration. It does nothing to improve ISA's limited bandwidth. Moreover, at this writing NT doesn't support Plug-and-Play (though future versions probably will), so there is little advantage in purchasing plug-and-play hardware for Windows NT.

Local Busses—VESA and PCI

The bandwidth limits of ISA have led many peripheral card manufacturers—especially video card makers—to look for a compatible alternative. They've found it in the concept of *local bus*, which basically extends the high-speed parallel bus used by RAM on the computer's motherboard to peripheral devices. Early local bus implementation were proprietary, varying from manufacturer to manufacturer—and in some cases between models in a single product line. Such busses should be avoided for obvious reasons.

The need to standardize on a nonproprietary local bus architecture for video cards drove the Video Electronic Standards Association (VESA) to define the VL-Bus (VESA Local) standard. VL-Bus provides a relatively high-speed 32-bit connection, initially optimized for 25MHz machines, and currently extended to support 33MHz.

VL-Bus is fine as far as it goes, but it has two problems: First, it is restricted in bandwidth. (Though that bandwidth is at least 6 times higher than the basic ISA bus!) Second, it's tied to the Intel x86 architecture. Intel developed a competing standard, Peripheral Connect Interchange (PCI), which eliminates those limits—and as of this writing, PCI seems to be emerging as the new industry standard for high-speed peripherals.

As always, when considering VL-Bus vs. PCI for NT, it is *essential* to consult the current NT hardware compatibility list. Make sure the system you are considering is supported, and make sure the peripherals you require are available for that system's bus. If the system is new, demand a demonstration running shrink-wrapped NT—not a customized beta version—and ask for a list of compatible peripherals.

EISA Bus

The Extended Industry Standard Architecture (EISA) bus was developed by a consortium of PC clone manufacturers led by Compaq, and is functionally a 32-bit extension of the 16-bit ISA bus architecture. It has two great advantages, the first of which is that by doubling the number of bits, it effectively doubles the system throughput. It also provides features that allow *bus-mastering* of certain devices. That is, that a hard disk controller or network interface card (or other peripheral) can effectively take the place of the CPU for some operations and operate independently of the CPU. This is a decided advantage, especially in servers where the bottleneck introduced by shoving data across the bus and waiting for it to be processed by a peripheral can be significant. A further advantage is compatibility: 32-bit EISA bus systems will accept 8- or 16-bit ISA bus cards, although the introduction of such cards will introduce a significant performance hit into the system and, therefore, should be avoided.

The major disadvantage of EISA bus systems is cost, both for the system itself and for the peripheral cards—and in competition with the VL and PCI variants of Local Bus, this has led to a decline in the availability of EISA systems and peripherals.

MCA Bus

The Micro Channel Architecture (MCA) used in IBM's Personal System/2 line of PCs was their answer to the EISA bus development and an attempt to replace the ISA bus that they had originated with the AT computer. MCA is a from-the-ground-up redesign of the computer bus with many advantages, the principal ones being significantly higher system bus data rate (25MHz), as well as provisions for bus mastering and for burst data transmission at high speeds. The MCA bus is a good choice for both workstations and servers, but it has one great limitation—cost and availability of components. At this writing, MCA is available only in a limited range of PS/2 systems from IBM—and it is likely that those systems will be discontinued in the near future. We regretfully do not recommend the purchase of new MCA-based systems (a pity, because in many ways MCA is a superior architecture, and we suspect that when a true sucessor to ISA and Local Bus emerges, it will bear more than a passing resemblence to MCA in its fundamental design).

Other Choices

There are several other bus options available, especially in the more exotic computers, such as the Symmetric Multiprocessor (SMP) and Reduced Instruction Set Computer (RISC) machines discussed in Appendix 5. A variety of approaches have been used—including multiple parallel memory bus architectures, proprietary local bus architectures, and whatnot. If you are considering any computer using such a proprietary bus architecture, there are two things you should examine with great care. One is what availability there is for peripherals on this bus architecture. The other is what provision has been made for using an auxiliary bus, such as MCA, EISA, or PCI, for peripheral interface cards. Be very careful when you look at the system configuration. As with using ISA bus interface cards in an EISA bus computer, any EISA, MCA, or PCI bus cards in a proprietary bus computer will impact performance.

How noticeable that performance impact is will depend on the devices in use. A tape drive, for example, or CD-ROM drive, might slow performance *while you are using that device*. On the other hand, in a network server, if the network interface card is sitting on the EISA bus, this means that every time a network request is transmitted the system has to operate at the lower bus speeds. This can have a significant impact and it should be investigated closely.

Backup

Every Windows NT server *requires* a backup device. This is not an option. Can you configure a Windows NT Server without a backup device? Yes, and you will pay for that choice. You do not even want to consider configuring a server system without providing backup.

Windows NT has a simple backup program built into it, which is covered in more detail in Chapter 3. The system's basic limitation is that it supports only tape-drive devices with SCSI interfaces, and a limited range of other tape drives (such as QIC-40 and -80 compatibles, and 4mm DAT drives). Therefore, to use NT's built-in backup, you'll need a compatible tape device from the Windows NT hardware compatibility list. A wide range of NT-compatible tape drives are available—consult the latest Windows NT hardware compatibility list.

In larger networks, NT's built-in backup is really inadequate. If you need to maintain backup data for a network of any size, we recommend investigating *Backup Alternatives* in Chapter 3.

UPS

As with the backup device, an uninterruptible power supply is *mandatory* on all Windows NT Servers (and desirable on workstations). Windows NT includes a *UPS Service* that can be used with a compatible UPS, *provided it is equipped with a serial port that can be used to signal power/fail conditions.*

In selecting a UPS for NT, it's important to consider three factors: 1) the switching time for the UPS to resume power after AC failure, which should be 4 milliseconds or less (ideally, zero); 2) serial-port signalling, so that the NT UPS service can be notified that a failure has occurred; and 3) capacity. UPSs are typically rated for capacity using two measures: peak power output in Volt-Amperes (VA or Watts), and a duration in minutes. You'll need a UPS with a peak power output sufficient for your complete system, and a duration long enough to complete critical tasks and shutdown gracefully. This varies from installation to installation, of course—a small departmental server can probably get by with 500 VA peak output and a ten-minute duration. The PDC of a large site, however, may need considerably more capacity.

Today's UPSs offer a wide range of optional features over and above those required for NT compatibility—among these are SNMP support, hot-swappable batteries, and significant monitoring and management capability.[10] The latter, of course, will help on an NT network only if it's NT-compatible (or at least Windows-compatible)—don't pay extra for NetWare-based management software if your UPS will be used only with NT!

Windows NT's UPS service depends on signalling through a serial port using a compatible cable. Table 2.1 presents a list of manufacturers who provide

---

10. The January 15, 1995 issue of *Network Computing* magazine has an excellent review of high-end UPS hardware.

Table 2.1 NT-Compatible UPS Suppliers

Company	Address	Telephone	Notes
American Power Conversion	132 Fairgrounds Rd. West Kingston, RI 02892.	(800)800-4APC (401)782-2515	Supplies are available with 400-2,000 volt-ampere capacity.
Best Power Technologies	N9246 Hwy 80 Necedah, WI 54646	(800)356-5794 (608)565-7200	BAA-0162. Supplies available with 500VA-18KVA capacity.

NT-compatible UPS devices, and lists the cables required.[11] Specifics of setting up the UPS service are covered in detail in Chapter 3.

CD-ROM

As with backup, CD-ROM should be considered essential for all Windows NT servers and it is highly desirable on workstations. Microsoft is distributing Windows NT on both CD-ROM and floppy disks. However, the server installation consists of some 24 floppy diskettes—not an installation that anyone would want to undertake lightly. The CD-ROM installation is much simpler, consisting of one CD-ROM and two floppy diskettes.

Having a CD-ROM available on the server also provides a variety of other interesting options, such as the availability of MS-Tech Net on CD-ROM, components of the Microsoft knowledge base on CD-ROM, and third-party products on CD-ROM. It should also be noted that placing the CD-ROM on the server and then sharing it over the network will permit you to carry out efficient over-the-network installations that cannot be easily carried out using floppy disks. Therefore, a CD-ROM should be considered a necessity on Windows NT servers, not an option.

As with tape drives, the major limitation here is that Windows NT supports a limited range of CD-ROM controllers—mostly ones based on SCSI. So, again,

---

11. This list is based on information from Microsoft's *Windows NT Hardware Compatibility List—Version 3.51 Beta Release*, and is up to date as of March, 1995. Consult the current NT hardware compatibility list for up-to-date information.

you're going to need a controller and CD-ROM from the Windows NT hardware compatibility list. As you may imagine, given that SCSI is the best supported controller type for both CD-ROM and tape backup, SCSI makes sense as the primary transport mechanism for your hard disks as well—allowing you to have just one disk controller for the entire system. Since SCSI also supports use of the various disk array options supported by Windows NT Server, we recommend SCSI as the standard disk controller type for all NT server installations. The number of NT-compatible CD-ROM suppliers is far too long for a table. Consult the latest Windows NT hardware compatibility list.

Floppy Disks

Floppyless operation of Windows NT is certainly possible; but while an over-the-network installation from CD-ROM is available, works beautifully, and is much simpler and easier to maintain than handing around floppy disks on each workstation, should the system's registry ever become corrupted, you will find it inconvenient to employ the standard Windows NT Emergency Diskette approach—the maintenance team will first have to open up the workstation and physically connect a floppy disk in order to boot the recovery diskette.

For fully secure operations, a better choice may be physically locking the floppy disk drive, or using the FLOPLOCK application supplied with the Windows NT Resource Kit. Providing one 3.5 inch 1.44 megabyte capacity floppy diskette on each workstation will save a great deal of trouble.

Miscellaneous Devices

The use of Windows NT Remote Access Services (RAS) to provide Wide Area Networking connections between isolated Windows NT machines and the network requires compatible modems at both ends, and for efficiency, the server requires an X.25, ISDN, or multiport card. These issues are discussed further in Chapter 7. Likewise, Chapter 7 is also the place to look for information on the necessary hardware to support the Macintosh file system, which may require either an Apple Talk card installed in the server or (preferably, for performance reasons) an EtherNet card in the server coupled to Ether Talk hardware on the Macintosh machines. The selection of appropriate UPS hardware is discussed elsewhere in this chapter. Remember that the first place to look when considering the selection of a particular hardware device is the current Windows NT Hardware Compatibility List.[12]

---

12. Available on CompuServe (in Download area 1 of the WINNT forum) or by calling Microsoft.

Portables

It may seem ridiculous after talking about 16-megabyte RAM and 100MB hard disk requirements to even consider running Windows NT on a portable. Yet it can be done—and it has some interesting advantages. Windows NT runs reasonably well on a 486SX25 or better CPU portable with 12MB of RAM (it works better with 16MB) and 100MB of hard disk (it works better with more).

The most convenient approach to configuring such a portable is to employ a Xircom Pocket LAN adapter (or PCMCIA network card) to give the portable access to a shared CD-ROM for an over-the-network install using the WINNT.EXE file. One thing to watch out for in such an installation is that when you add any drivers, you will find that you cannot use the floppy disks—since the .INF file format used on the floppies differs from that on the CD. You can get around this by renaming all the CD-based *.INF files in the WINNT\SYS-TEM32 directory to *.INC, then copy all *.INF files from all floppies (they may be stored in compressed format as *.IN_, in which case you'll need to expand them with NT's EXPAND.EXE—since you can't tell what the last letter is supposed to be, you may accidentally convert some *.IND files, but you can eliminate them later by comparing a list of *.INC files to *.INF, and eliminating any of the latter that don't have a match). Once this is done, device driver/service installations will request the relevant floppy disk rather than the CD. To reverse the process, rename the *.INF files to *.INX, and then rename the *.INC files to *.INF. Fortunately, this procedure is *much* easier than it sounds!

The biggest problem to watch out for in this kind of installation is a situation where NT doesn't automatically recognize your network card. If that happens, your best bet is to skip the network installation (you can try to bull through the installation, but with no network adaptor set up, you'll probably crash NT when you shut it down). One alternative at this point is to install the MS Loopback adaptor, (which is a dummy), finish the rest of the NT install, then boot back to DOS. Once back in DOS (with access to whatever network WINNT.EXE was started from), you can copy all of the NT 3.5 installation files from the CD's \i386 directory—they take up only about 30MB. You may also want to copy the CD's \drvlib\netcard\i386 directory, which contains additional drivers for less common cards—it's another 5MB.

In any case, after the files are copied, reboot to NT and select Control Panel / Networks. You can then install the network card manually.

You can save time and trouble when installing and configuring a Windows NT portable system by installing Remote Access Services on the first pass. This will allow you, using null-modem serial cable connections (or a compatible modem), to communicate with the server computer, and is an effective alternative to installing from floppy disks. Given a RAS connection and access to a phone line or null-modem cable it is, of course, always possible to update drivers and so forth from the CD-ROM at the central site.

Printers

The printing situation in Windows NT is good news indeed. Windows NT supports every printer that is supported by Windows 3.1 and also, using the built-in DLC (Dynamic Link Control) driver, supports network printers, such as the Laser Jet IIIsi. The latter can be extremely convenient, since it can be plugged into the network at any convenient location without requiring a direct physical connection to the print server.

All Windows NT machines can function as print servers (though NT Worksations are limited to a maximum of ten simultaneous connections—to support more users, an NT Server is required). You need not dedicate a machine to this task, nor do you need to necessarily connect all the printers to the file server. In general, you have as wide a choice of printers as you could ask for. Selecting a printer will largely be a matter of speed, reliability, and cost. For desktop publishing and other graphics work, PostScript printers remain desirable because of the tremendous infrastructure of PostScript-compatible software. For most other applications, any laser printer that supports TrueType will provide a perfectly acceptable result.

One issue that does bear some consideration is the implication of mixing RISC and x86-type computers in a Windows NT network. The over-the-network printer driver approach used by Windows NT has the great advantage that each workstation does not have to have its own print driver. It does have the slight disadvantage that the print server has to have all types of printer drivers that might be requested of it. Therefore, if you are running a network that includes x86-based workstations, MIPS R4000-based workstations, and DEC Alpha AXP workstations, any print server that is made available to all of these will require all three types of print drivers.

This is not difficult to do. It is merely necessary on the print server to first install the native print driver for the print server CPU, then bring up the Properties dialog for the printer in question, select Other from the list of print drivers, and designate the directory from which it can obtain the print servers for the foreign types (the \MIPS directory on the installation CD-ROM, for instance). The Windows NT Print Spooler automatically determines whether the request is coming from a RISC workstation, as opposed to an x86 system, and will employ the proper print driver at that time.[13]

Simultaneous use of multiple print driver types on a high-capacity print server does not require additional memory. As noted earlier, 4MB of memory is generally considered sufficient for a Windows NT print server that services up to six printers—but NT print servers execute only native print driver code (non-native driver code is transported over the network to the printing station and executed there).

---

13. Implemented as a separate service in NT versions from 3.5 on.

Beginning with version 3.5, NT Server has also supported a UNIX-compatible Line Printer Daemon (LPD) service for plain-text and PostScript printing on TCP/IP networks. Consult Chapter 6 for further information on the LPD service.

Limitations

Note that Windows NT cannot be run on all systems. Specifically excluded are those that use the DoubleSpace compression algorithm from DOS 6, as well as competing products, such as Stacker (Stac Electronics) or SuperStor (AddStor). This is a pity, as the disk space requirements for Windows NT are such that it could undoubtedly benefit from a compatible compressor.[14] Hopefully some third party will fill this need in the near future. Compression *can* be used with the NTFS file system, as described later in this chapter and in Chapter 4.

Hardware

The major problem with hardware support on Windows NT occurs when you want to upgrade existing equipment to run Windows NT—at which point you will discover every piece of proprietary or otherwise incompatible hardware in your inventory. A useful first step is to examine the hardware requirements section earlier in this chapter, as this will give you a good working understanding of what to watch out for. In the meantime, here are a few situations that we *know* will cause problems.

CD-ROMs

A variety of manufacturers (notably Creative Labs in the Sound Blaster series of add-on cards) have produced multimedia upgrade kits in which a sound board is provided with a proprietary CD-ROM interface. Generally this is a partial SCSI interface. Windows NT is not compatible with such boards, and the CD-ROM drives associated with them will not work *unless* a compatible device driver is provided—as, indeed, is provided in the *Windows NT Device Library* disk supplied with Microsoft TechNet. Unfortunately, only a limited range of such devices are supported—thus, for example, some Creative Labs and Mitsumi multimedia kits and CD-ROMs are supported, while MediaVision's generally equivalent kits may not be. An alternative to provide reuse of this hardware within a Windows NT network is to install these boards into systems that will run DOS and Windows for Workgroups or Windows 95. The drives can then be

---

14. Indeed, usually reliable sources tell us that a DoubleSpace/DriveSpace-compatible compressed file system for NT *does* exist, and may ship with future versions.

shared from Windows for Workgroups using the /s parameter on the MSCDX CD-ROM support software provided by Microsoft, and the drives can then be accessed over the network by Windows NT machines (consult Microsoft's current documentation to determine the equivalent procedure on Windows 95 systems). But there is no way you can install and use such unsupported CD-ROM drives using Windows NT Workstations or servers.

Tape Drives

Make sure any tape device you purchase for use with NT is on the Hardware Compatibility List—or that the manufacturer provides an appropriate driver. As mentioned earlier, most SCSI-interface drives will work, as will QIC-40 and -80 compatibles.

Motherboards

This can be one of the most serious limitations with Windows NT, and any organization embarking on a Windows NT pilot project (more so on a wholesale conversion to Windows NT) should examine this with care. Many early 386 motherboards are expandable only up to maximum of 8MB of RAM and will not run Windows NT properly. (It is *possible* to run Windows NT in an 8MB configuration.[15] It is not recommended by Microsoft; and we discourage it. The performance is, frankly, terrible and it is, in general, not worth the effort. Machines that cannot be upgraded beyond 8MB should be used with Windows for Workgroups, Windows 95, or other software, rather than attempting to run Windows NT on them in a crippled state.)

Some motherboards can be upgraded only to 16MB. Some—in particular, some earlier 486 motherboards from Dell, and certain Packard-Bell models— will operate more slowly if more than 16MB is introduced. Another major issue is the availability of cache RAM, as many early 386 and 486 motherboards not only didn't ship with cache RAM, but made no provision for adding it. And, as noted earlier, Windows NT does not reach its full performance capability until significant amounts of cache RAM are introduced into the system. The only way to deal with this situation is to inspect the manufacturer's information for the motherboards for each computer in the organization.

Obviously, when buying new equipment, avoid any system that has these kinds of problems. Make sure the system is expandable to at least 32MB of RAM (64MB for servers), and that it will accommodate at least 256KB of on-chip SRAM cache. You can save yourself significant time and trouble if you are

---

15. Indeed, it's *possible* to run NT in just 4MB—at the expense of swapping continuously. This doesn't provide a useful configuration, though it might be an interesting torture test for hard disk manufacturers!

investigating the potential for upgrades within your organization by spending time in CompuServe's Microsoft Knowledge Base , checking to see what motherboards have been reported as having problems with Windows NT.[16] Finally, a useful reference that will save time by identifying systems that you don't need to worry about, is the downloading of the current Windows NT Hardware Compatibility List.[17]

Planning Your Installation

Before you install Windows NT, there are several decisions you need to make and pieces of information you need to gather. In this section we'll look at what you need to know before you begin.

File Systems

The primary decision you need to make is which file system to use. Windows NT introduces a completely new file system, NTFS (New Technology File System). If you select NTFS, file names can be 256 characters long, Windows NT can automatically recover in the case of problems (you no longer have to run CHKDSK—though it's still available), auditing and security features found in Windows NT can be enabled, and (beginning with version 3.51) file compression is available.[18]

During installation you will need to decide which file system you want to use. If your C drive is currently formatted as an MS-DOS drive and uses a file allocation table (FAT) file system (the kind normally used by DOS), Windows NT refers to this as a FAT drive. If you select this drive as the destination drive, Windows NT can be installed on this drive, or the installation program can convert the drive to an NTFS file system drive, then install the program.[19] Windows NT can do the same with drives formatted to the OS/2 High Performance File System (HPFS). Here's what you need to consider when selecting a file system.

---

16. Go to the CompuServe MSKB (Microsoft Knowlege Base) area. This contains up-to-date technical notes on Windows NT issues, including installation. A periodic search of this area, using the keywords "Windows NT" and "motherboard," will provide you with a wealth of valuable information—and may save you from making a serious mistake.

17. Available in download area 1 of the CompuServe WINNT forum.

18. Beginning with NT version 3.5, DOS-compatible FAT partitions also support long file names, which are compatible with the long filenames used by Windows 95.

19. However, if a drive has seen heavy use, it may be preferable to reformat it rather than to convert it—conversion may yield a suboptimal NTFS layout (since NTFS has to retain the previous filesystem's cluster size), and if the drive is seriously fragmented, both performance and reliability may suffer. This is particularly true for server disks being converted from the OS/2 HPFS format.

Security

Only NTFS drives can be made secure according to the C2 security specifications. You can create access control lists locally and remotely with NTFS, but only remotely for other file systems. Auditing on NTFS drives can monitor which users access which files. Furthermore, you can set a variety of file permissions on NTFS drives, such as restricting which users can rename files or directories. By comparison, files and directories on FAT drives can be shared or not shared, but you cannot restrict a user to read-only access, as you could if the file were located on an NTFS drive.

Access by DOS Applications

During installation you can also select the dual-boot option, which allows you to select which operating system you want to use—the one originally installed or Windows NT. You cannot convert your C (boot) drive to an NTFS drive if you still plan to use the original operating system (such as MS-DOS), as it will not be able to boot from an NTFS drive. Furthermore, if you choose to install NT on a drive other than your boot drive, such as the D drive, and select the NTFS file system for that drive, the drive and all its files will be invisible when DOS is loaded.

File Names

Both NTFS and (from NT version 3.5 on) FAT allow you to create file names with up to 256 characters, including spaces but excluding special characters (such as question or quotation marks, forward and backward slashes, less than and greater than symbols, and so on). The file extension is separated from the file name by a period (.). To maintain DOS compatibility, NT also creates a DOS-compatible file name. The algorithm for this, fully explained in the printed NT user guides, takes the first non-blank eight characters for the file name. If a duplicate name results, NT uses the last character in the file name as a numeric serial number, incrementing the number until a unique file name is created. Thus, though you can use both the NTFS and FAT file systems on the same system, you will need to be prepared for handling converted file names.

OS/2 HPFS File System

In addition to the FAT and NTFS file systems, Windows NT supports the High Performance File System (HPFS) used by OS/2. HPFS has many features in common with NTFS, including long file names, but is generally less sophisticated and reliable. The only reason to retain HPFS partitions is if they already exist on a system being converted from OS/2 (or dual-booted to run both NT and OS/2); and it will probably pay to bite the bullet and convert those partitions to NTFS at some point.[20]

Apple Macintosh File System and POSIX Support

The Windows NT Server supports a Macintosh-accessible directory format on NTFS partitions. You'll find this subject covered in more detail in Chapter 7, but for now you need to be aware that you'll need at least one NTFS partition on an NT Server if you intend to support Macintosh computers on your network. Similarly, NTFS is required if you expect to use NT's POSIX subsystem with applications that expect a UNIX-style file structure.

Network Information

Before you begin installing Windows NT, you also need to have network information and the settings you'll use for your computer.

You must know the name of your computer and the name of the workgroup or domain the computer will be part of. If the computer is already part of a Windows for Workgroups group, you may use the same name.

You must also know the type of network adapter card installed, as well as the card's interrupt number (IRQ) and its base address. While the installation program will do its best to automatically sense these settings, it is best to have the information available in order to know if the derived settings are incorrect.

You can install NT without network settings, then add or change the settings through the Control Panel's Network icon—but it's generally much simpler to set up the network when the system starts. In particular, systems being added to a Windows NT Server domain cannot be logged in and used as domain members until a network card has been installed and configured—which is as good a time as any to address the issue of domains-vs.-workgroups.

Domains and Workgroups

All new NT users (and many NT network administrators) are confused by the distinction between workgroups and domains. In a nutshell, there are people who want to run centrally managed NT networks, and other people want to run NT systems on a stand-alone basis. If you are running an NT network, you want to put your machines in a *domain*. A domain is an administrative unit

---

20. Indeed, HPFS support has been eliminated from beta versions of the NT 3.51 *format* command, and it's possible (though unlikely) that HPFS support will be removed altogether from future versions of Windows NT. This isn't as serious as it sounds—the OS/2 subsystem treats NTFS as though it were HPFS (the OS/2 extended attribute data is stored in an NTFS data stream).

with centralized user account information stored on a Primary Domain Controller (PDC). The account information may then be replicated by secondary Domain Controllers (DCs). When a user logs in to an NT system (be it a Workstation or Server), the logon request is validated by whatever DC is available. If none is available, the user may be logged in locally using account information cached on the particular workstation or server he's logging on to.

The advantage of a Domain setup is that *all* NT systems in a domain are managed as a single unit. Domain-wide user accounts and policies (created using User Manager for Domains from the NT Server's Administrative Tools group—see Chapter 3 for details) apply to *all* servers and workstations in the domain—not to just one machine. This concept can even be extended to multiple domains using Inter-domain trust relationships, covered in Chapter 7. Thus, when using NT servers in a large organization, organizing them into domains is clearly the preferred approach.

The alternative to centralized domains is *workgroup security*—in which each individual NT system, be it a Workstation or Server, must maintain its own set of user accounts. This is far from optimal in any but the smallest LANs, and we recommend it only for stand-alone NT systems. On such systems there's no benefit to the overhead of making the isolated server a DC. Finally, groups of NT Workstations operating without any NT Servers cannot be a domain, because only NT Servers can be operated as Domain Controllers. (Hint: In such a situation, you should have at least one NT Server!) In all other cases, set up a domain.

Why spend so much space discussing this issue in a chapter on installation? Because on NT servers, the decision to support domain vs. workgroup security *must* be made when the system is installed (on workstations, you can change the security model at will).

Network Protocols

By default, NT 3.1 was installed with the Microsoft-standard NetBEUI (NetBIOS Extended User Interface) protocol. Beginning with NT 3.5, this changed—NT Servers now install with TCP/IP as the base protocol, while NT Workstations (and Servers, for that matter) that are installed in a NetWare-compatible environment get Microsoft's NWLink IPX/SPX protocol by default. All three base protocols can be selected for installation, and there are add-in protocols available from third parties (see Chapter 10 for details). This entire subject is extremely complex, and we will not attempt to cover it in detail here—see Appendix 2 for detailed information on Windows NT protocols and drivers; Chapters 6 and 7 for information on using TCP/IP for internetworking; Chapter 8 for information on interoperating with other Microsoft network products; Chapter 9 for information about using Windows NT with Novell NetWare; and Chapter 10 for information on using Windows NT with other types of networks.

If that seems like too much reading, stick to installing the default protocol(s) selected by NT's Express installation option on the first pass, and add another protocol later if your situation requires it.

Printer Information

Unlike Windows 3.1 and Windows for Workgroups, you need install a printer driver only on the server machine in Windows NT—you do not need to define a printer on any computer that does not have a computer directly attached. In NT, you change the printer configuration using the Print Manager, not the Control Panel; and you can add a printer at a later time. If you want to install a printer during the NT installation process, you need to know the printer make and model, as well as the communications port (LPT1, etc.) used.

Passwords

You will need to know the name of the user you want assigned to this copy of Windows NT, and you will be asked for a password. You can press the Enter key to bypass setting up a password, though this defeats a major security feature. Passwords are case sensitive, and they can be changed later. An administrator can also force the expiration of passwords at regular intervals, such as every 30 days (see Chapter 3 for more information).

Updating Your Current Windows Installation

The NT installation program will look for an existing Windows or Windows NT installation, and offer to update the version of Windows. If you select this option, NT will maintain your program groups and other settings. However, if you use the Dual Boot option, you will be unable to run NT from DOS, for example. Thus, if you are evaluating NT, it is probably wise to install NT in a separate directory until your evaluation is complete, then reinstall over your Windows 3.1 or Windows for Workgroups program.

Installation Overview

As with Windows and Windows for Workgroups, the installation of Windows NT occurs in two phases. The first phase is a text-based application, asking you for the basic parameters and settings NT needs in order to be installed on your hard disk. In the second phase, the installation process turns graphical as Windows NT copies additional files and actually sets up and displays new program groups.

The installation process also varies by your response to the questions asked by the setup program. As all machines and environments vary, there is no foolproof description we can offer to all users.

As with most Microsoft application setup programs, there are two installation options at the outset. The first, Express Setup, makes most of the decisions for you, and substitutes defaults (such as the destination directory name) for you. If you select Custom setup, you will have more control over the exact details of the installation. Because of the complex nature of Windows NT, novice users will probably prefer, and I recommend, the Express Setup option.

The Installation Process

By far the easiest way to install Windows NT is by using a CD-ROM drive that is directly attached to the computer. However, there are other methods that also allow NT to be installed if you do not have a CD-ROM drive, and they will be described here. You should allow at least 30 minutes for a Windows NT installation, a period that varies according to the speed of your hard disk and CD-ROM; and assuming there are no problems during the installation process. If you are installing from floppy diskettes, allow at least 75 minutes for the installation.

Floppy-Based Installation

In all honesty, if you're going to install NT, you should have a CD-ROM (or access to one). The normal NT Workstation and Server shrink-wrap kits include only the CD-ROM boot floppies. If you have no other way to install NT than via floppy disk, you'll have to special-order the floppies from Microsoft, who will send you back 3.5-inch diskettes. If you don't have a 3.5-inch drive, you are out of luck—Microsoft supports *only* 3.5-inch disks for the floppy-based install in NT versions from 3.5 on.

If you install from floppies, you get only the base NT Workstation or Server installation—additional features (driver library, online documentation, service and debugging tools) provided on the CD version are not available when NT is installed from floppies. Since the NT Workstation shrink-wrap doesn't include *printed* documentation, you will need to order that as well.

CD-ROM Installation

NT versions 3.5 and 3.51 come with three (3) floppies and a CD. Boot the first diskette, and you will be prompted to insert the others when appropriate. If you lose the diskettes, you can still do an over-the-network-style installation using WINNT32.EXE, which has an option to create the floppies (which it does in a separate thread while continuing to copy files from the CD to your hard disk), or use the /B option to eliminate the need for the setup floppies altogether. But make no mistake; you need to make—and keep—at least one set of those install disks.

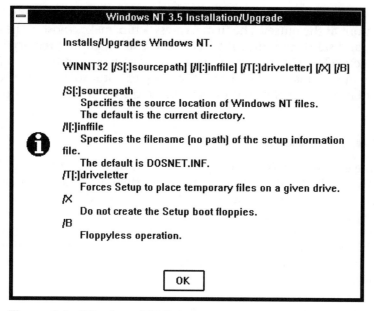

Figure 2.1 Windows NT Setup.

The WINNT32.EXE over-the-network setup program provides a number of useful options for Windows NT installation.

Without the first (boot) diskette, you cannot use an NT emergency diskette. And being able to use the emergency diskette can be a lifesaver.[21]

Over-the-Network Installation

On machines that lack a CD-ROM, the easiest way to install NT is over the network. There are two ways to do this—on machines where NT is already running, use WINNT32.EXE (see figure 2.1).

Just running WINNT32 (from the command line or Program Manager) will start the process. It will prompt for the location of the source files (the \i386 directory of the installation CD for intel systems; \mips, \alpha, etc. for RISC systems)—otherwise, it's pretty much like running the CD-based install locally. One nice option is the /B switch, which eliminates creation of the boot floppies

---

21. One of the authors once accidentally deleted a registry key on an NT system. The system had been installed using a floppyless installation, and no emergency disk—which would have allowed the damage to be repaired—was available. The only solution was to completely reinstall NT—in the process a complete NTFS partition (and about a month's work) was lost. Having a backup copy of the registry might have prevented this—especially if the boot partition is FAT-formatted and is compatible with DOS-based disk tools. Don't let this happen to you! —JDR

and the emergency disk—but as mentioned earlier, you won't know how badly you want that emergency disk until you *really* need it.

Of course, WINNT32 is useful only if NT (3.1 or 3.5) is already installed.[22] What about installing NT over the network on DOS systems? You'll need some sort of network connection to the shared directory on the CD (the client software provided with NT server, for instance—or a NetWare redirector running against FPNW or GSNW on an NT server). Once that's done, run WINNT.EXE—which is basically a 16-bit version of WINNT32. Like its 32-bit sibling, WINNT.EXE has several options:

```
D:\i386winnt /?
Installs Windows NT.


WINNT [/D[:]winntroot] [/S[:]sourcepath] [/T[:]tempdrive] [/I[:]inffile]
      [/O[X]] [/X | [/F] [/C]] [/B]
/D[:]winntroot
        Removes Windows NT system files from the installation in winntroot.
/S[:]sourcepath
        Specifies the source location of Windows NT files.
        Must be a full path of the form x:\[path] or
        \\server\share[\path].
        The default is the current directory.
/T[:]tempdrive
        Specifies a drive to contain temporary setup files.
        If not specified, Setup will attempt to locate a drive for you.
/I[:]inffile
        Specifies the filename (no path) of the setup information file.
        The default is DOSNET.INF.
/O      Create boot floppies only.
/OX     Create boot floppies for CD-ROM or floppy-based installation.
/X      Do not create the Setup boot floppies.
/F      Do not verify files as they are copied to the Setup boot floppies.
/C      Skip free-space check on the Setup boot floppies you provide.
/B      Floppyless operation.
```

Most of these are the same as WINNT32; but WINNT.EXE adds an /O option to create just the boot disks, plus the options having to do with free space. The latter are necessary because WINNT.EXE copies the NT setup files onto the target system's hard disk, then boots into NT to run the rest of setup—so a fair amount of disk space (about 56MB) must be available in order for it to run.

---

22. It doesn't support Windows 95 or OS/2, as of this writing (March 1995).

With appropriate use of the options, WINNT setup can be extremely powerful. For example, a typical command line that would carry out a complete installation over the network (assuming that the Windows NT installation CD-ROM is shared as disk-d of \\mips-lab-server) would be:

```
WINNT /s:\\mips-lab-server\disk-d\i386 /t:c /i:\\mips-lab-server\
install\dosnet.inf /x /f /c
```

This will carry out a complete installation using the files in the i386 directory of the CD device on MIPS lab server, with temporary file storage on the local C drive, getting the DOSNET.INF file from the install share on MIPS lab server. It will not create, verify, or perform a free space check on a boot floppy (which would assume that you are carrying a boot floppy with you). This is probably the fastest way to do an installation for small to medium-sized networks. For larger networks, you should see the forthcoming section on computer profile setup.

Upgrading from NT 3.1

There are some special considerations when upgrading from NT 3.1 to later versions. First and foremost, the file system drivers have changed. Beginning with version 3.5, NT includes a FastFAT driver that supports long file names on DOS-compatible File Allocation Table (FAT) partitions. NT 3.5 introduced minor changes to the NTFS driver, and NT 3.51 introduced compression in the NTFS driver.

The FAT driver is not really an issue—NT 3.5 will install over whatever FAT partitions you have and simply add new capabilities—but the modifications to NTFS are more serious.

For a one-way upgrade (from NT 3.1 to a later version), the situation's essentially the same as for FAT partitions—all of the regular setup options (floppy, CD, or network) will present a prompt asking if the NTFS partion(s) should be upgraded—answer Yes, and it will be handled automatically.

Those wanting to retain a capability to dual-boot between NT 3.1 and the later version (migration testing, for instance) can opt to retain the older version of NTFS. This requires the use of an UPDATE.EXE program in the distribution CD's \FS31UPD\i386 (or \mips or \alpha, as appropriate) directory, which updates the NT 3.1 file system drivers.

Hints, Tips, and Tricks

While working on this column and on our recent review of NT 3.5 Workstation and Server, I found a few interesting things that may save you time. First, don't try to run WINNT.EXE from Windows—it gives you a "Setup cannot run in a

386 Enhanced Mode Windows MS-DOS Command Prompt. Exit Windows and run Setup again" message. Do as the prompt says—exit to DOS and run it from there. This seems a mite silly (you have to run the Windows NT installation program from a DOS prompt ?!), but is apparently necessary because of the way WINNT.EXE forces a reboot halfway through the setup process.

One more thing: If you install NT on a system that already has Windows on it, you'll be given the option of installing NT in the existing Windows directory. *Accept that option!* It automatically migrates all of your installed Windows applications for you—which is a great time-saver.

Computer Profile Setup

For departmental network installations, where a large number of machines with a common configuration will need to be set up for Windows NT, Microsoft has provided a fourth installation option: Computer Pofile Setup (CPS). CPS is included in the Windows NT Resource Kit (you'll find a reference to that at the end of the chapter).

CPS has two parts. In the first, an administrator creates a computer profile for the standard workstation configuration used in his organization using a *computer profile editor* provided in the Resource Kit. This provides the administrator with a way to specify a standard configuration for all workstations that will be set up for Windows NT, including the network card used, disk drivers, file systems, and so on. The administrator then executes a *computer profile installer* on the target workstation, (again, supplied with the Resource Kit) which performs a custom over-the-network installation using the information provided by the computer profile editor.

This approach provides what amounts to a customized batch-mode installation—all of the configurable parameters are preselected by the administrator and always come up in a standardized manner. This is clearly advantageous for a large organization. It's possible to do something similar using a custom .INF file in conjunction with the over-the-network WINNT or WINNT32 installation programs discussed earlier—but given the availability of this approach, we strongly recommend that administrators responsible for larger sites investigate the Windows NT Resource Kit and CPS.

Installing Windows NT, Step by Step

Though every environment is different, here is the typical sequence of events that occur during installation:

1. After placing the special boot disk in the A drive and booting your machine, the installation program determines if it can run from a

CD-ROM.[23] If not, you can choose to run WINNT.EXE or WINNT32.EXE from a network drive (or shared CD-ROM) provided by your administrator, or you can use the floppy diskette installation. In any case...

Note: If you're installing NT for the first time, skip to step 4.

2. If you're upgrading from an ealier version of NT, Setup first requests that you specificy the location of Windows NT system files, then carries out a check of available space on your hard disk. It may refuse to install if it cannot find enough space. If this happens, you'll need to remove files to make sufficient space available. (Hint: Resizing and/or moving NT's system page file, PAGEFILE.SYS, can help when upgrading NT systems.)

3. After copying the necessary files to your system's hard disk, NT will ask you for permission to restart the system. This is necessary in order for installation to complete.

4. Windows NT Setup will execute in character mode, and ask what type of installation you want to perform. For most purposes, the Express Installation is preferable, as it's standardized and fast. Alternatively, you can set up Windows components you select (such as accessories, games, screen savers, and wallpaper bitmaps), set up a network, set up locally connected printers, and set up applications NT will find on your hard disk. Check the box(es) for the tasks you want NT to perform. With these options, such as installing accessories, NT provides you with another dialog box and asks you to make further selections, such as which accessories you want to install.

5. Setup will detect any built-in disk controllers. It will also allow you to specify any additional controllers you may have (including ones requiring a device control diskette). If Setup cannot locate a recognizable disk partition, it will present you with an option to create and format a partition as FAT, HPFS, or NTFS. See the discussion on file systems earlier in this chapter for the pros and cons of each.

6. If you're upgrading from an ealier version of NT (or DOS/Windows, for that matter), Setup will search for a previous NT installation, and if present, offer to upgrade it. Accept the option unless it's necessary to install multiple versions for testing. If no previous NT installation is found, Setup will propose a directory for the NT system files—typically a WINNT directory or WINNT35 directory. On x86 systems that have past versions of Windows installed, it will offer to install in the WINDOWS directory—this is a preferable option (especially on desktop

---

23. In some cases, it may detect the CD immediately—in others, it won't be apparent until the second and third setup floppies have been used.

systems) because your existing program manager groups and .INI file setting will be automatically migrated. In any case, accept the proposed directory unless there is a special reason not to do so.

7. Setup will perform an automatic inspection of your hard disk(s), and will then begin copying files into the directory structure designated in the preceding step. When the files are copied, it will direct you to press Enter, at which point the system will be restarted and you'll enter graphics mode.

8. If you're installing NT for the first time, Setup asks for your Name and Company. When the next dialog box displays your entry, press Continue if all information is correct.

9. On NT Servers, you'll need to designate whether the system should function as a Domain Controller (DC) or Server. If you are setting up a Windows NT Server domain (see the "Domains and Workgroups" section earlier in this chapter for an explanation), the first NT Server installed in a new domain must be domain controller—and by default, will become the primary domain controller (PDC). To assure that logon accounts are properly replicated, in a multiserver domain you should designate at least one additional server as a backup DC. All other servers in the domain can be servers. If you are setting up a Windows NT Workgroup, then the system cannot function as a domain controller— so designate it as a server.

10. If you're installing NT for the first time, the installation program asks for your computer name. Enter the name of the computer as used in an existing workgroup or on an existing network, or enter a new computer name if this is a new node.

11. If you're installing NT for the first time, you'll need to select a language/locale. The language/local selection affects the formatting of some text, such as date, time, and currency. This setting can later be changed using the International option from the Control Panel.

12. If you asked to set up a printer in step, NT asks you to enter a printer name. This name is displayed in the Printer Manager window and is displayed for all users that share the printer. Select the printer make and model from the pull-down list, and choose a port in the Print to list.

13. If you asked to configure the network settings, the install program finds and displays the network adapter card on your computer. Press Continue to move to the IRQ level and I/O port addresses. The installation program prefills these text boxes with the values it has determined are correct. You may change them, and they can also be changed later by using the Network facilities of the Control Panel (see figure 2.2). The

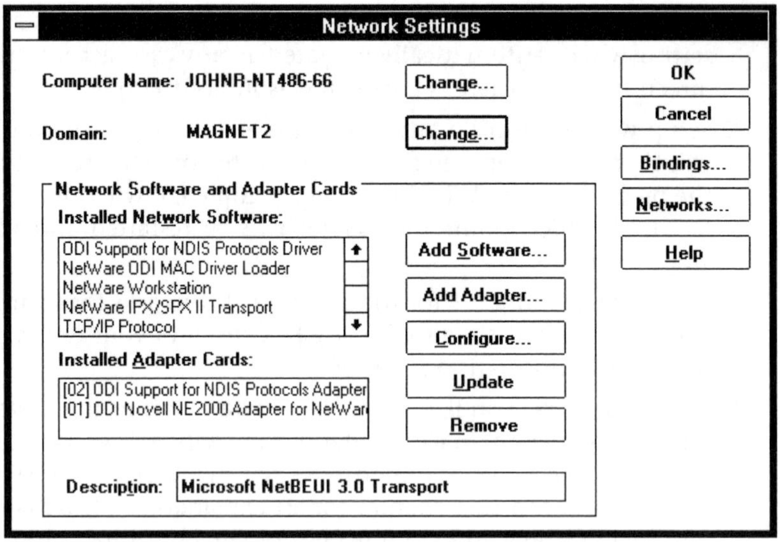

```
┌──────────────────────────────────────────────────────────────┐
│ ─                    Network Settings                          │
├──────────────────────────────────────────────────────────────┤
│                                                                │
│  Computer Name:  JOHNR-NT486-66    ┌─────────┐   ┌──────────┐ │
│                                    │ Change… │   │    OK    │ │
│                                    └─────────┘   └──────────┘ │
│  Domain:         MAGNET2           ┌─────────┐   ┌──────────┐ │
│                                    │ Change… │   │  Cancel  │ │
│                                    └─────────┘   └──────────┘ │
│  ┌─Network Software and Adapter Cards──────────┐ ┌──────────┐ │
│  │ Installed Network Software:                 │ │Bindings… │ │
│  │ ┌──────────────────────────────────┬─┐      │ └──────────┘ │
│  │ │ODI Support for NDIS Protocols Driver│▲│  ┌──────────────┐│Networks…│
│  │ │NetWare ODI MAC Driver Loader     │ │  │Add Software… │││          │
│  │ │NetWare Workstation               │ │  └──────────────┘│ ┌──────────┐
│  │ │NetWare IPX/SPX II Transport      │ │  ┌──────────────┐│ │   Help   │
│  │ │TCP/IP Protocol                   │▼│  │ Add Adapter… │││ └──────────┘
│  │ └──────────────────────────────────┴─┘  └──────────────┘│
│  │ Installed Adapter Cards:                 ┌──────────────┐│
│  │ ┌──────────────────────────────────────┐│ Configure…   ││
│  │ │[02] ODI Support for NDIS Protocols Adapter│└──────────────┘│
│  │ │[01] ODI Novell NE2000 Adapter for NetWar│┌──────────────┐│
│  │ └──────────────────────────────────────┘│   Update     ││
│  │                                          └──────────────┘│
│  │                                          ┌──────────────┐│
│  │                                          │   Remove     ││
│  │                                          └──────────────┘│
│  │ Description:  ┌─────────────────────────────────────────┐│
│  │              │ Microsoft NetBEUI 3.0 Transport          ││
│  │              └─────────────────────────────────────────┘│
│  └──────────────────────────────────────────────┘          │
└──────────────────────────────────────────────────────────────┘
```

Figure 2.2 Windows NT Network Control Panel.

Once Windows NT is installed, it is necessary to confirm the network card and software choices, using the Network Control Panel interface.

installation program may also ask you which additional protocols it should install, which will depend on the specifics of your network setup.

Note: for Windows NT Workstation installation, skip to step 16.

14. On Windows NT Server systems, you're asked to choose a *licensing mode*. The options available are Per Seat (this is the information access license model discussed in Chapter 1) and Per Server (the concurrent connection license model). If you choose the latter model, you will need to designate a maximum number of users. *This must not exceed the number of client licenses you've purchased for the server—otherwise you will be in violation of your license agreement and potentially liable for prosecution.* If you're confused about which agreement should be used, click the Help button and review the options. Click the Continue button *only* when you're sure you've selected the right licensing mode—Microsoft provides only a one-shot upgrade from Per-Server to Per-Client licensing, and has no provision to change in the other direction short of reinstalling!

15. On Windows NT servers, a license agreement dialog will be displayed. This will explain the selected licensing model, and require you to select an "I agree that: I have read and agree to be bound by the license

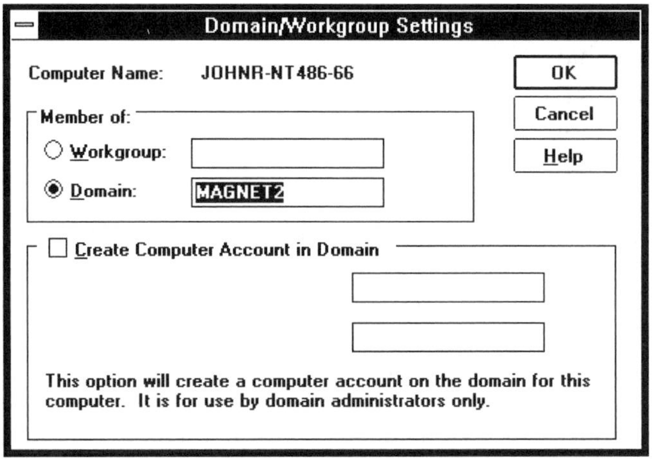

Figure 2.3 Domain/Workgroup Settings dialog.
You can set up Windows NT to log into a domain or workgroup as appropriate. If a domain is selected, time can be saved by creating a computer account in the Primary Domain Controller during installation.

agreement for this product." Check-box before proceeding. As mentioned previously, make sure you've selected the right licensing model—then check the box and click OK.

16. If you are setting network parameters, the Network Settings dialog box shows the installed network software and installed adapter cards. You may add software or adapters at this time, or configure the settings (use the bindings button to see or change the configuration). On portables, this is the time to add Remote Access Services (RAS) to enable serial-port or modem-based connections later on. This may also be the proper time to add support for an additional network protocol or third-party networking if needed.

17. The Domain/Workgroup Settings dialog box appears (see figure 2.3). You are asked to select whether the computer is a member of a workgroup or a domain (Windows NT Servers will ask whether they are to be configured as the Primary Domain Controller—see Chapters 3 and 7 for more information). You should select Domain if you are adding the machine to a Windows NT Server Domain, or Workgroup otherwise. If you select Domain, the dialog box expands to ask if you want to create a computer account in a domain; the dialog box also provides room for the domain administrator's user name and password. The administrator, by filling this information in, will cause a computer account to be added at the primary domain controller, adding the system to the

domain's database automatically. This will save time, as this step will otherwise have to be completed manually.

18. Windows NT will build (or upgrade) program manager groups. You'll note that Program Manager displays an NT AUTHORITY\SYSTEM login during this phase—that's a special security logon account used only locally for NT system setup.

19. The installation program assumes that you are an administrator, at least for your own computer. The user name is filled in (Administrator) and is not changeable. Enter a password of no more than 14 characters, and do not include spaces in the password. Passwords are case sensitive.

20. The Local Account Setup dialog box appears. Enter a user name of no more than 15 characters. As with the previous step, the password must be no more than 14 characters, cannot include spaces, and is case sensitive.

21. If you're installing NT for the first time, you must next select the location of the Virtual Memory Paging file. Select an appropriate drive from the pull-down list. The installation program updates the display with the space available, the minimum size, and the recommended size. You are asked to enter a value in the Size Chosen box. The value in the Recommended Size text box is already entered. In general, follow the recommendation unless you have a good reason to do otherwise, and never set the paging file size to less than the size of physical memory in the computer—otherwise Windows NT will not run properly.

22. If you've installed NT in the WINDOWS directory to upgrade from an earlier version of Windows, you're asked to select a directory from which to migrate applications, and migrate those applications into the NT program manager (as it does so, the appropriate .INI and .PIF files will be migrated as well).

23. The Date/Time dialog box appears, asking you to correct the system date and time and to select a time zone. Check the box Automatically Adjust for Daylight Savings Time if you are located in an area that observes Daylight Savings Time.

24. The installation program asks if you want to create an Emergency Repair disk—we highly recommend that you answer Yes. If you do so, Setup asks you to insert a blank disk in the A: drive marked Emergency Repair Disk. This disk will be formatted with the default configuration settings. All existing data on the diskette is lost. Once this disk has been created, it should be kept someplace safe but ready at hand—in the event that there is a problem with the system's configuration, the emergency disk provides the only way to recover short of installing NT again from scratch (see Chapter 5 for details)!

25. The installation program is now complete. Remove the Emergency Repair Disk from the A drive. NT Setup now removes temporary files and presents a Restart icon—select it to complete the installation.

26. The typical Windows NT Logon prompt appears.

Installation on RISC Computers

The only installation mechanism currently supported for RISC-type computers is the CD-ROM-based installation and/or WINNT32.EXE, which are similar to those employed for x86 computers. The floppy-based installation and the WINNT.EXE installations are only supported for x86-based computers and, based on the early documentation available to us, it would appear that the NT Resource Kit's Computer Profile Setup (CPS)—which is talked about later in this chapter—is x86 only as well.

The instructions that follow are representative. Details for specific configurations may vary—see the hardware manufacturer's specifications for details.

RISC Installation, Step by Step

Note: If NT is already installed on the machine and you're only attempting an upgrade to the most recent version, then use WINNT32.EXE as described previously.

1. NT may require a particular processor stepping or firmware upgrade—consult the Windows NT installation guide and SETUP.TXT provided in the \mips, \alpha, or \ppc directory, as appropriate, of your installation CD. If necessary, contact your hardware manufacturer to upgrade the CPU hardware and/or system firmware. In particular, all versions of NT on MIPS R4x00 systems require R4000 version 2.0 or later, and Digital Alpha systems require upgrading to the latest firmware version.

2. If necessary, configure the system for *little-endian* mode. If it displays the ARC boot loader when you start or cold-boot the system, then it's already configured for little-endian mode. If not, you need to get the boot floppy that came with the machine, insert it in the floppy disk drive, reboot the computer, and when the boot floppy executes and asks you if want to configure a Windows NT PROM, answer Yes. It will then make the necessary changes in the system's Programmable Read-Only Memory, and on a reboot the system will display an ARC boot loader prompt with a number of options, the most important of which, from our point of view, is Run a Program.

3. If necessary, format a system partition. RISC systems require a system partition to hold the OSLOADER.EXE and HAL.DLL files. This partition must be a FAT (File Allocation Table) partition, even if you don't want to store anything else that way and you want to run a fully configured system using NTFS. In the latter case, the system partition need be no larger than 2MB. Alternatively, you can make that partition the size of the hard disk and use it as the single drive partition for the system, or you can do any variation in between that suits your particular needs.

In general, using a small system partition just for those files and formatting the rest of the disk as NTFS will be beneficial. There's little advantage for providing a FAT partition on RISC-based systems, since they are incapable of running DOS, anyway. In any case, to partition the disk, select Run a Program from the ARC boot loader menu and enter:

```
SCSI()CDROM(0-7 as appropriate)fdisk()\mips\arcinst.exe
```

This will run the ARC system installation program and ask if you would like to create a partition. Answer Yes and you can create a system partition of any desired size, minimum of 2MB, to store the necessary files.

4. Start setup. Again, from the ARC boot loader select Run a Program, and then enter the path name:

```
SCSI()CD-ROM(0-7)fdisk()\setupldr.
```

This will start the setup loader, which performs the same function as the boot sector on the Windows NT CD-ROM boot disk for x86 based systems. This in turn will start the Windows NT setup program from the CD-ROM, and the installation will proceed exactly as it proceeds for CD-ROM installation on x86-based computers.

Required Files

For Intel-based systems, the installation program adds BOOT.INI, NTLDR (NT Loader), and NTDETECT.COM to the root directory of your boot drive. If you selected the dual-boot option (to select among operating systems at boot time), you will also have a BOOTSECT.DOS file in the root directory of your boot drive, which is used to boot the previous operating system.

If you install NT on a SCSI disk drive, the installation program will also copy NTBOOTDD.SYS to the root directory of your boot drive. RISC-based systems will find HALL.DLL and OSLOADER.EXE loaded to the \OS\NT directory of the boot drive. The files are all *required* for NT. If any one of them is missing, NT cannot be loaded.

Of course, the files in the /WINNT or /WINDOWS/SYSTEM32 directories (depending on whether you've installed Windows NT from scratch or added it in an installation to an existing Windows system) are also required. NOTE: when upgrading from one version of Windows NT to the next, it is critically important that you examine the documentation that comes with the new version to determine whether it is necessary to remove the previous installation before carrying out the new installation. *Do not assume that simply installing the new one over the old one will necessarily give you a working installation.* If you have any doubts on the matter, it may well be better to back the old installation off onto a tape drive, delete it, delete all files, and start the new installation all over fresh.

Starting Windows NT

After the installation process is completed, the installation program will ask you to boot the system. The Boot Loader program appears and asks you to select which operating system you want to use. Windows NT will be listed first, and your previous operating system will be listed next. Press Enter. The Windows NT logon dialog then appears (Figure 2.4) and asks you to press CTRL+ALT+DEL to begin NT. You'll be prompted for a password (which is case sensitive).

Installation Troubleshooting

Typically, installation problems encountered with Windows NT fall into one of two categories: Those in which the system succeeds in booting but doesn't operate properly, and those in which the system refuses to boot.

The first category is by far the simpler. If the system boots and Windows NT starts but other things don't seem to work properly for you, log in using the administrator account, run the Event Manager, and examine the system Event Log. The odds are quite good that this will show error messages referring to specific devices. For example, if you are coming up but failing to log on to the network, you are quite likely to see an Event Log with a series of network error messages, indicating that your driver has failed to bind. This generally indicates that either the wrong network card driver has been used or the settings on the

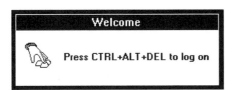

Figure 2.4 Windows NT Logon.

The Windows NT logon dialog is the most visible sign of operating system security. The CTRL+ALT+DEL sequence is required in order to assure that no *password stealer* program is running in the foreground.

network card do not match the settings provided to the network in the control panel's networks applet.

If the system fails to boot, then the situation is generally more complex and either indicates that the system as configured is incompatible with Windows NT or that inappropriate information has been provided to Windows NT during the setup process. The following is a list of some of the most common errors. No such list can be all inclusive. It is recommended that you examine the release notes for your version of Windows NT as well as this list. If you are unable to resolve the problem using the release notes, the Windows NT manuals, and this list, then consult the hardware manuals that came with your system. Finally, you may wish to call the system vendor or Microsoft for more assistance.

Common Installation Errors

A list of some common installation errors follows.

RAM

If the setup program indicates that memory is insufficient to load the system when you know in fact that there is enough memory to load the system, then the odds are quite good that the system configuration has not been reset since the memory was upgraded. This is particularly true on EISA and MCA systems. It can also happen with certain ISA systems. Run the system configuration utility supplied by your hardware manufacturer. If you are attempting to install Windows NT on a system that does not have sufficient memory (12MB) to run the graphical install program that comes with the Windows NT CD-ROM, then you may be able to accomplish an installation using the WINNT.EXE MS-DOS-based CD installation. However, it should be noted that Windows NT in its present configuration, while it will run in 8MB, will not run acceptably in less than 12MB. This is why Microsoft does not recommend this configuration. If, regardless of these facts, you decide to do an installation in an 8MB system, consult the section earlier in this chapter on over-the-network installation using WINNT.EXE.

If the BIOS is unable to recognize RAM above 16MB (a problem known to happen on some ISA-bus computers, including early model Dell 486 systems, among others), then it will be necessary to upgrade the BIOS on the particular system. Contact your hardware manufacturer for further information.

If you have any memory parity errors, Windows NT will refuse to run. The best approach, unfortunately, is to try swapping RAM chips or SIMMS until the system starts, at which point you throw away the offending RAM chip or SIMM because it has a hard error on it and is useless. This error is not a bug in Windows NT—you've had a hardware error all along. If you have had unpredictable system crashes that you have been attributing to Windows, it is entirely likely that after changing the offending RAM chip, you will find that your 16-bit DOS and Windows system has become more reliable.

Finally, you should disable any *shadow RAM* on the system—it has no effect on Windows NT, since the BIOS is never employed in Windows NT after the initial system start. Whatever memory is used for shadowing either the BIOS or video BIOS is not available to the system and is therefore completely wasted when Windows NT is running. In case of memory checksum errors, try swapping the RAM chips. The error number is F002 Parity error. Windows NT is extremely sensitive to system RAM and will not operate at all in situations where other operating systems may permit the systems to run in a crippled mode.

Network Interface Card (NIC)

The most common problems are related to the I/O address, interrupt (IRQ), and jumper settings. Interrupt conflicts are likely to cause the system to crash with an error number 0X000000A—IRQ expected to be less than or equal. Windows NT is extremely sensitive to interrupts and it will fail to load in situations that would be perfectly tolerable in the same hardware for DOS or Windows 3.1. In particular, Windows NT will not allow two hardware devices to share the same interrupt.

This typically is a problem in systems where a network interface card or other device has been configured to use IRQ 3, which is also typically used by COM2. In such a situation, it will be necessary to disable COM2, either using the CMOS setup built into your machine, manufacturer's utility programs, or by physically removing the COM2 port card. Alternatively (and much more easily), you may wish to consider using a different IRQ setting on your network card. Similar problems can be seen with I/O address and card jumper settings, either in a situation where the I/O address duplicates an I/O address for another device or where the jumper settings on the card do not match the settings that were provided to Windows NT during the installation.

These problems will usually allow the system to boot, in which case you will observe the problems in the Event Manager. The best solution at that point is to shut down Windows NT, turn off the system, remove the card that is suspected to be the problem, inspect the jumper settings, and inspect the hardware documentation that came with the card to see what settings, in fact, are set. A number of cards that are supposed to be software-configurable may not work properly with Windows NT with a software setting for which the cards have never been programmed, and it may be necessary to run a DOS-based configuration utility to reconfigure the card, and then run Windows NT.

One helpful approach is to examine the Adapter Card Help (NTCARD35.HLP) file supplied with the Windows NT Resource Kit. This file provides a complete description of NT-compatible network cards, including online diagrams showing the jumper settings, relating these to the IRQ, and jumper addresses. This can be an enormous time-saver in debugging network card problems. Note that other common IRQ conflicts include COM2, as described previously, blind printer ports, and so on. Again, Windows NT absolutely will *not* permit you to share interrupts.

If the system is starting and the Event Manager indicates that there are no hardware errors in the driver, then check to make sure that there is no duplicate computer name on your network, and also to make sure that the computer name is different than the workgroup or domain name that has been set on your system. The workgroup name cannot be the same as the computer name, or you'll get no network connection.

Video

If a video card refuses to operate at the specified video resolution, you may want to check and assure that the video card has sufficient video RAM for the specification. Also check to see that any hardware switch settings on the card match the settings that were provided to Windows NT installation. Normally, if Windows NT cannot otherwise determine how to control the video card, it will default to VGA, 640×480×16 color VGA, which works with most modern video cards. And, in general, on a system where the video has been set to an incorrect resolution, you can solve the problem by using the emergency repair disk.

Unfortunately, there is one major exception. The JZSETUP program used on MIPS and other RISC systems has a series of settings, allowing you to set a variety of video resolutions. On early MIPS R4000 workstations with fixed-frequency monitors, setting any of these resolutions other than the system default will have the effect of producing a totally screwed up video display. There appears to be no solution to this other than complete reprogramming of the system PROM on the R4000 systems. Should this happen to you, call MIPS technical support. You won't believe what they tell you to do but, amazingly enough, it *will* work.[24]

Certain specific video cards can create problems when used with NT—examples have included S3 video cards that have an address conflict with other peripherals, Weitek-based video cards that are not compatible with Microsoft's Weitek driver, and incompatibilities with a wide range of older Diamond and ATI cards (the latter can be handled using NT's 8514/a-compatible driver). Consult your Windows NT release notes for up-to-date information.

Microsoft strongly recommends upgrading any NT 3.1 video drivers to NT 3.5 (or later), as earlier drivers provided substantially lower performance. That matches our experience as well—at least in most cases.

---

24. Do we know something? Yes. Do we believe it? Well, we take the Fifth on that....

CD-ROM

If Windows NT loads from the CD but fails to recognize the CD-ROM after the graphical install has started, or if Windows NT goes through the installation correctly but refuses to recognize the CD-ROM after installation is complete, then you may want to first check the SCSI ID setting to see if the system's configuration is such that 0 and 1 are reserved for hard disk addresses, in which case you may wish to set another CD-ROM ID. Most CD-ROMs will come from the factory configured for ID = 6. If Windows NT fails to detect this, try setting it to 0 or 1.

You may also need to check to see that your CD-ROM is terminated—that in the chain of SCSI devices the last device connected has a termination plug attached or has a termination switch thrown. Consult your hardware manufacturer's specifications for details. And on some SCSI controllers, you must check to see that the bit interrupt is specified. There are controllers that have a *no interrupt* specification that is incompatible with Windows NT.

Boot Failure

First check to make sure there is enough space on the boot device for the paging file. That is, a minimum of 20MB and it may be larger depending on what you specify during the installation. Windows NT will not start if the paging file cannot be created. Make sure that BOOT.INI points to the correct path. BOOT.INI is a hidden file that will normally be in the root of the boot device. You can unhide this using the DOS ATTRIB command and then examine the file that is in text format. It will list the path using ARC system-style addressing. You must check to make sure that the path it is pointing to indeed exists on your system.

Multiple Operating Systems

In a multiple operating system environment, such as DOS-OS/2 -Windows NT, NT should always be the last operating system installed on the system. The reason for this is that some operating system boot systems, such as OS/2 multiboot, will interfere with the operation of the Windows NT boot system. The Windows NT Boot Manager, on the other hand, will generally permit other boot options to be executed. From the Windows NT Boot Manager menu, you select the option for previous operating system on drive C; the system will reboot and you will be presented with whatever the Boot Manager subsystem was that had previously been installed. This is known to work with the OS/2 Boot Manager approach, for example, and it provides a high degree of compatibility and flexibility in multiple boot situations, such as those used by system developers.

For dual-boot between NT and Windows 95, it's safe to install NT first, but then install Windows 95 from the distribution CD's SETUP program. If you install from a boot floppy, the Windows 95 boot program will overwrite NT's boot sector—and you'll have a major problem.

Hard Disk Controller

If the system is unable to recognize your hard disk after installation, then it is entirely possible that the disk is not recognized by the BIOS, which makes it impossible for the AT loader to determine that it's there and functioning. In that case you will have to manually edit the BOOT.INI file and replace the path name with the fully qualified ARC name path. There is a special tool (NTDETECT.COM) provided with the Windows NT Resource Kit that may be of some help in diagnosing this sort of problem—see Appendix 4 for details.

1,024 Cylinder Limit

Prior to version 3.51, Windows NT uses the BIOS to determine the hard disk geometry on AT-compatible disk controllers. In some cases this information is limited to 10 bits and the cylinders larger than 1,024 cannot be addressed. You may be able to use part of the disk by setting a custom configuration employing only the first 1,024 cylinders, or you may be able to use an approach, called *head doubling*, in which you state that the hard disk has ten times the number of heads physically present and half the number of cylinders; the geometry table information in the hard disk controller translates this to the actual physical dimensions of the drive. Finally, you may need a BIOS upgrade or a different hard disk controller.

From NT 3.51 on, NT supports Integrated Drive Electonics (IDE) and Enhanced IDE drives with more than 1,024 cylinders by providing support for Ontrack Corporation's *Disk Manager* program. Disk Manager is supplied with most high-capacity IDE and EIDE drives—it provides a customized boot sector and (in DOS) remaps the disk BIOS so that the additonal cylinders are recognized. NT cannot create the required boot sector, but it *can* recognize such a sector once it's created. To do so, use the Disk Manager boot disk, and follow instructions to create the boot sector—then install Windows NT.

Common Error Messages

Error 0x0000000A—IRQ expected to be less than or equal. This indicates an interrupt conflict. See the sections on network interface card, COM port, and other interrupt conflicts earlier in this section.

Error 0x00000067 or 0x00000069—Initialization error. This generally indicates a problem with the hard disk controller. On AT controllers try running at a lower DMA transfer rate. This generally will require a jumper switch change. On SCSI systems check to verify that the SCSI chain is terminated. On any system, check the IRQ, check for memory address conflicts, and check to see that the NTDETECT.COM file is in the root of the boot device. Absence of other NT files can also cause error 69, and if you find that a significant group of files is missing from the hard disk, this probably indicates a sector error on the hard disk. You will need to clean up the hard disk using a DOS-based disk maintenance utility, such as the Norton Disk Doctor, and reinstall Windows NT from scratch, unfortunately.

System Error F002—This generally indicates a hardware problem—typically, parity error on the RAM. It could also indicate a hardware problem machine check exception with the math coprocessor. It might conceivably be caused by a machine check exception on a Pentium-based system, indicating an overheat. It may also be caused by hardware problems with the accessory cards. You will need to use whatever hardware diagnostics are supplied by your system's manufacturer. If you formatted an NTFS partition on the system, you will have to use the DOS FDISK utility to deactivate the partition, reassign it, and reformat it as a FAT partition. An alternative way to do this is to use the Windows NT Setup program, select custom installation, refuse the Setup suggested path, select the NTFS partition, select p to delete the partition; then re-create the partition as a FAT partition and either continue on with the Windows NT setup, or exit. Use the DOS FDISK and FORMAT commands to replace the partition with a DOS-recognized FAT partition.

Error 00000001E—This error indicates something is wrong in the file system. You'll need to run CHKDSK or a DOS-based utility, such as Norton Disk Doctor.[25]

Couldn't Find NTLDR—This message indicates that the NT bootstrap (NTLDR) is missing from the root directory of the boot device. You can copy it directly from the CD-ROM's \I386 (or \mips, \alpha, \ppc) directory, or use EXPAND.EXE to uncompress NTLDR.$ from Setup diskette number 2.

Uninstalling Windows NT

Should you wish to completely remove NT from your system and return to a DOS-based system, it's possible—using the following steps:

---

25. The latter approach, obviously, works only on DOS-compatible FAT partitions. On HPFS you can use a compatible OS/2-based tool; for NTFS this error indicates a major problem. As of this writing (March, 1995) no low-level disk tools for NT are commercially available. However, there is a freeware disk editor from *WINDOWS Magazine*, and this—along with an NT-formatted boot diskette—can be a lifesaver. See the "Disk Maintenance" section of Chapter 5 for details.

1. Shut down and restart the system—and boot DOS (if you installed NT on a DOS system, this will probably be an option on start; if not, use a boot floppy).

2. From DOS, create a boot diskette using the FORMAT /S command, and copy CONFIG.SYS and AUTOEXEC.BAT on it.

3. Delete the entire WINNT35, WINNT, or WINDOWS\SYSTEM32 directory—whichever was used (it depends on whether NT was installed fresh, over NT 3.1, or into an existing DOS/Windows setup), and all subdirectories—from the boot partition on the target system's hard disk (this is most easily done using Windows file manager).

4. Delete the following files from the root of the boot drive:

```
pagefile.sys
boot.ini
ntldr
ntdetect.com
bootsect.dos
```

(Some of these files are hidden—use the DOS ATTRIB command to unhide them.)

At this point, attempting to boot your machine will give the error message "BOOT: Couldn't find NTLDR please insert another disk." To get around this, take the boot floppy you made earlier, then do a SYS to your boot disk (typically, sys c:) to transfer DOS and make the hard disk bootable.

Additional Notes for Servers

NT Server versions from 3.5 on contain some additonal installation tools that may be of interest once the operating system itself is installed. One of the nicest is the new Network Client Administrator—this is a complete, NT-based program that makes setup disk sets for Microsoft's NT-compatible DOS, Windows, and OS/2 clients (see Figure 2.5). It also can make an update disk with new network support for WFWG clients. Using this in conjunction with the over-the-network WINNT.EXE can just about automate installing NT Workstation on desktops—build a DOS client disk, install it on the target system, connect to the shared CD, and run WINNT to complete the installation.

There are also Windows-based NT administration tools (finally!) so that it's no longer necessary to have an NT Workstation on your desk if you want to remotely manage an NT Server. Those are in the \clients\srvtools\windows directory of the CD—just connect to it over the network, and run the SETUP.EXE in that directory.

NT 3.5 Servers also have the new Dynamic Host Configuration Protocol (DHCP) and Windows Internet Name Service (WINS) services, which make

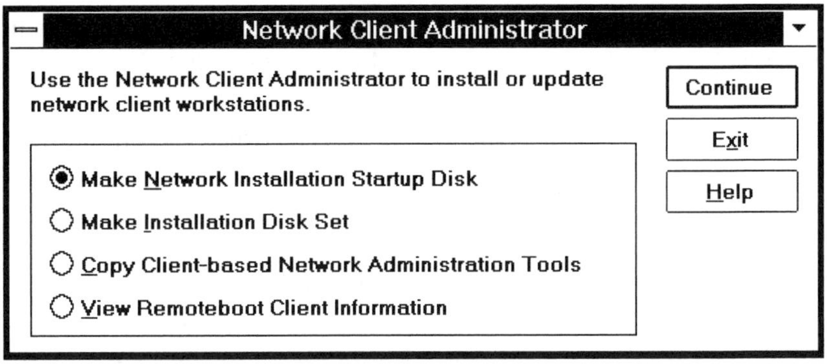

```
┌────────────────────────────────────────────────────────────┐
│ ━     Network Client Administrator                    ▼    │
├────────────────────────────────────────────────────────────┤
│ Use the Network Client Administrator to install or update  │
│ network client workstations.                    ┌──────────┐│
│                                                 │ Continue ││
│                                                 └──────────┘│
│  ┌──────────────────────────────────────────┐  ┌──────────┐│
│  │ ◉ Make Network Installation Startup Disk  │  │  Exit    ││
│  │                                           │  └──────────┘│
│  │ ○ Make Installation Disk Set              │  ┌──────────┐│
│  │                                           │  │  Help    ││
│  │ ○ Copy Client-based Network Administration│  └──────────┘│
│  │   Tools                                   │              │
│  │ ○ View Remoteboot Client Information      │              │
│  └──────────────────────────────────────────┘              │
└────────────────────────────────────────────────────────────┘
```

Figure 2.5 Network Client Administrator.
Windows NT Server includes this application, which is used by administrators to create client installation disks, copy client-based administration tools, and control the remote boot service for diskless workstations.[26]

administering TCP/IP-based networks much easier (see Chapter 6); a remote boot service that lets you support DOS and Windows on diskless workstations; and other powerful features, such as Microsoft's Migration Tool for NetWare (see Chapter 9).

Summary

You've learned how to carry out a Network Needs Analysis, how to select appropriate hardware for your needs, where to locate that hardware, and how to install and configure Windows NT on it. The next step is to establish the user accounts database, security policies, and access rights that will make the network useful to your end users—which will be covered in Chapter 3.

For More Information

Microsoft Staff (1995), *Windows NT Server Concepts and Planning Guide*. Redmond WA: Microsoft Corp. This guide, which comes with complete Server systems (or you can get them in a Windows NT Server documentation kit), is invaluable—it's the best place to start. (Other than right here, of course!) The complete NT server kit (or documentation kit) also provides an informative video that helps in understanding concepts like domains-vs.-workgroups, pri-

---

26. But not, as of this writing (March 1995), Windows 95. Special versions of the server management tools for Windows 95 have been supplied with prerelease versions of the Windows 95 resource kit, and presumably these will eventually replace the Windows-based tools altogether.

mary domain controller, and so on. If you do nothing else before installing an NT Server, at least skip the guide and watch the video. They make things a *lot* less confusing for the first-time NT user!

Microsoft Staff (1995), *Windows NT System Guide.* Redmond WA: Microsoft Corp. This guide contains all the specifics you'll need to get set up.

Microsoft Staff (1995), *Windows NT Resource Kit, Volumes 1-4.* Redmond WA: Microsoft Press. Volume 1, which includes setup information, and the Computer Profile Setup (CPS) is especially helpful.

Microsoft Staff, *TechNet CD (monthly).* Redmond WA: Microsoft Product Support Services (PSS). *TechNet* is a monthly publication on CD-ROM, containing a digest of topics from the Microsoft Knowlege Base, the *Net News* publication, Resource Kits, and other information. It's available from Microsoft sales—a one-year subscription (12 CDs) costs $295 and is worth every penny.

Microsoft Staff, *Books Online.* Redmond WA: Microsoft Product Support Services (PSS). Books Online is a feature of the Windows NT distribution CD. It essentially duplicates the printed documentation in online .HLP format, and may be found in the \SUPPORT\BOOKS directory of both Workstation and Server CDs.

Microsoft Staff, *Windows NT Workstation Evaluation Guide (version 3.5).* Redmond WA: Microsoft Product Support Services (PSS). The evaluation guides are floppy diskettes containing a wealth of information on NT Workstation and NT Server. They're available for download from Microsoft's Internet site (ftp.microsoft.com), the WINNT forum on CompuServe—or may be ordered from Microsoft Sales (800-426-9400) for a nominal fee.

CHAPTER 3

Administrative Connections

Administering Windows NT Networks

When you have read this chapter, you will understand the basic concepts of system administration, user accounts, and system security, including:

- ❑ **Why and how to create administrative user groups**
- ❑ **How to create and manage user accounts**
- ❑ **How to assign user permissions**
- ❑ **Formatting and management of system volumes (including spanned volumes)**
- ❑ **Administrative monitoring using the built-in performance monitor, event viewer, and alert tools**

You should feel comfortable carrying out the basic tasks of system administration on a Windows NT network, and be prepared to set up and use a small single-workgroup (or domain) network on your own.

System Management and the Network Administrator

All Windows NT systems are servers, and as such there are administrative tasks that have to be carried out on them. As a secure operating system, Windows NT requires all users—even local users logged in on the system console—to have a valid user account and password. The user's account, in turn, will determine what *user rights* and *resource access permissions* the user will have on the system—in effect, controlling what the user is allowed to do. Setting up, maintaining, and controlling these accounts is the job of the Network Administrator—you.

The Network Administrator

The role of *network administrator* is part systems technician, part shop foreman, part traffic cop—and more. It is the responsibility of the network administrator to provide access to the server and networked services on the LAN that is always available and—this is very important—*invisible* to the users.

A network that is always available is easy to understand, if not easy to provide. It means that the server and networked services on the LAN must be ready for users whenever they need to work. Of course hardware will need to come down for maintenance, and software must be upgraded; but it is the network administrator's job to manage these activities around users' peak production periods. You want to *plan* for maintenance, rather than fight fires as they occur.

Providing a network that is *invisible* to the users is more difficult. This means that users must have access to the server and peripherals, such as printers and network modems, without having to be aware of the way in which they are provided. In the movie *Running Scared* two policemen ask their vehicle maintenance officer for a car that is fast, powerful, and invisible.[1] He gives them a cab. This is perfect—the car is quick, the engine powerful, and in Chicago, nothing is more invisible than another yellow cab.

Your network should be a lot like that cab. It should be quick—users should be configured to have access to the things they need without resorting to searching through endless directories. It should be powerful—users must be able to print and store files on the server with confidence that their printouts will be processed quickly and their data will be backed up daily. But most of all, using the network should be familiar. Users should work on the network the way they do on their own systems. Understanding the few network facilities they use should be as easy as pointing and clicking.

This is where Windows NT lends a hand to the network administrator. Since Windows NT is based on the familiar look and feel of Windows 3.1 and Windows for Workgroups, your users will be in familiar territory when they log in to your server and access data from it. But configuring and managing your users to do so is the responsibility of the network administrator.

There are many items that go into a properly configured network to ensure that it is both available and invisible. First is network reliability. This takes into

---

1. Metro-Goldwyn-Mayer, 1986.

account server performance monitoring, fault tolerance of the system, UPSs and proper backup and recovery systems. Windows NT Server provides you with many of the tools that you'll require. For example, using the Performance Monitor you can get a quick overview of the server's current performance and even set up particular items that you want to view plotted as charts. You can also set alerts to warn you when various thresholds are exceeded.

Second is user management. This means installation and configuration of desktop equipment, creation and maintenance of user accounts and account groups, monitoring the performance of desktop systems, user training, providing user backups, and properly preparing and anticipating for user growth. It also means providing for an automated method of user and group creation via templates. This will help you save time and avoid making simple errors when granting access permissions.

Third is establishing procedures. Once procedures for providing both network reliability and user management are in place, it becomes easier to provide a stable and usable network environment. Setting up or terminating user accounts, performing daily backups, and maintaining printers should all become documented and repeatable procedures.

Performing a function one day without the ability to duplicate the steps is like cold fusion in a bottle—it may work great once but it's not at all useful. You need to have documentation in order to provide a full-time network. Who knows? You may find yourself on the phone trying to explain to a user how to retrieve a file from a backup tape. It's a lot easier if he or she has a document to refer to, for both of you, rather than trying to remember a series of dialog boxes in the correct order.

Fourth is looking toward the future. This covers many items. A properly planned network allows the network administrator to easily add additional users and additional storage to the server.

Don't think that the job is over when you have provided your group with the network they requested. If you've done a great job, your users will expect more from you. More nodes, more user directory space, more remote connectivity. The list is never-ending. It's actually simple: Your users have needs and desires related to your network, which will help them be more productive. Your task is also simple: you must be prepared to provide for their requests.

Fifth, and perhaps most important of all, is proper documentation. Network documentation is often considered an oxymoron, but its usefulness can't be overstated. It is imperative that you document every stage of your LAN for future reference. *Network Computing* magazine lists six excellent suggestions for network documentation that you can follow *now* to avoid headaches in the future:[2]

---

2. Franks, Mike; "Documenting Your Network (When You Don't Have Time)," *Network Computing*, August 1992, pgs 128-130.

Cross reference users with node addresses. This is especially useful if you are assigning IP (internet protocol) addresses to your users. Otherwise, put together a list showing your users' logins with their computer names.

Network diagrams are worth 1,000 words. You can get as fancy as you have time and patience for here. The items that you must include in your diagram are approximate locations of shared network resources (servers, concentrators, printers, network faxes, etc.), approximate locations of desktop PCs, basic cabling, and the location of any bridges, routers, or WAN (wide area network) services to which your network is connected. This diagram should be documented as fully as possible to include such items as disk capacities and amount of installed RAM for your servers and desktop systems, user names and titles, user phone numbers and modem numbers if applicable, and NIC MAC (machine access code) addresses for servers and desktop systems. In addition, include the concentrator patch number for each node next to the node location. This will help solve many of the endless mysteries usually associated with the phone wiring closet.

Document user and security information. Your list should contain the groups that each user belongs to, including global and local groups. Any special access should be noted here.

Document software on servers. When you install software, document the title, version, and publisher; give a description, show the directory location; and list the groups and users who have access to this software. Also, add a few lines that include the serial number, physical location of the disks, and the technical support phone number for the product.

Document software information online. Take this a few steps further and organize all of the information into a simple database. This will help you to locate that single item you need to know in an emergency. In fact, if you create your network diagram using your computer, you should be able to incorporate it into your database as well. That way you can also put together all of your physical location data with your user information in one place.

Document network policies and procedures online. With proper planning, the database you created in the previous step can contain all of the information you need to run your network, including your policies and procedures.

One last thought: Make hard copies of all of your documentation, place a copy with your server, and distribute the copies to the appropriate IT departments.

The Network Administrator's Responsibilities

The network administrator has a series of responsibilities that fall into nine categories. These categories may be thought of as a pyramid. The bottommost responsibilities are tasks that consume most of the network administrator's time, but are continuous activities, spread out over time. The topmost tasks are not as frequent, but they can consume an entire day in one shot.

Network Administrator's Pyramid of Responsibilities

Putting out fires
Training users
User account management
Group account management
User desktop configuration and maintenance
Backups, performance monitoring, network security
Server and network hardware and software maintenance
Backup and recovery
Disaster planning
Growth planning

For example, *growth planning* consists of listening to users and anticipating their future network and server requirements. Realistically, this occurs all the time; as the network administrator you are constantly planning for future growth of your network. Windows NT Server provides you with many ways to monitor performance, and it's your job to put these things together and draw conclusions about them that will assist you when making future acquisitions of hardware and software.

Putting out fires, on the other hand, is a shorter, more concentrated task that has immediate consequences. When a fire occurs, such as a failed NIC (network interface card) in your server, you aren't just storing away data for later use. You are going into action now! You'll have to down your server, replace the card, bring the server back up, test the new card, and make the server available to users. If you've built your server with fault tolerance and failsafes in mind, and if your budget permits, you may have a backup server on standby. In that case, you may only have to migrate users to the new server and replace the other when your users have met their deadlines.

The items in the pyramid fall into daily, weekly, and monthly tasks. This isn't a strict rule, but for an established network, most of the work that you do can be planned along these lines. New user creation, for example, might occur only twice a year with our original accounting department example. When it does, this task becomes a daily item, but we'll leave it under the monthly tasks due to its frequency.

Whether the network administrator is you or someone you hire, here are a few guidelines that you can refer to when managing your server and LAN.

Daily Tasks

Check Error Logs—All error logs should be checked for new entries, which should include those from *both* the Windows NT Event Manager and

Performance Monitor (covered later in this chapter). All warnings should be followed up—see Chapter 4 for troubleshooting and performance-tuning information.

Check Help Desk E-Mail—Read and prioritize user help requests.

Check Volume Free Space—Look for anomalous disk space loss and potential space shortages (you may want to consider automating this process using Performance Monitor *alerts*, a procedure covered later in this chapter).

Perform Daily Backups (if used)—If you are performing daily backups (and you must back up either daily or weekly, or both) and are having the backup performed automatically (using the scheduler service with NT's built-in backup, or a third-party backup product), remember to check that a new tape or the correct tape is ready in your tape drive. If necessary, periodically check and tension the tape drive mechanism.

Confirm Overnight Backups (if made)—If daily backups are performed overnight, ensure that they were successful. You can do this either by running a full verify pass, or by retrieving a sample set of files (in the latter case, don't always try to retrieve the same set of files). Remove and store the tapes. *Do not* store your only set of backup tapes in the same room as your only server—doing so *risks losing all of your data* in a single event, such as a fire.

Weekly Tasks

Clear Errant Temporary Files—Remove dead temporary files from user and mail directories (you might wish to automate this task using the Windows NT *at* script command covered at the end of this chapter).

Create and Distribute User Space Lists—Look for excessive disk space use, and distribute memos to responsible users, requesting that they either delete or archive the files.

Check Mail System Status—Look for excessive mail message archiving—dead backup files and other temp files that should be deleted.

Perform Weekend Backups (if used)—If you are performing weekly backups (and you must back up either daily or weekly, or both), remember to check that a new tape or the correct tape is ready in your tape drive. Periodically, check the tape drive mechanism. Be sure to confirm the backup, as specified in Daily Tasks given previously.

Monthly Tasks

Archive and Delete Dead Files—Check files for activity, and delete or archive files that have not had any activity for more than a month.

Perform Disaster Drill—During off time (yes, I know, "ha ha, very funny"), perform *disaster drills* to test your disaster recovery plan and backup strategy. This is *very* important and can mean the difference between being able to recover from a problem during peak periods and not being able to recover at all.

Perform Month-End (or Cycle-End) Backups (if used)—These are different from both daily and weekly backups, and should be performed for use as an archive if your data is cyclical in nature. For example, you might perform backups in the middle of every other month if that is when your production cycle ends. The data that you archive will contain the final report from each of your cycles. This data should be archived off-site as a disaster recovery tool.

Creating Groups and Users

The name of this section is Creating Groups and Users, rather than the other way around, for a reason. As you discovered while conducting your network needs assessment (in Chapter 2), it is possible to collect your users into similar groups who share the same access and security requirements. For example, you may have a directory that contains network applications. Not all of the users in your network will require access to all of these subdirectories containing applications. The directory containing a CAD/CAM application should be accessed only by the engineers who use the program. The directory that contains a word processing application is probably required by everyone on your network. You should build groups according to these access requirements.

Domains and Workgroups

Before looking into the details of user account and group management, we need to understand the concept of *domains* and *workgroups*. In a Windows NT network, a workgroup is a collection of computers that are grouped together for convenience when browsing network services. The network administrator designates a workgroup for each Windows NT system, and this name appears to other systems on the local area network.

The major limitation of a workgroup is that each server in the workgroup must maintain its own database of user accounts, independently of other servers in the workgroup. This means that users with a need to access more than one server will require separate accounts on each—a situation that can quickly become an administrative nightmare on a large network.

The Windows NT Server expands on this with the concept of a *domain*. Like workgroups, domains appear in the browse list, and they group servers and workstations together logically. However, domains expand on this by maintaining a single account database that applies to all servers in the domain. All account information is maintained in a single database on the *primary domain controller* (PDC). Other servers that are configured as domain controllers (DCs) on the network (which can include Windows NT Servers and LAN Manager 2.0 or higher servers) maintain a copy of this central database, in which changes are updated every five minutes (a process called *replication*, which will be covered in more detail in chapter 7).[3] Any server can validate a log-on request.

The great advantage of a domain over a workgroup is that users need only one account to access any system in the network. Indeed, through a process called *interdomain trust* (see Chapter 7 for details), this approach can be applied between domains so that a user with an account in one domain can access servers in other domains.

As a practical matter, however, you need not worry too much about the division between workgroups and domains—if your network includes a Windows NT Server, then you are using domains. If not (even if you are joining a Windows NT Workstation to an existing LAN Manager Domain) then you are dealing with a workgroup. In situations where the difference between these is more than just semantics, we will point it out—for now, just assume that the workgroup is a lightweight domain, and you'll get the gist of it.

You should choose your domain (or workgroup) name to reflect its primary function. TIM1 is not a good choice for the accounting department, even if the vice president of accounting is named Tim. ACCT_DEPT is a better choice. It is easy to understand what department this server belongs to and it takes into account the possibility of growth to ACCT_DEPT_2. Another possibility, which may make sense in very large networks, is the use of geographical domain names. Indeed, Microsoft uses this approach itself—as you will see in Chapter 7.

Working with Groups

The process of creating and managing user accounts and account groups is basically the same whether you are operating a stand-alone Windows NT server for a workgroup or an enterprise-wide multiserver network. It is perfectly allowable for one user to belong to more than one group—in fact, it is essential to planning your network. Windows NT Server provides for the creation of two types of groups.

Local groups are groups of users and global groups that have access to servers from their own domain. *Global groups* (NT Server only) are groups of users that have access to servers and workstations from their own domain or other domains that *trust* their home domain.

---

3. Unlike NTAS 3.1, NT Server 3.5 does not have to be installed as a DC—it can be installed as a stand-alone server that acts like NT Workstation where user accounts are concerned.

Predefined groups in the basic Windows NT product include Administrators, Users, Power Users, Backup Operators, and Guests. Windows NT Server adds Domain Admins, Domain Users, Account Operators, Print Operators, Server Operators, and Replicator—and eliminates the Power Users group. Some of these groups, as you can see from their names, involve special functions and rights that you may assign to particular users. Not every one of these groups is a stand-alone group. Some of them are, by default, members of other groups.

Administrative Tools

Both Windows NT Workstation and Server provide a basic set of tools for system management. All are found in Program Manager's *Administrative Tools* group. The *User Manager* application is used to create and modify both local and global groups. Once these groups have been created, File Manager is used to grant directory permissions to members of these groups. The *Performance Monitor* application provides a way to track the performance of NT services and applications, while the Windows NT *Event Viewer* is used to examine the system's log files. Windows NT also includes a simple built-in *Backup* application. We also cover Windows NT Server's *Licensing* application.

Windows NT Server provides more sophisticated versions of these tools for domain management, including *User Manager for Domains, Server Manager,* and *User Profile Editor*. Since these are used primarily in larger networks, we cover them in Chapter 7. NT Server also provides a set of client-based administration tools that run on NT Workstations, Windows for Workgroups, or Windows 95 systems—which are also covered in Chapter 7.

User Manager

The User Manager application helps you add, change, and delete accounts for individuals and groups. It also sets the server (or domain) security and audit policies.

Individual users are assigned a user type that correspond to security levels. For example, users who are part of the Administrators group may perform all User Manager tasks, and have the most control over a network. Users who are part of the Users group can create groups, then modify or delete them, and can give user accounts memberships in the groups created.

To start User Manager, click on the icon in the Administrative Tools program group, or select File/Run and type MUSRMGR.EXE in the Command Line text box and click on OK. The main window of User Manager is shown in Figure 3.1.

To exit User Manager, select User/Exit.

```
┌─────────────────────────────────────────────────────────────────────┐
│ ─                          User Manager                         ▼ ▲ │
├─────────────────────────────────────────────────────────────────────┤
│  User   Policies   Options   Help                                   │
├─────────────────────────────────────────────────────────────────────┤
│ Username          Full Name          Description                    │
├─────────────────────────────────────────────────────────────────────┤
│ 👤 Administrator                      Administrative User Account    │
│ 👤 Guest                              Guest User Account             │
│ 👤 JEP                                                               │
│ 👤 jpowell          JPOWELL                                          │
│ 👤 JR               John Ruley                                       │
│ 👤 RES              Rick Scott                                       │
│ 👤 RM               Roberta Morales                                  │
│                                                                     │
├─────────────────────────────────────────────────────────────────────┤
│ Groups                    Description                               │
├─────────────────────────────────────────────────────────────────────┤
│ 👥 Administrators          Members can fully administer the system  │
│ 👥 Backup Operators        Members can assign file backup and restore privileges │
│ 👥 Guests                  Guests of the domain                     │
│ 👥 Power Users             Members can treat the computer as their own - set time, set sharepoints, etc │
│ 👥 Replicator              Members can administer domain controller replication functions │
│ 👥 Users                   Ordinary users of the domain             │
│                                                                     │
└─────────────────────────────────────────────────────────────────────┘
```

Figure 3.1   User Manager.

The Windows NT User Manager (and User Manager for Domains, in the Windows NT Server) is the primary administrative tool for controlling user accounts, groups, access permissions, and user rights.

Adding a Group

You can create your own local groups (Domain Administrators in Windows NT Server domains can also create global groups). To do so:

1. Select the user accounts you want added to a group, or select a user group so that no user accounts are selected. Choose User/New Local Group. The Local Group Properties dialog box shown in Figure 3.2 appears.

2. Type in the name of the group and its description at the top of the New Local Group dialog box.

3. If you want to see the complete names of the users you chose in the first step, click on Show Full Names.

4. Select Add to add members to the group. Click on OK when all users are added.

5. Select OK to exit the dialog box.

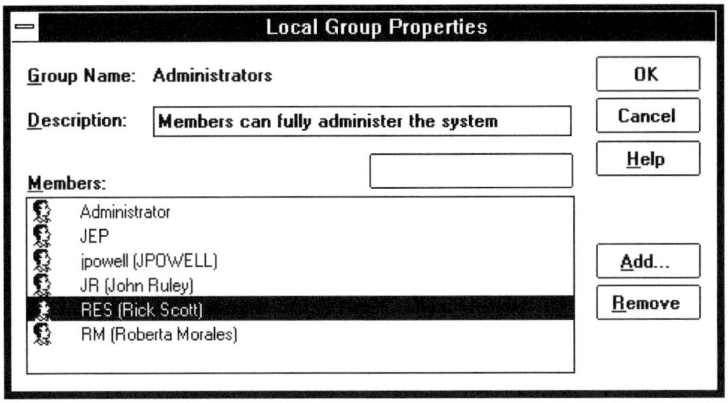

Figure 3.2 Local Group Properties.
Administration of Windows NT (and Windows NT Server) networks can be greatly simplified by exploiting the local and global groups. Assigning access permissions and user rights to groups automatically allocates the same permissions and rights to users within the group.

Deleting a Group

If you want to delete a local group, select the group from the User Manager window. Select User/Delete. If User Manager displays a confirmation message, click on OK. Click on Yes to delete the group.

Adding a User Account

A user account is a set of information about a user, including rights and membership in groups. Several user accounts come predefined within Windows NT, and are arranged in a hierarchy by default.

To add a user account to the system:

1. Select User/New User. The dialog box shown in Figure 3.3 is displayed.
2. Enter the user name in the Username box. User names must be unique, cannot exceed 20 characters, and cannot contain any characters except:

   " / \ ; : [ ] < > | = + , * ?

3. You can optionally enter the full name (first, middle initial, and last name) of the user in the Full Name box.
4. Optionally enter a text description in the Description box.

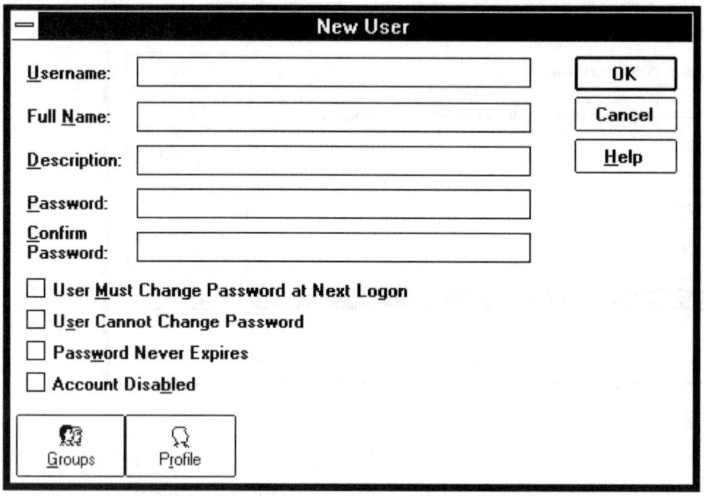

Figure 3.3 New User dialog.

You add a new user to your network using the New User dialog from the Windows NT User Manager.

5. Enter the same password in the Password and Confirm Password text boxes. Passwords must not exceed 14 characters and are case sensitive.

6. To require a user to enter a new password when he or she logs on for the next session, check the User Must Change Password at Next Logon check box. If selected, be sure the User Cannot Change Password check box is *not* checked.

7. If you want to prevent the user from changing the password you assign, check the User Cannot Change Password check box.

8. To override the Maximum Password Age in the Account policy setup (see Managing Security Policies following) check the Password Never Expires box.

9. Select Account Disabled to temporarily disable an account, a useful option for setting up multiple users in advance of their use of the system (users can be activated individually when they actually join the workgroup).

10. To administer a group or profile, select the option from the bottom of the dialog box and fill in the information as necessary.

11. Click on OK.

Note that sometimes it is actually faster to copy an existing user account and make changes as necessary. To copy a user account, select the user name from the list in the User Manager window, then choose User/Copy. The Copy Of dialog box requests information similar to that asked for new users. Complete it and click on OK.

Changing User Accounts

When a user forgets his or her password, or when conditions change within your organization, you may need to change information about a user account. To change the information in a single user account, choose the user account from the list in User Manager, then select User/Properties (alternatively, double-click on the user account name). Make the necessary corrections.

You can change more than one account simultaneously in a similar fashion. Select the user accounts from the list in User Manager by clicking on each one, then select User/Properties. If the users you selected share a common description, the description is displayed in the Description text box. You can enter a new description or edit the description if you wish. Next, set the Users Cannot Change Password, Passwords Never Expire, and Accounts Disabled check boxes as needed, and select the Groups or Profile options if desired. Finally, select OK.

It's also possible to rename, disable, and delete user accounts—which brings up an important point: User account references are stored by Security Information Descriptor (SID), *not* by name in permissions and group memberships. Thus, renaming an account leaves permissions and group membership intact, while deleting an account and creating a new one requires all permissions and group assignments to be rebuilt from scratch. Similarly, disabling an account and reenabling it later leaves permissions and group memberships intact, saving time and effort over deleting an account and then creating a new one.

To rename a user account:

1. Select the user account.
2. Select User/Rename.
3. In the Change To text box, enter the new user name. The same naming conventions used for creating new accounts are in effect here.
4. Click on OK.

To remove one or more user accounts:

1. Select the user account(s) from the User Manager window.
2. Select User/Delete.
3. If you are asked to confirm the delete, click on OK.
4. Select Yes to delete the account name displayed in the dialog box. Select Yes to All to delete all user accounts (if multiple accounts were selected in step 1).

An alternative to deleting accounts is inactivating them. Such inactivation keeps the underlying user information, but temporarily disables their user account. To disable an account:

1. Select the user account.
2. Select User/Properties.
3. Check the Account Disabled box, and click on OK.

Connecting Users to Groups

Once you have established user(s) and group(s), you need to attach (connect) a user to a group. Maintaining user and group connections is simple. To perform the update:

1. Select the user, then click on the Groups button at the bottom of the dialog box. The Group Membership dialog box, shown in Figure 3.4, is displayed.
2. The groups to which the selected user belongs are displayed in the Member Of list box. The groups to which the user is excluded (does not belong) are displayed in the Not Member Of list box.
3. To add a user to a group, select one or more groups from the Not Member Of list, then click on Add.
4. To remove a selected user from one or more groups, select the group(s) from the Member Of list, then click on Remove.
5. Select OK to exit the dialog box.

Adding, changing, and removing multiple users simultaneously is very similar. To do so:

1. Select the user accounts from the User Manager window.
2. Select User/Properties.
3. Click on Groups.
4. The groups to which all users belong (the common groups) are displayed in the All Are Members Of list box. The groups to which one or more members *may* be a part is shown in the Not All Are Members Of list box.
5. To add *all* selected users to one or more groups, select the group(s) from the Not All Are Members Of list, then click on Add.
6. To remove *all* users from one or more groups, select the group(s) from the All Are Members Of list, then click on Remove.
7. Select OK to exit the dialog box.

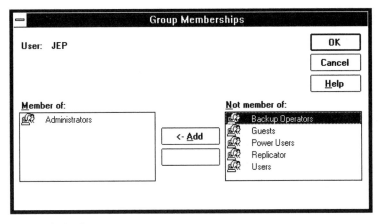

Figure 3.4 Groups.

Once the user is added, designate the groups to which he (or she) belongs—by doing so, you automatically assign all necessary access privileges and rights.

Managing Security Policies

User Manager allows you to define and configure policies that control user rights, how events are audited, and the method of password use.

Setting Account Policies

To manage the way passwords are used:

1. Select the User Account.
2. Select Policy/Account. The Policy/Account dialog box shown in Figure 3.5 appears.
3. Select the password policy or policies that are required. Select a maximum password period (up to 999 days), minimum password age (up to 999 days minimum), minimum password length, and password history options.
4. Click on OK.

Setting Audit Policies

To manage the events that are added to the audit log:

1. Select Policy/Audit.
2. To turn off all auditing, click on the Do Not Audit. To audit one or more events, select Audit These Events, then select the event you want to

```
┌──────────────────────────────────────────────────────────────────┐
│ ▬                          Account Policy                          │
├──────────────────────────────────────────────────────────────────┤
│  Computer:  WINNT                                    ┌──────────┐  │
│                                                      │    OK    │  │
│  ┌─Maximum Password Age──────┐ ┌─Minimum Password Age──┐          │
│  │ ◉ [Password Never Expires]│ │ ◉ Allow Changes Immediately│ ┌──────────┐ │
│  │                           │ │                        │ │ Cancel   │ │
│  │ ○ Expires In [    ][▲▼] Days│ │ ○ Allow Changes In [ ][▲▼] Days│ ┌──────────┐ │
│  └───────────────────────────┘ └───────────────────────┘ │   Help   │ │
│                                                           └──────────┘ │
│  ┌─Minimum Password Length───┐ ┌─Password Uniqueness────┐          │
│  │ ◉ Permit Blank Password   │ │ ◉ Do Not Keep Password History│      │
│  │                           │ │                        │          │
│  │ ○ At Least [ ][▲▼] Characters│ │ ○ Remember [ ][▲▼] Passwords│      │
│  └───────────────────────────┘ └───────────────────────┘          │
└──────────────────────────────────────────────────────────────────┘
```

Figure 3.5 Policy/Account.

You can enforce an appropriate security policy on your Windows NT network by setting appropriate policy settings on your system or Domain. The Windows NT Advanced Server adds a capability to force disconnection of users who operate outside their designated log-on periods.

audit. Check whether you want to log a successful event, a failed event, or both.

3. To stop Windows NT when the audit log is full, check the Halt System when Security Event Log Is Full check box.

4. Select OK.

The following describes the events that can be audited and what they mean:

Events	*Triggers*
File and Object Access	Access a directory, printer, or file set for auditing (see File Manager for details).
Logon and Logoff	Log into or log off a computer system, or connect to a network.
Process Tracking	This covers a wide variety of events, including starting a program.
Restart, Shutdown, and System	Restart or shut down a computer, or trigger an event that impacts the security log or security of the system.
Security Policy Changes	Changes to rights of users or to audit policies.
Use of User Rights	Using a user right.
User and Group Management	Add, modify, or delete a user account or group account; rename, disable, or enable a user account; or change a password.

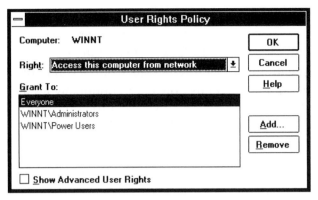

Figure 3.6 User rights.

Security is further assured by allowing the administrator to selectively assign user rights to particular groups of Windows NT users. This assures that only users who have a need to carry out sensitive operations (such as account maintenance, backup and restoration, or shutting down the system) can do so.

Setting User Rights

To manage the authorization for a task:

1. Select Policy/User Rights. The User Rights Policy dialog box shown in Figure 3.6 appears.

2. Select the right from the Right pull-down list box. The users and groups granted the right are listed in the Grant To box. To display the advanced user rights, check the Show Advanced User Rights at the bottom of the dialog box. Rights are detailed in the following. For a more detailed explanation, see the User Manager chapter of the Windows NT System Guide.

3. To remove a user or group from the list of the right, select it and click on Remove.

4. To add a user or group to the list, select Add. Complete the Add Users and Groups dialog box, and click on OK.

5. Select OK.

User Right	*Permissions Granted*
Access this computer from network.	Connect to the computer (via a network).
Back up files and directories.	Permission to back up files and directories; this overrides file and directory permissions.

Bypass traverse checking.	An advanced right allows user to change directories and move through a tree regardless of any existing directory permissions.
Change the system time.	Set internal clock of the computer.
Force shutdown from a remote system.	Shuts down (and optionally restarts) Windows NT. This right isn't used by any of the administration tools supplied with NT, but is employed by *Systems Management Server* (SMS) and some third-party tools.[4]
Log on as a service.	Register with the system as a service (used for Replicator local group's Replicator service).
Log on locally.	Log on to the computer using the active computer's keyboard.
Manage auditing and security log.	Specify the events and file access that can be audited; furthermore, this right permits a user to view and clear a security log.
Restore files and directories.	Permission to restore files and directories; note that this right overrides file and directory permissions.
Shut down the system.	Shut down Windows NT.
Take ownership of files and other objects.	Assume ownership of files and directories.

In our earlier example we looked at two groups, one that needed access to the CAD/CAM application, and another that needed access to the word processing application. Using the File Manager, you can highlight the directory you need to work with and choose Permissions from the Security menu (or choose the Permissions button on the toolbar). In the Directory Permissions dialog box you can allow particular access to the selected directory. First you highlight a group or user, then choose Special Directory Access from the Type of Access pull-down menu. You'll open the Special Directory Access dialog box, where you can grant either full control or choose a combination of six permissions.

Managing Profiles

Windows NT optionally stores a *profile* as part of a user's account information.[5] The profile associates a logon script name and the home directory with a

---

4. Including a public-domain shutdown command-line application, available for download from the Windows NT section of CompuServe's WinShare forum.

5. Windows NT Server includes much more sophisticated User Profiles, which are managed using a separate *User Profile Editor* tool covered in Chapter 4.

particular user account. This can speed up the login process, or help you as an administrator control the login process of your users.

To set a profile for a user account:

1. When adding, copying, or changing a user account, select the Profile button at the bottom of the dialog box.

2. Optionally enter the logon script in the Logon Script Name box.

3. If you want to use a local path as the home directory, enter the local directory in the Local Path text box. Use *%user name%* to substitute the username for a subdirectory name.

4. To use a network directory as the home directory, click on Connect. Enter a drive letter (or select one from the pull down list), then enter the network path in the To text box.

5. Select OK.

Monitoring Performance

As we noted earlier, in our discussion of the Network Administrator's responsibilities, day-to-day performance monitoring is critical. Windows NT provides a powerful set of tools for this that include *Performance Monitor* and *Event Viewer.*

Performance Monitor

The Performance Monitor utility of Windows NT lets you observe the performance of your current system, viewing information as charts or reports. You can also create charts and log files, and set warnings about activity levels on your system. While Performance Monitor provides data on the current performance, it does not offer suggestions for improving performance.

You can create up to four simultaneous views, one each for charts, alerts, logs, and reports. Each of these views can be customized, and each view's settings can be saved and recalled for future sessions. Setting and working with each of these views is quite similar. You can save the performance statistics from any of these views and use the data at a later time.

To start Performance Monitor, select its icon from the Administrative Tasks program group. To exit the utility, select File/Exit.

Views

There are four views in Performance Monitor:

Alert View provides information about events that exceed user-defined limits. You can monitor more than one condition at a time, and when an

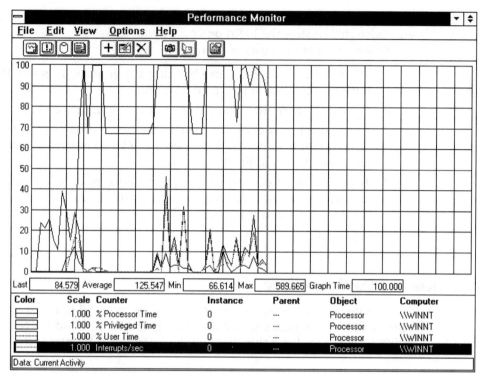

Figure 3.7 Performance Monitor.

The Windows NT Performance Monitor application provides a powerful capability to monitor system operations. You can observe system performance and display it graphically, set alerts when variable limits are exceeded, and log data to a file for later analysis or historical use.

event occurs Windows NT can run a program to take corrective or preventive action, or alert you to the existence of the condition.

Chart View allows you to display information graphically, which helps you spot system problems immediately. A sample chart view is displayed in Figure 3.7.

Log View sends key information to a separate disk file for later analysis.

Report View displays a simple report of event values you select to display.

To switch between alert, chart, log, and report view, select View, then select:

Alert to move to alert view. Shortcut: press Ctrl+A.

Chart to move to chart view. Shortcut: press Ctrl+C.

Log to move to log view. Shortcut: press Ctrl+L.

Report to move to log view. Shortcut: press Ctrl+R.

To clear a view, select Edit/Clear Display.

Working with Performance Monitor

The toolbar at the top of the Performance Monitor is shared by the four views. The buttons are all used in essentially the same way; only the information changed within each view is different. For example, to remove an element from a display, select the event being monitored, then select Edit/Delete, or click the Delete button from the toolbar.

On the toolbar, the plus sign button lets you add items to be monitored (charted, logged, reported, and so on). The next button (a pencil eraser moving across a screen) lets you edit values of parameters already set. The third button (an x) is used by all views to delete an element from the monitor.

The next button on the toolbar, a camera, is used to tell Windows NT to take measurements immediately. This is the Update Now button. You can also select Options/Update Now to update the display. To change the method of updating the display, select Options, then choose either periodic or manual updating. If you select periodic updating, enter a value for the frequency for periodic updates in the Interval text box. Finally, click on OK.

The button with the open book picture on it tells Windows NT to place a bookmark at the current measurement. The last button on the toolbar provides quick access to the monitor's options.

Specific instructions for each view are provided in the following section.

Alert View

To add items to be monitored to the alert view, switch to the alert view, then:

1. Select Edit/Add To View or select the Add to View button from the toolbar. The Add to Alert dialog box, shown in Figure 3.8, appears.

2. Select an object type from the Object pull-down list.

3. The Counter list box changes to display the elements of the selected object type that can be measured. Select one or more items from this list. (To read more about a counter, select Explain. Performance Monitor displays a text box that provides more information about the selected counter.)

4. Select an instance if this is appropriate to the object type you have selected.

5. The Color box is automatically updated with the next available color. To change the color, choose one from the pull-down list.

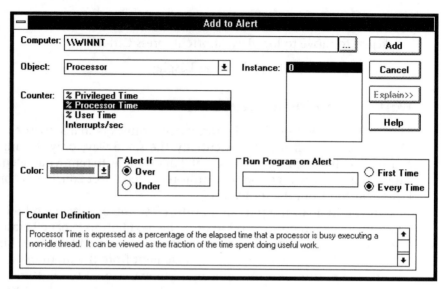

Figure 3.8 Performance Monitor Alert/Add.

Setting alerts on selected performance variables can give an early warning of system problems or security issues.

6. Enter the alert condition in the Alert If box. Enter a value that sets the minimum or maximum condition that will trigger an alert.

7. Windows NT can run a program when the alert condition is detected. To trigger this, type the full path name to the program in the Run Program on Alert text box. Select First Time to run the program once, or select Every Time to run the program each time the condition is detected.

8. Select Add.

9. Repeat steps 2 through 8 until all alert conditions have been added, then click on Done.

10. To save these settings, select File/Save Alert Settings. To create a new settings file, select File/Save Alert Settings As. Enter a file name, then select OK.

To change any alert conditions:

1. Double-click the element in the legend, select Edit/Edit Alert Entry, or select the Edit Alert Entry button from the toolbar.

2. Change the desired values: color, Alert If, and/or Run Program on Alert.

3. Click on OK.

Changing Alert Notifications

To change how an alert notifies you when a condition is detected:

1. Select Options/Alert or select the Options button from the toolbar.
2. Select a notification option. Windows NT can switch to the alert view when the condition is met. To set this property, select Switch to Alert View.
3. Select Send Network Message to notify you of a condition. Enter a computer name (do not include backslashes in the name) to be sent the notice in the Net Name box. Both Switch to Alert View and Send Network Message options may be selected at the same time.
4. Select the Update Time option: Choose either Manual Update or Period Update. If you select Periodic Update, enter the time interval in the Interval text box. If you select Manual Update, select Update Now to check for alert conditions.
5. Click on OK.

Chart View

To add items to a chart view, switch to this view, then:

1. Select Edit/Add to Chart or click on the Add to Chart button from the toolbar.
2. Select an object type from the Object pull-down list.
3. The Counter list box changes to display the elements of the selected object type that can be measured. Select one or more items from this list.
4. Select an instance if appropriate to the object type you have selected.
5. The Color box is automatically updated with the next available color. To override the selection, choose a color from the pull-down list. Likewise select a line scale, width, and style.
6. Select Add.
7. Repeat steps 2 through 6 until all items have been added. Select Done.
8. To save these settings, select File/Save Chart Settings. To create a new settings file, select File/Save Chart Settings As. Enter a file name, then select OK.

To change a chart's characteristics:

1. Select Options/Chart or click on the Options button from the toolbar.
2. Select the option you want to display from the Chart options dialog box.
3. Update the values desired, then click on OK.

Changing Items in a Chart

To change the options of an item in the chart:

1. Select the element you want to change from the legend.
2. Double-click on the element, select Edit/Edit Chart Line, or click on the Edit Chart Line button from the toolbar.
3. Make your selection of color, scale, width, or style; then click on OK.

Log View

The log file lets you record information on specific objects, then view these events later. The log file keeps an informational record, and sends this information to a separate disk file for analysis by other programs. In addition, log files can be used as input to the other views, which can then display the values captured in the log file.

To select which events are recorded in a log file, switch to Log View; then:

1. Select File/Open and enter the name of the file (log setting files have the extension .PML). To create a new log file, select File/New Log Settings.
2. Select Edit/Add to Log or click on the Add to Log button from the toolbar to add items to an existing log file. The Add to Log dialog box, shown in Figure 3.9, appears.
3. Select the type of object you want to add to the log from the Objects box, then click on Add. Repeat this step until all items are added.
4. Click on Done.

To change how events are recorded in the log file:

1. Select Options/Log or click on the Options button from the toolbar.
2. Enter the name of the log file in the Log File text box.
3. Enter the new values as appropriate.
4. Click on OK to record the options but *not* start the logging process. Otherwise, select Start Log to begin immediate logging of the selected events.
5. To stop logging events to the log file, select Options/Log and select Stop Log.

Sublog Files

You can create a log file that contains only *some* of the information of a full log file, thus allowing you to analyze a limited number of events using a smaller file.

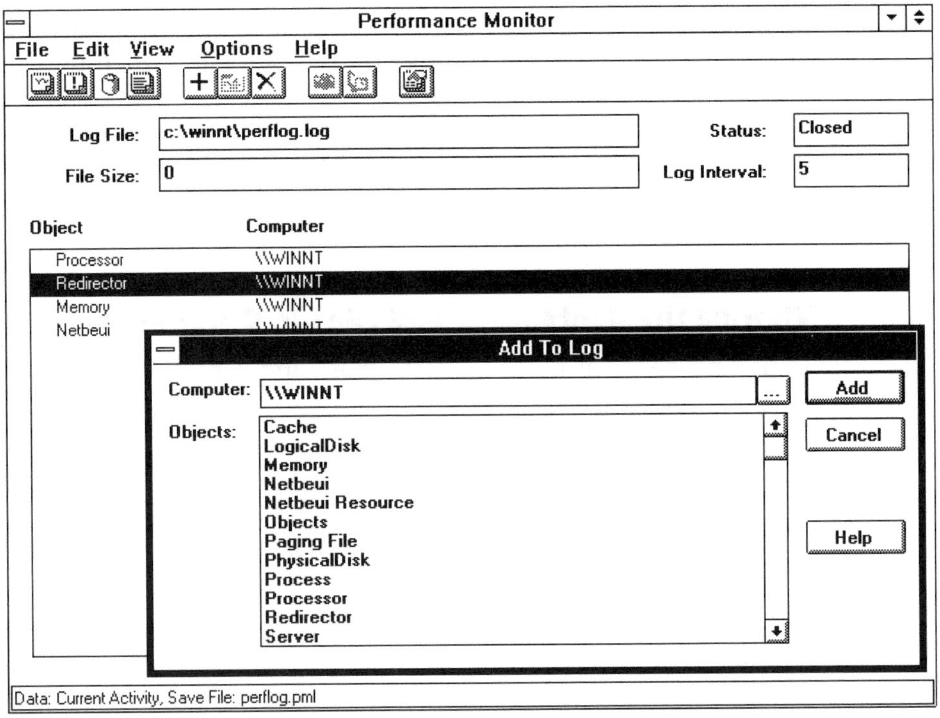

Figure 3.9 Performance Monitor Log/Add.

Writing data to a permanent log file allows you to analyze it offline and retain it for maintenance histories and auditing.

To create a smaller log file, a process called relogging a log file:

1. Select Log View.

2. Select Options/Data From.

3. Enter the name of the full log file.

4. Select Edit/Add to Log (to select which objects should be relogged), Edit/Delete from Log (to prevent an object from being relogged), and/or Edit/Time Window (to change the starting and stopping time points of the selected activity).

5. Select Options/Log and type the name of the new log file. Select a new log interval if desired, then select Start Logging.

Bookmarks in a Log File

Bookmarks, available in all views, are probably most useful in a log file. Bookmarks allow you to find key locations within the file; bookmarks are free-form text you can place anywhere within the log. Bookmarks are useful for noting the beginning and ending points of a log file when the file is used as input to a Chart, Alert, or Report view.

To add a bookmark to a log file, select Options/Bookmark or click on the Bookmark button from the toolbar (the icon that looks like an open book). Type the text of your bookmark in the Bookmark Comment text box, then click on Add.

Viewing the Contents of Log Files in Other Views

To use the log file as input to Alert, Chart, and Report views:

1. Switch to the view you want to use.
2. Select Options/Data From.
3. In the Data Values Displayed From box select Log File.
4. Enter the log file name and select OK.

Use the options within the view to limit what events are displayed. Unless otherwise specified, an Alert, Chart, or Report view will use the entire log file. To limit the analysis to specific beginning or ending points, select the view you want to use, then follow steps similar to the following, which explain how to control the values within a specified starting and stopping point.

1. Select Edit/Time Window.
2. Drag the beginning or ending point of the time frame to a new location. As you move it, the dialog box displays the new time.
3. To use a bookmark as a starting or ending point, select the bookmark, then select Set as Start (to use the bookmark as the beginning point for analysis), or select Set as Stop (to use the bookmark as the end point).
4. Click on OK.

Use the Edit menu and other editing tools for each of the appropriate views to analyze data from the log file. The steps are identical to those used for analyzing live performance data.

Report View

To add items to a report view:

1. Select Edit/Add to Report or click on the Add to Report button from the toolbar.
2. Select an object type from the Object pull-down list.

3. The Counter list box changes to display the elements of the selected object type that can be measured. Select one or more items from this list.

4. Select an instance if appropriate to the object type you have selected.

5. Select Add.

6. Repeat steps 2 through 5 until all items have been added, then click on Done.

7. To save these settings, select File/Save Report Settings. To create a new report file, select File/Save Report Settings As. Enter a file name, then select OK.

The most common change you will make to a report is to change the frequency with which it is updated. To change the frequency, select Options/Report or click on the Options button from the toolbar. Select Manual Update or Periodic Update from the Update Time section. Note that if you select Periodic Update, you *must* enter a time interval in the Interval text box. Click on OK.

Reusing Settings

In each view you can save the events being monitored (and critical values if any). These settings are created using the File/Save or File/Save As settings.
To use one of these settings for future monitoring:

1. Select the view you want to use.

2. Select File/Open.

3. Select the existing activity file. Alert files use the .PMA file extension, Chart files use .PMC, Log files use .PML, and report files use .PMR. You can select a work-space file (.PMW) that contains settings for all four views.

4. You may change any settings at this point and use File/Save to update the settings if you wish, or use File/Save As to create another settings file.

Analyzing Performance Data

To export performance data for analysis by another program, such as a spreadsheet:

1. Select the view whose data you want to export.

2. Select File/Export.

3. Select either the tab or the comma delimited format for separating data in fields in a record, according to the format your analysis tool can import.

4. Enter the full path name of the export file.

5. Click on OK.

Event Viewer

An event is any significant occurrence in the computer system or from an application that requires notification of a user, either using a pop-up alert message or by writing a message to a log file for later review by an administrator. Windows NT makes a record of these events in an event log.

There are three types of event logs:

1. The *System Log* tracks events triggered by the Windows NT system components, such as when a component doesn't load during startup. Another common message in the System Log is a power fluctuation involving the Uninterruptible Power Supply (UPS). A sample System Log appears in Figure 3.10.

2. The *Security Log* tracks *audit* events triggered by security violations, such as illegal logons to the system, or unauthorized file opens.

3. The *Application Log* tracks events that are written by an application program. These vary by the application.

You specify the type of events that are logged to the Security Log by selecting the Audit option from the Policies menu in User Manager (see User Manager

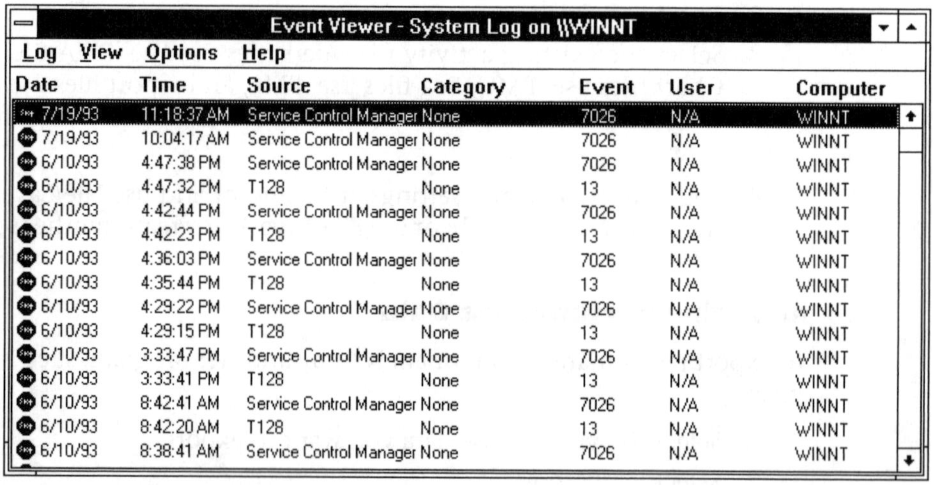

Event Viewer - System Log on \\WINNT						
Log View Options Help						
Date	Time	Source	Category	Event	User	Computer
7/19/93	11:18:37 AM	Service Control Manager	None	7026	N/A	WINNT
7/19/93	10:04:17 AM	Service Control Manager	None	7026	N/A	WINNT
6/10/93	4:47:38 PM	Service Control Manager	None	7026	N/A	WINNT
6/10/93	4:47:32 PM	T128	None	13	N/A	WINNT
6/10/93	4:42:44 PM	Service Control Manager	None	7026	N/A	WINNT
6/10/93	4:42:23 PM	T128	None	13	N/A	WINNT
6/10/93	4:36:03 PM	Service Control Manager	None	7026	N/A	WINNT
6/10/93	4:35:44 PM	T128	None	13	N/A	WINNT
6/10/93	4:29:22 PM	Service Control Manager	None	7026	N/A	WINNT
6/10/93	4:29:15 PM	T128	None	13	N/A	WINNT
6/10/93	3:33:47 PM	Service Control Manager	None	7026	N/A	WINNT
6/10/93	3:33:41 PM	T128	None	13	N/A	WINNT
6/10/93	8:42:41 AM	Service Control Manager	None	7026	N/A	WINNT
6/10/93	8:42:20 AM	T128	None	13	N/A	WINNT
6/10/93	8:38:41 AM	Service Control Manager	None	7026	N/A	WINNT

Figure 3.10 System Log.

Windows NT provides automatic logging of significant system events, including errors.

for details). You can control the file and directory events logged in File Manager by using the Auditing command from the Security menu.

The event log shows the following information:

Computer	The name of the computer on which the event occurred.
Category	A classification of the event; this varies by the event source.
Date	Date of the event.
Event ID	A unique number that identifies the event.
Source	The application or system resource that triggered the event.
Time	Time of the event.
Type	Windows NT classifies the event as: error, warning, information, success audit, or failure audit.
User	The user name that was logged onto the computer when the event occurred. If this column contains ***, the event triggering the log record did not capture the user name (as may be the case with application programs).

To open the log file for viewing, select the Event Viewer application in the Administrator program group.

Viewing a Log File

To select which log file you want to view, select Log from the main menu. Select System, Security, or Application to display the type of log file you want to view.

By default, the event log displayed when you start Event Viewer is that of your own computer. Administrators can view events for another computer. To select another computer, Select Log/Select Computer. Type the name of the computer in the Computername text box, or select one from the list provided. Click on OK.

In addition to the date, time, source, type, category, event ID, and user and computer name of each event, you can also view a description and the binary data logged by the event, usually created by an application.

To view detailed information about an event:

1. Double-click the event in the event list, or select the event and select View/Detail.

2. Click on Next to move to the next event in the sorted event order. Click on Previous to move to the previous event in the sorted event order.

3. Click on OK to return to the event log list.

Managing a Log File

You can change the amount of space allocated for each type of log and settings for event retention. To do this:

1. Select Log/Settings.
2. Select the log file from the Change Settings for Log pull-down list.
3. Enter the maximum space (in number of kilobytes) for the log file in the Maximum log size box. The default is 512K.
4. Select an Event Retention Period option to specify how or how long events are retained in the log. Select Overwrite Events as Needed to write new events over the oldest entries in the log (generally this option should be used for all logs to prevent losing recent events at the expense of uninteresting older events). If you select Keep Events, you must select the number of days to retain events in the log. If you select Never Overwrite Events (preferable for secure servers—especially for the security log, where evidence of hacking will be most likely to appear), you must clear the log manually. An option also exists to force a system halt when the security log is full—which may be of interest to users in secure environments.
5. As an alternative to steps 3 and 4, select Default and all settings will be restored to the system-defined default.
6. Click on OK.

To erase the log file and begin with a new, empty file, select the type of log file you want to clear. Select Log/Clear All Events. You are asked if you want to save the current log file. Select Yes and you will see the Save As dialog box. Enter the file name and click on OK.

Managing Events

You can display only a desired type of event (called *filtering*), search for a specific event, or sort the list of events.

Filtering Events

The log file records all events according to other settings in the Windows NT system, but you can view only the desired events by setting a filter.

To view a subset of the events in the event log:

1. Select View/Filter Events. The Filter dialog box is shown in Figure 3.11.
2. In the Filter dialog box enter the options you want. Events that meet these specifications will be displayed. A complete description of events

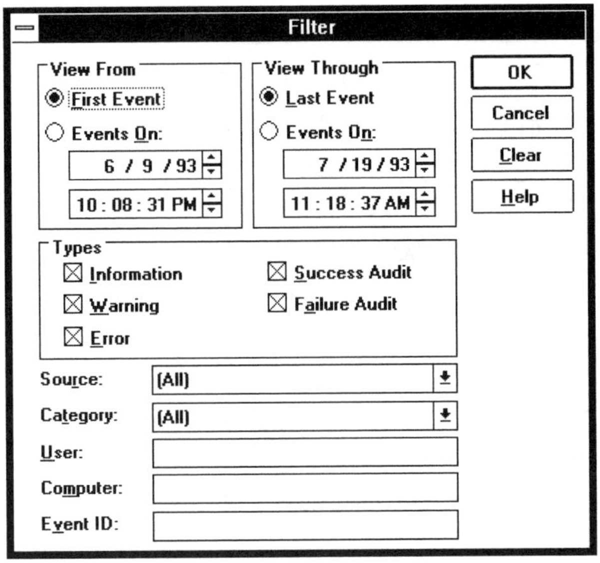

Figure 3.11 Filter dialog.
Inspection of a complex log file can be greatly simplified by filtering—selecting only the events you're immediately interested in.

can be found in the Event Viewer chapter of the Windows NT System Guide.

3. Click on OK.

To remove the filters, select View/All Events.

Searching for Events

To locate specific event, use the Find feature of Event Log. To search for a specific event or range of events:

1. Select View/Find. The Find dialog box shown in Figure 3.12 appears.

2. Select the options you want to use in the search in the Find dialog box. Select the direction (Up or Down) to search from the current event forward (Down) or backward to the beginning of the log (Up). Other options are detailed in the Event Viewer chapter of the Windows NT System Guide. (Most are self-explanatory.) If multiple Types are selected, the search will look for any event that meets *any* of the criteria.

3. Select Find Next to find the event that meets your criteria.

4. Press F3 to find the next event using the same criteria.

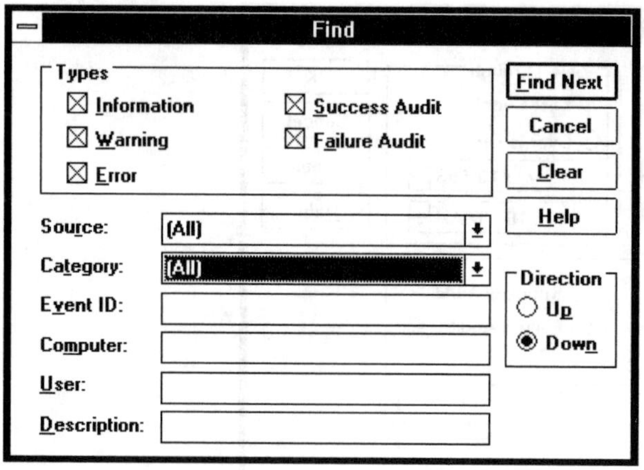

Figure 3.12 Find dialog.

Beyond filtering, a straight search capability is provided—giving you the tools to get the information you need from the log quickly.

Sorting Events

To sort the order of events in the log file, select View/Newest First to see the most recent events at the top of the list, or select View/Oldest First to see the oldest events at the top of the list.

Archiving a Log File

As log files grow, you may wish to save the event log to another file. You may also wish to perform this function as part of regular maintenance, such as every week or once each month. Archiving a log file is also useful if you want to export the data to another application, such as a database or spreadsheet, for further analysis.

When you archive a log file, the complete contents are archived and the filter options are ignored. The archived file does retain the sort order based on the export file format you select.

You can archive a log file in one of three file formats:

The *standard log file format* allows you to use the Event Viewer to view the contents of the archived file. The sort order of the events is ignored.

In an *ASCII text file*, the sorted order of the events is used. The binary data associated with an event is not included in the new file.

A *comma-delimited format* may also be selected. Comma-delimited format is used most often when you are exporting the data to a database or spreadsheet. As with ASCII text files, the sorted order of the events is used, but binary data associated with an event is not included in the new file.

To archive a log file:

1. Select Log/Save As.
2. Select the file format you want from the Save File as Type list.
3. Enter the file name in the File Name text box. If you select the standard log file format, the file extension assigned is .EVT. The file extension .TXT is used for text and comma-delimited files.
4. Click on OK.

To view an archived log file (for log files using the standard log file format) with the Event Viewer:

1. Select Log/Open.
2. Enter the log file name in the File Name box, or select it from the list of existing files.
3. Click on OK.
4. Select the type of log file you want (Application, Security, or System) in the Open File Type box, then click on OK.

Managing Disks

Disk (and more generally, *storage*) management is a major headache for system administrators. Windows NT simplifies disk management with a graphical *disk administrator*, and related tools.

Disk Administrator

Windows NT's *Disk Administrator* program provides tools for managing disks, allowing you to create partitions on hard disks, create volumes and stripe sets, read status information (such as partition size), and assign partitions to drive letters.

To start Disk Administrator, select the Disk Administrator icon from the Administrative Tools group in Program Manager, or select File/Run and enter WINDISK on the Command line. The main Disk Administrator dialog box is shown in Figure 3.13.

Once you have requested changes to your disk partitions, then quit Disk Administrator normally; Disk Administrator will remind you of your request and note which changes cannot be reversed. At this point you can change your mind and cancel the changes. In many cases you may also want to notify all

Figure 3.13 Disk Administrator.
The Windows NT Disk Administrator program provides a graphical view of disk partitions, along with central location of all disk management/maintenance functions.

users of your changes, as some modifications, such as deleting partitions, may directly impact users on the system.

Assigning Drive Letters

In many computer systems, adding a new hard drive disrupts the order of existing drive letter assignments. In Windows NT, Disk Administrator allows you to statically assign drive letters so that this does not happen. Once assigned, drive letters are maintained when another drive is added to the system.

To assign a drive letter:

1. Select the partition or logical drive you want to assign to a letter.
2. Select Tools/Drive Letter.
3. The Assign Drive Letter dialog box appears. Select the assignment option you want.
4. Click on OK.

Drive letters for CD-ROM drives may be set with the Tools/CD-ROM Drive Letters… command.

Primary and Extended Partitions

A primary partition is a subdivision of a physical disk; up to four primary partitions can be created per disk. A primary partition cannot be subdivided. In x86 systems, the primary partition of your C drive is the partition from which you boot the system. Only one of the four primary partitions can be designated an extended partition (explained in the following).

In contrast, an extended partition is created from free space on your hard disk and can be sub-partitioned into logical drives.

To create a primary partition on a hard disk:

1. Select the free space area on a disk.

2. Select Partition/Create.

3. The Create Primary Partition dialog box displays the minimum and maximum size for the partition. It also displays a text box labeled Create Partition of Size, in which you should enter the new partition size.

4. Click on OK.

On Intel x86-based computers, the system partition that contains the hardware specific files needed for booting must be marked as active. In contrast, RISC-based computers do not use such markings, but are controlled by a configuration program supplied by the computer manufacturer.

To mark a partition as active for x86-based computers, select the partition that contains the necessary startup files. Select Partition/Mark Active, then click on OK.

An *extended* partition can be set up and used to create multiple logical drives, or as part of a volume set.

To create an extended partition:

1. Select the free space area on a disk.

2. Select Partition/Create Extended.

3. The Create Extended Partition dialog box displays the minimum and maximum size for the partition, and displays a text box named Create Partition of Size. Enter the appropriate size, then click on OK.

To create logical drives *within* an extended partition, select the space in the extended partition, select Partition/Create, enter the size of the logical drive in the Create Logical Drive dialog box, and click on OK.

To delete a partition, volume, or logical drive:

1. Select the partition, volume, or logical drive you want to remove.

2. Select Partition/Delete.

3. Select Yes to confirm your delete request.

Formatting Partitions

Once a partion has been created, it must be formatted for use. This may be done using the *format* command-line function, or using the Tools/Format... command. Note that beginning with NT 3.51, no support is provided for formatting partitions with OS/2-comptible HPFS format, though NT continues to recognize such partitions (they must be formatted from OS/2). OS/2 subsystem users may want to investigate NTFS, which appears to be HPFS so far as OS/2 applications running on NT are concerned.

Volume Sets

A *volume set* is a method for allocating free space on several partitions as though the resulting set was a single partition itself. All space in the first area of a volume set is filled before space in the second area is filled; all space in the second area is used before space is used from the third area, and so on, until all areas (up to a maximum of 32) are used.

Free space from partitions can be of unequal size, and several areas can be on the same drive, in contrast to a stripe set, in which all areas must be on different drives. Volume sets also help you allocate the I/O across drives in an effort to improve overall system performance.

To create a volume set:

1. Select two or more areas of free space (up to 32 areas can be selected). Select the first area, then press and hold the Ctrl key as you select the remaining area(s).

2. Select Partition/Create Volume Set.

3. Enter the size of the volume you want to create. If the size you enter is less than the total space of the selected free space, Disk Administrator attempts to divide the total space by the number of areas, and to allocate the same amount of space from all areas to the volume set.

4. Click on OK.

To delete a volume set, select the volume set. Select Partition/Delete. Click on Yes to confirm your delete request. All data is deleted from the selected areas.

Extending Volumes and Volume Sets

If you are using NTFS volumes or volume sets, you can expand their size by using current free space. Doing so automatically logs you off the system and then formats the new area, a process that does not affect your existing data. Note that you cannot extend a volume if it is part of a stripe or mirror set.

To extend a volume or a volume set:

1. Select the existing volume or volume set.

2. Select one or more free space areas.

3. Select Partition/Extend Volume Set.

4. Enter the size of the new volume set that will be the result of combining the existing and new space.

5. Click on OK.

Stripe Sets

A *stripe set* is similar to a volume set. A key difference is that Windows NT fills one stripe of the first area, then one stripe of the second area, and so on, until one stripe from each area is filled. It then proceeds to fill the second stripe on the first area, the second stripe on the second area, and so on.

Each area of a stripe set must be on a different disk. Furthermore, Disk Administrator creates stripe sets with areas of uniform size.

To create a stripe set:

1. Select two or more areas of free space (up to 32 areas can be selected). Select the first area, then press and hold the Ctrl key as you select the remaining area(s).

2. Select Partition/Create Stripe Set.

3. Enter the size of the stripe set you want to create. Disk Administrator divides this number by the total number of areas, and allocates this uniform space from each selected area.

4. Click on OK.

To delete a stripe set:

1. Select the stripe set.

2. Select Partition/Delete.

3. Select Yes to confirm your delete request. All data is deleted from the selected areas.

Disk Configuration Information

You can save, restore, and search for information, such as the assigned drive letters, stripe sets, and so on, using the Disk Administrator's configuration settings. This is particularly useful when installing a new copy of NT on a previously configured machine. This information is also stored on the Windows NT *emergency repair disk* (although if you only create the emergency disk during system setup, and never update it, the information on the disk may be out of date—see "Making and Updating Boot and Emergency Repair Diskettes" in Chapter 5).

To save the current configuration settings, select Partition/Configuration. Note that changes to the configuration made during the current session are not saved. To save the changes, you must log off and log back in to the system.

To save the settings, select Configuration/Save and place a floppy disk into the A: or B: drive. Click OK, and Disk Administrator will write the information to the diskette.

To restore the disk configuration information, select Partition/Configuration. Select Configuration/Restore, then insert the floppy containing the configuration information into the A: or B: drive and click on OK.

To search disk configuration information:

1. Select Partition/Configuration.

2. Select Configuration/Search.

3. Click OK to acknowledge the warning message. *The search procedure erases your current disk configuration information, as well as any changes made during the session.*

4. Windows NT searches for other installations. When it finds one or more, it displays them in a list. Select the installation you want, then select OK.

Backup

The Windows NT *Backup* program lets you copy data from your hard disk (or across the network—provided a local disk letter has been assigned) to a tape cassette, protecting you from loss from accidental erasure, hardware failure, or damage resulting from power interruptions. Backup uses a graphical environment that is similar to the File Manager; you can select which files are backed up or restored by clicking on files, directories, and/or drive letters.

Backup can work with FAT, HPFS, and NTFS file systems. You can back up files from different drives and select from several of backup techniques. For example, you can back up only those files that have changed since the previous backup.

To start Backup, double-click on the Backup icon in the Administrative Tools program group, select NTBACKUP from the File Manager, or select File/Run and type NTBACKUP in the Command Line text box.

Selecting Files to Back Up

You can select all files on a drive, all files in a directory, or individual files. The technique is similar to the method used for selecting files in File Manager. The major difference is that in File Manager you select files by highlighting them. In Backup a check box is used for selecting files.

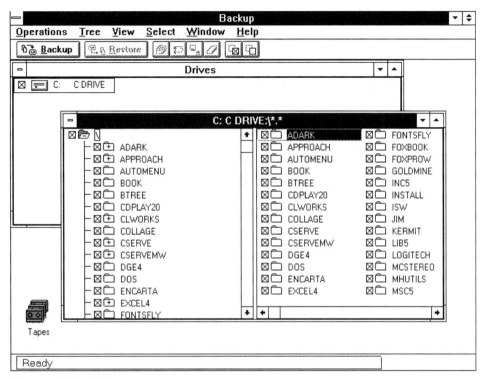

Figure 3.14 Backup program.

Windows NT includes built-in support for tape backup, a necessity for servers and highly desirable on high-performance workstations.

To select files to back up:

1. Select the Drives window and double-click on the disk drive icon or letter of the drive that contains the files you want to back up. The Backup program opens a window for the selected drive, as illustrated in Figure 3.14.

2. To select all files, choose Select/Check. You can also select all files by clicking on the Check button on the toolbar, or check the box for the drive from the Drives window.

3. To select a single file, select the box positioned before the file you want to select.

4. To select multiple files, press *and hold* the Ctrl key, then select each file. When all files are selected, release the Ctrl key.

5. To select a range of files that are listed contiguously, select the first file, then press *and hold* the Shift key and select the last file in the range.

Choose Select/Check to select each file's check box. Alternatively, select the Check button on the toolbar.

Backing Up Files to Tape

The backup process uses three pieces of information: The files you want to back up, the type of backup you want (full, only changed files, etc.), and optionally a description of the backup, which is useful for identifying the right backup when files must be restored.

Backup graphically shows its progress and prompts you when it is time to insert tape cartridges.

To back up files:

1. Select the files (see the preceding section), then click on Backup. The Backup Information dialog box appears.

2. Enter a description of the tape in the Tape Name text box, to a maximum of 31 characters.

3. Select Append to add the backup to the end of an existing tape set, or select Replace to erase the information already on the tape and replace it with the current backup. If you select Replace, Backup asks you to confirm your request.

4. To protect the tape contents from unauthorized use, check the Restrict Access to Owner or Administrator box. Only the tape's owner or administrator with Backup rights can read, write, or erase the tape. If you restrict access, the file will have to be restored using the same user account that created the tape originally.

5. To add a verification step to the backup (to compare the original with the copy on tape), check the Verify after Backup box.

6. To add the Registry files to the tape backup, select the Backup Registry check box.

7. Select the type of backup you want (see Table 3.1).

8. Select an option that describes how you want to log the backup session. Choose Summary Only to log the major events (loading a tape, for example). Choose Full Detail to list all operational details, including the full path name of the files backed up. Select Don't Log if you don't want information added to a log file.

9. Click on OK. The Backup Status dialog box appears and shows the activities as they occur. The dialog box also displays the number of directories, files, bytes being backed up, the elapsed time, and the number of files it could not back up because of security considerations.

Table 3.1 **Types of Backup**

Backup Type	What Backup Will Do
Normal	Back up selected files; files are marked as backed up (the archive bit is turned off).
Copy	Back up selected files, but files will not be marked as backed up (the archive bit is unchanged).
Incremental	Back up selected files modified since the last backup (the archive bit is on); files are marked as backed up (the archive bit is turned off).
Differential	Identical to incremental, but files are not marked as backed up (the archive bit is unchanged).
Daily Copy	Back up files that have been modified on the current date; files are not marked as backed up (the archive bit is unchanged).

10. If the backup requires more than one tape, you will be prompted to insert a new tape when appropriate.

11. To stop a backup operation at any time, click on Abort.

Restoring Files from Tape

The restore operation is the converse of the backup operation. You can restore all files on a tape or just selected files.

To restore files:

1. Insert the tape into the tape drive unit and click on the Tapes icon.

2. Backup displays the tape information on the left side of the Tapes window. It shows the drive backed up, the backup type, and the date and time of the backup. Select the tape containing the file(s) you want to restore: Double-click the tape's icon, select Operations/Catalog, or click on the Catalog button in the toolbar.

3. Backup displays a list of the backup sets in the Tapes window. A question mark is displayed with each icon, meaning the catalog (list of files) has not yet been read from the tape's directory. Select the backup set you want: Double-click on the backup set's icon, select Operations/Catalog, or click on the Catalog button in the toolbar.

4. The program displays the list of directories and files in a hierarchy in the Tape File Selection window. To restore all files, select the check box for the tape and select Select/Check or click on the Check button in the toolbar.

5. To restore an individual file, select the file's check box.

6. To restore multiple files that are not listed contiguously, press *and hold* the Ctrl key while you select each file.

7. To restore multiple files listed contiguously, press *and hold* the Shift key and select the first and last files. Choose Select/Check or click on the Check button in the toolbar.

8. Click on Restore. Restore may ask you to enter the drive to which you want to restore the file(s).

9. To force Restore to compare the data on the tape with the data restored to the hard drive, check the Verify after Restore box.

10. Select the log option you want. Choose Summary Only to log the major events (such as loading a tape or completing a backup). Choose Full Detail to list all operations and the fully qualified (path and filename) of all restored files. Choose Don't Log to bypass writing information to a log file.

11. To restore the Registry files, select the Restore Local Registry check box.

12. Click on OK to start the restoration. If the program needs additional tapes, you will be asked to insert a tape when necessary.

13. You may be asked to confirm replacing an existing file that has been modified since the backup with a file on the backup tape. Answer Yes to replace the file and No to restore the next selected file.

14. To stop the restore operation at any time, select Abort.

Tape Maintenance

In addition to installing a tape drive and periodically using it for backup, an administrator may have to perform periodic maintenance, including retensioning tapes and erasing old tapes so that they may be reused.

Erasing a Tape

There are two types of tape erasure. The Quick Erase method erases only the tape header, which contains information about the name of the tape, and the Backup process considers the tape empty and rewrites over all of it. The process is usually very short (typically under one minute). However, the files backed up to the tape remain on the tape. A Secure Erase overwrites the entire tape, and hence may be a very long process.

To erase a tape, insert the tape into the tape drive unit, then select Operations/Erase Tape or click on the Erase Tape button in the toolbar. Select Quick Erase or Secure Erase, and click on Continue to begin the tape erasure.

Retensioning Tapes

Older backup devices used tapes that required periodic retensioning to reduce slippage and improve reliability. The retensioning process fast forwards the tape to the end of the reel, then rewinds it.

To retension a tape, insert the tape in the tape drive unit and select Operations/Retension Tape, or click on the Retension Tape button in the toolbar.

Newer tape devices don't require retensioning—in which case the Retension Tape item will be disabled.

Backup Limitations

Microsoft is to be commended for including Backup with all NT systems, but in all honesty NT backup has some fairly severe limitations—the worst of which (in in our opinion) include: 1) no support for backup from one server's hard disk to another; 2) no support for dynamically connecting and disconnecting network drives during a backup operation. In effect, it's good only for backing up the local machine to tape—but you can get around this by writing your own backup script. See the section on "Scripts" at the end of this chapter for details.

Backup Alternatives

In all candor, on an NT network of any size, you do not want to use the built-in backup. It allows you to back up only devices which have been assigned drive letters (it has no support for NT-standard UNC names), is not multithreaded, does not support compression, and lacks any form of scheduling (this can be gotten around—to some extent—by writing a command script and executing it with NT's AT command-line schedule service. See the section on "Scripts" at the end of this chapter for details.) Quite simply, the built-in backup is inadequate for serious network-wide use. Fortunately, alternatives are now available (see Table 3.2).

All of these solutions use NT's standard tape API and drivers—so check the NT hardware compatibility list before buying tape backup hardware. In general, you should buy a tape device with a capacity equal to (or for growth, greater than) the total hard disk capacity of your system. Some of the third-party batch languages covered later in this chapter offer UNIX-style *tar* and *cpio* backup as well, which may be useful for those running NT in a mixed environment with UNIX systems.

Table 3.2 Third-Party Backup Applications for NT

Product	*Company*	*Address*	*Telephone*	*Notes*
ARCserve for Windows NT	Cheyenne Software	3 Expressway Plaza, Roslyn Hts, NY 11577	800-243-9462 516-484-5110	NT version of popular cross-platform backup. Tape format is identical across platforms.
Backup Exec Storage Exec	Arcada Systems	37 Skyline Dr. Lake Mary, FL 32746	407-262-8000	Enhanced backup from the maker of NT's built-in backup. Tapes are format-compatible with built-in NT backup.
ES/Backup MasterMind	Qstart Techologies	Jefferson Plaza 600 East Jefferson St. Rockville, MD 20852	301-762-9800	Multilevel client/server backup with Optical device support.
Network Archivist (BETA)	Palindrome Software	600 E.Diehl Rd. Naperville, IL 60563	708-505-3300	NT version of NetWare backup.[6] Tape format compatible with NetWare version.
SQLStor	SQL Business Systems, Inc.	17171 Park Row, Suite 350 Houston, TX 77084	713-578-7410	Automated backup for Microsoft SQL Server.
Wayback 1.0, InterTape for Windows NT	Cool Technologies	P.O. Box 158 Cool, CA 95614	916-889-1160	NT-based 9-track / 3840 tape services, and tape interchange utility that supports IBM (EBCDIC/ASCII), ANSI, and TAR formats.

Uninterruptible Power Supply (UPS)

An uninterruptible power supply is a battery-powered power supply that maintains power to a computer when the main power source is interrupted, such as during power failures. The UPS allows for the safe shutdown of the system until the main power source is restored (rationale for using UPS and factors for selecting an appropriate one are covered in Chapter 2).

Windows NT allows you to configure the UPS and how it works with the operating system. The main UPS window is shown in Figure 3.15.

---

6. In beta test as this was written (March 1995).

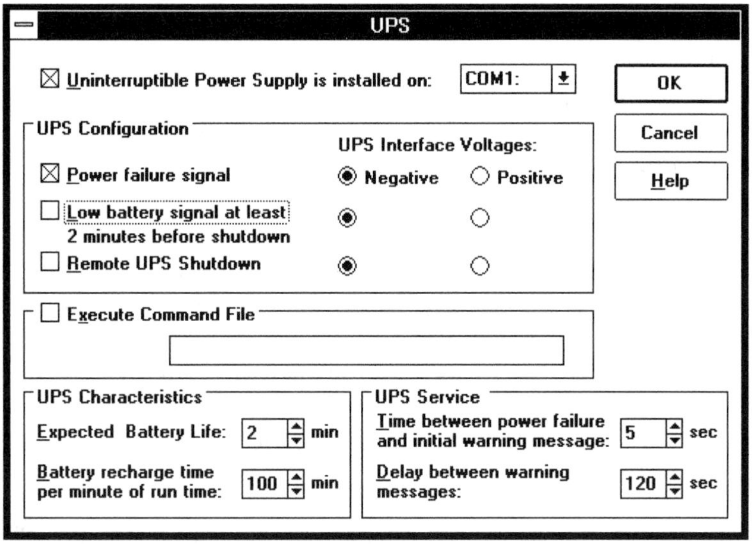

```
┌─────────────────────────────────────────────────────────────┐
│ ─                          UPS                               │
├─────────────────────────────────────────────────────────────┤
│                                         ┌────────┐  ┌───────┐│
│ ☒ Uninterruptible Power Supply is installed on: │COM1:  ±│  │  OK   ││
│                                         └────────┘  └───────┘│
│ ┌─UPS Configuration─────────────────────────────┐  ┌───────┐│
│ │                    UPS Interface Voltages:     │  │Cancel ││
│ │ ☒ Power failure signal    ⦿ Negative ○ Positive│  └───────┘│
│ │ ☐ Low battery signal at least  ⦿       ○       │  ┌───────┐│
│ │   2 minutes before shutdown                    │  │ Help  ││
│ │ ☐ Remote UPS Shutdown     ⦿       ○            │  └───────┘│
│ └────────────────────────────────────────────────┘          │
│ ┌─☐ Execute Command File──────────────────────────┐         │
│ │  ┌──────────────────────────────────────────┐   │         │
│ │  └──────────────────────────────────────────┘   │         │
│ └─────────────────────────────────────────────────┘         │
│ ┌─UPS Characteristics─────┐ ┌─UPS Service───────────────┐   │
│ │ Expected Battery Life: 2│ │ Time between power failure 5│sec│
│ │                     │min│ │ and initial warning message:  │ │
│ │ Battery recharge time   │ │ Delay between warning    120│sec│
│ │ per minute of run time:100│min│ messages:               │ │
│ └─────────────────────────┘ └───────────────────────────┘   │
└─────────────────────────────────────────────────────────────┘
```

Figure 3.15 Main UPS window.

Built-in support for Uninterruptable Power Supply (UPS) assures that Windows NT servers need never experience a total power failure without the opportunity to execute a controlled system shutdown procedure.

Setting Up a UPS

To establish the software connection between a UPS and Windows NT, select the Control Panel icon from the Main program group. Click on the UPS icon, then check the Uninterruptible Power Supply installed on box. Choose the port from the pull-down list box, then click on OK.

Once set up, you need to specify how the UPS will interact with Windows NT once it is triggered. Select the UPS icon from the control panel. Then:

1. Check the Power Failure Signal box if the UPS is capable of sending a message to Windows NT when it detects a problem. Select the Negative or Positive interface voltage value according to your UPS hardware instructions (this varies by make and model).

2. If you checked the Power failure signal box in step 1, enter the value in the UPS Characteristics box. The Expected Battery Life values can range from 2 to 720 (2 is the default). The setting is used in messages to notify you of the time remaining. The Battery recharge time per minute of runtime values range from 1 to 250 minutes (100 is the default).

3. Check the Low Battery Signal at Least 2 Minutes before Shutdown box if your UPS can send a message when it detects a low battery. Select the

Negative or Positive interface voltage value according to your UPS hardware instructions.

4. Check the Remote UPS Shutdown box if your UPS can respond to a signal to shut itself off. Select the Negative or Positive interface voltage value according to your UPS hardware instructions.

5. Enter the number of seconds between the moment a power failure is recognized and the display of a warning message. Enter the value in the UPS Service area in the text box labeled Time between Power Failure and Initial Warning Message. Valid values are between 0 and 120 seconds; the default is 5 seconds.

6. Enter the number of seconds between warning messages in the Delay between Warning Messages box. Valid values are between 5 and 300 seconds; the default value is 120 seconds.

7. Click on OK.

Once the settings have been established, you can test your UPS's ability to recover your system. To test the system, disconnect the power from the UPS to simulate a failure. Windows NT displays a warning or alert message, and the battery will begin to run down (you may want to allow this to continue the first time so that you can get a feel for exactly how long the system can stay up.) When the UPS battery reaches its low level, the system will begin its shutdown. At this point, reconnect power to the UPS. Use the Event Viewer to see that all actions were properly recorded and that none caused an error.

Services

Many server-side programs act as *service* routines, running in the background and providing support for other applications. On Windows NT such applications are called *services*, and they're handled differently from other applications. An NT service typically has no user interface of its own—instead, it's controlled through NT's *service control manager*, which is exposed through the Services applet in the NT Control Panel (see Figure 3.16).

This interface allows services to be started and stopped, allows their startup mode to be configured (whether they're started automatically on system boot, or manually), and to be started using a different account than the one currently logged in. In general, services are installed and preconfigured by Windows NT setup (or the installation routine used to install the service), but from time to time administrative intervention my be required (for example, it may be necessary to stop NT's *Remote Access Service* if you need to use a RAS-configured device for other purposes).

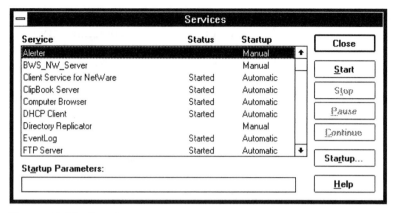

Figure 3.16 Services.
Windows NT provides a class of applications called *services* that run as background processes. They are controlled through the Services icon in the Windows NT Control Panel.

Starting and Stopping Services

To start or stop a Windows NT Service, select the Control Panel icon from the Main program group. Click on the Services icon, and choose the service you want to stop or start from the list. You can then click the Start or Stop button, as required (note that in general any user may *start* a service, but administrative privilege is required to *stop* a service).

Pausing and Continuing Services

Many services offer the additional option of being paused and continued. This offers some advantages—the service remains in memory and can continue without having to be reloaded. On the other hand, depending on how the service is set up, any service-controlled resources may not be released when the service is paused. Click on the Services icon, and choose the service you want to stop or start from the list. You can then click the Pause or Continue button, as required (note that in general, any user may *start* a service, but administrative privilege is required to *stop* a service).

If you're logged in on an account with administrative permissions, you can control services startup parameters—in particular, what user account the service initially logs in under. That can be important for certain services, such as Microsoft's SMS, which require a special user account. (*Note: if you change the password on such an account, you may have to reinstall the associated service! At a minimum, you will need to bring up the service's startup dialog box in the Services applet and type in the new password.*) You can also configure a service to permit desktop interaction, which can be useful for debugging services (internally, services are basically old-fashioned command-line programs with a thin layer of additional code that interacts with NT's Service Control Manager—see Appendix 1 for details), and it may be necessary for certain services. NT's scheduler service, for example, *must* have permission to interact with the desktop if it's to be used with Windows (16- or 32-bit) software, such as NT Backup, since the Win32 and Win16 subsystems interact with the desktop by definition.

Batch Files and Logon Scripts

Microsoft's documentation is strikingly silent on the topic of logon scripts—indeed, at one point in the original NT 3.1 documents, there was a statement to the effect that scripts are obsolete, replaced by User Profiles.

Hogwash!

Logon scripts are as valuable—and necessary—on NT as they are on any other network operating system. While NT *reduces* the need for logon scripts by maintaining a list of permanent network connections (designated as such in File Manager—see Chapter 4) and automatically reinstating them, scripts are nonetheless necessary to assign a home directory, carry out tasks automatically on login, or to reinstate network connections when multiple user names and passwords are employed.

Scripts are fundamental tools in any client/server networking environment. They're what an administrator uses to assure that users will see a particular configuration when they log in. They're also the key to fully exploiting some of NT's features—especially if you run an NT server unattended. You can set a login script to be executed automatically when a user logs in to a Windows NT server (using NT's User Manager—select the account you want to set a script for, then select Properties, click the Profile button, and you can type in a script file name).

NT Scripts—Basic Syntax

To begin with, NT gives you pretty much all the command-line capabilities available in either DOS or OS/2 1.*x* though it lacks the OS/2 2.*x* built-in REXX command language. (As we went to press, Microsoft announced that future versions of the NT resource kit would include the PERL script language used by NCSA Mosaic. Consult our electronic update for details.) Typical command-line functions, such as *copy* and *move*, are supported, as is the use of command-line parameters. For instance, to implement the *unix mv* and *cp* command syntax instead of NT's DOS-style *copy* and *move*, the following scripts would work.[7] For cp.bat:[8]

```
copy %1 %2
```

As in DOS, the *%1* and *%2* will be replaced by the first and second arguments that you type on the command line. When the user types *cp test1.txt test2.txt*, test1.txt replaces %1, and test2.txt replaces %2—so what's executed is: *copy test1.txt test2.txt*. Similarly, we can create an mv.bat file:

```
move %1 %2
```

That works the same way. As in DOS or OS/2, NT provides conditional statements — the *if* statement detemines if an error has happened, checks existence of a file or directory, or compares strings. For instance:

```
if "%2"=="" goto usage
if exist %2 goto fail
copy %1 %2
goto done
:fail
echo ERROR-%2 exists!
goto done
:usage
echo usage: cp  fromfile  tofile
:done
```

Now if the user attempts to copy one file over another using cp, it will print an error message and fail. To override that, we can add a third parameter:

```
if "%2"=="" goto usage
if "%3" == "FORCE" goto doit
if exist %2 goto fail
:doit
copy %1 %2
goto done
:fail
echo ERROR-%2 exists!
goto done
```

---

7. UNIX mavens will no doubt observe that these implementations are exceedingly primitive— among other things, providing no support for multiple command-line arguments. Serious users of UNIX-style commands should check out the Hamilton C-shell, MKS toolkit, and Toolbuster—all covered in Table 3.3—or the POSIX tools included in the NT resource kit (see Appendix 4).

8. While NT itself accepts either the .BAT or .CMD extension for command scripts, DOS and Windows-based clients expect the .BAT extension, while OS/2 clients expect .CMD—in a mixed environment, it may be necessary to provide both and to use the %OS% environment variable to determine which is used.

```
:usage
echo usage:  cp  fromfile  tofile  [ FORCE ]
echo (use FORCE to overwrite an existing file)
:done
```

Now the user can override the error message for an overwrite by using FORCE as the third parameter on the command line.

Administrative Net Commands

While most administrative functions in Windows NT are performed using one or the other of the graphical applications, User Manager, Server Manager, and so on, discussed elsewhere in this chapter, there is a very powerful set of command line functions for administrative control that are essentially an extension of the basic *net* commands discussed at the end of Chapter 4.

In this section we will discuss these commands and how they can be of considerable administrative use, because they can be employed in batch files and logon scripts. The basic *net* commands for control of file sharing, printer sharing, attaching two shared directories, and the like was discussed at the end of Chapter 4. In addition to those commands there are a set of commands that are intended for administrative use only. By using these commands in a batch file or logon script you can generally accomplish all the same tasks that would otherwise be performed in User Manager, Server Manager, and so on.

When Windows NT 3.1 was in beta, there was much dispute over how *new* NT really is—many people pointed out that it was originally planned as OS/2 3.0. NT's kernel design really *is* new, but most of the networking functionality is actually a ported (and improved) version of Microsoft LAN Manager. For script writers this means that most LAN Manager commands work in Windows NT. The most important of these are the *net* commands and the *at* command scheduler.

To get a list of *net* commands, just type *net* at a command prompt:

```
The syntax of this command is:

NET [ ACCOUNTS | COMPUTER | CONFIG | CONTINUE | FILE | GROUP | HELP |
     HELPMSG | LOCALGROUP | NAME | PAUSE | PRINT | SEND | SESSION |
     SHARE | START | STATISTICS | STOP | TIME | USE | USER | VIEW ]
```

To get a better explanation of any command, type *net help* followed by the command name. For instance, *net help view* gives:

```
The syntax of this command is:
NET VIEW [\\computername | /DOMAIN[:domainname]] [/NETWORK:networkname]
```

We present a complete list of the Windows NT *net* commands in the following.

Setting System-Wide Security Policy: *Net Accounts*

This command may be used to control the account policies for single servers or for all servers within a domain, provided the command is used by a domain administrator (NT Server domains only). The syntax of the command is *net accounts* followed by any of several command switches. Issued by itself the command displays the current account policy for the server in which it is activated:

```
C:\users\default>net accounts
Force user logoff how long after time expires:     Never
Minimum password age (days):                       0
Maximum password age (days):                       42
Minimum password length:                           0
Length of password history maintained:             None
Machine role:                                      WORKSTATION
The command completed successfully.
```

Or, through the use of the /domain switch it will display the domain-wide policy set by the PDC. All major factors of the server account policy may be directly controlled using the following switches:

/force logoff—This command controls whether a user will be forcibly logged off of a system when his account password has expired or when his allowed time on the system is exceeded. The default value is No, which will not force a logoff. The alternative is to set a time in minutes. For example, the command *net accounted/force logoff: 10* will give a user ten minutes in which to change his account password if he logs in with an expired account, or will give him ten minutes after notification that he has exceeded his permitted time on the system, in which to finish up his business.

/minpwlen—Minimum password length. This command sets the minimum length for passwords for the server. Permitted values are in the range 0 to 14 characters, where a value of 0 will permit users to have a blank password. By default, Windows NT Server requires a six-character minimum password length. *Note*: The entire NT security system depends upon proper use of passwords. Setting */minpwlen:0* is functionally equivalent to disabling the majority of the Windows NT security system.

/maxpwage—Maximum password age. This command is similar in function to the force logoff function. It determines the maximum age of a password before the user will be required to change passwords. Legal values are a range of days from one to slightly over 40,000, or the keyword UNLIMITED, which allows passwords to be used indefinitely. *Note*: Again, the Windows NT security system depends upon effective use of passwords. Setting an unlimited password makes it technically possible, though perhaps not feasible, for passwords to be hacked. It is better to force passwords to be changed on a regular basis. For example, once a month would be */maxpwage:30*.

/minpwage—Minimum password age. Functionally the opposite of the /maxpwage command, /minpwage could set the minimum number of days that must pass before a user is permitted to change his password. This may seem like a ridiculous setting. After all, why not provide a minpwage of 0 days, which is the default, and allow people to change the password at will? The reason for setting a minimum password age is to foil intruders who temporarily change the password and then try to change it back, and to enforce the password history mechanism by preventing users from using a program to cycle through however many passwords are kept in the history in quick succession, then change back to the original. Legal values are in the range of 0 to slightly over 40,000. The default, again, is 0 days.

/uniquepw—Unique password. This command requires the user's password to be unique through a specified number of changes ranging from 0 through 8. Thus, for instance, setting uniquepw:2 will require that a user's password be unique through the last two passwords. That is, he cannot repeat an earlier password until he has used at least two new ones. This will prevent users from repeatedly entering the same password and thus functionally defeating the use of the */maxpwage* command.

/domain—The domain switch. Use of the /domain switch in conjunction with any of the other *net accounts* commands will make the command refer to the entire domain rather than just to the server on which it is executed. You have to have domain administrative permissions and be logged in to a Windows NT Server Domain to use this command. The command will be remote executed on the PDC and will then affect domain-wide account policies—not merely single server account policies. For example, *net accounts /minpwage:2 /domain* will set a domain-wide account policy requiring a minimum password age of two days. *Note*: This parameter has an effect only if it's executed from a Windows NT computer that is a member of a Windows NT Server domain but is not functioning as a Domain Controller. The /domain switch has no effect if it is executed on a Domain Controller.

/sync:—User account database synchronization. This switch, usable only on a Windows NT Domain Controller, forces an update on the user accounts database to synchronize database information across the domain. It may be used only by a domain administrator and then only on a Domain Controller. It cannot be executed remotely.

Adding Computers to a Domain: *Net Computer* (NT Server Only)

This command can be used to add computers to a domain database, and is the primary command that needs to be executed by domain administrators in order to add new computers to an NT Server domain. The syntax of the command is *net computer \ \name of computer to add*, followed by either an */add* or */del* switch. The /add switch adds the computer to the domain. The /del switch deletes it. This command can be executed only on a Domain Controller. It cannot be executed remotely. Functionally the command determines which computers will be affected by domain-wide updates. The same effect as this command can be accomplished using the network settings section of the Windows NT control panel. By creating a computer account in the domain you are functionally performing the same thing as a *net computer \ \computername /add*. You can also add computers to (and remove them from) a domain using Windows NT Server Manager, covered in Chapter 7.

Viewing the System Configuration: *Net Config*

This command displays information related to the operation of the server and workstation services. The command has two variants:

```
net config server
```

displays the following information:

```
C:\users\default>net config server
Server Name                        \\JOHNR-NT486-66
Server Comment

Software version                   Windows NT 3.10
Server is active on                Nbf_ODINSUP02 (00001b48d2aa)

Server hidden                      No
Max Logged On Users                Unlimited
Max. open files per session        256

Idle session time (min)            15
The command completed successfully.
```

or

```
net config workstation
```

which displays the following information:

```
C:\users\default>net config workstation
Computername                       \\JOHNR-NT486-66
Username                           jruleynt

Workstation active on              Nbf_ODINSUP02 (00001B48D2AA)
Software version                   Windows NT 3.10

Workstation domain                 MAGNET2
```

```
Logon domain                            MAGNET2

COM Open Timeout (sec)                  3600
COM Send Count (byte)                   16
COM Send Timeout (msec)                 250
The command completed successfully.
```

This command may be useful, for example, in running a periodic automatic maintenance report to a central logging facility. See the example later in this section.

Controlling Services: *Net Start, Net Stop, Net Pause,* and *Net Continue*

All of these commands are used to control the various services which are built into Windows NT. These services include the alerter service, the computer browser service, the directory replicator service, the event log, the rpc locator, messaging, net logon, rpc subsystem, schedule subsystem, the server service, the uninterruptible power supply service, and the workstation service. In other words, the very same services that one controls from the services applet in the Windows NT Control Panel.

The syntax of the commands is *net start*. By itself, the *net start* command will list all of the services that are started in the system. *Net start service* will start the service in question. For example, *net start clipbook* starts the clipbook service. *Net stop service* will stop a particular service. The service may then be restarted using the *net start* command. *Net pause service* will temporarily suspend a service or resource. This command can be used only with the *netlogon, schedule, server,* or *workstation* services. The suspension amounts to putting the service on hold. That is, it will not accept new requests until this command is overridden by a *net resume*. And, of course, *net resume* undoes what was done with the *net pause*. Despite what is printed in the Windows NT System Guide, *net pause* does not appear to have any effect when used in association with printers or shared directories.

Controlling User Groups: *Net Group, Net LocalGroup*

These commands allow you to add and remove user account groups from a Windows NT server or Windows NT domain. User groups are among the most basic fundamental features of the Windows NT administrative account system and are covered earlier in this chapter. (See the section on the Windows NT user manager.) The *net group* and *net localgroup* commands allow you to add or delete user groups from the accounts system. The *net localgroup* command affects the local Windows NT server on which it is executed. *Net localgroup group-name /add* adds a group to the account database. *Net localgroup group-name /delete* removes the group. The /domain switch causes this function to be executed domain-wide (it must be executed by a domain administrator). The command is actually executed on the primary DC. The *net group* command may only be executed on a Windows NT Server and sets domain-wide groups. Again, *net group group-name /add* adds the group and *net group group-name /delete* deletes an entire group.

Note that the /domain switch from the *net localgroup* command has no effect when it is executed on a Windows NT Server, since Windows NT Servers by default carry out their operations on the primary DC. However, you should not make the mistake of thinking that a net localgroup and a net group command are the same when executed on a Windows NT Server. NT Servers maintain separate domain groups and local groups. Domain groups are user groups that are employed for domain administration and apply to all machines within the domain, whereas local groups apply to individual machines whether they are NT Server machines or standard Windows NT machines. You can also add or delete individual users from groups and local groups using the *net group* and *net localgroup* commands. For example, the command:

```
net group "Domain Admins" jruleynt /add
```

adds the account *jruleynt* to the group of Domain Admins for a Windows NT Server domain. The command

```
net localgroup administrators fred /delete
```

deletes the user account *fred* from the local group of administrators on a local Windows NT server. If the user name is not specified the *net group* and *net localgroup* commands will list the groups or the members of a particular group. For example, the command

```
net localgroup
```

without other arguments will list the groups within the Windows NT account database:

```
C:\users\default>net localgroup

Aliases for \\JOHNR-NT486-66

_____

*Administrators        *Backup Operators        *Guests
*Power Users           *Replicator              *Users
The command completed successfully.
```

Then typing:

```
net localgroup administrators
```

will list the user accounts that are members of the administrators group:

```
C:\users\default>net localgroup administrators
Aliasname      administrators
Comment        Members can fully administer the system

Members

_____

Administrator            MAGNET2\Domain Admins
The command completed successfully.
```

Individual user accounts can be added, deleted, or controlled using the *net user* command covered later in this section.

Note: While the *net group* and *net localgroup* commands will allow you to add or delete administrative groups both for individual servers and for NT Server domains, you cannot control permissions, the user rights granted to groups, or for that matter individual users using the command line. User rights can be issued only from the Windows NT User Manager (from the User Rights item of the Policies menu), and then only by a Windows NT administrator or domain administrator (where domain accounts are concerned). The absence of any capability to set permissions from the command line does present a limitation from the standpoint of writing batch files; for example, to create a mass migration of accounts. This is unfortunate but it apparently was considered a security feature by the Windows NT designers. Therefore, you can create the accounts and you can create the groups in a batch file, but when it comes to setting the permissions you have to go to the User Manager and set them manually.

Controlling Who Gets Messages: *Net Name*

As described in Chapter 4, Windows NT provides a reasonably powerful system for the issuing of system-wide messages through the *net send* command. Normally *net send* can be used either with individual computer names, with individual account names, or through the /domain switch it can send messages that will be received by all computers within a domain. It can sometimes be desirable, however, to send a message alias, that is, a name of convenience that can be used to identify a particular user or a particular computer without using the actual computer name or the actual user name. This can be accomplished by using the *net name* command. The syntax of the *net name* command is:

```
net name alias /add
```

to add the name, or

```
net name alias /delete
```

to delete the name. If neither the /add or /delete switch is used a /add switch is assumed—thus the command

```
net name boss
```

is functionally equivalent to

```
net name boss/add.
```

This command must be issued at a particular workstation. It is most conveniently done as part of a logon script and can be convenient if one uses long, descriptive computer names. Instead, one can issue a short name or a more friendly name. For instance, as opposed to sending a command to the jruleynt account, one could send a message to John—assuming that net name John has been executed on the same workstation as jruleynt is logged into. This may seem rather pointless but a certain degree of informality is often useful. An administrative message addressed to John will appear to be much more personal than an administrative message delivered to jruleynt for instance. Note that message aliases must be unique. You cannot add net name John on *two* workstations in the same network.

Checking Performance: *Net Statistics*

This command provides a concise report of system information for either the server or workstation service. It can be used as part of an automatic maintenance reporting system; see the example later in this section. The command has two forms:

```
net statistics server
```

displays statistics for the server service, for example:

```
Server Statistics for \\JOHNR-NT486-66

Statistics since 07/30/93 03:20pm

Sessions accepted          1
Sessions timed-out         1
Sessions errored-out       1

Kilobytes sent             262
Kilobytes received         722

Mean response time (msec)  25

System errors              0
Permission violations      0
Password violations        0
```

```
Files accessed                136
Comm devices accessed         0
Print jobs spooled            0

Times buffers exhausted

  Big buffers                 0
  Request buffers             0

The command completed successfully.
```

while:

```
net statistics workstation
```

displays statistics for the workstation service, for example:

```
Workstation Statistics for \\JOHNR-NT486-66

Statistics since 07/30/93 03:20pm

  Bytes received                              50734
  Server Message Blocks (SMBs) received       429
  Bytes transmitted                           58320
  Server Message Blocks (SMBs) transmitted    429
  Read operations                             0
  Write operations                            8
  Raw reads denied                            0
  Raw writes denied                           0

  Network errors                              0
  Connections made                            13
  Reconnections made                          1
  Server disconnects                          9

  Sessions started                            17
  Hung sessions                               0
  Failed sessions                             0
  Failed operations                           429
  Use count                                   20
  Failed use count                            0

The command completed successfully.
```

Note that any Windows NT system with file sharing enabled will have both. The server service is necessary in providing browsing functionality to a Windows NT system, so even though the system is not in fact used as a server, do not assume that there is not a server service running. The command *net statistics* by itself simply lists the services for which statistics may be requested; that is, server and workstation:

```
C:\users\default>net statistics
Statistics are available for the following running services:

Server                    Workstation
The command completed successfully.
```

Controlling User Accounts: *Net User*

This command allows user accounts to be added or deleted on a Windows NT server or domain server. It also allows control of certain features of the account, including a text comment, a descriptive comment, country code, expiration date, home directory, and so on as described below. As with the *net group* and the *net localgroup* commands, you can add users and assign users to existing groups. However, you cannot control other than by group assignment; you cannot control the permissions assigned to a user account from the command line. This has to be done in the Windows NT User Manager. The syntax of the net user command is:

```
net user user-name password (or asterisk)
```

and one or more switches. *User-name* is the name of the user account to add, delete, modify, or view. *Password*, if present, will assign or change the password for the user account. It must satisfy the minimum length set with the /minpwlen option in the *net accounts* command. The asterisk character, if used, will produce a prompt for a password, rather than putting the password in manually. This can be used if one wishes to set up a batch file requiring new passwords to be entered, for example, and one wishes to avoid the inherent security breach that would be represented by having the clear text password present in the file.

The */domain* switch will cause the operations employed in the *net user* command to be carried out on the primary DC in a Windows NT Server domain. As with other places where a domain switch is used, this has no effect if it's executed on a Domain Controller, since by default DCs carry out all operations on the PDC. On a Windows NT Workstation, or an NT Server that's not configured as a DC, *net user* commands issued without the /domain switch affect only the local machine. Also, the /domain switch can be used only by a domain administrator (or account operator).

The */add* switch will add a user account to the database. The */delete* switch eliminates a user account from the database. A variety of options may be added following the /add switch. These include /active:, which takes the arguments yes or no. This will activate or deactivate the account. If the account is not active the user cannot access the server using the account; however, unlike the /delete switch this does not remove the account from the database. This can be useful if a user has intermittent access to a server.

You can use the */active:no* switch to prevent the user from having access until some formal action is taken.

The */comment:* switch followed by a text message with a maximum length of 48 characters will provide a descriptive comment about the user account. You should enclose the comment text in quotation marks. For example:

```
net user jruley /add /comment:"John D Ruley's account"
```

The */countrycode:* switch, which takes a number as an argument, will use the operating system country code specified by that number to set the user's help and error messages. The default is country code:0, which uses whatever the default country code is for the Windows NT server in question. This can be useful in an international system, where users may be logging in who will expect to see different languages. You can custom configure using this logon system which language base is employed once the user logs in. Unfortunately this will affect only the help and error messages. It will not affect the primary Windows NT language set at the workstation. This has to be controlled manually.

The */expires:* switch takes a date or the keyword *never*. This will determine when the account expires. A /expires, for example:

```
net user jim /add /expires:12/25/93
```

will create a *jim* account expiring on Christmas Day. The keyword *never* will create an account that never expires.

The */fullname:* switch followed by a string in quotes sets a user's full name. For example:

```
net user jim/add/fullname:"James M. Ruley"
```

sets my brother's full name in association with the jim account.

The */homedir:* switch followed by a path name will set the path for a user's home directory. Note that the path must exist so that when a batch file is creating and setting home directories for one or more users it, will be necessary to create the directories *first* before setting the home directories. The home directory is the directory that will be set as the default directory during a remote logon.

The */homedirreq:* switch followed by a Yes or No specifies whether a home directory is required. If so this should be used in association with a /homedir switch to set the directory.

The */passwordchg:* switch followed by a Yes or a No specifies whether the user can change his own password. Saying */passwordchg:no* will require administrative change in a password and can be used in systems where for some reason users are not trusted to set their own password.

The */passwordreq:* switch followed by a Yes or a No specifies whether a user account must have a password.

The */profilepath:* switch followed by a path sets a path for the user's logon profile. This is functionally equivalent to the logon profile information that is set using the User Manager.

The */scriptpath:* switch followed by a path name sets the location of a user's logon script. Again, functionally the same as set in the User Manager.

The */times:* switch followed by either a time or the keyword *all* sets the hours during which the user is permitted to log on. The times are formatted as day-day,day-day,time-time,time-time, where time is limited to one hour increments. The days may be spelled out or abbreviated. Hours can be 12 or 24 hour notation. For example:

```
net user jim /times:monday-friday,8 a.m.-5 p.m.
```

will set the *jim* account with the permission to log in on weekdays during normal working hours. Attempts to log in at other times or on other days will fail.

The */usercomment:* switch followed by a text string lets the administrator add or change the user comment for the account; the comment being displayed is a text message that is displayed when the user logs in.

The */workstations:* switch command followed by computer names lists which workstation the user is permitted to log in on. If this string is absent then the user is assumed to be able to log in from any workstation.

You should note by this time that the *net user* command provides a considerable—not to say enormous—degree of administrative control. You can determine the time of day a user can log on, you can determine which days the user can log on, you can force the location of a home directory, force the execution of a logon script, present information to the user on logon, and determine which machines he is permitted to log on from. As described in chapter 1, Windows NT is a fully secure operating system. Your opportunity to effectively use this security is largely controlled by *net accounts*, *net user*, and their equivalents in the Windows NT User Manager.

Net user typed by itself simply provides a list of the user names defined for a particular system:

```
User accounts for \\JOHNR-NT486-66

-----------------------------------------------

Administrator          GuestJimFredJruleyJruleynt
The command completed successfully.
```

An interesting intellectual exercise would be to consider what it would take to write an application that would first issue a net user command, then parse the results, identifying each user and carrying out some operation on each user in sequence. But we digress....

Viewing, Controlling, and Unlocking Shared Files: *Net File*

When shared files are open on a Windows NT system it is possible to view a list of which files are in use to see specifics on the use of the file; that is, who has the file open, whether it is locked, what permissions are in use, and if necessary eliminate sharing on the file using the *net file* command. The syntax:

```
net file
```

prints a list of which shared file names are in use, whether they are locked, who has them, and what the file ID is:

```
C:\users\default>net file

ID        Path                          Username         # Locks


_____--

43        d:\netnt\uuencode             administrator       0
The command completed successfully.
```

Net file followed by an ID number prints a more specific display for the particular file:

```
C:\users\default>net file 43
File ID      43
Username     administrator
Locks        0
Path         d:\netnt\uuencode
Permissions  XA
The command completed successfully.
```

Net file ID number /close will close the file—terminating the share. This can be useful in two situations. Obviously one is if there is unauthorized use of a file, although in that situation it would probably make the most sense to kick the user off the system, rather than simply disconnecting the file. It can also happen that certain applications, particularly 16-bit applications, may not do a proper job of cleaning up after themselves. A file may be opened at the beginning of an application session and not closed when the application shuts down. If this happens the user will then attempt to reconnect to the file but not be permitted to do so. He will receive a message indicating a sharing violation or indicating that the file is otherwise in use. In this circumstance it can be useful to issue a *net file*, view the list of files, probably identify the file in question, then issue a

```
net file ID number /close
```

to close the file, disable sharing, and permit the user to use the file again. Unfortunately, there is no such thing as *net close all*, which could be useful in some emergency situations. If one does wish to eliminate a user completely from a system, force them off, one can use the *net session* command, which is described next.

Controlling Logon Sessions: *Net Session*

The *net session* command lists or disconnects logon sessions connected to the server. Issued by itself the *net session* command presents a list of the computers that are logged into the server:

```
C:\users\default>net session

Computer                User name           Client Type     Opens Idle time
_____

\\MIPS-LAB-SERVER    administrator          NT                 1      00:30:28
The command completed successfully.
```

Issuing the command:

```
net session \\computer name
```

for a particular computer lists statistical information about the session, including which users are using the session and which shares are open:

```
C:\users\default>net session \\mips-lab-server
Username        administrator
Computer        MIPS-LAB-SERVER
Guest logon     No
Client type     NT
Sess time       23:43:28
Idle time       00:31:24

Sharename       Type      # Opens
_____

disk-d          Disk       1
The command completed successfully.
```

The */delete* parameter will force the session to log off and will disconnect the session. For example, *net session\ \mips-lab-server /delete* will disconnect *mips lab server* from the current session and terminate all connections. This should be used only as a last resort and is functionally equivalent to employing the disconnect button from the user session's dialog in the server portion of the control panel.

Time Synchronization: *Net Time*

One problem that often occurs in networking is assuring that all workstations within a domain have their system clocks synchronized. This can, for example, cause substantial problems in carrying out a distributed backup in the event that some random event, such as a change to daylight saving time or hard reset on a computer, has inadvertently changed the system clock. A particular machine may then carry out a backup at an unwarranted time. You can use the *net time* command to provide synchronization between computers and the network. The command

```
net time
```

with no arguments will print the time determined by the currently defined time server in the network, if any, while:

```
net time \\computer name
```

will print the time on the selected computer. The command:

```
net time /domain
```

will print the time on the current primary domain server.

```
net time /domain: domain name
```

will print that time for any specified domain server that is on the network. Any variation on this can be followed by the keyword */set* which will set the time at the machine on which the *net time* command is executed to match the time on the machine from which the time was requested. Thus, for example:

```
net time/domain/set
```

will synchronize the workstation by setting the local workstation time to be the same as the time of the DC. This command should normally be executed as part of a logon script.

Scheduling Commands for Execution: *At*

Up to now we have been concerned with commands within the *net* series of commands that are specific to Windows NT networking. In order to understand how commands can be executed at a specified time, we now need to understand the *at* command, which is a unique feature of the Windows NT Batch command set. The *at* command allows you to schedule commands for execution at a particular time. It also allows you to schedule these commands for execution on remote computers. It is a very powerful command for use by system administrators. The command has the following syntax:

```
at\\computer-name time "command-string"
```

where *computer-name* refers to the computer at which the command is to be executed. If this is omitted then the command is assumed to refer to the local computer. *Time* refers to the time for execution and may be used in conjunction with the flag */every:*, which may be followed by a date of the week or month or with */next:*, which will run the command the next occurrence of the day. So, for example, the command */every:Monday* will cause the command to be executed the set time every Monday. The command */next:Monday* will cause the command to be executed on the next Monday.

The command-string in quotes is a string that will be executed on the machine in question. For example, the command:

```
at\\mips-lab-server 10:28a.m. "net send jruleynt the time is 10:28"
```

will execute a *net send* command at 10:28 sending jruleynt a message that the time is 10:28.

This command requires the schedule service to be started (*net start schedule*) on the machine on which it is to be executed. Just typing *at* on a machine will list any jobs which are currently scheduled, and their ID numbers. The */delete* keyword will delete a particular ID number, or if no ID number is set will delete all jobs on the specified computer. For example:

```
at \\mips-lab-server
```

will print

```
C:\users\default>at
Status ID    Day           Time         Command Line
            ─────────────────────────────────  -
         0   Tomorrow      10:30AM      net send ADMINISTRATOR It's 10:30!
```

the command

```
at\\mips-lab-server 0 /delete
```

will delete this job. The command

```
at\\mips-lab-server /delete
```

without any ID number will delete *all* jobs. The command string can include any valid Windows NT command—including *start* commands—to cause a separate process (or batch command) to start. Thus, using the *at* command, it is possible to schedule remote execution of processes, such as backups, administrative maintenance reports, or whatever, and to have them occur at a specified time on a specified date repetitively. This is in addition to Windows NT's basic capability to support logon scripts.

As an example, it can be very helpful to back up really critical information to a central directory on one server. You can do this for any number of other servers/workstations with a simple combination of *net use* and *xcopy*:

```
net use z: \\ncr_nt\disk-c
xcopy z:\data c:\backup\ncr_nt /d /v
net use z: /DELETE
```

will copy files from the \data directory on \\ncr_nt to the c:\backup\ncr_nt directory—copying only files that have been updated since the last backup (that's what the /d switch is for), and verifying that the copies are good (the /v switch). You could repeat this process for other systems using similar commands, and then just run NT's tape backup on the local c:\backup directory—backing up all the systems at once.

Obviously, it would be nice to have a log for something as critical as this. That can be handled by redirecting the console output from xcopy to a file:

```
xcopy z:\data c:\backup\ncr_nt /d /v >BACKUP.LOG
```

But what do you do with the file once you've got it? Here's what: *Run*, don't walk, to your system, and download Martin Heller's *mailfile* command-line e-mail utility (MAILFILE.ZIP) from one of *WINDOWS Magazine*'s software libraries.[9] That allows you to send the log off via e-mail:

```
mailfile BACKUP.LOG to ADMINISTRATOR
```

will send the log as an MS-Mail message. The same approach lets you run a daily status report:

```
net statistics >net.log
mailfile NET.LOG to ADMINISTRATOR
```

To have this done autmatically at noon five days a week:

```
AT 12:00pm EVERY monday tuesday wednesday thursday friday REPORT.CMD
```

The resource kit includes a graphical interface to the scheduler service that gives you an alternative to the *at* command—WINAT.EXE does everything the *at* command-line interface does—but does it in a window, which makes it a bit easier to see what's happening—as illustrated in figure 3.17.

From its second edition on, the resource kit also includes a universal service (SRVANY) application that allows any NT program—including scripts—to be treated as NT services. This has several advantages and should be considered for mission-critical scripts. See Appendix 4 for more information.

Environment Variables

Windows NT provides a powerful capability to simplify administrative script creation through *environment variables*. These are character strings that can be referred to by name in a logon script, or using NT's *set* command. Typing *set* at the command line with no arguments gives a list of the current environment variables:

---

9. Available from the WinMag forum on CompuServe, WinMag on America On-Line, or via FTP from ftp.winmag.com.

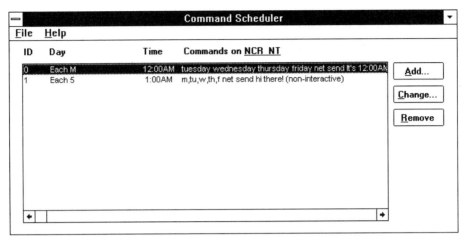

Figure 3.17 Command scheduler.
WINAT.EXE from Microsoft's Windows NT Resource Kit provides a graphical interface to the scheduler service, as an alternative to the *at* command-line program.

```
C:\ >set
COMPUTERNAME=COMPAQ-LTE
ComSpec=C:\WINDOWS\system32\cmd.exe
HOMEDRIVE=C:
HOMEPATH=\users\default
OS=Windows_NT
Os2LibPath=C:\WINDOWS\system32\os2\dll;
Path=C:\WINDOWS\system32;C:\WINDOWS;C:\;C:\DOS;C:\MOUSE
PROCESSOR_ARCHITECTURE=x86
PROCESSOR_LEVEL=4
PROMPT=$P$G
SystemRoot=C:\WINDOWS
SystemDrive=C:
TEMP=C:\temp
tmp=C:\temp
USERDOMAIN=MAGNET2
USERNAME=jruleynt
windir=C:\WINDOWS
```

As you can see, there's a wealth of information here. To use these variables in logon scripts, enclose them with the % character. For instance:

```
%username%
```

would evaluate to *jruleynt* in this case. In the examples at the end of this section, we will see how to exploit environment variables—among other things, dynamically assigning a local printer, depending on which workstation a user logs in to.

Setting Environment Variables

Environment variables can be locally set using NT's *set* command. For instance:

```
C:\users\default>set homepath=\
C:\users\default>set
COMPUTERNAME=COMPAQ-LTE
ComSpec=C:\WINDOWS\system32\cmd.exe
HOMEDRIVE=C:
HOMEPATH=\
...
```

However, such local settings apply only to a particular command-line session (and child sessions). If you start another session, you'll still find homepath set to \users\default.

You can *permanently* set some (but by no means all) environment variables with the *user profile* portion of NT User Manager, as described previously, and/or the *net user* command described in the following.

NT-Specific Commands

Besides the DOS- and LAN Manager-style commands, there are some commands that are specific to Windows NT. These are documented in the Command Reference section of Windows NT Help (the help icon in the Main program group). The sections on "What's New or Different from MS-DOS" and "What's New or Different from LAN Manager" provide lists with details. Some of the new commands are rather esoteric—the *ipxroute* command used for routing on NetWare-compatible LANs, for instance. Others are quite useful—the *start* command, for instance, will start a program running in a separate session from the one where the command line is executing. The *pushd* and *popd* commands are for changing the current directory and getting back to where you started from.

Some commands aren't documented in the NT Command Reference—in particular, a command-line option to dial out using NT Remote Access Services (RAS) that's ideal for making economical use of Wide Area Network (WAN) links. RAS is implemented as a service, so it can be controlled using *net start* and *net stop*. Dialing the phone is accomplished using the undocumented *rasdial* command (type *rasdial /?* on the command line for a very limited amount of documentation). As an example, if you've upgraded your system to have a full MS-Mail postoffice (see Chapter 7), and want to perform transfer messages in the middle of the night, you might want to use RAS.CMD:

```
net start remoteaccess
rasdial mail_server
net use w: \\mail_server\MAILDATA
m:external.exe -A -Ww
```

```
net use w: /DELETE
rasdial mail_server /DISCONNECT
net stop remoteaccess
```

where EXTERNAL.EXE is the Microsoft Message Transfer Agent (MTA) that's used to transfer data between postoffices (discussed in Chapter 7). The script starts the remote access service, creates a temporary connection to the other mail server's MAILDATA directory, runs the MTA over that temporary connection, then disconnects and shuts down.

To have this run five days a week at midnight:

```
AT 12:00am /EVERY: monday tuesday wednesday thursday friday RAS.CMD
```

Fortunately, the days may be abbreviated; for example:

```
AT 12:00am /EVERY: m,tu,w,th,f RAS.CMD
```

It's also possible to execute NT's built-in backup software from the command line—and thus from a script—using the *ntbackup* command (documented in the Helpfile for the NT Backup application—run Backup from the Administrative Tools group, Execute the Search for Help On... command from the Help menu, and type in *batch*). This can be combined with the *net use* command to get around Backup's inability to handle dynamic drive assignments by assigning a drive before running Backup:

```
NET USE X: \\mips-lab-server\vb
NTBACKUP backup X:  /A
NET USE X: /DELETE
NET USE X: \\ncr-nt\disk-c
NTBACKUP backup X: /A
```

This script will first back up the vb directory on \\mips-lab-server, and then the disk-c directory on \\ncr-nt—appending them to the existing tape (via the /A switch on NTBACKUP). Data must be restored using the graphical interface—NTBACKUP doesn't provide a command-line restoration capability.

Finally, there are some very powerful (even dangerous) command-line programs included in the NT resource kit (described in Appendix 4). Probably the most useful of these is CHOICE.EXE from the resource kit, which enables you to create interactive scripts—ones where the batch file can ask for input from the user. This is key to writing real (if simple) programs using scripts. For instance, our unix-style *safe* copy script can now ask the user whether to overwrite a file:

```
if exist %2
goto ask_user
do_copy:
copy %1 %2
exit
```

```
ask_user:
choice /c:yn File exists, overwrite it
if ERRORLEVEL 1 goto do_copy
```

If the user types *cp this that*, and *that* exists, a prompt is displayed:

```
File exists, overwrite it [Y,N]?
```

If the user hits a Y, then the file will be overwritten. If not, the command aborts.

The most powerful and *dangerous* of the additional tools is REGINI.EXE, which is included in the \SUPPORT directory of all NT CD-ROMs, as well as in the resource kit. It is a command-line interface to the configuration registry, and allows registry settings to be changed from the command line. Like the registry editor, REGINI.EXE is powerful because it lets you change almost anything—and also like the registry editor, it's dangerous. Use it with care!

Examples

Several example scripts are shown below.

Example 1—Automatic Server Maintenance Report

report.cmd

```
REM This is a 3 time-per-week maintenance report
REM
REM First, get to the \temp directory:
c:
cd \temp
REM
REM delete any old stuff:
REM
del a b c d
REM
REM run NET CONFIG and NET STATISTICS, piping output to files:
REM
net config server >a
net statistics server >b
net config workstation >c
net statistics workstation >d
REM
REM copy the results to the administrator's system:
REM
copy a+b+c+d R:\reports\system1\reptnew.txt
REM
```

```
REM It is the administrator's responsibility to see that REPTNEW.TXT is
REM copied or otherwise taken care of before the next night, so that
REM it won't be overwritten—he can run another scheduled process
REM to do this—or transfer the file using e-mail, as described below
```

To cause this script to be executed nightly, it is only necessary that:

1. The administrator place it in the path on each server
2. The following *at* command is issued for each server:

```
at  \\server_name 3:00am /each:monday,wednesday,friday "report.cmd"
```

Obviously, the file should be edited slightly for each system, with the copy placing the file in reports\system2 for the second system. It would be awfully nice to have this report *mailed* to the administrator, rather than copied. This is technically feasible—see the following Example 6.

Example 2—Workstation Logon Script

As mentioned at the start of this section, Microsoft's NT documentation could easily lead you to believe that logon scripts are obsolete. Nothing could be further from the truth—here's a script that performs the following functions:

❏ Sets a message alias for the current user
❏ Synchronizes system time with the PDC (*this is essential for use of scheduled commands accross multiple systems*)
❏ Starts the Scheduler service (this could be done automatically using the NT control panel)
❏ Announces the logon to other users in the domain
❏ Assigns a network drive letter

Note that all this is done without hard-coding a user name. This allows the same login script to be used by all users (or at least many users) on a given server—and *that* greatly simplifies maintenance. For example, the assignment of the M: drive in the following example allows an administrator to move the mail directories to another drive (or server), and by making the change in *one* logon script, all users will be automatically connected to the proper server and drive.

logon.cmd

```
REM
REM Add a message alias for the user (we use the user's name—by default
REM the only name stored is the computername):
REM
net name %username% /ADD
REM
REM Synchronize time with the domain server
```

```
REM
net time /DOMAIN /SET
REM
REM Start the Schedule service (so remote at... commands will work)
REM
net start schedule
REM
REM Announce the log-in to the domain
REM
net send /DOMAIN:%userdomain% %username% is logged in
REM
REM Set M: to the mail directory (doing this in a logon
REM script makes it maintainable)...
REM
net use M: \\win1\msmail\maildata
```

Example 3—Converting a list of NetWare users into Windows NT accounts

In the first edition of *Networking Windows NT*, we talked about how this might be done. Since then, Microsoft has provided a *Migration Tool for NetWare Servers* with NT Server, which does a far better job than any script. So, the example has been deleted from this chapter, and we recommend using the Migration Tool instead. You'll find more on it in Chapter 9.

Example 4—Wandering Users

This example was suggested to us by an NT adminstrator with a real-world problem: The administrator runs an NT-based network at a major hospital. His users are the hospital's doctors, nurses, and support staff. The problem: Doctors and nurses don't always access the same computer. When a patient is brought to the emergency room, his doctor may need to access the patient's chart from a computer in the ER. The patient may then be moved to intensive care—and the doctor follows the patient, needing to log on from there. The doctor may then need to log on from his office, and... you get the picture.

NT's profiles certainly help in this situation. Using them, the doctor can be given his personal preference of desktop, program groups, and so on, while forcing a home directory on a particular server—but How, the administrator asked, can the doctor's default *printer* be handled? When the doctor's in the ER, printing to a printer in the physician's lounge isn't too helpful.

The answer: a logon script—and nothing else. There is no way to assign location-dependant printer connections from a user profile or Print Manager! A logon script, however, makes the problem easy to solve: First, the location the doctor logs in from can be determined using the %computername% environment variable, and based on that, an appropriate printer can be assigned via the *net use* command:

```
If %computername%==\\ER_NT net use lpt1: \\ER_Laserjet
If %computername%==\\ICU_NT net use lpt1: \\ICU_Laserjet
...
```

Of course, in Print Manager, the default printer is just LPT1:, and an appropriate print driver has been installed for that port. The one limitation of this approach is that all the printers have to be identical—or at least compatible with a single standard print driver.

The same approach can be used to maximize efficiency in large networks by assigning the user's home directory to an appropriate local server—data integrity can be assured using the replication service (see Chapter 7) to replicate data from a single location to all servers in the domain.

Example 5—Weekly Backup

The Windows NT Backup application can be controlled through the *at* command scheduler and a command script, as described previously. To execute a daily backup on the server, start the scheduler service, and type:

```
AT 10:00pm /EVERY mo,t,we,th,f,sa,su backup.cmd
```

This will cause the BACKUP.CMD script to be executed every night at 10:00. Since *at* also supports specifying what computer you want the command to be run on, you can use the same approach to command remote backups on other systems:

```
AT \\mips-lab-server 2:00am /EVERY m,w,f backup.cmd
```

will cause a three-day-per-week execution of BACKUP.CMD on \\mips-lab-server.

To backup multiple machines on the network, a temporary drive connection can be established and backup executed on that temporary drive—as discussued earlier—but a better approach may be a *multistage backup*, in which critical information is regularly copied to a central directory on one server, and then backed up from there. This can be accomplised with a combination of *net use* and *xcopy*:

```
net use z: \\ncr_nt\disk-c
xcopy z:\data c:\backup\ncr_nt /d /v
net use z: /DELETE
```

This will copy files from the \data directory on \\ncr_nt to the *c:\backup\ ncr_nt directory*—copying only files that have been updated since the last backup (that's what the /d switch is for), and verifying that the copies are good (the /v switch). You could repeat this process for other systems using similar commands, and *then* run NT's tape backup on the local c:\backup directory—backing up all the systems at once.

Obviously, it would be nice to have a log for something as critical as this. That can be handled by redirecting the console output from *xcopy* to a file:

```
xcopy z:\data c:\backup\ncr_nt /d /v >BACKUP.LOG
```

And, as with Example 1, it's then possible to transfer the file via e-mail—as described in the following.

Example 6—E-Mail and Scripts

Microsoft's myopia about use of the command-line generally—and scripts in particular—is especially obvious when you realize 1) that NT provides e-mail as a basic feature, but 2) no command-line interface to mail is provided. That's ridiculous, as Examples 1 and 5 make clear: What *should* happen at the end of those scripts is that the log files should be e-mailed to an administrator. That way you have a log and tracking information available whenever and wherever you need it.

To fill this gap, download Martin Heller's MAILFILE command-line e-mail utility from *WINDOWS Magazine* listings.[10] This will allow you to send off the logs via e-mail:

```
mailfile BACKUP.LOG to ADMINISTRATOR
```

The same approach can be used with the three-time-per-week status report in Example 1:

```
mailfile REPTNEW.TXT to ADMINISTRATOR
delete REPTNEW.TXT
```

Example 7—SMS Logon Script

Curiously enough, despite Microsoft's tendency to ignore the command line and scripts in the NT documentation, the singlemost extreme example of NT batchfile complexity we've seen (by far!) is the logon script used by Microsoft's Systems Management Server (SMS) application. The script is far too long to reproduce here (even if Microsoft would permit us to do so), but it's discussed in Chapter 7, as is Microsoft's use of its TEST application to extend the concept of command scripts to graphical applications.

---

10. MAILFILE.ZIP from any of the download locations specified in the Electronic Updates section of the Introduction.

Extending NT Scripts with a Command Language

As the previous examples show, NT's built-in batch language is actually a good bit more powerful than most people think—but there are still situations where it's inadequate. There are also people who cringe at the idea of using a direct descendant of the DOS (and OS/2) batch language for enterprise applications.

For those who want a more powerful (or simply a more elegant) solution, there are several alternatives available; see Table 3.3.

Table 3.3 Third-Party Batch Languages for NT

Product	*Company*	*Address*	*Telephone*	*Notes*
4DOS for Windows NT	JP Software, Inc.	PO box 1470, E. Arlington, MA 02174	800-368-8777	Improved command-line interpreter with batch processing.
Batch Services for Windows NT	Intergraph Corp.	Huntsville, AL 35894-0001	800-345-4856	Priority-based, network-wide scheduling of noninteractive jobs. Resubmits jobs automatically if the network is down.
Event Control Server (ECS) for Windows NT	Vinzant, Inc.	600 E. Third St, Hobart, IN 46342	219-942-9544	High-end, multiplatform batch sceduler with remote dispatch.
Hamilton C-Shell	Hamilton Labs	21 Shadow Oak Dr. Sudbury, MA 01776-3165	508440-8307 fax: 8308.	Multithreaded NT port of OS/2-based UNIX shell toolkit (primarily useful for programmers). Includes both TAR and CPIO. *Highly Recommended for those familiar with UNIX-style shell tools.*
MKS Toolkit	MKS, Inc.	35 King St. N. Waterloo, ON, Canada N2J2W9	519-884-2251	UNIX-style toolkit (primarily useful for programmers). Includes UNIX-compatible Tape Archive (TAR) bundled by Intergraph Corp. with their NT-based Technical Workstation line.
Oriel Plus for Windows NT	LeBlond Software	10921 Reed Hartman Hwy, Suite 314, Cincinnati, OH 45242	513-745-9990	Advanced batch language that supports direct access to NT's graphics subsystem (software packaged with book).

(continues)

Table 3.3 (*Continued*)

Product	Company	Address	Telephone	Notes
Queue Manager	Argent	49 Main St., Torrington, CT 06790	203-489-5553	Job queuing and scheduling with workload support.
Systems Management Server (SMS), MS-TEST	Microsoft Corp	One Microsoft Way, Redmond WA, 98052	800-426-9400 206-882-8080	MS-Test is a graphical scripting tool originally written for use in regression testing during software development. SMS is Microsoft's network-wide client management tool, which uses MS-Test for automated software installation. See Appendix 4 for more information.
VX/DCL	Sector 7 USA, Inc.	2802 W. 50th St, Austin, TX 78731	512-451-3961	NT implemention of VAX print and batch queue manager with DCL support.
WinBatch	Wilson WindowWare Inc.	2701 California Ave SW, Suite 212, Seattle, WA 98116	800-762-8383 206-938-1740	Advanced batch services for Windows applications—can send keystrokes to graphical apps. Supports DDE and OLE.

Summing up NT Scripts

The ultimate future of scripting in NT doubtlessly is OLE2 automation and a universal command language. But in the meantime, creative use of NT's built-in batch language and environment variables—augmented if you like with a third-party script language—provides a very workmanlike alternative.

NT Administration—Still Not Perfect

While the enhancements provided in NT 3.5 and 3.51 (not to mention SMS!) has greatly improved NT's manageability, there are at least three serious limitations NT Servers suffer from in comparison to other network operating systems: Changing drivers still generally requires a reboot, and there are still no per-user accounting and no way to set per-user resource quotas.

These are serious limitations, especially at large sites. If you've spent the money to buy fault-tolerant hardware that supports hot-swapped hard disks and tape drives, it's a bit much to be forced to reboot every time you install a new driver (especially so for printers—a problem that Microsoft solved with the *spooler* service in NT 3.5. SCSI devices, and network protocols *ought* to be handled the same way). If you're supporting users from many organizations, the lack of a way to track how much time each is spending online can make cross-departemental charging all but impossible, and the lack of quotas makes NT all but unusable in educational institutions—if the system permits students to fill a hard disk, you can count on 'em to do so.

Still, all network operating systems have *some* problems, and we would rather worry about these than have to deal with server crashes when one more user is added than the server's memory supports—as still happens on one of today's most popular NOSs. Moreover, every one of these limitations is an opportunity for an ambitious third-party developer—let's hope some of them get the message!

Conclusion

In this chapter, you've learned what the responsibilities of the Network Administrator are, how to create user accounts and account groups, how to assign user permissions, how to monitor performance and log events, and how to write command scripts. You should be ready to get your users online, and we will next look at how users can exploit the networking features of Windows NT in Chapter 4.

For More Information

Microsoft Staff (1993-1994), *Windows NT Server Concepts and Planning Guide*. Redmond WA: Microsoft Corp. Included with NT Server (full version) and the NT documentation kit. Electronic version included on NT Server CD. Excellent overall coverage of Windows NT concepts from the administrator's point of view.

Microsoft Staff (1993-94), *Windows NT System Guide*. Redmond WA: Microsoft Corp. Included with NT Workstation. Basic information on administrative tools, including User Manager, Performance Monitor, and so on. Note that the similar *Windows NT Server System Guide* adds information for the domain-management tools, including User Manager for Domains, Server Manager, and so on.

Microsoft Staff (1995), *Windows NT Resource Kit, Volumes 1-4*. Redmond WA: Microsoft Press. Volumes 2 and 3 are especially helpful.

Farris, Jeffrey L. (1988), *Saber LAN Setup Guide—a Guide to Network Planning*. Dallas TX: Saber Software Corp., ISBN: 1-878092-69-3. While oriented toward a particular vendor's LAN Administration products, this book gives a good overall introduction to the concepts an administrator must deal with.

Using NT Networking Features

After reading this chapter, you should understand the basic networking features that are included with Windows NT. You will understand how to share resources (including directories and printers) with other network users, how to use shared resources, and how to create and maintain user accounts. You will also be introduced to the utility programs that are bundled with Windows NT, including File Manager, Mail, Chat, Schedule+, Print Manager, ClipBook, and the NET Command Interface. You should feel comfortable performing basic network operations, such as file/device sharing, using mail, and scheduling a group meeting, after reading this chapter.

File Manager

Like Windows 3.1, Windows NT contains a File Manager application that lets you manage files on floppies or on your hard drive. The File Manager application looks more like that in Windows for Workgroups: It contains a toolbar for fast access to common tasks.

Besides basic file management, NT's File Manager is responsible for setting file permissions for NTFS drives, and setting the audit parameters for such files. It is also used to share directories across the network.

To start File Manager, double-click on the File Manager icon in the Main program group window. Alternatively, select File/Run from the main Program Manager menu and type WINFILE.EXE in the Command Line box; then click on OK.

The File Manager Window

The main File Manager window, shown in Figure 4.1, contains a directory panel that displays in hierarchical order the directories on the selected drive, as well as the files and subdirectories in the selected directory. If both windows are not displayed, select View/Split. For NTFS drives, the file name displayed is the DOS equivalent (that is, a filename of 8 characters or less and a file extension of 3 characters or less).

File Manager's main screen can contain several windows, each displaying a separate directory or drive. To add a window for a drive and directory, select Window from the main menu, then select New Window from the pull-down menu. Alternatively, click the New Window button on the toolbar. To close the

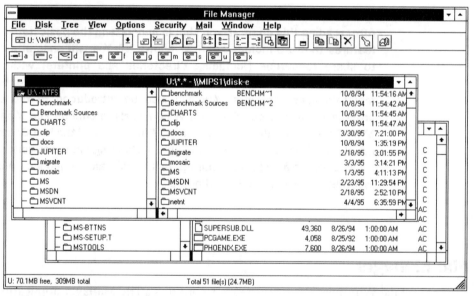

Figure 4.1 File Manager.

Windows NT file operations can be carried out using the familiar File Manager interface. This gives users a simple, graphically illustrated, and intuitive way to manipulate files, eliminating any need to resort to the command line. Windows NT 3.51 enhanced this interface with Windows 95-style user interface elements (not the textured *grab bar* in the lower right corner) and compression support.

active directory window, double-click the Control menu box (the minus sign in the upper left corner).

To work with files on another drive, click on the drive icon you want. Then click on the subdirectory name. If the subdirectory icon contains a plus sign (+) inside it, you can double-click on the subdirectory and expand the tree to show all subdirectories. The icon changes to an open folder and contains a minus (-) sign inside. Double-clicking on an expanded directory listing collapses the hierarchy.

The icons that precede file names provide information about the type of file listed:

❑ A folder icon indicates a directory.

❑ A folder held by a hand indicates the directory is shared.

❑ A rectangle with a small band at the top indicates a program, batch, or Program Information File (PIF) file.

❑ A page with lines on it indicates a document file associated with an application, such as a spreadsheet or word processing file.

❑ A page with an exclamation mark inside indicates a system or hidden file (by default, such files aren't shown—you must enable the Show Hidden/System Files check box in the View/By File Type menu).

❑ A page that is blank is a file that does not fit into any of the preceding categories.

The icons are illustrated in Figure 4.1.

Sharing a Directory

Sharing a directory makes the files in the directory available to other users on your network. You must also have sufficient rights to share a directory. You can also share directories on your local hard disk.

To share a directory on a network:

1. Select the directory you want to share. You can select the directory by clicking on it in either the directory panel or the file name panel. Select Disk/Share As or click on the Share Directory button if it is on the toolbar. File Manager displays the Share Directory dialog box shown in Figure 4.2.

2. Enter the name you want other users to see in the Share Name box. By default, File Manager displays the name of the directory. Enter the full path name in the Path box. By default, File Manager fills this box with the full path name you have selected. Optionally, type a comment in the Comment box. Users will see this comment when they attempt to connect to the directory.

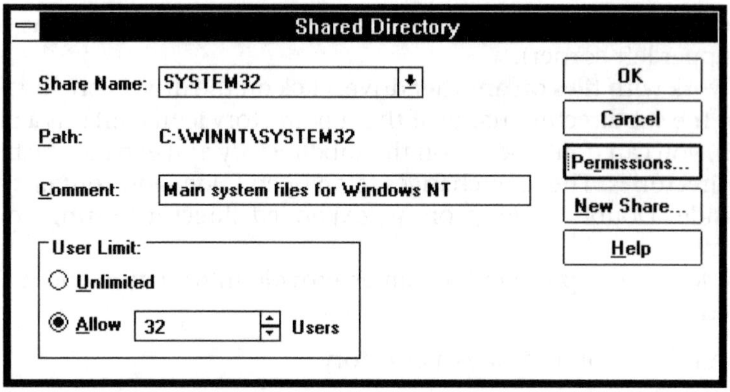

Figure 4.2 Share dialog.

Sharing directories and files is achieved by selecting the file/directory, and clicking a single toolbar button. This dialog then appears, allowing definition of the Share Name, assignment of a comment, and control of who is permitted to access the share.

3. Set the maximum number of users who can share this directory at any one time. Enter this number in the User Limit box or click on the up and down arrow buttons until the correct user limit is reached. If you do not want to restrict the number of users, select the Unlimited button. Setting the maximum number of users ensures that performance will not be degraded for those using the directory.

4. Click on Permissions if you want to specify permissions for the directory. This option is available only if the drive is an NTFS drive.

5. Click on OK.

Working with Shared Files

While a directory or file is shared, you can view which users are currently using the file(s). While anyone can see the total number of opens and locks on a file, only an Administrator or Power User can stop sharing a file.

To view the file statistics, select the file, then select File/Properties. Click the Open By button. The file name, total number of opens and locks, and list of users using the file is displayed.

If you have proper security rights, you can stop the sharing of the file. Select the user(s) you want to prevent from using the file and select Close Selected. To close the shared file for all users, click on Close All.

Click on OK to return to the File Manager.

Stop Sharing a Directory

Before you stop sharing a directory, be sure that all users currently using the directory are notified and asked to stop using the directory. Otherwise, if you stop sharing a directory that is in use, those users connected to it could lose data (in particular, users of 16-bit applications run from the server will see a *Segment Load Fault* error).

To stop sharing a directory, you must be an Administrator or Power User, or the user who shared the directory. Select the directory you want to stop sharing. Select Disk/Stop Sharing, or click on the Stop Sharing button in the toolbar if it is present. File Manager displays the Stop Sharing dialog box. The directory you selected is already selected. Click on OK.

Connecting to a Network Drive

File Manager can connect to other drives on the network. Once connected, you can specify whether you want Windows NT to reconnect you to the drive(s) in all future sessions.

To connect to a network drive:

1. Select Disk/Connect Network Drive. You may also begin by clicking on the Connect Network Drive button in the toolbar if it is present.

2. The Connect Network Drive dialog box appears, which is shown in Figure 4.3. The Drive box contains the next available letter for your computer. To change this value, click on the down-pointing arrow key or press Alt+Down Arrow and select the drive letter you prefer.

3. If you have connected to this drive before, the path may be listed in the Path pull-down list. The Path list shows the previous ten paths you have selected. If the path you want to connect to is displayed, select it and proceed to step 5.

4. There are two options for selecting the path.

   ❑ If you have not connected to this drive before, or your drive is not listed in the Path list box, enter the path name directly. Be sure to enter the network path of the drive, followed by the directory name. Network path names include a computer name and the name of the shared directory, such as \\MAINPC\BUDGETS.

   ❑ Alternatively, select the shared directory from the Shared Directories box. The networks, domains, servers, user names, and shared directories are listed in a hierarchical tree structure similar to that used in the directory panel of File Manager. When you make your selection, File Manager displays the shared directories of your selection in the box at the bottom of the dialog box. Select the shared directory. File Manager displays the path in the Path box.

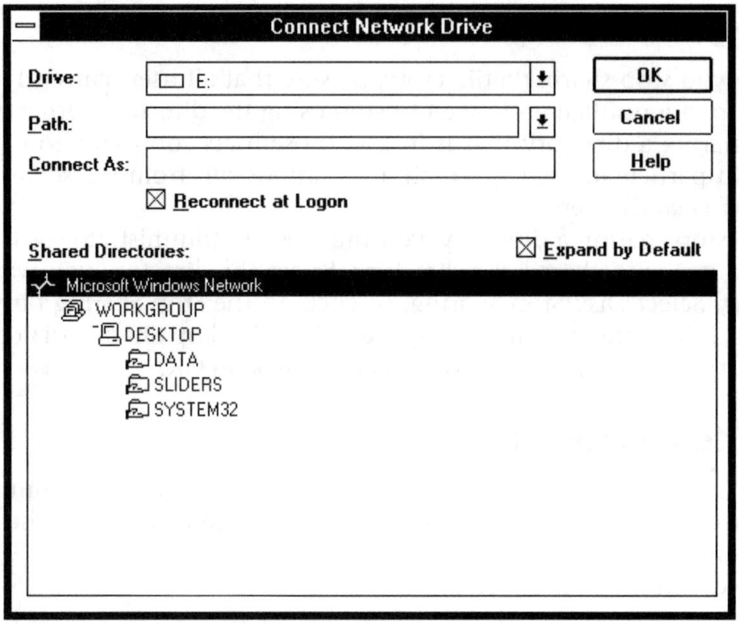

Figure 4.3 Connect Net Drive.

Connecting to shared directories on network servers is achieved by selecting the server and share in this browse dialog. The user can also determine what local drive letter is assigned.

5. If you want to reconnect to this directory automatically when you begin Windows NT, be sure to check the Reconnect at Logon box. Caution: If the directory is on a computer that is not the server and is not certain to be running when you start Windows NT again, you will get a warning message asking if you want to proceed with connections. Therefore, we recommend that you check the Reconnect at Logon box only if you are connecting to a directory on the server for which there is a strong likelihood of availability when you log in.

6. If you are attempting to connect to a shared directory on which you have a valid account that is different from the one you are logged in with, enter the account name in the Connect As: field. Windows NT will prompt you for the associated password. Note: If you are connecting across domains (or using a master domain account that is not recognized by the particular system you are connecting to), you will have to use the *domain\username* syntax; for instance: *magnet2\jruley*.

7. Finally select OK.

Disconnecting from a Network Drive

To disconnect from a network drive, select Disk/Disconnect Network Drive. Select the drive(s) you want to disconnect from. To select more than one drive, press and hold the Ctrl key and click on each drive. Click on OK to perform the disconnect.

Setting Directory and File Permissions

You can control who has access to your files and directories, as well as the extent of that access, using what Windows NT has named *permissions*. You can limit access on any *shared directory*, but you can restrict access to *files* only on New Technology File System (NTFS) partitions.

Windows NT's set of standard permissions can be set for files and directories.

For Directories

Standard Permission	Access allowed.
No Access	None.
List	Display a directory's files and a directory's attributes; user can move to any subdirectory within the directory.
Read	All rights from List permission, plus user can display the owner and permissions of a directory; this permission also allows the same Read permissions as for file permissions for all files in the directory (see the following).
Add and Read	All rights from Read permissions, plus user can create subdirectories, add files to the directory, and change the attributes of a directory.
Change	All rights from Add and Read, plus user can delete the directory or any subdirectories below it. This permission also allows the same Change permissions as for file permissions for all files in the directory.
Full Access	All rights from Add and Read and Change permissions. In addition, users can change permissions for a directory, or delete subdirectories and the files in them (no matter what their permissions). User can also take ownership of the directory. Full Access also allows the same Full Access permissions as for file permissions.

For Files

Standard Permission	Access allowed.
No Access	None.
Read	Display the file's data; view the file's attributes.
Change	In addition to Read activities, user can launch program files, change the file's attributes, and display the file's owner and the permissions assigned to the file.
Full Access	In addition to the Read and Change activities, users can change or append data to the file.

To set permissions on a *directory*:

1. Select the directory from the directory panel. Select Security/Permissions or select the Permissions button from the toolbar (the button with the key). The Permissions dialog box shown in Figure 4.4 appears.

2. Note that whether the changes you make affect subdirectories and files depends on the setting of the Replace Permissions on Subdirectories and Replace Permissions on Existing Files check boxes.

3. You can change permissions, add new user permissions, or delete existing permissions.

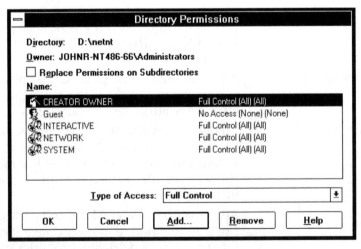

Figure 4.4   Permissions.

On New Technology File System (NTFS) partitions, total control over user access is provided for both local and network users. The security information is built directly into the directory structure, and will follow a drive if it is physically moved to another system.

❏ To change a permission, select the name of the user group or the individual user you want to change. Select the permission type from the Type of Access pull-down list. Then click on OK.

❏ To add a user permission, click on Add. Select the name(s) of the users or user groups you want to add and click on Add. The name(s) are added to the Add Names box. When all users have been added, click on OK.

❏ To delete a user permission, select the user, then click on Remove.

4. Click on OK to return to the File Manager window.

Setting file permissions is similar to setting directory permissions. By default, the File Permissions dialog box shows the permissions that are inherited from the directory in which it is contained. Managing file permissions is almost identical to managing directory permissions. Instead of selecting a directory, select one or more files from the file panel of the File Manager. Select Security/Permissions or select the Permissions button from the toolbar (the button with the key). Select the user(s) you want to remove or change, or click on Add to grant user(s) permission to the selected file(s).

Special Access Permissions

If the standard permissions are not sufficient to limit access to files or directories, you can use a set of special access permissions.

The special access permissions are:

D   Delete

O   Take Ownership

P   Change Permissions

R   Read

W   Write

X   Execute

To set a special access permission:

1. Select the directory from the directory window to set permissions on a directory. Select the file(s) from the file name panel to set permissions on individual files.

2. Select Security/Permissions or click on the Permissions button in the toolbar (the button with the key on it).

3. Select the user or user group you want to grant special access. Then select the appropriate Special Access button. For example, to set permissions

on a directory, click on Special Directory Access; for files click on Special File Access.

4. Select the check boxes for the access(es) you want to grant. Then click on OK.

5. Click on OK to return to File Manager.

Permissions on a Shared Directory

Permissions on shared directories are slightly different. You must be an Administrator or Power User to manage permissions on shared directories.

Permissions on a shared NTFS directory are cumulative with those set for sharing over the network (for users connecting over the LAN). If the permission is less extensive on the directory, the directory's permission takes precedence.

For shared directories, the standard permissions are:

No Access   Nothing.

Read   Display the files (including data) and any subdirectories, all attributes, launch programs, and move to any subdirectory of the selected directory.

Change   In addition to Read activities, create files and subdirectories, change or append data to files in the directory, change file attributes, and delete files and subdirectories.

Full Access   Same as Change.

To *add* or change the security permissions on a shared directory:

1. Select the shared directory from the directory panel. From the main menu select Disk/Share As, or select the Share Directory button from the toolbar.

2. Click on Permissions.

3. Select the user or name to be changed. Then select the permission from the Type of Access dialog box. When a check box contains an X, the permission is granted. When the check box is empty, the permission is not granted.

4. Click on OK.

To *remove* permissions already granted for a shared directory:

1. Select the shared directory from the directory panel.

2. Select Security/Permissions or select the Permissions button from the toolbar.

3. Select the name of the user or user group that will have the permissions removed, then click on the Remove button.

4. File Manager asks to confirm your request. Select Yes, then click on OK to return to File Manager.

Auditing Files

Auditing provides a view of which users or user groups are using your files or directories. The volume containing the file(s) must be an NT File System volume (NTFS volume).

To audit a file or directory:

1. Select the file in the file name panel, or select the directory in either the file name or directory panel. Then select Security/Auditing. The dialog box shown in Figure 4.5 appears.

2. Set the Replace Auditing on Existing Files and/or Replace Auditing on Existing Subdirectories check boxes if you want to audit existing files and/or directories. Leave the box empty (unchecked) if you want to audit only new files and subdirectories.

3. Select the user or user group you want to view.

4. Choose the events you want to audit. A check in the corresponding box means that File Manager will audit the event; an empty box means that File Manager will not audit the event.

5. Click on OK.

You can easily modify the user list. For example, to add a user to the audit list, choose Security/Auditing, click on Add, and select the user or user group you want to add. To remove a user from the audit list, select Security/Auditing, select the user, and click on Remove.

Ownership of Files

When you create a file or directory, you are the designated owner of it. This allows you to grant permissions. You can grant permission to another user so that he or she can act as an owner and, in turn, set permissions. When you grant another permission to take ownership of a file or directory, and that user takes ownership, you give up that ownership.

If you are using an NTFS partition, you must have adequate permission to take ownership.

To take ownership of one or more files, select the file(s) from the file name field. To take ownership of one or more directories, use the directory or file

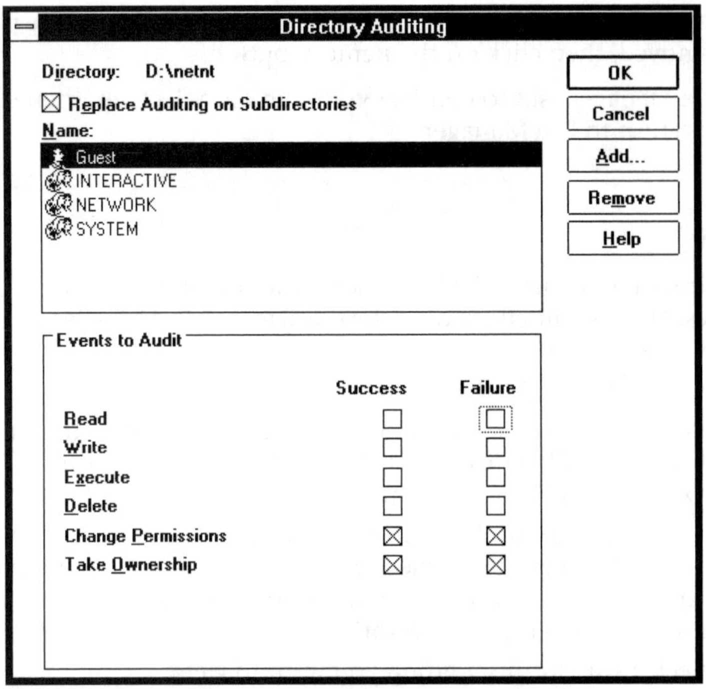

Figure 4.5 Security/Auditing.

If required, auditing may be enabled, allowing direct tracking of the use (or misuse) of system resources. Audit information is stored in the security log and may be viewed using the Event Viewer application. Auditing is also affected by the Audit Policy set using the User Manager application—for example, auditing of file events will happen only if the Administrator has auditing turned on for a given file or directory, and has audit policy selected for file events.

name field. From the main menu choose Security/Take Ownership. Click on the Take Ownership button. If multiple files or directories were selected, File Manager asks if you want to take ownership of all selected items. Select Yes.

Controlling Compression

Beginning with version 3.51, Windows NT provides file compression on NTFS partitions. This is controlled through File Manager's new File/Compress... and Uncompress... items. To compress a file, group of files, directory, or an entire disk, simply select the files and directories in question and click File/Compress. File Manager will ask if you want to compress all files, and if you answer Yes, compression will proceed automatically (uncompression works in exactly the same manner).

If you compress a directory, and decline when asked if you want to compress files in the directory, then the directory is marked for compression, while existing files remain in their uncompressed form. Files will still be compressed automatically when copied or moved to the directory. Similarly, you can mark a compressed directory as uncompressed without decompressing the files it contains.

Alternatively, you can control compression using the *compact* command-line function:

```
C:\>compact /?
Displays and alters the compression of files or directories.

COMPACT [/C | /U] [/S[:dir]] [/A] [/I] [/Q] [filename [...]]

    /C       Compresses the specified directory or file.
    /U       Uncompress the specified directory or file.
    /S       Performs the specified operation on matching files in the
             given directory and all subdirectories. Default "dir" is the
             current directory.
    /A       Do not ignore hidden or system files.
    /I       Ignore errors.
    /F       Force the operation to compress or uncompress
             the specified directory or file.
    /Q       Be less verbose.
    filename Specifies a pattern, file, or directory.


Used without parameters, COMPACT displays the compression state of
the current directory. You may use multiple filenames and wildcard.
```

Running *compact* on a typical directory yields the following results:

```
C:\users\default>compact
 Listing C:\users\default\ [Compress new files]


        0 /         0 = 100% C .
        0 /         0 = 100% C ..
    17408 /     59873 =  29% C DREAMS.MID
    46897 /     46897 = 100% C NEWTIPS.ZIP
     1024 /      1087 =  94% C README.TXT
```

```
   264704 /    346880 =  76% C WINROIDS.EXE
    19968 /     24379 =  81% C WINROIDS.HLP
    19968 /     67715 =  29% C WINROIDS.MID
   220445 /    220445 = 100% C WROIDS10.ZIP
    84370 /     84370 = 100% C WTNSRC.ZIP

Of 10 files within 1 directories
10 are compressed and 0 are not compressed.
674784 bytes are being used to store 851646 total bytes of data.
The data occupies 79% of its uncompressed size.
```

Files are automatically decompressed when accessed over the network—so compression is completely transparent to client applications; however, you cannot assume that files copied to a partition will be compressed automatically unless you've marked the partition itself for compression.

Leaving File Manager

To exit File Manager, select File/Exit from the main menu, or double-click on the Control Menu button in the upper left corner of the File Manager window.

Microsoft Mail

Windows NT includes Microsoft Mail (MS-Mail), an electronic mail application that lets you send and receive messages with other users on your network. In addition to text messages, you can send files by attaching them to messages. You can save messages in a folder, delete them, or forward them to others.

The version of MS-Mail bundled into Windows NT is sufficient for a single-server workgroup, but lacks store-and-forward capabilities that would make it useful for electronic mail in a large organization. Microsoft offers an upgrade to this package, which we'll discuss in Chapter 7. Most procedures described here apply equally to either version.

MS-Mail uses Postoffices, collections of users and a storage location on hard disk for their messages. Incoming messages appear in an inbox, though messages can be moved to other folders for better organization. Each incoming message includes the sender's name, a subject, and the date and time the message was received. An icon to the left of each inbox message provides information about the message: An exclamation point indicates a high-priority message; a paper clip indicates there is an attachment to the message.

MS-Mail is also used by other applications within NT, such as Schedule+, which uses MS-Mail messages for scheduling and notification of meetings .

Start MS-Mail by selecting the Mail icon from the Main program group.

Exiting the MS-Mail application can be done in one of two ways. Since MS-Mail may be in use by other applications, such as Schedule+, you may log out of the current session but keep the MS-Mail application running (so you can send meeting requests in Schedule+ via MS-Mail), or exit MS-Mail and terminate the application completely. To keep MS-Mail running, select File/Exit. To quit MS-Mail and stop the application, select File/Exit and Sign Out.

Setting Up a Postoffice

When you create a new Postoffice, you are added as the administrator for the account. This allows you to add or delete users as well as change their passwords.

To create a new Postoffice and an administrator account, select Mail from the Main program group. Select Create a New Workgroup Postoffice and click on OK. MS-Mail reminds you that by creating a Postoffice you will be responsible for managing it. Select Yes to create the Postoffice.

Select the directory for storing messages and user files for the Postoffice. This can be on a local hard disk, but is more usually set up on a network server. To select a network server, choose the Network button and network server and shared directory name, then click on OK. (You can create a Postoffice on a NetWare server if you grant full trustee rights to the NetWare directory in which the Postoffice is being created.) Then click on OK.

MS-Mail will now ask you for the administration details, using the dialog box shown in Figure 4.6. An explanation of the administration data is shown in the following. When they have been entered, click OK. Be sure to share the directory if it not already shared.

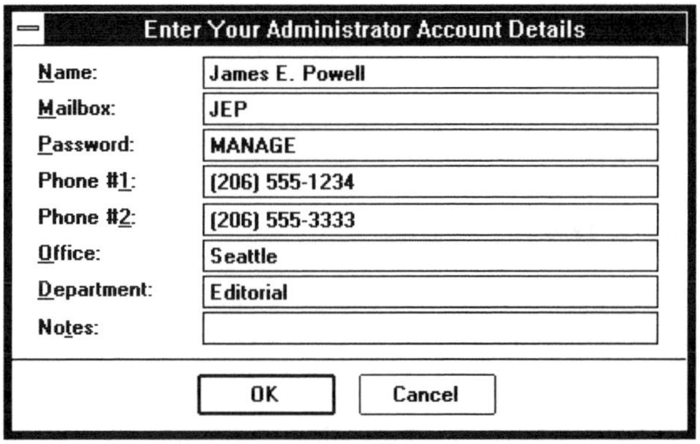

```
┌─────────────────────────────────────────────────────┐
│ ▬        Enter Your Administrator Account Details    │
├─────────────────────────────────────────────────────┤
│  Name:        │ James E. Powell                    │ │
│  Mailbox:     │ JEP                                │ │
│  Password:    │ MANAGE                             │ │
│  Phone #1:    │ (206) 555-1234                     │ │
│  Phone #2:    │ (206) 555-3333                     │ │
│  Office:      │ Seattle                            │ │
│  Department:  │ Editorial                          │ │
│  Notes:       │                                    │ │
│                                                       │
│              ┌────────┐   ┌────────┐                 │
│              │   OK   │   │ Cancel │                 │
│              └────────┘   └────────┘                 │
└─────────────────────────────────────────────────────┘
```

Figure 4.6 Mail Admin.

A post office manager can create an address list and manager users from this dialog.

User Information Needed by MS-Mail

Name	Enter your full name (typically in first name, last name order).
Mailbox	A unique abbreviation for your mailbox, such as the first letter of your first name and your complete last name. The Mailbox name must be no more than 10 characters long, and will be used to log on to the mail system when you want to perform administrative duties. The name is not case sensitive. Enter letters or numbers only.
Password	To password-protect access to your mailbox, enter a password of no more than 8 characters, using letters and numbers only.

The following information is optional:

Phone #1	Your telephone number, up to 32 characters long.
Phone #2	An alternative telephone number, such as a cellular phone, fax, voice mail number; also up to 32 characters long.
Office	A description of your office location; 32 characters maximum.
Department	A description of your department; 32 characters maximum.
Notes	Any text you like, to a maximum of 128 characters.

Once you've added a Postoffice, the next step is to add users. Users can actually add themselves to a Postoffice, but you can save them the trouble by adding them during your administrative work. To add a user to a Postoffice, select Mail/Postoffice Manager. Choose Add User and enter the new user's information. See the preceding lists for details. Finally, click on Close.

To remove users from a Postoffice, select Mail/Postoffice Manager. Select the user you want to delete and click on Remove User. Select Yes to confirm your request, then click on Close.

Adding a Computer to a Postoffice

As a user, you are usually added to a Postoffice by an Administrator. However, you can add your own account this way.

1. Start the MS-Mail application.
2. Select Connect to an Existing Postoffice, and click on OK.
3. MS-Mail displays the Network Disk Resources dialog box. Type the name of the network path directly in the Network Path text box. If you do not

know the name, select the computer name from the Show Shared Directories on List box, then choose the shared directory name on that computer from the Shared Directories on List box. The standard name for the MS-Mail directory is WGPO (Workgroup Postoffice).

4. Click on OK.

5. The next dialog box asks if you have an account. If you do, select Yes and enter your password. If not, enter your account information in the Enter Your Account Details dialog box. Enter the details as shown previously.

Creating an Address List

Once a Postoffice has been established, you'll want to get started creating messages. MS-Mail provides an address book for you to store the most frequently used addresses. To maintain an address book, select Mail/Address Book.

To select an address book, select the Directory button (the first button in the Address Book dialog box shown in Figure 4.7). To select your personal address book, select the Personal Address Book button (the second button in the Address Book dialog box) or press Ctrl+P.

To modify an existing name, click on Details.

To find a name, click on the magnifying glass button or press Ctrl+F.

To add a new address to your personal address book, click on the last icon in the Address dialog box or press Ctrl+N. Enter the Name, E-Mail address, E-Mail type, and optionally a comment, then select the Personal Address Book icon. MS-Mail sets up a heading for this user. Select Cancel to return to the Address Book dialog box.

To remove a name from an address book, select the name, then click on Remove.

Creating and Sending a Message

To create and send a message to one or more users in your MS-Mail system:

1. Select Mail/Compose Note, or click on the Compose button in the toolbar. The Compose dialog box shown in Figure 4.8 appears.

2. If you know the name(s) of the recipient(s), enter them in the To and Cc (carbon copy) boxes and go to step 4. If you do not know the names of the recipients, click on the Address button.

3. MS-Mail displays the Address dialog box. It contains the names of the people in your Postoffice (the users to whom you can send a message) at the top of the window. Highlight the name you want to send the message to and click on To (to add the name to the To: line) or Cc (to add the name to the list of carbon-copy recipients). If you need to see

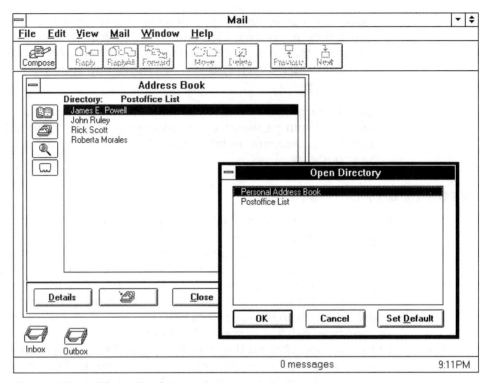

Figure 4.7 Address Book.

Every user has access to the main address list for his (or her) post office. Users can also create their own personal address books.

the details of any user in the address list, click on Details. When all recipients have been entered, click on OK.

4. Type the subject of your message in the Subject line. This heading will appear when your message is displayed in the recipient's inbox.

5. Type the message in the area below the heading.

6. You can specify that MS-Mail take action when you send your message. To set optional message handling options, click on Options. Choose Return Receipt and Save sent messages if you wish MS-Mail to send you a message indicating receipt of a message, or if you wish MS-Mail to save the message (for possible later resending to the same or other users). Select the priority (high-priority messages are displayed with a different icon in the recipient's inbox). Select OK.

7. To send the message, click on Send.

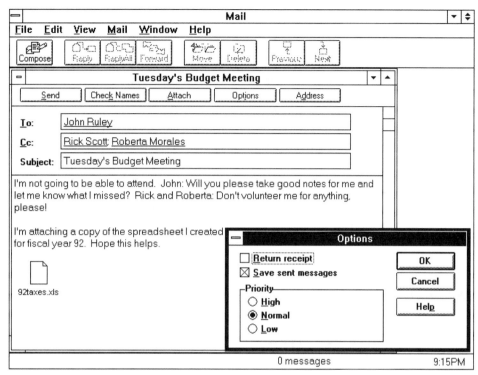

Figure 4.8 Compose Note.

Creating a message is done using MS-Mail's built in text editor. Using OLE, a wide variety of data objects may be added, and binary files can be attached as well.

Attaching a File to a Message

Besides sending plain text, you can attach one or more files to a mail message. Files can contain anything you like: sound, graphics, word processing or spreadsheet documents, and so on. MS-Mail represents attached files by displaying an icon within the message area wherever you have positioned a file.

To attach a file to a message, compose the message text in the message area as previously described; then select Attach. Enter the name of the file you want to attach, or select it by navigating through the Drive/Directory listing. Select OK. MS-Mail displays an icon of the file, which you can reposition within the message area. For large files, a better option may be to use the Object Packager application from Windows NT's accesories group to create an icon linked to the UNC name for the file in question.

Replying to Messages

To read a message, select the message then double-click on it to open the MS-Mail reader. After reading the message, you can send a reply to the sender or, if the message was sent to multiple users, to all of the recipients of the original message. To reply to a message, select Mail/Reply or click on the Reply button to send a message *only to the original sender*. Select Mail/Reply All or click on the Reply All button to send your message to *all recipients of the original message*. MS-Mail automatically fills in the To name with the sender's name. The original message is also displayed in the message section, which you can edit or delete if you wish.

You can *add* names to the address list (either the To or Cc areas) by entering the names directly by selecting the Address button, as you would when creating a new message.

Enter your text in the message area, then click on Send to send the message.

MS-Mail Administration

Several tasks can be handled by the administrator of a Postoffice. These tasks include changing a password, reducing disk space, and moving a Postoffice to a new location.

Changing a User Password

To change an MS-Mail user's password, select Mail/Postoffice Manager. Select the user name, then click on Details. Enter the new password in the Password box and click on OK. Then click on Close.

Managing Postoffice Space

As the number of users in your Postoffice grows, or as message volume increases, you will want to manage how much disk space is being used. You can also compress a Postoffice to recover some disk space.

To manage disk space, select Mail/Postoffice Manager, then click on the Shared Folders button.

To compress disk space, notify all MS-Mail users with access to the folder, and ask each to close the folder on his or her workstation. Do not begin the compression until all users have closed their folders or loss of messages could result. Click on Compress to begin the disk compression. When MS-Mail tells you that the compress is complete, click on Close.

Moving a Postoffice

As a network changes or a Postoffice grows, you may find it necessary to move a Postoffice to a new location. To move a Postoffice to another drive or directory, notify all users of the Postoffice that they must sign out of the MS-Mail system. Failure to have all users out of the MS-Mail system could result in losing messages.

Open File Manager and select the WGPO directory of the drive where MS-Mail is installed. WGPO is the standard (default) location of MS-Mail systems. Select File/Move. Enter the new location in the To box, then click on OK.

Share the Postoffice: Select the WGPO directory, select Disk/Share As, and enter the name of the Postoffice in the Share Name box. By default, File Manager uses the name WGPO. Check the Reshare at Startup check box, then select Full Access in the Access Type section. If you want to password-protect the directory, enter the password in the Password text box. Click on OK.

Using the Configuration Registry Editor (REGEDT32.EXE), edit the server computers' HKEY_CURRENT_USER\Software\Microsoft\Mail\Microsoft Mail registry key, and change the ServerPath entry to reflect the new location.

Renaming a Workgroup Postoffice

To change the name of a Postoffice, you must first notify all users of the Postoffice that they must sign out of the MS-Mail system. Message loss will result if this is not done.

Select the WGPO directory from the File Manager, then select Disk/Share As. Enter the new Postoffice name in the Share Name text box and click on OK. Use a text editor, such as Notepad, to edit MSMAIL32.INI. Change the Server-Path= entry in the [Microsoft Mail] section to reflect the new name. Delete or edit the password entry if the directory was password-protected.

Chat

The Chat application lets you conduct an interactive conversation with another person on your network. Unlike MS-Mail, in which users send text messages and await a reply, Chat provides two windows for immediate, real-time conversations. One window is used by you for entering text; the other window displays what the other user is typing.

To start the Chat application, click on the Chat icon in the Accessories window. The main Chat window is shown in Figure 4.9.

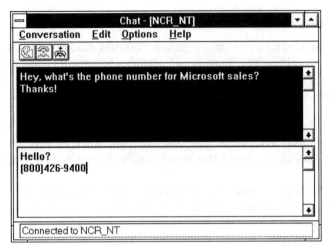

Figure 4.9 Chat.

The surprisingly useful Windows NT Chat utility provides interactive one-on-one communication between any two Windows NT or Windows for Workgroups workstations on the network. A multiuser Chat is expected to debut in later versions of Windows NT and Windows for Workgroups.

Starting a Chat Session

To start a chat session (conversation), click on the Dial button in the toolbar or select Conversation/Dial. Enter the computer name of the person you want to talk with in the Select Computer box. If the person answers, Chat displays a message in the status bar. You may begin typing in the top or leftmost window. The response from the other user is displayed in the other window. Note that the NetDDE service on which Chat depends is not started by default, as it may have an adverse performance inpact.

Answering a Call

If you are the party being called, you will hear a short sound and a message will appear in the Chat status bar. If you are not running Chat, the program begins running as an icon, indicating that someone wants to start a conversation. To answer a call, click on the Chat icon if necessary to open the application, then click on Answer in the toolbar, or select Conversation/Answer. Both you and the person you are chatting with can enter text at the same time. As you type, your letters are visible to the other user, and vice versa. You can jump between windows—for example, you can copy text from the other user's window and paste it in your window. (To move between windows, select the other window with the mouse or press F6.)

The standard Windows NT text selection procedures (for example, highlight the text using the mouse or keyboard) are used in the Chat windows.

Ending a Chat Session

To end a conversation, click on the Hang Up button on the toolbar or select Conversation/Hang Up. Either party can end a session at any time. If the other user hangs up before you do, Chat displays an informational message in the status bar.

To end the Chat application itself, select Conversation/Exit.

Schedule+

Schedule+ is a workgroup and individual scheduling program. It can help you plan your day, find the first available meeting time for people or resources (such as meeting rooms), send meeting requests (using MS-Mail), and help you plan tasks and to-do's.

Schedule+ lets you work with the online schedule, or work offline (for example, on your laptop), then synchronize your work.

The main Schedule+ screen contains a daily appointment calendar, a monthly calendar, and an area for notes. Four tabs run vertically down the left side of your screen. By clicking these you can go to the current day's appointments, appointments for another day, a time planner that displays all scheduled and available time, and a list of prioritized tasks.

Another part of Schedule+ is the Messages window, which displays messages sent by others connected to your Postoffice (see the section on MS-Mail), and is available *only* if you are connected to a Postoffice.

To begin Schedule+, select the Schedule+ icon from the Main program group. The program displays the Sign In dialog box, which asks you for your name. Enter the same name used for the MS-Mail system, and your MS-Mail password (if any), then press Enter.

Creating an Appointment

You must be viewing the Schedule window in order to add an appointment. If it is not visible, select Window from the main menu, then select your name from the pull-down menu.

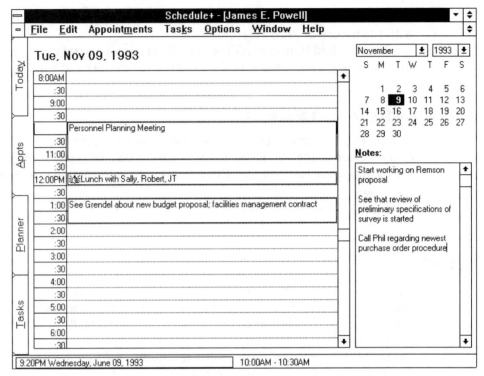

Figure 4.10 Schedule Plus.

Like Windows for Workgroups, Windows NT includes a built-in appointment book with group scheduling capabilities.

Adding an Appointment with the Mouse

To add an appointment by highlighting the appointment duration in the Schedule window, select the Appts (Appointments) tab (then select the day from the calendar or select Edit/Go To Date), or the Today tab (to add an appointment for the current date). The Schedule window is shown in Figure 4.10.

Select the time of the appointment. Using the mouse, click on the beginning time and drag the mouse to the ending time. This action will highlight each block of time as the mouse is dragged through it. You can also use the keyboard and press Shift+Tab to move to the appointment list, press the up and down arrows until you select the beginning time, press Shift+DownArrow until you highlight the ending time.

Enter the text for the appointment.

To set reminders (alarms) for appointments, see the following section on "Setting Reminders."

Using Precise Appointment Times

You can add appointments with more precise control over the starting and ending times, for example. To do this, select Appointments/New Appointment or press Ctrl+N. Type the start time and date in the When box, or click on the spin buttons (the up- and down-pointing arrow keys) to change the values that are currently displayed. Likewise, enter the end time and date in the When box, or click on the spin buttons to change the displayed values.

Enter the appointment description in the Description box. To set a reminder (alarm), check the Set Reminder box and enter the time and increment unit values.

Adding Recurring Appointments

As with regular appointments, the Schedule window must be displayed in order to add a recurring appointment.

Select either the Appts or Today tab. From the main menu, select Appointments/New Recurring Appointments or press the shortcut keys, Ctrl+R.

Click on Change in the This Appointment Occurs box, shown in Figure 4.11. Select the appointment frequency from the Change Recurrence box, and choose the detailed frequency information in the box to the right. The contents of this box change based on the frequency you select. When multiple check boxes appear, be sure to check every box on which the appointment can occur.

Choose the starting and ending dates for the recurring appointment in the Duration box. By default, Schedule+ fills in an ending date that is one year from the start date. If the recurring appointment is to occur indefinitely, select the No End Date option. Click on OK.

Adding Reminders

To add a reminder to an appointment, double-click on the appointment or select the appointment and choose Edit/Edit Appt. Check the Set Reminder For box and enter the time period in the adjacent box. Click on OK. A bell icon appears to the left of the appointment, indicating that an alarm has been set.

To automatically add reminders for all *new* appointments and notes, select Options/General Options. In the Reminders box, check the Set Reminders for Notes check box to automatically set reminders when new notes are added. Check the Set Reminders Automatically box. Enter the number of time units and the time units (minutes, days, etc.) from the pull-down list. To create a noise when the alarm is triggered, check the Sound Audible Alarm box.

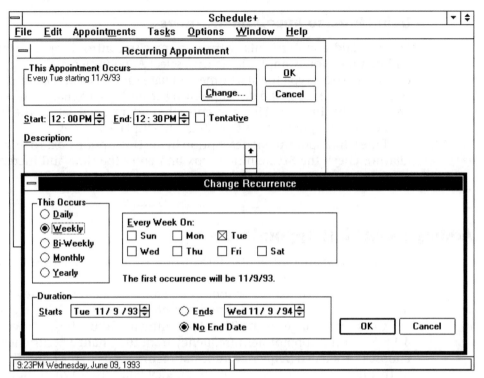

Figure 4.11 Appointment Occurs.

Designation of the time for a meeting is accomplished using this dialog.

Managing Appointments

To copy an appointment, select it from the Appointment list, then select Edit/Copy Appointment or press Ctrl+Y. Select a new appointment date and time, then choose Edit/Paste or press Ctrl+V.

To reschedule an appointment, select it from the Appointment list, then select Edit/Move Appointment or press Ctrl+O. Enter the new appointment date and time and click on OK. If the appointment was a meeting scheduled with others, Schedule+ asks if you want to notify the other attendees of the change, so click on Yes. Optionally, add a message in the Meeting Request form. Click on Send.

To delete an appointment, select it from the Appointment list, then select Edit/Delete Appointment or press Ctrl+D. If the appointment is for a meeting scheduled with other attendees, Schedule+ will ask if you want to send a notice to the other attendees of the cancellation. Select Yes. Optionally, add a message in the Meeting Request form. Click on Send.

To remove an appointment to an archive file (which can be opened later and appointments retrieved from it), select File/Create Archive. Enter the last date of appointments—all appointments before this date will be archived. Click on OK.

Working with Tasks

A task list is simply a list of things to do. Items listed can be assigned a priority and due date; Schedule+ displays unfinished, past-due tasks in red.

Adding Tasks

To add a task, open the Task window by clicking on the Tasks tab or by pressing Alt+T. Select Tasks/New Task, and in the New Task box enter the task description. Click on Add.

Next, double-click on the task in the task list, or select the task and click on the Edit button at the bottom of the task list. Schedule+ displays the Task dialog box. If the task is assigned to a project, select the project from the pulldown list or enter a new product name. By default the project name is None.

To enter a due date for the task, click on the By button in the Due Date box and enter the date, or use the up and down arrow buttons to choose the date. To specify the day the task should become active, enter the number of time units (1, 2, 3...) and select the time units (days, weeks, or months) in the Start Work text box.

You can set a reminder by clicking on the Set Reminder box and completing the reminder information.

Tasks can be assigned priorities, which are useful for viewing high-priority tasks first. Enter the priority or use the up and down arrow buttons to choose priority value. Priorities are 1 (highest) to 9, then A through Z (lowest).

To make the task hidden from other users, check the Private box. Click on OK.

To add time to your schedule to work on the task, select Add to Schedule. Select the time you want to reserve for working on the task, and click on OK.

Deleting Tasks

To remove a single task from the task list, select the task and click on the Delete button, press Alt+L, or press the Del key.

If the task is a recurring task, select Tasks/Edit Recurring Tasks, select the task to delete, click on Delete, then click on Close.

Sorting Tasks

To sort the task list, select Tasks/Sort by Priority, Tasks/Sort by Due Date, or Tasks/Sort by Description.

You can also sort tasks within a given project. Select Tasks/View by Project, or press Ctrl+Shift+V. Tasks are arranged by priority within project. Tasks with no project assigned appear at the top of the list.

Scheduling Meetings with Multiple Resources

To set up a meeting with others in your group, follow these steps:

1. You must be using the Planner window. If it is not displayed, click on the Planner tab or press Alt+P.

2. Select the date of the meeting you want to schedule, then click on Change.

3. Select the address book you want by clicking on the book icon at the top left of the dialog box, then select the name of the person you want to invite and select Add. The name is added to the Attendees list. Repeat this step until all attendees are listed. Note that if you do not know a name, you can find it by clicking on the magnifying glass icon.

4. Click on OK.

5. Unavailable time periods are shown with colored bars. Overlapping time periods may have two colors. See Figure 4.12.

6. Select an available time slot (a time slot that has no color). Drag the mouse across the desired time segments, or use the keyboard and press the Shift+arrow keys to select a time period.

7. Choose Request Meeting. Schedule+ displays the Send Request dialog box with the date, time, and attendee list already filled in. Type in the meeting description in the Subject box. To request attendees reply to your meeting request, check the Ask for Responses box.

8. Click on Send. Schedule+ adds the meeting to your schedule and sends mail to the potential attendees using Windows NT's MS-Mail application.

Responding to Meeting Requests

The Messages window in Schedule+ is available if you are connected to a Postoffice. The window contains both meeting requests and meeting responses. To open the Messages window, select Window/Messages.

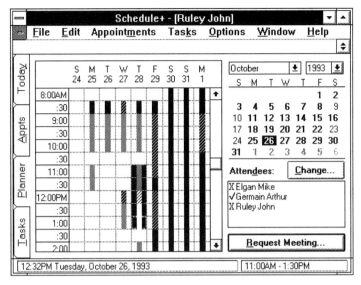

Figure 4.12 Meeting Time Conflict.

Resolution of the inevitable conflicts when scheduling meetings between several people is eased with a grapical display.

Messages are listed by attendee name. A check to the left of the name indicates that the person has accepted your invitation. A question mark to the left of the name indicates that the person might or might not attend. An X indicates the person will *not* attend.

When you read an invitation sent to you, you can reply in one of three ways:

1. Accept the invitation; Schedule+ will add the meeting to your schedule.

2. Decline the invitation; Schedule+ will notify the sender of your answer.

3. Tentatively accept; Schedule+ will add the meeting to your schedule but mark it as tentative, meaning you have not firmly committed to it.

Appointment and Task Security

You can grant another user on your network access to your appointments and tasks. To do so, select Options/Set Access Privileges. If the user's name is displayed in the Users box, select it. Otherwise, select Add and select the user's name, click on Add, then click on OK. Select the privilege you want to grant from the Privileges box. An assistant can add, change, and delete all your appointments and tasks except those marked Private. Click on OK.

To manage appointments and tasks of another person (one who has granted you access), select File/Open Other's Appt. Book. Choose the name of the user whose appointment book you want to manage (if the name isn't listed, click on Add, select it, click on OK, then select the user's name from the User box). Click on OK. Next, perform the scheduling tasks as needed. To work with your own appointment book, double-click on the control menu to close the window.

Print and Printer Management

Print Manager is used to view the status of documents waiting to be printed, to connect to or disconnect from a network printer, or to set up a new printer. Print Manager starts automatically when you print a document in Windows NT, or you can start it by selecting its icon from the Main program group.

The Print Manager screen, shown in Figure 4.13, includes a window for each of the printers installed on your computer, including printers on a network.

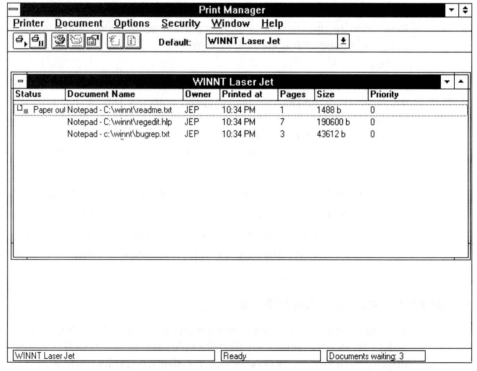

Figure 4.13 Print Manager.

Printer connections, drivers, and queues are all managed from this dialog. Even print *pools* can be handled.

The toolbar, located at the top of the window, lets you access frequently used commands with your mouse. A status bar, displayed at the bottom of the screen, displays the name of the current printer, its status, and the number of documents waiting to be printed. If the status bar is not displayed, select Options/Status Bar. A check mark to the left of the menu option indicates that the status bar is to be displayed.

Within each window you'll find a list of the documents being printed or in the print queue; Print Manager also lists the time the documents were generated and their size (the number of pages and the print file size in bytes).

Document Information

To see detailed information about a job waiting to be printed, select the document, then select Document/Details or click on the Details button in the toolbar.

Managing the Print Queue

When you open a window associated with a printer, Print Manager shows you a list of the documents waiting to be printed, listed in the order in which they will be printed. To change the order, and hence the priority of a document, select it, then drag it to the new position in the queue. Alternatively, use the keyboard: Select Document/Move Document Up to give the document a higher priority, or Document/Move Document Down to give it a lower one.

You can also change the document's print priority by selecting Document/Details, then entering a high priority number to print a document sooner. Select OK to set the new priority.

To stop the printing of a *single* document, select the document, then choose Document/Pause or click on the Pause button in the toolbar. Print Manager displays *Paused* after the document description. To resume printing, select Document/Resume or click on the Resume button in the toolbar.

To stop printing a document *and* remove it from the print queue, select the document, then choose Document/Remove Document, press the Delete key, or click on the Remove Document button on the toolbar. To remove *all* documents in the print queue, select Printer/Purge Printer.

You can temporarily stop printing *all jobs* by selecting the printer, then selecting Printer/Pause. Alternatively, you can select the Pause button from the toolbar. Print Manager displays *Paused* after the printer description in the Print Manager list. To resume printing, select the printer, then select Printer/Resume or click on the Resume button in the toolbar.

Note: To see the most current print information, press F5 or select View/Refresh.

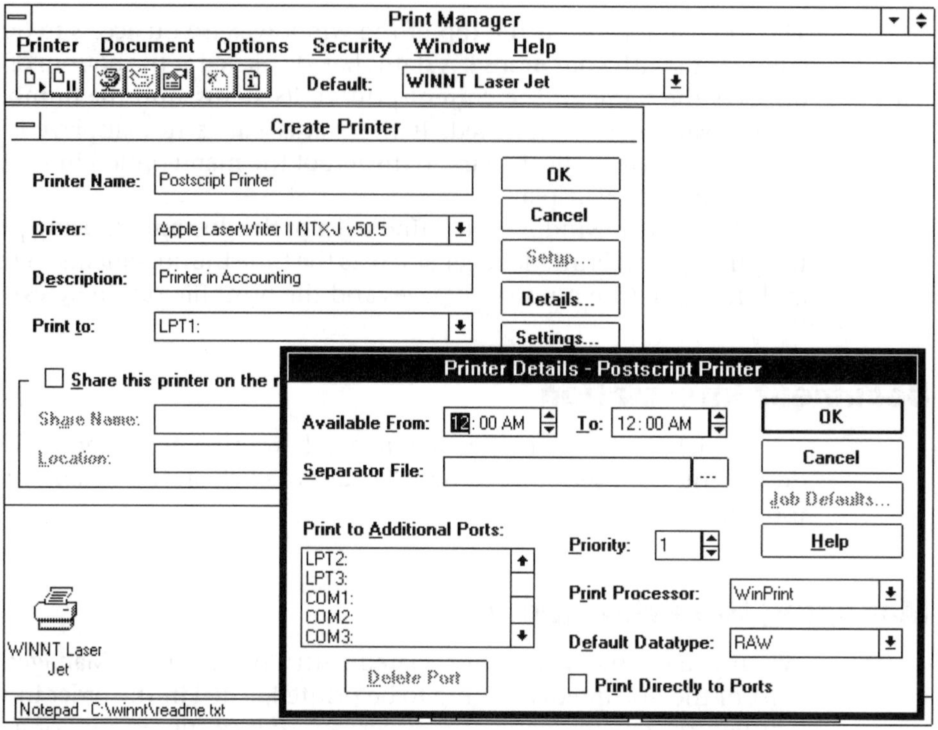

Figure 4.14 Create Printer.

Adding a new printer is done using the *create printer* command.

Creating a Printer Definition

You cannot print a document to a printer until you have created a printer definition. This is equivalent to installing a printer driver in other versions of Windows, such as Windows 3.1.

To create a new printer definition:

1. Select Printer/Create Printer. Print Manager displays the Create Printer dialog box shown in Figure 4.14.

2. Enter the name of the printer in the Printer Name text box. This name is used in the title bar of status windows. The maximum size of a printer name is 32 characters, although only 12 characters are viewed by workstations running MS-DOS.

3. Select the printer driver in the Driver pull-down list box. If the driver is not installed, select Other, then enter the complete path where the printer driver is located (usually A:\ or B:\) in the Install Driver dialog box, then click on OK.

4. Enter a printer description in the Description text box. This description is displayed to users connected on the network.

5. Select a destination in the Print To text box. The pull-down list includes the standard parallel (LPT) and serial (COM) ports. You can also specify that Windows NT send the printing to a file (Windows NT will prompt you for the file name when printing begins). Select the LPT or COM port if the printer is physically connected to your computer. If you are installing a printer that exists on the network, select the printer's network name or its network address. If you are creating a printer controlled by a LAN Manager 2.x server, select Network Printer, select LAN Manager Print Share in the Print Destinations dialog box, and click on OK. Other printer destinations—including Digital Network Port on DECnet or TCP/IP lans, UNIX lpd/lpr ports, local printer ports (provided by FAX software, for instance) may be accessed by selecting Other... from the list.

6. To share the printer you are creating, check the Share this printer on the network box, then type a name for the printer in the Share Name text box. By default, the share name is the same as the printer name.

7. To set the port time-out options, click on Settings. Select the number of seconds that must pass before Windows NT recognizes that your printer is not responding. Enter the number of seconds Print Manager will wait before determining that the printer is not available in the Device Not Selected text box. Enter the number of seconds Windows NT must wait before trying to send more data to the printer in the Transmission Retry text box. Click on OK.

8. You can specify descriptive information, such as the location of the printer, and control printer availability and separator file name by clicking on Details. Consult the Windows NT System Guide for more details.

9. Click on OK.

Removing a Printer

To remove a printer from your system, *including the printer driver*, select the printer you want to remove, choose Printer/Delete Printer or click on the Remove Printer button from the toolbar. Select Yes to confirm your request.

Connecting to a Network Printer

To connect to a printer already defined on your network so that you can print a document to that printer:

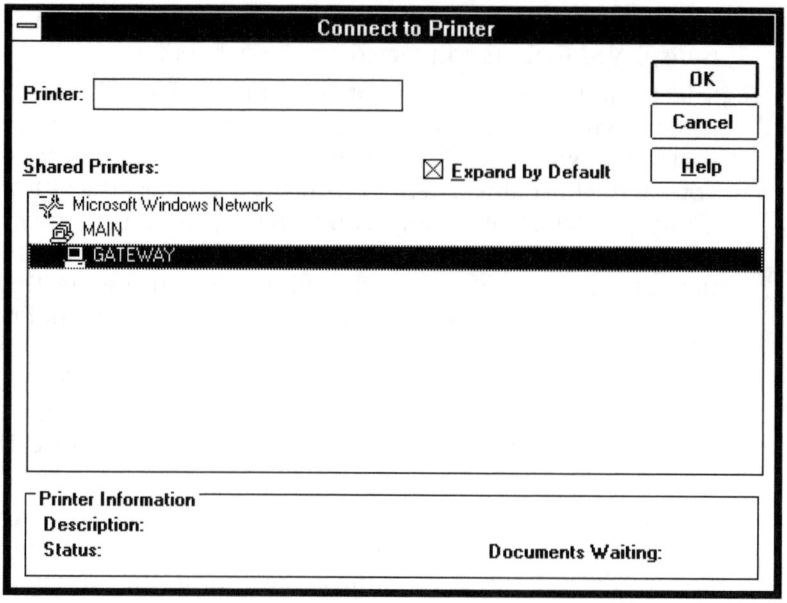

Figure 4.15 Connect Printer.
Network printers are connected using a browser similar to that used for network directory access.

1. Select Printer/Connect to Printer or select the Connect Printer button on the toolbar. The dialog box shown in Figure 4.15 appears.

2. Enter the name of the printer in the Printer text box. If you do not know the name of the printer, select one from the list in the Select Printers box. The printers are displayed in a hierarchical list, which can be expanded to show the printers, domains, and workgroups by double-clicking on an entry. Select a printer and the name appears in the Printer text box. Select OK.

3. If the printer is shared by a Windows NT computer, you can now use the printer. The steps that follow should be followed if the printer is shared by a computer *not* running Windows NT (or running NT on a different CPU architecture).

4. Print Manager prompts you to install a driver. Select OK, then choose the driver from the Select Driver dialog box. Enter the location (drive and directory) of the Windows NT printer drivers, then select Continue.

5. Windows NT will install the driver for you.

Disconnecting from a Network Printer

To disconnect from a printer on your network, select Printer/Remove Printer Connection, or click on the Remove Printer Connection button on the toolbar. Select Yes to confirm your request.

Sharing a Printer

To share a printer that is connected locally on a network, select the printer you want to share, then choose Printer/Properties. Check the Share This Printer on the Network check box.

Next, enter the printer name that will appear in the list of available printers for others on the network if different from the default name Windows NT supplies. Then type the description of the location of the printer. This name will be displayed in the Connect to Printer dialog box when other users try to connect to a network printer. Click on OK.

Setting the Default Printer

To set a printer as the default printer, causing all document output to be directed to this printer, select the printer and select Printer/Set Default Printer or click on the Set Default Printer button on the toolbar. Print Manager displays the default printer in a bold font.

Security Options for Printers

A unique feature of Windows NT is the ability to track which users or groups are accessing a printer. To audit a printer, select Security/Auditing. Choose the user or group name you want to monitor. If the name is not listed, select Add, select the Names and Type of Access, then select Add.

Next, select the events you want to monitor using the check boxes in the Events to Audit box, then select OK.

You can also change the permissions granted to a printer. Select the printer, then choose Security/Permissions. To add a user or group name to the permissions, select Add. Select a name from the Name list, and an access from the Type of Access pulldown list box, then click on OK.

To change the permission of a user or group, select the user or group name from the Name list in the Printer Permissions dialog box. Select the permission from the Type of Access pull-down list.

To delete a permission, select the user or group name from the Name list and select Remove. Select OK.

Working with Printer Drivers

RISC-based and Intel x86-based systems use different print drivers, so if you wish to share a printer for use by users on both x86 and RISC systems, you may wish to install both versions on your system.

To install a printer driver, select the icon for the printer, then choose Printer/Properties or click on the Properties button in the toolbar. Select Other in the Driver box, then enter the drive and directory where the driver is located, typically A:\ or B:\ if the driver is supplied on a diskette. Choose OK and Windows NT will load the driver.

Fax Applications

One major problem area for those upgrading from Windows for Workgroups (WFWG) to NT is the lack of any fax support built into the operating system. From version 3.11 on, WFWG has provided at-work fax support—and of course, there are many fax applications for DOS and 16-bit Windows. With rare exceptions, none of these applications work under Windows NT. They depend on providing a *print-to-fax* driver, and NT's print driver architecture differs significantly from that in 16-bit Windows or DOS.

Fortunately, this was seen as an opportunity by several independent software vendors; and over the last year quite a few third-party fax solutions have appeared for Windows NT. They range from single-user systems all the way up to automated fax-back servers and enterprise fax routing solutions. A list is provided in Table 4.1, below.[1]

1.Current as of this writing (March 1995).

Table 4.1 Fax Applications for NT

Product	Company	Address	Telephone	Notes
FacSys	Optus	100 Davidson Ave. Somerset, NJ 08873	813-539-7429	32-bit fax server with 16- and 32-bit clients. Supports most e-mail systems. Class 1 and 2 fax modems. Single-user version under development.
Fax Sr.	Omtool	2 Manor Pkwy, Salem, NH 03079	800-886-7845	Multiuser fax print server. Multiplatform clients. Supports most e-mail systems. Requires class 2 fax modem.

Table 4.1 (*Continued*)

Product	Company	Address	Telephone	Notes
FaxFacts Server	Copia International	134 Avalon St. Wheaton, IL 60187	800-689-8898 708-682-8898	Extremely high-end fax-on-demand server. Many options.
Faxination Enterprise Server (BETA)	Fenestrae Inc.	6525 The Corners Pkwy, Suite 400, Norcross, GA 30092	404-729-6878	High-performance fax gateway.
FAXport WINport (BETA)	LANSource	221 Dufsrein St., Suite 310A, Toronto, ONT, Canada M6A3J2	800-677-2727 416-535-3555	Network fax and modem sharing servers. Supports many mail systems.
HyperKit	Response Logic	One Kendall Square S2200 Cambridge, MA 02139	215-558-2523	Development tools for voice, telephone and fax services. Integrates with MS-Access database.
LanFax Redirector	Alcom Corp USA	1616 North Shoreline Blvd. Mountain View, CA 94043-1316	415-694-7000	High-end 32-bit client/server fax, with inbound routing and server-based shared phone book. Supports DDE.
Message Port/NT 1.0	Siren Software Corp.	1609A S. Main St.Milpitas, CA 95035	800-995-2166 408-262-2225	Multiport fax- and modem-pooling via serial port translation. Supports faxing from Windows and DOS applications; supports e-mail.
Print2Win	LA Business Systems	1866 Sheridan Road, Suite 216 Highland Park, IL 60035	708-433-6477	Combination of 16-bit client and 32-bit print driver that allows WinFax to run under NT.
Telcom FAX	LTC	328 Fitch St. Syracuse, NY 13204	315-455-1003	32-bit fax server. Supports class 1 and 2 fax modems. *Demo version downloadable from CompuServe.*
UltraFAX	Wordstar	201 Alameda del Prado, Novato, CA 94948	404-514-6387	Single-user fax app with OCR/scanner support.

ClipBook

Like its Windows and Windows for Workgroups cousins, Windows NT's clipboard is an intermediate area used for cutting or copying data within or between applications. Windows NT takes this further by letting you save the contents of your clipboard in a storage area called the Local ClipBook. Each item is stored in a separate ClipBook page, and pages can be arranged in several ways. In addition, you can share the contents of your Local ClipBook with those on your network, and access the contents of other shared ClipBooks.

Windows NT provides a ClipBook viewer that lets you examine what is on the clipboard and what you have saved to the Local ClipBook.

To start the ClipBook Viewer application, click on the icon in the Main program group. When the application starts, you will see the Local ClipBook window and a Clipboard icon, as shown in Figure 4.16.

The Clipboard

Most Clipboard content is created when you select Edit/Copy from within an application. To save information from a character-based DOS or OS/2, open the application's control menu box (the minus sign in the upper left corner) or press Alt+Spacebar. Select Edit/Mark and mark the data you want to copy by using the arrow keys until the selection is highlighted. Select the control menu box again and select Edit/Copy.

To copy the contents of the Clipboard into a Windows NT application, move to the application and select Edit/Paste from the application's main menu. To paste the contents of the Clipboard into a character-based DOS or OS/2 application, switch to the destination application and position the cursor or insertion point at the location where you want the Clipboard contents to be placed. Press Alt+Spacebar to display the Non-Windows-NT application's control menu. Select Edit/Paste.

You can also save screen images to the Clipboard. To save the contents of the currently displayed window to the Clipboard, press Alt+PrintScreen. To save the contents of the entire screen, press PrintScreen.

To delete the current contents of the Clipboard, activate the Clipboard Viewer, then select Edit/Delete (or press the Del key). Click on Yes to confirm your request.

To copy a page from a ClipBook to an application, you must first copy it to the Clipboard. Select the page you want from the ClipBook, then select Edit/Copy or click on the Copy button in the toolbar.

By default, the Clipboard viewer displays the data in its native format. You may wish to view the data in another format, such as to view the embedded

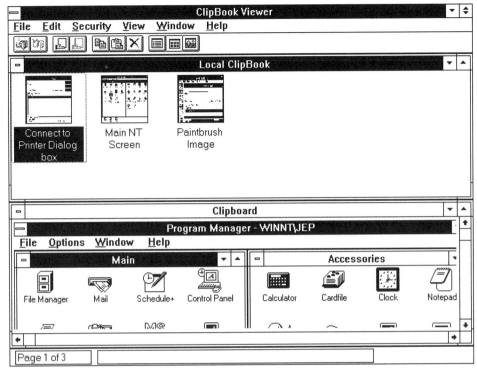

Figure 4.16 Clipbook.

Windows NT borrows the *clipbook* metaphor from Windows for Workgroups, providing a simple but powerful form of *ad hoc* client/server connectivity that can be exploited by end users.

codes in a word processing file. To view the contents of the Clipboard in a different format, select Display from the main menu. Choose the desired format from those listed in the pull-down menu. To view the contents in its original format, select Display/Default Format.

To save the contents of the Clipboard to a file, select the Clipboard viewer and choose File/Save As. Enter a file name with the .CLP file extension and click on OK. To open a Clipboard file, select File/Open, select the file and click on OK. If the Clipboard is *not* empty, the viewer asks if you want to clear the contents of the Clipboard. Select No and save the Clipboard, or select Yes to discard the contents and display the selected file.

You can also save the contents of the Clipboard to your local ClipBook. To do so, select the Local ClipBook window. Select Edit/Paste (or click on the Paste button in the toolbar) to place the image in the ClipBook. Type the name of the page in the Page Name text box. This name is used when sorting pages using the Table of Contents option. To share the page with other users, check the Share Item Now check box. Click on OK. If you opted to share the page, the Share ClipBook Page dialog box is displayed. Enter the options and select OK.

ClipBook Pages

To share a page from your ClipBook with other computers, select the ClipBook page, then select File/Share (or click on the Share button in the toolbar). Enter a password if you wish to protect the share, then click on OK.

To stop sharing the page, select it and choose File/Stop Sharing (or select the Stop Sharing button in the toolbar).

To use pages from another ClipBook that is shared on another computer, select File/Connect (or click on the Connect button on the toolbar). Type the name of the computer, or select it from the Computers list, then click on OK.

To disconnect from the ClipBook, select File/Disconnect (or click on the Disconnect button on the toolbar).

In addition to sharing ClipBook pages, you can also protect them. To set the access permissions for a ClipBook page, select the page, then choose Security/Permissions. Select the user or group name whose permissions you want to change, select the permission from the Type of Access pull-down list, and select OK.

To remove all ClipBook permissions for a group, select the user or group name and select Remove. To add permissions, select Add, select the user(s) and/or group(s), and select the permission you want to grant, then click on OK.

You can also take ownership of a ClipBook page. To take ownership, select the page you want, choose Security/Owner, and select Take Ownership.

Arranging ClipBook Pages

You can arrange your ClipBook pages in three ways. To view ClipBook pages alphabetically by name, select View/Table of Contents. To view small images of each page, select View/Thumbnails. To view the entire contents of a ClipBook page, select View/Full Page.

Auditing ClipBook Pages

Auditing allows you to keep track of who is using images in *your* ClipBook. To audit a ClipBook page, select the page, then choose Security/Auditing. Select the group or user name you want to track. Choose the event(s) you want to audit, then select OK.

To add a user or group to an existing audit list, click on the Add button, select the group(s) or user name(s) you want to add, and click OK. To remove a user or group, select the user or group and click on Remove.

Network Operations from the Command Line: The *Net* Command Interface

While it's usually easier to use the graphical utility programs, such as File Manager and User Manager, there are times when a command-line interface is more convenient. The Windows NT *net* commands fill this need—essentially, every network operation that can be conducted from a graphical program can be done in this way. Aside from simple convenience, the *net* interface has two major advantages: The syntax is consistent across all LAN Manager-derived networks, so users familiar with the LAN Manager, LAN Server, MS-Net, or Windows for Workgroups *net* commands will immediately be comfortable in NT; and the *net* commands can be employed in batch files.

Five of these commands are helpful for general use as command-line alternatives to the functions normally accomplished from File Manager, Print Manager, or the Control Panel—and one, *Net Send*, has no graphical equivalent. These end-user commands can be used as follows:

Listing the Available Network Commands—*Net*

Just typing *net* at the command prompt will print a list of the available commands on the display screen. This is handy when you can't remember the particular command you want, and can be used in conjunction with *Net Help* to quickly find the command you want. A slightly better formatted list of commands will be printed if you type *net help* without any arguments.

Getting Help for Network Functions—*Net Help* and *Net Helpmsg*

When you know you want to use a particular *net* command, but can't remember the command syntax, typing *net help <command>* will provide a brief description of the command and its arguments. For instance, *net help view* prints the following message:

```
net help view
The syntax of this command is:

NET VIEW [\\computername | /DOMAIN[:domainname]]
```

```
NET VIEW displays a list of resources being shared on a server. When
used without options, it displays a list of servers in the current
domain.
```

```
\\computername          Is a server whose shared resources you want
                        to view.
```

```
/DOMAIN:domainname      Specifies the domain for which you want to
                        view the available servers. If domainname is
                        omitted, displays all domains in the local area
                        network.
```

Just type _net help_ without arguments for a formatted list of the _net_ commands.

Note: Many of the screens displayed by _net help_ are quite long. If material goes by too fast for you to read, you may find the _|more_ command helpful. For instance, _net help use |more_ will display Help on the _net use_ command, but will do so one screen at a time.

Viewing and Browsing the Network—_Net View_

You can view lists of servers and browse shared network resources from the command line just as easily as you can from File Manager. Type _net view_ without any arguments for a list of servers. To view shared resources at a server, type _net view <server name>_. In a multidomain/workgroup network, type _net view /DO-MAIN_ for a list of domains and workgroups, and _net view /DOMAIN:<domain name>_ to see a list of servers in the specified domain or workgroup.

Net view is most often used in conjunction with the _net use_ command to access shared resources on other computers. A typical use begins with _net view_ (no arguments) to get a list of server names, then one views the resources on a server, and finally employs _net use_ to access the shared resource in question. For instance:

```
net view

Servers on MAGNET1:
\\MIPS-LAB-SERVER
\\JOHNR-NT486-66

net view \\JOHNR-NT486-66

Shared resources at \\johnr-nt486-66:

Sharename   Type    Used as     Comment
_____

disk-d      Disk    Z:
PUBLIC      Disk                Public Shared Space
```

One could then employ *net use* to access the Public share, for instance, by typing:

```
net use Q: \\johnr-nt486-66\public
```

Sharing Directories—*Net Share*

Sharing directories from the command line is done with the *net share* command. To share a directory, type *net share <sharename>=<directory to share>*. For instance, the command *net share disk-d=d:* will share the entire d: disk (and all subdirectories) with the share name disk-d. Other users (provided they have user accounts on your system) will be able to access this directory using the *net use* command, or by appropriate actions in file manager. To designate how many users can access the share at any one time, set the */USERS:<number>* switch—this can be useful if, for instance, you are sharing data files that only one user can safely access at a time. Or you can use the */UNLIMITED* switch if there is no upper limit you wish to enforce (this is the default). If you want an explanatory remark to be associated with a share, you can use the */REMARK: "<your text here>"* flag. Be sure to type the quote marks.

Sharing printers cannot be done the same way—you must use the Print Manager for this (Windows NT's printers are tied very closely to the Win32 subsystem, so a Windows driver must be selected before a printer can be shared).

Both shared directories and shared printers can be deleted from the command line by typing *net use <sharename> /DELETE*. This will eliminate the share—and terminate any outstanding connections (functionally, this is the same as performing a *Stop Sharing* command in File Manager or Print Manager).

Typing *net share* without any arguments will display information on the shares currently active (including administrative shares if you are logged in with administrative privilege). For example:

```
net share

Sharename      Resource        Remark


_____

ADMIN$      C:\winnt        Remote Admin
A$      A:\         Default share
C$      C:\         Default share
D$      D:\         Default share
E$      E:\         Default share
IPC$                    Remote IPC
NETLOGON        C:\winnt        Logon server share
Public      E:\Public       Advanced Server NTFS Volume Set
```

Connecting and Disconnecting Shared Directories and Printers—*Net Use*

Just as File Manager and Print Manager allow you access to shared directories and printers graphically, the *net use* command gives you this capability from the command line. Without arguments, it will display a list of whatever resources are currently connected, for example:

Displaying Currently Used Shares

```
net use
New connections will be remembered.


Status Local name     Remote name


OK Q:             \\johnr-nt486-66\Public
OK Z:             \\johnr-nt486-66\disk-d
Disconnected\\johnr-nt486-66\IPC$
```

Terminating Shares

The keyword */DELETE* will terminate use of a shared resource, so the command *net use /DELETE Q:* would terminate sharing on *johnr-nt-486-66\Public*, and make the Q: device name available for other use. To reuse this device name for the \\mips-lab-server\Public directory, for instance, one could type: *net use Q: \\mips-lab-server\Public*.

Persistent Shares

If a connection is meant to be retained in future sessions, you can add the */Persistent:* keyword, which is followed by *Yes* or *No* to indicate whether sharing is to be persistent or temporary. These keywords act as a toggle, and will continue in force until changed—that is: */Persistent: YES* makes connections persistent by default, while */Persistent: No* makes them temporary. For example: *net use Q: \\test_server\a_share /Persistent: YES* creates Q: as a persistent connection to the home directory defined in User Manager. All further connections in the session will be assumed to be persistent until a *net use* command is issued with the /Persistent:NO keyword, such as: *net use R: \\test_server\temp /Persistent: NO*, which will create R: as a temporary connection to \\test_server\temp.

All further connections in the session will be temporary until a /Persistent: YES is issued.

Passwords

If the device one connects to is password-protected (a passworded Windows for Workgroups share, for instance) the share name should be followed by the password—or by an asterisk place holder, which will cause the system to prompt you for a password to be typed in. The latter is especially useful in batch .CMD files. For example, the command *net use Q: \\accounting\first_quarter ** will connect me to the accounting server's first_quarter share if I type in the correct password when prompted to do so.

Connecting as Another User and Across Domains

In some situations, it may be desirable to establish a connection under another user name—for instance, while my user name may be *jruley* on one system, it might be *jdr* on another. In such a case, the */User:* keyword allows you to connect to a share using another user name. For instance, while logged in as jruley, I can issue the command *net use Q: \\accounting\financials /USER:jdr* to gain access under my *jdr* account on the \\accounting system. If the *jdr* account is a domain account for the CFO domain, then the command *net use Q: \\accounting\financials /USER:cfo\jruley* would be used.

The Home Directory

The */Home* keyword connects a user to his home directory, as defined in the User Manager. Thus, the command *net use Q: \\accounting /HOME* would connect Q: to my home directory on the accounting server.

Sending Messages—*Net Send*

MS-Mail and Chat are the usual methods for communicating between NT users, but there are times when it's preferable to reach many users with a single command. *Net Send* meets this need—it causes a pop-up window to appear immediately on the systems to which a message is addressed, carrying your message (which must be one line of simple text).

The simplest form of the command assumes that you want to send a message to only one user, and that you know that user's name, in which case the command is, for instance *net send jruley Hi There!* which will send *Hi There!* to the user named *jruley* on the network.

Sending a Message to All Members of a Workgroup

If you want to send a message to everyone in your workgroup, just use an asterisk instead of the name. For instance, *net send * Who has my copy of Networking Windows NT* would be an efficient way to see who in your workgroup has borrowed your copy of a very interesting book.

Sending a Message to All Users in a Domain

It's often necessary to send messages to users of a particular Domain or Server. In a Windows NT Server Domain, you can send a message to all other domain users by using the /DOMAIN keyword. For instance, *net send /DOMAIN Warning: Server 2 almost out of disk space* would let everyone in your domain know that Server 2 has a problem. You can follow the /DOMAIN keyword with the name of a domain if you want to send a message to users in that domain. For instance, *net send /DOMAIN: accounting Backup System is Down for Maintenance* would alert all accounting domain users to the status of the Backup System.

Sending a Message to All Users Connected to a Server

There are times when you may want to reach everyone else attached on your server—especially if you are the administrator and you know there is a problem. The */Users* keyword meets this need, sending the message to all users of the system. Thus, the command *net send /USERS Server going down in 5 minutes* would perform the traditional service of scaring the wits out of everyone connected to your server.

Logon Scripts and Batch Files

Of course, the availability of the net command-line interface makes possible quite sophisticated network-aware batch files and scripts in Windows NT. Indeed, there are additional administrative commands beyond those documented here. Since the most frequent use of these commands is in logon scripts created and maintained by system administrators, they're documented in the "Batch Files and Logon Scripts" section of Chapter 3.

In Conclusion

The basic networking features of Windows NT run the gamut from file and printer sharing through electronic mail, group scheduling, and ad hoc client/server links (with Network DDE). You can perform most network tasks from the File Manager, Print Manager, and Control Panel, although the *net* command interface gives you a character-mode alternative.

With this chapter completed, you're ready to begin looking into the details of maintaining your Windows NT connections—which we will cover in Chapter 5.

For More Information

Custer, Helen (1993), Inside Windows NT. Redmond WA: Microsoft Press, ISBN: 1-55615-481-X. Chapter 6 (on NT's networking features).

Feldman, Len (1993), Windows NT: The Next Generation. Carmel IN: Sams Publishing, ISBN: 0-672-30298-5. Curiously enough, the networking coverage is in Chapter 6.

Microsoft Staff (1993—95), Windows NT System Guide. Redmond WA: Microsoft Corp. This is the basic reference guide to Windows NT, and comes with all Windows NT systems.

CHAPTER 5

Keeping Connected

Troubleshooting and Performance Tuning Windows NT

When you have finished reading this chapter you should understand:

- ❑ **The principles of preventive maintenance**
- ❑ **Performance monitoring and tuning procedures**
- ❑ **Basic mechanisms of Windows NT troubleshooting**
- ❑ **Windows NT Registry**
- ❑ **Special tools provided with Windows NT and the NT Resource Kit**
- ❑ **Getting technical support**

You should *not* feel comfortable facing the diagnosis of a fault in a Windows NT system on your own. No competent technician *ever* feels so confident. But you should feel comfortable taking a crack at it. You should understand the preventive maintenance techniques that will help you avoid trouble whenever you can, and you should know when to cry Uncle! and call for professional help.

Read This First

The odds are quite good that if you've turned to this page you're faced with a system that is not operating as it should and you are desperately seeking help. This is the worst possible time to read about troubleshooting procedures, but we're all too aware that it's often the only time we do. If you look carefully at the edge of the book you will see that some pages have been tinted. These pages, later in this chapter, constitute a troubleshooting section listing the most common errors in Windows NT, their symptoms, and the steps you need to take to correct them. So, read the rest of this paragraph and then go to the tinted pages, and the best of luck to you. But when you've finished that, when your bug is fixed, come back and read the rest of this chapter, because it will tell you how to avoid having to go through this again.

The preceding sentence will strike some readers as an appallingly bad joke; it is not!

In many situations a complex piece of equipment or complex piece of software (such as Windows NT) is installed by someone whose most urgent consideration is bringing the thing up as fast as he can. Once installed it will run until it breaks, at which time that same individual will be desperately looking for help—and that's the reason for that first paragraph. But those of us who have taken the trouble to read a chapter like this ahead of time will know that there's a much better approach. This is the approach that the United States Air Force taught me at some expense in 1976.[1] It's called *preventive maintenance,* or *PM.* The principle of PM is simple: Don't wait until the system breaks—fix it before it breaks. Replace parts that you know will wear out before they wear out.

How do you find out which parts of the system are wearing out and need replacement? By applying *actuarial statistics* and *the mathematics of fault prediction* (see Appendix 6 for details). Basically, you need to keep a maintenance log for the system, recording how performance varies over time, along with the date and time of any failures. By examining the log, it's generally possible to predict the overall reliability of the system, and to perform maintenance tasks in advance of an actual failure.

There's a second benefit to PM—since it forces you to undertake regular, scheduled, maintenance, it also gives you the foundation for *performance tuning*—keeping throughput as high as possible by tweaking the system to eliminate bottlenecks. Windows NT gives us some particularly sophisticated tools with which to determine system throughput. For example, it's not necessary to go through any complicated calculation to determine the Packets/Sec. the server is handling. It is necessary only to go to the Performance Monitor and look at it. With this theory under our belts, we'll now take a look at the specifics in performance tuning and troubleshooting in Windows NT systems.

---

1. The author of this chapter is John D. Ruley, formerly a Radio Relay Equipment Repair Specialist (AFSC 30470) with the Ohio Air National Guard and Reserve Air Forces. In other words, an old-fashioned, get-your-hands-dirty technician; and this chapter is written from that point of view.

Performance Tuning in Windows NT

As discussed in Appendix 6, the overall throughput of a system is an end-to-end process, a chain in which total system throughput is no greater than the throughput of the slowest individual component. So performance tuning generally amounts to the process of determining this component, referred to as a *bottleneck* that's *bogging* the system, and increasing its throughput either by changing system settings or by replacing the component with a faster one. In individual Windows NT systems the components that can be performance tuned (aside from components that will be tuned to suit individual preferences, such as the keyboard and the mouse) include the central processor, memory, disk, video, and network.

General Methods of Performance Tuning

The principal tools an administrator or technician will use to perform routine performance monitoring/tuning on Windows NT systems are the Windows NT Performance Monitor (covered in Chapter 3) and the Windows NT Configuration Registry Editor (covered later in this chapter). In the sections that follow we will discuss which performance monitor counters to track, what threshold values to look for, and what steps you should take when a threshold value is reached. In some cases there will be little that you can do short of moving the user to a faster machine—for instance, you detect a CPU-speed bottleneck. In other cases it may be possible to modify various Window NT configuration values to produce a performance improvement. You will generally perform this using the Windows NT Configuration Registry Editor (a.k.a. REGEDT32.EXE), illustrated in Figure 5.1.

You should be forewarned that the Configuration Registry has some features in common with a nuclear reactor. It is potentially an immensely powerful tool. It is also fairly dangerous. No, it won't irradiate you and leave you with three-headed progeny—but if it's not used with care it can render a system unusable. (effectively irradiating your career!) So you should always take great care when making a configuration change using the registry. And in particular, you should make sure you have the *emergency repair diskette* for the system you are working on close at hand (this diskette is created during the installation process, and may be re-created or updated using the *RDISK* utility described later in this chapter).[2]

---

2. Sometimes even the Emergency Disk won't help. Since this section was originally written (1993), I've had the miserable experience of accidentally deleting the entire SYSTEM key on a Windows NT Server. That turned out to be more than even the Emergency Disk could recover from, forcing me to reinstall NT—and losing access to an NTFS partition in the process. Based on that experience, I recommend using the Resource Kit's REGBACK and REGREST utilities (see Appendix 4) to keep

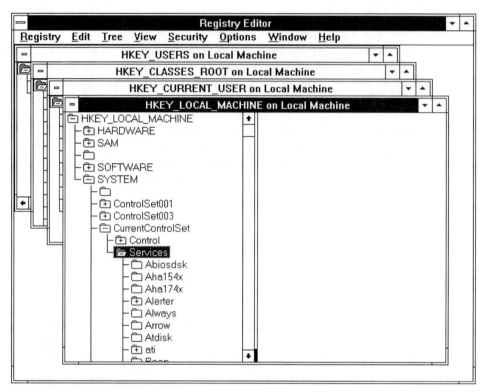

Figure 5.1 Registry Editor.

Windows NT's configuration registry editor (REGEDT32.EXE) provides an interface to the *registry*—a redundant database of configuration information for the system, software, and users.

Performance Monitor

In what follows, we will be constantly referring to Performance Monitor (see Figure 5.2) *objects*. To review (remember, Performance Monitor is covered in detail in Chapter 3), these are selections from the Objects pull-down list that appears in the Add to Chart (or Add to View) dialog after selecting Add to Chart (or Add to View) from the Edit menu. The pull-down lists all system objects that have registered themselves with the Performance Monitor service. Each object has an associated set of *counter* variables that can be charted, or on which alerts can be set. In the sections on subsystem tuning that follow, we will refer to these counters and to their parent objects.

separate copies of registry data in a nice safe place. You'll never know how much you need it until it's way too late!

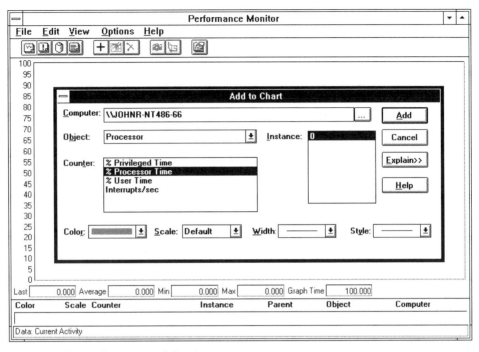

Figure 5.2 Performance Monitor.

The Windows NT Performance Monitor application gives administrators and support personnel the ability to observe, monitor, and record data on a wide variety of system (and application software) components.

CPU Tuning

For the most part, it's not possible to tune the CPU for maximum performance. You can, however, employ Performance Monitor to detect CPU bottlenecks, and then either modify the software configuration (perhaps moving some applications to another system) or the hardware (by installing a faster CPU).

❑ *System Object*—Since the central processing unit (CPU) is the *brains* of the system, it is not surprising that monitoring CPU performance is one of the most important functions an administrator can undertake. Windows NT provides a very high degree of capability to monitor the CPU, including measuring total CPU utilization, percent of time in privileged (operating system) mode, percent of time in user (application) mode, and how frequently the system is *context switching* between tasks. All of these can be extremely useful, and most can be monitored not only for the entire system but on a per-processor basis on symmetric multiprocessor (SMP) machines. The relevant counters to monitor are:

- *% Total Privileged Time*—This is the percentage of the total system time (time for all processes in the system) that is being spent in *privileged* (that is, in operating system) mode. This generally is a reflection of how much time the system is expending performing system-level tasks, such as disk I/O, video display operation, and so on. If the system is bottlenecked at the CPU and this counter is high, there is a configuration problem in your system. To diagnose the problem further, see %Total DPC Time, below.

- *% Total User Time*—The percentage of system time that is being expended running user-level or application code. If the system is bottlenecked at the CPU and this counter is a high percentage, then it may conceivably be possible to improve performance by changing the way applications are being used on the system. You can consider having in-house vertical applications rewritten in a more efficient way, for instance; or you may want to examine the way a user is operating on the system to see if there is any possibility that some additional efficiency can be achieved.

- *% Total Processor Time*—Indicates the percentage of system time that the processor is spending doing useful work, and is effectively the total of the percent privileged time and the percent user time. When this percentage approaches 100 percent it indicates that the processor has become a bottleneck in the system. Windows NT will then be forced to suspend certain tasks in order to give others time to run, and the system will slow down in much the way a time-sharing system slows down when too many users are logged in to it. At this point, the alternatives are: 1) increase the number or speed of processors in a scalable processor system, or 2) move the user or server, as the case may be, to a faster CPU.

- *% Total DPC Time*—Measures the percentage of time that the processor is spending in *Deferred Procedure Calls*. DPCs are a mechanism for efficiently handling interrupts—rather than executing interrupt code immediately, NT may elect to handle it in a DPC. DPCs run at a lower priority than hardware interrupts, so deferring execution can allow higher interrupt rates to be handled—but a *very* high interrupt rate can still bog the processor. Related counters worth checking include Processor Queue Length and Interrupts/sec.

- *Context Switches/Sec.*—Indicates how frequently Windows NT is performing a *context switch* between one task and another task. By default, Windows NT will switch between tasks several times each second to give each task in a system a chance to run. Should this counter become *very* high, (on the order of 1,000 Context Switches/Sec.) it may indicate that Windows NT is blocking on one or more shared resources in the system—quite possibly a video resource. To diagnose this, observe the

Percent Total Privilege Time and Percent Total User Time counters of the System object. If both of these are at or near 50 percent and the total processor time is at or near 100 percent, then what's happening is that multiple threads within the system are contending for a single shared resource, and are doing so with such frequency that the resource can't keep up (a form of *contention*—a topic described more fully in Appendix 5). This can happen, for example, if intensive use is being made of a video application and the video card is not fast enough to keep pace.

❑ *Processor Queue Length*—Indicates the number of threads queued for execution on a processor (you must also monitor at least one Thread counter in order to generate Queue Length data—otherwise it always indicates zero). Sustained values higher than 2 indicate congestion— you'll need to identify which process is causing the congestion, and either reconfigure the process, switch to a faster system, or (if you have the capability) add an additional processor to your system.

❑ *System Calls/Sec.*—Indicates the frequency of calls to Windows NT system routines, not counting the graphical routines. If the preceding values are high, including Processor Queue Length, Percent Total Privileged Time at or near 50 percent, Percent Total Processor Time at or near 100 percent—but the System Calls/Sec. is low—then in all probability you have a video problem, particularly if you are running graphically intensive applications. See the section on video performance troubleshooting for more information.

❑ *Total Interrupts/Sec.*—Indicates the rate at which interrupts are being generated by hardware in the system for all processors. This indicator should tend to closely track with the System Calls/Sec (with the exception of high mouse, keyboard, and serial port activity). If it does not, then it may indicate that some hardware device is generating an excessive number of interrupts. Attempt to determine whether the device in question is the video card, the network interface card, the hard disk driver, or perhaps some other device, such as the mouse.

❑ *Processor Object*—Like the System object, the Processor object provides indications of % Privileged Time, % Processor Time, % User Time, and Interrupts/Sec. However, this is done on a per-processor basis rather than on a system-wide basis. On a single-CPU system, the Processor counters should yield the same results as the System counters. On a symmetric multiprocessor (SMP) system, the Processor object will have multiple instances—and you can examine these instances (in particular, % Processor Time for all processors) to check the load balancing of applications across processors. All processors in the system should tend, on average, to achieve approximately equal loadings, with all processors reporting approximately equal utilization—if this isn't happening, you likely have a problem with one of your processor boards (or, if you only observe an imbalance when running certain applications, such as MS SQL Server version 4.*x*, it might possibly be a programming problem) and should investigate further.

Floating-Point (FPU) Performance

Unfortunately, Windows NT does not provide a direct counter for floating-point operations, which would be useful in determining whether the system is being bogged by floating-point performance when running applications such as Computer Aided Design (CAD). However, in general, if a system is performing an application known to be floating-point intensive, and is indicating a CPU bogging condition (% Processor Time at or near 100 percent) with no other indication of a bogging condition (such as a high number of System Calls/Sec., high number of Interrupts/Sec., etc.), then the odds are quite good that the system is floating-point bogged. A typical Performance Monitor trace for such a condition is shown in Figure 5.3:

You should investigate to see whether the system in question, in fact, includes floating-point processor hardware.[3] No 386-based or 486SX series Intel computers have built-in floating-point hardware, but all 486DX computers, all Pentium series processors, and most RISC processors will have built-in floating-point hardware. If a user is experiencing a CPU-bogged condition of this type and is operating on a 386 or a 486SX workstation, you may want to consider moving that user to a 486DX, Pentium, or RISC-based workstation to see if the problem clears up.

Windows NT *does* provide a performance counter for floating-point *emulation*: It's the System object's Floating Emulations/Sec. If the system shows signs of processor bogging (high %Total Processor Time) and Floating Emulations/Sec. is high, then you are running a floating-point intensive application on a processor that lacks hardware floating-point support.[4]

---

3. You can test for the presence of an FPU—and profile its performance—using a 16-bit benchmarking tool, such as *WINDOWS Magazine*'s Wintune®; or use Martin Heller's NTHELL benchmark. Both are available for download from any of the sites mentioned in the "Electronic Update" section of the Introduction.

4. Or (on NT 3.51 and later systems) you may have a system that has a floating-point unit, but has been configured to *emulate* floating-point operation (e.g., an older model Intel Pentium chip, in which the FPU has been disabled because of the infamous divide flaw). You can check and change the emulation mode with the *Pentnt* command, covered in Appendix 5. Alternatively, you can edit the relevant registry entry: HKEY_LOCAL_MACHINE\System\CurrentControlSet\Control\Session-Manager\ForceNpxEmulation. This is a REG_DWORD that accepts values of 0 (hardware floating-point), 1 (Pentium Only, *may* emulate FP divide instructions *if* a defective Pentium CPU is installed), 2 (emulates all floating-point instructions).

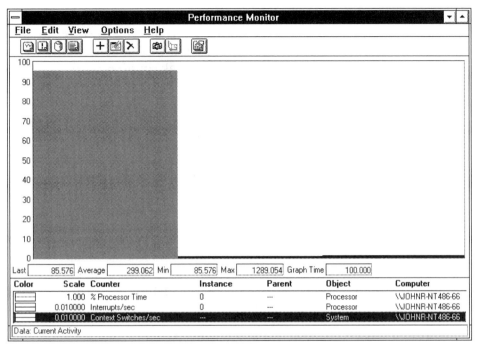

Figure 5.3 Performance Monitor.

This Performance Monitor display illustrates the *signature* of floating-point bogging—very high % CPU Time, with low Context Switches and Interrupts.

Memory Tuning

As with the CPU, tuning NT's memory performance mainly involves monitoring memory performance to detect bottlenecks.

❑ *Memory object (big surprise!) Pool Nonpaged Bytes*—This counter measures the total number of bytes in the pool of nonpaged memory. Nonpaged memory is memory that is *reserved* and cannot be paged out into virtual memory (disk space) on demand. In effect, it's the total amount of memory the system is using that must at all times remain in the physical RAM. If this value rises to within 4MB of the total amount of memory in the system (for example, if it rises to over 12MB in a system that contains only 16MB of memory), then performance is compromised.

Whenever an application is launched from Windows NT, Windows NT temporarily requires a substantial amount of space for buffers, for loading subsystems (such as the 16-bit WOW system for 16-bit applications), and so on—in an instantaneous state where less than 4MB of nonpaged pool is available, Windows NT will begin to *swap* severely in an effort to free up enough memory to get a new application started. In this situation, the best thing to do is provide the user with more memory in the system. You can also use this value in conjunction with the Working Set and Working Set Peak counters of the Process object(s) to determine the total amount of memory required by a particular user. See the section on the Process object for further details.

❑ *Commit Available Bytes, Committed Bytes, and Commit Limit*—Together serve as indicators of the state of the virtual memory management subsystem. Commit Available bytes is an instantaneous indicator of the *available* virtual memory in the system (i.e., virtual memory not being *used* in the system). This value fluctuates with time and is interesting to monitor, but does not provide a reliable indicator of total memory available. The Committed Bytes value, on the other hand, is an instantaneous indicator of the *total* amount of virtual memory committed— reserved memory space for which there must be backing store available. Commit Limit is the total amount of space that is available for committing, and is generally equal to slightly less than the size of physical memory plus the size of the page file (just slightly less because of memory the system reserves to itself).

Note: If the Committed Bytes counter approaches the Commit Limit, then the system is running out of virtual memory and it will become necessary to expand the page file. You can use this as an indicator to expand the page file *manually*—avoiding an automatic page file expansion and the associated deterioration of system performance.

❑ *Pages Per Second*—An indicator of the total paging traffic in the system; the rate at which memory pages are being swapped between the paging file and physical memory. Systems with lots of physical memory will tend to show a 0 value for Pages/Sec. Systems operating with a minimal amount of physical memory (16MB in workstations, 24MB in servers) will generally show 0 Pages/Sec. in an idle state, but may show paging activity (on the order of 100 Pages/Sec. or less) as applications are opened and closed in the system. Should the Pages/Sec. rise to a sustained value above 100 Pages/Sec., this will indicate a *thrashing* condition, in which the system has reached a state where the demands made on the virtual memory manager exceed its capacity—indicating that more RAM is needed. Therefore, when the Committed Bytes indicator approaches within 10 percent of the Commit Limit, you should begin watching the Pages Per Second to see if the system is thrashing—in fact, this seems as good a place as any to take a bit of time out to explore the entire subject of virtual memory in a bit more detail.

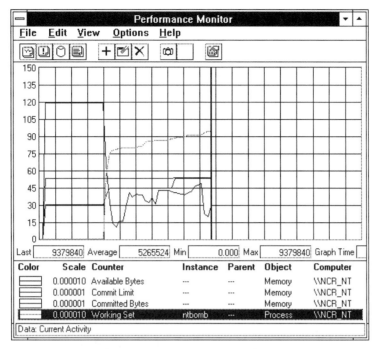

Figure 5.4 Performance Monitor, Working Set.

Performance Monitor can be very useful in diagnosing memory hogs. Now that NTBOMB has been identified as the errant process, it can be shut down.

> ❑ *Process object Working Set*—This counter measures the total number of bytes used by an application. It's particularly helpful in detecting memory hogs, as illustrated in figure 5.4.

Memory hogs are, unfortunately, all too common in Windows NT—all versions of Microsoft's 32-bit compilers for Intel CPUs currently implement a nonstandard runtime memory allocator that does not return memory allocated by applications to the OS unless specifically instructed to do so. As a result, applications can exhaust system memory—*even virtual memory*—if they continually allocate and deallocate large memory blocks. Real-world applications that exhibit such behavior include, I am sorry to say, some of the more commonly used NT backup software.

If you encounter a memory hog (the symptoms are pretty obvious—excessive memory paging; when doing normally innocuous things, such as moving the mouse; appallingly low Memory/Available Bytes, and Memory/Comitted Bytes appallingly high; possibly also the dreaded Low Virtual Memory message later in this chapter), you can isolate which application is causing the problem with Process/Working Set—then simply shut that process down. *It is not necessary to restart Windows NT.*[5]

Virtual Memory and Swapping

As described in Chapter 1, Windows NT is a virtual memory operating system, meaning that it can employ hard disk space as auxiliary memory to hold information that is not immediately required in RAM. The strategy that Windows NT uses to do this depends upon the operation of several sections of memory, known as *memory pools*, in conjunction with the cache manager. To begin with, there is a *nonpaged pool* that stores memory which cannot be paged out to disk—that is, memory required to be immediately on hand in order for Windows NT system components and applications to perform their functions. This memory generally appears to run in a pool of 2 to 3MB in most configurations. There is also a *paged pool* of memory that is pageable and can be swapped to disk, but is kept ready at hand for immediate access. This generally will contain the memory pages that are being most frequently requested by system components or applications. Paged pool may vary in size from a few megabytes up to the total capacity of physical memory, depending upon the configuration and available free space.

Windows NT also caches disk activity within the virtual memory space, *and can employ up to one half of the physical memory's space to store disk cache information.* That is, on a 16MB system, up to 8MB will be employed for cache, and so on. When the physical memory becomes exhausted—so many applications and system components are running and requesting memory that the system cannot fulfill those requests from within the range of pages available in the Physical Page Pool—the system will begin to *page* less frequently used pages out to hard disk—freeing up these less frequently used pages to fill those requests. This process will continue until the *commit limit* is reached. The commit limit specifies the total amount of memory that can be committed— that is, for which data space is required in either the physical memory or the virtual memory paging file—without expanding the paging file. When the commit limit is reached, Windows NT will attempt to expand the paging file.

Notice that we have two separate threshold situations involved here, where the paging file becomes a consideration. In the first, Windows NT is paging information into the file without the commit limit being affected. In this situation, disk I/O is *special cased* in a manner analogous to that used by the Windows 3.1 permanent swap file. That is, if you have a 16MB system with 24MB set as the initial size for your paging file, the commit limit for the memory

---

5. In the OS/2 1.x environment, rebooting servers nightly was a common practice due to a system-wide memory fragmentation problem. NT has no such problem, so while it may be necessary to shut down an ill-behaved application, it should *never* be necessary to reboot the computer.

system will be about 37MB (24MB plus the physical memory—16MB—less the space reserved for the Paged and Nonpaged Pools, which must be retained in physical memory). Until that commit limit is reached, Windows NT will perform *special case* I/O—essentially raw reads and writes within the paged file space—a relatively efficient process. Paging will occur but the impact on system performance will tend to be minimal.

When the commit limit is reached, however, Windows NT is forced to expand the paging file—and a completely different situation occurs, analogous in many respects to the temporary swap file in Windows 3.1. It is now necessary for Windows NT's system software to carry out *create* operations in an attempt to find more room on the disk. As a result, once the commit limit begins to increase, performance becomes abysmal. This situation should be avoided at all costs—particularly in file servers—because it can rapidly reach a point where the system becomes totally bogged and almost useless. But we haven't quite hit the ultimate limit. That happens when Windows NT either reaches the maximum size of the paging file (set in the Control Panel/System/Virtual Memory), or worse, if Windows NT runs out of physical disk space because application and data files on the disk partition containing the paging file don't leave enough room for the page file to grow to its maximum size.

At this point it becomes impossible for Windows NT to fill the application and system requests for memory, and you may expect a series of events, beginning with a System Low on Virtual Memory alert that will escalate through various error messages until the system crashes. This need not happen. When multiple page files are available, Windows NT will distribute paged virtual memory more-or-less equally across all of them—allowing for more total paging *and* improving performance—provided that each swap file exists on a separate physical disk. Note, however, that creating multiple paging files on a *single* physical disk will slow the system down—page file I/O alternates between two separate locations on the same disk, keeping the disk head in constant motion.

The best performance can be achieved if the page file is on a partition or disk by itself—indeed, the ultimate performance can be achieved if a separate controller is available for the page file, as this will allow page file operations to occur independently of other disk operations—something to consider when setting up large, multivolume file servers.

Why Not Just Add More RAM and Forget about Paging?

You might think that the solution to all these paging problems is simply to add enough RAM to the machine to prevent it from ever carrying out paging operations—on servers particularly. We know from experience that this is probably not a wise strategy where Windows NT is concerned. Windows NT has been designed to be efficient—nay, stingy—in its use of memory resources. It likes to run with just a few megabytes of RAM available as a ready reserve pool for emergency use. It does this in order to maximize disk performance—which in Windows NT is outstanding.

Essentially, the Windows NT cache manager takes over as much as possible of the free physical RAM to use for disk caching. Even on systems with what one would expect to be rather large amounts of memory, for example, 32MB, it turns out to be relatively easy to force Windows NT to engage in some swapping behavior, particularly during application start. When applications are loaded, Windows NT attempts to load the full binary image of the application in memory, and in doing so, begins to release pages from its pageable pool (with resulting flush operations on the disk cache). This is one reason that first-time users of Windows NT may *think* it's slower than Windows 3.1 (or OS/2 2.1)—it really *is* slower, where application launch is concerned. Steady-state performance of applications after they're launched, however, is quite another matter.

It's not possible to configure Windows NT so that it won't engage in this behavior (although it *can* be minimized by adjusting the Control Panel/Network/Server configuration). As long as sufficient virtual memory is available to handle peak cache loads without exceeding the commit limit, this doesn't have any significant impact on performance. In fact it will not be noticed at all unless you have a situation in which applications are continually started and stopped. Applications that just run in a steady state for the most part will be completely unaffected—indeed, they benefit from significantly higher effective disk performance because of the large disk cache size.

The one major performance situation to watch out for is where page file limits are not sufficient and Windows NT starts raising the commit limit. The way to avoid this is to run Windows NT systems during a burn-in period for the first few days (or weeks) of operation, observe the commit limit, and note any increase in the page file size. If the page file size has increased over and above the preset size during the burn-in, you should reset the Initial Page File Size in the Control Panel, increasing it by 20 percent. This will take care of most peak loading situations, give you a little *head room*, and minimize any performance impact due to further page file growth. You needn't do this if Windows NT has not expanded the page file during the burn-in period, as it's probably already big enough.

In either case, observe the Commit Limit using Performance Monitor. Add 10 percent to that value and set it as a Performance Monitor alert. This should be done on all servers—and it's advisable on workstations. As an example, if the commit limit is 60MB, set an alert at 66MB. Make sure, of course, that the maximum page file size is *more* than 66MB—and that there is sufficient free space on the partition containing the page file to store the additional space should it become necessary.

Essentially, this will set a trip wire. When the system begins to expand its paging file, as soon as that 10 percent threshold is crossed the alert will be transmitted and you'll likely have a chance to react to the problem. You'll want to react *quickly*, particularly if it happens on a server. Expansion of the commit limit doesn't indicate an imminent crash—but it indicates a fairly severe problem that will become a *very* severe one if you leave it alone.

Paging on Workstations

The situation on workstations is a little different. The most common situation encountered is where a Windows NT workstation over time starts seeing a sufficient load that the page file starts to increase—and an adequately configured system starts subjecting its user to severely frustrating behavior because whenever the user does *anything* the page file grows (with associated thrashing).

Again, the way to anticipate this situation is to set an alert based on a 10 percent growth in the commit limit. This isn't a crisis situation—let's explore how this can happen. Let's say that you have a basic Windows NT workstation outfitted with what would appear up front to be plenty of memory, say 20MB—not the 12MB Microsoft recommends but the 16MB we recommend, plus an additional 4MB because the system is being used as a print server or perhaps as a TCP/IP router. Initially, the system will be just fine—its user will be delighted with its performance. The user may be running a suite of applications, including MS Mail, Microsoft Schedule Plus, and two or three additional programs. Initially the user's going to employ the system very much the way he or she would employ a Windows 3.1 or Windows for Workgroups station. That is, the user will perform *task-switching* rather than *multitasking* on the system.

Mail and Schedule Plus may be autostarted and minimized, but for the most part the user will run Word for Windows or Excel for Windows or Power Point. Over time the user finds that it's much more convenient to start *all* of applications first thing in the morning, iconize the ones not immediately being used, and just work away with the one on top. This works fine, of course, in Windows NT. It is a preemptive multitasking system, and the intelligence built into the Virtual Memory Manager is such that the applications that are iconized (and not in use) take up a minimal amount of memory.

At some point, however, your user will find the threshold for the commit limit. It doesn't matter how high you set this initial threshold—believe me, your user will find it! In fact, the risk here is of a more severe situation. If the user *doesn't* find the commit limit, he's likely to run out of disk space on the hard disk; that situation probably deserves to be looked into with some care. Assuming that the user finds the commit limit, he's going to complain of poor performance. Even on a system with 20MB of memory and perhaps a 486/66 or Pentium processor (and heaven knows what else), which you would expect to be an excellent performer, you're going to find that System/% CPU Time is relatively low—but that System/Pages Per Second is intermittently hitting a relatively high value (in the hundreds of Pages/Sec. at least) and this is happening pretty much whenever a new application is started, often when an application is closed, and so on.

This happens because the *Working Set* for the user's applications now totals more than the memory available in the system with the page file at its default size. Windows NT now starts expanding the page file. It does this in a very stingy manner, expanding only a little bit at a time—which means it buys just enough room to have the crisis come again ten seconds later (it would be awfully convenient if the system were designed so that administrators could selectively control the growth of the paging file, or cause an alert to be displayed, suggesting to the user that he might want to use his paging file or call the administrator).

Unlike the server situation—where this presages a crisis—for end users it's probably not an urgent situation. Moreover, it's likely that the commit-limit problem will grow slowly over time. Since Windows NT workstations can be inspected remotely, you can sit on any workstation, and (using administrative privileges) open a Performance Monitor session on any other user's station. The most desirable approach is probably to log Commit Limit and Working Set sizes for users on an infrequent basis—say once a week or so, observe users who are approaching their commit limit, and (when time is convenient) expand their page file for them. In this way they will never see the problem. You can also take advantage of this situation to observe the free space availability on the disk that holds the paging file, and suggest to the user that he might want to move some files around if he's getting himself in a situation where there's not going to be sufficient room should the page file begin to expand. In this way you achieve that ultimate goal of administration that we talked about in Chapter 3, invisibility.

Controlling Memory Use

In most respects, Windows NT is a self-tuning operating system. At installation, certain configuration settings will be made to optimize performance for the amount of memory in the system. In most cases, these settings will provide the best performance—but there are exceptions.

By default, Windows NT Servers run a Large System Cache model, in which all available RAM not otherwise used by applications or the system is available for disk caching. Windows NT Workstations, by contrast, run a Small System Cache, in which the cache manager will page out least recently used memory in an attempt to keep 4MB of RAM free for application launch.

In some circumstances, you may want to change this behavior—for instance, if an NT Server is being used in nondedicated mode by someone running it as a desktop system, using the small cache model may speed local application performance (at the expense of Server performance). Likewise, NT Workstation users who spend most of their time running a preloaded set of applications—but rarely launching new ones—may benefit from a large cache model (especially on systems with limited RAM).

To control which model is set, use the NT configuration Registry Editor and reset HKEY_LOCAL_MACHINE\System\CurrentControlSet\Control\Session Manager\Memory Management\LargeSystemCache (this is a REG_DWORD value). A value of 1 sets large cache mode, a value of 0 sets small cache mode.

Virtual Memory Settings

Aside from large/small cache mode, NT's virtual memory subsystem can be tuned using the Control Panel/System icon's Virtual Memory settings (see Figure 5.5)—this lets you set the initial and maximum page file sizes, set which disk(s) page files reside on—as mentioned earlier, systems with multiple physical disks can benefit from having multiple page files—and control growth of the Windows NT configuration registry database.

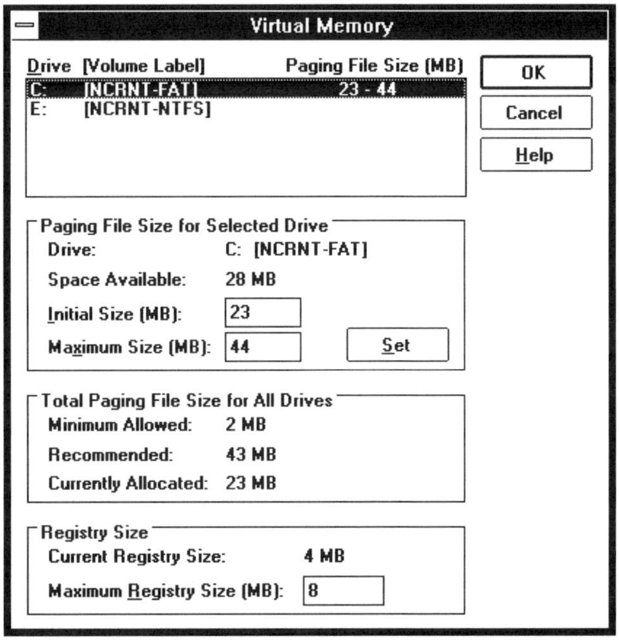

Figure 5.5 Virtual Memory.

Windows NT's Paging File and Registry settings are adjusted in the Control Panel, as shown here.

Video Performance

The Windows NT Performance Monitor includes no specific video object.[6] It is nonetheless possible to get an indirect indication of video activity in the Windows NT system. The most convenient way to do this is with the Process Object—examine the instance called *CSRSS*, and use the *% Processor Time, % Privilege Time*, and *% User Time* counters:

CSRSS

CSRSS is a subsystem of the Windows NT Executive which carries out graphical activities on behalf of applications. It contains one thread for each application that employs on-screen graphics, and is generally a reliable indicator of graphical activity. If CSRSS % Processor Time is continually absorbing a very high proportion of the overall system activity—that is, if one observes a high percent of processor time on the system and then traces this high percent processor time to CSRSS (as shown in Figure 5.6)—then in all probability, your system is being limited by its video bandwidth and a faster video card would produce a performance improvement.[7]

Disk Performance

Microsoft recommends monitoring two counter values when attempting to determine disk performance. The first is *Average Disk Sec./Transfer* from the *Logical Disk Object* on any logical disk. The second is *Disk Queue*. Average Disk Sec./Transfer gives a direct measure of disk access speed, although determining a transfer *rate* will also require you to look at the *Average Disk Bytes/Transfer* to estimate the size of the block being transferred. Disk Queue gives direct indication of the number of disk transfer requests that are being stored tempo-

---

6. At least, no such object has been available in NT versions from 3.1 to 3.51. We expect that later versions of NT will move the video subsystem into the NT kernel—at that point CSRSS will probably disappear and a video object may be added to Performance Monitor.

7. It's possible to demonstrate CSRSS tracking of video performance using an undocumented (but cute) feature of the Free Cell game that's included with all Windows NT systems. To do so, start Performance Monitor and add an entry for % Processor Time in the CSRSS instance of the Process Object. Set the Chart Scale to a maximum of 100 percent. If you move the mouse you'll observe a high indication on the graph, because the mouse is one of many graphical activities. However, you should see no more than a 10 percent-20 percent maximum that settles to zero as mouse movement stops. Now start a Free Cell game, start a New Game, then hold down the Control and Shift keys while hitting the F10 key. A rather interesting alert message will appear. You can select either abort or retry—then pick any card and drag it to any empty card slot. The Free Cell game will automatically play to completion—and as it does so you will observe a very high peak in the CSRSS subsystem (because of all the graphic activity as the game automatically plays itself to completion).

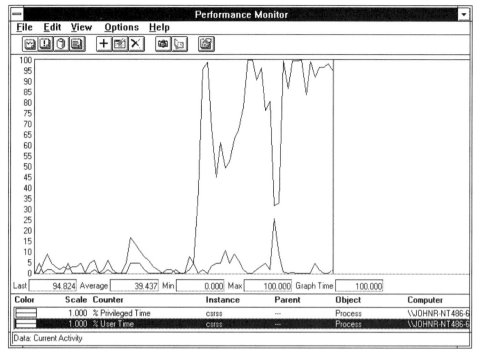

Figure 5.6 Performance Monitor, CSRSS process.

Performance Monitor does not include any counters or objects specific to video performance—but monitoring % User Time and % Privileged Time in the CSRSS process provides a workable substitute (% Privileged Time indicateds time spent in the system's internal routines—in this case, the low-level graphics component of Win32). This display illustrates a system that's experiencing an extremely heavy video load.

rarily because the disk is unable to respond to the request. A sustained Disk Queue above 1 probably indicates that the disk is becoming a bottleneck in the system.

Note: It is not possible to measure any of these values without turning on disk counters. These are turned off by default in Windows NT, because the overhead involved in disk performance monitoring will reduce overall disk throughput by 10 percent to 15 percent. To turn them on type diskperf -y at the command line and then restart the system.

Because disk performance monitoring incurs a 10 percent to 15 percent overhead, it should not be permanently turned on unless it's absolutely necessary. Disk performance monitoring is something that you want to do only during maintenance intervals or when problems are suspected. It *may* be left permanently on servers if, in fact, you can determine that a 10-percent disk performance hit will not materially affect overall responsiveness of the system.

Logical Disk object—the *Percent Free Space* and *Free Megabytes* counters indicate, respectively, the percentage of disk space that is not filled and the number of megabytes of disk space that are not filled. If Free Megabytes falls near to or below the space needed to hold the page file at its maximum size, then the system might be unable to grow the paging file and will start giving you Out of Virtual Memory indications. In general, it is probably wise to set alerts on Percent Free Space less than 5 percent on all drives on servers.

% Disk Time indicates the activity of the disk drive including both reads and writes as a percentage of total elapsed time. This is a good indicator for excessive disk activity. If this value achieves a sustained level greater than 50 percent it indicates that the disk is approaching a full duty cycle and may indicate a thrashing condition, indicating that some corrective action needs to be taken. You may wish to examine Percent Disk Drives on all of the volumes of a server to see how load is being balanced across the disk drives, and consider moving files as necessary (particularly in database server applications) to try to equalize load on the drives on the system.

The *Physical Disk* object provides a set of counters similar to those used for the Logical Disk objects. These will give you information about performance of a physical disk platter, but will not give you information that can be broken down by partition and therefore is probably less useful in most circumstances. However, Microsoft does make one interesting recommendation—which is to observe Average Disk Access Time for physical disks.[8] If you have multiple platters available, particularly in a SCSI disk system, where the disks could be striped, striping will probably improve disk performance if average disk access time for the physical disk is less than average disk time divided by the number of disks available striped.

With respect to setting alerts on disk performance counters, again, bear in mind that turning on disk performance counters (using the *disperf-y* command syntax) will extract a 10 percent to 15 percent performance penalty on disks for which performance monitoring has been enabled. Having said that, on servers where you suspect that disk performance may represent a system bottleneck, it might well be advisable to turn on disk performance monitoring as a debugging aid, and then set an alert on the Disk Queue value in the Logical Disk Object for any disks on which you suspect that performance may be a problem. Set the alert to trip if a sustained value greater than 1 is achieved. This will indicate that disk transfer requests are being received faster than the disk can accommodate them. Monitoring this value might indicate when a particular disk is accessed more frequently than the physical disk hardware can sustain, in which case you should consider moving files around on the disk, or replacing the existing disk setup with a stripe set.

---

8. In the Resource Kit—see chapter 4 of Volume 4, "Optimizing Windows NT."

You should also be concerned if you see a Disk Queue higher than 1 and cannot account for it. If the level of traffic is such that the disk ought to be able to handle it, then consider monitoring Average Disk Bytes/Transfer and Average Disk Sec./Transfer. You can use this information by dividing Average Disk Bytes/Transfer by Average Disk Sec./Transfer. You will get a *transfer rate* in Bytes/Sec. Comparing this with the specifications for the disk drive may give you an indication if a disk drive is starting to lose performance due to wear, fragmentation, and so on. Periodic monitoring of this value and historical logging of this information on a month-to-month basis may give some indication of when a disk needs to be reformatted to eliminate fragmentation, or when the disk hardware is beginning to have problems.

Network Performance

Up to now we've been concerned with monitoring other parts of the system to detect and overcome system bottlenecks—but the plain fact is that this is a book about networking and as any network administrator knows, the odds are much higher that you will experience performance bottlenecks on your network than on almost any other component. The classic approach to this problem (other than guesswork, jiggling the network cables, and so forth—always a good idea if you're having a network problem on a workstation) is to break out the Protocol Analyzer—and this remains the preferred method of dealing with a wide variety of network problems.[9]

Where NetBIOS is used (NetBEUI, NBT, NetBIOS on the NWLink protocol), Windows NT actually provides built-in performance tuning that will give you almost (but not quite!) the same information you'd get from a protocol analyzer. You can't get down into the wire and actually look at the bits in the packets, but you can look at data rates and collisions—you can in fact perform a sophisticated level of system performance monitoring in the software itself. There are also performance counters that can be used in monitoring performance of some of the critical software components, including the LAN Manager workstation and the LAN Manager server. We'll examine all of those in what follows.

NetBEUI Object

The two basic counters you can monitor to determine NetBEUI throughput on a system are *Bytes Total/Sec.* and *Packets/Sec.*—which represent, respectively, the total data transfer for all packets containing data and the total number of

---

9. Incidentally, Microsoft's Systems Management Server (SMS) includes what amounts to a software sniffer for NT. See Chapter 7 for more information.

packets transmitted. You can work out the packet size by dividing an average of the Bytes Total/Sec. by Packets/Sec.—and if that number begins to change (particularly if it begins to drop), it probably indicates a *collision* condition where you have a large number of packets that don't contain any data.

From a performance-tuning standpoint, there are two additional values you might wish to monitor, particularly if you are seeing slow traffic on a heavily loaded network. The *Piggyback Ack Time Out* counter indicates time outs on acknowledgments that are piggybacked onto data packets to the remote system. If this value rises to above 10 percent of the total number of packets sent (monitored by the Packets/Sec. counter), then you may want to consider increasing the DefaultT1Timeout value in the HKEY_LOCAL_MACHINE/SYS-TEM/CurrentControlSet /Services/NBF/Parameters section of the registry.

Similarly, you may also need to monitor *Expirations Ack*, which will indicate the number of NetBEUI acknowledgments that have expired. If this is greater than 10 percent of the packets transmitted, you will need to decrease the DefaultT2Timeout value located in the same section of the registry previously mentioned. Note that this value must always be less than T1.

Finally, if you're increasing those other values, consider increasing the DefaultTiTimeout, which is the wait time before polling an inactive host. This will avoid having repeated polling packets sent before a slow host can respond to the initial packet—at the expense of taking longer to respond when attempting to access a server that's not on the network.

TCP, UPD, Appletalk, and NwLink IPX Objects

These provide similar counters to the NetBEUI object, but support other protocols. The values can be monitored in much the same way as NetBEUI.

Redirector Object

As you will recall from Chapter 1, the Redirector is a software component in the Windows NT Executive, which essentially acts as a traffic cop and determines when data transfers need to be handled by local resources (such as hard disks) and when they need to be handled over the network. It is, therefore, the component that sits nearest the center of the Windows NT network and is a good place to look for network bottlenecks. Several parameters can be monitored here that may prove useful in problem detection and network turning. The first of these is Redirector Current Commands. This indicates the number of commands queued, and it should never be more than 1 for every network card in the system. If it rises and stays at a number greater than 1 for any network card in the system, then there is a bottleneck either in the Redirector software—or (more probably) in the network hardware.

The Redirector can be a bottleneck if the network is slow or if you're getting slow response to a server—in which case you may need to increase the *Maximum-NumberOfCommands* parameter in the HKEY_LOCAL_MACHINE/SYSTEM/CurrentControlSet/Services/LanmanWorkstation/Parameters section of the registry. This defaults to a value of 50. It can be raised as high as 255 and may need to be raised (obviously) if the Current Commands counter is within 10 percent of 50. On the other hand, again, this invariably indicates that there is a problem somewhere in the system—otherwise the Redirector would not be queuing commands to that extent. A better solution, at this point, will be to determine *why* the commands are being queued. Either the network itself is bogged (which can be checked by a counter we'll mention shortly), or the *server* performance is extremely slow for some reason—and you will want to investigate the cause.

The *Network Errors/Sec.* counter indicates the number of serious network errors (generally collisions) being experienced in the system. You can look for further information in the System Error Log (using Event Viewer), because there will be an entry every time a network error is generated. In any case, if Network Errors/Sec. rise above zero on a well-behaved network (or above some small background value in a heavily loaded network), you've got a problem somewhere in the subnet and you'll need to trace it down.

The *Reads Denied/Sec.* and *Writes Denied/Sec.* counters indicate that a remote server's refusing to accommodate requests for *raw* reads or writes. Raw reads or writes are a technique that Windows NT uses to increase data rates in large data transfers. Instead of transferring packet frame information for each data packet, a *virtual circuit* connection is opened and a whole stream of raw data packets is transmitted, maximizing the throughput rate for the duration of the virtual circuit connection. If the server is running low on memory, it may refuse to participate in this kind of a connection because it cannot allocate the necessary local buffer space. Therefore, the Reads Denied/Sec. and Writes Denied/Sec. counters are a direct indication of memory problems at the file server.

Obviously, the preferred solution to this problem is to increase the memory in the server (or at any rate, examine the file server and determine why it is running so low on memory that it's refusing to allocate space for raw reads and writes). If it is impossible to fix this problem promptly (i.e., you haven't got extra RAM to put in the server, or cannot immediately take it offline), you can set the *UseRawReads* and *UseRawWrites* parameters of the LANManWorkstation entry in the system registry to False. This will stop futile attempts to use raw I/O, thus increasing throughput. Again, however, the preferred way to deal with this is to correct the problem at the server.

One further registry setting that might help in situations where networks are heavily used is to set the *UseNTCaching* parameter in the LanmanWorkstation registry subkey to True. This will cache I/O requests during file writes, reducing the number of requests transmitted across the network. In effect, repeated writes will be cached locally, and then a single request for transfer will transmit all the information across the network. When a network is heavily loaded, this may improve performance.

Server Object

All Windows NT systems are to some extent servers, irrespective of whether they are dedicated as file servers or whether they are functioning as desktop work-stations. And operations in which services are provided, resources are shared, and so on, are managed by the Server Object. This can be monitored from the Server Object in the Performance Monitor. Appropriate counters and indicated performance are as follows:

❑ *Bytes Total/Sec.*—This value provides an overall indication of how busy the server is and should probably be monitored on file servers, because an increase on this over time indicates a need to expand server memory (or perhaps even to consider upgrading your server hardware).

❑ *Errors Access Permissions, Errors Granted Access, Errors Logon.* All of these indicate security problems. These may be as innocuous as someone forgetting their password, but *could* indicate that someone's attempting to *hack* your system. In particular, a high value for Errors Logon may indicate that someone is trying to hack the system using a password-cracking program. You will want to examine the system security log (using Event Viewer) and you may want to enable auditing (from User Manager) to track what's happening.

❑ *Errors System* will indicate the number of unexpected system errors that the server is experiencing, and this will indicate that there is a problem with the server. You should probably, at this point, investigate the server to see whether it is running out of memory, and the system error log to see if you have a hardware problem. If neither is indicated, then call a Microsoft-certified professional technician, or Microsoft technical sup-port.

❑ The *Pool Nonpaged Bytes* and *Pool Nonpaged Failures* counters will give an indication of the physical memory situation with respect to the Server Object. Pool Nonpaged Bytes indicates the amount of nonpageable physical memory that the server is using, while Pool Nonpaged Failures will indicate the number of times it attempts to allocate memory that is not available. The latter indicates that the physical memory in the system is too small. One thing you can do in an attempt to recover from this is to reset the Server Object in the Control Panel/Network settings, and consider using the Minimize Memory Used optimization setting. However, this will reduce system performance. It may prove inadequate in a situation where you are attempting to establish connections with more than five systems. Increasing the physical memory is always the preferred solution to this problem.

❏ The *Pool Paged Bytes* and *Pool Paged Failures* parameters give a similar indication for pageable memory used by the server. In this case, the solution to the problem may be to increase the page file size on the system (set in Control Panel/System Virtual Memory).

❏ The *Sessions Errored Out* and *Sessions Timed Out* parameters give an indication of the number of times that network errors are causing a session to be disconnected or, alternatively, the number of times that an administrative autodisconnect setting (from User Manager), is disconnecting users with idle connections. The latter may be a useful thing to do on a system with a heavily loaded server that's experiencing memory problems.

❏ Finally, the *Work Item Shortages* counter indicates that you need to tune the InitWorkItems or MaxWorkItems parameters in the LANmanServer Object of the System Registry. If you are seeing a work item shortage only during system start, then probably the InitWorkItems number needs to be increased. If not, it's the MaxWorkItems number that needs to be increased.

❏ You can select any one of four optimization settings for Server operation (from Control Panel/Network Settings, select Server from the list of installed software, and then click on Configure, as illustrated in Figure 5.7). The four optimization settings are *Minimize Memory Used, Balance, Maximize Throughput for File Sharing*, and *Maximize Throughput for Network Applications*. The first setting is obvious; it is designed for a maximum of five network connections and is suitable only for lightly used workstations. This setting should *never* be selected on a file server (unless it's doing local file services on a *very* small—five clients or less—network). The Balance setting allocates memory initially for up to ten sessions and is primarily useful for small servers or for Windows NT workstations providing local *ad hoc* file sharing or functioning as print servers. Maximize Throughput for File Sharing allocates memory initially for up to 128 connections, and is the basic setting for Windows NT Servers. Maximize Throughput for Network Applications detunes the Windows NT Virtual Memory System to be less aggressive in reserving physical memory to provide a buffer for application launch. This reduces swapping in systems and is a good choice for servers that primarily run network applications (such as SQL server). Indeed, this is probably the *optimal* setting for Server installations that have adequate memory (greater than 32MB).

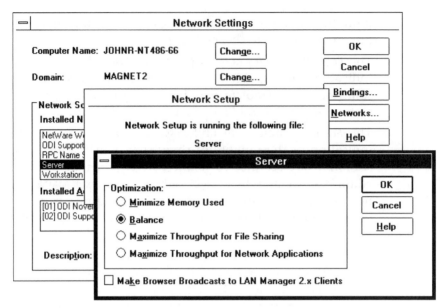

Figure 5.7 Server Object in Control Panel Network.

The Server Configuration dialog, shown here, allows you to control the memory optimization settings of Windows NT's built-in network services. The effect of the four settings is described in the text. This dialog is reached from the Control Panel/Network Settings by selecting the Server object and clicking the Configure button.

A Final Word about Performance Tuning, Logging, and Maintenance History

The built-in tools (such as Performance Monitor and the configuration Registry Editor) in Windows NT are quite powerful and can make life much easier for a support professional who needs to maintain multiple servers and workstations. They can also, however, lead you into making a grave mistake. It's all too easy to install a Windows NT system, conduct some initial performance tuning, and then forget about it until something breaks, at which point one goes back to do the performance tuning and is left with no more information than that which I have just described, and that provided in the Microsoft documentation.

Whenever a server is put in, you should carry out an initial performance tuning. You should also write down the performance results you eventually achieve in a *performance history*. This can either be a log document that is kept on the server (although, if it is in electronic form, you should keep a copy somewhere else—because if the server goes down, you want to still be able to access the maintenance information), or it can be a separate physical record.

The point of the maintenance history is that the next time you need to conduct a performance tuning or routine check on the system, you have a *base of comparison*. That is, you know what the system performance was when you conducted the initial tuning, and you know how it differs when you look at it later. This can be enormously valuable in detecting problems. A routine performance tune-up once per month, for example, is probably a good idea. Values for basic performance criteria, such as Nonpaged Pool and Paged Pool sizes from the Memory Object, Total Processor Time from the System Object, Logical Disk Available Space, Free Space, % Free Space, Average Disk Bytes/Transfer, Disk Queue and Average Disk Sec./Transfer, Netbeui Bytes Total/Sec. and Packets / Sec., and so on, will make it possible when comparing these values to identify when something is going on with the system that's going to need to be corrected eventually.

For example, if you find that the Nonpaged Pool is rising continuously, you know that eventually you're going to have to increase the physical memory in the system. If you find that the Paged Pool is rising consistently, you might need to expand the size of the paging file, consider adding more virtual memory to the system, consider distributing the paging file over multiple disks to improve performance, and so on. Use your common sense. Keep a record of this information. Look at it periodically, think about it. That way you will not have to resort to using the troubleshooting information that we are about to present.

Windows NT Configuration Registry

Windows NT provides an advanced approach to configuration tracking and maintenance that can be an absolute godsend to system administrators. This approach is mediated through a special tool called the Configuration Registry Editor (REGEDT32.EXE), which is a full-featured software tool for the examination and manipulation of configuration information.

WARNING! The Registry Editor is one of the most powerful administrative tools provided with Windows NT. It is also potentially one of the most dangerous. Editing registry entries, and making changes to the registry blindly may render the system completely unstable. Use this tool with care.

The Configuration Problem

How many times have you been faced with this problem?: A Windows user comes to you and says "My system won't work." You say "What did you change?" Your user says "Nothing!" You examine the system and find that it won't boot. You know that however sincere the user may be, *something* changed in the system, because it booted before. On talking further to the user you find that he or she recently added some software, removed some software, and in all probability edited the CONFIG.SYS file, AUTOEXEC.BAT file, and/or any of the dozen or so *.INI files in the Windows\SYSTEM directory (or the protocol.ini file on a Windows for Workgroups or LAN Manager system). You are now faced with the nightmare of system administrators the world over—trying to correct configuration problems in the absence of any backup information at all. The odds are quite good that the solution of the problem will be to reinstall Windows, reinstall networking, reinstall applications—in any case, to reinstall something, because there really isn't anything else you can do.

Windows NT attempts to solve this problem with a *Configuration Registry*—a true database organized as a multiple tree structure and maintained individually on every Windows NT Server or Workstation. This database contains all (well, in theory *all*, in practice *most*) of the information that is contained in the AUTO-EXEC.BAT, CONFIG.SYS, *.INI files of a Windows systems or in the enormous CONFIG.SYS file of an OS/2 system, or in the PROTOCOL.INI file of a LAN Manager system. Furthermore, the data is inherently backed up—multiple copies are maintained and a special tool is provided for manipulating the data, which, among other things, organizes the data in a logical structure and makes it possible to access the data remotely, a dream come true for many system administrators. This tool is called the Configuration Registry Editor (REGEDT32.EXE).

The Bad News

The availability of a centralized configuration database and a proper tool for managing it is a dream come true for system administrators—up to a point. Unfortunately, the current implementation of the Registry Editor is less than perfect. It looks and behaves much like File Manager—neither the best nor the worst thing that one could think of to use as a model—but its most unfortunate feature is that (much like the various *.ini files it replaces), the Registry continues the system management tradition of providing configuration information in the form of thousands of incomprehensible key values that are not documented anywhere.[10] This is extremely frustrating and potentially dangerous. It means that when you first examine the Registry, you need to be very careful not to change anything—as you're going to find that if you do, it's almost impossible to get the initial value back because there's no place to look it up. It also means that finding the appropriate values to modify in a system is difficult.

Configuration Registry Structure

As mentioned previously, the Configuration Registry is organized as a multiple tree database. This is stored in such a manner that it is fully backed up in a

---

10. Except in the Windows NT Resource Kit. See Appendix 4 for details.

system, as we will see. Changes to the Registry are made through a Registry Editor, which enforces a high degree of *atomicity* in the database—you are guaranteed to see either an old or a new value for any registry key. You will never see a mixture of an old and new value even if the system crash occurs. That's the good news.

Physical Data Structure

Physically the Registry is organized as a set of files stored in the WINNT (or WINDOWS)\SYSTEM32\CONFIG directory on the boot volume of every Windows NT system). If you examine this directory you will see files named *system, software, default, system.alt, security, sam,* and *userdef.* Each of these files corresponds to a logical tree structure in the Registry Editor, as we will see in a moment. If you attempt to examine any of these files either by typing them out or by examining them in a bitwise editor, you will quickly find that they are incomprehensible, because the data is stored in binary format. There is, therefore, currently no alternative to the use of the Registry Editor provided with Windows NT.

With backup of the Registry information, you should note that the system.alt file contains a complete alternate copy of the system file, which the system will employ automatically in the event that the System Registry file is corrupted. One could conceivably back up the Registry files manually and attempt restoration of an old Registry in the event that system problems occur. This is probably a questionable procedure, given that in the event that the Registry is corrupted, you're not going to have a way to access the system to restore the files.

Fortunately, Windows NT goes to considerable lengths to make sure that the Registry doesn't become corrupted, and it provides *last known good* configuration recovery during system start. So you will usually be able to recover at least to a previous known state in a system reboot (provided, of course, that nobody has been making dramatic Registry changes in an ill-thought-out manner).

Logical Data Structure

Because you are invariably going to access the Registry through the Registry Editor, the data structure of most importance is the logical data structure that you see when observing the Registry Editor. This is organized at the top level into four registry *keys*; that is, four entry points into the four major tree structures that contain the system Registry information. HKEY_LOCAL_MA-CHINE is the tree structure describing the hardware and software configuration of the machine whose Registry Editor you are running or whose Registry you have loaded remotely. HKEY_CURRENT_USER is the Registry information applying to the currently logged-in user of the system. HKEY_CLASSES_ROOT is Windows NT's OLE database. HKEY_USERS maintains the list of users in the local machine's local login database and the security identification number (SID) for each user, along with the program groups, control panel settings, environment variables, and so forth, associated with each user's login.

Of these, by far the most useful for system maintenance is HKEY_LO-CAL_MACHINE, which contains, again, the actual description of the system and the settings that would formerly have been found in CONFIG.SYS, AUTO-EXEC.BAT or *.INI file. This is the Registry key with which we are going to be most concerned in this chapter.

The HKEY_LOCAL_MACHINE Key

Starting from the HKEY_LOCAL_MACHINE entry there are five subkeys. These are HARDWARE, Security Account Manager (SAM), SECURITY, SOFTWARE, and SYSTEM. Of these the SAM and SECURITY section are of interest to us only in knowing that they exist. They cannot be accessed except through the appropriate APIs (in the case of SAM—the SECURITY entry cannot be accessed at all). These Registry entries contain the security information used to validate logons into the system and to validate privileges and user access rights. They cannot be edited manually.

The HARDWARE key contains a description of the system, which is updated every time the system restarts. This is done using a *hardware recognizer*—one component of the Windows NT boot process. Examining the HARDWARE key you'll find subkeys for DESCRIPTION, DEVICEMAP, and RESOURCEMAP. A subkey of the DESCRIPTION will be System—and this will contain information about the central processor (or processors), the various adapters in the system, and so on. The DEVICEMAP subkey will contain a list of the I/O devices in the system—as will the RESOURCEMAP subkey. This information is used by the various Windows NT system software components, such as the network components and the Control Panel, which will examine the HARDWARE key in the Registry to identify any or all network cards in the system and test their settings. It can be used by an administrator to examine what hardware is in the system and the status of the hardware—but obviously it can't be changed (other than by changing the hardware and restarting the computer).

The SOFTWARE subkey contains, first of all, the subkey called Classes, which provides the software class associations used by File Manager (the same data is pointed to by HKEY_CLASSES_ROOT); that is, it associates a three-letter file extension with a program. This is followed by a Program Groups subkey listing common groups that apply system-wide. There will also be subkeys for each vendor that supplies software to the system. In Windows NT systems today you are certain to find a subkey called Microsoft—and there is some small probability that you will see subkeys called Lotus, Borland, or whatnot in the future (if you have the NetWare Requester for Windows NT installed, for instance, you'll see a Novell subkey).

In the event that a vendor employs this technique, within each vendor subkey you will see subkeys for particular products, and within those product subkeys, subsubkeys for versions of the products and within those subsubkeys you might find information about the product, product settings, and so on. From an administrator's point of view, the value of this information lies solely in the fact that it does provide a central resource for determining the versions of software currently installed in the system. You can examine the SOFTWARE entries for each vendor and if you click, for example, on the LAN Man Server entry under Microsoft, you'll see a subkey called Current Version. Clicking on that will list description and installation date, major version, minor version, and so on. For instance, we know that we are looking at LAN Man Server version 3.1 with an installation date.

In any case this could be used (and over time will be used) by software, such as Microsoft's forthcoming Hermes configuration maintenance tool, to automatically track and update software versions across the network. The SOFTWARE key will also contain a Secure subkey—the purpose of which is not clear at the moment—and a Windows 3.1 migration subkey. This subkey will indicate the status of any migration information for systems providing dual boot between Windows 3.1 and Windows NT that have been upgraded from a Windows 3.1 or Windows for Workgroups installation to a Windows NT installation. After the SOFTWARE subkey, there is only one more subkey of the HKEY_LOCAL_MACHINE, the SYSTEM subkey. This is the one that contains practically everything of interest to a support professional.

The SYSTEM Subkey

Opening the SYSTEM subkey we find a number of subsubkeys. The most important are the *ControlSets*: CurrentControlSet, ControlSet001, ControlSet002. A ControlSet is a tree structure containing information on all of the main services of a Windows NT system—including parameter settings. The system maintains a CurrentControlSet, which is the one currently being used in the system, and two fall-back copies, representing previous configurations. During shutdown the CurrentControlSet will be copied into ControlSet001, so that always contains the ControlSet in use when the system was last shut down; that, in turn, replaces ControlSet002 during system start if the system starts correctly. In the event that the system fails to start correctly, an attempt will be made to start using the earlier configuration. You could also have the option of doing this manually using the *Last Known Good Configuration* menu, which comes up during a Windows NT system start. This feature alone is immensely valuable to system professionals, because it means the system automatically protects users from themselves. If you have a system that starts to misbehave, there is a very good chance that by reverting to one of the two last known good configurations, you will be able to recover.

The Select subkey of the SYSTEM key tells you which of the Control Sets is in use. Examining this you'll see entries for Current, Default, Failed, and LastKnownGood, which (by default on a system operating normally) will have a Current value of 1, Default value of 1, LastKnownGood value of 2, and a Failed value of 0. In the event that a configuration corruption has been detected during startup, the Failed value will rise and the system will attempt to use the last known good entry as the current entry instead of using the default entry.

The Setup subkey of the SYSTEM key contains information about the Window NT system setup that was performed when the system was installed. This includes the network card, the type of setup performed, and the setup command line employed. There is an entry for system setup in progress. If you ever examine this and it is other than zero, something has gone dreadfully wrong and it will indicate the path to the system setup files. The Disk subkey to the SYSTEM key contains a basic set of information about the disks in the system. But by far the most important information—again, from a support professional's point of view—is the information contained in CurrentControl-Set, which we will examine next.

The CurrentControlSet Key

CurrentControlSet contains two subkeys, the first called *control* and the second called *services*. The services subkey refers to particular subsystems or hardware devices within the Windows NT system, each subsystem or hardware component having a subkey within the services key; within that subkey the linkage of the subsystem to other parameters appears in a subkey, and there may be a parameters subkey, which will have any user-stable parameters for the component. Some subkeys will also have an autotuned parameters key associated with them, which will incorporate parameters dynamically tuned by the component itself.

The Control subkey, on the other hand, contains information, such as the load order for the device drivers and services (in the GroupOrderList and ServiceGroupOrder subsubkeys), much of the Control Panel and Setup data, and so on. This will rarely be edited directly by an end user or administrator, but will simply reflect the settings set for the computer using other tools. So from an administrator's standpoint it is the services subkey, finally, which contains the parts that are a matter of concern.

The Services Subkey

As mentioned previously, the Services subkey contains, in turn, key entries (or subtrees) for each software subsystem or hardware component that is part of the Windows NT system under inspection. Each key entry, in turn, can contain subkeys for autotune parameters, linkages to other subsystems, parameters, and perhaps security information. Of these the most immediately interesting is the Parameter subkey, which lets you control certain features of the system. Perhaps an example will make this clear.

If you start the Registry Editor (by typing REGEDT32 from the command line), you will see the Registry Editor display containing within it the four windows containing the four Registry keys. Select the one called HKEY_LO-CAL_MACHINE and double-click the HKEY_LOCAL_MACHINE key entry to list its subkeys; double-click the SYSTEM subkey; double-click the CurrentControl-Set subkey; double-click the Services subkey. This will give you a list of all of the services and hardware components in the system. If you now double-click on the Browser subkey, you'll see Parameters, Linkage, and Security. Double-click-ing on Parameters will give you a list of parameters for the subkey.

It should be noted that this list is not necessarily complete—and this is one of the problems with the Registry as it currently exists. It's possible for a parameters entry in a subkey entry for a component to be empty. This does not mean that there aren't any parameters. It means that the component is using the default parameters, whatever those might be.

On the Windows NT Server system I'm inspecting as I write this, the Parameters for Browser are: IsDomainMaster, which is a parameter of type REG_SZ (a string data type) that is set to False; and the parameter MaintainSer-verList, which is again of type REG_SZ and is set to Yes. Possible values for *IsDomainMaster* would be True, and for *MaintainServerList* would be No. These settings, in fact, determine the operation of the system browser—the compo-nent that determines the response to a *net view* command or to clicking to the Connect Net Drive icon in File Manager. *ThisIsDomainMaster* determines whether the system in question stores the *browse list*—the list of systems that can be accessed on the local workgroup or domain.

In this case—despite the fact that the system in question is primary domain control for the Windows NT Server logon domain in question—it is *not* the domain Browse Master. In fact, one of the workstations on the system is functioning as Browse Master. However, because *MaintainServerList* is set to *Yes* the system does maintain a list of the available systems and can act as fall-back to the Browse Master in the event that the Browse Master does not respond to a browse request from other workstations. (If none of this makes sense, see the section on browsing in Chapter 8).

To edit any of these entries, for example the *IsBrowseMaster* entry, it is necessary only to double-click on it. An editor will then appear. Since these entries are of the type REG_SZ, the String Editor will appear, which will allow you to type in a character string. Again, at this point we have one of the unfortunate problems with the Registry database. Obviously only certain strings will provide acceptable entries for string data types—yet there's nothing to indicate how a string should be typed. In fact, the True and False values are uppercased; Yes and No values are lowercased. You must find this kind of information by examination (for that matter, as this is written, we are unsure whether the choice of case is even significant—it may not be).

Other data types are REG_DWORD, the double-word data type, which contains a 32-bit binary value. Double-clicking on one of these, such as the LMAnnounce parameter in the LAN Man Server subkey, you will be presented with a Dword Editor, which will show the data in question in your choice of a binary, decimal, hexadecimal representation. This can be of some use to you in setting a particular value, because you can type it in using the most convenient form. Again, however, there is no explanation of what the acceptable values are. The *LMAnnounce* value, in fact, has legal values of 0 or 1, a 1 indicating that the system is to perform LAN Manager 2.x-compatible system announcements, and a 0 indicating that it is not. Fortunately, as with most entries in the System subkey, it is not necessary to edit this value from the Registry Editor. You can edit the value, in fact, by using the Control Panel / Network Settings, selecting the Server from the list of installed network software, and clicking the Configure button. You will then see a screen offering a choice of four possible optimizations, and a check box for Make Browser Broadcasts. Checking this box and clicking OK will change the Registry value from 0 to 1—and if you return to the Registry Editor, you'll see, in fact, it updates itself and the *LMAnnounce* value will now be set to 0x1 as type REG_DWORD.

You will also notice a *Size* value in the LAN Man Server subkey. Size, which is a REG_DWORD, represents which of the four possible server optimization values has been selected from the Control Panel. Since the four possible values are 1 through 4, it is obvious that a value of 0 or 5, for instance, would be illegal—yet there is nothing in the Registry Editor that would indicate this.

Why Go On and On about the Limitations of the Parameter Settings?

Why do we keep harping on this? Because it's *dangerous* to edit settings in the Registry Editor! You should *never* do this if there is an alternative. Do not change the LMAnnounce setting with the Registry Editor—change it from the Control Panel. Do not change the server size from the Registry Editor—change it from the Control Panel. Whenever you examine a setting in the Registry Editor and consider changing it, try to find an alternative way to change it first. And these ways are usually available in one of the Control Panel components on a Windows NT system.

In my opinion, there really *ought* to be a button associated with the Registry Editor that would examine the LMAnnounce parameter and tell you that it can be changed in Control Panel/Network Settings. And since that way of changing it is available, the ability to edit it directly ought to be disabled. There are, of course, circumstances in which you have no choice.

The Registry also allows you to configure systems *remotely.* From the Registry menu of the Registry Editor, you can perform a Select Computer, select another Windows NT server or workstation on the network, and edit that computer's Registry. If you want to set the LMAnnounce parameter remotely, that's the only way to do it. But this is something that must be done with extreme care—when you use the Registry Editor to make a parameter change, you run the risk of typing an illegal parameter, or deleting a value and not being able to remember what it is. Possibly the worst thing that you could do would be to delete a value; then wish to reestablish it—and reestablish the wrong type.

Suppose, for example, we delete the LMAnnounce parameter. Blindly looking at the registry Editor and thinking about the LM Announce parameter—remembering that it only has two possible states, on or off—we might very well tend to restore it as LMAnnounce type REG_SZ with a value of True or False. That would not work properly. Worse, it might cause the browser to malfunction, rendering the system unstable. We repeat: *Do not make parameter changes using the Registry unless you have no alternative.*

Registry Value Types

The types of entries that can be accepted in a Registry value include:

- ❑ *REG_DWORD*—A double-word value that can be represented as a decimal, hexadecimal, or binary number. By default, when displayed in the Registry, it will be displayed in hexadecimal format.

- ❑ *REG_SZ*—A Registry string value, and this will be a data string.

- ❑ *REG_EXPANDSZ*—A special string type used when you need to include environment variables within the string. For example, a legal REG_EXPANDSZ could contain the value *%system root%/SYSTEM32/whatever.* The *%system root%* environment variable will be expanded to the appropriate directory path at the time that the string is evaluated.

- ❑ *REG_MULTI_SZ*—A multiple string type. Double-clicking on a REG_MULTI_SZ value will bring up a multistring editor with scroll bars, allowing you to enter multiple strings, with one string on each line in the editor.

- ❑ Binary data is also supported in the Registry. This is represented as *REG_BINARY*, and the Binary Editor is necessary to edit it. Binary Editor can also be used to edit other types. It provides a bit-by-bit representation of the data similar to that used by the Dword Editor, with the binary type selected. You can use the Binary String Dword and Multistring options under the Edit menu in the Registry to select whether the Binary String Dword or Multistring Editor is used with a particular Registry entry; and all Registry entries are, in fact, 32-bit entries. Registry Names are not case sensitive, but they do preserve case and they are unicode compatible.

Registry Limits

One limitation of the current Windows NT Registry implementation is that it does not support *quotas*.[11]

That is, users and software applications and systems are not limited on what information can be entered into the Registry. This may change in future versions of Windows NT—and one hopes so, because one would not wish to exceed a system limit by adding and updating Registry information—and in fact there are some limits. By default, value entries in the Registry database cannot contain more than 1 megabyte of information, and the total size of the Registry is limited to 8MB.[12] Normal size in a small server will be more on the order of 1 to 2 megabytes, although this may expand dramatically as the number of users is increased.

One Last Time...

Finally, a reminder: The Registry is an extremely powerful tool. It's tremendously useful when properly controlled. But if you get in there and meddle around blindly you are going to mess up your system beyond repair. Treat it with care.

Troubleshooting Hit List

In any system as complex as Windows NT a broad range of errors and problems can occur. As we noted in Appendix 6, the potential for errors increase enormously when the system is networked. So it's impossible for us to present a comprehensive list of the errors you are likely to encounter, and directions for fixing them. Having said that, there are certain errors more likely to occur than others. What we present are some of the most frequently encountered errors,

---

11. Although the overall maximum size of the registry can now be controlled using Virtual Memory settings, as described previously.

12. As mentioned earlier, this can be set using Virtual Memory settings.

with suggestions about how to troubleshoot and fix them.[13] We've arranged them by general category.

Failure to Boot

In general, when a Windows NT system that has otherwise operated correctly suddenly refuses to boot (or recover from a reboot), you have to expect that one of two things has happened. Either there has been a major hardware failure or something has changed in the configuration. Major hardware failures or boot problems that occur when a system is first created are generally of the type that we covered in the "Troubleshooting" section of Chapter 2, and we urge you to look there.

Misconfigured System

It's worth remembering that many problems that appear to be due to boot failure can actually reflect misconfiguration—for instance, if you change the video type in Windows NT Setup to one that's not compatible with your particular hardware, you may have a completely successful boot (NT is still running) but find yourself looking at a blank screen. So the best initial step to take with *any* boot problem is to try selecting the previous configuration from the Last Known Good Configuration menu; or if that doesn't work, try using the Windows NT Emergency Diskette. Get the boot diskette originally supplied with Windows NT, insert it in drive A, reboot the computer, and when it asks whether you want to do an installation or attempt a repair, select Repair and insert the emergency disk. The odds are good that this will allow the system to *heal itself*—but if that doesn't work, some other boot problems that may occur include:

- ❑ *Unrecognized Partition Types and BOOT.INI*—When you install Windows NT on a system in which an unusual partitioning scheme is used, or a partition type is presented that Windows NT does not recognize, it is possible for Windows NT to install but for the system partition to be incorrectly identified—the boot subsystem may assume that system files are on partition 0 when they are in fact on partition 1, for instance. You should inspect the BOOT.INI file to make sure that it refers to the correct partition or logical disk drive and directory. You may also want to check

---

13. Information in this section is from a variety of sources, including the Microsoft online Knowledge Base (go MSKB on CompuServe), the Microsoft TechNet CD-ROM, reports from Windows NT users, and our own experience with Windows NT during the beta program. We can't claim to have personally experienced every problem (or tested every fix) reported here—but we've had quite a few!

and examine the arc system formatted syntax for the initial partition location. This will be in a format like:

```
SCSI(0)DISK(0)RDISK(0)PARTITION(1)\WINDOWS="Windows NT".
MULTI(0)DISK(0)RDISK(0)PARTITION(1)\WINDOWS="Windows NT".
```

(The format here is BUS(*number*)—where the bus can be SCSI or AT-bus; the latter represented by MULTI; the disk controller number—represented by DISK; the disk itself, represented by RDISK—where R stands for Rigit; and the PARTITION.)

PARTITION(1) is most likely to be the cause of a problem here; although, on some machines the controller, represented by DISK(0), could be the cause of the problem, as noted in the section on Installation. Try changing the partition number to 2 in this case (PARTITION(0) refers to the entire unpartitioned physical disk), or to another partition number, depending on the contents of your partition table (which can be examined using the *fdisk* program on DOS machines).

❑ *Boot NTLDR Not Found*—If for any reason the NTLDR file is deleted from the root of the C drive, Windows NT will be unable to boot. This can be cured by copying NTLDR back on the hard disk from the diskettes or from the CD.

❑ *NTDETECT.COM Deleted*—When Windows NT starts on x86 systems, it employs the NTDETECT.COM program to detect the hardware configuration on the system—which updates the hardware information in the Configuration Registry and begins to carry out the boot process. This insulates Windows NT from configuration errors that may occur when someone changes a hardware component. However, it also means that if NTDETECT.COM is deleted, the system will fail to boot, generally failing with a fatal general system error of 0x00000067-Configuration Initialization Failed. This can also indicate that an error has been introduced into the BOOT.INI file (an indicator for this is if an additional line appears in the BOOT.INI file besides those for NT and for any alternate operating systems that existed when NT was first installed). So this should be checked as well—but in the event that the BOOT.INI file is found to be correct, you will need to restore the NTDETECT.COM file from the installation CD or floppy disks.

❑ *Problems in the OS Loader*—In the event that the BOOT.INI is sufficiently correct for the OS to start loading but then presents a bad path, it's possible that the OS Loader blue screen will start but will then fail with one of these errors:

Could not read from the selected boot disk.

The system did not load because it could not find the following file: ...

Either of these errors, again, indicates a problem with the BOOT.INI file. A solution is to revert to an alternate operating system, boot from floppy disk, or on RISC machines use the built-in Monitor Program to inspect the disk directory structure and determine which directory or file has been marked incorrectly, and then manually edit the BOOT.INI file and try again.

□ *Failure to Boot Back to a Previous Operating System*—Windows NT uses a hidden file called BOOTSECT.DOS to store information about the physical layout of the hard disk so that the system can boot back into DOS (or other operating systems) from Windows NT. In the event that this file is inadvertently deleted or cannot be found during an attempt to boot to an alternate operating system, the boot process will fail with the message: Couldn't open boot sector file. Unfortunately, there isn't a good solution to this problem, because the file contains very specific information about the physical disk layout—which varies from machine to machine. If you have another machine with the *exact same physical disk, partitioning,* and *directory structure*, it *may* be possible to copy the BOOT-SECT.DOS file from that machine, install it on your machine, and the thing may boot back correctly. In the event that does not happen, your only solution is to revert to Windows NT, back off all the files, reformat the hard disk with the predecessor operating system, and start over (or live with the Windows NT-only installation).

□ *OS/2 Boot Manager Problems*—The Boot Manager that IBM supplies with OS/2 versions 2.0 and 2.1 attempts to perform very much the same functions that the Windows NT Flexboot performs. Unfortunately, each tends to compete with the other to a certain extent, so it's possible that a system that has been set up with the OS/2 Boot Manager will fail to operate properly after the Windows NT Flexboot has been installed. You can get around this problem by booting OS/2 from the installation disk, pressing Escape at the first opportunity to get to the OS/2 command line, bringing up the OS/2 fdisk, and reinstalling Boot Manager—adding entries for each of the bootable partitions in the system.

When Boot Manager is installed *after* the Windows NT Flexboot, it generally seems to operate correctly. OS/2 Boot Manager will give you the option either to boot DOS or OS/2—there won't be any mention of Windows NT, but don't fear! If you boot to DOS, you will then get the Windows NT Flexboot—giving you the option to use Windows NT or DOS. Another option is to avoid the use of the OS/2 Boot Manager entirely and instead use the OS/2 Dual Boot feature in conjunction with Windows NT—although this does not give the same flexibility in terms of booting from multiple partitions on the disk.

A related common problem with the OS/2 Boot Manager is that the Boot Manager and Windows NT Flexboot may disagree on which drive letters represent which partitions in the system. The simplest solution to this is to install the OS/2 Boot Manager in the *last* partition on the drive and put Windows NT on the *primary* (first) partition at the start of the drive. If this is done then both systems will agree on the drive letter assignments for all partitions (unless, of course, the "sticky drive letter" feature of Windows NT been used to modify the drive letters used with Windows NT).

CPU Problems

Generally, a problem with the Central Processor Unit in a Windows NT system will be detected during the installation process, and the system will fail to install properly. Again, there are a few things to watch out for. The first—which again is an installation problem—is to make sure you are installing on a CPU that supports NT. Windows NT requires a 25 MHz 386 or higher processor. Note that for the 386 processor it does not support version B1 and earlier 386 chips. If you have such a chip, you'll need a CPU upgrade.

Machine Check Exception on Pentium Chips

Windows NT machines equipped with Intel Pentium (P5) CPUs may experience a *machine check exception fault* during operation, particularly if they have been in heavy use over an extended period of time. A machine check exception on the Pentium processor chip is an indication that the processor self-test hardware has detected an internal fault. It most commonly indicates an overheating condition. This is not unknown on early model Pentium CPUs and it generally indicates a cooling problem in the system. The first solution, of course, is to turn off the computer and let it cool down. If the problem happens repeatedly, you may want to open up the case and make sure any on-chip cooling fan is operating and make sure that there isn't any obstruction in the airflow, and consider moving the system so that the airflow holes are not being obstructed by walls, desks, or other obstructions. Finally, contact your system manufacturer to see about some kind of an upgrade.

Poor CPU Performance

This is a topic that really refers back to the tuning section earlier in this chapter. If the computer is running but seems to be dead-slow, and the processor appears bogged with tasks that should not bog it, then you may want to check to see first if the *turbo switch* (if any) is depressed. Second, you may need to reboot the computer and examine the CMOS register settings to see if the computer is set for one or more memory wait states. A computer operating in a 1 wait-state condition effectively is operating at a half the stated CPU clock rate—because after every clock cycle involving a memory access it will idle or *wait* one cycle to give memory a chance to stabilize. In the event that your system is using one or more wait states, try resetting to a 0 wait-state condition. If the computer refuses to run, then your memory is physically incapable of operating at the processor full speed, and the solution is to buy faster memory chips. Beyond that, refer to the section on "Performance Tuning" earlier in this chapter for suggestions on how overall system throughput may be increased.

COM Port Problems

Attempting to Use One COM Port for Two Applications

Aside from the usual problems with improperly matched baud rate, parity, stop bits, and so forth, between an application and the device attached to a COM port, Windows NT presents one new class of problems. It absolutely, positively will *not* let you assign a COM port to another application or device when one is already using it.

You can see this by looking at the COM Port item in Control Panel. If you have a mouse installed on COM1 port for instance, then the COM1 port will not appear in the Control Panel listing even though it does exist in the system. The reason is that Windows NT has assigned the COM port permanently to the mouse, and it will not allow that port to be used by any other application or service until and unless the mouse releases it.

You can determine which COM ports are permanently assigned to physical devices in this way by inspecting the Windows NT Registry's HKEY_LO-CAL_MACHINE/hardware/descriptions/SYSTEMs/multifunction adapter/0/serial controller entry (this may say EISA adapter instead of multifunction adapter on EISA machines, etc.), as illustrated in Figure 5.8.

The COM port will be stored in a subkey numbered from 0 through 1 less than the number of COM ports; 0 through 3 respectively, for instance, represents COM1 through COM4. The device using the COM port will appear within the numbered subkey for the COM port in question. If no hardware device is using the COM port, the next thing to look for is the possibility that you have some application or service using the port.

An example of this would be if COM1 is physically attached to a modem and you attempt to use COM1 from a communications program at the same time that Remote Access Services (RAS) are running bound to COM1 through the network's Control Panel—Windows NT won't let you assign the port to the communications program. The solution to this is to stop RAS (or the other service in question) from using the Services applet in the Control Panel while you use the communications program, then close the communications program (or select another COM port temporarily) and start RAS again.

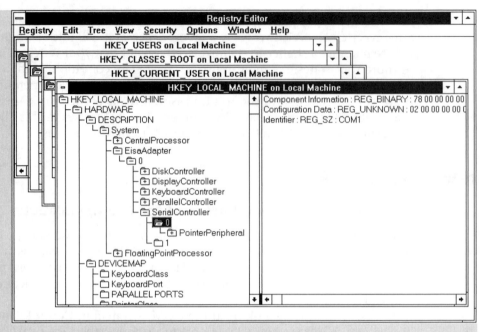

Figure 5.8 Registry Entry for Comm ports.

Determining which system component *owns* a commucications port can be extrememly confusing in Windows NT. You can find out by looking at the Registry Entry illustrated here, using the Registry Editor (REGEDT32.EXE). Note that the attachment of PointerPeripheral to the SerialController/0/ entry means that on this system a mouse is attached to the first Comm port (COM1).

Incompatible Hardware

Most other COM port problems will be either improper matches between the COM port settings and the external device, as mentioned previously, or in rare cases, you may run into a situation where a COM port is using a universal asynchronous receiver transmitter (UART) chip that is incompatible with Windows NT. The way to test for this is to attach a known good serial device (such as a dumb terminal or another computer running a terminal program) using a null-modem cable to the port; run the Windows terminal; select identical baud rates, parity settings, and word lengths on both ends of the connection; and then try typing on the Windows NT system's keyboard. If only one or two characters appears on the other screen, and then the port appears to hang up and refuse to transmit, you need a new UART chip. Machines known to have this problem include several models of DEC machines in the 300 and 400C series.

Some sytems with 16550 UART chips may be incompatible with NT's support for a FIFO buffer—if you have a 16550 and are experiencing COM port problems (you may note an event log entry saying A FIFO was detected and enabled), try disabling it with the Ports control panel applet (select the port in question, click Settings, then Advanced—and you'll find a FIFO check box).

COM3, COM4—COMn Problem

On machines that don't include a Micro-Channel adapter (MCA) bus—virtually all machines except IBM PS/2 computers—COM3 and COM4 support is provided by sharing the same interrupt as COM1 and COM2 with two different port addresses. That is, COM3 has the same interrupt number as COM1 but is at a different physical port address. COM4 is at the same interrupt level as COM2, but at a different port. This works fine until you try to use both COM1 and COM3 (or COM2 and COM4) at the same time. Windows NT supports interrupt sharing by the two sets of ports, but it cannot and will not permit devices to use the ports at the same time. As a result, you may find it impossible, for example, to attach modems to COM1 and COM3 and get two programs (for example, Remote Access Services and a terminal program or Microsoft Mail Remote) to work on both ports simultaneously. You can have one or the other, but not both.

Interrupt Conflicts

Just as Windows NT is intolerant of multiple applications or devices trying to share the same COM port, it is exceedingly intolerant of devices attempting to share an interrupt. In fact, the usual indication of an interrupt problem is the refusal of Windows NT to boot (on rare occasions, it can crash *after* booting correctly, during an attempt to perform a network login). The major symptom will be the Windows NT *blue screen* displaying error number 0x000000A: IRQ Expected to Be Less than or Equal. This indicates that two hardware devices in the system are set for the same interrupt level. It most probably will happen just after you've installed a network card or other physical device.

Remove the card that's most recently been installed and reboot the computer. Examine the hardware manufacturer's settings for the device and attempt to find an interrupt level that is not used by other devices. A common cause of this problem are interrupt cards that are predefined at IRQ3—the interrupt used by COM2 and COM4. Therefore, if you have a second COM port in your machine, IRQ3 is automatically disallowed. Common interrupts in most systems include:

- ❏ IRQ0 (timer)
- ❏ IRQ1 (keyboard)

- ❏ IRQ3 (COM2 and COM4)
- ❏ IRQ4 (COM1 and COM3)
- ❏ IRQ5 (LPT2)
- ❏ IRQ6 (floppy controllers)
- ❏ IRQ7 (line printer one)
- ❏ IRQ8 (system clock)
- ❏ IRQ13 (math coprocessor)
- ❏ IRQ14 (hard disk controller)
- ❏ IRQ15 (secondary disk controller)

You will need to select an interrupt number not used by any of these devices installed in your system.

Malfunctioning Disk Drives

Most common hard disk problems were covered in the section on installation problems in Chapter 2—check there. Aside from that, the problem that most frequently causes difficulties is failure to terminate a SCSI chain. Make sure that the last device in the chain is terminated, and that there is terminating power. Failing this, in the event that disk drives are misbehaving on Windows NT when they have been installed correctly and have been behaving themselves until now, you should check the BOOT.INI. Try reverting the configuration. Try using the emergency diskette. If none of that has any effect, then you probably have a disk hardware problem and need to employ conventional hardware troubleshooting techniques. Call your hardware manufacturer for details.

CD-ROM Problems

The most frequent CD-ROM difficulty with Windows NT is adding a CD-ROM into an installation that did not initially have a CD-ROM. Making Windows NT recognize the CD-ROM is fairly straightforward: Run the Control Panel Services applet, select the SCSI CD-ROM object, and set the startup value to automatic so that the service will start when the system boots. You may want to set the CD audio entry to automatic as well (for certain CD-ROMs, this may be required). And to avoid the necessity to restart Windows NT to get immediate benefit of the CD-ROM, you can, of course, start these services manually.

CD-ROM Impacting Windows NT Performance

Certain CD-ROM players, specifically including the NEC Intersect series players, may have a dramatic impact on Windows NT performance when the CD-ROM is playing. This will occur because of the setting of a jumper switch on the CD-ROM reader that disables disconnects during read operations. Disk read operations on CD-ROMs are very slow and if a disconnect is not available, then no other device has access to the SCSI interface card until the disk read is finished. Consult the hardware documentation for your CD-ROM reader and reset the jumper switch as necessary to enable disk connects during read operations.

Failure to Recognize Data on a CD

Windows NT supports the ISO9660 CD-ROM format but does not support any format extensions. A series of extensions known as the *Rock Ridge CD-ROM format* provide additional features that are used by CD-ROMs for some systems, in particular, UNIX systems that require long file names and a complex directory structure—and, unfortunately, the Macintosh Heirarchal File System (HFS) format. Windows NT's CD file system does not recognize these formats.

Printing Problems

Windows NT suffers from one unique set of printing problems in common with its COM port problems, which again arises out of the fact that only one device can own an interrupt. There are a number of sound cards, including the SoundBlaster Pro card, which by default use interrupt 7, the same interrupt that is typically used by the Line Printer 1 port. If Windows NT refuses to recognize a printer attached to LPT1, start a command line prompt and type *mode LPT1:* If you see the message Device Not Found, then IRQ7 is being subverted by another hardware device. You should be able to determine this using the System Registry in a manner similar to that previously described for communication ports. It will be necessary to either remove the offending device, change the settings on the device, or otherwise make an adaptation so that the interrupt conflict is eliminated.

Cross-Platform Network Printing

If RISC and Intel versions of Windows NT are mixed on a network, the usual Windows NT print driver approach, in which the remote printer takes advantage of the print driver installed, the print server will fail. The reason being that a MIPS RISC machine, for example, has no use for an Intel print driver. The indication will be an error message when you attempt to connect to the printer, saying that the server does not have a suitable print driver installed. You then have the option to make a temporary print driver installation on the local machine, or you can install print drivers for the other types on the print server.

For instance, if the print server is a RISC machine, you could install the Intel print driver. Alternatively, if the print server is an Intel machine, you could install one or more RISC drivers—as described in Chapter 2.

Network Problems

Disconnection

The most common symptom of a network card problem is that the user is unable to connect to the network. The most common cause is that the network cable is not plugged into the card. So, the first thing to do if you suspect a network card error is to check the connection between the network cable and the computer, and then the connection between the network cable and the wall. If it's a 10base2 (coax) EtherNet connection, check to make sure that the chain of connections isn't broken. The cable may be plugged in on the computer of the user who is reporting a problem, but it may be unplugged further down the line. Of course, this will usually be easy to spot—if such a break in a 10base2 cable exists, *all* users on that side of the break will be disconnected—not just one. But that good first step is to check and be sure everything's connected. The next step to take is to run the Windows NT Event Manager and look to see if it's reporting any network errors.

Misconfigured Network Card

If the network connection appears to be good and the other systems on the subnet are up, you'll need to check to see whether you have a hardware or software error. The easiest way to do this is with PING (on TCP/IP networks) or the *net send* command (on NetBIOS networks).[14] Use of PING is covered in a following section.

In either case, you will want to determine whether the computer is in fact talking to the network at all—from this you can then determine whether you have a software problem with misconfigured networking software, or a hardware problem in which the network is not working at all. In our experience the *net send* command is convenient for this, because it operates at a very low level on the system. You can reliably expect a *net send* command to tell you if the network is properly installed. If the network is installed and network commu-

---

14. In NT 3.1, it was possible to use *net send /BROADCAST* text without designating a target. This functionality has been removed from NT 3.5 and later versions. Assuming that you know the name of any one machine on the net, you can achieve the same effect with *net send MachineName text* or *net send /domain:domainname text*—for instance: *net send mips1 just testing* should print "just testing" on \\mips1—assuming nothing's broken.

nications exist, but the computer is not being logged in to the network properly, the *net send* will still reach the designated target system. For instance:

```
net send mips1 Can anyone hear me?
```

will print the message Can anyone hear me? in a pop-up window on the mips1 workstations or server. A second possibility is that *net send* will not give an indication on the target but will return with the message The message was successfully sent to MIPS1. In this case, the low-level Windows NT software, driver, and transporter are all working properly—they are getting proper indications from the card—but for some reason the transmission is not getting out on the network. This indicates that the network cable is bad, and the signal is being blocked somewhere outside of the computer.

TCP/IP Misconfiguration

If DHCP is not in use, inability to *see* hosts on TCP/IP networks may indicate that the HOSTS or LMHOSTS database files (described in Chapter 6) contain bad information. Try acessing a local host (or router) using the TCP/IP *ping* utility, *using the four—number IP address of the host (or router) in question.* The syntax of the command is *ping <ip-address>*, that is: *ping 127.119.13.213* for a node with address 127.119.13.213. Do *not* use a ping to a DNS or HOSTS name (at least, not at first) because this may not be definitive; for instance, the command *ping vax.cmp.com* will evaluate to the same command as ping 127.119.13.213 if and *only* if the vax.cmp.com DNS name properly evaluates to 127.119.12.213. By contrast, pinging "by the numbers" is an absolute—if it gives you no response, then there is a very deep configuration problem.

If a "by the numbers" ping gives a response, try a ping to the name. If that doesn't work, then check the Name Resolution settings in Control Panel/Networks TCP/IP Configuration to see whether DNS or HOSTS naming is in use, and then check the status of the DNS server (or HOSTS file), as appopriate.

If both pings work, but you still can't *see* the system in question using the built-in Windows NT networking, then check the LMHOSTS file settings, and the settings of any intervening routers. A useful diagnostic for systems that use Windows NT at each end may be to run the FTP Server Service on one end, and attempt FTP client access from the other. If that works, then the low-level linkage (and router if any) are properly set up, and the problem *must* lie with the LMHOSTS database or Windows NT domain settings.

Unfortunately, the TCP/IP settings files (HOSTS, LMHOSTS, etc.) are *not* part of the Windows NT configuration registry, so restoring a Last Known Good Configuration won't help in this situation—you'll have to figure out the problem using *ping*, and correct the problem by editing the files with a text editor.

Once you've done so, *save a backup copy* so that you won't have to go through the same experience the next time something changes!

Hardware (Interrupt) Problems

It is quite common to experience network problems on Windows NT machines if the network card is set to interrupt level 3. Normally, Interrupt 3 is used by the COM2 port and since Windows NT does not permit interrupt sharing if a network card is designated to use Interrupt 3, there are two possibilities: One is that you will see the infamous blue screen when NT boots up with Error 0x0000000A—IRQ expected to be less than or equal. This is the most severe version (the other case is that NT starts but the network refuses to run). In either case, take the network card out and reset it to a new IRQ setting. You'll also have to change the IRQ setting for the card in question in Control Panel/Networks.

It's possible that the computer will boot but the network card will refuse to function. In this case, again, you need to shut down the computer, take out the card, change the settings on the card, bring up the computer, change the settings on the Network Control Panel applet, and then shut down and restart Windows NT—and it should work. If it's not an interrupt problem and the network cables are believed to be good, then you need to begin troubleshooting procedures to determine whether you in fact have any connectivity to the network card, and try to determine where the break is occurring. This can be done using the *ping* application on TCP/IP networks or the *net send* on NetBEUI and other SMB networks.

On rare occasions, there are network cards with programmable interrupt and I/O settings in which the low-level network software can see what appears to be a perfectly good network connection, yet will not work initially. It may be worth trying the following procedure: Perform a warm boot by shutting down Windows NT and selecting the Restart; when shutdown is complete, switch and then try *net send* again. If it operates correctly after the reboot, then you have a network card that requires two passes to set the software configurations. You may want to consider reconfiguring the card with a hardware configuration (if that's possible), or you may need to tell the user that when he starts up in the morning he's going to have to do a warm boot before he can expect to see his network.

If *net send* reports that the message is not being sent because of a network problem, this invariably indicates that an error in the binding of the low-level network software to the network card. This *should* be accompanied by an entry in the System Event Log. (You did check the log, didn't you?) But in any case, the problem is a low-level one. It indicates that, for whatever reason, the software is not recognizing the card. This may mean that you're using the wrong driver for the particular network card you have, or that the network card may be misconfigured. In any case, take a close look at the network card. Verify that the network settings match the settings in the Network Control Panel. Verify that you are using the correct driver, and try again.

Sound Card Problems

As with network cards, the most usual symptom for sound board problems is the user reporting that no sound comes out of the speakers; again, as with network cards, the first thing to do is check to see that there is a speaker plugged in, that the speaker has power, that the speaker volume is turned up, and that in all other respects you have a situation in which sound should be coming from the computer. If it is not, then you may want to look at the following things:

- *Is the sound driver installed?* This may sound simple-minded, but Windows NT does not install sound drivers during installation by default, so you will very likely have to install a sound driver for each system. You do this through the Control Panel Sound Driver's applet. Check to make sure that you are using the right driver for the right sound card. In particular, with Creative Labs SoundBlaster cards you have to be careful, because there are several different versions of the SoundBlaster and the drivers are not interchangeable. For example, the driver for a SoundBlaster Pro will not work with a SoundBlaster version 1.

- *Do you have an interrupt conflict?* Check the interrupt and port settings that are set in the driver's applet and make sure they match the settings on the audio card. (Note the fact that the SoundBlaster by default uses IRQ7. This is also the setting for LPT1 and, as noted elsewhere, Windows NT does not tolerate interrupt overloading—so it is likely that if you've installed a SoundBlaster card and it refuses to work that you'll have to change the interrupt.) If you can play .WAV files (an easy way to check this is with the Control Panel Sound applet setting system sounds on and using the test button) but you can't play .MID (MIDI) files, then you may need to install the ad-lib MIDI driver. Because most sound boards have two independent audio chips on them, one for MIDI synthesis and one for wave audio, two drivers are typically required.

- If you are using a *Windows sound system* and have upgraded from Windows 3.1 or Windows for Workgroups, you may see the message: SOUND.CPL is not a valid Windows NT Image, and find that the Control Panel is not working properly. That's because the SOUND.CPL file installed by Windows is incompatible with Windows NT.

- As we noted in the section on CD-ROMs and SCSI, there are a number of sound card manufacturers who incorporate a *proprietary* CD-ROM interface on the sound card. Windows NT supports most of the common ones, either with built-in drivers, or ones from the installation's CD's DRIVERS library. See Chapter 2 for details.

Video Problems

The most common video problem arises when a user changes the video settings using Windows NT Setup to try to get a higher resolution, and is suddenly presented with an image that is either grossly unstable or completely blank. The solution in either case is the same. Restart Windows NT going through the shutdown procedure if you can (this is one case where pressing the reset switch may be your *only* option). When Windows NT starts, it will start with the character mode startup, which ordinarily will survive a change in video resolution and will present you with a Press Escape for Last Known Good Menu option. Immediately hit the Escape key and select Last Known Good Configuration. Hopefully, if the user has not repeatedly modified the installation (which is almost impossible with a video problem), this will get you back to the working video.

Another common problem with video drivers occurs when a user installs a new video board without resetting the driver—in which case, the only response is to use the VGA mode boot option, and then install the proper driver.

The Messages Database

Windows NT can produce a variety of messages during its normal operation, along with a wide range of error messages. If you purchase a Windows NT Server, then you will receive a Messages Guide, and you also can get the same information from the Windows NT Resource Kit. All CD versions of Windows NT include the Messages database in a runtime Microsoft Access format (which is one of the reasons we recommend having at least one CD-ROM available on *all* Windows NT networks).

The runtime Messages Database application is found in the SUP-TOOLS\WINNTMSG directory of the CD-ROM, and includes a Windows-based setup program that will automatically install the messages database on your hard disk. By installing the database on a server, and then sharing the database directories, you can enable remote users to access the database; and this is by far the most convenient way to get access to the Windows NT system messages. Incidentally, the runtime Access software used with the Messages Database is accessible not only from Windows NT systems, but also from Windows 3.1 and Windows for Workgroups systems—which may be convenient for support professionals.

You need not access the database from a Windows NT Workstation. To install the messages database on your Windows NT Server, insert the Windows NT distribution CD-ROM in the CD-ROM drive, and start a character mode command line; from the command line, find the disk that represents the CD-ROM—for example, disk D—and type the following:

CD d:\suptools\winntmsg

start setup.

The Windows NT Messages setup program will start. It will ask whether you want to join an existing workgroup for the server installation. Answer No. It will then propose a directory for the database to be set up, which you can change to another directory if you wish, and will carry out the setup for you automatically. To make the database accessible from other systems (including Windows NT systems, Windows for Workgroups systems, and Windows systems), simply go to File Manager and select the directory in which you installed the database, and share it on the network.

To access the database from other machines, it will be necessary to set up the Access runtime query engine on the other machine. To do this, you use File Manager and the Windows for Workgroups machine; whereas on a Windows NT machine, you will use File Manager to establish a virtual disk drive connected to the directory where you shared the database, and then from that directory run the setup program. This time when it asks if you want to join an existing workgroup, answer Yes and it will go on from there. An incidental point is that you could in fact set up the database on a Windows for Workgroups machine or a LAN Manager machine. It doesn't necessarily have to be stored on a Windows NT server.

Windows NT System Messages

As noted in the start of this section, Windows NT can produce a broad range of messages indicating system status or system errors. One of the most important functions that an administrator or support professional must carry out is determining the meaning of these messages and taking the necessary corrective action. The easiest way to do this is to use the Messages database included on the Windows NT CD-ROM, whose installation we just discussed. It is then necessary to perform a database search only for the particular message number or for some fragment of the message text to receive a detailed description of the message, along with recommendations for corrective actions.

Alternatively, if you have a Windows NT Server, you can look up the message in the Windows NT Server Messages manual, or if you have purchased the Windows NT Resource Kit you can look the messages up in Volume 3. In any case, the exact details of the messages and how to deal with them are beyond the scope of this book. We will present here only a brief introduction, describing the types of messages you may have to deal with and giving some general suggestions for how to quickly get the information and quickly take corrective action when such a message appears.

Character Mode, Stop, and Hardware Malfunction Messages

The ultimate worst-case situation you have to deal with in Windows NT is the blue screen crash. This happens when the Windows NT kernel encounters a completely unrecoverable error either in the kernel software or in the hardware. The system will stop and display a screen similar to that illustrated in Figure 5.9.

In a blue screen crash, the first line displayed on the screen will generally be of the form

```
*** STOP 0x000000nn DESCRIPTION
```

The 0x000...number is a unique hexadecimal identifier that identifies the STOP message number and will indicate the cause of the crash. The text immediately following it is a text description of the crash. This will be followed by a system trace, including an identification of the address areas in which the crash occurred, register dump, and a system call tree, indicating the various functions that are in the tree of system calls above the function in which the crash occurred. They are of value only to a system developer or hardware support engineer, but if the same crash occurs repeatedly, it may be worth writing it down—in particular the first two or three lines of information on the screen so that the information can be presented when Tech Support is called. The follow-up to a blue screen crash is generally going to involve making a change to the hardware settings in the system, removing hardware devices from the system, or other relatively drastic steps. The list of troubleshooting problems and work-arounds in this chapter will give some suggestions for certain well-known errors, such as the 0x0000000A IRQL problem, but the nature of this kind of crash is that it's pretty serious.

Hardware Malfunctions

If a low-level hardware problem occurs on a system at such a level that Windows NT kernel cannot handle it at all (technically, a nonmaskable interrupt, or NMI), then you're likely to see a message beginning "Hardware malfunction..." and ending "...call your hardware vendor for support." And the message says it all—call the vendor.

Status and Warning Messages

These messages will appear as a Windows alert and will generally indicate some specific matter of concern for the system. They may simply indicate some piece

```
*** STOP: 0xFF729E90 (0x00000000, 0x00000000, 0x00000000, 0x00000000)

eax=ffdff13c ebx=80100000 ecx=00000003 edx=80100000 esi=ffdff13c edi=00000000
eip=00000000 esp=00000000 ebp=00000000  p4=0300      nv up ei ng nz na po nc
cr0=00000000 cr2=00000000 cr3=00000000 cr4=ffdff13c irql:1f DPC  efi=00000000
gdtr=80036000   gdtl=03ff idtr=80036400   idtl=07ff tr=0028  ldtr=0000

Dll Base DateStmp - Name            Dll Base DateStmp - Name
80100000 2c51c0b2 - ntoskrnl.exe    80400000 2c3b5c01 - hal.dll
80400000 2c3b5c01 - hal.dll         80100000 2c51c0b2 - ntoskrnl.exe
80100000 2c51c0b2 - ntoskrnl.exe    80400000 2c3b5c01 - hal.dll
80100000 2c51c0b2 - ntoskrnl.exe    80400000 2c3b5c01 - hal.dll
80400000 2c3b5c01 - hal.dll         80100000 2c51c0b2 - ntoskrnl.exe
80400000 2c3b5c01 - hal.dll         80100000 2c51c0b2 - ntoskrnl.exe
80400000 2c3b5c01 - hal.dll         80100000 2c51c0b2 - ntoskrnl.exe
80100000 2c51c0b2 - ntoskrnl.exe    80400000 2c3b5c01 - hal.dll
80100000 2c51c0b2 - ntoskrnl.exe    80400000 2c3b5c01 - hal.dll
80100000 2c51c0b2 - ntoskrnl.exe    80400000 2c3b5c01 - hal.dll
80100000 2c51c0b2 - ntoskrnl.exe    80400000 2c3b5c01 - hal.dll
80400000 2c3b5c01 - hal.dll         80100000 2c51c0b2 - ntoskrnl.exe
80100000 2c51c0b2 - ntoskrnl.exe    80400000 2c3b5c01 - hal.dll
80100000 2c51c0b2 - ntoskrnl.exe    80400000 2c3b5c01 - hal.dll

Address  dword dump   Build [v1 511]                 - Name
80100000 2c51c0b2 80100000 2c51c0b2 80100000 2c51c0b2 80100000 - ntoskrnl.exe
80100000 2c51c0b2 80100000 2c51c0b2 80100000 2c51c0b2 80100000 - ntoskrnl.exe
80100000 2c51c0b2 80100000 2c51c0b2 80100000 2c51c0b2 80100000 - ntoskrnl.exe
80100000 2c51c0b2 80100000 2c51c0b2 80100000 2c51c0b2 80100000 - ntoskrnl.exe
80100000 2c51c0b2 80100000 2c51c0b2 80100000 2c51c0b2 80100000 - ntoskrnl.exe
80100000 2c51c0b2 80100000 2c51c0b2 80100000 2c51c0b2 80100000 - ntoskrnl.exe
80100000 2c51c0b2 80100000 2c51c0b2 80100000 2c51c0b2 80100000 - ntoskrnl.exe
80100000 2c51c0b2 80100000 2c51c0b2 80100000 2c51c0b2 80100000 - ntoskrnl.exe
80100000 2c51c0b2 80100000 2c51c0b2 80100000 2c51c0b2 80100000 - ntoskrnl.exe
80400000 2c3b5c01 80400000 2c3b5c01 80400000 2c3b5c01 80400000 - hal.dll
80400000 2c3b5c01 80400000 2c3b5c01 80400000 2c3b5c01 80400000 - hal.dll
80400000 2c3b5c01 80400000 2c3b5c01 80400000 2c3b5c01 80400000 - hal.dll
80400000 2c3b5c01 80400000 2c3b5c01 80400000 2c3b5c01 80400000 - hal.dll
80400000 2c3b5c01 80400000 2c3b5c01 80400000 2c3b5c01 80400000 - hal.dll
80400000 2c3b5c01 80400000 2c3b5c01 80400000 2c3b5c01 80400000 - hal.dll
80400000 2c3b5c01 80400000 2c3b5c01                   - hal.dll

Kernel Debugger Using: COM2 (Port 0x2f8, Baud Rate 19200)
Restart your computer. If this message reappears, do not restart,
Contact your system administrator or technical support group, and/or
peripheral device vendor.
```

Figure 5.9 Blue screen crash.

You should *never* see this display from Windows NT under normal circumstances—if you do, then the system has become completely unstable and will require a hardware reboot. The *** STOP 0x000000...message will identify the type of error involved, and is followed by a register dump that can be helpful in identifying what's gone wrong with the system.

of system information that is of general interest, such as Password too complex. They may warn of a problem with some components of the system, such as a Printer Out Of Paper message. They may indicate a more serious problem, such as the Access Denied message that indicates that an application has tried to do something for which it doesn't have the necessary security permissions.

Network Messages

Errors that occur within the network components of Windows NT and Windows NT Server will be identified as network errors and will have a four-digit number associated with them. In addition to the messages database, you can get a brief description of each error by typing *net helpmsg* and the message number; for instance:

```
C:\nwnt>net helpmsg 2102

The workstation driver is not installed.

EXPLANATION

Windows NT is not installed, or your configuration file is incorrect.

ACTION

Install Windows NT, or see your network administrator about possible
problems with your configuration file.
```

But the information in the NT messages database will be far more complete. To get the equivalent information from the NT messages database that you'd get from typing *net helpmsg*, start the messages database (by clicking on the Microsoft Windows NT Messages icon in the Microsoft Windows NT Messages group in Program Manager) and click the Find button, enter the network error number (such as 2102) in the Find field in the Search for field, and from the pop-up list of items to look at, select Net Message ID. Once you have the Net message ID field selected and the number typed in, click the OK button. The database will conduct a search and will then give you all of the relevant database records containing information about that error number (see Figure 5.10).

Other Maintenance Issues

Aside from the basic troubleshooting situations covered earlier in the text, there are some additional matters that may be of concern to the NT system adminis-

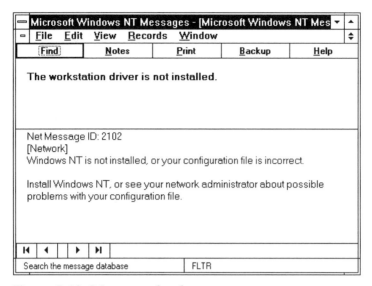

Figure 5.10 Messages database.

A runtime Microsoft Access database is provided on the Windows NT CD-ROM that contains definitions for all messages generated by the system. It can be run either locally or over the network—and doesn't require Windows NT as an over-the-network client.

trator or maintenance professional. The most common such concerns include disk fragmentation, update of the NT emergency diskette, accidental deletion of files, and recovery from server crashes.

Disk Fragmentation

Since NT was first introduced, Microsoft's position on disk fragmentation has been: 1) use NTFS because it doesn't require defragmenting; 2) if you run a DOS-compatible FAT partition, boot DOS and use a DOS-based defragmenter (or an OS/2 defragmeter on HPFS patitions); 3) as a last resort, back everything up on tape, reformat your disk, and restore the tape.

Of course, NTFS does in fact require defragmentation—we've seen a 2:1 performance improvement by using the third approach above to defragment heavily used machines, and other users (especially those running heavily used servers) report much the same results.

As it happens, this isn't the first time Dave Cutler and his ex-Digital crew have missed the boat on fragmentation. Cutler's VMS operating system had much the same problem on VAX computers, and Executive Software eventually filled the gap with a line of *Diskeeper* products.[15] In 1994 they brought the same technology to NT with *Diskeeper for Windows NT*, which is in beta as this is written. (The product manager assures us it will be shipping long before you read this!)

Making and Updating Boot and Emergency Repair Diskettes

You cannot create an old-fashioned, DOS-style boot into character mode for Windows NT, but you can nonetheless boot the operating system from a floppy (although the NT systems files will still have to load from the hard disk), which can be a lifesaver if the boot sector on your hard disk accidentally gets overwritten. This can be done using the NT installation diskette—or you can make a boot diskette.[16]

To do so, first format the floppy from NT, then (on Intel machines) copy the following files: NTLDR, NTDETECT.COM, BOOT.INI, and NTBOOTDD.SYS (they're hidden files—you'll have to use the ATTRIB command-line utility or the Show Hidden/System Files option in File Manager). On RISC machines, format the floppy and copy OSLOADER.EXE, HAL.DLL and JZSETUP.EXE.

If you add the NT version of CHKDSK.EXE and a copy of *WINDOWS Magazine*'s DISKEDIT.EXE (mentioned in the following) perhaps augmented with the Resource Kit's REGBACK and REGREST utilities, you'll have a crash diskette that *may* let you recover in situations where the NT emergency disk won't work.

Of course, a good support person covers all the bases—so having *both* a boot diskette *and* an emergency disk is a good idea. The latter is normally created during the NT setup process, but if you need to make one later (or update the data on the original—a good idea, especially after installing any software packages), you can use the RDISK utility provided with NT versions from 3.5 on (see Figure 5.11).

WARNING! If the Emergency Disk was created during the installation process and never updated, it contains the original Registry settings for the computer—which most likely will include only default user accounts. Restoring the Registry from such a diskette will destroy any user accounts created after the installation—and since NTFS tracks directory permissions based on security access rights, it can make accessing data impossible as well.

---

15. They can be contacted at 818-547-2050.

16. Much as it pains me, I have to give credit for this idea to Mark Minasi, who first described the procedure in his *Mastering Windows NT Server 3.5* (Sybex, 1994).

```
┌──────────────────────────────────────────────────────────────────┐
│ ▬                        Repair Disk Utility                    ▼ │
├──────────────────────────────────────────────────────────────────┤
│  ┌──┐   This utility updates the repair information saved when you installed the system, │
│  │👤│   and creates an Emergency Repair disk. The repair information is used to │
│  └──┘   recover a bootable system in case of failure. │
│                                                                    │
│                                                                    │
│  ┌──────────────────┐ ┌──────────────────┐ ┌────────────┐ ┌────────────┐ │
│  │ Update Repair Info│ │ Create Repair Disk│ │    Exit    │ │    Help    │ │
│  └──────────────────┘ └──────────────────┘ └────────────┘ └────────────┘ │
└──────────────────────────────────────────────────────────────────┘
```

Figure 5.11 Repair Disk utility.
The Windows Nt RDISK utility allows you to create—or update—an NT emergency repair diskette. Used in conjunction with a boot diskette, this allows recovery from a variety of serious system errors.

Undeleting Files

There are currently no simple undelete programs for NT available. However, there are three approaches that *may* retrieve an accidentally deleted file. First, if you're using the DOS-compatible FAT file system, you can boot your computer to DOS (either using NT multiboot or a DOS boot diskette) and use DOS undelete software (likewise, on HPFS partitions you may be able to use an OS/2 boot diskette and OS/2 undelete software).

Alternatively, try the DiskEdit application from the *WINDOWS Magazine* NT Disk Tools beta.[17] While this doesn't provide a simple undelete, it does provide a way to search the disk for data on *any* partition type, including NTFS. Finally, you can always restore a file from backup—provided you've been keeping regular backups.

Crash Recovery

Windows NT is a very reliable operating system, but it *can* crash due to errant drivers, hardware problems, or—rarely—undetected operating system (or application) bugs. Beginning with NT 3.5, you have some options for handling such crashes. The most important of these is the Recovery settings, controlled by the Control Panel's System object. Clicking the Recovery button on that object brings up the dialog shown in Figure 5.12.

The most obvious of these options is, of course, the one to automatically reboot after a crash. This would seem to be the obvious setting for servers, and in many cases, it is—but with a caution: If whatever problem caused the server

---

17. The NT disk tools can be downloaded from any of the addresses from the *Electronic Update* section of the Introduction.

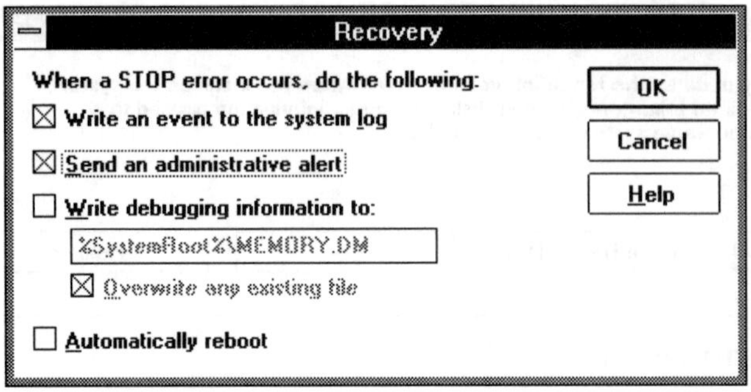

Figure 5.12 Recovery.
Beginning with version 3.5, Windows NT provides recovery options that may be used to control how an NT system behaves during and after a system crash.

to crash in the first place reccurs, you can put your server into an infinite loop: reboot, crash, reboot, crash....

Obviously, you should enable the options to write a system event (and possibly to send an administrative alert) if you're enabling the automatic reboot feature. Enabling the memory dump feature can also help—though decoding it will most likely require cooperation from a Microsoft support engineer.

Incidentally, the crash recovery behavior of NT is controlled—like so much else—through the configuration Registry. The HKEY_LOCAL_MACHINE\SYSTEM\CurrentControlSet\Control\CrashControl key contains entries that match all the control panel settings. As we've said before, making these settings in Control Panel is preferable to making them directly in the Registry—but if you're managing several servers on a LAN or WAN, you may find it simpler to set them using the Registry Editor.

Other Tools

The Windows NT Resource Kit includes a wide range of maintenance and support tools, including tools to back up and restore Registry files, monitor browser and domain servers, and even upgrade the single-CPU version of NT to a multiprocessing version. (The hardware, needless to say, is not included!) These are covered in Appendix 4.

Microsoft Systems Management Server (SMS) provides a wide variety of troubleshooting and maintenance tools, along with remote software installation/upgrade capability. It's primarily of interest to larger sites and is covered in Chapter 7. That's also where we cover troubleshooting and maintenance of Microsoft's Remote Access Services (RAS) and other wide-area networking issues.

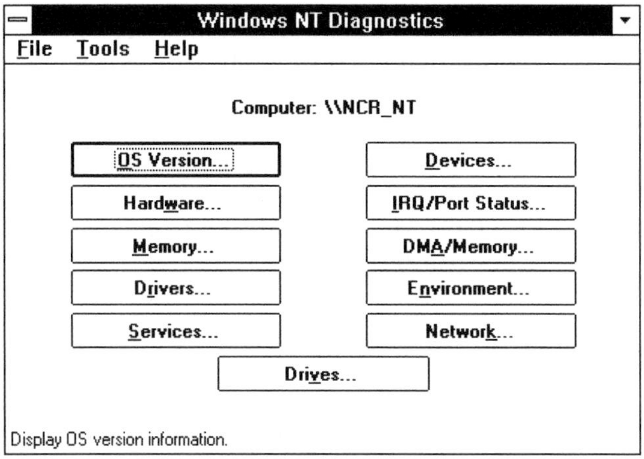

Figure 5.13 Microsoft system diagnostics.

Windows NT includes a Windows-based system diagnostics application as a standard component.

Microsoft System Diagnostics (MSD)

One of the most overlooked tools for troubleshooting NT systems ships with all versions of NT.[18] It is a 32-bit version of Microsoft's standard System Diagnostics (MSD) program. NT's version of MSD is actually implemented as a Windows application with a graphical interface (see Figure 5.13), and is therefore named WINMSD.EXE.

The graphical interface is useful for browsing, and gives an instantaneous view of information, including the NT revision, build number, and type; hardware configuration; memory (both physical and virtual); peripheral devices and drivers; services, including networks; and disks. You can also save or print a complete report.

How to Get NT Tech Support

There are times when even the best technician is in over his head, and it's time to call in the support engineers. Unfortunately, where NT is concerned, calling for support can be expensive. Microsoft provided 30 days of free support for installation problems with NT 3.1, but dropped all free support in NT 3.5.

The minimum level of support from Microsoft for all versions of NT is now $150 per incident (what Microsoft calls *priority support*.) Microsoft justifies this

---

18. We missed it completely in the first edition of this book!

by calling NT a Business Systems product rather than a personal product—but it seems excessive for NT Workstation. Fortunately, Unisys offers a $30 per-call support program for setup problems—and they cover all versions of NT on all platforms.[19]

Larger organizations that want to purchase a support contract or one of Microsoft's higher-end Premier support options should call Microsoft Product Support Services at 800-426-9400. Microsoft can also refer you to a local *solution provider* if you prefer to deal with someone in your area.

Summary and Conclusions

We've reviewed the basic principles of preventative maintenance (PM—covered in detail in Appendix 6), examined the steps necessary for performance tuning in a Windows NT system, reviewed the tools used for tuning and troubleshooting, and presented a list of the most likely problems—and their solutions. Hopefully, with this information at your disposal, you'll have a good idea of how to proceed when you're presented (inevitably) with your first Windows NT system crash—but we reiterate that it's *far* better to apply PM principles and avoid the crash altogether!

For More Information

Microsoft Staff (1993-1995), *Windows NT System Guide*. Redmond WA: Microsoft Corp. Includes a brief section on network errors and troubleshooting.

Microsoft Staff, *TechNet CD*. Redmond WA: Microsoft Product Support Services (PSS). TechNet is a monthly publication on CD-ROM containing a digest of topics from the Microsoft Knowlege Base, the *Net News* publication, Resource Kits, and other information. TechNet is available from Microsoft sales—a one-year subscription (12 CDs) costs $295 and is worth every penny.

Microsoft Staff (1993, 1995), *Windows NT Resource Kit, Volumes 1-4*. Redmond WA: Microsoft Press. The *only* source for detailed information on the Windows NT configuration Registry, and the best source of information on such topics as performance monitor counters.

Microsoft Staff (1995), *Windows NT Training*, Redmond WA: Microsoft Press. This is a two-volume set with a video and diskettes, covering Windows NT support and troubleshooting issues. It's marketed as a self-paced training guide for professionals studying to take the Microsoft Certified Professional (MCP) examinations.

---

19. Call 800-328-0440.

CHAPTER 6

Connecting to the World with TCP/IP

After reading this chapter, you should understand the basic elements of NT's TCP/IP services and how to install and configure them. You should also be able to build a Windows NT-based network using TCP/IP as the primary transport, and have a basic understanding of the TCP/IP applications provided with NT and how to use them to connect to UNIX and other TCP/IP hosts. If you're unfamiliar with TCP/IP concepts, such as addressing, subnet masks, and routing, you should read the TCP/IP section of Appendix 2 before proceeding.

TCP/IP is an extremely flexible set of protocols, and Microsoft has put that to its advantage by including the basic protocol suite with NT. You can take advantage of NT's TCP/IP capabilities in many ways, or in many combinations of ways. You can:

❑ Run Windows NT network services over TCP/IP, either instead of or in conjunction with NetBEUI.

❑ Use TCP/IP-specific utilities (such as Telnet and FTP) to communicate with NT and non-NT systems alike, either instead of or in conjunction with the NetBIOS-based built-in Windows NT networking.

There are two basic areas of operations where NT's TCP/IP support can be used. The primary method will be as a routable transport protocol for Windows NT networks. If you're unable to utilize NetBEUI in complex environments, then you will naturally turn to the built-in

281

support for TCP/IP as a way to get the most use of NT's networking capabilities. The secondary use of NT's TCP/IP support will be in heavily mixed environments (especially UNIX environments) that rely on TCP/IP-specific applications for host access. In this case you may or may not be using NT's built-in NetBEUI-based network services.

Among the sections in this chapter, "Installing and Configuring TCP/IP" covers the details of configuring NT to use TCP/IP, regardless of what upper-layer network services you plan to use with it. "Using TCP/IP with Windows NT's Built-In Networking" covers the issues specific to that environment. Finally, the section titled "Using Windows NT TCP/IP Utilities" introduces applications and services, such as Telnet.

The Network Stack

In NT's modular network design, each component acts like a LEGO® block, providing stubs and sockets for interacting with other components. Figure 6.1 shows a basic overview of the networking modules of NT. Since the uppermost layer for most of the bundled applications is geared toward NetBIOS, it is the most important layer from an end user's perspective. Applications, such as Chat, NetDDE, ClipBook, and Messenger, all rely on NetBIOS. If you wish to use any

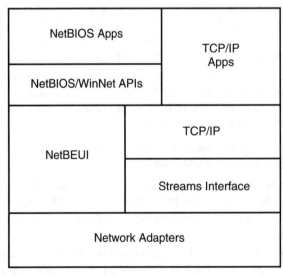

Figure 6.1 A high-level view of NT's network architecture.

of these services (or the Windows NT Workstation or Server), then you must have the NetBIOS interface installed. If you don't need these services, or if your applications are strictly TCP/IP-based, then you do not need the NetBIOS interface. Almost everyone will use the NetBIOS services, however, since most of NT's network functionality is dependent upon them.

As shown in Figure 6.1, the NetBIOS service can be bound to the TCP/IP protocol stack, allowing these applications to run across WANs and complex LANs. The result is known as NetBIOS-on-TCP/IP, or NBT. NetBIOS is not a *routable* protocol, meaning that it can communicate only with other devices on the same network segment. TCP/IP, however, is fully routable, allowing systems to communicate across just about any medium, from serial lines to satellite links. Since NBT rides on TCP/IP (technically, the NetBIOS packets are encapsulated within TCP/IP), NBT is routable to a limited degree.

Since NetBIOS is the protocol that applications use, there must be some way for TCP/IP to make NetBIOS act as though remote nodes were local. Likewise, there must be a facility for NetBIOS to hand TCP/IP a destination address that both can understand. NetBIOS uses workstation *names* to identify devices, an approach that works well in the small network environments for which Net-BIOS was designed. TCP/IP, however, uses 32-bit binary addresses (most commonly represented by four 8-bit digits), providing a large and flexible address space for large and complex networks.

The process of converting NetBIOS names into IP addresses used to be managed with a text database called LMHOSTS. With NT 3.5, however, the name resolution can be handled by a variety of mechansims, which we will discuss in detail later in this chapter. For now, let's move into installing the TCP/IP protocols.

Installing and Configuring TCP/IP

Beginning with Windows NT 3.5, Microsoft has made it easier to install TCP/IP support. However, they did this by robbing you of some configurability. With previous versions of NT, you could choose not to install some components to free up system memory (if you didn't need to bind NetBIOS to TCP/IP, you could choose not to install the NetBIOS Interface, for example). However, with NT 3.5 all of these previously separable options are installed whether you want them or not. Since 3.5's overall performance is much better than 3.1's, this isn't really all that big of a deal.

Also, NT 3.5 has a whole lot more TCP/IP stuff in it. There are still many choices that you have to make before you install TCP/IP onto your system, however, and we'll review each of the major areas throughout the rest of this chapter. It is strongly recommended that you read the rest of this chapter before you install the TCP/IP Services.

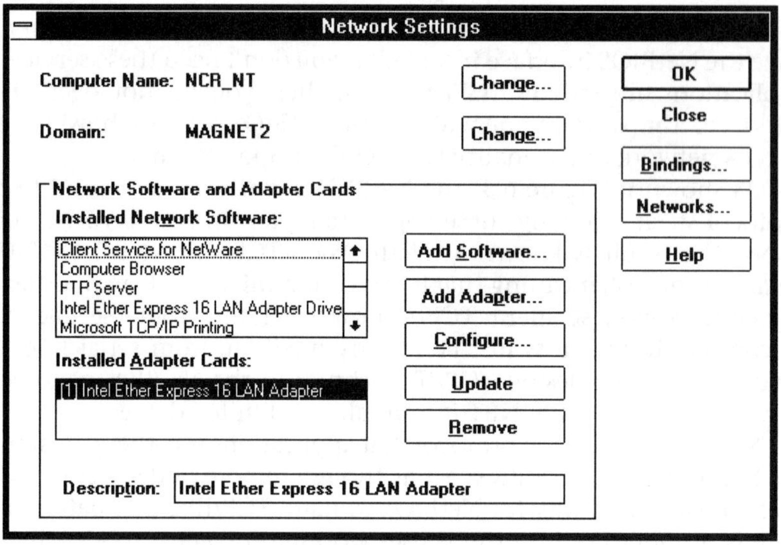

Figure 6.2 Network Settings dialog.
The Network dialog box from Control Panel is the central point for configuring all network-related Windows NT components, including TCP/IP.

The Network Control Panel

If you are configuring network services during installation, you will be presented with these options during the initial setup routines. If you are changing an existing installation, you need to load the Network control object from the Control Panels utility. Double-click Control Panels from the Main window in Program Manager, or type *CONTROL.EXE* in the File/Run menu of either Program Manager or File Manager. Likewise, you can type *CONTROL.EXE* from the command prompt. Once the Network control object has loaded, you will be presented with the dialog box shown in Figure 6.2.

By default, none of the TCP/IP services are installed, but the NetBEUI protocol is. To add the TCP/IP services, click the Add Software button, and select TCP/IP Protocol from the drop-down list. At this point, you will be presented with the dialog box shown in Figure 6.3.

You must make some choices here regarding what exactly you plan on using the TCP/IP services for. Take a few minutes to study the following list:

Service	*Description*
TCP/IP Internetworking	The TCP/IP protocol, NetBIOS over TCP/IP, and the TCP/IP diagnostic utilities (ping, etc.)
Connectivity Utilities	Telnet, FTP client, the R* services, and other TCP/IP utilities

SNMP Service	SNMP agent for use with SNMP management systems; also enables local monitoring of the TCP/IP stack from the Perfmormance Monitor
TCP/IP Network Printing	LPR and LPD printing support
FTP Server Service	FTP Server
Simple TCP/IP Services	TCP/IP daemons for CHARGEN, DAYTIME, ECHO, and QUOTE
DHCP Server Service	DHCP Server
WINS Server Service	WINS Server

If a DHCP server has already been set up to configure the system currently being worked on, then selecting the Enable Automatic DHCP Configuration will prepare the machine's configuration according to the network administrator's preferences and assigned settings. If you are not the network administrator, you should contact him to ask about this. Otherwise, continue reading for additional information about configuring TCP/IP services.

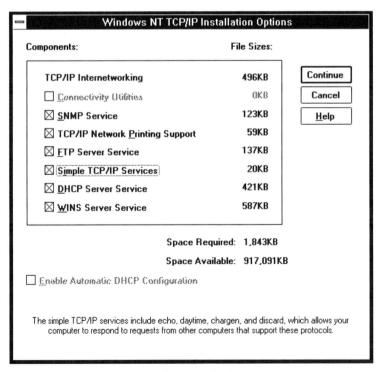

Figure 6.3 TCP/IP Installation dialog.

Windows NT includes a variety of TCP/IP-related components. You can determine which of these are installed during TCP/IP setup.

Installing TCP/IP Internetworking

When you first add the TCP/IP protocol, you cannot configure the software immediately. Instead, you must complete the installation, and NT will prompt you for the TCP/IP configuration details later. If this is a modification of an existing installation, you can select the Configure button to make changes to the TCP/IP protocol. Either way, NT will present you with the TCP/IP configuration dialog, illustrated in Figure 6.4.

You will mainly be concerned with three entries in this dialog: IP Address, Subnet Mask, and Default Gateway. These three parameters identify the logical location of your workstation. (For more information on IP addresses, see Appendix 2.) When you first add TCP/IP to a network adapter, this dialog box is empty. If you've already set these parameters in a previous install, then the dialog will show them instead. The various elements of the dialog box, and their meaning and potential values, are explained below.

- ❑ *Adapter*—This drop-down box lists all of the adapters in your system. If you have more than one network card, then you can set the parameters for each of them here. Simply fill out the information for the first adapter, then select the next one from this drop-down list. NT will remember the settings for all of the adapters. The number in parentheses

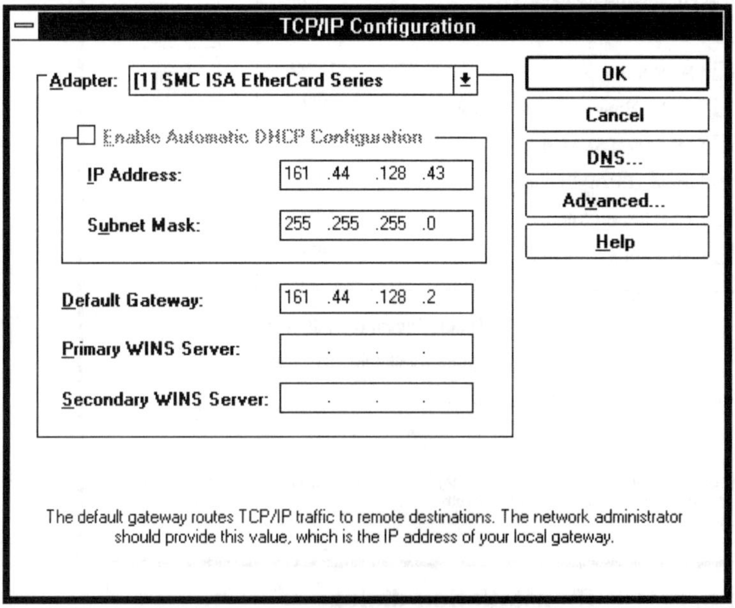

Figure 6.4 TCP/IP Configuration dialog.

TCP/IP is configured using this dialog box.

before the adapter description is the load order of all the adapters in the system. An adapter with a (1) means that it is loaded first, (2) means second, and so on.

❑ *IP Address*—This is where you put the network address for this specific adapter. Each adapter gets its own unique address. Other machines use this address to find you when they have network traffic to send. Get your address from the network administrator. If you are the network administrator, get a valid block of addresses from your Internet Service Provider. When you receive your IP address from your network administrator, be sure to copy it carefully and confirm that it is correct. Do the same when you enter it into the dialog box—duplicate IP addresses on a network can cause all sorts of problems, including lockups.

❑ *Subnet Mask*—This number is used to mathematically *mask* IP addresses on your network. In other words, it eliminates those parts of an IP address that are alike for machines on your network. It is absolutely essential that this number be correct. Treat this the same way you do the IP address—make sure it is right. If it is incorrect, you will not be able to *see* the other machines on your network. Once you've entered the IP address, NT will automatically guess the appropriate subnet mask, based on the *class* of the address. You will need to modify this value only if you are using nonstandard subnet masks on your network. All systems using the same addressing schemes must use the same subnet mask in order to see each other (refer to Appendix 2 for more details on subnet masks and how they can be useful).

❑ *Default Gateway*—This entry indicates where TCP/IP traffic should be sent when its address indicates that it needs to be forwarded to another logical or physical network. You must provide a default route for every adpater in your system. This address points to a router—either another computer, or a piece of dedicated hardware—that is responsible for forwarding packets to hosts that are not on the currently selected adapter's subnet. Get this information from your TCP/IP network administrator.

❑ *Primary (and Secondary) WINS Server*—Windows NT can run NetBIOS and Windows Networking over a TCP/IP network. The NetBIOS machine names must be mapped to the corresponding IP addresses for those machines, however. This mapping can be managed through the use of a text database called LMHOSTS, or by using DNS, or by using a Windows Internet Naming Service (WINS) Server, which is the easiest method to use. Since each adapter is on a different subnet, and WINS Servers work by sniffing the wire for NBT traffic, you should have at least one WINS Server on each of your subnets. You can specify up to two WINS Servers for each adapter to use. Refer to the "Windows Internet Naming Service" section later in this chapter for more information on WINS.

❑ *DNS...*—Pressing this button opens the dialog illustrated in Figure 6.5. The DNS Configuration dialog allows you to set the various parameters related to DNS (Domain Name Service). The DNS server on your network lets you use machine names (but not NetBIOS names) rather than numbers to connect to other machines. The only alternative to DNS is the HOSTS file. This is a list of IP names and addresses stored in a text file. The advantage of DNS over HOSTS is that central storage of names and addresses on a DNS server allows a single change or addition to be used by everyone on the network. For more information on DNS, refer to Appendix 2.

❑ *Advanced...*—Pressing this button opens the dialog illustrated in Figure 6.6. The TCP/IP Configuration dialog allows you to set nonstandard options for each of the network adapters installed on your system. You can assign multiple IP addresses per adapter, specify the routers you want to use, and select the NetBIOS-over-TCP/IP specific options that you need to use on your network.

If you choose to use DNS, you will be presented with the dialog box shown previously. The various elements of the dialog box, and their meaning and potential values, are explained in the following:

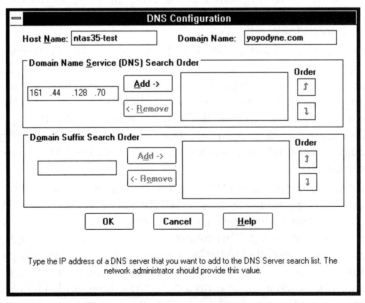

Figure 6.5 DNS Configuration dialog.

Windows NT's DNS participation in DNS is controlled with this dialog.

❑ *Host Name*—This is the name that others will use to connect to your workstation. By default, NT uses the system's workstation name (assigned during installation) as the TCP/IP host name. If you want to change it, type in the new value here, but make sure you tell the other users so that they can update their HOSTS and DNS files.

❑ *TCP Domain Name*—If you are in a TCP/IP domain, type in the domain name here (this is not the same as your Windows NT Domain or Workgroup). Get this value from your network administrator. (See Appendix 2 for more information on TCP/IP domain names.)

Combining the Domain Name and Host Name entries will give you a complete DNS name. For example, if your machine name is *colossus* and your domain name is *forbin.com*, your fully qualified domain name (FQDN)—equivalent through DNS to your numerical IP address—is *colossus.forbin.com*. Note that the *.com* part of this name indicates that this is a commercial enterprise. Other extensions are used to indicate other types of organizations; for example: *.edu* for educational institutions, *.org* for nonprofit organizations, *.net* for networks, and *.mil* for military.

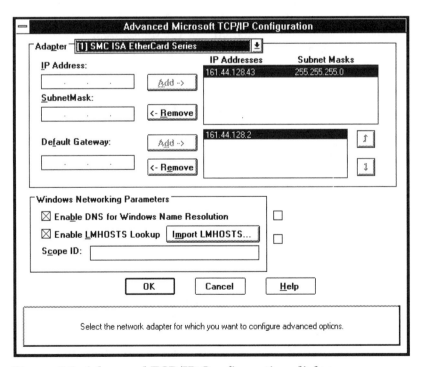

Figure 6.6 Advanced TCP/IP Configuration dialog.

A variety of more sophisticated TCP/IP settings are controlled with this dialog.

❑ *Domain Name Service (DNS) Search Order*—If you tell NT not to use DNS, this portion of the dialog box will be disabled. If you are using DNS, then you must tell NT the IP addresses of the name servers you wish to use, and their precedence. To add a DNS server to the list, type in the IP address in the edit box on the left and click the Add button. To change the search order for DNS queries, select the IP address from the listbox on the right, and click the up or down arrow buttons to move the server up or down the list, as desired.

❑ *Domain Suffix Search Order*—If you tell NT not to use DNS, this portion of the dialog box is grayed out. If you are using DNS, then you need to tell NT the TCP/IP domains that you want to search in. By default, NT will look in the domain you specify in the TCP Domain Name field discussed previously. To add other domains, type them in the edit box on the left and click the Add button. To change the search order for DNS queries, select the domain name from the listbox on the right, and click the up or down arrow buttons to move the domain name up or down the list, as desired.

If you choose the Advanced... button in the TCP/IP Configuration dialog box presented in Figure 6.3, you will be presented with the dialog box shown in Figure 6.6. The various elements of the dialog box, and their meaning and potential values, are explained in the following.

❑ *IP Address*—Each network adapter can have up to five IP addresses assigned to it. This is commonly used in networking environments with multiple domains and subnets sharing the same wire. Since IP is based on defined nodes, and is not reliant on broadcasting like NetBIOS, IPX, and AppleTalk, it is possible to have many different IP networks on the same physical wire that are invisible to each other. Another common use for multiple IP subnets on one wire is the benefit of having multiple *virtual* servers on one machine. You can have an FTP server look like several servers simply by mapping different IP addresses and their associated host and domain names to one physical machine.

❑ *Subnet Mask*—Each IP address may need a modified subnet mask.

❑ *Default Gateway*—Each IP address that is on a unique subnet will need a default gateway for that subnet.

❑ *Enable DNS for Windows Name Resolution*—Windows NT 3.5 allows you to convert NetBIOS names to IP addresses by using a text database called LMHOSTS, or with DNS servers, or with WINS servers, or a combination of the three. If you want to use DNS for the name-to-address mapping, enable this check box.

- ❏ *Enable LMHOSTS Lookup*—If you want to use LMHOSTS for the name-to-address mapping, enable this check box.

- ❏ *Import LMHOSTS*—Pressing this button allows you to use a predefined LMHOSTS database. For more information on the LMHOSTS file, refer to the "Using TCP/IP with Windows NT's Built-In Networking" section further ahead in this chapter.

- ❏ *Scope ID for Windows Networking*—The Scope ID allows you to set a filter on the NBT traffic you want the machine to see. By default, this field is blank, and unless you are instructed to provide a value by your network administrator, you should leave it that way. Like subnet masks, the Scope ID must be consistent across all machines for the systems to see each other.

- ❏ *Enable IP Routing*—Enabling this check box allows you to configure static routing tables on this machine. The static routing information you could enter would allow you to deterministically route traffic to routers other than the default router specified for this adapter. For more information on this subject, refer to the "Multiple Adapters and IP Routing" section later in this chapter.

- ❏ *Enable WINS Proxy Agent*—Enabling this check box allows you to establish this machine as a WINS Proxy Server. It would store remotely managed WINS databases locally, and answer queries on behalf of the remote WINS servers. You must have specified a WINS server in the main configuration screen before this check box is enabled.

HOSTS, LMHOSTS, NETWORKS, PROTOCOL, and SERVICES Files

Although most of the configuration settings for the TCP/IP services are managed by the Network Control Panel object, there are a collection of files that can make life easier for your users. These files are stored in the directory specified by the HKEY_LOCAL_MACHINE\CURRENT_CONTROL_SET\Services\Tcpip\Parameters\DataBasePath entry of the Windows NT system registry (\winnt\system32\drivers\etc by default). The file names and a description of their functions are listed below.

File Name	Description
HOSTS	Host name to IP address database
NETWORKS	Network name to network number database
PROTOCOL	Protocol name to protocol number database
SERVICES	Application/service name to port number database

WARNING!   Unlike most other Windows NT configuration and settings files, the HOSTS, LMHOSTS, NETWORKS, PROTOCOL, and SERVICES files are not maintained in the Registry database, and fall back data for these files is not part of the Last Known Good data available on system restart. It is essential that administrators maintain backup copies of these files!

HOSTS

People have a difficult time remembering 32-bit binary numbers, which is why the IP address is most commonly represented by four 8-bit numbers instead. But even then, remembering a bunch of obscure number sequences can be a mental strain. TCP/IP allows users to use host names for systems instead, making life easier for its human users. For example, to connect to a host named VAX, you could type *telnet vax* instead of *telnet 192.155.13.116.*, provided your host file is properly set up as shown in the following.

Windows NT TCP/IP uses a file called HOSTS to map IP addresses to well-known host names. The file is simple in structure, containing an IP address, the host name, and (optionally) a comment preceded by a pound (#) sign. An entry in the HOSTS database file to substitute *vax* for IP address 192.155.13.116 would look like this:

```
192.155.13.116 vax      #Mapping for local VAX mini
```

Hosts you connect with often can be added to this database at any time. TCP/IP will consult the database whenever a host name is passed to it (provided the proper Name Resolution Search Order setting has been selected, as described previously.

HOSTS File Tips

❑ Back up HOSTS before making changes. The copy can be placed in the same directory as the real HOSTS file and will protect you from inadvertent changes you might make during editing. HOSTS files can become large, with many entries, and they just won't work if the IP addresses are incorrect.

❑ Keep the HOSTS file up to date. Be sure to keep track of machines added to or taken from the network, and make sure your HOSTS file reflects these changes. To help automate this process, the administrator can use e-mail to send changes and updates that can be placed in the HOSTS file through copy and paste. If you can maintain exactly the same HOSTS file on all machines, the process of update is even simpler. The administrator can place the updated file directly into the machines directory with no user intervention, using NT's native networking capabilities.

Obviously, this is less critical if your network uses DNS—but be aware that the HOSTS file is the fall-back for DNS name resolution if the DNS server is down; so even on DNS networks, periodically updating HOSTS is a good idea.

❑ Keep HOSTS entries in order. Since HOSTS files are read in the order they're written, you should place the entries covering your most frequently used hosts at the top of the file to speed searches.

❑ Editing HOSTS. If you have a big HOSTS file, you might find it easier to maintain it in a spreadsheet. To do this, update the spreadsheet, then save it as text—not the native format—of your spreadsheet. This way you can use the database and organizational functions of the spreadsheet on your library of IP names and addresses.

LMHOSTS

This text file works just like the HOSTS file and uses the same format. The difference is that it is used to translate Windows NT names to numerical IP addresses for use by the NetBIOS-over-TCP/IP (NBT) protocol. It's covered in more detail in the following section on "Mapping NetBIOS Names to TCP/IP Addresses."

NETWORKS

Just as you can create alias names for hosts, you can create alias names for networks. If you are in a complex environment, creating aliases helps you keep track of different networks. For example, you can type the command *netstat -r*, and see that network Lab 10baseT is up, rather than having to remember that 192.155.12 is the IP number for that network. To do so, the NETWORKS file would need the following entry:

```
Lab10baseT      192.155.12
```

PROTOCOL and SERVICES

The remaining two TCP/IP files are not likely to require editing in normal use. PROTOCOL allows you to define the specifics of the IP, TCP, ICMP, and so on, protocol levels within the overall TCP/IP suite. If you replace (or augment) Windows NT's built-in TCP/IP protocol stack with a third-party stack, then you may need to edit this file. SERVICES provides a similar capability for mapping application-level communication requests to a well-known TCP/IP port number. More information on these files can be found in Appendix 2, and in the Microsoft TCP/IP documentation included with Windows NT.

Using TCP/IP with Windows NT's Built-In Networking

Since most of NT's network functionality is dependent upon the NetBIOS APIs, most users will need to incorporate the NetBIOS-over-TCP/IP (NBT) services into their configuration. Configuring NT to map NetBIOS machine names to IP addresses is a nontrivial task, although the payback can be great, especially in large networks.

An Overview of NetBIOS on TCP/IP (NBT)

NetBIOS (which, as we've seen, is used by Windows NT's built-in networking) uses machine names to identify nodes on the network, and for all exchanges of information between them. NetBIOS accomplishes this almost exclusively with broadcasting. When a new node comes on the net, it broadcasts its assigned name; and if no other node challenges the name (or claims to be using it already), it keeps the name for itself. It does not register the name anywhere, but instead each node is responsible for maintaining its own name tables. If a subsequent node comes on the net and claims the same name, it is the responsibility of the first node to challenge the new one.

Likewise, when a node needs to communicate with another node, it uses broadcasting to find the remote system. The remote system is responsible for responding to the broadcast with a directed reply. Once nodes have identified each other, they can communicate with directed messages.

An example that illustrates the broadcast-dependent nature of NetBIOS is the *net view* command. When you type *net view* from a command prompt, the Windows NT Workstation service issues a directed query to the domain Browse Master—unless it can't find the Browse Master, in which case it sends a broadcast on the subnet(s) it is attached to. After a specified amount of time, it lists the servers that responded to the broadcast. If you want to see a specific node, such as *mips-lab-server*, you can issue the n*et view mips-lab-server* command, and a directed query is sent to the known node.

The Windows NT NetBIOS implementation for built-in networking is protocol-independent. NetBIOS is just an API. It does not have to use any specific low-level transport protocol to communicate with other systems. However, all of the systems that wish to communicate with NetBIOS must use the same low-level transport protocol. Otherwise, they would never see each other, and the NetBIOS API would be useless.

By default, Windows NT uses NetBEUI as the transport protocol. NetBEUI is based on the X/Open standard Server Message Block (SMB) protocols, with a NetBIOS API, and using NBF as a transport protocol (refer to Appendix 2 for a detailed discussion of NetBEUI). NetBEUI is very small, fast, and efficient.

However, NetBEUI is a nonroutable protocol, meaning that it has no mechanism for identifying different network segments. The entire network must look like one big wire in order for NetBEUI to communicate with remote segments. Unfortunately, the number of nodes a single network organized in this way can handle is fairly limited, and bridging multiple segments into one large network—especially when wide-area links are involved—is a sure way to kill performance. Likewise, since NetBIOS names use a flat, nonhierarchical database, there are no mechanisms for targeting broadcasts to a remote segment. Thus it makes a poor choice for large, complex networks.

Fortunately, the NetBIOS APIs can be used with any low-level transport protocol—such as TCP/IP. Unlike NetBEUI, TCP/IP is completely routable. Indeed, it is predominantly a point-to-point protocol that avoids broadcasting whenever possible. Thus, using TCP/IP as a way to move NetBIOS-based data is an attractive alternative to NetBEUI, especially in large and complex environments. Although this is an improvement, it is still hindered by the need for NetBIOS broadcasts.

Since NetBIOS uses names for addressing purposes, while TCP/IP uses numbers, there must be some way to map the two so that both of them see what they expect. In order for NetBIOS-based applications to run over TCP/IP networks, the NetBIOS application must see names and the IP protocol must see numbers; yet neither can see the other. A layer between the two must map NetBIOS names to IP addresses, and convert IP addresses back to NetBIOS names. This layer is known as the NetBIOS-over-TCP/IP (or NBT) service. Figure 6.7 shows a high-level view of the various layers.

TCP/IP standards are defined by Requests for Comment, or RFCs. Anyone may submit an RFC for consideration as a standard (even you). Two such RFCs are 1001 and 1002, which define a standard method for running NetBIOS over

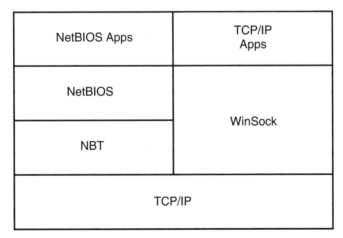

Figure 6.7 NBT.
Windows NT's NetBIOS-over-TCP/IP (NBT) layers.

TCP/IP. RFC 1001 defines a general overview, while RFC 1002 defines the detailed.

There are three types of NetBIOS nodes defined in these two RFCs. A *b-node* (broadcast node) is one that uses broadcasting to query nodes on the network for the owner of a NetBIOS name. A *p-node* (point-to-point node) uses directed calls to communicate with a known name server (not to be confused with DNS) for the IP address of a NetBIOS machine name. An *m-node* is a mixed node, one that uses broadcasted queries to find nodes, and failing that, queries a p-node name server for the address. Another type currently under review is an *h-node*, which reverses the m-node standard so that a directed query is executed first, and failing that, a broadcast is attempted. Remember that the node types apply only when a node is attempting to match an IP address to a NetBIOS node name. Once the device has discovered the IP address of the machine it's trying to communicate with, it no longer broadcasts information, but sends the IP traffic directly to the node associated with the NetBIOS name.

Windows NT 3.5 can use a variety of mechanisms for name resolution. The simplest conceptual and practical method is to simply rely on the default scenario. This calls for the server to issue broadcasts for every NBT query, and failing a response, to issue a directed query to the DNS server you have specified in the local configuration. However, this doesn't always work for a variety of reasons. When you need to be able to configure exacting name resolution patterns for your more complex environments, you will want to use one of the more powerful options available.

The LMHOSTS Database

The LMHOSTS format is identical to the HOSTS file described earlier, with a numerical IP address, a tab character, and a Windows NT name (and optionally, a comment); for example:

```
128.0.0.1        lm-machine
```

LMHOSTS is read by the NT system at startup and cached in memory, so any changes you make will not take effect until you either restart or execute NBSTAT-R from the command line.

Do not confuse the LMHOSTS database with the HOSTS database. Although they are similar in use and structure, they serve two entirely separate purposes. The HOSTS file is a database of TCP/IP host names and their corresponding IP addresses, while the LMHOSTS file is strictly for NetBIOS name to IP address mapping. Typically, the LMHOSTS file shows only a few systems. This does not mean that there are only a few nodes on the network, but rather that there are only a few remote nodes that must be addressed directly.

LMHOSTS simply acts to extend the realm of the broadcast area to include hosts that would otherwise be unreachable. By using this method, NT takes advantage of both the broadcasting and point-to-point architectures, without relying on a dedicated name server. Since broadcasting is necessary in the dynamic environments so typical of peer-to-peer LANs (because it's impossible to predict which systems will be available when), it is the preferred vehicle for name resolution. For example, if the primary domain controller were down, then another would respond to any broadcast-based query, such as a login request. This increases network reliability tremendously, without forcing users to place servers on every segment.

More specifically, name resolution takes the following steps to find a node's IP address:

1. NBT searches its internal cache for the NetBIOS name and IP address.

2. If the address is not found in the cache, a b-node broadcast is issued.

3. Failing a response from a local node, NBT searches the LMHOSTS file.

4. If no match is found, and if the client has been configured to use DNS servers in its name-to-address resolution scheme, it will then issue a DNS query for the NetBIOS name in question.

5. If a match is not found, a Name Not Found error is returned to NetBIOS.

By understanding the sequence of events, and also by knowing a few tricks that we're about to show you, you can customize your environment for both speedy responses and flexibility.

The Name Resolution Cache

Since NBT first checks the local name cache for entries, it is best to preload some names into the cache at boot time. Thus, your system won't have to wait for the local broadcasts to time out, nor go through the trouble of having to check the LMHOSTS file. Adding a name to the cache is done by adding a *#PRE* command to an entry in the file:

```
192.155.11.10      marketing1    #PRE    #Marketing Domain Controller
```

Preloading the *marketing1* server into NBT's cache speeds up the name resolution process considerably. Likewise it's worth preloading the *app1* and *app2* servers, if they're accessed frequently. In fact, you can preload every node on the network (up to a maximum of 100). There isn't much need to do this, however, since successful resolutions via broadcasts and lookups are also held in the cache for a while. If you need to preload more than 100 addresses (which you might in a really large network), here's how to do so:

1. Start the Registry Editor by typing *REGEDT32.EXE* in the File/Run menu of either Program Manager or File Manager, or from a command prompt.

2. When the Registry Editor starts, select the HKEY_LOCAL_MACHINE key, and find the SYSTEM tree.

3. Double-click the SYSTEM folder icon, and select the CurrentControlSet folder. Continue working down the tree until you get to the SYSTEM\CurrentControlSet\Services\Tcpip\Parameters folder, and then select it.

4. Select Edit/Add Value. In the Value Name field, type the keyword *MaxPreload* and then select a Data Type of REG_DWORD. Click the OK button, and type the desired number of preloaded entries into the String Editor dialog box.

5. You must shut down and restart the system after making these changes in order for routing to begin.

Items stored in the cache with the *#PRE* command never leave the cache unless forced. Using the NBTSTAT-R command will flush the cache and reload the first 100 #PRE entries from the LMHOSTS file.

Note that although the # symbol in the LMHOSTS file normally signifies a comment, Windows NT uses the #PRE string as a valid flag. This is for backward-compatibility with LAN Manager servers that do not support selective preloading. They will ignore the *#PRE* command because they will not see it.

Specifying Domain Controllers

Whenever a client attempts to log onto the network, broadcasting is used. Normally, a broadcast message follows the chain of events previously described, but where domain controllers are involved, it is sometimes necessary to bypass normal channels. We certainly don't want domain controllers broadcasting password changes to every node on the network and all the nodes in the LMHOSTS file!

To signify that a system is a domain controller, put the #DOM flag in the LMHOSTS file:

```
192.155.11.10   marketing1   #PRE   #DOM   #Marketing Domain Controller
```

The #DOM keyword activates a pseudo-backchannel for communication between domain controllers. All domain controllers should have entries in their local LMHOSTS files for all of the other controllers within their domain. Also, if trust relationships have been established across separate domains, then there should be entries for the primary controllers within the trusted domains (and perhaps for backup domain controllers as well).

In fact, you might want to set #DOM for all Windows NT Servers on your network. Otherwise, if the primary domain controller fails, then a server that promotes itself to domain controller will not be able to use the backchannel for domain administration.

Sharing LMHOSTS Files

Obviously, large networks with multiple trusted relationships and many hosts will have a hard time dealing with massive LMHOSTS databases. There are a couple of tricks that can help in this situation. One is to use the #INCLUDE flag, which tells NBT to read not only the local LMHOSTS file, but other files as well. This would allow you to point NBT to a shared LMHOSTS file on a departmental server or domain controller. For instance:

```
#INCLUDE \\marketing1\public\lmhosts
```

In this example, the local PC will incorporate any entries in the remote LMHOSTS file whenever a lookup is needed. Although you can point to as many remote databases as needed, you should keep the remote #INCLUDE list as small as possible. If you do this, make sure to give users at least read-only access to the shared file. Also, never reference drive letters for remote systems, but instead use the UNC names of the share point whenever possible. (Remember, remote drive letters can change!) For servers that need to share master copies, you can take advantage of NT's replication features to make sure that backups are always available (see Chapter 7 for details).

There are other tricks that you can do with the *#INCLUDE* command. For example, suppose that marketing1 was down. You would not be able to read the remote LMHOSTS file. You would not want to put multiple #INCLUDE statements for each of the servers in the marketing domain, as that would increase your search time with no foreseeable benefit (the data in each file would be the same).

However, by enclosing a block of #INCLUDES with *#BEGIN_ALTERNATE* and *#END_ALTERNATE* commands, you can tell NBT to search the first available LMHOSTS file. Thus, if marketing1 were down, NBT would search marketing2's LMHOSTS file:

```
#BEGIN_ALTERNATE
#INCLUDE \\marketing1\public\lmhosts
#INCLUDE \\marketing2\public\lmhosts
#INCLUDE \\marketing3\public\lmhosts
#END_ALTERNATE
```

The Windows Internet Naming Service (WINS)

When resolving IP addresses using an LMHOSTS file, broadcasts are issued first, and then the LMHOSTS file is consulted as a fall-back. When you use WINS however, the process is reversed. NBT queries are sent directly to a specified WINS server, and if that fails, then a broadcast is issued. This improves response time and overall reliability of the network considerably. In essence, a WINS server is a p-node server, as defined in RFCs 1001 and 1002.

More specifically, name resolution takes the following steps to find a node's IP address when WINS servers are used on your network:

1. NBT searches its internal cache for the NetBIOS name and IP address.

2. If the address is not found in the cache, a p-node query is issued to the WINS server specified in the TCP/IP Configuration dialog box.

3. If the WINS server doesn't respond with an IP address for the host requested, a broadcast is issued on the local segments.

4. Failing a response from a local node, NBT searches the LMHOSTS file if available.

5. If no match is found and the client has been configured to use DNS servers in its name-to-address resolution scheme, it will then issue a DNS query for the NetBIOS name in question.

6. If a match is not found, a Name Not Found error is returned to NetBIOS.

WINS servers have NetBIOS name-to-IP address databases that are built automatically from a variety of sources:

❑ If you are using DHCP servers, they will inform all WINS servers they know about of all NetBIOS names and IP addresses in their databases. This makes the entire network less reliant on static information stored in LMHOSTS database files scattered around the enterprise.

❑ WINS clients that come up on the network register their NetBIOS names and IP addresses with the WINS servers specified. If a name is duplicated, then it is rejected by the server, and the WINS client software informs the system manager of the error. This allows the WINS database to be centrally maintained and refreshed by clients scattered around the world.

❑ WINS servers also store local b-node query traffic so that they can answer on behalf of other devices. This means that nodes won't have to resort to broadcasts as often, since the WINS server will respond immediately with the cached information.

Since the WINS servers are populated by so many forms of network activity, they require almost zero administration, and are extremely reliable at the same time. This makes them the best choice for NBT mappings. A single WINS server that all clients point to can be used to enable browsing across an entire world-wide network, since the reliance on broadcasting has all but been eliminated.

Also, clients that do not have WINS software (and therefore rely on broadcasting) can take advantage of the WINS servers, since the latter will respond to a broadcast on behalf of a remote system. This means that all NBT nodes now can know about any other node that the WINS server knows about, increasing your network's overall reliability.

WINS Proxies

Depending on the size and geographical nature of your network, you may wish to have either a highly consolidated cluster, or a regionally distributed network, of WINS servers. If you choose to go with the consolidated architecture, you can increase your geographical coverage by taking advantage of WINS *proxy servers*.

WINS proxies query the primary WINS servers for new information on a regularly scheduled basis, cache the information locally, and answer queries on behalf of the primary WINS servers. These proxies contain almost all of the same information that the primary WINS servers have, with the exception of locally broadcast information.

This may or may not be of significance to you, depending upon your applications and your network topology. A WINS proxy can be established on any NT 3.5 system, meaning you don't have to have NT Servers at every location. However, you will also not have the same level of information available to your clients, so there is some trade-off.

Installing the WINS Server Service

You will need to load the Network control object from the Control Panels utility. Double-click Control Panels from the Main window in Program Manager, or type *CONTROL.EXE* in the File/Run menu of either Program Manager or File Manager. Likewise, you can type *CONTROL.EXE* from the command prompt. Once the Network control object has loaded, you will be presented with the dialog box shown in Figure 6.2 earlier in this chapter.

If you are installing the complete WINS Server Service, select the WINS Server check box, and click OK. You will not need to do any additional configuration, as WINS is completely self-maintaining. The only settings that you may need to make would be to set the TCP/IP Configuration utility to point to a DHCP server. Although this is not required, WINS does interact with DHCP servers to build its list of nodes.

If you are installing the WINS Proxy Agent, then you will need to open the TCP/IP Configuration dialog from the main list of services in the network control object. Under the Advanced button is the dialog box shown in Figure 6.6 earlier in this chapter. Select the WINS Proxy Agent checkbox, and click the OK button.

Dynamic Host Configuration Protocol (DHCP)

Without a doubt, the biggest single problem with TCP/IP is the fact that *every single node* must have a unique address number assigned to it. Once that's done, the list must be maintained so that the uniqueness is guaranteed. This can be (and *is*, for most people) an administrative nightmare. Almost every large network manager has had to track down duplicate IP workstation names at one time or another, and can attest to the great indignity of it all.

What would be really great, as most of these administrators will tell you, would be a database that not only tracks IP address assignments, but *makes* the assignments for you as needed. This is what the Dynamic Host Configuration Protocol (DHCP) is for. Microsoft, Sun, and others wrote a series of RFCs (1533, 1534, 1541, and 1542) for DHCP, which provides mechanisms for assigning IP addresses, host names, domain names, and other IP information to nodes dynamically.

Basically, at boot time, a client PC with DHCP software requests an address and other information from a DHCP server, stores the information for a certain amount of time, and periodically rerequests the information from the server. This provides administrators with a centralized address allocation tool, relieving them from having to manually make these assignments on a per-workstation basis.

Using DHCP servers provides several benefits to network administrators:

❑ Global network parameters, such as domain name, can be set for all nodes.

❑ Per-subnet parameters can be set (such as default router, etc.) for nodes on specific subnets.

❑ Pools of IP addresses can be set aside for use on a per-subnet or enterprise-wide basis.

❑ Lease terms can be established, forcing clients to renew their requests every so often.

There are also advantages at the client level:

❑ DHCP clients don't have to be configured for anything. When the node boots, it issues a DHCP broadcast request, which gets answered by all of the DHCP servers on the network. DHCP-enabled routers automatically forward these requests, so you don't have to have DHCP servers on every subnet to take advantage of this.

❑ If you move a client PC to another subnet, it will automatically get the new subnet information, since the server can tell what subnet the client request came from.

Installing the DHCP Server Service

You will need to load the Network control object from the Control Panels utility. Double-click Control Panels from the Main window in Program Manager, or type *CONTROL.EXE* in the File/Run... menu of either Program Manager or File Manager. Likewise, you can type *CONTROL.EXE* from the command prompt.

Once the Network control object has loaded, you will be presented with the dialog box shown in Figure 6.2 earlier in this chapter.

Select the DHCP Server check box, and click OK. You will not need to do any additional configuration at this point, although you will need to use the DHCP Manager utility to add scopes, nodes, and other information.

DHCP Scopes

DHCP groups nodes into logical entities called a *scope*. Every subnet on an internetwork has it's own scope, for example. You assign IP address ranges, subnet masks, and length of *leases* to each scope. You can also assign any of the DCHP options to each individual scope to be served, or you can assign them on a global basis. If a global setting and a scope-specific setting are both present, the DHCP server uses the scope-specific setting. If you assign these values to a specific node, then those node-specific settings override the scope-level settings.

To create a scope, load the DHCP Manager utility from the Network Administration group. Select a server from the list presented, and then select Scope/Create. You will be presented with the following dialog box (Figure 6.8), which you must complete.

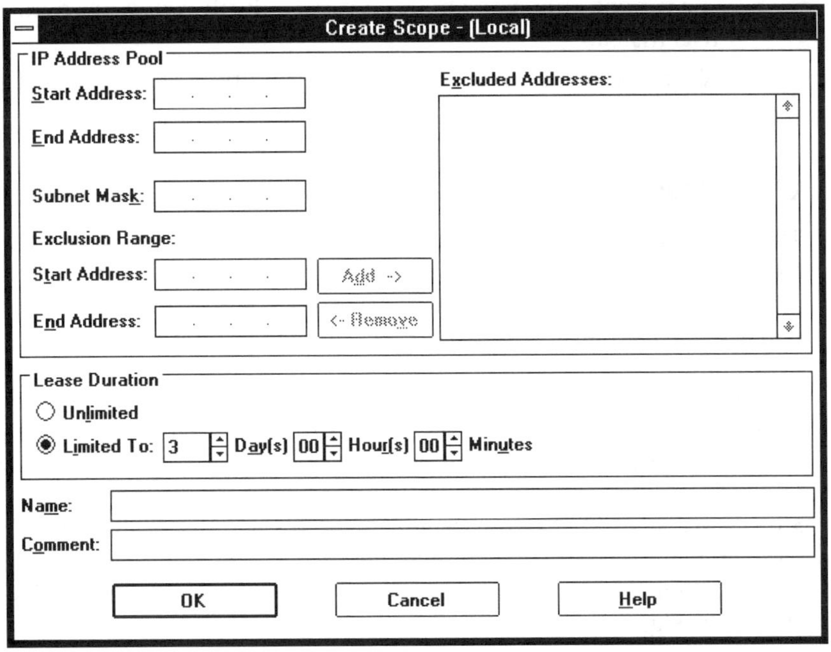

Figure 6.8 Create scope.

Ranges of TCP/IP addresses, called *scopes*, are created and managed using Windows NT's DHCP Manager application.

The various elements of the dialog box, and their meaning and potential values, are explained in the following:

- *Start Address*—This is the first IP address to be used in this scope's pool of available addresses. If you were to place the entire class C subnet 192.155.11.0 into this scope, you would start with 192.155.11.1.

- *End Address*—This is the last available IP address to be used in this scope's pool of available addresses. If you were to place the entire class C subnet 192.155.11.0 into this scope, you would end with 192.155.11.254.

- *Subnet Mask*—This is the subnet mask of the IP address pool. Since each segment contains a unique subnet mask per address block, this is a required field. If you have broken a subnet into multiple subnets, then you would need to create separate scopes for each of the resulting subnets.

- *Exclusion Range*—Just as you can specify a starting and stopping point for address ranges to include in the scope, you can exclude a block of addresses from the scope's include list. You can also exlude a specific address from the pool simply by defining the complete node address, and clicking the Add button. If you need to exclude multiple ranges from the subnet, then you should create multiple scopes with unique inlcude lists instead.

- *Name*—You can give a name to your scope by editing this field.

- *Comment*—You can attach a description of this scope by editing this field.

Client Reservations

There are some times when you want to always assign the same IP information to the same node. For example, if you have SMTP mail gateways, FTP servers, DNS servers, or other frequently accessed systems that must always have a consistent host name and IP address, then you would want to ensure that their information never changes.

One way to do this is to simply *not* configure these types of systems to use DHCP. However, there are many benefits to using DHCP beyond simple address assignment, as we'll see later in this chapter. In these instances, you would want to configure the node to use DHCP, but you would want to guarantee that it always received the same IP address. This is accomplished by the use of *reservations*.

To add a client reservation, select Scope/Add Reservations. The dialog box shown in Figure 6.9 will appear with the following elements:

- *IP Address*—The IP address to use with this client.

- *Unique Identifier*—This is the unique MAC (Media Access Control) address for the network adapter the client will use when requesting information from the DHCP server. The MAC address is the network-topology-specific address, such as the EtherNet address, or the Token Ring address of the network adapter.

❑ *Client Name*—This is the name you use to refer to the PC, and should not be confused with the host name or the NetBIOS machine name.

❑ *Comment*—You can assign a comment to this machine by editing this field.

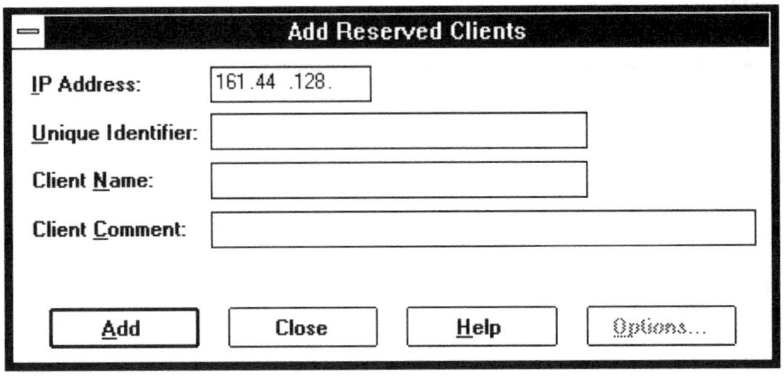

Figure 6.9 Add Reserved Clients.

Settings for DHCP clients that require a particular *reserved* IP address are made in DHCP Manager's Add Reserved Clients dialog.

Other DHCP Options

There are many DHCP options that can be defined beyond simple IP address assignment. You can make these assignments on a global basis, per scope, or per machine if you have defined any reserved clients. To set these options on a global basis, select a scope from the list of servers, and then select DHCP Options\Global menu. The dialog box shown in Figure 6.10 will appear.

There are several configurable options that can be assigned to any DHCP client on boot. These options can be assigned globally, on a per-scope basis, or per-node when client reservations are used. Microsoft's DHCP client software does *not* support all of the DHCP options that are defined in the DHCP RFCs. All those that it does support, however, are listed below:

❑ *Router*—You can add a list of default routers that you want the clients to use. This option is best set on a per-scope basis, since you wouldn't want to assign a remote subnet a local default route.

❑ *DNS Servers*—You can specify a list of DNS servers and their preference with this option.

❑ *Domain Name*—You can specify the domain name you want a client to use. If you have multiple geographically or deparmentally separated

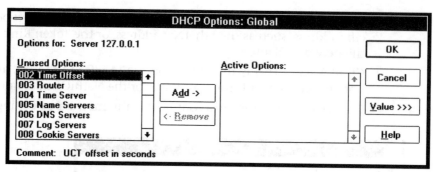

Figure 6.10 DHCP Options Global.

Network-wide DHCP settings are controlled from DHCP Manager's Global Options dialog.

domains, you would probably want to assign this value on a per-scope basis.

❑ *WINS/NBNS*—You can specify a list of WINS servers and their preference with this option.

❑ *WINS/NBT Node Type*—This option allows you to define the NBT node type (b-node, p-node, m-node, or h-node). For best operation, leave this setting alone.

❑ *NetBIOS Scope ID*—This option allows you to define the NBT Scope ID for the client.

Client Lease Times

DHCP clients request information from DHCP servers when they are booted. If the client has local storage capabilities, this information is retained locally. If not, the information is requested every time the client boots.

This information is kept for a certain amount of time, referred to as a *lease*. When the lease *expires*, the information is considered invalid. Rather than wait for the lease to expire, and then have to argue with the server and other clients over new lease information, the lease is renewed when 50 percent of the lease term has expired. Otherwise, the lease may expire, the client may not be able to get another address for some reason, and the user would be dead in the water until another lease became available.

After the client has renewed their lease, they attempt to rebind the information. Just as the clients don't attempt to renew their leases after the lease expires, they don't attempt to rebind the information when it is too late. By default, clients attempt to rebind their information after 50 percent of the remaining lease term has expired. If the lease was renewed at exactly 50 percent of the lease term, then this would first occur at 87.5 percent of the lease term (renewed at 50 percent of lease term—rebound at 50 percent of remaining term equals 87.5 percent of lease term). If another node contests the binding, then the process is delayed until 50 percent of the remaining time has passed, and so on, until the binding succeeds. This allows multiple nodes to phase information between themselves without human intervention.

Using Windows NT's TCP/IP Utilities and Services

If you are familiar with using TCP/IP utilities on a UNIX system, you will be right at home on an NT system. The utilities provided by Microsoft are of the standard variety with little difference from any others you may have used.

The utilities included with Windows NT allow you to take advantage of UNIX and other systems with TCP/IP server capabilities. There are a handful of TCP/IP client applications, such as Telnet, FTP, and Finger; and a couple of server services as well, such as an FTP server and a quote-of-the-day server.

The Telnet Client

Windows NT 3.5 provides a barely usable Telnet client application, about on par with TERMINAL.EXE. It's not meant to be a fully-functional application, but instead a usable tool for people who require Telnet capabilities but have not yet purchased a full-featured Telnet client. Typing *telnet* in a command window or from the File/Run menu of Program Manager will start the Telnet application running. Figure 6.11 shot shows the Telnet client's main window.

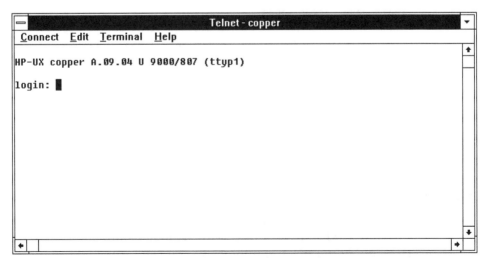

Figure 6.11 Telnet support is provided through Windows NT's Telnet application.

To connect to a remote host, click Connect\Host... menu, and enter the IP address or host name (if you are using DNS or have the host listed in your HOSTS file) of the host you want to connect to. For our example, we'll connect to RS.INTERNIC.NET, which is one of the main control centers for the Internet. Upon completing the connection, we are presented with the following information:

```
SunOS UNIX 4.1 (rs) (ttypd)

**************************************************************************
* - InterNIC Registration Services Center  -
*
* For wais, type:                    WAIS <search string> <return>
* For the *original* whois type:     WHOIS [search string] <return>
* For referral whois type:           RWHOIS [search string] <return>
*
* For user assistance call (703) 742-4777
# Questions/Updates on the whois database to HOSTMASTER@internic.net
* Please report system problems to ACTION@internic.net
**************************************************************************
Please be advised that use constitutes consent to monitoring
(Elec Comm Priv Act, 18 USC 2701-2711)
6/1/94
We are offering an experimental distributed whois service called referral
whois (RWhois). To find out more, look for RWhois documents, a sample
client and server under:
gopher: (rs.internic.net) InterNIC Registration Services ->
        InterNIC Registration Archives -> pub -> rwhois
anonymous ftp: (rs.internic.net) /pub/rwhois
Cmdinter Ver 1.3 Tue Apr  4 23:09:56 1995 EST
[vt100] InterNIC >
```

Obviously, each host you connect to using Telnet will present you with a different welcome message.

RSH and REXEC

If you don't need a completely interactive session with a host, you can use the RSH and REXEC utilities to execute a single command on a remote system. These are noninteractive utilities, so you can't run a text editor or the like in this manner; but you can retrieve a directory listing, or type out a file, or execute any commands that don't require interaction.

RSH and REXEC are virtually identical. In fact, they both provide the exact same service and even use the same command-line parameters. The difference between the two is based on authority. While RSH uses the concept of trust between remote hosts, REXEC does not. The latter requires a user name and password to pass to the host for authentication before executing the command.

For example, assume that there are two hosts named GRUMPY and DOPEY. GRUMPY *trusts* the NT system, using either the .rhosts or /etc/hosts.equiv files. A user on the NT system could list the files in his or her home directory on GRUMPY by issuing the command *rsh grumpy ls*. Since the host GRUMPY trusts the NT system, it accepts the RSH request, logs in with the user's account, executes the command *ls*, and returns the results. Then it logs the user out.

DOPEY, however, doesn't trust the NT machine. When a user wants to run a program on DOPEY, the user needs to use the *REXEC* command. This requires the user to provide a user name and password for the remote command. Thus, to list the files in the user's home directory on DOPEY, the user would type *rexec dopey -l username ls*. Then NT will ask for a password to go with the user name entered in the command line. The user name and password are sent over to DOPEY, which verifies the account; and if accurate, logs the user in and runs the command. Note that the REXEC utility will abort if no password is given; so if the remote user ID doesn't have a password, you can't use this program. RSH, however, allows you to use user names with no password.

In order for a host to provide remote command execution services, it must be running the appropriate remote server service programs. Currently, NT does not offer this functionality, so it can act only as a client. Furthermore, although the default action for the RSH command is to allow users to log in if no command has been passed on the command line, the RSH and REXEC utilities bundled with NT do not allow this. A command must be provided in order for the utilities to run.

For information on setting up trust between hosts, refer to the documentation provided with the system that will act as your server.

The Finger Client

Another way to interact with a remote system is through the *finger* command. *Finger* is, essentially, a way to query a remote system for information in the form of text. The principal use of *finger* is to identify users on the remote system (hence its name), but it has gained popularity as a way of distributing any sort of information that a system administrator wants to provide. The traditional use of *finger*—identifying users—is simple. At the NT command prompt type *finger username@host.domain.com.*

Depending upon how the remote system supports *finger*, your results will vary. For example, the Massachusetts-based public access UNIX system *world* run by Software Tool & Die takes a *finger* request pretty seriously:

```
finger bgaret@world.std.com
jgaret@world.std.com
[world.std.com]
world—The World—Public Access UNIX—Solbourne 5E/900 OS/MP 4.1A.3
5:14pm  up 24 days, 15:05,  69 users,  load average: 13.33, 15.51, 17.16
bgaret . Bill Garet          Login Fri 16-Jul-93 1:11AM from std-annex.sto
[3374,3374] </users/bgaret>;  Group: bgaret
Groups: hamradio bgaret
bgaret has new mail as of Fri 16-Jul-93 4:58PM
last read Fri 16-Jul-93 8:24AM
```

Clearly, world.std.com provides plenty of information about the user. On the other hand, some system administrators consider *finger* a security hole, and disable it.

The other way that *finger* is used is to provide specific text files, but from your point of view it works the same. For example:

```
finger weather@iugate.ucs.indiana.edu
```

will provide the text for the Weather Service forecast for central and southern Indiana.

Transferring Data between Hosts with TCP/IP

The TCP/IP client utilities included with NT offer three programs to move files between hosts. RCP, the remote copy program, is the simplest, providing the same functionality as the DOS copy command between hosts. The other two, FTP and TFTP, are the client side of the FTP server discussed later in this chapter. These two programs allow the transfer of files through the standard TCP/IP File Transfer Protocol (FTP) by interacting with the remote machine's server and creating the necessary communications channels.

RCP

RCP stands for *remote copy*, which is what this command is all about. You can exchange files with remote host—or even copy files from one host to another—without having to log onto them explicitly. RCP uses trust between systems, via either the .rhosts or /etc/equiv.hosts files on the remote systems. You can use explicit user names on the command line, but there must still be trust between the hosts and the NT system.

RCP also supports copying files on the local system, similar to the NT (or DOS) copy command line utility. To copy a file named SCHEDULE.TXT to the c:\accounting directory on the remote system, type the command *rcp schedule.txt c:\accounting\schedule.txt*.

To copy binary files, such as an executable program or a document with extended characters, use the *-b* option. To copy a file named PAYROLL.WKS from one directory to another, type the command *rcp -b payroll.wks c:\accounting\payroll.wks*. If the -b option is left out, RCP assumes that ASCII transfer is all that's needed.

To copy the same spreadsheet to the remote host GRUMPY, use the command *rcp -b payroll.wks grumpy:payroll.wks*. To copy the file from GRUMPY to the local NT system, type the command *rcp -b grumpy:payroll.wks payroll.wks*.

You can copy entire directory trees from one host to another using the RCP utility as well. If you need to move a bunch of files from a remote host to the local system, or vice versa, this is the quickest way to get the job done. To copy the entire accounting directory on GRUMPY to the NT system, type the command *rcp -b -r GRUMPY:/accounting c:\accounting*. This command will create a directory called c:\payroll on the local NT system, and copy all the files in all of the subdirectories in GRUMPY's /accounting directory.

Like the RSH and REXEC services, the RCP utility is implemented as a client service only. You cannot RCP to and from the NT system from another system. Also, remember that the remote hosts you exchange files with must trust the NT machine you are using. For information on setting up trust between hosts, refer to the documentation provided by the vendor of each system that you want to use.

The FTP Client

The FTP client software included with NT is of the simple command line variety. It lets you establish a connection to the remote machine, log in as a user, and then interact with the host to locate and transfer files. FTP can be used for upload or download, and while it has many subcommands, you need to know only a few to use FTP effectively. There are third-party FTP clients available that offer a friendlier Windows interface. If you find yourself using FTP as part of your daily Windows routine, a Windows NT version of one of these products is probably a good idea. For occasional use, though, the included utility is adequate.

Establishing a Connection

The first step in using the FTP client is to establish a connection. There are two ways to accomplish this. First, if you are not yet running the FTP program, is the command line:

```
ftp host name
```

where *hostname* is the name or numerical IP address of the host to which you wish to connect. This will execute the FTP program and initiate the connection to the named host. If the FTP program is already running, the open command will perform the same function at the FTP prompt:

```
ftp> open hostname
```

The prompt *ftp>* is displayed whenever the FTP program is running to indicate that it is active.

Logging In

Once the connection to the remote host is established, you will be prompted to log in. Frequently, FTP sessions are of the *anonymous* variety. Anonymous FTP is a way to allow users without accounts on a particular machine to access a public directory (usually called *public* or *pub*) to get or send files. Anonymous FTP is prevalent on the Internet. The first message you will see upon connecting is an informational message about the FTP server:

```
220 host name Windows FTP Server <Version 1.0>.
```

This message provides the name of the machine (*hostname*), and the operating system/server software. Note the number in front of the message: 220. Each message sent by the FTP server is preceded by a message number. These numbers are used by the client software to determine the meaning of the message. The numbers are standard and can be used to determine what the server is saying, with no ambiguity. The text messages are there for your benefit and may vary, depending upon the server.

Immediately after this informational message you will be prompted for a user name. This message comes from the client software, not the server. When you enter the name, the FTP program uses it as the argument for the *pass* command. For example, if you answer the login prompt:

```
User host name: anonymous
```

(where *hostname* is displayed by the client to remind you of where you are logging in, and *anonymous* is the user name that you entered), this is then translated by the FTP program and sent to the host as:

```
PASS anonymous
```

Before you saw the user prompt from the FTP program, the server sent a message asking for a login. It was intercepted before you saw it. If for some reason you want to see all the messages, you can use the *verbose* command; just enter it at the ftp> prompt as *ftp> verbose*. This will give you a full view of all the messages, which may be useful if you're debugging a system (or interesting if you're just curious). Here's what a successful login looks like:

```
C:\users\default>ftp 130.26.0.100
Connected to 130.26.0.100.
220 emsworth Windows NT FTP Server (Version 1.0).
User (130.26.0.100:): anonymous
331 Anonymous access allowed, send identity (e-mail name) as password.
Password:
230 Anonymous user logged in as ftpuser.
ftp>
```

In this example, the numerical address of the server named *emsworth* is used to connect directly from the command line. The user name *anonymous* is used; the password—which does not echo—is the real internet e-mail address for the user logging in. This is traditional, since it allows administrators to contact the user should some sort of problem occur. This is not enforced by the server, since it doesn't know who you are. The message that starts with *230* tells us that the login was successful, and for information, indicates that we were logged in as *ftpuser*. This is the account name that the system administrator assigned to anonymous FTP logins, and determines various access permissions. Most commonly this will say *guest*, but it can be anything. The return of the ftp> prompt indicates that the FTP client program is ready for the next command.

Navigating on the Remote Host

Once logged in you have access to the directory structure that the remote hosts administrator has made available to FTP users. If you know DOS or UNIX commands, FTP navigation will be old hat. The first thing you are likely to want to do is get a directory of the remote drive. You can do this in more than one way. The two simple ways are with the *dir* and *ls* commands. Which you will use will depend on the file system in use there. There are FTP servers running on just about every sort of machine that can be connected to the Internet. The most common type to see, though, is UNIX. Many FTP servers will even translate their non-UNIX file system into something that looks like one for FTP users. On a NetWare FTP server, the *dir* command returns:

```
- [RWCEAFMS] supervisor        20319      Aug 12 06:49    vol$log.err
- [RWCEAFMS] supervisor        10423      Aug 12 06:50    tts$log.err
- [RWCEAFMS] supervisor        20480      Aug 12 09:48    backout.tts
d [RWCEAFMS] supervisor          512      Aug 13 09:49    login
d [RWCEAFMS] supervisor          512      Aug 13 10:07    system
d [RWCEAFMS] supervisor          512      Aug 13 09:49    public
d [RWCEAFMS] supervisor          512      Aug 13 09:49    mail
```

This is a variation on a standard UNIX structure (the differences lie in the way the permissions are indicated). What's important to you, as an FTP user, is the lowercase *d* that precedes the letters in square brackets. This indicates that the entry is a directory, instead of a file. The UNIX-style *ls* command is a quick directory that eliminates everything except the names:

```
vol$log.err
tts$log.err
backout.tts
treeinfo.ncd
login
system
public
mail
```

In this NetWare example, there is no indication that an entry is a directory. On many UNIX systems, a directory will be followed by a forward slash:

```
file
file
directory/
```

One thing to keep in mind as you connect to remote systems is that the file system in use there may be something completely foreign to what you are used to. Some IBM mainframes, for example, use a flat system with no subdirectories, and are very hard to navigate.

Once you determine what is available in the root directory of the remote host, you'll want to switch to the directory of interest. You will almost always have to do this, since it is rare that any files will be in the root directory on an FTP server. Once again your DOS experience will help out. The *cd* command is used to move to other directories. Remember, though, the DOS convention of *(a backslash)* (\) as a separator is exactly the opposite of the UNIX world where *(a forward slash)* (/) is used. Just type *ftp> cd directory/directory* to switch the working directory. To find out where you are, use the *pwd* (print working directory) command:

```
ftp> pwd
257 "/sys" is the current directory.
Getting Files from the Remote Host
```

You have two choices in transferring files: one at a time or in a batch. The simple one-shot file transfer is done with the *get* command. The syntax is very simple:

```
get remote-filename local-filename
```

It works just the way it looks—getting the remote file and storing it in the local file you've named. For instance, the command *get myfile.dat c:\temp\myfile.dat* will cause the remote system to send MYFILE.DAT to your system's C:\TEMP directory. The batch method is very similar, using *mget* (multiple get). With *mget*, wildcards are allowed, which simplifies batch transfers. For example, to get all the files in the current directory that start with *my* use the command *mget my**.

Note that the wildcards are UNIX-style, so this will get everything that starts with *my*, regardless of extension. The FTP program will prompt you for an OK on each file it finds that matches the wildcard criteria.

Sending Files to the Remote Host

Sending files is done with *get*'s companion command, *put*. There is also an *mput* command, which (surprise!) does a batch-style (or multiple) put. These commands work the same way as *get*:

```
put local_filename remote_filename
```

that is:

```
mput c:\temp\myfile.dat myfile.dat
```

or

```
mput my*
```

just as in the previous example.

Manipulating Directories and Files

FTP offers a set of commands to manipulate directories and files:

mkdir directory—Make directory creates a directory on the remote host. This command will fail if you do not have sufficient permissions.

rmdir directory—Remove directory removes a directory on the remote host. This command will fail if you do not have sufficient permissions.

delete filename—Deletes a remote file. This command will fail if you do not have sufficient permissions.

mdelete filespec—Multiple delete deletes a set of files specified by a wildcard. This command will fail if you do not have sufficient permissions.

rename filename—Renames a remote file. This command will fail if you do not have sufficient permissions.

Configuration Commands

There are a few FTP commands that help to make the FTP environment more suitable to your particular use.

ascii—Puts FTP into ASCII mode for transferring text files. This mode is needed because, for historical reasons, American Standard Code for Information Interchange (ASCII) text files are stored differently on UNIX sytems than they are on other systems (including Windows NT). The UNIX convention is to follow each line of text with the ASCII linefeed (LF) character. Most other systems (including Windows NT) follow each line of text with a pair of characters—an ASCII carriage return (CR) and then an LF. (A few systems use just the CR, as if matters weren't complicated enough already!) This mode does automatic CR/LF translation where appropriate, which is great for text files, but inappropriate for binary file transfer.

binary—This companion to ASCII switches to binary mode, which transfers characters as a binary stream verbatim from the other system (without any CR/LF translation).

mode—Displays the mode—binary or ASCII.

bell—Toggles the bell, indicating completed operations. This is useful if you are doing long transfers and want to know when they are complete.

hash—Toggles the printing of a hash mark (#) for every 512 bytes of data transferred. This is useful if you have a slow connection or are transferring large files—it lets you know that things are progressing.

Ending an FTP Session

To end a session, simply type *close* at the ftp> prompt. This disconnects you from the remote machine. The *open* command can then be used to begin a new connection. To close the connection and exit the FTP program, type *bye*.

Getting Help

The help included with the FTP program is minimal, but still useful—at least as a reminder. Type *help* or *?* at the ftp> prompt for a list of available commands:

```
ftp> ?
Commands may be abbreviated. Commands are:

!            delete        literal       prompt       send
?            debug         ls            put          status
append       dir           mdelete       pwd          trace
```

```
ascii       disconnect    mdir      quit         type
bell        get           mget      quote        user
binary      glob          mkdir     recv         verbose
bye         hash          mls       remotehelp
cd          help          mput      rename
close       lcd           open      rmdir
ftp>
```

For a little information on any particular command, type *help command-name* at the ftp> prompt.

remotehelp

The nature of FTP is that it translates local commands into a set of standard commands. Not all FTP server software supports the entire command set. If a command does not seem to be working, typing *remotehelp* at the ftp> prompt might shed some light with a list of supported commands.

TFTP

The Trivial FTP program is a command-line FTP client that allows simple transfers from the command line. It is useful for quick transfer operations, and use in batch or command files. TFTP does not allow user logins, which means that the remote file/directory must allow *world* access. The syntax for TFTP is:

```
tftp [-i] hostname <put|get> source file destination file
```

The *-i* option tells TFTP to use binary (image) mode instead of the default ASCII, which performs translations of control characters. Use binary mode to move compressed and executable files. *Put* or *get* do just what their FTP counterparts do—transfer files to (put) or from (get) the remote host. The source and destination files are the name of the file on which the operation will occur (source) and where it will end up (destination). If no destination file is specified, the source file name will be used.

NT Server Services

Windows NT 3.5's TCP/IP suite not only includes client applications, but a handful of server services as well. The most dominant of these is the FTP Server that comes bundled with NT Server. Also of note is the inclusion of DNS, Gopher, and HTTP servers on the NT 3.5 Resource Kit CD. Although these services aren't world-class equivalents to what you get with UNIX or other well-established servers, they are more than usable in many environments.

Microsoft's own World-Wide Web server uses the HTTP Server Service that is on the Resource Kit CD.

The FTP Server

FTP (File Transfer Protocol) offers an easy way to share files stored on an NT system with other systems—UNIX workstations, for example. An FTP server can be used to allow other systems (non-NT) to place files where they can be shared by NT systems through NT's native networking. One additional advantage of FTP is its prevalence on the Internet. An NT server connected to the Internet can offer *anonymous* FTP to Internet users that can connect to it. This allows general distribution of files to users who do not have a normal account on the server machine (to maintain good security, the FTP directories should reside on an NTFS partition).

FTP is a client/server-based transfer protocol. The client package translates commands to FTP-compliant syntax, and translates data between file systems where incompatibilities exist. NT comes with a command-line-based FTP client, which is described earlier in this chapter.

Installing the NT FTP Server

The NT FTP Server is an optional component of NT, but installation is simple. Membership in the Administrator group is required to install and/or configure the FTP server. Because of the potential security risk the FTP server presents, be sure you understand the implications before making the FTP server available. To install the FTP server:

1. Launch Control Panel.
2. Double-click the Network icon in the Control Panel window. This invokes the Network Settings dialog box.
3. Press the Add Software button.
4. Locate the FTP Server entry in the Network Software listbox, and select it. Press Continue. A dialog box warning of the potential risk to passwords appears. This warning means that during the establishment of an FTP session, the password is sent by the client in plain text. This is a potential security risk if someone is listening to the traffic on the network. If this is an unacceptable risk, you can consider installing a separate NT machine just for FTP, and offering only anonymous FTP— that is, FTP where there are no privileged accounts. This arrangement can still be very useful.
5. Press the Yes button, unless you wish to abort the installation.

6. You will be prompted for the path to the NT distribution files; provide it in the Edit field, and press the Continue button.

7. NT will now copy the required files to your system; once this operation is complete you will be given a chance to configure the server—this must be done before the server will operate.

Configuring the NT FTP Server

Like installation, configuring NT's FTP server is a simple process, but before you begin, you should have some idea of what you intend to use the server for. There are two most likely scenarios for the NT FTP server:

1. The FTP server will be used to provide connectivity to an NT machine (or network) for UNIX-based workstations. If this is your main objective, there are a couple of things to consider. First, the security of FTP is not as good as the security of NT itself. You can do some things to ensure maximum security, but it will not match NT's native capabilities (this is probably an issue for only a small number of sites). If you must have maximum security:

   ❑ Use a separate NT machine to act as a server, and provide users with special accounts for that server only.

   ❑ Be sure that the passwords for these accounts are not the same as for the users' regular accounts.

   ❑ Make sure that the FTP server accesses only NTFS partitions, where the file system is secure.

   ❑ Use FTP to transfer only nonsensitive data; assume it is accessible.

      The second consideration in this scenario is that, by the time you read this, several implementations of NFS (Network File System) will probably be available for NT. NFS is a standard developed by Sun to allow *mounting* of remote volumes as if they were local, and is well supported throughout the UNIX world. Though not identical, it is the functional equivalent of NT's native networking. If this is what you need, NFS is a much better choice.

2. The FTP server will be used to provide anonymous FTP access to users with no accounts in your organization, as well as to some known users. The NT machine may even reside on the Internet. This seems the most likely scenario, and the best use of the FTP server. Paradoxically, this scenario actually makes security easier. By limiting FTP logins to user *anonymous*, there are no privileged accounts and no passwords to secure. Yet even with this limited access, the FTP server has a great deal of utility. If a user has native NT access—through NT's built-in networking—nothing prevents privileged access to the same directories to which FTP has

only minimal permissions. For example, through anonymous FTP, an outside user could upload or download only files in a particular directory, while an internal user with an account on the machine could delete or edit those same files. This allows the FTP server to act as a distribution and collection point for your organization.

It is most likely that you will wish to use FTP this way. In order to accomplish this, you must:

❑ Create an account with the appropriate permissions, which will be used for every user who makes an FTP connection.

❑ Limit FTP connections to *anonymous* only.

❑ Create a directory structure, accessible to the anonymous FTP user, which facilitates the server's intended application.

Selecting Configuration Options

If you are in the process of installing the FTP server, the FTP Service dialog appears automatically at this point. If you are reconfiguring the server, or if for some reason the dialog is not on-screen, you will find it in the Control Panel:

1. Launch Control Panel.

2. Double-click on the Network icon; this will invoke the Network Settings dialog.

3. Locate the FTP Server entry in the Installed Network Software listbox and select it.

4. Press the Configure button—this will invoke the FTP Service dialog, illustrated in Figure 6.12.

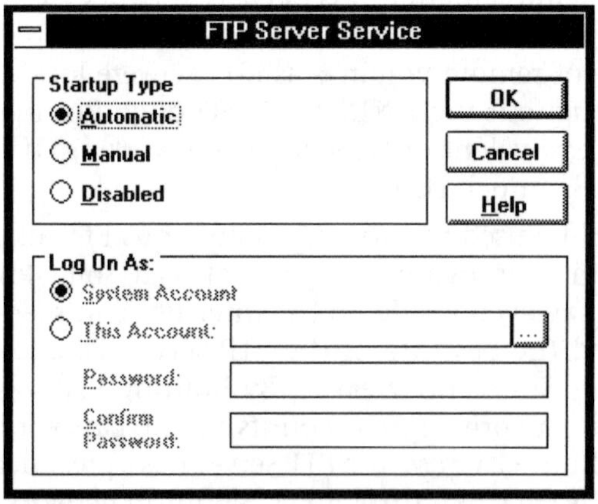

Figure 6.12 The FTP Service dialog.

❑ *Maximum Connections*—This setting determines the number of FTP connections the system will allow. This setting defaults to 20, which may be too large for your site. Remember that FTP sessions are data intensive, since they are purely file transfers. Determining the optimum value for your situation will take practical experience of what your particular users do with the FTP server. Watch for degradation of the machine's performance while many users are connected, as a sign that the number should be reduced. On the other hand, complaints from users that they cannot connect because of the limit is a clue to increase the number, which cannot exceed 50.

❑ *Idle Time Out*—This setting determines the length of time (in minutes) a user can remain idle before the server will disconnect that user. This setting is somewhat interactive with the maximum connections setting—if many idle connections are tying up the server, logging them out makes the slots available for other users. The ten-minute default time is reasonable and should serve most purposes. If, for some reason, you need to disable the time-out feature, set it to 0. The maximum value for this setting is 60.

❑ *Home Directory*—This entry determines the directory in which the user will be placed once connected. For a public system, it is wise to make this directory the root of whatever area the user will be allowed to access. If you're setting up an anonymous FTP server, remember that it is the account you specify for anonymous users that determines the permissions—and therefore the directories—the FTP user can access.

❑ *Allow Anonymous Connections*—This check box determines if the server will accept connections from the user *anonymous*. This is an Internet convention and will allow users who do not have an account on the system to access files specifically made available to them (see previous discussion). If you have no intention of providing access to your server to outside users, leave this check box blank.

❑ *Username*—This entry determines the account that will be assigned to the anonymous user. The default is the standard Windows NT guest account. It is probably best, though, to create an account specifically for this purpose and give it the permissions needed. You can name this account anything you wish, but it makes sense to use something logical, such as *ftpuser*. Keep in mind that this account will also be accessible from any machine on your network.

❑ *Password*—This entry is the password for the account selected in the user name entry, previously defined. Note that this is not required for anonymous FTP login. Instead, it is the password for the account when it is used as a normal login (the usual password for an anonymous FTP connection is the e-mail address of the user who is connecting).

❑ *Allow Only Anonymous Connections*—This check box limits connections to the FTP server to the user *anonymous*. It is strongly suggested that you run the FTP server in this fashion. If this checkbox is selected, no other account can be used to log into the FTP server. This eliminates the security problem of unencrypted user passwords being passed over the network.

Completing FTP Server Configuration

Once you have filled in the various fields and check boxes press the OK button in the dialog box. Another dialog will appear, explaining the requirement to restart NT for changes to take effect. If this is the first configuration, you do not need to restart the system. Instead, close the control panel and reopen it. You will now find an FTP Server icon in Control Panel. There is one more configuration operation that must be completed before the FTP server will operate.

1. Double-click on the FTP server icon in the control panel. This will invoke the FTP User Sessions dialog (this dialog is also available from the FTP menu in the Server Manager on Windows NT Servers). Press the Security button. This invokes the FTP Server Security dialog.

2. From the Partition combo box, select the partition(s) that the FTP server will access (remember that it is best to use an NTFS partition, not a FAT one).

3. Select read and/or write access from the check boxes provided. This determines whether the FTP server will allow upload, download, or both to the FTP user.

4. Press the OK button when finished, or cancel to abort the operation. Changes made in this dialog are immediate and do not require a system restart. The FTP server is now configured for operation.

FTP Server Administration and Control

Most of the administrator's job is done when the FTP server is configured, but there may be times when you'll need to take special steps. When you do, the most likely places you'll take them are in the FTP Server Configuration section of the Networks object in Control Panel, as discussed earlier; or in the separate FTP Server object in the Control Panel, illustrated in Figure 6.13.

The FTP Server Control Panel object simply lists the number of FTP sessions currently in use, and allows you to disconnect any or all of them. It also gives a limited capability to enable additional FTP security, through the Security pushbutton. This will give you access to the dialog illustrated in Figure 6.14.

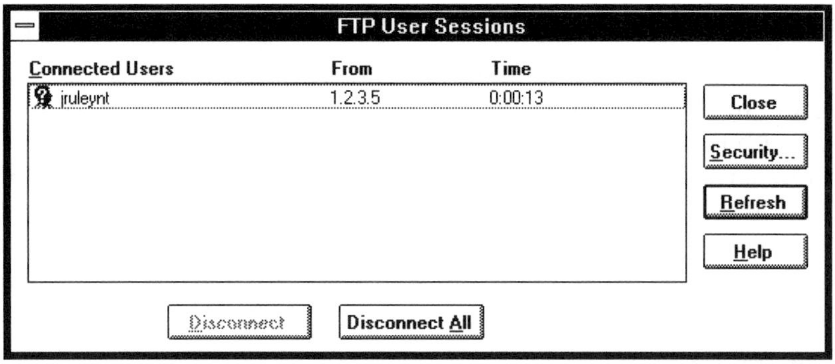

Figure 6.13 Windows NT's FTP Server Service is controlled through the FTP Control Panel Object.

This Security dialog lets you determine which volumes in the system FTP users are permitted to read from and write to. Obviously, this gives you a simple way to significantly enhance FTP server security: Create a separate volume (logical disk drive) for FTP users, and restrict their access to that volume.

A Separate FTP User Account?

As discussed earlier, the most convenient way to provide FTP users with access to a Windows NT system is with anonymous access—which normally uses the system's *Guest* account. The only trouble with this is that you may want to use the Guest account for other purposes—letting other NT and WFWG users from outside your domain or workgroup access shared directories, for instance—that conflict with the need to restrict FTP login. You can get around this by creating a separate FTP User account that is used only for FTP login, and not for other purposes.

Figure 6.14 FTP Security.

Security Settings for the FTP Server Service are set in the FTP Control Panel Object's Security Dialog.

Servers Bundled with Windows NT 3.5's Resource Kit

The Windows NT 3.5 Resource Kit also contains a variety of server services, including DNS, Gopher, and HTTP servers. These server services, while not on par with their UNIX counterparts, are generally satisfactory enough to be used for departmental or workgroup servers. The Resource Kit documentation contains information on how to install the services; it's a somewhat convoluted process, as they are not installed as other services are. The following sections contain general background and configuration information for these services.

The DNS Server

DNS is one of the most convoluted subjects on the planet. It takes weeks to understand, and a lifetime to master. However, once you set it up right, you rarely have to mess with it again. Also, the paybacks for running DNS servers are tremendous. You won't have to mess with HOSTS files scattered around your network anymore. If you're interested in DNS, there's a book called *DNS and BIND* (publisher information is listed at the end of this chapter) that is a must read.

Basically, DNS revolves around the concept of a client/server relationship similar to the WINS or DHCP architectures. A DNS client wishing to communicate with a remote host issues a lookup request to a specified DNS server. If the DNS server knows the information (i.e., has it cached), it will return it. If it doesn't know the information (i.e., a client is asking for information about a host in a remote domain), it will query the remote domain's DNS server for the information on behalf of the client and pass the resulting information back.

Each domain has a *Primary* server that manages information for that domain. The primary DNS server reads information from a series of text files. These files generally contain subnet-specific information, such as host names and corresponding IP addresses. The primary DNS server is the *authoritative* server for the domain.

There are also *secondary* servers that can read information from the primary servers, instead of from a collection of text files. Clients can point to these services for their interdomain name resolution. If a client requests a remote host be looked up, the secondary server will issue the request to the remote domain's primary server on behalf of the client, and return the information back. It also caches the information for future use.

There can also be *caching-only* servers, which simply forward requests and cache the information for future use. They don't know any more about the local domain than they do about the remote domains. However, since they are caching servers, they can retain the information for a long time, instead of having to constantly query other servers.

Every NT Server should be configured as a caching-only server, and local clients should be pointed to it. This will allow users to get fast response for their queries, with no overhead required on the primary and secondary servers. Obviously, you'll need at least one primary DNS server for your domain. If you have geographically dispersed or heavily laden networks, you'll also do well to distribute secondary DNS servers throughout your network.

One of the neat tricks with the DNS server that comes with the Resource Kit is the ability to map WINS servers into the DNS database. For example, if you know the NetBIOS name of a workstation you wish to PING or FTP to, but don't know the IP host name, then you can have the DNS server issue WINS queries on your behalf, and return the corresponding IP address to you. This is achieved through the use of the $WINS directive (similar to the PRIMARY or SECONDARY directives). This would tell the DNS server to match any host with the specified domain name to the specified WINS server.

The Gopher Server

The Gopher server that comes bundled with NT is an adequate one. If you are not familiar with Gopher, suffice it to say that it is a distributed menu system. It can provide a menu of files, links to other menus, or links to other servers' menus. It is somewhat similar to FTP, only distributed and more user friendly.

The Gopher server that comes with the Resource Kit is pretty restricted, however. It serves only files and directories, and doesn't appear to offer any links to other systems, or links to non-filesystem-based information. Still, it is functional enough for workgroups or departments to use on an informal basis.

One of the neat things about Gopher is that you can link a file type to an application. That is, you can tell the Gopher server that a file ending in .WAV is an *audio* file. Then when a client sees the list of available files using a Gopher client, they will only need to double-click on the entry, and the client will retrieve the file and play it using a user-determined audio utility. It's sort of a multimedia FTP, only better.

The Gopher server is configured with a Control Panel applet. Double-clicking on the Gopher control object displays the dialog box shown in Figure 6.15. You can add new file mappings as needed, and make other system-specific tweaks.

The HTTP Server

If Lotus 1-2-3 was the killer app for the PC, and Lotus Notes was the killer app for networking, then the Internet's killer app is the World-Wide Web. The cool browsers you see for NetScape and Mosaic are used to display HTML (HyperText

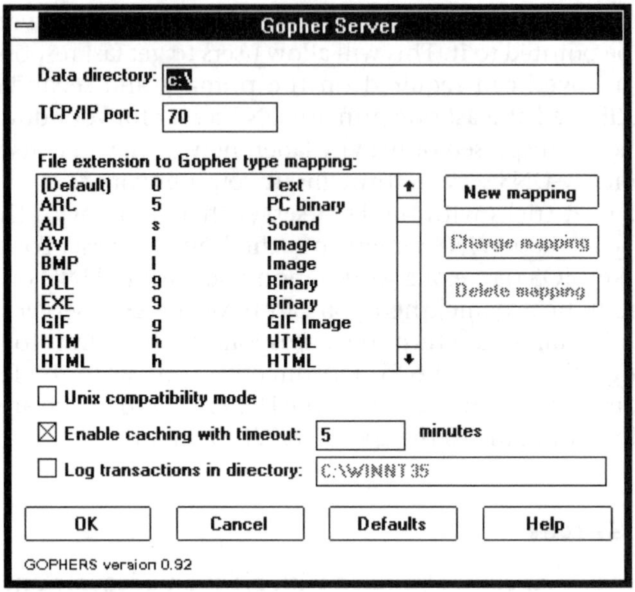

Figure 6.15 Gopher server.

The Windows NT Resource Kit (2nd Edition) includes a Windows NT Service implementing an Internet Gopher server.

Markup Language) documents located on HTTP (HyperText Transport Protocol) servers. This is a highly optimized, distributed document display system, with streamlined document layout formats and protocols. This narrow-function optimization is what allows these documents to be distributed so quickly across slow links.

The HTTP server that comes bundled with the NT Resource Kit allows you to share HTML documents using the HTTP protocol. Clients with HTTP browsers (such as NetScape and Mosaic) can connect to your server and view those files, but it will *not* help you to create them. You will need to get literature on the essentials of HTML or a tool to help you make them. Microsoft has made a Word-to-HTML converter available on their HTTP server (http://www.micro-soft.com).

In the real world, most HTTP servers also allow you to have background processes that can be called from the HTML documents, such as file searching, imagemap clicking (xy mouse coordinates are returned to the server for processing), and user authentication. The HTTP server provided with the resource kit has none of these capabilities; the only non-HTML support in this package is the ability to let users view the server's filesystem from outside of a document. That is, you can use the HTTP server as a psuedo-Gopher server.

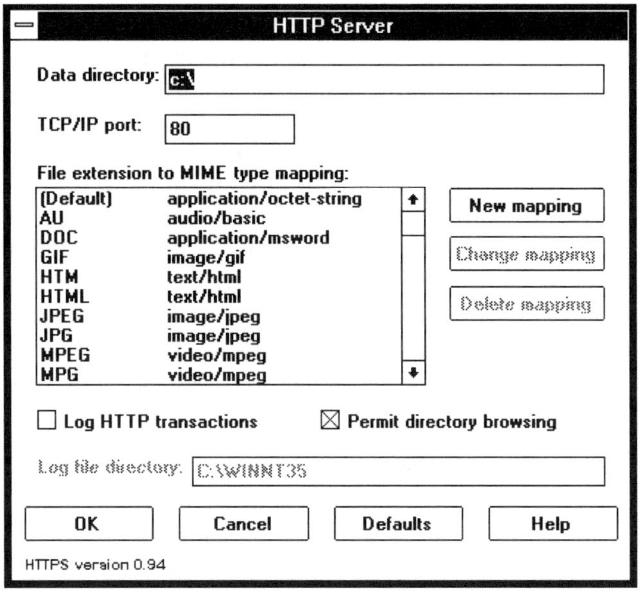

Figure 6.16 HTTP server.
The Windows NT Resource Kit (2nd Edition) includes a Service implementing a HyperText Transport Protocol server—used by World-Wide Web clients, such as NCSA Mosaic.

The HTTP server is configured with a Control Panel applet. Double-clicking on the HTTP Server control object displays the dialog box shown in Figure 6.16. You can add new file mappings as needed, and make other system-specific tweaks.

Advanced Topics—Routing and SNMP

Beyond the simple TCP/IP configuration, NBT, and IP-centric services, you may encounter difficulties when attempting to use NT in an advanced TCP/IP network. It's lack of support for most of the fundamental protocols (such as RIP) makes it difficult to integrate in some environments. The rest of this chapter focuses on what is required to go the *extra mile* when necessary.

Multiple Adapters and IP Routing

Although most TCP/IP systems support dynamic routing, the Windows NT implementation does not. You must tell each NT system explicitly how to get to other network segments. You can point all nonlocal traffic to a default router, or you can build route entries for specific remote networks. For complex networks with multiple paths to the same remote destination, you must use a non-NT system that supports dynamic routing.

NT can act as a very basic router for users who have only a few segments and do not need dynamic routing capabilities. In order to do this, you must have multiple network adapters with TCP/IP enabled on all of the ones you want to route IP traffic between. Then use the TCP/IP Configuration in the Networks control panel to turn on static routing between network adapters, and then use the ROUTE.EXE utility to create static routing maps between the adapters. For information on configuring TCP/IP on multiple adapters, refer to the "Installing TCP/IP" section earlier in this chapter.

Routing on Small Networks

After you have enabled routing and rebooted the system, your system will provide local routing services to the networks it knows about. You can then point other systems' default routes to the NT system. Any network segments that the NT system is not physically connected to must be entered into the route table manually.

ROUTE.EXE is a command-line utility that lets you add or delete static routes between networks or hosts. You can define multiple routes to a destination, and if the first one fails, the second will kick in. You must define routes to all intermediate points along the way. For example, let's look at the simple network illustrated in Figure 6.17.

There are two network segments (192.155.11 and 192.155.12) and 3 nodes (x.2, x.3, and x.4). When NT was installed on nodes 192.155.11.2 and 192.155.12.4, the default router was given as node x.3, meaning that all nonlocal IP traffic will be passed to the server in the middle. However, by default, x.3 is unable to route the traffic. The network administrator must enable TCP/IP on each adapter in node x.3, and then enable IP routing using the Registry Editor as previously described. At that point, the node at x.3 will be able to forward traffic from 192.155.11.2 to 192.155.12.4, and vice versa.

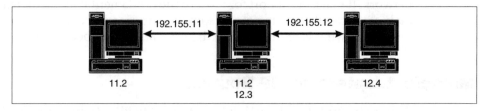

Figure 6.17 Routing-1.

Simple network layout and routing.

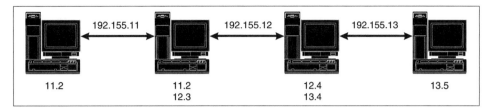

Figure 6.18 Routing-2.

Mildly complex network routing setup.

Routing in Mildly Complex Networks

Let's look at the more complicated setup shown in Figure 6.18. As in the example in Figure 6.17, node 192.155.11.2 points to 192.155.11.3 as the default route. However, node x.3 knows only about networks 192.155.11 and 192.155.12, since that's all it is directly connected to. Likewise, node x.4 knows only about networks 192.155.12 and 192.155.13. In order for packets from network 192.155.11 to reach network 192.155.13 (and vice versa), several things must happen.

First, nodes x.3 and x.4 must be configured to route, as in the previous example with node x.3. Then, static routing entries must be defined for nodes x.3 and x.4, telling them about the remote networks. For node x.3, the command would look like this:

```
ROUTE ADD 192.155.13.0 192.155.12.4
```

This command adds a static route to node x.3's routing table. Then, any packet coming from subnet 192.155.11 destined for network 192.155.13 will get passed to node 12.4 for handling. In order for x.4 to return packets to network 192.155.11, it must be informed about the route as well (remember that NT doesn't support dynamic routing). Therefore, the following command must be given to node x.4:

```
ROUTE ADD 192.155.11.0 192.155.12.3
```

Now packets will make it from any node on any net to any other node on any other net. Believe it or not, this is a very simple example, and serves to illustrate the complexity inherent in multiple-segment IP networks. The more segments you add, the more systems you must manually configure. The static routing model breaks down after about five segments, at which point the administration and configuration becomes overwhelming.

Routing in Very Complex Networks

A very complex network, more typical of large corporate sites, is illustrated in Figure 6.19, where there are many departmental routers throughout a company

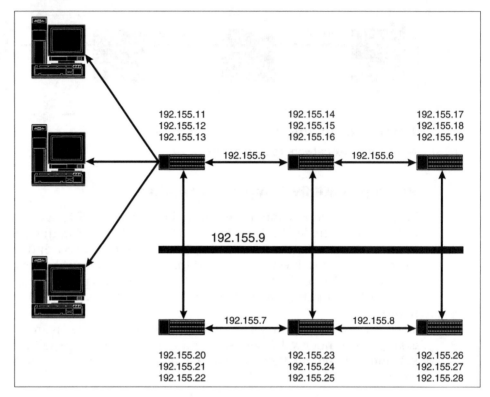

Figure 6.19 Routing-3.

Large corporate or campus network.

connected over a high-speed backbone with redundant links between the routers. All of these routers have separate interfaces for multiple small networks. Workstations on each of the smaller subnets have a single adapter running TCP/IP, and they identify the nearest backbone router as their default router.

This method is the simplest to configure and maintain, as each of the routers is capable of updating the others via RIP, OSPF, or some other router-to-router protocol. Since they are directly connected to each segment, the network numbers are seen automatically by the routers, and forwarded out with no maintenance or configuration required. If a node on network 192.155.11 sends a request to a node on 192.155.28, the routers are capable of automatically forwarding and rejecting packets as needed. The clients simply point to the closest router as their default, and let the network hardware do its work.

Purchasing and maintaining these dedicated routers is an expensive proce-dure, however, and many companies prefer to let other devices handle the routing work instead. Almost all of the UNIX and NetWare implementations

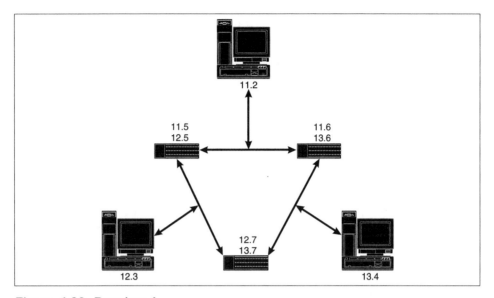

Figure 6.20 Routing-4.

TCP/IP Routing in a Redundant network.

support RIP or other dynamic routing protocols, and NT would benefit from this as well, allowing customers to use departmental servers as routers. Microsoft has hinted at the possibility of providing this functionality in the future (for more information on IP routing, refer to Appendix 2).

Secondary Default Routes

In some environments, users may see multiple routers on a single segment. This is similar to the example in Figure 6.19 earlier, where each router has multiple paths in the event that one fails. However, here we are speaking of multiple routers on the clients network, which might look something like Figure 6.20.

In this type of environment, users would need to be able to define multiple default routes. In the event that one router failed, another router would be used automatically. NT allows this by adding multiple default routes in the TCP/IP Configuration section of the Networks control panel. You must reboot the system after making these changes. You can also add additional default gateways after making the initial changes with the *ROUTE-S* command, although they are not permanently added to the registry.

It's important to note that you can have multiple default gateways for every network interface in your system. For example, if you have two dynamic routers on two different segments to which you are directly connected, you can have up to four default routers. In the event that one of your adapters or subnets fails, you will still have two routers on the other segment that you can use. This is an expensive and unlikely wiring scheme, but it is completely possible.

SNMP

SNMP stands for Simple Network Management Protocol, and that's exactly what it is. It provides basic administrative information about a device so that network administrators or SNMP management software can monitor the overall health of the network (as well as individual systems). In order to take advantage of NT's SNMP services, you must have an SNMP manager that can monitor and display SNMP alerts. Several such programs are available for a wide variety of platforms.

To install the SNMP service, load the Network control object from the Control Panels utility. If you are configuring the SNMP services during the original system installation, you will be presented with these options during the initial setup routines. If not, you need to load the Network control object manually. Double-click Control Panels from the Main window in Program Manager, or type *CONTROL.EXE* in the File/Run... menu of either Program Manager or File Manager. Likewise, you can type *CONTROL.EXE* from the command prompt. Then double-click the Networks icon to load the Network Settings dialog box.

To add the SNMP service, click the Add Software... button, and select SNMP Service from the drop-down list. After the system copies the necessary software to the hard drive, you are presented with the SNMP Service Configuration dialog illustrated in Figure 6.21.

There are two methods that SNMP management software can use to collect information about devices. One way is to have devices send alerts to an SNMP

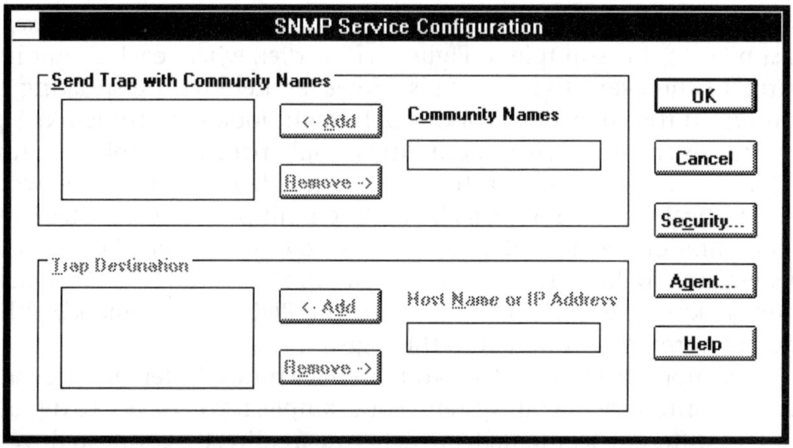

Figure 6.21 The SNMP Service Configuration dialog box.

manager, or to any manager in the community. Another method is to have the SNMP manager poll devices every few seconds (or minutes or hours). There are benefits to both strategies, and it is likely that both are in use within your organization.

For example, when an SNMP device can send an alert to a management station, that device can do so as soon as something starts to fail. By the time a polling management station gets to a node that has started failing, it may be dead altogether, leaving no clue as to the cause of death. Conversely, devices that are in good health clutter the network with unnecessary alerts, and it's better to let a manager poll nodes when needed.

By default, NT's SNMP service does not send alerts. It does, however, support SNMP queries from any device in the *Public* community (a community is a logical grouping of devices).

To enable the SNMP service to send alerts, select the Community Names edit box, type in the community name you wish to add, and click the <- Add button. Although Public is the default community for inquiries, it is not the default community for the sending of alerts. To make your system send SNMP alerts to devices within the Public community, add it here. If you have a departmental SNMP community, add it here as well. A node can be in more than one community at a time simply by adding additional community names as needed.

By adding the Public community to the alert list, any management station within the community will receive the alerts, and may also be able to make changes to your configuration. If you want to send alerts only to a specific management station, you can add it to the Trap Destinations listbox by selecting the Host Name or IP Address edit box, typing in the address or host name of the management station, and clicking the <- Add button. Then only that management station will receive the alerts.

Remember that by default NT will respond to any management station request that comes from the Public community. To disable this feature, or to add a new community name, click the Security button, and you will be presented with the dialog illustrated in Figure 6.22.

If you want to remove the Public community from the list, select it and click the Remove -> button. If you want to add another community to the list, then click in the Community Name edit box, and click the <- Add button.

If you want to restrict the management stations that can query your machine for SNMP statistics, click the Only Accept SNMP Packets from These Hosts radio button, and add the desired management stations to the listbox below it. To add a host, click the Host or IP Address edit box, type in the host name or IP address of the management station you want to add, and then click the <- Add button.

The Send Authentication Trap check box in the upper left corner is for alerting managers that an unauthorized host is attempting to pull statistics from

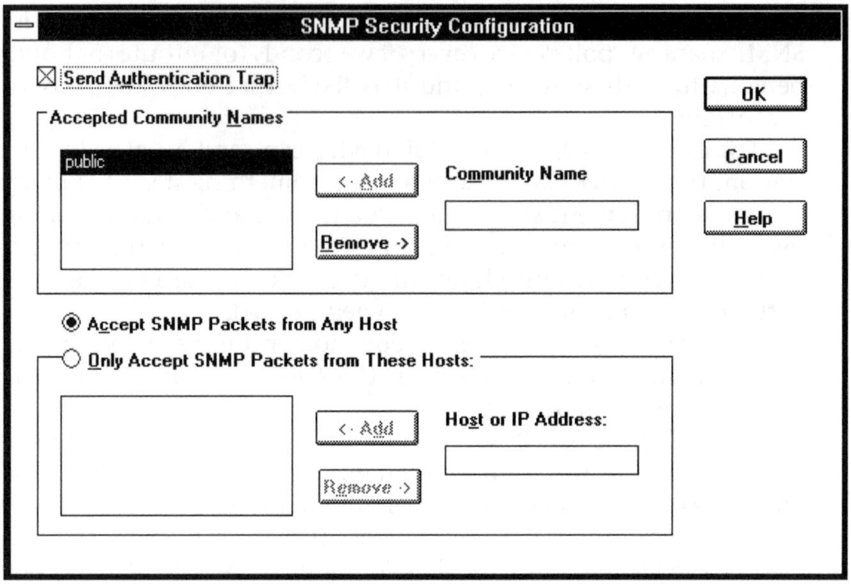

Figure 6.22 The SNMP Security Configuration dialog box.

your machine. If a management station that does not belong to one of the accepted communities queries your machine, and this option is checked, then the software will send an alert to the management stations listed in the Trap Destinations from the SNMP Service Configuration dialog box.

You can customize additional information about your system for inclusion with SNMP alerts and responses. From the SNMP Service Configuration dialog box, click the Agents button, and the dialog shown in Figure 6.23 will appear. Type in either your name or the name of the system administrator in the

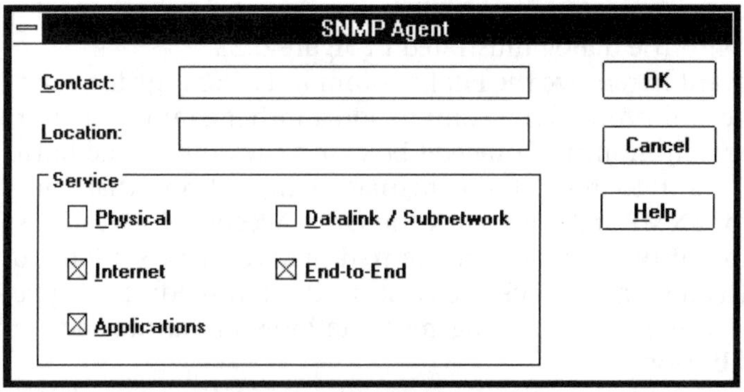

Figure 6.23 The SNMP Agent dialog box.

Contact edit box. Type in a location, such as building, floor, or room number, in the Location edit box.

The Service group box consists of several check boxes that allow you to detail various levels of specific information. The Physical check box pertains to the low-level wire and physical network statistics. If your node acts as a part of the physical network (i.e., a repeater, bridge, or router), then you should check this box.

The Datalink/Subnetwork check box applies only if you are acting as a part of a logical network, such as a bridge. The Internet check box applies only if you are acting as an IP router. Errors generated within the higher-level network software are passed to the management stations if these check boxes are enabled.

The End-to-End check box applies to devices that act as an end node on the network. If you're running TCP/IP, then you are acting as an end node at least some of the time. Application alerts have to do with TCP/IP-based application-generated errors, such as e-mail failures or FTP errors. All NT systems that use SNMP should have at least the End-to-End and Application check boxes enabled.

Conclusion

Windows NT's TCP/IP support, while not perfect, does provide a broad range of the most needed TCP/IP features, including FTP Service, Telnet (client) support, and the usual range of TCP utilities. In addition, Windows NT TCP/IP provides a routable alternative to NetBEUI for use in large networks—and this feature is augmented by NT's built-in static router support, which allows a single computer with two network cards to functionally replace an expensive dedicated router in some TCP/IP routing applications. Now that we've examined these pieces of the Windows NT network puzzle, we can put them to use in creating multidomain enterprise networks, the subject of Chapter 7.

For More Information

Arick, M. (1993), *The TCP/IP Companion*. Wellesley, MA: QED Publishing Group, ISBN: 0-89435-466-3. Good end-user-oriented discussion of TCP/IP and utilities.

Comer, D. (1991), *Internetworking with TCP/IP, Volume 1*. Englewood Cliffs, NJ: Prentice Hall, ISBN: 0-13-472242-6. Mandatory desktop reference for the TCP/IP administrator.

Black, U. (1992), *TCP/IP and Related Protocols*. New York: McGraw-Hill, ISBN: 0-07-005553-X. Mandatory desktop reference for the TCP/IP administrator.

Hunt, C. (1992), *TCP/IP Network Administration*. Sebastopol, CA: O'Reilly & Associates, ISBN: 0-937175-82-X. Mandatory desktop reference for the TCP/IP administrator.

Albitz, P. and Liu, C. (1992), *DNS and BIND*. Sebastopol, CA: O'Reilly & Associates, ISBN: 1-56592-010-4. Great book for learning Domain Name Service (DNS).

Allard, J. (1993), *Advanced Internetworking with TCP/IP on Windows NT* (tcpipnt.doc). Redmond, WA: Microsoft Corp. (downloadable via anonymous FTP from rhino.microsoft.com). This is a 34-page paper on networking that explains advanced TCP/IP topics for Windows NT, including static routing, in great detail.

Microsoft Staff (1993), *Microsoft Windows NT TCP/IP*. Redmond, WA: Microsoft Corp. (part of Windows NT documentation). Brief overview and reference on Windows NT TCP/IP functionality.

C. Liu, et al, *Managing Internet Information Services*, O'Reilly & Associates, Sebastopol, CA, ISBN: 1-56592-062-7. An excellent book for people setting up Internet servers; covers FTP, Gopher, WWW, and WAIS server management techniques extensively.

Enterprise Connections

After reading this chapter you'll understand:

- ❑ Why enterprise networks are different from simpler LANs
- ❑ The need for administration across multiple domains
- ❑ Wide-area networking issues
- ❑ The need for routers and gateways
- ❑ The central importance of e-mail
- ❑ Multivendor issues
- ❑ Troubleshooting enterprise networks

You'll have a basic understanding of the principles involved in creating, operating, and maintaining networks characterized by size, complexity, and the need for communications between multivendor platforms, and you'll have a good understanding of where to go for further information.

Introduction

Enterprise networks—this term has come into general use only recently and has tended to displace more descriptive technical terms like *internetwork*. Fundamentally, the idea behind an enterprise network is the idea of making all data from any network in an enterprise (that is, a corporation), available to users on all other networks, provided, of course, that they have the necessary security privileges. The idea leverages the total information resources of an enterprise

by making, for example, information from the shipping and receiving department available to management, an approach that is clearly essential if you are
looking at, say, just-in-time manufacturing and wishing to maintain minimum
inventory. These kinds of issues are becoming increasingly important as indus-
tries engage in downsizing or rightsizing operations.

From the system administrator's perspective, the central issues involved
with enterprise networks are really threefold. First is the issue of *communicating
across great distances,* because the odds are high that an enterprise network will
not exist within a single building. Second is the issue of *complexity,* because the
enterprise network by its nature involves many servers and users—and this is
closely related to the third and most complex issue, *multivendor connectivity*.

Enterprise networks almost never comprise components from a single
vendor, and it's unlikely that anyone will establish a totally Windows NT-based
enterprise network (even Microsoft hasn't done this). So, there are issues of
integrating the Windows NT networking components with existing networking
components.

Because of the complex relationship among these facts, and the need to
provide an administrative communications medium that includes them all, *we*
consider that there is a fourth overriding concern on enterprise networks—*electronic mail.* In our experience, only electronic mail can possibly be used to
provide reliable connectivity throughout the enterprise.

You can provide specific connections between different points in the
enterprise for specific purposes—and we'll talk about how to do that—but the
bottom line is that the only reliable way to connect *every* individual within the
enterprise is to use some form of e-mail that works across all platforms. Since
Microsoft Mail is incorporated in Windows NT (and at the moment is the *only*
e-mail system hosted on Windows NT), that's the main e-mail platform we'll
talk about.

Windows NT in Enterprise Networks

Microsoft clearly had enterprise networking issues in mind when the Windows
NT (especially Windows NT Server) networking architecture was conceived.
Windows NT incorporates some unique features for use in enterprise networks
that have never before been packaged into a single networking product. Among
these are Windows NT Server's domain-wide administration features, and a very
important additional feature, *interdomain trust*. This allows separate administrative domains of Windows NT systems to share user account information.

Windows NT also comes with Microsoft Mail workgroup clients preinstalled. This provides the essential electronic mail infrastructure just discussed.
Unfortunately, even on Server systems, Windows NT does *not* provide the
facilities necessary to connect multiple e-mail *postoffices*—so we're going to
discuss what is necessary to expand upon this. We'll also discuss the issues of

providing connectivity between the MS Mail system and other e-mail systems the company may already have installed, such as IBM PROFS or the UNIX-based Simple Mail Transfer Protocol (SMTP).

Windows NT also has a limited degree of wide-area networking support built in by its support for the Remote Access Service (RAS) which is provided in a single-user version on basic Windows NT workstations, and in a multiuser version on Windows NT Servers. This is important because the fact that enterprise networks normally span many local area networks combined within a larger geographical area makes it impractical to string wires and physically connect all the elements of an enterprise. There must be some mechanism provided for connecting across the wider area. RAS allows you to do this via multiprotocol dial-up phone lines, Integrated Services Digital Network (ISDN), or x.25 packet switching links.

Windows NT also provides a high degree of multiprotocol support (as discussed in Chapters 6, 8, and 9; and Appendices 2 and 4). In particular, the provision of support for the Tranmission Control Protocol/Internet Protocol (TCP/IP) provides the necessary foundation for creating an enterprise network. As we will see, it frankly is not practical to even consider constructing a Windows NT-based enterprise network without TCP/IP.

Finally, Windows NT and Windows NT Server support a very wide range of network clients, including DOS, 16-bit Windows, OS/2, Windows NT, UNIX, and Macintosh workstations. This makes Windows NT—and particularly Windows NT Server (which has Macintosh support built in)—*ideal* platforms for creating or expanding an enterprise network with a mix of client types.

The Search for Perfection

The preceding laundry list of features makes it sound like Windows NT and Windows NT Server are a one-stop shopper's dream for enterprise network problems. Don't make the mistake of believing this! Windows NT has an excellent network architecture and is based on some very advanced technology. It's a good design but the phrase, Jack of all trades, master of none, comes to mind.

There are major (though not fatal) issues with the Windows NT network architecture that become apparent when you examine enterprise connections. In particular, Windows NT depends upon the TCP/IP protocol to provide a routable enterprise backbone—yet it modifies that protocol by transporting NetBIOS packets over it. As a result, the Windows NT subcomponents of an enterprise net always make up separately a network within an enterprise. While you can, of course, incorporate Windows NT systems into an overall enterprise network management scheme based on IBM NetView or SNMP protocols, the NT portion of the network will remain somewhat separated from other platforms.

We don't mean to say that it's impossible or outrageously difficult to incorporate Windows NT into an enterprise network. Sadly, it will present many of the same difficulties that incorporating any other proprietary networking into an enterprise network will. It's greatly to Microsoft's credit that they have provided *some* of the essential infrastructure as part of the Windows NT and Windows NT Server packages.

Enterprise Network Architectures

As we said earlier, the central facts of life for an enterprise networking environment are: first, a network that commands a large geographic area where it is not practical to string physical wiring to connect all components of the enterprise; and, in all probability, the existence of myriad network hardware and software within the subnets that make up the network. To put this in perspective, let's consider a hypothetical example:

A small growing company has, up to a given point, grown its own local area network at the corporate headquarters (say, in New York), and then opens a branch office (say, in California). The existence of the branch office immediately creates some enterprise network issues. How are the branch office workers to be connected to the corporate headquarters? Some form of wide-area networking will be necessary. There's no realistic way to string private cable from New York to California—so dial-in support over modems will be needed. But will that be fast enough? If not, there are other possibilities extending all the way up to T-1 dedicated telephone circuits (which amount to buying the dedicated wire from New York to California from the phone company at a rather hefty price). Finding the right combination of network hardware and software to achieve this connection efficiently and economically is one of the keys to enterprise networking.

The situation is further complicated if the company grows over a period of time or, to take a modern example, gets taken over and integrated into another corporation. It's quite possible that our small company will have grown up using one networking system—for example, Novell Netware—and the acquiring corporation may have standardized on another networking system, perhaps DEC Pathworks. At this point, you are not only faced with the wide-area networking problems in connecting the new division into the corporate headquarters of the acquiring organization, but also with the problem of matching incompatible network protocols, transports, hardware, and heaven only knows what else.

When Windows NT enters this networking picture you're presented with some immediate opportunities, because Windows NT Server includes some enterprise features, in particular domain-wide management, interdomain trust, and built-in wide-area network support.

Administrative Domains

One of the essential decisions that will face the network administrator attempting to carry out an enterprise network situation, whether he is expanding an existing network to become an enterprise network incorporating new subnets that have been acquired through acquisition or in the creation of a branch office—or whatever, will be deciding when to use the features that have been built into Windows NT, *when* to go outside and acquire other components, and, most of all, deciding on the overall structure for the network. This is an administrative and management issue and a very important one. It has to do with the relationships between the *administrative domains* that make up the network.

As we learned in Chapter 1, Windows NT can support two different administrative architectures. One is a *workgroup* architecture, essentially an ad hoc collection of more or less independent machines that happen to reside on the same subnet. The second is an *administrative domain*, characterized by the existence of a single Primary Domain Controller (PDC), which must be a Windows NT Server. All users log on to the PDC, and the PDC stores account information for all computers in the domain. This greatly simplifies an administrator's responsibility, because it's possible to *centrally* manage those user accounts for all users in the domain.

Of course, when one starts to consider an enterprise network this begins to present some problems. It is possible, although unlikely, that an enterprise network can, in fact, be managed as a single account domain. However, as you reach a very large number of users connecting over a very large network, you'll run into some severe problems. The first of these is the basic bandwidth limitation of the network hardware that's currently in general use. The most common network media today is 10-base-2 or 10-base-T EtherNet, which has a band width of 10 million bits per second. That sounds like a lot but let's suppose an enterprise has built its entire network at its headquarters around a single EtherNet backbone (without routers).[1]

Our hypothetical enterprise has a thousand employees. They all arrive between 8:30 and 9:00 A.M. on a Monday morning, turn on their workstations, and attempt to log in to the primary domain controller. Now, assuming (for argument's sake) that the login sequence requires an exchange of ten data packets between the workstation and the server, each packet containing one kilobyte of information; the total information that needs to be transmitted through the company during this login *storm* will amount to just ten million bytes of information. Ethernet should be capable of handling this within 8 seconds, and we have half an hour—so it should be perfectly adequate. It isn't.

---

1. Nobody could be that dumb? Guess again—while this example is hypothetical, it's based on a real case!

We've neglected the fact that for each one of those user logons the primary domain controller must perform disk accesses to locate the user's records in the database, update them, and so on. Since Windows NT employs a very efficient caching architecture based on its virtual memory system, it may be able to keep up with this example. At some point—if we expand the number of users to 5,000 or 10,000—we're going to saturate either the server or the network itself. Worse, as we've discussed earlier, the odds are quite high that not all parts of the company are going to be connecting over a 10-megabit-per-second EtherNet. Branch offices are likely to be transmitting their login information over wide-area network channels that will have variable speeds ranging from 9600 baud telephone lines up to T-1 circuits that can approach EtherNet transmission rates.

If all of the users in a large branch office are attempting to transmit their login information over a single 9600 baud phone line, you may find yourself with a very frustrated branch manager on the telephone. You might think that the solution to this is to avoid the use of domains altogether and use the workgroup model instead. That won't work in an enterprise network—the administration problems involved in supporting user accounts across myriad servers will quickly become totally unmanageable.

Fortunately, Microsoft has provided a rather elegant solution to this problem. In Windows NT Server domains, while only one server can be the primary domain controller for the user accounts, *any* server can support a login request and can *replicate* the primary domain controller's account database. For instance, our hypothetical branch office might have its own login controller (a Windows NT Server set up to replicate the database on the primary domain controller). This *login server* would then handle all of the login traffic on Monday morning on its own over the local EtherNet. It would simply receive information from the primary domain controller on a regular basis (we'll discuss how do this shortly).

The one problem with this approach is that creating or modifying user accounts requires interaction with the primary domain controller, so the administrator will wind up bearing the burden of communication over the wide-area connection. A work-around for this situation (which also provides for more centralization and control of the network) is for all administration to be handled in the corporate headquarters, and for requests for changes in user accounts to be transmitted to the administrators by electronic mail.

There are variations on this approach—and Microsoft has taken these into account in Windows NT Server, which provides *interdomain trust*. The idea behind interdomain trust arises from the fact that it isn't always practical for an enterprise to have a single account domain.

Suppose that the branch office in our example grows to include several hundred people. At this point, even with the account database being replicated on the branch office server, there's going to be enough administrative traffic to become a real burden traveling across whatever the wide-area networking link is between the corporate headquarters and the branch office. If e-mail is used for communicating with the central MIS group that includes all the administrators, a certain amount of frustration and friction will likely attend dealing with that distant and seemingly unresponsive MIS department.

At some point, with a large branch office you're going to wind up having to have an administration group, essentially an MIS department in miniature, for the branch office. And the best solution, obviously, is to create a separate login domain and separate user accounts at the branch office. You then confront the same problem discussed when we defined the difference between workgroups and domains. A home office employee needing to access files on the branch office server will need *two* accounts, one at the branch office and one at the home office. For example, suppose the branch office handles west coast regional sales. Then the west coast branch office manager will probably need to have a user account at the home office—to communicate with other branch managers and the sales department chief. Similarly, the sales manager at the home office will need to have access to directories on the branch office server.

The traditional way to handle this is that the MIS heads at the branch office and the home office will communicate—and try to keep their user account databases in sync. Invariably, this results in problems. It means an increased overhead both at the branch office and at the home office; and if an organization has many branch offices, the overhead at the home office can become overwhelming.

To get around this problem, Windows NT provides interdomain trust. A *trust relationship* is created between the domain servers for two domains. The trust relationships are inherently *one-way*. Thus, the fact that the branch office trusts the home office does *not* imply that the home office trusts the branch office (although it is possible to arrange two-way trust). With two-way trust, our problem goes away—our west coast regional sales manager has an account on the branch office domain server. The home office server trusts the branch office domain server.

Since the regional sales manager is a member of the sales manager's group, and sales managers have read/write access to the sales data directories, this individual *automatically* has access to the data directory on the home office server, as well as on the branch server. With a trust relationship extended in the other direction, the head of the sales department at the home office will have the same kind of access on the branch server, not only in California, but also in any other branch the company has. The account management problem is essentially eliminated. The home office MIS group needs to maintain accounts only for people who have local access to the local server. Access to the remote servers is handled automatically. Only the trust relationships need to be maintained.

The one degree of coordination that is required between the MIS director at the home office and the branch office MIS directors is, first of all, to maintain the trust relationships and second, to agree on the group names. The need to manage separate user accounts for remote individuals is eliminated. This is a tremendous assist in a complex enterprise situation and particularly for organizations with many branch offices.

The only problem with interdomain trust is that it works *only* with Windows NT Servers, not only at the home office, but also at all branch offices. You cannot extend interdomain trust privileges to a NetWare server or a UNIX server or even to a LAN Manager server (in its current incarnation). Therefore, to provide interdomain trust capabilities, it will be necessary to install a Windows NT Server for domain control at each branch that needs to be trusted, or needs to trust the central office.

Windows NT Server Domain Administration Models

Given the existence of Windows NT Servers at the home office and all branch offices, trust relationships can be arranged a number of different ways to provide one degree or another of centralized administrative control over the network. Microsoft defines four basic models for trust relationships. They are:

Single Domain Model

This is the most obvious of the models and essentially is the baseline case. There is one user domain applying to one primary domain controller, which maintains *all* accounts for the entire enterprise. This provides, obviously, the maximum degree of centralized administration and control, and it can work for very large networks (up to around 10,000 user accounts) with judicious use of replication and fall-back servers to provide local logon server capabilities for remote offices and divisions. The network traffic, however, will become considerable on this kind of networking scheme, particularly for organizations with branch offices that must replicate the primary database controller over a wide-area networking link, and for organizations where user accounts (particularly remote user accounts) change frequently.

Master Domain Model

In this approach there may be more than one domain but there is a single domain to provide central control, probably the MIS domain at the central site. All other domains trust this master domain. This model is ideal for organizations maintaining a centralized MIS department but supporting users at many branch office sites, and it can be used with very large networks (this is the approach that Microsoft uses itself). Users are members of local domains. They are *not* members of the central MIS domain. All user accounts are created in the central MIS domain—but since the remote domains trust the MIS domain, users automatically have access privileges on their local servers.

The administrator can define which servers and workstations the user is permitted to use at the time the user account is created. Requests for user account modification are communicated by electronic mail to the central account operators in Redmond. Local system administrators do not have account operator privileges and cannot create or modify user accounts, but they do have the necessary permissions to administer servers and to administer groups of users.

This approach provides central MIS control over the network, and a single central authority for creating and granting user access rights (with a high degree of security), while minimizing network traffic between central MIS and the remote sites, and providing administrative flexibility at the remote sites. This scheme makes sense for large organizations.

Multiple Master Domain Model

This approach, recommended for very large networks (greater than 10,000 users), employs essentially the same logic as for the master domain but allows more than one master domain. Each subdomain trusts one or more of the master domains. The master domains might or might not trust each other (it will probably be most convenient if they do). In a very large organization this would allow a distributed MIS environment in which there are central MIS groups for several divisions within the organization, and would provide the benefits of the Master Domain Model without the necessity for centralizing all user accounts. Microsoft uses this approach—the central MIS department in Redmond WA (Microsoft's Corporate HQ) is the global master domain, but there are geographically oriented user account domains for each area in which Microsoft has a major presence. Management overhead is reduced by having locally controlled second-tier domains throughout the organization—all of which trust the central user account domains. Thus, Microsoft gains the benefit of decentralized operations while retaining central control over user accounts—and, because all user account domains trust each other, users throughout the organization have the benefits of enterprise-wide single login.

Complete Trust Model

The final model that Microsoft discusses is one that, in all honesty, appears to make *no* sense for an enterprise network. This is a model in which all domains operate independently, but all domains trust all other domains within an enterprise. The idea here is that there is no central MIS department. Instead, each server is separately administered, but (by the maintenance of the necessary interdomain trust links) users who have an account on any server will be able—with appropriate privileges—to use any other server in the enterprise.

The problem with this approach is that it depends *critically* upon the diligence of the network administrators supervising each of the trusted domains in the organization. Laxness on the part of any one administrator (for example, in closing obsolete user accounts or enforcing password changes) can propagate throughout the network via the trust relationships, creating a large opportunity for security breach.

Since this type of networking is inherently insecure, we do not recommend it.

A Mixed Domain Model

In addition to the four models that Microsoft recommends, it's likely (especially as Windows NT capabilities are added onto existing networks—or as subnetworks are acquired and incorporated into an enterprise running a Windows NT network) that a need to *mix* the various models will arise. In particular, a model we think makes some sense is a combination of the Single Domain and Master Domain Model. In this approach, one would have a more or less independent account domain with a local administrator, which also trusts a central Master Domain. Account control can be accomplished either locally *or* from the Master Domain. Local user accounts can be created locally; local or remote user accounts can be created by the Master Domain (i.e., the central MIS department).

This approach may be advantageous in several situations. When Windows NT networks are initially added to an existing enterprise, it's unlikely that there will in fact *be* a Master Domain for the local domain to trust. Therefore, it will make sense to create an independent domain. Later on, if the company accepts Windows NT as a standard, you're faced with the problem of grafting these independent subnetworks into the Master Domain Model. This can most conveniently be done by trusting the Master Domain—servers then begin life with local user databases that can be supplanted (or augmented) by a remote account database at the Master Domain. There is no need for users who only use a particular domain server to have an account in the central MIS account database, and it may simplify things initially if they do not.

Similarly, when a remote site needs to be added to an existing Windows NT Master Domain or Multiple Master Domain network, it may not be possible (initially) for that branch network to be administered using the Master Domain Model—probably because the remote domain does not in fact *have* a Windows NT Server available initially as domain controller. In this situation, it may be convenient to allow the domain to operate more or less independently, and transport the foreign accounts from the existing network onto a Windows NT

Server. Again, you're faced with essentially an independent network. By having this network trust the central Master Domain, you gain the opportunity for remote administration and for access by users who have accounts in the remote network.

There is a problem with this approach—synchronizing account database information between the local network administrators and the administrators in the Master Domain. It's possible in this kind of model to wind up having multiple user accounts, one presented from the MIS domain and one from the local domain. Cooperation between the administrators can prevent this from becoming a significant burden, and the overall security risks reflected by the complete trust model do not occur, because the trust relationships in this approach are essentially *one-way*. A variation on this approach would be to have the remote domains not only trust the Master Domain but be trusted by the Master Domain. It's not necessarily required for each of these domains in turn to trust each other. Such a two-way trust model will present something of a security risk—but not as great a one as the Complete Trust Model discussed earlier.

Selecting a Domain Model

From the preceding discussion, it should be clear that many factors—including company policy, location of branch offices, and the underlying network infra-structure—affect the choice of a domain model. Selecting the right model for your organization can be a complex task. Microsoft does provide some help with this—a *Domain Planner* is included with the Windows NT Resource Kit. It's a *wizard* appliction that queries you for information about your network and how you plan to use it, and then recommends a model—and provides instructions for how to install it. See Appendix 4 for more information on the Resource Kit.

Now that we've examined the basic administration models for Windows NT, let's take a look at the specific steps involved in creating the necessary interdomain trust links:

Setting Up Interdomain Trust Linkage Relationships

Microsoft packages an excellent video on domain management with the Windows NT Server documentation kit (number 227-074-410, $69.95), which also includes eight volumes of printed NT documentation. Any NT Server site should have one of these kits (the full NT Server package with documentation includes the tape), and the tape will show you all the details on domain management in much greater detail than we can describe here.

With that said, the basic steps for establishing interdomain trust links (assuming that you have administrative status on both the domain to be trusted and the trusting domain) are:

1. Start User Manager for Domains. Select Select Domain from User menu. The Select Domain dialog appears. Select the Domain to be Trusted from the list (or type it in if you can't see it).

2. Select the Policies/Trust Relationships from User Manager for The Domains. Trust Relationship dialog appears (see Figure 7.1).

3. Click the Add... button on the lower (Permitted to Trust this Domain) list box and add the Trusting domain to the list. The Permit Domain to Trust dialog appears. At this point you will also have to type in (and confirm) an Initial Password for the trust relationship. This will be used only the first time the trusting domain is attached—at that point the system automatically changes the password on both systems, and the modified password (which you cannot change) will be used for further connections. Click Close to dismiss the dialog.

4. User/Select Domain, and select (or type) the *trusting* domain name.

5. Policies/Trust Relationships. The Trust Relationships dialog appears again. Click the Add button on the upper (Trusted Domains) listbox. The Add Trusted Domain dialog appears. Type in the Domain name to be trusted and the password from step 3.

6. Assuming steps 1 through 5 work properly, an infobox will appear with the message "Trust relationship established with domain <domain name>." If not, examine the Event Log to see if an error occurred and carefully repeat steps 1 through 5.

Once these steps have been accomplished, administrators in the trusting domain can assign permissions to users and groups in the trusted domain at

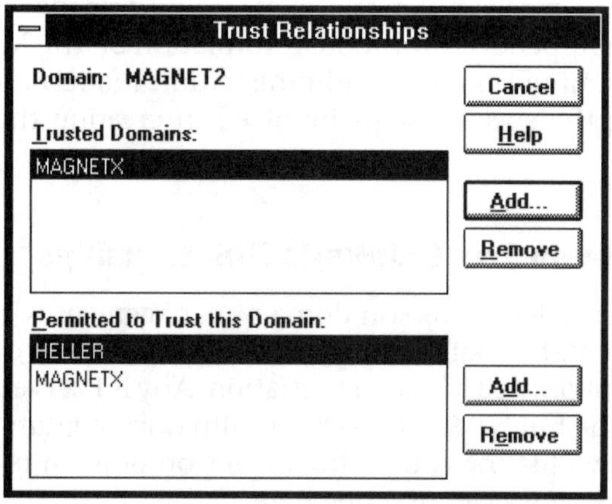

Figure 7.1 Trust Relationships dialog.

Interdomain trust relationships in Windows NT Server are set using this dialog from User Manager.

will. Administrators cannot, however, create or delete user accounts in a domain other than their own, nor can they assign rights to resources in the other domain (unless granted the right to do so by an administrator from the trusting domain). Some coordination between administrators is necessary to make the system work, but it's still a vast improvement over separately administering each server.

Performance Tip: Isolate Domain Controllers[2]

Login performance on enterprise networks can be improved by setting aside a separate server (it doesn't have to be a very big one) as the Primary Domain Controller. Don't run any other services on that machine—don't even share directories on the network (other than for administrative access).

The PDC is a very busy server on a big network, since it validates most logons and provides the master database that's replicated by other servers. If the PDC is busy validating logon requests, then the performance of other services will suffer—and vice versa. In fact, one of the few ways to seriously impair an NT Server network is to run SQL Server on a PDC, with the Boost SQL Server Priority box checked in SQL Server Setup/Set Server Options. That setting gives SQL Server exclusive priority over all other system tasks, including logon validation. It can render the PDC completely useless, or (at worst) crash the PDC. That's why Microsoft recommends running SQL Server on a separate machine from the PDC. If you're running a very small network, you can go ahead and run both services on one machine; just don't check the boost box!

It may seem extreme to dedicate a server to handling user accounts; but if you're running a large network, the additional cost involved is—to use one of our coauthors' colorful phrases—*chump change*!

Replication

The mechanism Windows NT Servers use to provide for users to log on to machines other than the primary domain controller is called account replication. The way this is done is actually relatively simple: Every five minutes, the primary domain controller examines its account database to see if any changes have occurred. If they have, then it transmits these changes to *every other Windows NT Server in the domain*. In this way all Servers within a domain maintain directory information that is within five minutes of being current across all servers. This also means that if for any reason there is a network failure that blocks out the primary domain controller, users can continue to log in using the information in their local servers (although changes to the user

---

2. A tip from the MIS department at Sequent Computer Systems, Inc.

accounts—which have to be accomplished through the primary domain controller—won't work until the linkages are reestablished). While Windows NT workstations within the network do not replicate the account database, they *do* cache the account information for the most recently logged-on user, so (even if no logon server is available when the user next logs in) the system will identify the user based on the information stored from the last logon and will permit the user to use the computer if the information matches.

With that information under our belts, let's examine the specifics of setting up the replication service in Windows NT:

Replicating Directories

In addition to replicating the user account structure, you can exploit the *replicator service* to copy other information between servers. This is necessary in a Server domain that employs *logon scripts*, because (obviously) you want to have users log on to any server in the network but still use the same script that you maintain on the primary domain controller. It can also be desirable if you need to maintain centrally controlled information that has to be broadcast to all servers in the network (policy statements, etc.).

Each Windows NT Server can maintain an *export* directory structure and an *import* directory structure. These directory structures normally include the logon scripts and data. You can add additional subdirectories into the directory structure if you want. However, *only one directory tree may be exported from each server*. Windows NT Workstations cannot export but can *import* through the replication system. With replication in place, changes within the directory tree will be transmitted to other systems on the network, either immediately when they occur or (at the administrator's discretion) after a two-minute stabilization period.

Proper operation of the replicator service is absolutely key to efficient use of logon scripts in NT Server networks. If replication is set up correctly, login scripts from the PDC can be automatically duplicated on servers throughout the enterprise—but if replication isn't properly set up, you have no way of knowing who does and does *not* have up-to-date scriptfiles. This problem becomes especially important if you deploy an enterprise-wide application, such as Microsoft SMS (covered later in this chapter), which depends on login scripts.

Replication provides a transparent method for replicating the script information throughout a domain. It also can be employed to provide *automatic backup* of information. For example, one can replicate the critical data directory structures of a server, export that information, and import it on a backup server. You can use this in a variety of ways.

You should not view this replication approach as a panacea for providing automatic near line backup of user directory information. One site that attempted to do this by replicating all user directories on backup servers every six minutes found that it almost immediately saturated a 100-megabit-per-second FDDI backbone.[3] It is simply not practical to use the replication mechanism for frequently changing data at existing data rates.[4] You should use it only on data that changes *infrequently* or data so important that you can't afford to risk its loss. For user information that changes on a minute-by-minute basis, you should consider some other mechanism for critical data backup; such as a near line magneto-optical storage system.

Given that you've decided to exploit replication for cross-server account maintenance or for some other purpose, here's how to get it running:

Step-by-Step Instructions for Setting Up Replication

To set up replication export (assuming you have domain administrative privileges):

1. Start Server Manager from the Admin Tools group

2. Select View/All (this will show both servers and workstations in the domain).

3. Select the server you wish to have export directories (typically the Primary Domain Controller). The Properties for <Machine Name> dialog will appear (see Figure 7.2) (functionally, this is the same as running the Control Panel Server object locally on <Machine Name>).

4. Click the Replication button. The Directory Replication dialog (see Figure 7.3) appears.

5. Click the Export Subdirectories radio button. The default path for export (typically \WINNT\SYSTEM32\REPL\EXPORT) appears in the From Path field. You can edit the path if needed (note that you can export directories from only one directory).

6. If needed (to control replication of subdirectories and record-locking within the replication path), click the Manage... button. The Manage Exported Directories dialog appears. This allows you to add or remove subdirectories from the export list, determine whether the entire subtree or only the top-level subdirectory is exported, whether replication can occur while the contents of the export directories are being changed, and to *lock out* specific directories that you do *not* want to export (the

---

3. See *Enterprise Connectivity in a Multivendor Environment*, paper from 1992 TechEd conference, included on Microsoft's TechNet CD.

4. It might conceivably be possible if data can be transmitted over a *very local area network* (VLAN)—essentially memory space in each computer that's tied together using fiber-optic cable. The memory-mapped files described in Chapter 1 might well have something to offer in this regard.

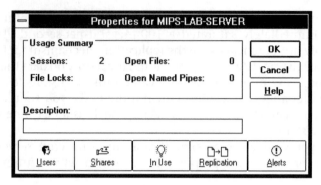

Figure 7.2 Properties dialog (from Server Manager).

The properties dialog from Windows NT Server's Server Manager application duplicates the Server component in Control Panel—but from Server Manager, you can control servers over the network.

first time through, you're well advised to click the Help button for a more detailed explanation). When you're satisfied with the export management settings, click the OK button.

7. By default, the system will export replicant directory data to *all* importing systems in the *local* domain. If that's what you want, then click the OK button now and skip ahead to step 9.

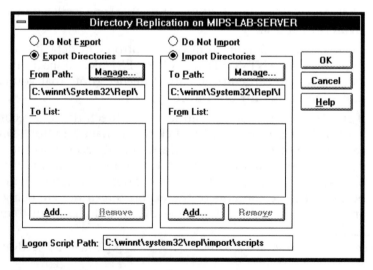

Figure 7.3 Directory Replication dialog.

Directory replication is set using this dialog from Windows NT Server's Server Manager application.

8. If you want to limit which systems are permitted to import replicant data, or if you want to export data to systems outside the local domain, then you will need to add these systems explicitly in the To List. You can do so using the Add button, which will display the Select Domain dialog. You may select just a domain name to export to all systems in the domain, or you can select specific systems (Note: in wide-area network systems selecting the domain may not be sufficient—you may need to select each system to be exported to explicitly).

9. Click the OK button. The replicator service will be started if it was not already running. If import has not been set up on any system(s), you will now need to set up replication import on the relevant system(s)—see the instructions that follow.

To set up replication *import* (assuming you have domain administrative privileges):

1. Start Server Manager from the Admin Tools group

2. Select View/All (this will show both servers and workstations in the domain).

3. Select the server you wish to have import directories (typically all Backup Domain Controllers). The Properties for <Machine Name> dialog will appear.

4. Click the Replication button. The Directory Replication dialog appears.

5. Click the Import Subdirectories radio button. The default path for import (typically \WINNT\SYSTEM32\REPL\IMPORT) appears in the To Path field. You can edit the path if needed (note that you can import to only one directory, although that directory can be loaded with information from multiple *export* servers).

6. If needed (to control replication of subdirectories and record-locking within the replication path), click the Manage... button. The Manage Imported Directories dialog appears. This allows you to add or remove subdirectories from the import list, determine whether the entire subtree or only the top-level subdirectory is imported, whether replication can occur while the contents of the import directories are being changed, and *lock out* specific directories that you do *not* want to import (the first time through, you're well advised to click the Help button for a more detailed explanation). When you're satisfied with the import management settings, click the OK button.

7. By default, the system will import replicant directory data from *all* exporting systems in the *local* domain. If that's what you want, then click the OK button now and skip ahead to step 9.

8. If you want to limit which systems the system will import from, or if you want to import data from systems outside the local domain, then

you will need to add these systems explicitly in the From List. You can do so using the Add button, which will display the Select Domain dialog. You may select just a domain name to import from all, or you can select specific systems (Note: in Wide-area network systems, selecting the domain may not be sufficient—you may need to select each system to be imported from explicitly).

9. Click the OK button. The replicator service will be started if it was not already running.

Enterprise Connectivity One—The Local Area Networks

An enterprise network is made up of one or more local area networks (typically many *local* area networks) connected together through a backbone system or across wide-area network (WAN) links. The structure of the individual LANs that make up the enterprise network is similar to an isolated small business local area network—but there are some differences that come into play when multiple local area networks must be connected. In particular, protocol selection (a rather arbitrary choice in an isolated LAN) becomes a critical issue when applied to large-scale enterprise networks, and this is especially true for Windows NT and other Microsoft networking products, because they depend so heavily upon NetBIOS broadcasts.

TCP/IP as the Backbone Protocol

TCP/IP connectivity was discussed extensively in Chapter 6 and some readers may find it confusing that we chose to discuss TCP/IP networking *before* introducing the enterprise issues. The reason we did this is a simple one: If you are doing enterprise networking with Windows NT, you *must* use TCP/IP as the backbone protocol. You have no other choice.

The reason for this is also simple: TCP/IP is the only protocol that Windows NT can use for its native networking that is fully routable. You can connect two local area networks to each other using TCP/IP routers, and traffic will be routed between the two TCP/IP networks, including the NBT (NetBIOS over TCP/IP) packets necessary for Windows NT native communications involving the Network Browser (File Manager or the administration tools, or so forth). The other protocols supported by Windows NT (e.g., NetBEUI and NWLink IPX) are not routable.[5] This is particularly true of NetBEUI, whose virtual circuit archi-

---

5. Actually, NWLink is routable to a limited degree—it generally will route one hop: That is, you can have machines on either side of a router that will *see* each other. If two routers are involved, however, it fails to route the essential NetBIOS broadcast messages. Hopefully, this problem will be eliminated in future versions of Windows NT.

tecture inherently limits it to operation over a single subnet. The reason for this should be obvious when you think about it. Were the NetBIOS broadcasts to be routed, a large-scale network could quickly be saturated by routed broadcasts not intended for any particular subnet; and since broadcasts are inherently not addressed to a particular location, it isn't possible to route them selectively. Therefore, the broadcasts are blocked at the router—and any subsystem requiring broadcasts (in particular the browser) cannot function across the router.

TCP/IP avoids this problem, because the HOSTS and LMHOSTS databases (or a Domain Name Service or Windows Internet Name Service server) provide addresses for any and all message traffic.[6] This eliminates the need for broadcast announcements to locate a given machine, and allows Windows NT to operate effectively through quite complicated routing situations. Because of this fact, *any* Windows NT system that involves routers *must* use TCP/IP as the backbone protocol.

Does This Mean No Other Protocol Can Be Used?

The fact that TCP/IP is required as the backbone protocol does not mean that it must be the only protocol used in an enterprise network. There are significant advantages to using a multiprotocol solution. TCP/IP is quite complex (which is why we've devoted an entire chapter to it), and setting up and maintaining TCP/IP protocols is a significantly more complex task than setting up more standardized protocols, such as NetBEUI or IPX. The reason for this is the complicated addressing scheme that has to be manually set up and maintained using the HOSTS and LMHOSTS database files. There's also a performance implication.

The NetBEUI protocol that Windows NT 3.1 used by default is designed as a high-efficiency protocol for small networks.[7] It provides a *virtual circuit* scheme for high data rate *raw* I/O transmissions between the server and the client. This works well on small subnets and delivers higher performance than TCP/IP (although it obviously militates—along with the broadcast issues discussed earlier—against use of NetBEUI over wide-area network links, where error handling can be a severe restriction). The NWLink IPX protocol has similar (though lesser) limitations—and is even faster than NetBUEI. Again, however, it does not provide any provisions for NetBIOS broadcasts to be forwarded, and thus cannot be used in a routed situation (with certain exceptions that we'll get to shortly).

---

6. See Chapter 6 for more information.

7. Beginning with NT 3.5, IPX is the default protocol for NT Workstations, and either IPX, TCP/IP, or both are typically used by NT Servers. NetBEUI, while retained for compatibility with earlier versions of NT and other Microsoft networking systems, is clearly on its way out.

What you *can* do is set up a mixed protocol network. Consider a network situation in which a central office local area network backbone needs to communicate with a remote office for account information. Obviously it's necessary for the central office backbone to run TCP/IP, which will also be the preferred protocol for a wide-area network connection between the central office and the remote server. Now, does this mean that one should run TCP/IP for *all* of the clients on the remote network? The answer is probably no, both for performance reasons and for simplicity of administration. Rather than doing so, you should run *two* network stacks in the remote server. The TCP/IP stack will be used for communications with the central office (including the necessary traffic for maintaining the account databases and communicating interdomain trust links). The second protocol should be either NetBEUI or NWLink IPX, depending on the needs of the particular site. This will be used for connections between the remote server and clients on the remote LAN.

The implication of this is twofold. First of all, it means that the remote clients will *only* be able to see the remote server and will not be able to establish connections across the wide-area network to the central office. If such connections are necessary, then a particular client will need to have TCP/IP protocols installed either as a replacement for, or augmentation of, NetBEUI (or IPX) in that client. Alternatively, a Remote Access Services (RAS) connection could be established directly from the remote client into the central office—this may be preferable in certain situations.

Using dual network stacks in Windows NT computers presents no particular problems—it's simply a matter of loading and configuring the necessary protocols. Moreover, you can choose to manipulate the bindings using the Control Panel/Networks object, and can place the most heavily used bindings first in the list. This would mean, presumably, the NetBEUI (or IPX) bindings for the local traffic. This will have the effect of performing what amounts to a primitive routing function. Any traffic that can be sent over the NetBEUI (or IPX) links will be sent that way. Traffic that cannot be sent over the local links will automatically go to the next step in the bindings to the TCP/IP and NBT portions of the stack for transmission that way. The result is effectively a TCP/IP network extending between the remote server and the central office, which overlaps a local area network running either NetBEUI or IPX between the remote server and its clients on the remote LAN.

The advantages of this approach are: first, better performance—with a fast local protocol for all traffic on the LAN and TCP/IP for remote connection only when needed; second, it makes for a much reduced administrative burden. The network administrator at the remote site only needs to maintain TCP/IP connections between the remote server and the central site. Most workstations on the LAN don't require TCP/IP addresses, since they will use principally the much simpler local protocol stack. This makes it easier to plug and unplug computers, as necessary. If a few users need connections extending into the central office, they can be provided with TCP/IP stacks—but the number of addresses needing maintenance will be minimized. And, while it's true that today's DHCP and WINS-enabled TCP/IP implementation dramatically reduces the administrative burden traditionally imposed by TCP/IP, the higher performance of a local protocol more than makes up for the additional complexity of running two protocol stacks. (Especially so if there's a problem with your DHCP or WINS server!)

Windows NT has an additional advantage in this kind of environment. The *static routing* capability it provides for TCP/IP is suitable for use at many branch offices. Rather than installing an expensive hardware router, one of the Windows NT servers can have two network cards installed and maintain a static routing table for connections to the central office (see Chapter 6 for details).

Moreover, beginning with version 3.5, Windows NT provides support for TCP/IP WAN links. The TCP/IP point-to-point protocol (PPP) and serial link interface protocol (SLIP) are supported, and no special hardware is required to connect the subnets (though you may want to use custom router hardware for optimal performance). See the "Remote Access Service" section later in this chapter for more information on NT's built-in WAN support.

If you're setting up a network with TCP/IP as the backbone protocol, and NetBEUI or NWLink IPX as the local protocol, you'll need to tune the bindings appropriately. Here's how:

Step-by-Step Instructions for MultiProtocol Binding Tuning

1. Start the Windows NT Control Panel, and select the Network Settings icon. Then click the Bindings button to display the Network Bindings dialog (see Figure 7.4).

2. Bindings at the top of the list are executed first, so in a mixed NetBEUI (or NWLink IPX) local protocol and TCP/IP environment, make sure that the local protocol bindings are at the top of the list (especially so, for the Workstation bindings—or Client Service for Netware; you can simplify matters by picking the service in question from the Show Binding For list). If the local protocol is not at the top, select the appropriate binding and click the Up Arrow button to *promote* it as necessary.

3. You can disable unused bindings (a step that may prove helpful in troubleshooting) rather than removing them. To do so, click on the binding step in question and click the Disable button. The lightbulb icon for the binding in question will be dimmed.

4. Click the OK button. You will be returned to the Network Settings dialog. Click OK again to exit to the Control Panel. You will need to exit and restart Windows NT to apply the new bindings.

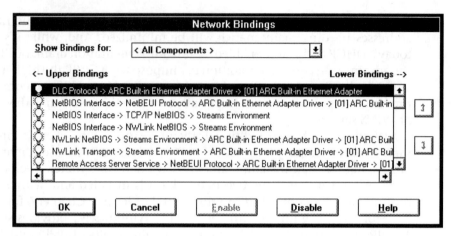

Figure 7.4 Network Bindings dialog.

In multiprotocol environments, you can control the order in which network bindings are executed using this dialog from Control Panel/Networks.

Services for Macintosh

Microsoft provides another unique capability in Windows NT Server by supporting Apple Macintosh computers as network clients out of the box. This is done using *Services for Macintosh* (SFM), a combination of a Windows NT server, file system driver, and network protocols that provides:

- Macintosh-compatible namespace on NTFS volumes
- Native (and fully routable!) support for AppleTalk network protocols
- PostScript emulation on non-PostScript printers (allowing Macs to leverage non-PostScript printers already on the network)
- Access to Apple LaserWriter (and compatible PostScript printers on the AppleTalk network) by Windows NT, Windows 3.x, DOS, and OS/2 clients

SFM is included with Windows NT Server—there is nothing additional to buy (with the possible exception of a compatible AppleTalk card for the server if you want to use LocalTalk cabling to the Macintosh workstations).[8] It requires

---

8. LocalTalk is the native form of networking built into all Macintosh systems since the 512KB *Fat Mac*. It is less than one quarter as fast as EtherNet, but for many users this lower performance is more than offset by its low cost. It's also possible to put EtherNet cards into most newer Macintoshes—or to use a LocalTalk/EtherNet router to bridge Macintoshes into an existing EtherNet. Windows NT is compatible with all of these solutions, although (as always) it's wise to check that any AppleTalk or EtherNet cards you're thinking about buying are listed in the current *Windows NT Hardware Compatibility List*.

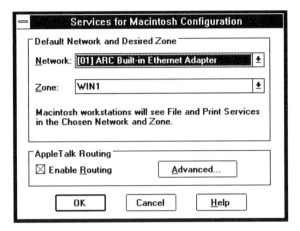

Figure 7.5 Services for Macintosh Configuration dialog.
Windows NT Server's Services for Macintosh are configured using this dialog.

no additional software on the Macintosh (although it can provide better security if a Microsoft authentication package is used in place of the Macintosh default authenticator—this is included with Windows NT Server). SFM does require approximately 2MB of additional disk space in the server, and directories to be made available to the Macs must exist on an NTFS drive (or CD-ROM).

Installing SFM

SFM is installed from Control Panel/Network settings, as follows:

1. Click the Add Software button, select Services for Macintosh from the list, and click Continue. You will be asked to specify the source directory for installation, which may be A: or the appropriate directory on a Windows NT Server CD. The SFM files are then copied to your hard disk.

2. The Services for Macintosh Configuration dialog appears (see Figure 7.5). This is where you will designate the network card and AppleTalk Zone to use for SFM.[9] You can also control AppleTalk routing by checking the Enable Routing box and clicking the Advanced button.[10] When you're satisfied with the network and Zone settings, click OK.

3. Click OK again from the Network Settings dialog. You will need to reboot the computer to start Services for Macintosh.

9. AppleTalk Zones are used for routing in much the way Windows NT uses *domains*.

10. Details of AppleTalk routing are beyond the scope of this text—see *Windows NT Server—Services for Macintosh* (listed in "For More Information" at the end of this chapter) for a detailed discussion of this topic.

After it's installed, SFM can be started, stopped, paused, or continued from Control Panel/Services (or Server Manager/Services) like any other Windows NT service. You will also find that MacFile menus have been created in File Manager and Server Manager—and that a MacFile icon has been placed in the Windows NT Control Panel. You will use these new features to control operation of the SFM service.

Creating SFM Volumes

Once SFM is installed, it's neccessary to create an SFM-compatible *volume* that Macintosh clients can mount. This is done as follows:

1. Create the directory tree you want Macintosh systems to access, using File Manager (or the equivalent command-line functions) on an NTFS disk volume. Note: SFM volumes include *all* subdirectories of the root directory that's made accessible to Macs, and SFM volumes cannot overlap—you cannot share only part of a directory subtree, nor can you share a directory and also share its subdirectory with a separate volume name).

2. Select the root of the directory tree you want to make accessible to Macs, using File Manager; then choose MacFile/Create Volume. The Create Macintosh-Accessible Volume dialog appears (see Figure 7.6). You may now declare the volume name, edit the path, and specify a password that Mac users will have to issue for access to the volume.[11] You may also designate a maximum number of users for the volume (the default is unlimited). Note that none of this affects the status of the NTFS directory that contains the volume—it's still a valid NTFS directory and can be accessed by PCs in the usual way.[12]

3. Click the Permissions button. This will bring up the Mactosh View of Directory Permissions dialog (see Figure 7.7), which you will use to decide which users have permission to access the volume (this is in addition to the regular NTFS security settings—however, be aware that Macs see access controls on a directory-by-directory rather than file-by-

---

11. This *volume password* is a separate, additional security measure for Macintosh users—it is *not* the same as the user name and password, which still must be issued in order for Mac users to access the volume.

12. SFM extends the existing file name translation scheme that NTFS uses to present 8.3 names to DOS users to Macintoshes as well. Macintosh-created long names are treated as native NTFS file names (with the exception of certain illegal characters, which are replaced). These are then translated into 8.3 DOS-compatible names for PC users. Windows NT users see the long file names. NTFS file names will appear exactly as created to Mac users, *provided* the names are 32 characters or shorter—if not, NTFS converts them to 8.3 names for the Mac users.

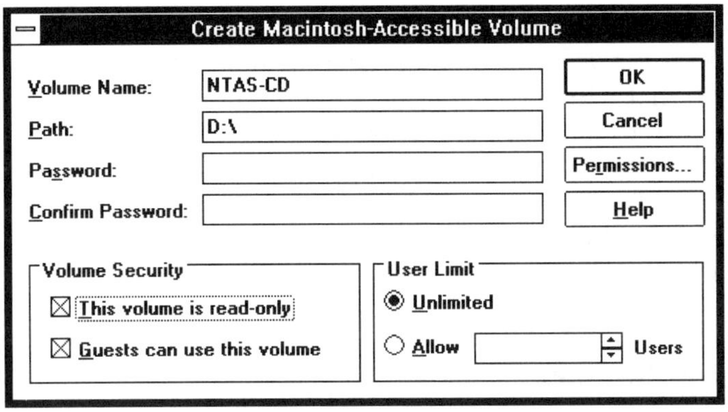

Figure 7.6 Create Macintosh-Accessible Volume dialog.

MacFile volumes are created within the filespace of an NTFS disk using this dialog from Windows NT Server's File Manager.

file basis). When you're satisfied with the permission settings, click OK to exit the MacFile Permissions dialog.

4. Click OK to exit the Create Macintosh-Accessible Volume dialog. The volume is now available for access from Macintosh clients.

Once a MacFile volume is created, you can modify its settings by selecting it in File Manager and selecting MacFile/View-Modify Volumes. You can elimi-

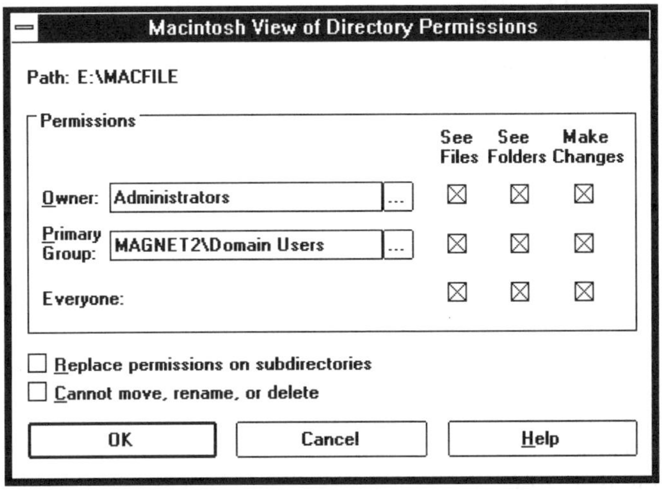

Figure 7.7 Mactosh View of Directory Permissions dialog.

MacFile directory permissions are set using this dialog, from Windows NT Server's File Manager.

nate Macintosh access to the volume using MacFile/Remove Volumes (note that this removes the MacFile volume associated with the directory, *not* the directory itself—you do that with File Manager in the usual way).

You can use exactly the same procedure to make CD-ROM directories available to Mac clients–just skip the first step (it's usually most convenient to share the entire CD, starting from the root directory, specifying read-only access; this allows you to change discs in the CD player without having to reset the MacFile volume sharing).

SFM Printer Support

As mentioned previously, SFM provides *PostScript emulation*, so that Macintosh users can take advantage of non-PostScript printers (such as the HP LaserJet); and also makes Macintosh printers accessible to PCs. SFM does this by exploiting the Windows NT Print Manager (and the associated print spooler), along with a little trick called *capturing* the Macintosh printers.

To understand how this works, you need to be aware that Macintosh printers are usually connected to the *AppleTalk Network*, rather than to any particular Macintosh—they're *network printers* in much the same sense as HP's LaserJet IIIs (which contain their own EtherNet card) are.[13]

By capturing LaserWriter printers, Windows NT Server assures that the administrator has control of all print jobs dispatched to that printer—it accepts jobs only from the Server (which in turn makes a *logical* printer available to both Macintosh and PC users). This has the additional benefit of avoiding the *LaserPrep Wars* that can result from incompatible versions of the LaserWriter print drivers on Macintoshes attempting to access the same printer—instead, Windows NT sends its own LaserPrep code with each print job.

Of course, using PC printers with Windows NT Server doesn't necessarily involve any form of capture—the printer is connected directly to the print server (or at least controlled by it). DLC printers *are* captured in exactly the same way as Macintosh printers.

To set up SFM printing on your Windows NT Server:

1. Start Print Manager, and select Printer/Create Printer. This brings up the Create Printer dialog (see Figure 7.8). Type a name for the printer in the Printer Name field, and select an appropriate printer driver (for PCs this will be the native driver for the printer, *not* PostScript—unless, of course, you're using a PostScript-compatible printer). You can also type in an optional description.

---

13. We are referring here to Apple's LaserWriter (and compatible) printers—not the various dot-matrix printers made by Apple.

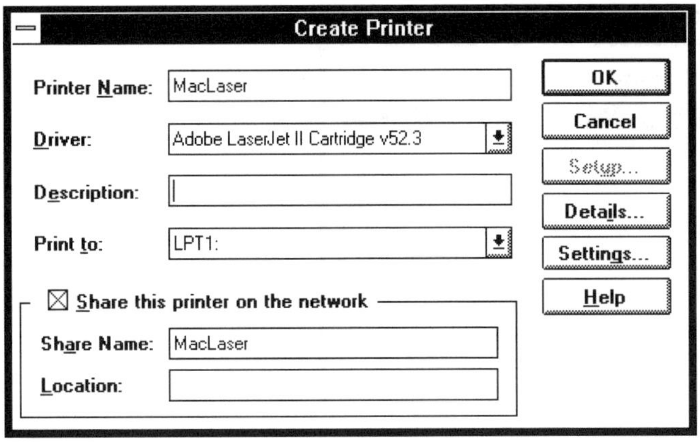

Figure 7.8 Create Printer dialog.

Adminstrators create logical printers using this dialog from Windows NT Server's Print Manager. Once created, the printers can be made accessible to either (or both) Macintosh and PC clients on the network.

2. Select an appropriate device for printing from the Print To list. For a printer connected directly to the server, this will be an appropriate LPT port. For a LaserWriter (or other AppleTalk printer), choose the Network Printer entry in the Print To list. This will present a Print Destinations dialog (see Figure 7.9), from which you can select AppleTalk Printing Devices.

3. Assuming you are connecting to an AppleTalk printer, you're now presented with an Available AppleTalk Printing Devices dialog (see Figure 7.10). Select the Zone and printer from this list, and click OK. The printer will be captured by the Server by default—meaning that instead

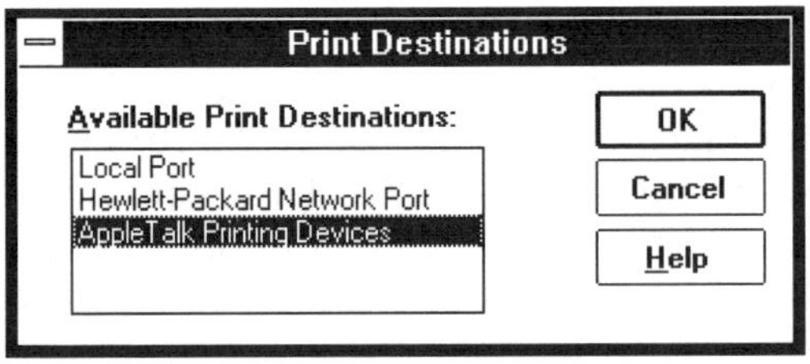

Figure 7.9 Print Destinations dialog.

This dialog, from Windows NT Server's Print Manger, allows administrators to *capture* AppleTalk (i.e., Macintosh-compatible) printers for control by the Windows NT Server. Captured AppleTalk printers can be made available to PC users as though they were connected to the server itself.

Figure 7.10 Available AppleTalk Printing Devices dialog.

This dialog lets an administrator designate an AppleTalk printer to capture.

of printing to it directly, Macintosh users will have to print to the logical printer you create in the next step. If you do *not* want to capture the printer (warning: Not capturing the printer means you cannot control which jobs it prints in what order, and runs the risk of LaserPrep wars), you'll need to click the Settings... button, which will bring up the AppleTalk Port Configuration dialog. Unchecking Capture, this Apple-Talk Printing Device box will eliminate capture of the printer.

4. To make the printer available to other (Macintosh and/or PC) users, check the Share This Printer on the Network box, and enter a share name and (optionally) location.

5. The printer should now be available to PC clients in the usual way. To make it available to Mac clients, one further step is needed: A user account for Mac printers must be created. Start Control Panel /Services, select Print Server for Macintosh, and click the Startup button. A Print Server for Macintosh dialog will appear. Click the Choose This Account button, and type in a user account name (and optional password) for Mac print jobs. Then click OK. Macs should now have access to the printer just as PCs do.

Accessing SFM Volumes and Printers from Macintosh Clients

Before a Macintosh client can access an SFM volume, it must log in to the server in question. This is done using the Macintosh Chooser. Click the AppleShare icon, then the Zone where the server is located. This will present a list of file servers, from which the Mac user selects the name of the Server.

At this point, a Connect to the File Server... dialog appears. If Guest access has been enabled on the Server, then the Guest button can be clicked. Otherwise, the registered user button must be clicked, requiring the entry of a valid Windows NT user name and password.[14] Once this is done, a list of available volumes is presented and the Mac user can mount one by selecting it and clicking the OK button—at which point an icon appears on the Mac desktop that represents the shared volume. The Mac user then accesses this icon in the usual way (see Figure 7.11) Macintosh workstations access Windows NT Server printers (including captured AppleTalk printers) through Chooser in exactly the way they use any other AppleTalk printer—there is no difference at all.

A Final Word about SFM

In summary, SFM is one of Windows NT Server's best-implemented features. By simply installing SFM and configuring it properly, you can provide full file-and-printer sharing to Macintosh clients, while giving Windows NT, Windows, OS/2, and DOS clients access to the very same printers and files. To the enterprise network administrator, this represents a significant advantage over other network servers, which require add-on software or bridging to connect Macs and PCs to the same directories. The Windows NT Server approach to this is completely seamless, leverages the advantages of NTFS (including excellent performance and fault tolerance), and is extremely easy to set up.

Unfortunately, there are limitations. One of the most serious is that RAS *still* doesn't support AppleTalk. MS-Mail can support Macintosh clients—but the necessary client software must be purchased separately (you'll also need an MS-Mail Upgrade Kit—Mac clients aren't compatible with the workgroup version of Mail bundled with NT). Macintosh clients logged in to a Windows NT Server also do not execute login scripts and cannot take advantage of User Profiles—nor can they participate in interdomain trust relationships or *see* resources from other Windows NT systems (unless those systems also run SFM and have access to the *same* Appletalk or AppleTalk/EtherNet network as the clients).

With all that said, however, SFM is by far the *cleanest* approach we've seen for giving Macs and PCs simultaneous access to the same files. We consider it one of the best reasons for buying a Windows NT Server, and hope that

---

14. And here we run into a security problem—AppleShare passwords are sent in clear text over the network, which violates Windows NT's C2 security standards. All is not lost, however—Microsoft provides an alternate Microsoft UAM sign-on with password encryption. Its installation is detailed in the *Windows NT Server—Services for Macintosh* manual that's included with Windows NT Server full packaging.

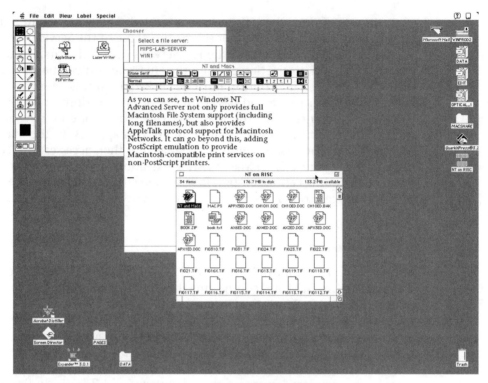

Figure 7.11 Macintosh Access to Windows NT Server.

Macintosh users *see* Windows NT Server files and directories as icons and folders on the Macintosh desktop.

Microsoft will improve the support for Macintosh clients in future versions of Windows NT.[15]

Enterprise Connectivity Two—Electronic Mail

The most general method of connecting up the LANs that make up an enterprise network is to connect them via one form or another of wide-area networking link, or through an enterprise backbone. However, as we will see when we begin discussing WANs, the assumption that one can simply extend a network connection across low data rate media and get tolerable results is often false.

15. We suppose it's too much to hope that Microsoft might see fit to exploit the SFM technology to give Windows NT *native* access to AppleTalk. That's a pity—it's completely routable yet avoids the incomprehensible addressing problems of TCP/IP. An optional native AppleTalk capability for Windows NT would go far toward making the dream of Mac-like plug-and-play connectivity a reality for PCs.

Wide-area networking links are orders of magnitude slower than local EtherNet networks, slower still by comparison with say FDDI backbones. They're also expensive—in WANs you must pay for use of the wire, rather than having (essentially) free use of the wire once you've paid for installation, as is true of LANs.

This being the case, the least expensive and most flexible way to connect people in an enterprise system is often e-mail. This has the following advantages:

❑ Low-cost wide-area connections are possible by modem.

❑ Disparate systems can be connected with gateways.

❑ Connections are *asynchronous*—they don't require continuously operating links.

Windows NT includes built-in e-mail, which we discussed in Chapter 4. Unfortunately, the built-in e-mail that's included is not suited to enterprise use. It's a Windows for Workgroups-style *workgroup postoffice* that cannot be connected to other postoffices—the key requirement for enterprise systems.

As we saw in Chapter 4, the postoffice is the basic building block of Microsoft Mail (which is included with Windows NT)—it's the central storage point for messages, which are communicated between the postoffice and the clients. To create an enterprise mail system, you need a capability to *forward* messages between postoffices, along with some sort of *directory*, so that postoffices know what to do with messages intended for users outside the local postoffice. The workgroup postoffice built into Windows NT lacks this *store-and-forward* capability—but you can get it by upgrading to a full MS-Mail 3.*x* postoffice.

MS-Mail 3.*x* is a true store-and-forward system that uses a DOS-OS/2-, or (in version 3.5) NT Server-based EXTERNAL.EXE program (or EXTERNAL *service* in version 3.5) to copy mail between postoffices (EXTERNAL functions as a *Message Transfer Agent* or MTA). To do this, you must set up a machine (known as a *mail server*) that runs the MTA, and that can *see* both postoffices, either using a network connection or via modem. On a preset schedule, the MTA copies files from one postoffice to the other. If you can't rig things so that a single copy of the MTA can see both postoffices, then you use two copies of the MTA—one for each postoffice—and connect them by modem. It's a simple (you might almost say crude) approach, but it does work—provided you have the MTA.

To get it, you can use the *MS-Mail and Schedule Plus Extensions for Windows for Workgroups* to upgrade the workgroup postoffice. This is a $695 product that changes the postoffice directory into MS-Mail 3.*x* form, and it includes that much-needed MTA program (unfortunately, it's currently a DOS version).

The most convenient approach to using the Extensions with Windows NT is to:

1. Create a Workgroup Postoffice on the Windows NT system in question per the procedure for "Setting Up a Postoffice" from Chapter 3. This will create a Workgroup Postoffice in a directory named WGPO by default.

2. Follow the instructions for "Upgrading a Workgroup Postoffice in Place" that are given in the *Microsoft Mail Administrator's Guide* (included in the Extensions). This will give you a complete MS-Mail postoffice in the same WGPO directory you created in step 1.

3. Share the WGPO directory on your network. Workstations will most conveniently access the directory if they access it as local disk M: (because the MS-Mail client and the MTA expect to see mail files on disk M:).

With this done, you have a full store-and-forward postoffice that can be connected to other MS-Mail postoffices, or to other mail systems using an additional piece of software called a *gateway*.[16] Connecting postoffices together is a fairly simple process; one simply configures the MTA to see both postoffices and configures it for periodic update. This is most easily done as follows:

1. Select a workstation that can function as the *mail server* (i.e., run the MTA). This may be the same system that has the postoffice set up, or it may be another system.

2. Configure the mail server to see the postoffice directory as drive M:, for instance, by the *net use* command:

   ```
   net use M: \\mips-lab-server\WGPO
   ```

3. Or use the equivalent File Manager steps. Do this even if the postoffice is physically on the mail server—it expects to see mail files on drive M:.

4. Configure the mail server to see the other postoffice as drive N: (assuming that it is on the network), for instance:

   ```
   net use N: \\mailhost\maildata
   ```

   (The MSMAIL\MAILDATA directory on MS-Mail 3.0 systems is functionally equivalent to the WGPO directory on Windows NT systems that are upgraded in place using the Extensions).

5. Run the MTA on the mail server, using the -a switch to disable modem operations, and the -d switch to specify drives to search for mail files; for instance (assuming that the MTA is itself on drive M:):

   ```
   M:external -A -dMN
   ```

---

16. Gateways are beyond the scope of this book—each e-mail system requires its own MS-Mail gateway, as each has its own unique file structure. In general, gateways will be separate DOS programs that function in much the same manner as EXTERNAL.EXE. Microsoft has a catalog of gateway products—request it from Microsoft sales (800-426-9400).

6. The MTA will now run and will poll the two postoffices for mail needing to be moved to the other postoffice. When it finds any mail that needs to be moved, it will move it.

If your setup doesn't permit a single machine to see both postoffices, you'll need to run one MTA on *each* postoffice, and connect the two via modem, according to the instructions given in the *Microsoft Mail Administrator's Guide.* This will also give you some alternatives; for example, the -w switch lets you specify wide-area network (WAN) connections that are to be used only at a specified time. You can use this in conjunction with Remote Access Services (RAS) to create a low-cost forwarding scheme for low-priority mail messages—an example of which is given in the section on wide-area networking later in this chapter.

A Critique of MS-Mail and Windows NT

By the time you read this, MS-Mail 3.5 should be available, featuring a Windows NT-based MTA.[17] This is available in two forms: The first is essentially a clone of MS Mail 3.2's OS/2-based command-line appliction (itself a near-clone of the DOS version). As a character-mode application, it must be run from the command line, with all the security and autostart implications that implies. The second option is a complete NT-based service, and this is what we recommend that you run (we can't give detailed instructions here because the NT-based MTA wasn't available when this was written). The availability—at long last—of this product should greatly simplify the integration of MS-Mail into NT networks.

That's a good thing, because the next step up from NT's built-in Mail looks to us like a less than ideal proposition....

Microsoft Exchange

In the first edition of this book, we expended two paragraphs talking about all the wonderful things Microsoft's Enterprise Messaging Server (now Exchange) would do—and we firmly expected that our instructions on Mail 3.*x* would be completely out of date by now. The fact that those instructions still hold—with minor modifications—makes us a bit less sanguine about Microsoft's mail strategy.

That strategy is to move from a store-and-forward mail architecture to a true client/server messaging system, which (to repeat what we said in the first edition) "will be NT-based, graphically administered, x.400/500 *standards-*

---

17. Mail 3.5's NT-based MTA was just entering beta testing as this was written.

based, and network-independent....Since EMS will be MS-Mail 3.2-compatible, gateways built to the current MS-Mail File API (FAPI) and clients written to the Messaging API (MAPI) will work with it, too—and a new Gateway API (GAPI?) will make it easier to *roll your own* solutions for special e-mail problems. It all sounds great, but it's six to nine months off as this is written. For the moment, integrating Windows NT mail beyond the local postoffice requires either a DOS or OS/2 form of EXTERNAL.EXE, per the preceding instructions...."

The trouble is it's *still* six to nine months (or more!) off as *this* is written.[18] Exchange is only in limited beta test at this time—and what we know of the product gives us little cause to expect that it will ship in the immediate future. Microsoft *has* shipped an Exchange *client* with the Windows 95 Preview program. Problems with that client include inability to connect using existing MS Mail Remote protocols by modem—leaving you to choose whether you want to support existing Mail Remote users or Exchange users; one-way conversion of mail files from the MS Mail 3.*x* format to Exchange format—making it impossible to revert if the Exchange client won't do what's expected; and incompatible attachment formats.

Microsoft has also distributed a white paper on migration from MS-Mail 3.*x* to Exchange, which points out some additional issues to be faced by those marching to the client/server drum:

- ❏ Mail 3.*x* clients are incompatible with Exchange servers.

- ❏ Exchange clients are incompatible with Mail 3.*x* servers.

- ❏ For compatibility, all message text from Exchange clients to foreign mail systems (including Mail 3.*x*) must be sent *twice*: once in Rich Text Format (RTF) and once as plain text for mail clients that do not understand RTF.[19]

- ❏ For *complete* compatibility in mixed Exchange and MS-Mail 3.*x* networks, binary attachments must be sent *twice*: as OLE 1.0 attachments for older clients, and as OLE 2.0 attachments for the new ones.

- ❏ Remote mail is accomplished via Remote Access Services (RAS—described later in this chapter). There is no compatibility with existing Microsoft Remote Mail servers.

Against all that, Exchange *does* offer powerful inducements—in particular, the standards-based X.400/500 messaging mentioned earlier, and a built-in, UNIX-compatible SMTP gateway. Unfortunately, the difficulty of migrating to

---

18. This was written in April, 1995. The first edition was completed in December, 1993. Given the small apparent progress made in that period, I'm not especially hopeful that things will be any simpler by the time our (projected) third edition comes out—JDR.

19. The really ugly thing is that *this* is a solvable problem. The issue with binary attachments is something of a necessary evil, but sending all the message text twice is ridiculous!

Exchange from earlier editions of MS-Mail renders those inducements some-what difficult to reach.[20]

Other Mail Systems

Of course, if you're working for a corporation that's standardized on another mail system—UNIX Simple Mail Transfer Protocol (SMTP) or cc:Mail, for in-stance—the preceding discussion will have struck you as weird. Couldn't we just ignore MS-Mail, and substitute another mail system instead?

In principle, the answer is *yes*—provided, of course, that the necessary client, MTA, and Gateway software run under Windows NT. Since most such software is DOS- or Windows 3.*x*-based, it will probably work under Windows NT (and cc:Mail, at least, is planning to support Windows NT as a client platform directly, although the software was not available as this was written). Users of such e-mail sytems may want to investigate running their existing client software on Windows NT.

RAS—Windows NT's Built-In WAN

LANs are fine for local connections, and e-mail can help with certain kinds of connections at any distance; but there comes a point when you're going to need direct connection and you can't find (or buy) a long enough wire. That's when you must resort to *wide-area networking*, in which LAN-style connections are extended across phone company lines and other elements of the larger tele-communications system. Uniquely among today's operating systems, Windows NT comes with a limited-use WAN built-in. It's called *Remote Access Services* (RAS).

In NT 3.1, RAS was a *NetBIOS router* using a proprietary asynchronous extension of Microsoft's NetBEUI protocol. In NT 3.5 (and later versions) this was extended to a protocol-independent routing over Point-to-Point Protocol (PPP).[21] In effect, it takes the network connections of the *RAS Server* (the machine on which RAS dial-in services are running) and extends them over a WAN connection to the *RAS Client* (a machine that's connecting to the RAS server using RAS client software).

---

20. You may well wonder how Microsoft transports e-mail among the thousands of employees at its Redmond, WA, headquarters. Sad to say, as of this writing Microsoft does *not* use what it sells (see the "Windows NT" column of the May, 1995 *WINDOWS Magazine* for details). In fairness, I expect this to change over time—and as Microsoft itself migrates to Exchange (and experiences the problems caused by that migration) the problems described here will presumably be addressed.

21. Microsoft's proprietary AsyBEUI protocol continues to be supported for backward compatibil-ity—and Serial Link Internet Protocol (SLIP) is now supported as an alternative to PPP for TCP/IP networks. The change betweeen RAS in NT 3.1 and 3.5 was nothing short of astonishing!

Two different RAS servers are provided: a single-user version with Windows NT, and a multiuser version with Windows NT Server (the client software is the same in either case). Both NT Workstation and Server can function as RAS clients—a local user logged in to the system console can connect over the WAN to another RAS server. The single-user RAS Server provided with Windows NT Workstation allows one user at a time to access the Windows NT system remotely over the WAN, while the Windows NT Server version supports multiple users logged in at one time.[22]

Both versions of RAS are installed from Windows NT's Control Panel/Network Settings, using a procedure that we'll examine shortly; but first, there are some things you need to know about the different kinds of WANs that RAS can support.

Modems

The first and least expensive option is connecting by an asynchronous MOdulator/DEModulator (MODEM). Modems are widely available today that will work at data rates up to 48 Kbps, which is actually faster than most telephone systems can handle—the maximum data rate available on standard phone lines that are digitally switched (most offices) is currently 28.8 Kbps (some older systems are limited to 9.6 Kbps).

RAS works well with modems, although given the limitation of the low data rate the resulting connection is mostly useful for transferring data files or administrative information on an intermittent basis. The major issues of concern in using modems with RAS are:

❑ Get fully compatible modems—preferrably identical ones—at each end of the link.

❑ Get modems that work *symetrically*. Some high-speed modems use a low data-rate *back channel* for receiving that can be overwhelmed by RAS traffic.

❑ Get modems that are compatible with Windows NT, for which the Windows NT Hardware Compatibility List is indispensible.[23]

Since modems can be used with normal telephone lines, you need only pay the usual telephone company connect charges for use of the line; which makes this approach by far the most economical if you don't require continuous high-speed connection. If you do, then one of the other choices will probably suit you best.

---

22. NT Server 3.1 supported up to 64 users. NT Server 3.5 and 3.51 support up to 256—assuming you can come up with that many ports!

23. Available online in the CompuServe WINNT forum, as well as in the Microsoft Windows NT documentation.

RS-232 Null Modem—NT's Zero-Slot LAN

One interesting way to use RAS isn't really *wide*-area networking at all: If you replace the modem used for asynchronous communication with a widely available RS-232 *null-modem* cable, you get a wired connection good for speeds up to 115,000 baud (about 10 percent of EtherNet) that *doesn't require a network card*. This kind of approach can be useful in several situations—for one thing, given the fact that all Windows NT systems (not just Servers) can use RAS to support one user at a time, it makes a very convenient way to connect a portable computer running the DOS-based (LAN Manager) or Windows for Workgroups version of RAS. Another possible application for RAS with null modems would be to provide a low-cost *zero-slot* LAN connection for up to 64 users to a Windows NT Server. Given the low cost of EtherNet cards and cable today, this probably won't be a common solution—but many sites have *miles* of serial cable left in the walls and ceilings from the 1970s and 1980s, when connecting terminals to host mainframes was common. Multiuser RAS on Windows NT Server offers an effective way to reuse that cable, where full EtherNet data rates aren't required.

Multiport RS-232 Cards

Windows NT Server can support multiple simultaneous remote WAN users on RAS, as mentioned earlier. Of course, it can't do this with just the communication ports built into most PCs. If more ports are needed, the solution is a multiport serial communications (RS-232) board.

Multiport boards include their own coprocessors and memory, offloading the main CPU from the need to oversee all communications between the system and the outside world. You can use a multiport board to connect Windows NT RAS with modems, or (using a *null-modem cable,* as mentioned above) as a zero-slot LAN for local systems.

In any case, the vital issue in selecting a multiport board for Windows NT is to get one for which a Windows NT driver is available. Check the Windows NT Hardware Compatibility List (availaible in the CompuServe WINNT forum, from microsoft's *ftp.microsoft.com* Internet site—and packaged in the Windows NT shrinkwrap) before buying.

X.25 Links

If asynchronous modem data rates (14,400 baud) aren't sufficient—or if users spend so much time connected that long-distance telephone bills become a major expense—consider an *X.25 packet-switching network.* X.25 is a communications standard for digital switching of customer data over long distances. It provides data rates as high as 56 Kbps, or multiplexes many low data-rate connections together into a single high-speed connection. There are two ways that Windows NT can use X.25—directly, through a *smart card*; or indirectly, through a *Peripheral Access Device* (PAD).

PAD's are generally used for client connections, and usually connect to a standard asynchronous modem. This makes it possible for remote clients to dial into a PAD but have their data transmitted over the X.25 packet switch to the server, which can use either a PAD or a smart card. Since modem connections to PADs are limited to the usual data rates for asynchronous communication, you might think this is a waste of time; but it isn't.

To understand why, consider what's involved in connecting five remote users to a RAS server using conventional modems. Each user requires a modem and telephone line, and the server will need five modems (and a multiport serial card, described in the following). The total investment in equipment alone will run into the thousands of dollars, and if the phone lines get a lot of use (and remember that they're limited to just a few percent of EtherNet data rates, so things will happen slowly), the connection charges—especially if they're long-distance—will become quite a burden.

By using X.25, you can save money in this situation. The server gets a single X.25 smart card, and a leased line from the local telephone company connects it to an X.25 provider (such as Tymnet, Sprintnet, or Telnet). Client systems connect to the server by modem, making a local telephone call to the X.25 provider's PAD in their area. The cost will be lower (*if* the system is heavily used), because the hourly charge by the X.25 provider is typically much less than that from the telephone company; and the line conditions are better (so the connection is more reliable).

For Windows NT clients, there's another advantage to X.25—by using a smart card at both ends of the connection, you can get much higher data rates (typically 56 Kbps) than from modems. For applications that require such data rates (and use of RAS for more than intermittent copying of small data files certainly qualifies!), these data rates can be not just convenient but *essential*.

ISDN

The final option for using Windows NT RAS is *Integrated Services Digital Networking* (ISDN). In contrast to X.25 and standard telephone lines, ISDN was designed from the beginning for computer use, and provides throughput as high as 128 Kbps.[24] By comparison with X.25, ISDN is generally cheaper (at the maximum data rate) and gives higher throughput. It's almost certainly a better choice for remote clients who need high-speed connections. On the other hand, X.25 PADs offer great flexibility—a server with an X.25 smart card installed can support a single high-speed client (itself connected with a smart card) or a

---

24. ISDN typically provides two channels, each supporting a maximum of 64Kbps. RAS supports using both channels at once, but be aware that most providers will bill for each channel separately.

Table 7.1 RAS Hardware

Vendor	Address	Telephone Number	Products
Comtrol Corp.	2675 Patton Rd. St. Paul, MN 55113	(800)926-6876	Multiport Controllers
DigiBoard	6400 Flying Cloud Dr. Eden Prairie, MN 55344	(800)344-4273	Multiport Controllers, ISDN cards
Star Gate Technologies, Inc.	29300 Aurora Rd. Solon, OH 44139	(800)782-7428	Single slot serial/parallel controllers
Link Technology Inc.	P.O. Box L-127 Langhorne, PA 19047	(215)357-3354	ISDN Basic Rate Adaptor
Eicon Technologies	14755 Preston Rd., Suite 620, Dallas, TX 75240	(214)239-3270	X.25 smart cards

number of low-speed clients (using dial-in PADs). ISDN is also limited to the larger metropolitan areas, and is not generally available overseas.

Companies that make multiport boards, X.25 smart cards and ISDN interfaces for use with Windows NT RAS include those seen in Table 7.1.

Installing Windows NT Remote Access Services (RAS)

Now that we've looked into the various WAN options that RAS supports, let's see how it all works out in practice. To install the RAS server:

1. Start the Windows NT Control Panel and select the Network Settings icon. The Network Settings Dialog appears.

2. Click the Add Software button. The Add Network Software dialog appears, containing a list of items you can install. Select Remote Access Service from the list, and click the Continue button. You will be asked to type a path for the installation disks (or CD). As several disks are involved, the CD is far more convenient if available. Once you've entered the path, Remote Access Service Setup copies the necessary files to your hard disk.

3. The Add Port dialog appears. You will need to select a communications port to use from this list. Once the port is selected, RAS setup attempts to detect your modem, and the Configure Port dialog appears (see Figure 7.12). Depending on whether autodetection works (if it doesn't, check to see that the modem is plugged into the correct port and is turned on—then click the Detect button to try again), you may need to select

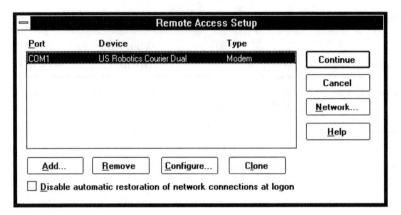

Figure 7.12 Configure Port dialog (RAS).

Windows NT Remote Access Service requires selection of a communciations port for operation. This is done using this dialog.

an appropriate modem (or X.25/ISDN card) from the list. The Hayes Compatible 9600 setting works with most 9600 baud modems, but does not take advantage of V.32 compression on advanced modems—you're better off to select the precise model of modem you have. You will also have to select one of the three possible Port Usage settings—Dial out only, Receive calls only, or Dial out and receive calls. Servers should generally be set to Receive calls only, and Workstations to Dial out only. You can adjust low-level settings using the Settings button, but start with the default settings, as these are most likely correct (in particular, note that Enable Hardware Flow Control *must* be checked for RAS to operate properly). When the port is properly configured, click the Continue button.

4. The Remote Access Setup dialog appears. Click the Network button to bring up the Network Configuration dialog (see Figure 7.13), which allows you to decide whether RAS will allow access to the entire network or only to the local computer. In the former case (the default for Windows NT Server), RAS will function as a *gateway* to the LAN for remote users, while in the latter case (the *only* option for NT Workstations), it provides access only to the resources of the local computer.[25] When you are satisfied with the setup, click the OK button. Note that protocol support for outgoing and incoming calls is completely separate—you can, for instance, arrange to dial out using only TCP/IP, but

---

25. It's a sad commentary on Microsoft's thinking that the option to have access to the entire LAN, which existed in all versions of NT 3.1, was *removed* from NT 3.5 Workstation.

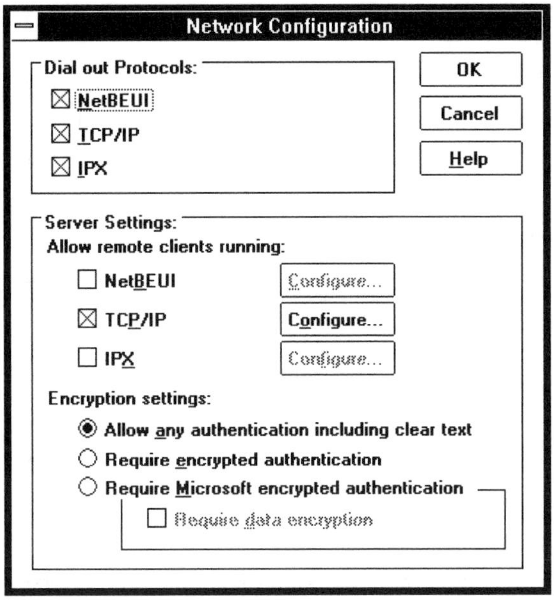

Figure 7.13 Network Configuration dialog (RAS).
Remote Access Services Network configuration settings are controlled from this dialog.

receive calls only on IPX. This dialog also allows you to control the authentication method used, with options varying from Allow Any Authentication, which is useful if you are setting up a RAS server that will be dialed into by a variety of clients, to Require Microsoft Encrypted Authentication, which provides the highest level of security. You may also select the Require Data Encryption check box, in which case data transported over RAS will be encyphered. Once you have selected the appropriate protocols and authentication, click OK.

5. For each selected Server Protocol, RAS will display a Server Configuration dialog—the most complex of which is the one for TCP/IP (see Figure 7.14). At this point, you can determine whether dial-in clients have access to the entire network (default for NT Server) or just the local computer (default for NT Workstation). You will also need to make some protocol-specific settings—for TCP/IP, determining whether IP addresses are determined by DHCP (assuming, of course, DHCP is enabled on your LAN—see Chapter 6), or a static address pool is used. For IPX, you'll need to determine how IPX network numbers and node numbers are assigned (online help is available to explain the various options). When you are

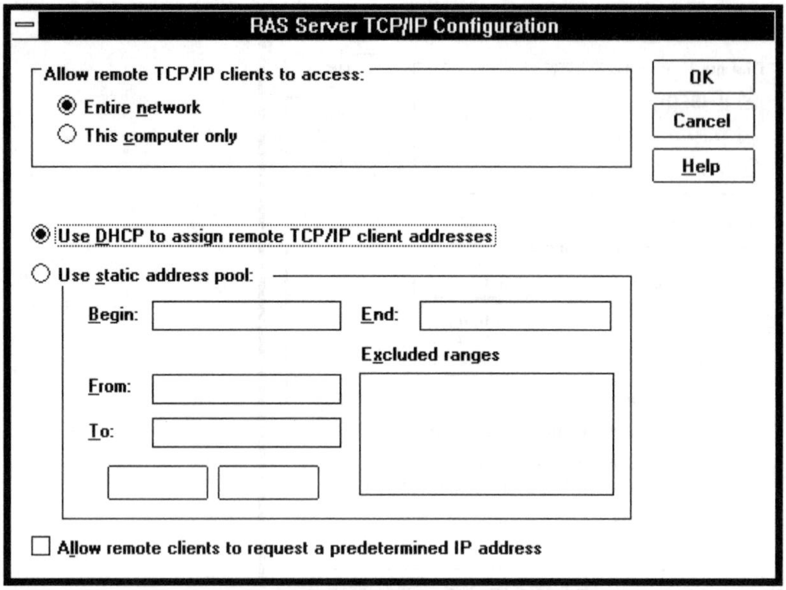

Figure 7.14 TCP/IP Configuration dialog (RAS).

TCP/IP configuration for Remote Access is controlled from this dialog. Similar dialogs allow configuring NetBEUI and NWLink IPX for remote operation.

satisfied with the protocol configuration, click the OK button to return to the Remote Access Setup dialog. Click Continue to complete the setup.

6. Setup creates a Remote Access Service common group in Program Manager. You will use the icons in this group to run RAS after it's installed. Setup then informs you that RAS has been installed, and suggests that you configure it using the Remote Access Administration program. Click OK to complete the setup—a binding analysis will be performed, and depending on the options selected, one or more configuration dialogs may appear. When Network Setup is complete, you will be prompted to restart the computer. Do so.

Using RAS

Once RAS is installed, it's necessary to configure it using the Remote Access Admin program (see Figure 7.15) from the Remote Access Service group. You can start RAS using the Server/Start Remote Access menu (or it can be started from Control Panel/Services).

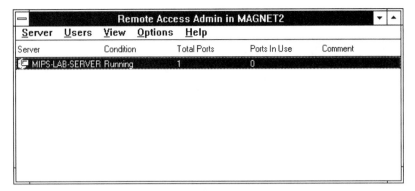

Figure 7.15 Remote Access Administration program.
Administrators control access to Remote Access Services (and settings such as dial-back) from the Windows NT Server's Remote Access Administration program.

Users/Permissions allows you to grant or revoke remote access permissions to any user of the server, and also allows you to specify whether a *callback* option is specified for any caller. Callback is both a convenience and a security mechanism—it's convenient because the *set by caller* option lets a remote user dial the RAS server, then hang up and have the RAS server call him (or her)—which puts the burden of telephone connect charges on the server rather than the client. For people who will use RAS from home or the road, this can be a great convenience.

As a security feature, the *Preset to Callback* option assures that only authorized personell connect, by hanging up on dial-in and then calling back to a preset number. This makes it practically impossible to hack RAS (unless the hacker has physical access to a RAS client).

With access permissions granted and dial-back set, you can access the system from other Windows NT, Windows, or DOS systems that support a remote-access client. To do so, install RAS on the client system, and then run the Remote Access program (called RASPHONE.EXE in earlier versions) from the Remote Access Services group (see Figure 7.16). The first time this is done, you will be prompted to add an entry, which can be done using the Add toolbar button. This brings up an Add Phone Book Entry dialog that allows you to type in an entry name, phone number, and description—and designate whether RAS is to log in using the user's current user name and password (if not, you will be prompted for the user name and password when RAS makes a connection).

If the default modem settings (entered when RAS is installed) are to be used, then this is all that's required, and you can click the OK button to complete creation of the entry, and then click the Dial button to initiate a connection. However, if a nonstandard setting is to be used (modem connection on a system

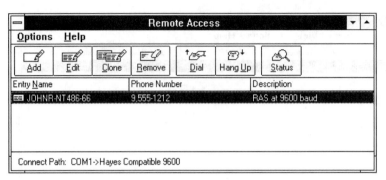

Figure 7.16 Remote Access program.

Remote users access Windows NT Remote Access Services through the Remote Access application.

where ISDN is the default RAS connection type, for instance), or a different port is to be used (outgoing dial through a single modem on COM1 while incoming calls are handled by a multiport board, for instance), you'll need to click the Advanced... button. This will expand the Add Phone Book Entry dialog to show advanced feature buttons, which allow you to designate the specific type of connection you want associated with this phone book entry. Again, when the entry is complete, the OK button returns you to the main Remote Access screen, from which you can initiate a RAS connection (using the Dial button); terminate it (with the Hang Up button); Add, Edit, or Clone phone book entries; and examine the status of an entry.

When a connection is initiated (with the Dial button), the RAS client initializes the modem (or other connecting device), dials out (or performs the other steps necessary to make the connection), and waits for a response from the RAS server. The server and client then exchange user-name and password information (note that the password is not transmitted in cleartext—instead a hashed password is sent, which is based on an encryption scheme) at which point, you're prompted for a user name and password if the Authenticate Using Current User Name and Password check box was not checked. Assuming that the user name and security identifier match at both ends, the connection completes—at which point you have a complete network connection between the client and server (and a gateway to the rest of your network if the server has been configured to permit access to the entire network).

Several things can go wrong with this process—in particular, if you haven't properly configured the RAS client or server for the modem's they're using—or if the modems do not match (especially on high-speed connections), then you're likely to get a message that RAS failed to authenticate. Our experience with this situation is that you should drop both the server and client back to a known connection state (we've found the Hayes-compatible 9600 baud setting to work for most modems) and try again. If it still doesn't work, check the configuration settings for RAS at both ends, check that the user who's attempting to dial in has in fact been granted remote access permissions at the RAS server, and check for RAS-related error messages using the Windows NT Even Log (note that login errors will often show up in the *Security* log)—and refer to the RAS documentation included with Windows NT for further suggestions.

RAS on the Internet

Since RAS supports PPP and SLIP protocols for TCP/IP networks—and TCP/IP is the core protocol for the *Internet*, it's possible to connect NT systems to the Internet using RAS. How this is done varies, depending on whether you're primarily interested in using RAS on NT as a platform for Internet *client* software, such as FTP or Mosaic, or whether you want to use RAS to create an Internet *gateway* using NT Server.

To connect NT Workstation (or Server) to the Internet as a client, you must set up RAS with TCP/IP, and arrange an account with a local Internet *provider*. Providers are local Internet hosts that provide access (typically via dial-up modem lines) for a fee—Microsoft provides a list of providers in a *Remote Access and the Internet* helpfile that's installed with Windows NT Remote Access.[26] You'll need to arrange for an account that provides PPP or SLIP access, and configure RAS to use that access. You'll probably also need to set up DNS support in your TCP/IP configuration, designating the provider's host system as your DNS server—and depending on how your provider works, you may need to designate a static IP address given to you by the provider. You'll also need to set an appropriate security authentication mode (typically Accept Any Authentication) as specified by your provider.

If your provider supports PPP, connecting should be automatic, once everything is properly configured. If your provider supports SLIP, you may have to type commands in a terminal window to complete a login sequence (it may be possible to automate this by entering the login commands in a \WINNT\SYSTEM32\RAS\SWITCH.INF file—consult the *Remote Access and the Internet* Help file Microsoft supplies with Windows NT RAS for more information).

Using NT Server RAS to provide an Internet *gateway* is somewhat more complex. You'll need to arrange some form of *leased line* service from your provider—this will be a higher-bandwidth connection than simple dial-in modem lines (typically 56 Kbps frame relay, or a T-1 digital telephone connection), which will typically terminate in a router. The router is then connected to your local network (or to part of it), either directly or through a security host (called a *firewall*). In either case, a Windows NT Server with RAS installed is

---

26. Another good source is Paul Gilster's book *The Internet Navigator*, listed in "For More Information" at the end of this Chapter.

connected to the router. Users dial into the NT Server using RAS, and the server extends those connections to the router (and thus, to the Internet). Similarly, users on the Internet can access services on the NT Server (such as FTP) through the router.

Setting up such an Internet server is somewhat complex—and carries a certain security risk. We urge you to read one of the standard works on Internet security, and consult volume 2 of the *Windows NT Resource Kit* before attempting such an installation.[27]

Advanced Uses of RAS

Besides providing interactive WAN connections for end users, RAS can be invaluable to administrators. As mentioned earlier in this chapter, using Windows NT Servers at remote locations invariably requires some sort of connection between servers to exchange user account information (and other replicated data). RAS is ideal for this, provided you can live with the available data rates. RAS is also a useful adjunct to MS-Mail: Instead of having the Mail Transfer Agent (MTA) on your local postoffice dial another MTA directly (thus subsidizing your local telephone company), you can use RAS to create a WAN connection and have the MTA use that. In fact, Microsoft's EXTERNAL.EXE provides a special class of WAN device setting for just this purpose—and you can even configure the MTA so that it will use the WAN for routine messages, while retaining the ability to use a modem connection for messages that can't wait.

The key to using RAS *economically* for administrative or mail connections is to have it connect only at preset times of the day—typically times when the telephone (or other connection) charges are low, say between midnight and 4:00 A.M. You can do this by exploiting the fact that RAS is implemented as a Windows NT *service*, which can be started and stopped using either the Service Control Manager application in the Windows NT control panel, *or* using the *net start remoteaccess* command-line syntax from a command prompt or script file. Dialing from the command line is accomplished using the *rasdial* command. Since the replicator service can also be started and stopped using *net start* and *net stop*, we have here the makings for a completely effective periodic replication script:

```
net start remoteaccess
rasdial replicant_server
net start replicator
net accounts /sync[28]
```

27. Firewalls and Internet Security-Cheswick L. Bellauin, Addison-Wesley, 1994.

28. Per Chapter 3, the /sync option on net accounts (equivalent to Server Manager's Synchonize Entire Domain command) *must be executed locally on the Domain Controller. Therefore this script must*

The only problem with this is determining when it's safe to terminate the connection. It will be remembered that the replicator operates every five minutes, so we suggest having a separate script that reverses these steps:

```
net stop replicator
rasdial replicant_server /DISCONNECT
net stop remoteaccess
```

If the first script is named REPLISTART.CMD, and the second REPLISTOP.CMD, then the commands:

```
at 12:00 am /EVERY Monday Wednesday Friday REPLISTART.CMD
at 12:15 am /EVERY Monday Wednesday Friday REPLISTOP.CMD
```

will get the job done. Similarly, you can use command-line starting (and dialing) for mail connections, using a script something like this:

```
net start remoteaccess
rasdial mail_server
net use w: \\mail_server\WGPO
m:external.exe -A -Ww
```

Again, the trick is knowing when to disconnect. Since EXTERNAL.EXE can be configured to transfer mail on one pass and then quit, it isn't necessary to have two scripts, as are needed for replication. Instead, just allow EXTERNAL.EXE to finish, and end the script with:

```
net use w: /DELETE
rasdial mail_server /DISCONNECT
net stop remoteaccess
```

As with the replication script given previously, this script is most conveniently executed using a Windows NT *at* command. Since the -w option on EXTERNAL.EXE is designed for automatic transfer of low-priority mail each day at 3:00 A.M., it's probably best to start this script a bit early and allow five to ten minutes for it to make the connection before EXTERNAL tries to send mail. Thus, if the script is named RASMAIL.CMD, you'd need to execute:

```
at 2:50 AM /Every Monday Wednesday Friday RASMIAL.CMD
```

---

be executed on the Domain Controller—or there should be another at command that forces synchronization (e.g., at \\domain_controller 12:05 AM net accounts /sync).

Bridging

In the first edition of this book, we made much of NT 3.1 RAS limitations—in particular, its support only for Microsoft's proprietary, nonroutable NetBEUI protocol, and its inability to *bridge* between LANs. The former limitation has been eliminated. The latter can be gotten around by two methods: Either use *two* RAS servers, each of which dials the other (obviously, this requires two WAN channels—be they phone lines, X.25 links, or ISDN lines), or change the HKEY_LOCAL_MACHINE\CurrentControlSet\Services\RemoteAccess\Parameters\NetBIOSGateway\RemoteListen paramater from 1 to 2 in the Configuration Registry. This causes RAS to function as a *bidirectional* gateway, and effectively bridges LANs over a single link—but it does so by forwarding all network traffic, which is virtually guaranteed to saturate the link on a busy network.

As a practical matter, if you're running anything but a very small WAN, you'll want to run a dedicated router—RAS works, but it loads the server that's running it proportionately to the network traffic. It's a good solution for small-scale applications, but if you need more bandwidth, the way to get it is with specialized hardware.

Dedicated Multiprotocol Routers

The principle alternative to RAS for Windows NT wide-area networking is use of a *multiprotocol router*. This is essentially a special-purpose computer whose sole mission is to take traffic in one protocol—for instance, NetBEUI, IPX, or TCP/IP—and convert it to (or from) another protocol, such as X.25, PPP, or frame relay. By using a pair of such routers, one can achieve higher-performance wide-area networking than that provided by Windows NT RAS.

An optimal multiprotocol router setup for Windows NT involves TCP/IP as the primary protocol (because, as noted earlier, this is the *only* Windows NT protocol that is fully routable), and whatever secondary protocol is best suited to your particular needs. Determining the best protocol for your situation is beyond the scope of this book, but the general rule in WANs is that you pay for speed: Low data-rate dial-up lines (up to 14,400 baud) are relatively cheap, while high-speed circuits tend to be extremely expensive.

Aside from the protocols needed, selecting a router is largely a matter of features and price—you can pay from $2,000 to $25,000 for a router, depending on the features it provides. Aside from multiprotocol support, some routers provide simple network management protocol (SNMP)-compatible remote maintenance features, out-of-band (generally RS-232) console features, and varying degrees of upgradability. You would be wise to request literature from *all* the firms listed in Table 7.2 before selecting a router for your network.

Table 7.2 Multiprotocol Router Vendors

Vendor	Address/Phone	Comments
Advanced Computer Communications	10261 Bubb Rd. Cupertino CA, 95014 (408)864-0600	Routers
Cabletron	P.O. Box 5005 Rochester, NH 03867 (603)332-9400	Routers, hubs
Cisco Systems	1525 O'Brien Dr. Menlo Park, CA 94025 (415)326-1941	De-facto standard central router for TCP/IP environments
Clearpoint Research	35 Parkwood Dr. Hopkinton, MA 01748 (508)435-2000	Routers
David Systems	701 East Evelyn Ave. Sunnyvale, CA 94088 (408)720-8000	Unique Windows-based graphical management system
Digital Equipment	146 Main St. Maynard, MA 01754 (508)493-7161	OSI-protocol routers for European applications
Hewlett-Packard	Roseville Networks Div. 8000 Foothills Blvd. Roseville, CA 95747 (800)752-0900	Routers, NetView LAN Management system
IBM	One Old Orchard Rd. Armonk, NY 10504 (800)772-2237	SAA/DLC routers for mainframe connectivity
Network Systems	2001 Gateway Pl., #700 West San Jose, CA 95110 (408)452-8400	Routers
Novell Internetworking Products Division	2180 Fortune Dr. San Jose, CA 95131 (800)638-9273	IPX/SPX routers, mainly for use in NetWare LAN environments
Proteon	Nine Technology Dr. Westborough, MA 01581 (508)898-2800	Routers

(continues)

Table 7.2 (*Continued*)

Vendor	Address/Phone	Comments
3Com	5400 Bayfront Plaza Santa Clara, CA 95052 (408)764-5000	Routers, network cards, and other network components
Xyplex	330 Codman Hill Rd. Boxborough, MA 01719 (508)264-9900	Routers
Welfleet Communications	15 Crosby Dr. Bedford, MA 01730 (617)275-2400	Routers

Since NT 3.5 and later support PPP and SLIP multiprotocol connectivity, getting a router that supports dial-up connections over any of these protocols will provide an additional level of flexibility—an NT-based client can use RAS to dial directly into the router! That can be a cost-effective approach in some situations: Use dedicated routers for the home office and larger offices, and NT RAS for smaller offices.

Shiva Netmodem

Another alternative that may work in smaller applications is the Shiva Net-modem. This is a high-speed modem with internal hardware that enables it to function as a network bridge. Models are available for both NetWare IPX/SPX and NetBIOS networking—the former is suitable for use with Windows NT's NWLink IPX protocol, and the latter with NetBEUI. Unfortunately, while the Netmodem will *bridge*, it will not *route*—so all network traffic is transmitted from one net to the other regardless of whether it's intended for nonlocal recipients. This makes the Netmodem useful only for very small networks unless one can combine it with a separate router (in the IPX case—NetBIOS, of course, is not routable in this sense).

Management and Maintenance Issues

Managing and administering enterprise networks is not fundamentally different from managing LANs, although the complexity of the network tends to make the administrator's job a bit harder—troubleshooting, on the other hand, takes on its own character where enterprise networks (especially WANs) are involved.

Microsoft provides a number of advanced administration tools with Windows NT Server that can make life for the administrator easier. These include *User Manager for Domains, Server Manager, User Profile Editor,* and *Remote Access Services Admin.* Client-based versions of these tools are available for NT Workstation, Windows for Workgroups, and Windows 95—see the following section on "Client-Based Administration Tools." There are other administration tools that are specific to third-party add-ons, such as those for SQL Server (see Chapter 11) and SNA Server (see Chapter 10); but the tools included with Server—building on those included with the base Windows NT product (Disk Administrator, Backup, Event Viewer, Performance Monitor, and Registry Editor), of course—provide most of what you need to get an enterprise network up and running.

Server Manager

The most important of the Server administration tools is the Server Manager (see Figure 7.17). From this program, you can add computers to your Server domain, remove them from the domain, inspect the users, shares, replication and alert status of any computer in the domain, synchronize user accounts accross all servers in the domain, send messages (such as the ever popular "Server going down in 3 minutes!"), or promote a server to be the Primary Domain Controller.

All of these tasks are performed pretty obviously—you select a computer from the list (which may be brought up to date at any time using the View/Re-

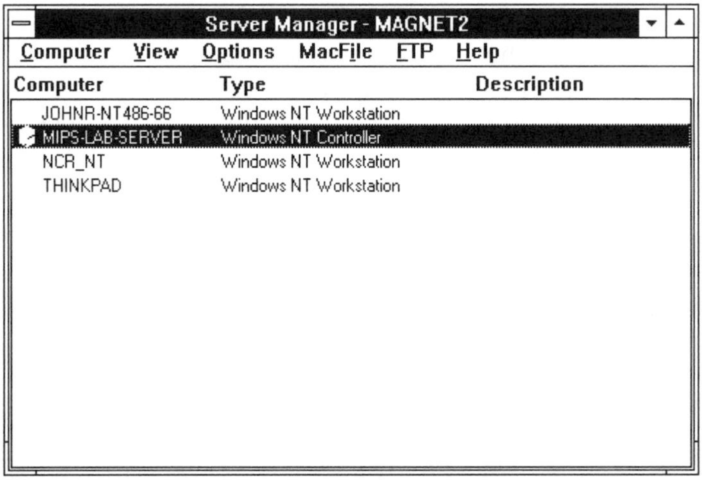

Figure 7.17 Server Manager.
Adminstrators can view and control all servers (and Windows NT workstations) in a Windows NT Server domain from the Server Manager.

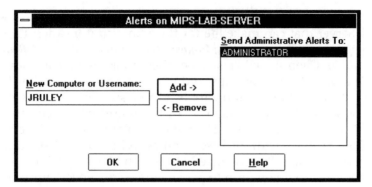

Figure 7.18 Alerts dialog Server Manager.

The Alerts dialog, accessed from Server manager's Computer/Properties menu, allows an administrator to determine where alert notifications are sent on the network.

fresh menu item), then either select a command to execute from the Computer menu, or double-click the entry (equivalent to Computer/Properties) to bring up a Properties—it's equivalent to the Server dialog in the Control Panel, and allows you to inspect (and control) logged-in user accounts, shared resources, connections, replication, and administrative alerts in exactly the same way. Perhaps the most critical use you'll make of this is controlling administrative alerts—clicking the Alerts button brings up an Alerts dialog (see Figure 7.18) that lets you send administrative alert information to specified computer or user names. This can be particularly convenient when the server's locked up and you want alerts to show up on your workstation.

Services on the remote system(s) can be controlled by selecting Computer/Services, which brings up a Services dialog that's identical to that from the Control Panel. This allows you to start/stop/pause/continue services on any Windows NT system in the domain, and to determine the startup parameters (if any).

User Manager for Domains

As we've discussed, the management of user accounts in Windows NT Server differs from that in NT Workstation—especially when interdomain trust is involved. Not surprisingly, Microsoft provides a different version of User Manager for Server administrators. User Manager for Domains looks almost identical to Windows NT's User Manager, but provides several additional features.

The first is that you can select a domain to administer, from the User/Select Domain menu item. You will need administrative access in the domain you

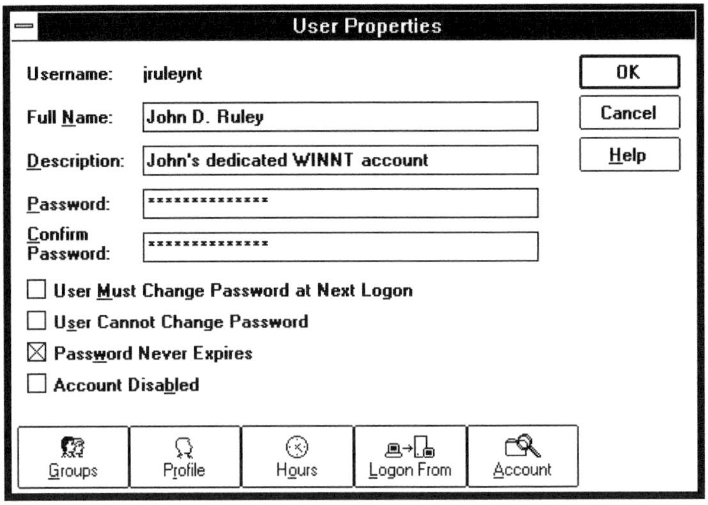

Figure 7.19 User Properties dialog.
This dialog, from Windows NT Server's User Manager for Domains, allows administrators to control most aspects of a user's access to Windows NT servers and workstations in the domain.

want to administer, of course. Once that's done, the list of user names in the main User Manager screen will update, showing users and groups in the selected domain. Double-clicking on a user name brings up a User Properties dialog (see Figure 7.19) that appears similar to the single-server version—except for the additional buttons on the bottom of the dialog. These buttons allow you to specify the hours during which a user may log in, the systems they're permitted to log in on, the date that the account expires (this differs from the date the account's *password* expires), and whether the account is *global* or *local*.[29] In all other respects, User Manager for Domain operates identically to the single-server version of User Manager (covered in Chapter 3).

User Profile Editor

One of Windows NT Server's nicest features is the availability of per-user login profiles that span the entire domain rather than just applying to a single machine. These profiles (which differ from the *user environment profile* set in User Manager), are set with the User Profile Editor (see Figure 7.20). This tool lets you control many features of a Windows NT user's environment, including what features are enabled (or disabled) in Program Manager and File Manager,

---

29. See Chapter 3 for an explanation of *local* and *global* user accounts.

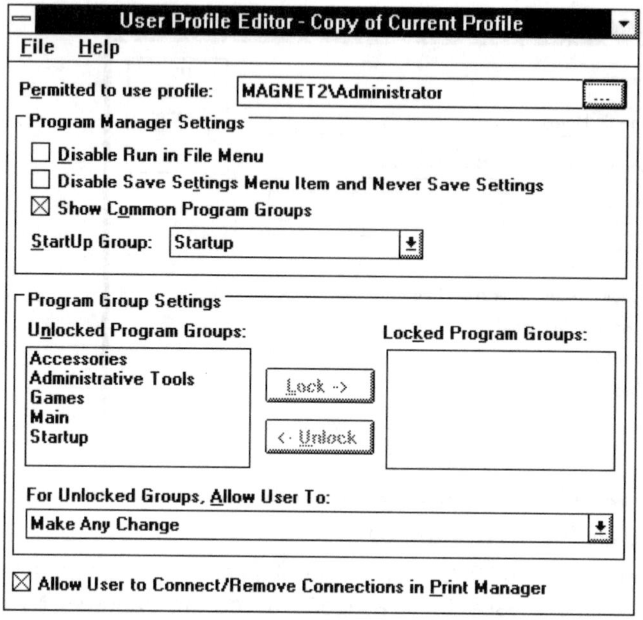

Figure 7.20 User Profile Editor.

Windows NT Server administrators can control user access to specific Program Manager, File Manager, and Print Manager features using the User Profile Editor.

what startup group is set in Program Manager (it need not be named Start Up), whether program groups are locked (the user cannot change them) or unlocked (can be changed at will), and so on. Used in conjunction with the user environment profile and user rights set in User Manager, and (if necessary) a login script; this allows you a very high degree of control over the environment of your users.

Remote Administration

Although the tools just mentioned are shipped with Windows NT Server (and require one to be present on the network and configured as Primary Domain Controller), they do *not* have to be run from one. Indeed, you can run them from any Windows NT workstation on the net—even remotely, using RAS.

There are two ways to do this. The obvious one is to exploit the hidden ADMIN$ share that provides administrators access to the \WINNT\SYSTEM32 directory on all NT systems. Server Manager (SRVMGR.EXE), User Manager for Domains (USRMGR.EXE), User Profile Editor (UPEDIT.EXE), and so on, can be run remotely over the network (you could even set up a Remote Admin program group for this in User Profile Manager) from that location. We don't recommend this approach on slow WAN links (like RAS over modems).

There is one more setting that will help if you administer a Windows NT domain remotely—Server Manager and User Manager for Domains both support a Low Speed Connection option that saves time on slow data links by not displaying the full list of servers, users, and so on. This option is also available on the RAS Admin program, and on many other tools.

Client-Based Administrator's Tools

Beginning with version 3.5, Microsoft added a long-needed (and much appreciated) set of client-based administration tools to Windows NT. The tools provided (in both NT and Windows 3.*x* varients) include User Manager for Domains, Server Manager, Event Viewer, Print Manager for Windows NT Server—and an option to add a Security menu to the standard Windows 3.1/3.11 File Manager that lets you control access to directories and files on the NT server. The Windows 3.*x* versions of the tools are Win32s-based, and require Windows (or WFWG) 3.1/3.11 enhanced mode. A comparable set of tools is made available for Windows 95 in the *Windows 95 Resource Kit*.

The practical implication of having such tools on client platforms is that remote administration of an NT Server no longer requires an NT Workstation—a distinct advantage, given the high cost of setting up a reasonably well-configured Workstation for administrative use. There's also something to be said for running on the same client system as your end users. The client-based administrative tools do lack some of the full NT management features. There are (as yet) no Windows-based versions of NT's Performance Monitor, Disk Administrator, User Profile Editor, and Backup applications; and they currently provide no support for remote access to the NT command line.

Running a Windows NT Server in a Locked Closet

Locked-closet servers are of interest to both domain-wide and single-server administrators, of course; but the issue is such a no-brainer for domain-wide administration that we decided it was best covered here.

The main problem with locking up an NT server is that it normally requires human intervention to start up—specifically, the Ctrl+Alt+Del sequence that's used to log in. Until this has been done, any command scripts or autostarted programs (from the Start Up program group) won't run.

Microsoft's recommended solution to this problem is to exploit Windows NT's *services* interface, which *does* allow for automatic startup before any user logs in. Any Windows NT service can be designated for automatic startup from Control Panel/Services (or Server Manager/Properties) Startup button. The resulting dialog allows you to select *Automatic* startup, which will happen immediately on system start.

The one problem with this approach is that it works *only* for Windows NT services—and as yet, there are many critical system tasks (Microsoft's own EXTERNAL.EXE mail transfer agent, for instance) that are not yet implemented as services. To get those programs started automatically on system start, it's necessary to defeat Windows NT's logon security system. To do so:[30]

1. Start the Registry Editor, select HKEY_LOCAL_MACHINE\Software.

2. Select Microsoft\Windows NT\CurrentVersion\Winlogon, and enter values for DefaultDomainName, DefaultUserName, and DefaultPassword.

Of course, entering the user name and password into the Registry means that anyone with administrative access can see them (using the Registry Editor)—but administrators have the ability to *change* the password, anyway. And the fact that the system comes up automatically logged-in doesn't seem like much of a security risk if it's already locked up. We *do* recommend that you use a specially created user account—*not* the Administrator account—for such an automatic login account. This minimizes the security risk to the system, since a person who jimmies the lock to the server room will not thereby gain automatic administrative access to the server. If Administrative access is required, it can be obtained by using Registry Editor on another system to eliminate the DefaultUserName and DefaultPassword entries set in the preceding procedure; then log off from the server's console and log back in as the administrator and reset the defaults when you're done (you could even write a script for this using the REGINI.EXE program provided in the \SUPTOOLS directory of the Windows NT CD).

However, the most important things to do in support of a locked-up Windows NT server don't require meddling with the Registry—just use Control Panel / Services (or Server Manager / Properties) to verify that the *Workstation* and *Server* services are set for automatic startup. That way, even if the system doesn't come up properly, you can control it from an administrative workstation. You may want to set the Remote Access Server service for automatic startup, too, so that you can get into the server using dial-in. And, of course, locked-up servers (like any NT servers) should have a UPS installed, and the UPS service properly configured, per Chapter 3.

Systems Management

Many observers expressed dissapointment when NT 3.1 first appeared, noting that it lacked the kind of high-end systems management software required of

---

30. Our thanks to Microsoft's Dave Hart for pointing out this procedure—it's documented in Microsoft Knowlege Base article Q97597.

a true enterprise operating system. Systems Management Server (SMS), formerly known by the code name *Hermes* is Microsoft's answer—a powerful (and, surprisingly, multiplatform!) enterprise management service.

SMS stores management information in an SQL Server database, which is accessed using a specialized SMS administrator's program (essentially a highly customized query tool). Data is collected for the database automatically through client software executed in conjunction with system login scripts. This data constitutes basic *configuration* data on all SMS-managed clients and servers, *inventory* data on software installed on the clients, and *audits* of specified software packages.

Each SMS site must contain a *site server*—an NT Server running SMS software—as well as an SQL Server (which may or may not run on the same physical machine). Clients execute the SMS client software (a complex logon script) as part of their normal network server logon—and as necessary, receive software updates and provide inventory/audit data in response to commands incorporated in the logon script. Inventory/audit data from the clients is stored in Management Information File (MIF) format files that propagate back to the site server through the logon (and optionally, helper) servers. Finally, the site server stores the collected data in an SQL Server database.

Basic inventory data—such as the operating system version, processor type, free disk space, and so on, on clients and servers is collected automatically at logon. Optionally, this can be expanded to include searching for specific files by name, size, and/or modification date—and files may be collected as well as detected. Once data is collected, queries may be executed against the resulting database—finding all copies of WINWORD.EXE with a date prior to 31/03/94, for instance, to generate a list of workstations that have not been upgraded to Word 6.0.

SMS also allows automatic (or nearly so) installation and upgrade of both locally installed applications and server-based network applications. This is accomplished by creating a *package*, which consists of all files required for the installation, including an installer (.BAT file, SETUP.EXE, or Microsoft Test script—SMS client software includes a Test runtime, and predefined packages for a host of Microsoft's own applications and operating systems are supplied with the product). Shared network applications are supported through the creation of program manager groups and icons that access applications installed in and shared by a file server.

Once a package is created, SMS will automatically propagate the package to all designated clients—as simply as dragging an icon representing the package to a particular client, group of clients, or result of an explicit query against the site database.

SMS inventory and remote installation features are complemented by an impressive set of troubleshooting tools that (for Windows 3.*x* clients) include examination of available DOS and Windows memory, a network PING test, remote file copy, remote execution of programs, remote control of the client console—and even remote reboot.

SMS also ships with an NT-based Network Monitor (formerly code-named *bloodhound*) that has most features of a network *sniffer*. It records network traffic, decodes it, and permits the troubleshooter to search captured packets in a wide variety of ways. It runs as an NT service, and can be installed on any NT system on the network.

Unfortunately, these extremely handy remote troubleshooting features are currently available *only* on DOS/Windows clients—not on Windows NT, OS/2, or Macintosh clients (or servers). Other limitations of SMS include its dependence on Microsoft SQL Server for Windows NT (Microsoft justifies this by pointing to SMS membership in its Back Office suite), the requirement that a Windows NT-based system be used to run the Administrators tools, and lack of support (as of this writing) for Windows 95 clients.

While SMS doesn't provide true software metering (particularly for server-based network applications), its inventory and audit features do allow generation of a list of clients that have application components installed. In many cases this is just as valuable, and Microsoft is working with a third party to provide add-on metering capability for those who demand it.[31]

Experience with a small (three servers, less than a dozen clients) SMS test site showed that once the complicated installation process is completed (the release notes alone make up a 77KB Windows Help file!), it's quite easy to use—and extremely powerful. Indeed, some might say *too* powerful. SMS provides managers with a level of control over client PCs that may offend some end users. It needs to be deployed with some care.

SMS does *not* provide the kind of *network management* that's provided by such products as IBM's NetView and SNMP-based systems. Microsoft's position is that there are plenty of other products available for such uses, while the issue of managing network *clients* hasn't been generally addressed.

Troubleshooting Enterprise Networks

As we mentioned earlier, while administration of an enterprise network is much like administering a very large LAN, troubleshooting problems in an enterprise environment is a different matter altogether. The reason for this is that enterprise networks are so much more complex than LANs—if a user can't see a server in a LAN environment, there are only really four possible causes: The server's gone down, the wiring's bad, the network card's bad (more likely, the cable *to* the network card is unplugged—always check this first), or (*most* frequently)

---

31. Express Systems, Inc.—they may be contacted at 206-728-8300.

the software in the user's workstation is having a problem. There really isn't anything else to break!

Add a couple of routers and a WAN link to the connection, however, and you greatly multiply the possible causes of trouble. The WAN link might be down—or just having line noise problems. One of the routers may have failed. A power glitch may restart a router with a bad routing table—and the list goes on and on.

As it happens, there's a fairly simple approach to troubleshooting these problems that we feel confident in recommending: It's used twice a year by the *network warriors* of INTEROP, who accomplish the amazing feat of creating a large (hundreds of routers, an FDDI backbone, and thousands of nodes) TCP/IP network, called ShowNet, *in just a few days*. That approach is to use the standard TCP/IP PING.EXE utilty—and little else.[32]

The reason the INTEROP folks do this is that the huge network they put in really represents something of a worst-case multivendor net—each node on the network terminates in a booth on the show floor, where vendors plug in whatever network hardware and software they're trying to sell. By using PING to get underneath whatever software the vendors are using, the ShowNet team isolates themselves from the details of a particular vendor's software. This lets them concentrate on making sure that the cabling is good and the routers are properly configured. They start looking at the software *only* after checking the hardware with PING.

We think this makes good sense for NT networks—especially since (as we discussed at the start of this chapter) *all* routed NT networks *must* use TCP/IP as the backbone protocol. We do think it makes sense to leverage NT's built-in tools as well (in particular, using Performance Monitor to check on network throughput, per Chapter 5), and it's *always* a good idea to look at the event log when a problem occurs; but if the cause of the problem isn't immediately apparent, we suggest that a good place to start is to use PING from the workstation to the server. If PING gets through, then you know the hardware's good—and you can start looking at the software. If not, then you have a hardware (or router configuration) problem that's got to be solved before looking at any higher-level issues.

We also recommend that you look carefully at *out-of-band signaling* in enterprise networks—especially big ones. Out-of-band signaling means that you don't lock yourself into sending all administrative data and commands over the network itself—because otherwise, if there's a hardware problem, it will stop the administrative data just as it stops the network traffic. There are basically three ways to get an out-of-band capability in a Windows NT-based enterprise network:

---

32. It's particularly instructive that they do this even though *most* nodes on the INTEROP ShowNet support SMTP, NetView, or any of a dozen proprietary network management schemes.

1. Use RAS on your servers—set up a separate dial-in *only* modem and line on each server (or one server in each closet), and grant access rights *only* to administrative users. This gives you a reliable *back door* to get into that server remotely, and doesn't compete with user traffic on other RAS links you may have.

2. Configure a non-NT PC on the network to run a DOS- (or Windows-) based remote control program, such as PCanywhere for Windows— again, with a dedicated modem line configured only for dial-in, and with access restricted to administrators. This gives you access to the local network, and can be especially useful in resetting a balky router (when you're on the wrong side of the router).

3. If you buy a multiprotocol router, get one with an RS-232 port, and (again) put a dedicated modem on that port for administrative access. This gives you direct control of the router from a remote location (if you're using Windows NT's built-in static router feature, setting up RAS on the routing machine gives you the same capability).

In any case, the point is: *Give yourself a back door!* It doesn't matter whether your operation is standardized on NetView or SNMP or what have you; make sure there is a network-independent way to get in. This will save you from the need to go in yourself on an emergency call.

One more thing to consider—on a really large enterprise system, there may be unattended servers (and routers) in locations that aren't easily accessible. Clearly these are candidates for one of the back-door dial-in approaches we've just listed, but there's also a need for these systems to get the word out that they're in trouble.

One way to handle this is to reverse the RAS-based back door we've just discussed: Make sure that your own administrative workstation runs RAS with a modem set up for dial-in, and configure the system you're worried about with RAS set to dial-out. You can then set up alerts (in Performance Monitor) to execute a script like this one:

```
rasdial trouble_line
net send Admin1 Help! Router in trouble!
rasdial trouble_line /DISCONNECT
```

This way, the router calls *you*, and you can then call it back (assuming it has a dial-in line) to find out the specifics and fix the problem.

If you're in charge of a truly mission-critical system that has to operate 24 hours a day, the ultimate way to handle this is, of course, the inevitable pager. Two applications that allow NT to interface with these useful (if annoying) little beasts will be found in Table 7.3, as will some other products of special interest to enterprise network managers.

Table 7.3 Windows NT Network Management Apps

Product	Company	Address	Phone	Comments
LanAdmin *Lan Licenser*	ABC Systems and Development	The Carriage House 28 Green Street Newburg, MA 01951	508-463-8602	Simplified network administration and license management with encrypted auditing
Notify!	Ex Machina	45 East 89th St. Suite 39-A New York, NY 10128-1232	800-238-4738 718-965-0309	Alphanumeric pager support for Window NT; supports TAPI and various DMTF pagers; supports DDE and MAPI
WinBeep	Fourth Wave Software	560 Kirts Blvd. Suite 105 Troy, MI 48084	313-362-2288	Wireless messaging to users of full-text pagers; personal, SDK, and Server versions available
AppMeter	Funk Software	222 Third Street Cambridge, MA 02142	617-497-6339	Application usage metering and logging
NMC 4000 Network Manager	Network Managers	Stirling House, Stirling Rd. The Surrey Research Park Guilford, Surrey GU2 5RF (UK)	508-251-4111	Configuration-, fault-, and performance-management; supports SNMP; can integrate with SMS
Carmel Anti-Virus for Windows NT	Carmel Software	20 Hahistadrut Ave POB 25055 Haifa, Israel 31250	972-441-6976	Client/server antivirus product
InocuLAN for Windows NT	Cheyenne Software	3 Expressway Plaza, Roslyn Heights, NY 11577	516-484-5110	NCSA-certified LAN-wide antivirus product
Systems Management Server(SMS)	Microsoft	One Microsoft Way, Redmond, WA 98052	800-426-9400 206-882-8080	Described earlier in this chapter
Polycenter AssetWorks	Digital Equipment	151 Taylor Street, Littleton, MA 01460	800-DIGITAL	Enhances SMS by providing multiplatform support to legacy systems
Quota Manager for Windows NT	New Technology Partners	15 Constitution Drive, Suite 176 Bedford, NH 03110	603-472-4000	Caps user files and directories at a fixed maximum size; requires (and supports) NTFS
Tivoli/Courier for Windows NT	Tivoli Systems	9442 Capitol of Texas Highway North, Arboretum Place North Austin, TX 78759	800-2-TIVOLI	Automatic, unattended software installation/update

Is NT Really Ready for the Enterprise?

You may find it interesting to compare this chapter with what we wrote in the first edition of *Networking Windows NT*. In the intervening year and a half, NT has gained client-side administration tools, an add-on management package (SMS), considerable third-party support (see Table 7.2) and *greatly* improved built-in WAN connectivity. On the other hand, the mail situation hasn't improved much, and NT still lacks some enterprise essentials, such as per-user chargeback accounting. On the whole, we think that while NT has made great strides and is eminently suitable for use *in* the enterprise, it isn't—yet—the system we'd recommend as the *backbone* of the enterprise.

That's bound to change, however. Big-system features are coming for NT—and from a variety of sources. For example, Digital Equipment Corporation carried out a demonstration of NT-based *clustering* at the 1994 fall Comdex trade show. Clusters have been used in the VAX world for years as a cost-effective way to combine fault-tolerance and scalability. In a cluster, several servers are tied together, sharing certain resources (in particular, hard disks), and are treated as a unit. For example, two servers can share two disk drives—using standard SCSI. Each server has a controller on *both* disks. Users see the two disks as part of a single virtual device, so a NET USE shows just see one entry, called (for instance) Cluster1. The disks are accessed as though both are connected to a single server called Cluster1; that is, \\Cluster1\disk1 and \\Cluster1\disk2.

With both servers operating, disk performance is enhanced, because each drive is *actually* handled by a separate server (the cluster software masks this from users). However, if one server goes down (Digital demonstrated this at Comdex by physically disconnecting power on one server *during a disk access*), there's a short delay—and the other server takes over.

The beauty of this technology, as compared to such alternatives as proprietary ultrareliable systems (NetFrame, for instance), is that it's *cheap*. Standard servers and disks are combined to create a redundant cluster. If all goes well, Digital should have Clusters for NT in beta test by the time you read this, and it should ship some time in 1995.

As big-system technologies such as clustering become available, we think the issue of whether NT is *really* an enterprise operating system will answer themselves!

Summary and Conclusion

We've examined the challenge represented by enterprise networks, and seen how the features of Windows NT—and especially Windows NT Server—can be used to ease the implementation of enterprise networks. We've explored what makes an enterprise network different from a LAN, and determined that the governing factor is *complexity*.

Beyond sheer complexity, enterprise networks are characterized by geographic dispersion—they extend beyond one building or office complex (often beyond even one city, state, or country) requiring WAN connectivity. We've examined RAS, Windows NT's built in WAN, which provides a reasonable alternative to dedicated multiprotocol routers in departmental applications. We've also examined some special issues of interest to enterprise administrators, including Windows NT Server's built-in support for Macintosh computers; and issues involved in managing and maintaining enterprise networks, including remote administration and complex network maintenance.

By now, you should have a good feel for the features built into Windows NT. The next three chapters will extend these concepts beyond Windows NT's built-in networking, as we examine what's involved in connecting Windows NT to other Microsoft SMB networks (Chapter 8), Novell NetWare (Chapter 9), and other networks—including IBM's LAN Server and SNA sytems and Banyan VINES (Chapter 10).

For More Information

Microsoft Staff, *Windows NT Server—Services for Macintosh*. Redmond WA: Microsoft Corp. The best (and only) reference on SFM.

Microsoft Staff, *Windows NT Server—Remote Access Service*. Redmond WA: Microsoft Corp. All the details of RAS, including specifics of use with modems, multiport cards, X.25 smart cards, and ISDN.

Microsoft Staff, *Windows NT Server—Concepts and Planning Guide*. Redmond WA: Microsoft Corp. Detailed coverage of domain management, interdomain trust, printer services, and so on.

Microsoft Staff , *32-bit Applications Catalog*. Redmond WA: Microsoft Corp. This is an electronic document (a large Windows Help file) that lists dozens of Windows NT applications in categories ranging from desktop utilities to enterprise management. It's downloadable from Microsoft's Internet server (ftp.microsoft.com).

Renaud, Paul. (1993), *Introduction to Client/Server Systems*. New York: John Wiley & Sons. ISBN: 0-471-57774-X. Among other things (it's no accident we've cited him elsewhere in this book), Renaud has good coverage of end-to-end system management that's as applicable to Windows NT as it is to UNIX systems.

Gilster, Paul. (1993), *The Internet Navigator*. New York: John Wiley & Sons. ISBN: 0-471-59782-1. An outstanding introduction to the Internet, including descriptions of most common services, and extensive lists of local providers. The book's one flaw is inadequate coverage of Mosaic/World-Wide Web issues, but everything he has to say about getting connected to the net still applies.

CHAPTER

Microsoft Connections

When you finish this chapter, you should understand how Windows NT's networking features arose from the old MS-Net/LAN Manager products, and how to achieve interoperation between NT, LAN Manager dialects, Windows for Workgroups, and Windows 95. You should feel comfortable connecting NT clients and servers into LAN Manager, LAN Server, and Windows for Workgroups or Windows 95 networks; understand what's involved in operating a mixture of LAN Manager and Windows NT servers; and should understand the difference between workgroups and domains.

Microsoft Networks

Although Windows NT Workstation and its companion Server version are the most ambitious network products that Microsoft has ever built, they are not the company's only network products. Microsoft also offers its Windows for Workgroups product as a peer-to-peer network for sites with modest networking needs. Its successor, Windows 95, is in the final stages of beta testing as this book is being written. And, despite Microsoft's coolness to OS/2, their OS/2 LAN Manager was Microsoft's high-end networking solution until NT arrived.

All Microsoft network products can use the Server Message Block (SMB) protocol (see Appendix 2), which gives them a baseline level of interoperability. In practical terms, that means you can usually share a printer or a directory subtree between any two Microsoft-based networks. However, the differences

401

between the products often mean that advanced features, including security and system administration, are not fully interoperable.

Microsoft's Early Networks

Microsoft is far from a newcomer to networking. It has been in the business since the early 1980s, when it offered its MS-Net product. Instead of selling MS-Net directly to end users, Microsoft licensed MS-Net to vendors, who then modified it—sometimes in incompatible ways—and resold it under many names. For example, IBM sold MS-Net as the IBM PC LAN Program, while 3Com's version was called 3Plus.

LAN Manager

When Microsoft and IBM announced OS/2 in 1987, they also announced an OS/2-based network solution compatible with MS-Net. Microsoft called the product OS/2 LAN Manager. As with MS-Net, Microsoft licensed OS/2 LAN Manager to vendors—such as IBM (LAN Server), 3Com (3+Open), and DEC (Pathworks)—who made their own enhancements and modifications.

In 1990, Microsoft made an important change in the way it sold networking products. It began to offer OS/2 LAN Manager as a retail product under the Microsoft name, but continued the licensing agreements with such vendors as IBM, 3Com, and DEC. Since then, Microsoft has moved its networking emphasis from licensing to retail sales, capitalizing on the familiar Microsoft name.

Windows for Workgroups

Today, Microsoft offers Windows for Workgroups (WFWG) as its low-end peer-to-peer network. WFWG is essentially Windows 3.1 with networking built in. In addition to having file sharing features built into File Manager, Print Manager, and common dialogs, WFWG includes versions of Microsoft Mail and Schedule+ scheduling software in the box.

Windows 95

Microsoft's choice for a mass-market desktop operating system successor to Windows for Workgroups is Windows 95. It extends the networking capabilities of that earlier product, but most sigificantly replaces the Windows 3.1 look with a very different user interface. Windows 95 is in *final beta test* as this chapter is being written, so some of the detailed information may still be subject to change. However, many aspects of Windows 95 networking are not likely to change, and we'll concentrate on those capabilities in this chapter.

Using Windows NT with LAN Manager

As you would expect, since Microsoft wrote both LAN Manager and Windows NT, and the networking features in Windows NT are derived from those in LAN Manager (one can think of Windows NT Server as LAN Manager 3.0), this all works together rather better than some of the third-party networking issues that are discussed in Chapters 6, 9, and 10. Windows NT workstations can utilize the resources of LAN Manager servers pretty much seamlessly. LAN Manager workstations can make use of Windows NT servers pretty much seamlessly. There are a few rough edges—particularly when one tries to mix LAN Manager and NT servers in the same domain—but there are work-arounds for this. On the whole it's a very usable system.

It's All the Same...

The networking features in Windows NT are advanced 32-bit versions of the networking features that Microsoft has built into the LAN Manager 2.x series. Windows NT and LAN Manager share many features in common, including: being based on SMB networking, use of NetBEUI as the principal protocol (with TCP/IP as the enterprise protocol), and use of NDIS device drivers. Many of the APIs and the data structures and even the syntax of the commands are the same. The systems are generally quite compatible and the migration process moving from LAN Manager to Windows NT is not a difficult one.

Except When It's Not

The LAN Manager/NT situation is something of a good news/bad news story. The bad news is, first, that the structure and operation of the administrative domains differ and, as we will see, this can become a real problem when you start to mix LAN Manager (OS/2) and NT servers. There's also a difference in the way that network browsing and announcement is handled. This is easy to get around in that Microsoft has made it possible to reset Windows NT to use the LAN Manager-style browser service, but unfortunately, there are very good reasons that they changed it—so this is not a permanent solution, either. There is also a difference in the way the passwords are handled in the two systems (a problem that LAN Manager and NT interoperation shares with Windows for Workgroups and NT interoperation). Finally, the directory replication mechanism differs, and in large networks this can be a major issue. But having said all that, take heart—you can get there from here. Microsoft was not foolish enough to build a totally incompatible networking architecture into its new operating system.

With that as an introduction, let's begin at the beginning—in all probability, if you have an established LAN Manager system, your first experience with NT will be adding workstations.

Windows NT Workstations with LAN Manager Servers

Windows NT workstations work well with LAN Manager servers. The one major issue of concern is the browsing service—the service that is activated when you go into the file manager and select Connect Net Drive or type net view from the command line.

Network Browsing in Windows NT

This is as good a place as any to discuss the browse service. To understand the Windows NT situation, we should begin by understanding some basic facts about server message block (SMB) networking and the way LAN Manager works. Network browsing in the SMB system depends on a *broadcast* mechanism that uses APIs called *mail slots*. In the broadcast situation, whenever a LAN Manager server or workstation is joined to the network, it begins by sending a class-2 mail slot message to all other machines on the local network segment, looking for a server. Any servers will respond with a message directed back to the workstation, announcing who they are. The workstation looks for the Primary Domain Controller (PDC), which is the center of administrative control in a LAN Manager network.

There is a major problem with this approach in that *broadcast announcements cannot be routed beyond the local subnet.* Otherwise, a complicated internetwork with many routers would spend most of its time doing nothing but broadcast announcements. Therefore, routers do not pass the broadcast announcements—creating a *double hop* problem. If you connect more than one LAN together, the LAN Manager-style browsing breaks down. Workstations in one subnet cannot see servers outside their subnet.

A variety of mechanisms have been attempted to get around this problem—and the cold fact of the matter is that Microsoft is still working on it. The ultimate solution appears to be use of TCP/IP as a standard internetworking protocol for multiple-hop networks (and you'll find detailed coverage of this in Appendix 2 and Chapter 6). Aside from the double-hop problem, the use of broadcasts as a method of network browsing creates two difficulties. The first is that whenever a workstation logs into the network, it has to broadcast its presence on the subnet. It will then sit for up to a minute waiting for a response from the domain controller. This can be extremely annoying. On a heavily loaded network it may be necessary for the workstation to make several broadcast announcements before the server will respond—a very frustrating situation for end users. Worse, on large LANs with many stations, *race conditions* can exist, where so many stations are attempting to logon at once that it's impossible for the server to keep up with them. This can actually have a significant impact on the overall network traffic.

Beginning with Windows for Workgroups and with the first beta versions of Windows NT, Microsoft began to eliminate the use of broadcast announcements during login. Instead, Windows NT and Windows for Workgroups employ the concept of a *browse master*. In the browse master scenario, one station within the subnet (the primary domain controller and a Windows NT Server domain, or an elected Windows NT or Windows for Workgroups machine in a Windows for Workgroups/Windows NT Workgroup) maintains a list of all the other servers and workstations in the workgroup or domain. During login, instead of sending a broadcast message to all systems on the subnet, a workstation needs to communicate its presence only to the Browse Master, which in turn communicates the location of other systems—including the domain controller, to whom the system sends a login message. No broadcasts are required.

Unfortunately, difficulties can still occur in this kind of networking. The whole thing comes unglued if the machine that has been selected as Browse Master is not turned on. In this condition, the machines that are turned on will attempt to contact the Browse Master, but *time out* after a preset interval and then conduct a *Browse Master election* (which involves the same broadcasts we were trying to get away from in the first place), in which they identify each other; the machine with the best performance characteristics will generally elect to be the new Browse Master.

To avoid having constant Browse Master elections, it is possible to force a machine to be a Browse Master. On Windows NT machines this can be accomplished using the Registry Editor (REGEDT32.EXE) by opening HKEY_LO-CAL_MACHINE\SYSTEM\CurrentControlSet\Services\Browser\Parameters, and creating an IsDomainMaster value, defining it as type REG_SZ and specifying the text TRUE for the value of the string. This will cause a machine to maintain the browse list irrespective of whether it is elected as a Browse Master. This is essential in a situation where a remote workgroup does not have a domain controller associated with it.

While Windows NT and Windows for Workgroups have migrated to a new manner of maintaining browse information, the existing installed base of LAN Manager 2.x systems have not. So whenever Windows NT is used in conjunction with LAN Manager computers, it is necessary to make a few adaptations. The most important of these is a parameter called *Lmannounce*. (LAN Manager announce) which essentially forces a Windows NT (or Windows for Workgroups) machine to engage in the same behavior that a LAN Manager machine would. This doesn't mean that you will automatically wind up waiting one minute every time you log in on a Windows NT workstation. The Windows NT machine continues to employ the Browse Master principle. It just adds the periodic broadcast messages the LAN Manager machines will need in order to see the Windows NT system.

To set LAN Manager-style broadcast announcements under Windows NT, run Network Settings in the Windows NT Control Panel, select Server, press the Configure button, and check the Make Browser Broadcasts to LAN Manager 2.x Clients check box at the bottom of the Server dialog. Alternatively, run the Registry Editor. (REGEDT32.EXE), select HKEY_LOCAL_MACHINE\SYSTEM\ CurrentControlSet\Services\LanmanServer\Parameters, and create an Lmannounce keyword, defined as type REG_DWORD with a value of 0x1. Just as with the much simpler Control Panel setting, this will cause you to broadcast.

LAN Manager Domains Are Windows NT Workgroups

Here we get into a really unfortunate piece of semantics. The concept of an administrative domain is a simple one. This is a logical grouping of servers and workstations that are treated as a single administrative unit. In the LAN Manager environment all domain members share a centralized security account database that is controlled by the primary domain controller (PDC).

Unfortunately, in Windows NT we have a completely different type of domain controller and an incompatible domain system. As we'll see a little bit later on, in a Windows NT Server domain, LAN Manager systems are essentially second-class citizens and the PDC *must* be a Windows NT Server. Windows NT Workstations can participate in Windows NT Server domains only as domain members.

Does this mean that a standard Windows NT system cannot participate in a LAN Manager domain? No. Just as in Windows for Workgroups or Windows 95, the solution is to operate the Windows NT machine with a workgroup name but to set the workgroup name to the same name that is used for the LAN Manager domain. At this point, everybody's happy and they can all talk. The Windows NT machine believes that it is part of a Windows NT workgroup. The LAN Manager machine sees the Windows NT machine as a workstation, not a server, in the domain. Everything works fine until the Windows NT machine tries to behave as a server by sharing files and printers.

Windows NT Systems as Servers in LAN Manager Domains

Since Windows NT machines cannot participate as domain members, they cannot share security account information with the PDC and its cohorts. Therefore, a Windows NT machine takes the role of a stand-alone server or *peer* in a LAN Manager environment. That is, it must maintain its own user account database. This is very similar in principle to the existence of Windows for Workgroups machines within the domain. However, it incurs a greater responsibility and more difficulty on the part of the Windows NT system operator, in that you have to have a true account database. There must be an account name and password for every individual who is going to attempt to use the shared directories and printers on the Windows NT machine. Therefore, stand-alone Windows NT machines present a significant administrative problem as part of LAN Manager domains—so if you want to employ Windows NT servers, you should upgrade at least one LAN Manager server to a Windows NT Server (and as we'll see by implication, that means you will have two).

However, for light-duty purposes and for such things as printer sharing, you certainly can operate with the base Windows NT machine as a stand-alone server in a LAN Manager domain. As mentioned earlier, you must set the Lmannounce parameter to 1 using one of the two methods defined in the preceding section to avoid browsing problems. If you do not do this, LAN Manager workstations, be they OS/2 or DOS machines, within the domain will find it impossible to locate the Windows NT machine or its shared resources. Again, you must think of any such stand-alone NT system administratively. Windows NT machines sitting within LAN Manager domains are best thought of as *peers* (version 2.0 of LAN Manager supported a special category of OS/2 machines as peers, stand-alone machines capable of resource sharing). This is very much the same situation that a Windows NT machine takes. It will work—albeit with some difficulty.

There are generally two approaches. One is to simulate share-level security. Windows NT does not support the Windows for Workgroups- or Windows 95-style of resource sharing, in which any user can access a shared resource, assuming he has the necessary password; but Windows NT does support a *guest account,* which is very similar to that used by LAN Manager systems. If you set the guest account to have a null password and give the guest account privileges for a shared printer, for example, then everyone will be able to access the shared printer, irrespective of whether they have a user account on the print server (if the server does not recognize the user name at login, it will log you in as a guest). This approach is fine for printers, but it's completely insecure and therefore may not be a good idea for shared directories.

The alternative is to maintain a full user-name and password list on the Windows NT machine. This represents a pretty substantial job to expect an end user to perform. It is, I suppose, theoretically feasible to construct some kind of a batch file system that would automatically export account information from the LAN Manager server to a Windows NT system (possibly using some of the same techniques that were discussed at the end of Chapter 4, where we introduced a batch file for automatically converting NetWare accounts to Windows NT accounts). However, Microsoft does not provide any such capability in the Windows NT box—and in any case it represents a significant maintenance problem. Therefore, we do not recommend this approach.

It is possible to mix the two approaches—enable the guest account on Windows NT servers for nonsecure access, and augment this by maintaining user accounts *only* for users who require access to secure resources: But, again, this quickly can become a major administrative burden, since you must maintain these user accounts separately on each NT server. If you must enforce user-level security from within Windows NT servers that are part of a LAN Manager domain, it's time to upgrade the domain to a Windows NT Server domain.

Windows NT Server and LAN Manager

Microsoft has a special version of the Windows NT Server (Windows NT Advanced Server Upgrade for LAN Manager) that includes additional migration tools for converting the user accounts, access controls, and even directories to work with NT.

Now we begin to see the method in Microsoft's madness—it's all very straightforward if instead of thinking *NT Server* you think *LAN Manager 3.0*. As LAN Manager has migrated from version to version, it has acquired new features while retaining a certain degree of backward compatibility. Administrators have consistently been in the position of needing to upgrade the primary domain controller to the latest version. The current situation is no exception—even though the name of the product has changed.

Windows NT Server functionally is the latest version of LAN Manager, and there is a definite need in a mixed environment to upgrade the primary domain controller to a Windows NT Server system. Fortunately, you don't need to upgrade *all* the servers in the system. It is perfectly possible to apply an NT Server as a domain controller and have it work with OS/2 LAN Manager 2.0 machines as backup controllers.

Note, however, that a significant issue arises if only one Windows NT Server functions as primary domain controller in a LAN Manager domain: What happens when the domain controller fails? Although the LAN Manager machines can participate as backup controllers and can *replicate* the user account database, they cannot export it to another Windows NT system. For this reason we strongly recommend that you upgrade *two* of your OS/2-based LAN Manager 2.x servers to Windows NT Servers. The second machine should be regarded as the fall-back controller in case something goes wrong with the primary. The other LAN Manager servers can continue to participate in the domain as well (although only a Windows NT Server can authenticate login requests from Windows NT Workstations participating in the domain).

Pass-Through Permissions and Interdomain Trust

The issue of interdomain trust and multidomain administration is discussed in more detail in Chapter 7. Suffice it to say that Windows NT Server brings a new and very powerful concept to enterprise system administration—a domain can be set to *trust* the users of another domain—providing a mechanism for account management that spans many domains and (potentially) many subnets. That's the good news. The bad news is that LAN Manager does not support this capability—so when you mix LAN Manager and Windows NT servers you immediately create a problem. Fortunately, of course, existing LAN Manager systems do not employ interdomain trust (since they don't support it), so converting from a LAN Manager server to a Windows NT Server as primary domain controller does not immediately create this problem.

However, when interdomain trust services are instituted from the Windows NT Servers, or if an attempt is made to tie a LAN Manager domain to a Windows NT Server domain, then you'll have problems. As a work-around, since the LAN Manager machines cannot support interdomain trust , you can create *local* user accounts for the interdomain trusted users. Essentially this amounts to resorting to the LAN Manager-style of administration (which was to maintain duplicate accounts on each primary domain controller). This is clumsy but it's better than not working at all.

As described earlier, it is also necessary to employ Lmannounce=1 on the Windows NT machines that will be talking to the LAN Manager machines. Finally, with respect to *directory replication* (duplication of critical data on more than one server to maintain an ultimate degree of fault tolerance), as described earlier, LAN Manager machines can *import* replicate data but they cannot *export* it to the Windows NT machines—so it's not really practical to use LAN Manager Servers as a backup to Windows NT Servers.[1] As a result, again, we recommend that if the primary domain controller is converted to an NT Server, another machine also be converted to a Server (in effect, convert them in pairs). That way it is possible to step immediately from the NT Server primary to an NT Server fall-back and not miss a beat.

In the event that all Windows NT Server primary domain controllers fail, you can have the replication data on a LAN Manager server and can then manually go through the necessary steps to restart the system using LAN Manager user accounts. The major issue here, of course, is that the LAN Manager user account database and the Windows NT account database are incompatible. As we will discuss a little further on, migration tools exist that will automatically convert between the OS/2 LAN Manager account database and the Windows NT Server account database. The tools do not exist, however, going in the other direction, so the fact that the replication data exists on an OS/2 machine does not mean that it's going to be easy (although in principle it is always possible) to reestablish the system with an OS/2 domain controller. In effect, converting from an OS/2 LAN Manager domain to a Windows NT Server domain is a one-way process.

---

1. See Chapter 7 for replication details.

These incompatibilities relate to another issue. Obviously, in implementing pilot programs many sites will wish to minimize the initial investment in the new technology. In these situations, it certainly makes sense to convert one LAN Manager machine to an NT Server, convert one more as a fall-back, and see how things work out. However, once it has been decided that Windows NT is an environment that everyone is comfortable with, the incompatibilities with the OS/2 machines will render it increasingly cumbersome to deal with them in the environment. It's also unlikely that Microsoft will see fit to significantly enhance the OS/2 based server products over time.[2] Administrators with large-scale systems are advised to contact Microsoft and ask about quantity pricing.

LAN Manager Workstations and Windows NT Servers

Here the situation is generally much cleaner than it is for servers. In general, LAN Manager workstations see Windows NT servers, including both base product NT machines that are sharing resources and Windows NT Server machines, just as if they were LAN Manager servers. There's little difference in the way they're handled. It is necessary to employ the Lmannounce parameter, as discussed earlier, so that the DOS, Windows, and OS/2 workstations will be able to see the NT systems.

Compatibility Issues

While operation of LAN Manager workstations and NT servers is generally a clean process, there are a few things to watch out for. The first of these is passwords. Windows NT systems employ a password validation mechanism that is case sensitive. That is, *PASSWORD* and *password* are not the same in a Windows NT environment, and if the uppercase PASSWORD has been employed for a resource or a user account name, typing in the lowercase one will generate an error. To support backward compatibility with LAN Manager, Windows for Workgroups, or Windows 95 systems (which are not case sensitive), Windows NT detects during login the fact that it is talking to a foreign, non-Windows NT system and uses a case-insensitive validation technique.

This can lead to one unfortunate situation if a user employs both Windows NT and LAN Manager systems to access a Windows NT server. If the system has validated his login from a non-Windows NT machine, it will begin employing the case-insensitive logic and will continue to do so *even when the user transfers to a Windows NT machine*. But the Windows NT machine will transmit different characters, and the server may produce an error—even though the proper password has in fact been typed. The solution to this is simply to suggest to

---

2. As this was written (1993), we were told that OS/2-related development at Microsoft has stopped.

users that they always type the password the same way. If you always type the password in lowercase or you always type it in uppercase (or you always type it in one particular combination, as long as the combination stays the same), everything will work fine.

Another item to watch out for is login scripts from Windows and Windows for Workgroups machines. When a Windows or Windows for Workgroups user logs into a Windows NT (or, for that matter, LAN Manager) system in which the administrator has defined a login script, the Windows 3.x machine initiates a virtual DOS session in which to execute the script. However, the virtual DOS system remains *live* for only approximately 30 seconds—and this is not a configurable parameter. Therefore, if a script takes more than 30 seconds to execute, it will fail. The user will see an error message that the script has violated system integrity, and will come to the system administrator (bearing gifts, one might say).

The solution for this is to keep your scripts short—or disable script operation entirely when you have Windows users logging in. This is probably a particular issue for remote users logging in over Microsoft's Remote Access Services (RAS) or through a remote TCP/IP gateway traveling over async modem lines—all operations are going to be slow over such a connection. The script support feature in the Windows control panel can be disabled. To do so run Control Panel, choose the Network icon, choose the Networks button, select Microsoft LAN Manager in the Other Networks in Use box, choose Settings, and clear the Logon to LAN Manager Domain check box. This is not an ideal solution but it will get the job done.

Finally, watch out for DOS and Windows workstations that hang during login because multiple processes are attempting to address the network adapter card while the card is handling an MS-DOS command. Microsoft supplies a TSR program called *COMNDIS.COM* that solves this problem. It's on the LAN Manager 2.2 installation disks in the LANMAN.DOS/NETPROG directory. If COMNDIS.COM is used, it should be the last thing loaded in AUTOEXEC.BAT and it must start before any LAN Manager commands (except *net bind*).

COMNDIS.COM is not necessary with Windows for Workgroups, which uses a protected mode protocol stack and does not have the problem (unless it's used with real-mode drivers, in which case COMENDIS might be desirable). In any case, try this solution only on those workstations with a demonstrated propensity to hang when running with Windows NT (or LAN Manager) servers.

How LAN Manager Clients Access Windows NT Servers

In general, a LAN Manager client will see a Windows NT server as if it were a LAN Manager server—and the same operations that are normally used on the client (File Manager from Windows, File Manager or the *net* command-line interface from OS/2, the NET.EXE program from DOS) will be used to access the

Windows NT server. All of these procedures work very much the same for Windows NT as LAN Manager—and in general you should see the LAN Manager documentation for details.

We present here a very limited subset of the commands that are portable between (so far as we know) *all* versions of LAN Manager, Windows for Workgroups, Windows 95, and Windows NT. It's useful for a system administrator to be able to walk up to any station and carry out a minimal set of steps with a known response. However, there are better solutions for each individual environment and we encourage you to consult the documentation for the system in question. Our portable command-line subset is as follows:

1. To use a shared resource from a LAN Manager, Windows NT or Windows for Workgroups server:

   net use *device \\server name\share name*

   Net use will permit you to redirect a network resource on a particular server and see it as a local device. Network resources include both shared directories and (LAN Manager only) printers. The syntax of this command is generally similar to the equivalent Windows NT command that is defined in Chapter 3. It works almost identically on all systems. As an example:

   net use m: \\mips-lab-server\WGPO

   will redirect the WGPO shared directory on \\mips-lab-server to local drive M. Just typing *net use* by itself, with no arguments, will list any shared resources currently in use at the local workstation.

2. To browse shared resources (directories and printers) on LAN Manager, Windows NT and Windows for Workgroups, or Windows 95 servers:

   net view
   or
   net view *server name*

   Without arguments, *net view* displays a list of servers on the local subnetwork. *Net view\\server name* displays a list of the shares on the server. Thus the process of command-line browsing on any form of Microsoft network is generally to type *net view* to see the list of servers, *net view* and the name of a server to see the list of resources at the server, and *net use local device name \\server_name\resource* to access the resource. When resource sharing is finished, you can type *net use device name /delete* to terminate use of a shared resource.

3. To send messages on LAN Manager and Windows NT networks:

   net send *name message text*
   or

net send /DOMAIN:*domain name message text*
or
net send /BROADCAST *message text*

Net send provides basic messaging capabilities using class-2 mail-slot broadcasts, as we described in the introduction to this section. In general, the form of the command is net send *name text*. For example:

net send Administrator How do I use this blankety-blank thing?

will send the text "How do I use this blankety-blank thing?", which will appear in a pop-up display on the workstation that Administrator is logged in to.

4. To share resources on LAN Manager, Windows for Workgroups, and Windows NT systems:

net share *sharename=local path*

The syntax of the *net share* command is *net share sharename = directory specification*. Thus, for instance:

net share disk-D=D:\

will share the D:\ device (and subtrees) with the share name *disk-D*. This is a completely portable syntax among all versions of LAN Manager. There are various switches and flags, which will vary from version to version. On all versions of LAN Manger that support sharing, you can also type *net share* without any parameters to get a list of any shared devices, and *net share sharename /DELETE* to terminate sharing of a device.

Portable Administration

With these four commands an administrator can pretty reliably get things done, moving from system to system in a mixed LAN Manager network. LAN Manager DOS workstations; LAN Manager DOS workstations running Windows; Windows for Workgroups systems, whether version 3.1 or 3.11; Windows NT systems, whether Workstation or Server flavors; and LAN Manager OS/2 systems—be they stand-alone servers, peers, or domain servers—all handle these four commands in generally the same way. It is one of the nicest, if least understood, features of the entire LAN Manager system.

Integrating WFWG with Windows NT

Although Windows for Workgroups and Windows NT look very similar, there are differences at almost every level. Architecturally, Windows for Workgroups is built on top of DOS and inherits many DOS limitations. That makes it less robust than NT, which is designed from the ground up as a secure and robust operating system. On the positive side, WFWG supports many more systems and peripheral devices than Windows NT, since vendors have been working with DOS for many years.

WFWG does take advantage of the 386 architecture to a great extent. For example, network drivers are implemented as 32-bit Windows device drivers, which leaves more low memory for running DOS applications. Although WFWG does offer a standard-mode implementation that can run on 286 systems, it has many differences and limitations in capabilities compared to running WFWG in 386 enhanced mode. The discussion here assumes you're running WFWG in the preferable 386 enhanced mode.

From the network standpoint, the most important difference between WFWG and NT is that WFWG always uses share-level security to share resources between stations on a network. This approach is less secure and harder to centrally manage than the user-level security primarily used by NT. For compatibility reasons, NT also offers share-level security. If you already have a Windows for Workgroups LAN installed, you can add one or more NT systems and use share-level security equivalent to that used in Windows for Workgroups.

Workgroup or Domain?

Taken on its own, Windows for Workgroups is a completely decentralized network that emphasizes sharing rather than security. You configure each WFWG system to be a member of a workgroup, which is primarily an organizational convenience. For example, when you browse the network within a File Open dialog in WFWG, you see the other users arranged in a two-level hierarchy based on the workgroup to which they belong.

Workgroups do not figure into the WFWG security scheme. In fact, the only security options you have when sharing a directory on a WFWG PC is to either make the directory read-only or to protect access (either read-only or read-write) with a password. All other WFWG-, Windows NT-, or LAN Manager-compatible systems can connect to the shared directory, irrespective of whether they're in your workgroup. The only way you can control who accesses the resource is by controlling the password for it.

The casually cooperative and decentralized nature of WFWG and its workgroup scheme lets users share files and devices with a minimum of hassle. However, if you're planning to use WFWG with Windows NT, you may want to make WFWG users part of a domain.

With Windows NT Server, a domain is a group of servers that use the same set of user accounts. Domains, unlike workgroups, are an important contributor to security and system administration. The details of how to configure WFWG users for either workgroups or domains are presented later in this chapter.

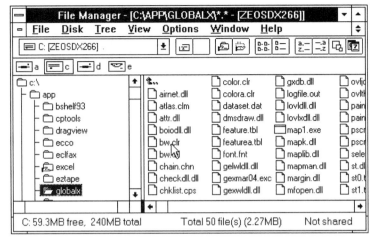

Figure 8.1 File Manager.

The Windows for Workgroups File Manager is very similar in appearance and function to the Windows NT File Manager.

Chapter 7 contains a complete discussion of domains and their operation in Windows NT Server.

File Sharing

To set up file-sharing connections in Windows for Workgroups, you use File Manager. The WFWG File Manager is visually very close to the one in NT (see figure 8.1). Both share the toolbar that is lacking in the Windows 3.1 version.

Sharing a Directory

When you share a directory on a WFWG system, you can access the directory from any WFWG-, Windows NT-, or other LAN Manager-compatible system on the network. In addition to the obvious use in sharing a hard disk directory, you can also share floppy drives, Bernoulli removable disks, or CD-ROM drives this way.

From File Manager, select Disk/Share As from the menu or click on the toolbar icon of a hand holding a folder. You'll get the dialog box shown in Figure 8.2. Enter the name of the directory you want to share. The share name must be unique for this system, but does not need to be unique network-wide. That is, other computers could share a resource with the name *excel*, since each share name will always be associated with (and qualified by) a particular computer name.

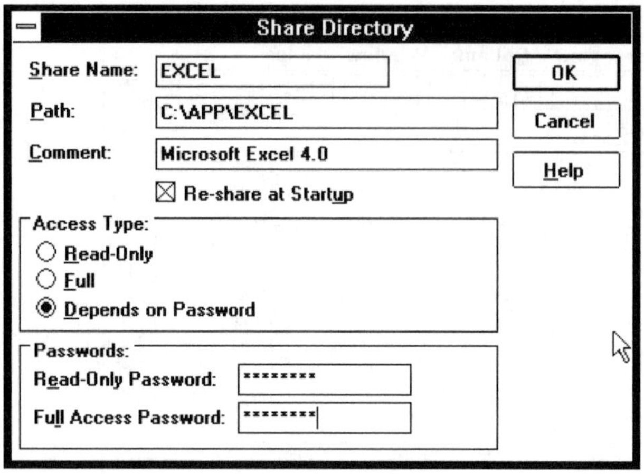

Figure 8.2 Share Directory dialog.

Directory sharing in Windows for Workgroups is controlled through this dialog, which appears when the Share As menu item (or speedbutton) is selected in File Manager.

If you want to share the directory only temporarily—for example, for someone to copy a few files—then clear the Reshare at Startup check box. If this box is checked, WFWG will automatically reshare the directory each time you restart your system.

WFWG offers only two levels of access: read-only and full. You can require that someone who wants to use the directory provide a password for either or both types of access. Remember that full access allows anyone to delete or rename files and subdirectories below the shared directory. Also, although NT lets you share a directory multiple times by different names (and potentially different passwords), WFWG lets you share a particular directory only once.

Once you've shared a directory, File Manager's directory tree will give you a visual clue that the directory is shared by using the folder-in-hand icon, rather than the standard folder icon. Also, if you click on a directory that is shared, the right side of File Manager's status bar will show you the share-name mapping.

Stop Sharing a Directory

Before you stop sharing a directory, be sure that all users currently using the directory are notified and asked to stop using the directory. Otherwise, if you stop sharing a directory that is in use, those users connected to it could lose data. You can find out who is using files in one of your shared directories by selecting the directory, choosing File/Properties from the menu, then clicking the Open By button.

You can either select Disk/Stop Sharing from the menu or click the toolbar icon of a hand holding a grayed-out folder. Select the directory you want to stop sharing from the list in the dialog box. If other people are currently using the directory, you'll get a warning that they might lose data if you continue, and be asked for confirmation.

Using a Remote Directory

Windows for Workgroups is flexible about letting you make connections to other PCs. You can either set up these connections from File Manager ahead of time, or wait until you need a file and make the connection at that point.

To connect to a remote directory from within File Manager, select Connect Network Drive from the Disk menu, or click the toolbar button showing the network drive icon. You can also get to this dialog through the File Open and File Save dialogs used by most applications. If the application uses the standard dialog, there will be a button labeled Network... you can click to bring up the Connect Network Drive dialog (see Figure 8.3).

Regardless of how you get to the Connect Network Drive dialog, it works the same way. If you click on one of the system names in the upper box, the

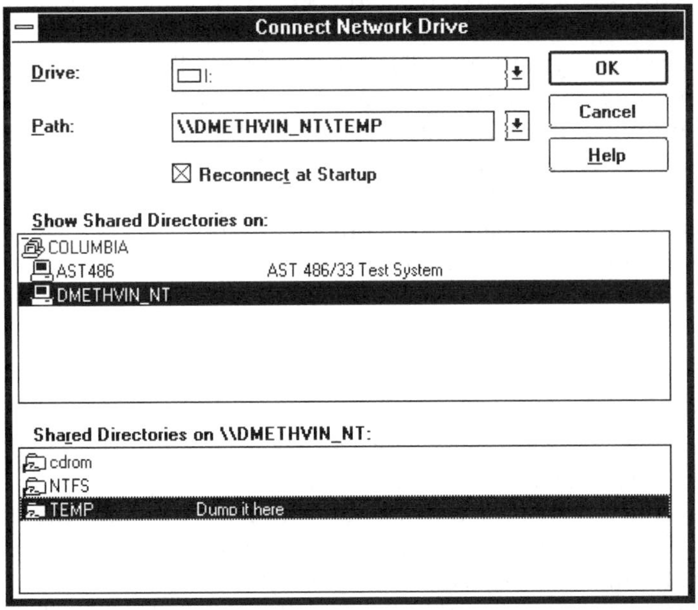

Figure 8.3 Connect Network Drive dialog.

Using a shared directory on a Windows for Workgroups system is done using this dialog, which appears when the Connect Net Drive menu item (or speed-button) is selected in File Manager.

shared directories on that system are displayed in the lower box. You can double-click one of the directories to establish the connection. Before you do, though, be sure the Reconnect at Startup check box is set the way you want it. If this box is checked, WFWG will reestablish the connection each time you restart the system. If it's not checked, the connection will end when you exit Windows, and never come back to bother you.

Stop Using a Remote Directory

To stop using a remote directory, select Disk/Disconnect Network Drive from File Manager's menu, or click the toolbar button that shows an X over a grayed-out network drive. You'll get a list of your network connections; just double-click the one you want to disconnect. You can also select multiple connections by Control-clicking on them, and then click OK to disconnect them.

When you disconnect a network drive, it's disconnected for good even if you checked the Reconnect at Startup check box when you were in the Connect Network Drive dialog originally. That option applies only when you exit Windows with drives connected, then restart Windows. It's logical when you think about it.

What's not so logical is that File Manager has a little bug. If you have File Manager running and then create your first connection outside of File Manager—for example, through a batch file or File Open dialog inside an application—you won't get a drive icon for that connection inside of File Manager. Also, the menu option and button to disconnect drives stay grayed out, which of course makes it pretty hard to disconnect anything. If you exit File Manager and restart it, though, you'll see all your connections and be able to pull the plug on any of them.

Printer Management

A Windows for Workgroups system can share any printers that are locally attached to it. However, each PC that wants to share a printer must install the Windows printer driver for that printer locally. It's usually easiest to install drivers for all your printers on every PC when you install WFWG, so you won't be hunting for installation disks when you'd rather be printing.

Print Manager is a vital part of the WFWG printer-sharing scheme, not just for establishing connections, but also for maintaining them. You must start Print Manager and keep it running to share printers. This is different from the situation with File Manager, which establishes file shares but does not need to be running for those shares to work. If you're connected to a printer that many

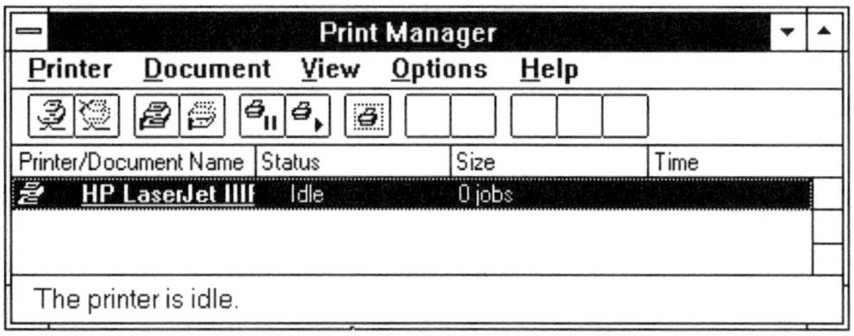

Figure 8.4 Print Manager.

The Windows for Workgroups Print Manager application controls the use of network printers in much the same manner as the Windows NT Print Manager. The two systems differ, however, in their use of printer drivers.

other people use, it would be a good idea to put a Print Manager entry in your Program Manager StartUp folder.

Figure 8.4 illustrates a typical Print Manager window.

Sharing a Printer

To share a printer, select File/Share Printer from Print Manager's menu, or click the toolbar icon that shows a hand holding a printer. You will then see the dialog box shown in Figure 8.5.

Select the printer you want to share, and assign it a name. You can optionally assign a password that other users must enter before they can use the printer. Select Reshare at Startup if you want the printer to be shared each time you start Print Manager. If you clear this check box, the printer will be shared only until the next time you exit Print Manager.

Stop Sharing a Printer

You can use either the menu selection Printer/Stop Sharing Printer or the toolbar button showing a hand with a grayed-out printer. Either way, you'll then get a

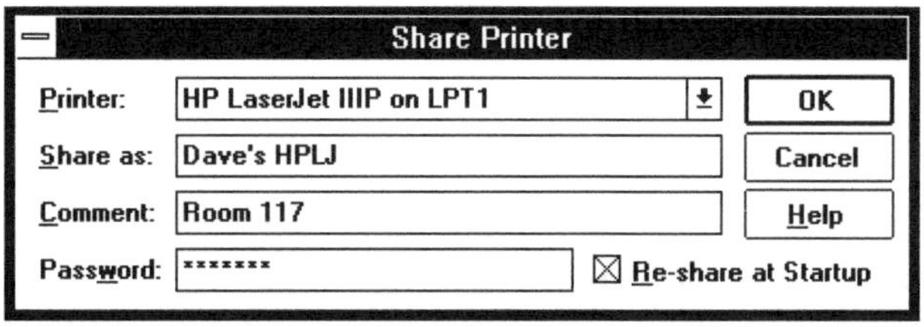

Figure 8.5 Share Printer dialog.

Printer sharing in Windows for Workgroups is controlled from this dialog, which appears when the Share As menu item (or speed-button) is selected in Print Manager.

dialog box showing all the printers you are currently sharing. Select the printer you want to stop sharing, then click OK.

Using a Remote Printer

Again, note that to use a remote printer you will need to have a driver for that printer on your local system. (This isn't true for Windows NT, which can automatically obtain the driver from the system that shares the printer.)

To make the connection, select Printer/Connect Network Printer from the menu or click on the toolbar icon showing a printer with a network wire connected to it. There might be a slight delay while Print Manager polls the network for available printers, then you will get the dialog box illustrated in Figure 8.6.

Many applications will also let you select a network printer from a Print dialog or Print Setup menu selection. This is the most convenient option if you use a certain network printer only occasionally. You will need to check the specific application to see if it supports network printers directly.

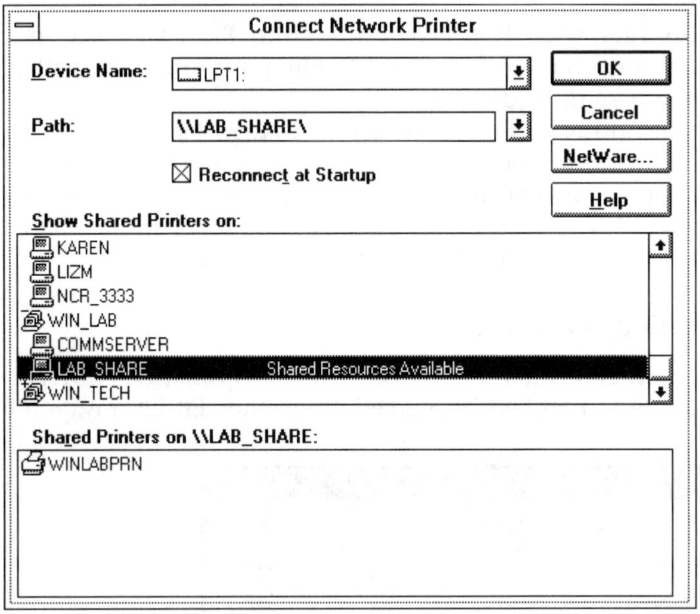

Figure 8.6 Connect Network Printer dialog.

Use of network printers by a Windows for Workgroups system is controlled from this dialog, which appears when the Connect to Printer menu item (or speedbutton) is selected in Print Manager.

Stop Using a Remote Printer

To terminate a remote printer connection, select Printer/Disconnect Network Printer from the menu, or use the toolbar button that depicts a network-connected printer with an X next to it. You will get a dialog box with your current network printer connections. Select the printer you want to stop using, then click OK.

Windows for Workgroups Utilities

In addition to the bread-and-butter utilities, like File Manager and Print Manager, there are other applications that make it easier to exchange data and messages with other users, and to diagnose problems.

Mail and Schedule+

The versions of Microsoft Mail and Schedule+ that are provided with WFWG work fine with the Windows NT versions. It's usually best to set up the mail postoffice on a Windows NT system, then share the postoffice directory so that the WFWG systems can use it.

ClipBook Viewer

The WFWG ClipBook operates very much like its namesake utility in Windows NT. The big difference is in the area of security; WFWG can protect shared pages with a password, but doesn't offer the user-based security of Windows NT.

Chat

The WFWG Chat utility is a split-screen message utility for point-to-point conversations over the network. It interoperates with and looks identical to the Windows NT version. At present, WFWG does not come with a broadcast messaging utility that would let you receive a note, such as "Main server going down in 5 minutes," from a Windows NT system.

NetWatcher

NetWatcher (illustrated in Figure 8.7) lets you see what connections other PCs have to your PC and when those connections were last active. You can also forcibly break connections.

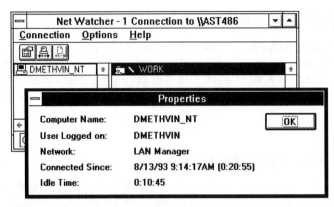

Figure 8.7 NetWatcher application.

The Windows for Workgroups NetWatcher application provides a degree of control over remote network connections similar to (but more limited than) the Server applet in the Windows NT Control Panel.

WinMeter

Winmeter (illustrated in Figure 8.8) shows the CPU time use on a computer. One color is used for local applications, and another for the server component. This is a quick way to see if a PC is being bogged down by access from remote users. You can control the amount of CPU time remote users can get through the Network section of Control Panel.

Integrating Windows 95 with Windows NT

In its networking aspects, Windows 95 is an evolutionary step from Windows 3.1 and Windows for Workgroups. The core of the Windows 95 operating system still has some 16-bit code so that it can be maximally compatible with Windows

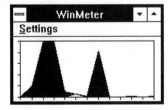

Figure 8.8 WinMeter application.

The Windows for Workgroups WinMeter application provides a visual indication of system activity similar to (but more limited than) that provided by the Windows NT Performance Monitor.

3.1 and DOS, but most of the core functions are now implemented as 32-bit protected mode software. As a result, Windows 95 should offer greater reliability, better performance, and easier setup than Windows 3.1. However, its robustness and security are still below the level of Windows NT, a point that even Microsoft emphasizes as one of the advantages of NT.

In contrast to the evolutionary architecture changes from Windows for Workgroups, the look and feel of Windows 95 will be a big change. The procedures for accessing and configuring network functionality have changed dramatically, and it's a change for the better. In this section, we'll just concentrate on the most important changes you'll need to understand when integrating Win95 workstations into your network.

Choosing a Protocol

Out of the box, Win95 supports most of the networking environments and configurations you're likely to want. In addition to support for Microsoft's own NetBEUI and SMB protocols, Win95 supports IPX/SPX and Novell's NCP protocols so that you can easily connect to NetWare servers. Multiple protocol stacks can be used with a single networking card, so you can use NetBEUI/SMB for peer sharing with NT and IPX/NCP for NetWare. Win95 takes care of all the details after you've set up the protocols.

If you prefer, you can use TCP/IP as your transport protocol with Win95. Drivers are included in the box, as well as interfaces for sockets (WinSock) and remote procedure calls (DCE RPC). If you have WINS and DHCP servers on your network, Win95 workstations can be configured to query these servers to obtain their network addresses and names.

For absolute compatibility, Windows 95 does offer you the ability to use 16-bit real-mode client drivers, such as Novell's NETX. You might be tempted to use this solution if you have an unusual TSR or DOS program that depends intimately on Novell's driver, but don't do it. First, the 16-bit software will give lower performance and be less reliable than the built-in support. Second, you can have only one protocol stack per network card if you use real-mode drivers. Finally, Win95's remote management capabilities aren't available if you use a real-mode driver. All of these are serious drawbacks, so it's better to remove or replace the offending code that requires old drivers.

You would expect Win95 workstations to work very well with Windows NT, but they also work well with Novell NetWare. With either type of server, you can configure a Windows 95 workstation so that it will pass the user name and password on to the server for verification. The support for Novell's NCP API is good enough that you can run Novell's own DOS-based tools from Win95 to configure a NetWare server connection. Fortunately, you won't often need to do that because common operations, like attaching to a NetWare printer, are supported through Win95's graphical interface. NetWare servers aren't second-class citizens anymore.

Managing Windows 95 Users

As with WFWG, Win95 can use pass-through security to validate logons, using the server's password capabilities. The trade-offs associated with this approach are described in the section labeled "User Account Management" later in this chapter. Because many Win95 network administration features depend on user-level security, it's highly recommended for all but the smallest networks.

Once you have set up user-level security, you can use the *user profiles* feature to greatly simplify management of Win95 workstations. On a user-by-user basis, you can control whether the user can use, change, or even *see* many features of Win95's interface. For example, you can prevent the user from changing the screen-saver options so that a password-protected screen saver can't be defeated. You can disable peer services so that users can't share their personal printers or hard disks. And, if you have users that share a pool of PCs, such as a classroom environment, settings will follow the user as they log in from PC to PC.

File Sharing

The new Explorer interface in Windows 95 is very different from the one used by Windows for Workgroups or Windows NT 3.5. For a new user it's often easier to use, especially because it provides many ways to access the same features. If you think semilogically and don't mind experimenting by right-clicking and double-clicking, you can probably find a way to do everything you formerly did in File Manager.

Sharing a Directory

When you share a directory on a Win95 system, you can access the directory from any system on the network that has a protocol stack compatible with yours. You can share directories, floppy drives, Bernoulli removable disks, or CD-ROM drives.

To share a directory or device, right-click on it in Explorer and select Sharing. You'll get a dialog that lets you select the share name and type of access (see Figure 8.9). Remember that Win95 clients that share resources do not employ user-level security, you must use share-level security.

Using Remote Files

The simplest way to use shared files in Windows 95 is to simply use the full UNC name when you are inside an application. So, instead of mapping the U drive to \\ATT3360\DATA and then specifying a file name of U:\MYFILE.DAT,

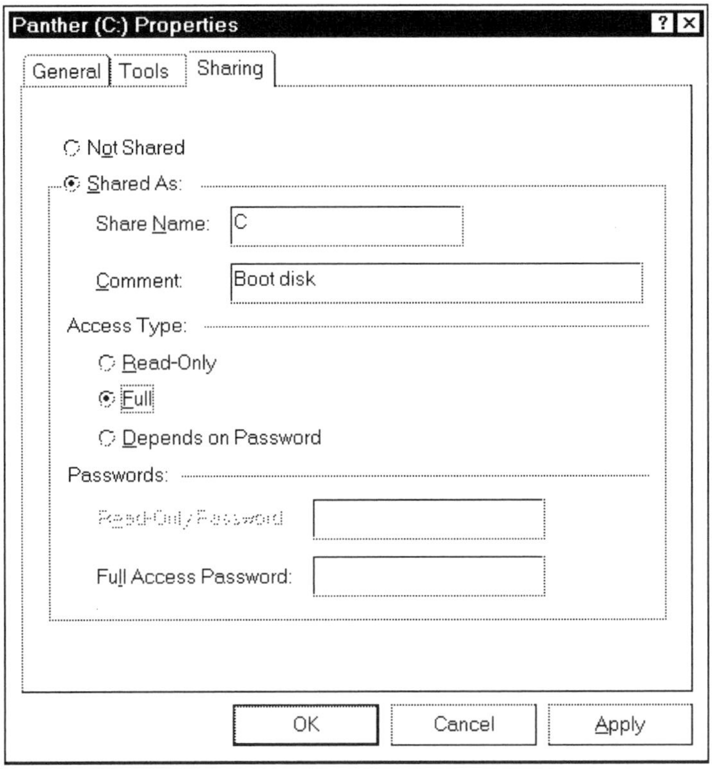

Figure 8.9 Windows 95 file sharing.
File sharing in Windows 95 is handled through the Properties/Sharing dialog for whatever disk or directory you're sharing.

just type the name *ATT3360**DATA**MYFILE.DAT*. If you don't know the entire path but know the share name, most file dialog boxes will let you type *ATT3360**DATA***.**, then click OK and you can browse from there.

However, you probably have older 16-bit Windows or DOS applications that won't take kindly to newfangled UNC names. In this case, you can set up a drive mapping. In Explorer, select the directory you want to map and click the Map Network Drive button. Alternatively, you can right-click the My Computer icon and map drives from there. You can unmap the drives from the same two locations. Drive mappings are shown under the My Computer window, which is usually the most convenient place to examine and remove them.

If you have a remote file or folder that you use frequently, you can put a shortcut to it on the desktop. To do this, double-click the Network Neighborhood and browse the network for the item you want to access. Using the mouse, click and drag the item out onto the desktop. On the menu that appears, click

Create Shortcut Here. You can now double-click this icon to access the file or folder.

Printer Management

Windows 95 makes many improvements over Windows for Workgroups in the management of shared printers. First, you do not need to have Print Manager active to share or use remote printers. Second, the drivers for network printers can be dynamically downloaded to the workstation when you connect to the printer. This eliminates the need for the system administrator to install printer drivers on every workstation.

In Win95, Connections to networked printers are implemented essentially as temporary shares that are active for only as long as it takes to send the file to the network printer. This is particularly important for NetWare servers, where every attached user counts against the license limits for that server.

Sharing a Printer

To share a printer on a Win95 workstation, click the Start button and select Settings>Printers. (You can also get to this window through Control Panel or My Computer.) Right-click on the printer you want to share and select Properties. Go to the Sharing tab and set the information for how you want to share the printer (see Figure 8.10).

If you have a NetWare network, there is another alternative you have for sharing a printer attached to a Win95 workstation. With Peer Services for NetWare Clients installed, you can set up the workstation to despool print jobs from a queue on a NetWare server. That way, you can subject the print jobs to the standard NetWare user restrictions but still have the printer attached to the workstation.

Using a Remote Printer

To use a remote printer, open the Network Neighborhood and find the printer you want to use. Then right-click on it and select Capture Printer Port from the menu. Then select which printer port (such as LPT1) you want to assign to this printer. Alternatively, you can create a shortcut for this printer on your desktop. To print a file, you can either open the application, load the file, then select File/Print from the application's menu; or just drop the file onto the printer shortcut.

If you use a Win95 workstation that is connected to a network only sporadically, such as a notebook PC, the deferred printing capability may prove useful. If you print to a printer that isn't currently available, the print job will

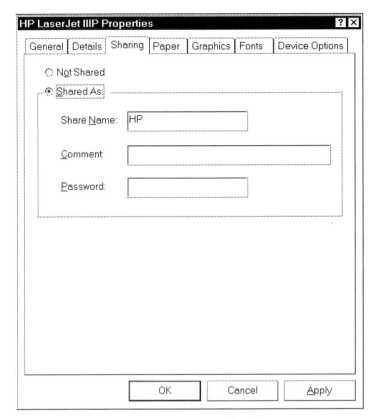

Figure 8.10 Windows 95 printer sharing.

Printer sharing in Windows 95 is handled through the Properties/Sharing dialog for the printer you're sharing.

be spooled on the local PC. When the PC is reconnected to the network, the print job will restart and be sent to the printer.

User Account Management

Although neither Windows for Workgroups nor Windows 95 provides user name-based security when used by themselves in a peer-to-peer arrangement, either can be integrated nicely into the Windows NT security scheme. There are essentially three options you can choose when integrating WFWG/Win95 users and NT Workstation or NT Server systems. Your decision in implementing user accounts should balance the need for security against convenience and hassle-free access to resources. Also remember that a very secure system will require someone to administer the user accounts and set permissions appropriately.

Option 1: No Accounts, Share-Level Security

If you have an established WFWG system, or if security is not a critical issue, you can add Windows NT Servers to your network and use share-level security to make their resources available to the network. These new servers will simply show up in the browse lists like all the WFWG/Win95 computers. To users, it just looks like you've added another machine to the network but there's no change at all in their work habits.

This option works because of the behavior of the Windows NT *Guest* account. If the user name and password for a WFWG/Win95 user don't match exactly with the user name and password of the NT system, you are granted Guest access anyway.

On an NT Server, the Guest account is disabled by default to increase the security of the network. If you want to use this option, you'll need to enable the Guest account. To do this, run User Manager and double-click on the account named Guest. By default, the Account Disabled check box will be checked. Uncheck it to make shared resources available to those who don't have accounts on this system (or domain, depending on how you've set up security). Now, any shared resource for which the group *Everyone* has been given access in File Manager will be accessible to all users on the network.

Option 2: Windows NT User Accounts

If you require more security than option 1 allows, you can get it by creating an account on each of your Windows NT systems for every WFWG user. The password should be the same password they use to log in to their WFWG system. Whenever a WFWG user connects to a resource on a Windows NT system, it will use that user's name and password to validate security, rather than the Guest account.

You can, of course, have a hybrid between options 1 and 2, where most of the users use the Guest account permissions and you create a few accounts only for users who need more (or less) access. For example, to restrict access to certain shares, give the Everyone group the No Access permission, and override this by giving Full Access (or other) Permissions to specified groups of users. Be warned, however, that this can become unwieldy if you have many users and/or NT systems. At some point, you may want to move to option 3 not for security, but for simplicity of account management.

Option 3: Domain Login

This is the most secure way to run a WFWG system with NT Server. You actually set up the WFWG/Win95 system so that it logs on to your network domain when WFWG starts. To implement this, you should first create the domain and user accounts under NT Server. The user accounts should match the names of the users of the WFWG/Win95 systems you want to add.

The next step is to set up the clients. On a WFWG system go into Control Panel and open the Network dialog. Click on the Networks button at the bottom of the dialog; a list of installed networks should appear. Select LAN Manager from the Other Networks in Use list and click on the Settings button. The Dialog illustrated in Figure 8.11 will be displayed. Check the check box labeled Log On to LAN Manager Domain, and enter the domain name. Wind your way out by clicking OK on all the dialog boxes.

On a Win95 client, right-click the Network Neighborhood icon and select Properties. Under the Access Control tab, select User-Level Access Control. In the box under this setting, type in either the server name in UNC style *(\\servername)* or the domain name if you are using domain-level security.

Although option 3 is the most organized and secure approach, it does have its share of caveats. Users need to come to this dialog to change their passwords

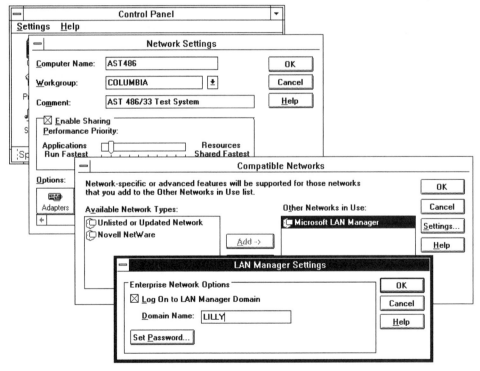

Figure 8.11 LAN Manager Settings dialog.

This dialog, accessed from the Windows for Workgroups Control Panel/Network Settings, allows the specification of a LAN Manager (or Windows NT Server) logon domain and associated password.

so that the domain controller is informed of the change. (You can also use the *net password* command from a DOS prompt; see the section in this chapter on the *net* command.) Don't depend on domain login to keep local information on a WFWG system safe. A knowledgeable person can disable domain login and boot the system by removing the LMLogon entry in the [network] section of SYSTEM.INI. At the very least, someone could boot the system into DOS and copy sensitive files.

Command-Line Network Interface

Windows for Workgroups includes a DOS command-line interface (NET.EXE) that gives you access to many of the resource sharing features. They are particularly useful inside automated batch files. A nearly identical NET command-line interface is also included in a product called Microsoft Workgroup Connection (MWC). MWC lets a DOS-only system use files or printers that are shared by a WFWG or Windows NT system. However, the DOS system running MWC cannot share resources; it is client-only. Even on WFWG, the *net* command-line interface does not include any commands to actually share resources on the current system.

A summary of the most useful NET commands are listed here. You can get a complete list of commands and their options by typing *NET /?*, or details on a specific command by typing *NET <command> /?*.

NET CONFIG

This command gives you a summary of this PC's network information, which is very useful while you're trying to debug things. A typical display looks like this:

```
C:\WFWG> NET CONFIG
Computer name              \\AST486
User name                  DMETHVIN

Software version           3.1
Redirector version         2.50

Workstation root directory C:\WFWG
Workgroup                  COLUMBIA
The command completed successfully.

C:\WFWG>
```

NET LOGON

This command logs this system into the workgroup. If you don't supply a user name or password on the command line, you will be prompted for them. Any NET USE commands that you specified as PERSISTENT (and the ones specified as Reconnect at Startup inside File Manager) are reconnected at this time.

NET LOGOFF

This command logs you off the workgroup and breaks any network connections.

NET PASSWORD

This command changes your logon password. If you don't enter the old or new passwords on the command line, you'll be prompted for them. You can specify computer, domain, and user names if you also want to change your password at an NT Workstation or an NT Server domain. Otherwise, the password will be changed only in your local password file (<systemname>.PWL in the \WINDOWS directory).

NET PRINT

This command lets you display the print queues on printers you are sharing, and also lets you delete a print job that you have submitted to a printer but that hasn't yet printed.

NET TIME

This command lets you synchronize your computer's clock with the clock on a Windows NT system or Microsoft LAN Manager time server. This is especially handy as part of each system's AUTOEXEC.BAT file to make sure all the clocks on the network are in sync.

NET USE

The NET USE establishes or breaks connections to network files and printers, and has numerous options that are explicitly documented in the online help. If you enter NET USE with no arguments, it will display your current connections.

You can make a connection persistent by specifying the option /PERSIST-ENT:YES. This means that WFWG will reestablish the connection each time the network is started. Normally, NET USE will save the password along with the persistent connection. If you prefer to reenter the password each time the computer starts, then specify /SAVEPW:NO.

Other options of NET USE let you manage your persistent connections. You can display your persistent connections that will automatically be created the next time you start this system, clear the list of persistent connections, or make all your current connections persistent. This last option is useful so that when you get your connections set up the way you want them, you can *snapshot* that for later sessions.

Migration from LAN Manager to Windows NT Server

If you're running LAN Manager Servers today, how do you go about moving to Windows NT? First of all, you'll notice that the heading of this section says "Migration from LAN Manager to Windows NT *Server*." It doesn't say Migration ... to Windows NT Workstation, because you can't do that. To retain LAN Manager's centralized account management it is essential to move to an NT Server environment.

As stated previously, Windows NT servers cannot participate as members of OS/2 LAN Manager domains. They can participate only as members of a Windows NT Server domain. So you're going to have to upgrade at least one system to a Windows NT Server, and as we've recommended earlier, if you upgrade one, you had better upgrade two. The first matter then is to set up a machine as a Windows NT Server. You probably won't want to do this with the machine being used as the primary domain controller in the OS/2 network, for obvious reasons. The accounts from the OS/2 LAN Manager system can be converted to NT Server accounts using the PORTUAS.EXE utility included with Windows NT Server software. This command has the syntax:

portuas file name

where *file name* specifies the LAN Manager 2.x NET.ACT file. Of course, the file name is always NET.ACT but you have to use the full network path name. For example:

portuas \\primary_server\admin\net.act

There are two flag variables that can be used: -u followed by a user name will specify a single user or group to port if you don't want to port the entire user account base. This makes sense, particularly in setting up a pilot project, where only a certain group of people are initially going to be exposed to the Windows NT Server environment. The second is -v, which displays all messages and which we recommend. This will give you a notification if there are any problems.

You must have administrative privileges to run portuas. Further information on portuas can be found in the online help system for the NT Server and in the NT Server documentation.

Once the user accounts are converted, it is necessary to restore the OS/2 access control list to Windows NT access rights. At this point, of course, we have a major issue with respect to the file system, because access rights at the directory and subdirectory level require NTFS on Windows NT. Therefore, when migrating from an OS/2 LAN Manager system to a Windows NT Server it is necessary for the NT Server to have an NTFS volume for the administrative information. This conversion is done using the ACLCONV.EXE utility. This command has the syntax:

aclconv /data: datafile /log:logfile

where *datafile* specifies the full path name for the OS/2 LAN Manager BAC-CACC.ACL datafile (created using the OS/2 LAN Manager BACKACC command), and *logfile* specifies a file where *aclconv* will log information about failed conversions. For example, the command:

aclconv /data:\\primary_server\admin\baccacc.acl /log:error.log

will convert the BACCACC.ACL file in the ADMIN directory on the OS/2 LAN Manager primary server to directory permissions on the current NTFS volume and will store information about failed conversions in the ERROR.LOG file. You would then inspect the ERROR.LOG file and carry out any missing conversions manually. Note that the drive letter for the NTFS volume where the ACLs are being restored must be the same as the drive letter on the original machine—you cannot restore the permissions from a C: drive on a LAN Manager OS/2 server onto a D: NTFS volume on a Windows NT Server.

In summary, the steps necessary to convert from a LAN Manager OS/2 server primary domain controller to a Windows NT Server as primary domain controller are:

1. Take the primary domain controller offline. You will probably want to do this after hours when fewer users will need to be forced off the system.

2. Back up access permissions using the LAN Manager for OS/2 *Backacc* command.

3. Share the administrative disk drives on the OS/2 system and make them accessible to the Windows NT system.

4. From the Windows NT system, issue the *portuas* command to port the user accounts from the LAN Manager for OS/2 system,

5. Use the OS/2 LAN Manager *Backacc* command to back up the permissions on the directories on the server.

6. Transfer them to the Windows NT system using the ACLCONV command.

Windows NT Server Upgrade for Microsoft LAN Manager

For LAN Manager users migrating to Windows NT Server, Microsoft includes an additional set of tools to make upgrading even easier. These include:

❑ BACKENV—A tool to back up the complete LAN Manager server environment (network card, network address, shared files and printers, etc.).

❑ BACKAT—Copies prescheduled *at*-command events.

❑ HCOPY—Tool to copy files from LAN Manager server across the network.

❑ BACKACC—Tool to back up user accounts and permissions.

❑ ACLLIST—Tool to list off-access control lists (permissions).

❑ BACKUP—Tool that backs up data to tape.

❑ CONVERT—Tool that converts FAT and HPFS partitions to NTFS.

❑ PORTUAS—Tool that ports the LAN Manager user account database to Windows NT.

❑ USERCONV—Tool that automatically converts multidomain LAN Manager user accounts and permissions into a single database for integrated cross-domain management.

❑ ACLCONV—Tool that converts access control lists (permissions) to Windows NT format.

❑ RESTENV—Tool that restores the server configuration under Windows NT.

❑ ACLCOMPARE—Tool that detects changes between the permissions before and after a LAN Manager-to-Windows NT conversion has been carried out.

❑ SMFCONV—Tool that converts Macintosh File System volumes from LAN Manager to Windows NT.

❑ A complete, graphically oriented, step-by-step application that guides you through the use of these utilities on both LAN Manager for OS/2 and the Windows NT Server.

Details of the LAN Manager Upgrade for Windows NT Server are beyond the scope of this book, but the combination of this impressive set of tools, and step-by-step instructions, makes the Upgrade an extremely attractive package. We urge anyone considering switching from LAN Manager to Windows NT Server to call Microsoft for more information.

Conclusion

What used to be called LAN Manager networking (and Microsoft would now like to call Windows networking) is in a state of flux—as represented by the changed names, browsing specification, APIs, and so on. Anytime there's change there's a certain amount of confusion—and no doubt we've added to that confusion here.

It's worth noting that the migration problems introduced by Windows NT are certainly no worse than those faced by people upgrading from NetWare 3.*x* to NetWare 4.*x*. And it also seems clear that LAN Manager/Windows networking has a bright future. The Windows NT Server has been embraced as a database application server by every major vendor of client/server database software. Hardware manufacturers are lining up to supply platforms for servers and for high-end workstations.

The move to TCP/IP as the standard networking protocol, which began with LAN Manager 2.1, is accelerating under Windows NT—driven in part by NT's rapid acceptance as an alternative to UNIX on the Internet. On the whole, the advantages of incorporating Windows NT into LAN Manager and Windows for Workgroups networks far outweigh any disadvantage. This is a system you can migrate to with confidence.

For More Information

Microsoft Staff (1993) *Windows for Workgroups Resource Kit*. Redmond, WA: Microsoft Corp. The encyclopedic guide to every setting in every initialization file in Windows for Workgroups. Also discusses the overall WFWG architecture and the differences between real and enhanced mode operation of WFWG.

Microsoft Staff (1993). *Windows NT Server Upgrade Guide for Microsoft LAN Manager*. Redmond, WA: Microsoft Corp. This guide gives detailed planning information for administrators planning to upgrade a LAN Manager system to Windows NT Server. If you have a LAN Manager system and are looking at Windows NT, this should be your first point of reference.

Microsoft Staff (1993). *Windows NT Server Concepts and Planning Guide*. Redmond, WA: Microsoft Corp. A solid and well-written introduction to Server issues, including administration, replication, fault tolerance, and user environment management. A bit weak on the details of migration from LAN Manager but essential information. If you begin an NT Server installation without reading this book you are making a serious mistake.

Microsoft Staff (1993). *Windows NT Server System Guide*. Redmond, WA: Microsoft Corp. All the gory details.

Novell Connections

Windows NT and NetWare

After reading this chapter, you will understand the fundamental similarities and differences between Windows NT's built-in networking and the networking services provided by Novell NetWare. You will understand six distinct approaches that may be taken to establish connectivity between Windows NT and NetWare:

❑ **Microsoft's NWLink IPX/SPX Protocol, which lets NetWare clients access Windows NT** *services* **in exactly the same way they would normally access** *NetWare Loadable Modules* **(NLM)—an especially useful approach for client/server applications, such as multiuser databases.**

❑ **Microsoft's Client Services for NetWare (CSNW), which uses the NWLink IPX/SPX Protocol stack (see the next item) to provide access to shared directories and printers on NetWare servers with standard (for Windows NT) NDIS drivers. Besides shared file and printer access (like Novell's NetWare Client for Windows NT), CSNW also provides command-line access to NetWare resources through the Windows NT** *net* **command interface, and supports most DOS-based NetWare utilities.**

❑ **Novell's NetWare Client for Windows NT, which lets NT clients access shared directories and printers on NetWare servers and supports** *both* **nonstandard (for Windows NT)** *Open Datalink Interface* **(ODI) drivers,** *and* **Windows NT standard** *Network Device Interface Specification* **(NDIS) drivers.**

437

❏ **Microsoft's Gateway Service for NetWare (GSNW) and NetWare Migration Tool,** server-side utilities that simplify integrating NT Server into NetWare environments.

❏ **Beame and Whiteside's** *BW-Multiconnect for Windows NT,* and Microsoft's *File and Print services for NetWare* (FPNW)—add-on packages that provide full IPX/SPX *and NetWare Core Protocol* (NCP) capability, effectively allowing a Windows NT system to function as a NetWare *server.*

❏ **UNIX services (including FTP and NFS)** that allow limited connection of NT to NetWare for file sharing without using any form of NetWare IPX protocol—a preferred method for connecting to NetWare over *wide-area network* (WAN) links.

As you can see, the flexibility of Windows NT makes it possible to connect to NetWare—but as must be expected in any multivendor internetworking situation, the connection is not an easy one.

The NetWare Story

It's a fact of life, probably obvious to everyone reading this book, that the story of local area networking is very much the story of one company, namely Novell—just as the story of desktop graphical user interfaces is very much the story of one company, Microsoft. Novell's great contribution was to eliminate the link between proprietary network hardware and software that characterized virtually all networking systems in the 1970's. Instead, they introduced the notion of a Network Operating System (NOS) that could work with hardware from many vendors.

Today, Novell's *NetWare* NOS covers some 70 percent of the local area networking market. And there is no way that any desktop operating system can exist in today's commercial environment without providing some degree of NetWare connectivity. In this chapter we will examine what this means to Windows NT.

Windows NT and NetWare are quite definitely competitors—especially as application servers—but the idea that *any* other operating system will replace NetWare as the *de facto* standard for file/printer sharing in the next few years is naive. Indeed, Novell has demonstrated versions of NetWare running on a variety of RISC- and SMP-based servers—a clear indication that NetWare will continue to evolve even as NT gets into its stride.

So finding effective ways to exploit Windows NT in a NetWare environment is not only important *today,* but we can also expect it to be just as critical *tomorrow.*

And Now, a Warning

We know that if you're reading this chapter, you probably have a NetWare server and need concrete advice on how to connect a Windows NT system to it. We will do our best to help you do that. In the process, we will recommend some things that do not have the blessing of either Novell or Microsoft. This entire subject area is an extremely complex and fluid one for reasons that will become apparent. The relationship between Microsoft and Novell is complex and, as of this writing, less than amicable.

In view of this, please bear in mind that this is the one chapter of this book most likely to be overtaken by events.[1] You are *strongly* advised to check what we have to say *for yourself*. At each stage, wherever possible, we have given you reference information to direct you to where you can get the very latest and most up-to-date information. Please treat this chapter as a starting point. It's vitally important, if you are to succeed in establishing and maintaining a good NT-to-NetWare relationship, that you develop and maintain your own active up-to-date sources of information.

Why Connecting Windows NT to NetWare Is Difficult

The facts of life are sometimes unpleasant. One unpleasant fact of life for Microsoft is that while Windows was becoming the dominant desktop environment, NetWare was becoming the dominant NOS. This is unfortunate from the point of view of the Windows NT user because Microsoft proceeded to make a number of rather engaging attempts in the networking field over the last few years. A whole series of products described in Chapter 8 were introduced over the last few years with little success, ending with the technically impressive—but commercially unsuccessful—LAN Manager 2.x series.

The reason for this is simple: NetWare provides a *shared resource* networking environment that in many respects is very similar to the kind of desktop operating system Microsoft has provided with DOS, while Microsoft made the mistake of trying to deliver something that might be better *technically* but didn't work as well for the end user.

NetWare NOS Advantages

In the formal sense of the word neither DOS nor NetWare is a modern operating system. There are many features that we demand of a modern operating system

---

1. Indeed, this chapter was revised *nine times* during production of the first edition, revised again for adaptation as a magazine article (*Network Administrator*, September/October 1994)—and promptly had to be revised again for this edition when Microsoft released its FPNW beta!

(such as Windows NT) that NetWare does not provide. In particular, it lacks virtual memory, preemptive multitasking, or any kind of a memory protection scheme.[2] The cognoscenti among programmers are often inclined to say that DOS is not an operating system; it's a monitor.[3] By the same standard, neither is NetWare. In many respects, NetWare is effectively DOS scaled up to run a network.

What NetWare *does* have is an incredibly efficient low-level I/O architecture employing special techniques, such as *elevator seeks,* that make it extremely efficient as a file-and-print server. In effect, NetWare exploits its own limitations—it may not provide virtual memory or preemptive multitasking, but it also doesn't have the overhead associated with such high-end features. As a result, NetWare gives good performance in memory configurations, where a Windows NT Server won't run at all.

The performance of Windows NT and Novell NetWare on a given single-processor Intel-based machine is always likely to favor the NetWare machine: First, if the machine has enough memory to run Windows NT, then it has *more* than enough memory to run NetWare. And second, NetWare will get better advantage from whatever disk drives and controllers are built into the machine than NT will. The fact that NT can offset this with such features as symmetric multiprocessing, or by abandoning the Intel processor to another line of CPUs is all well and good—but it falters on a basic fundamental fact. Windows NT's built-in *Server Message Block* (SMB) networking is inherently incompatible with Novell's *NetWare Core Protocol* (NCP).

Even though the packets Windows NT transmits can be received by a NetWare server (assuming a NetWare-compatible IPX stack is in place), the NetWare server does not understand the SMB packets or UNC-formatted requests issued by the NT machine—and even if it did respond, the NT machine would not understand the NCP formatted results.

Therefore, any approach to connecting NetWare to Windows NT has to take account of the fact that they are designed to operate with completely different protocols. At the same time, one should not stop at this point, drop the buck, and assume that Windows NT is not important because it won't talk to NetWare (or equally assume that NetWare is useless because it won't talk to Windows NT). There are, in fact, no less than *six* ways (as of this writing) to connect Windows NT systems to NetWare servers. We will go through all of these approaches in the sections that follow.

---

2. Memory protection is provided in NetWare 4.0, but as of this writing it is rarely used.

3. Monitor: A term used by hackers in denigration of an operating system. It refers to a kind of *operating system* typically loaded into a single-board computer with less than 1 *kilobyte* of memory during the 1970s.

Microsoft's NWLink Protocol Stack

Beyond redirecting simple shared files and printers, there's the larger matter of providing seamless client/server connectivity (in NetWare-speak, the function usually provided by an NLM). Microsoft's NWLink protocol stack takes care of this—while providing the low-level infrastructure needed by Microsoft's CSNW.

For obvious reasons, Novell does nothing to accommodate servers by other companies. Microsoft has, therefore, provided its own solution. NWLink is a NetWare-compatible protocol stack that provides full 32-bit IPX/SPX connectivity from an NT server. In effect, it lets existing NetWare DOS, Windows, and OS/2 clients access Windows NT in much the same way that they access NetWare servers—up to a point.

NWLink does not provide any file or printer sharing (unless you add the Microsoft CSNW). Instead, the full NetBIOS protocols are supported, the various levels of the Windows Network and Sockets APIs are supported, and Named Pipes are supported. Since all of these are implemented on top of an IPX/SPX stack (mostly using NetBIOS calls), a simple NetBIOS redirector in the client machines, such as Novell's IPX/NETX combination, provides a surprisingly high level of connectivity.

This is more than sufficient for use as an *application server*—the role traditionally filled in NetWare environments by an NLM executing in the NetWare server. For example, consider a company that runs its financials or customer service database using a high-end product, such as Novell's SQL NLM or Microsoft SQL Server. In that sort of environment, access to shared directories is meaningless—what you want is a way to link the client software in the workstations to the host database, exactly the capability that NWLink provides.

For all practical purposes, you can think of this approach primarily as a means for Microsoft to provide NetWare users with access to *network applications* running on Windows NT servers. Aside from the lack of file and print services (unless Microsoft's own client software has been added), which renders NWLink suitable only as an application server and *not* as a general purpose server; the only limitation is that the IPX implementation supported by NWLink is not truly routable (when used to provide SMB-based file and print services to Microsoft networking clients), because it encapsulates nonroutable NetBIOS broadcasts (see Appendix 2 for details). As a practical matter, this is probably insignificant, since the deployment of NWLink servers is likely to be aimed at only a local segment—and in any case, even when used for file-and-print sharing, NWLink NetBIOS packets *do* route over one hop (again, see Appendix 2 for details).

NT versions from 3.5 on have a rewritten NWLink stack that gives much better performance. In NT 3.1, both NWLink and the TCP/IP implementation were based on an NT port of a UNIX-style Streams interface, which was easy for

Microsoft to get running but didn't give great performance. The new protocols are pure NT-native implementations. NWLink in NT 3.5 also supports multiple networks and SPX-II.

But the fact remains that what most NT users want is a way to access their NetWare server(s), and while NWLink provides the all-important low-level plumbing for such a client requester, it doesn't understand NetWare Core Protocol (NCP) packets. Translating the NCP packets requires another piece of software, called Client Services for NetWare (CSNW), described later in this chapter.

Instructions

NWLink is supplied on both Windows NT and the Windows NT Server as part of the standard Network Services package. To install, it's necessary to:

1. Launch Control Panel.
2. Double-click the Network icon in the control panel window. This invokes the Network Settings dialog box.
3. Press the Add Software button.
4. Locate the NWLink IPX/SPX Compatible Transport entry in the Network Software listbox, and select it. Press Continue. You will be asked to designate a source for the software (the installation disks or CD), and Windows NT will then copy the NWLink files to your local hard disk.
5. Click the OK button.
6. Windows NT will configure the network and perform a binding analysis. When it reaches the bindings for the NWLink transport, an NWLink Configuration dialog will appear, as shown in Figure 9.1. Check this to

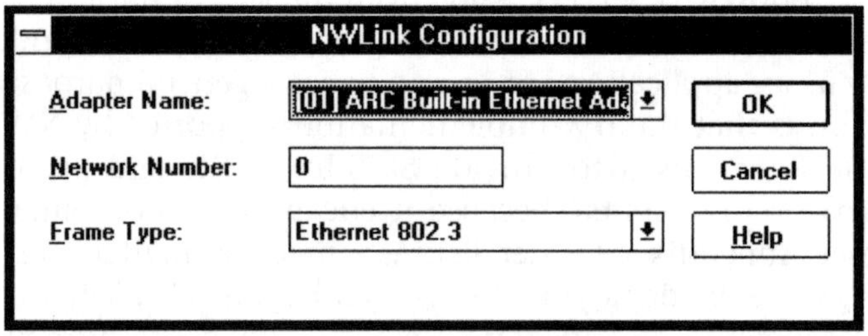

Figure 9.1 NWlink Configuration.

Microsoft's NWLink IPX/SPX protocol may be configured directly from Control Panel/Network Settings by picking the protocol from the list and clicking the Configure button. This dialog is then displayed, allowing you to select the network card bound to the protocol, the network number, and the frame type. It's also possible (though not recommended) to set these parameters using the Registry Editor (REGEDT32.EXE).

see that NWLink is bound to the proper adapter card (if more than one is installed), and that the Network number and frame type are correct (it defaults to Network 0 and an 802.3 EtherNet Frame—both correct for most installations—see "Configuring NWLink" later in this chapter for other options). Then click OK.

7. NT will prompt you to restart the system in order to start NWLink.

Connecting to an NWLink-serviced application varies from application to application, so we can't make any specific statements about that here (see Chapter 11 for a detailed example using Microsoft SQL Server for Windows NT). In general, an application that exploits NWLink will need to set itself up using a name recognized by the NetWare *bindery*. Microsoft SQL Server for Windows NT ships with a DLL that does this by sending out a Service Advertising Protocol (SAP) packet via IPX that gets picked up by a NetWare server. The server loads the SAP information into the bindery. Client applications can then use standard NetWare APIs for a list of servers to see the NT Server.[4]

Configuring NWLink

The basic NWLink configuration that's performed as part of the installation can also be performed later by running Control Panel/Network, selecting NWLink Transport from the list of installed software, and clicking the Configure... button. Aside from determining which adapter the protocol is bound to (note that while Windows NT supports having multiple network cards in the system, NWLink can be bound to only one network card at a time), you can set the network number and the frame type.

The *network number* will be 0 by default—and should be left at 0 in all but the most unusual circumstances. IPX network numbers are comparable to TCP/IP subnet addresses, but are set up dynamically at runtime. Setting the network number to zero initially causes NWLink to send a RIP (Routing Information Program) broadcast message, which will be responded to by the local subnet server (which will send the network number). If no server responds, the default setting of 0 will be retained, indicating that IPX packets are intended for the local subnet, which is compatible with the client software in most IPX implementations.

The only case where the network number should be reset to anything other than 0 arises if you're using NWLink to provide application services for a *different* subnet than the one it's on—and if you can't rely on RIP routing to get the job done for you. In this case you'll need to find out the 4-byte IPX network number for the subnet you're trying to send to, and set that in the control panel.

---

4. Programmers interested in implementing this kind of system should see the article on Windows Sockets in the July, 1993 issue of *Microsoft Systems Journal*.

The *frame type* will be set to 802.3 EtherNet Frame by default, which is standard for most EtherNet systems. If your hardware supports EtherNet II, then you can set this frame type. If you're running a Token Ring or FDDI network card, you'll need to set either 802.2 or SNAP as the protocol type, depending on your hardware. The final selection, ARCnet, would be used only with ARCnet-type cards (ARCnet is an obsolete competitor to EtherNet), which are not supported by Windows NT at this writing.

NWLink Performance Tuning and Advanced Settings

Besides the three settings for NWLink in the Control Panel, there are a number of parameters that can be set for NWLink in the Windows NT Registry. A detailed description of these parameters (and their uses) is beyond the scope of this book, but you'll find them detailed in Microsoft's online Knowledge Base on Com-puServe (go MSKB) and on Microsoft's TechNet CD (see "For More Information," at the end of this chapter). Settings are available for controlling the use of NetBIOS-over-IPX traffic (used if NWLink is employed for interconnecting Windows NT systems, as well as for application services to NetWare clients), controlling a variety of low-level IPX and SPX behaviors, and controlling RIP (or static) routing of NWLink traffic. NWLink also makes a variety of *performance counters* available for use with the Windows NT Performance Monitor application—including packet-level performance of IPX, SPX, and NetBIOS packets transmitted over NWLink (see Figure 9.2). These can be used for performance tuning and maintenance in much the same manner as the other network parameters detailed in Chapter 5.

Microsoft's CSNW for Windows NT

Originally, Microsoft expected Novell to provide NT's client requester—which they eventually did (see the following). But Novell's requester was late into beta (it still hasn't actually shipped as of this writing), and had more than its share of problems.[5] As a result, for its first few months on the market, NT had no clean way of connecting to a NetWare server. When it became apparent that Novell wasn't going to ship an NT requester in NT's first few months, Microsoft stunned the industry by announcing that it would develop its own NetWare client for NT.

The clumsily named NetWare Workstation-Compatible Service (NWCS) was the result. Right from the start it offered considerable advantages over Novell's client. Hosted on NWLink, it worked cleanly alongside NT's built-in network-ing. It also mapped NetWare servers directly into the NT filesystem so that you could access NetWare resources transparently from File Manager or the com-

---

5. True for *both* the first and second editions!

```
┌─────────────────────────────────────────────────────────────────┐
│ ─                        Add to Chart                            │
├─────────────────────────────────────────────────────────────────┤
│ Computer: \\MIPS-LAB-SERVER                        [ ... ]  [ Add ]│
│                                                                   │
│ Object:  [NWLink IPX              ↨]  Instance: [\Device\Streams] [Cancel]│
│                                                                   │
│ Counter: ┌──────────────────────────────┬─┐   ┌────────────┐  [Explain>>]│
│          │ Bytes Total/sec              │↑│   │            │           │
│          │ Connection Session Timeouts  │ │   │            │   [ Help ]│
│          │ Connections Canceled         │ │   │            │           │
│          │ Connections No Retries       │ │   │            │           │
│          │ Connections Open             │ │   │            │           │
│          │ Connections With Retries     │↓│   │[←][    ][→]│           │
│          └──────────────────────────────┴─┘   └────────────┘           │
│                                                                   │
│ Color: [▨▨▨▨▨ ↨]  Scale: [Default ↨]  Width: [──── ↨]  Style: [──── ↨]│
│                                                                   │
│ ┌─ Counter Definition ──────────────────────────────────────────┐│
│ │ Bytes Total/sec is the sum of Frame Bytes/sec and Datagram Bytes/sec.  This is the total rate of bytes [↑]││
│ │ sent to or received from the network by the protocol, but only counts the bytes in frames (i.e., packets)││
│ │ which carry data.                                                                                   [↓]││
│ └────────────────────────────────────────────────────────────────┘│
└─────────────────────────────────────────────────────────────────┘
```

Figure 9.2 Performance Monitor NWLink object.
Microsoft's NWLink IPX/SPX protocol provides a number of useful Performance Monitor counters that can be exploited by Network Administrators in NetWare environments.

mand line. In fact, NWCS was so good that—even in beta—it all but killed off Novell's competing requester.

Beginning with NT 3.5, Microsoft integrated NWCS—renamed CSNW (Client Services for NetWare)—with all Windows NT Workstation systems. A companion product, Gateway Services for NetWare (GSNW), covered later in this chapter, is shipped on Windows NT Servers.

CSNW Details

In contrast to Novell's approach, Microsoft uses standard (for Windows NT) NDIS network drivers, avoiding at a stroke all the driver problems that dogged Novell's beta redirector. Instead, Microsoft's client uses the NWLink IPX/SPX driver stack (covered in the next section of this chapter).

Besides using NDIS drivers, CSNW provides two major advantages over Novell's redirector: First, it allows you to use Universal Naming Convention (UNC) names to transparently access *both* Microsoft (Windows NT, LAN Manager, and Windows for Workgroups) servers *and* Novell NetWare servers. For example, the command:

net use x: \\server\sharename

works for both Microsoft and Novell servers if you use Microsoft's CSNW—which makes it very convenient for writing network-independent scripts. Second, CSNW provides limited support for DOS-based NetWare command-line utilities, such as SLIST, SYSCON, and SETPASS.

Installing CSNW

As CSNW uses the NWLink driver stack, you first need to install NWLink, and then add CSNW itself. You can install CSNW from the Control Panel/Network applet (you need to be logged in with administrative privileges to carry out this operation). Installation typically involves the following steps:

1. Run the Windows NT Control Panel/Networks applet, and click the Add Software button.

2. Select Client Service for NetWare from the pick list, and click the Continue button.

3. CSNW will load. Click OK to exit Control Panel/Network Settings. You will be prompted to restart the computer—do so.

4. Windows NT restarts and presents a Select Preferred Server for Netware dialog. Select the server you use most often from the list.

5. If your Windows NT and NetWare login passwords are different, you'll be prompted to enter your NetWare password (if your NetWare and NT user names are different, then you'll get a "User does not exist" error message, and you'll need to make connections manually using the Connect As field in File Manager's Connect Network Drive dialog or the /USER: switch on a *Net use* command line).

6. If you don't want to use Windows NT's built-In network services, follow the instructions given in "Eliminating Windows NT's Built-in Networking" later in this chapter.

Configuring CSNW

Once CSNW is installed, it's very easy to use. There are a couple of configuration settings you may need to set, depending on your installation: They are the *preferred server* for NetWare login (normally set in the first login after installing CSNW), and the *print options* for NetWare printers.

To set a preferred server for NetWare login, or print options for NetWare printers:

1. Start the Control Panel/CSNW applet. The NetWare Workstation Compatible Service dialog appears (Figure 9.3).

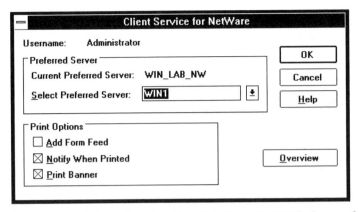

Figure 9.3 Client Service for NetWare (CSNW) Control Panel.

Microsoft's CSNW provides this dialog, available from Control Panel/CSNW. It allows control of a preferred NetWare server and of options for printing to NetWare printers.

2. To set a preferred server, pick the server you most frequently use from the list in the Select Preferred Server field. You can pick None if you have no preference.

3. The printer options you can select include whether a form feed is added at the end of each job, whether you are notified with a NetWare message when a print job is completed, and whether a banner page is printed at the start of each job. These are controlled using the Add Form Feed, Notify When Printed, and Print Banner check boxes, respectively.

4. Click OK to exit Control Panel/CSNW. Your changes will take effect immediately (if you changed your preferred server, Windows NT will immediately send your user name and password to the selected NetWare server for authentication). There is no need to restart the system.

Using CSNW

In most respects, using CSNW is no different than using Novell's Netware Client for Windows NT—or using Windows NT's built-in networking, for that matter. You can access NetWare volumes (shared directories) or printers from File Manager or the command line, and you can access NetWare printers from Print Manager or the command line. The instructions given in "Using NetWare Files and Directories," "Using NetWare Printers," and "ReSharing NetWare Printers" elsewhere in this chapter apply to CSNW just as they do to Novell's NetWare Client for Windows NT. Where CSNW goes beyond the Novell Client is in command-line access to NetWare resources, and the ability to use DOS-based NetWare utilities.

From the command line, you can view NetWare servers using the Windows NT *net view* command with the /NETWORK:NW switch. For instance, the command:

net view /network:nw

Gives the following response on our network:

```
Resources on NetWare(R) Network

_____

\\OPTICAL1
\\WIN1
The command completed successfully.
```

Net view also lets you inspect shared resources available on a server; for example, the command:

net view \\win1 /network:nw

gives this response:

```
Shared resources at \\win1

_____ -

Disk          \\win1\BOOKSHELF
Disk          \\win1\CDROM
Disk          \\win1\DATA
Disk          \\win1\SYS
The command completed successfully.
```

To access shared directories, you use the *net use* command in much the same way as it's used with the built-in Windows NT networking (documented in Chapters 3 and 4). For example, \\win1\bookshelf can be associated with the drive letter W: with the command:

net use w: \\win1\bookshelf

If your NetWare and Windows NT accounts have different user names, then use the /USER switch to set your NetWare user name, for example:

net use s: \\win1\sys /user:jruley

See the "Network Operations from the Command Line: The *Net* Command Interface" section of Chapter 4 and "Administrative *Net* Commands" in Chapter 3 for more information on command-line network access in Windows NT.

Access to NetWare Utilities

Unlike Novell's NetWare Client for Windows NT, CSNW allows you to access DOS-based NetWare utilities from the NT command line. Utilities like SYSCON, SLIST, WHOAMI, SEND, and so on, can all be run from a Windows NT command prompt with CSNW running. Here's an example of a CSNW session:

```
C:\users\default>net use z: \\win1\sys
The command completed successfully.



C:\users\default>z:

Z:\public>slist
Known NetWare File Servers          Network   Node Address Status
_____                 ___ _     ____ __

OPTICAL1                            [    122][           1]
WIN1                               [    112][           1]Default


Total of 2 file servers found

Z:\public>whoami
You are attached to server WIN1, connection 20, but not logged in.
Server WIN1 is running NetWare v3.11 (100 user).
```

For more information on how to use CSNW, including command-line control of NetWare print queues, see the CSNW documentation or the NWDOC.HLP file that ships with CSNW. Microsoft has not made CSNW generally available as this is written, but has announced that CSNW will be made available on CompuServe (presumably in the WINNT forum), and will be distributed free of charge.

Gateway Service for NetWare

Microsoft didn't stop with NWCS/CSNW. One major complaint about early versions was that you couldn't use it remotely—the NT 3.1 version of Remote Access Services (RAS) wouldn't extend NCP packets over phone lines. As a work-around, Microsoft provided a gateway feature in beta versions of NWCS that translated between NCPs and NT's native Server Message Block (SMB) protocol. The result was that you could dial into an NT server using RAS, and access a NetWare directory that had been *reshared* as an NT directory.

In NT 3.5 this feature is called Gateway Service for NetWare (GSNW)—and it's included with Windows NT Server but not with Windows NT Workstation.

GSNW provides the same functionality as CSNW, but it also breaks the link between the server and client protocol drivers. Before GSNW became available, all client systems in mixed (NT and NetWare) environments had to run two network protocol stacks: one for NetWare (NCP) and another for NT (SMB). This was true even if *both* networks ran the same underlying protocol—you could use NWLink as NT's only protocol driver, which meant that all the traffic for both NT and NetWare went over the wire as IPX packets, but every client still needed two requesters—one for NetWare and another for NT.

With GSNW, you can eliminate the need for dual stacks—all the clients run NT requesters, and all access to the NetWare server is through the gateway (an NT server that talks to the NetWare server using NCPs). It's a pretty slick idea—but it has one serious limitation: Since every request made of the NetWare server has to be translated, there's a pretty substantial performance hit. Thus, GSNW isn't something you'd want to use as the only way for a large number of users to connect to NetWare—but it does make sense in a number of special situations.

Installing and Configuring GSNW

GSNW is installed in exactly the same way as CSNW—through Control Panel/Network. Once installed, it can be configured as follows:

1. Start the Control Panel/GSNW applet. The Gateway Service for NetWare dialog appears (Figure 9.4).

2. Set a Preferred Server and Print Options exactly as previously described for CSNW.

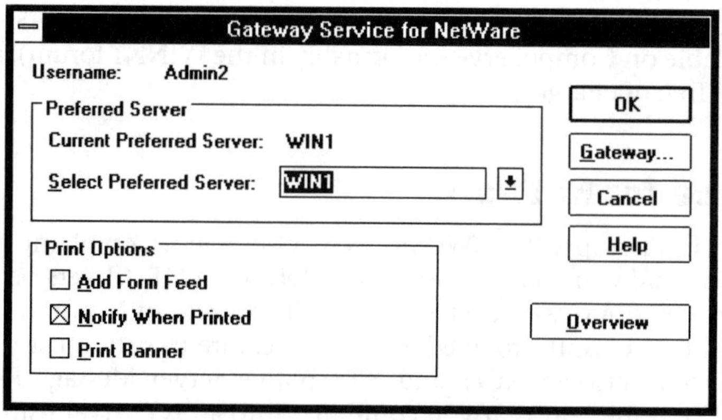

Figure 9.4 Gateway Service for NetWare (GSNW) Control Panel.
Microsoft's GSNW is managed from this dialog. In addition to the preferred server and printer options supported by CSNW, gateway functionality is supported.

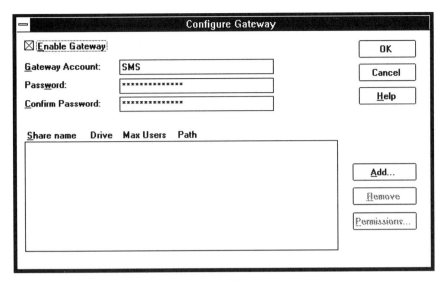

Figure 9.5 Configure Gateway dialog.

GSNW gateway functionality is controlled using this dialog.

3. To control Gateway operations, click the Gateway button. The Configure Gateway dialog appears (see Figure 9.5).

4. To reshare a NetWare volume, click the Enable Gateway check box. Then enter a valid NetWare account name and password into the appropriate fields (confirming the password in the field supplied for that purpose), and click the Add button. The New Share dialog appears (Figure 9.6).

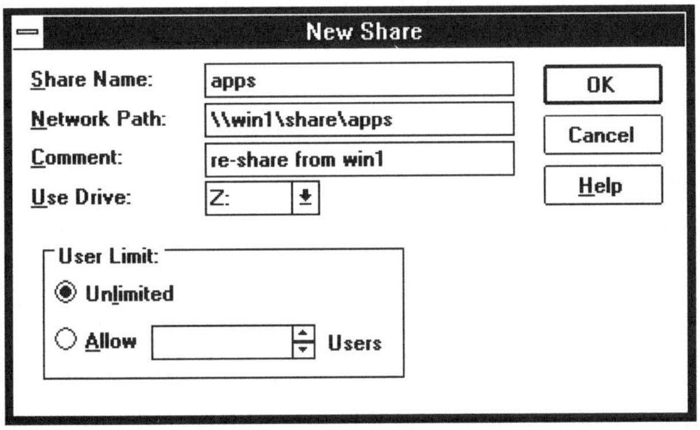

Figure 9.6 GSNW New Share dialog.

Once gateway functionality is enabled, it becomes possible to reshare NetWare directories using this dialog.

Note that the account used in this step will be used by all NT/WFWG/ Win95 users when attached to the NetWare server! This account must be a member of the NTGATEWAY group on the NetWare server. The currently logged-in NT user account must also have permission to access the NetWare server, and must have permission to create a share on the NT server.

5. You may now create a Windows NT share name for a NetWare volume. Enter a share name in the appropriate field, and a properly formatted UNC name in the Network Path field (it helps to have a command prompt window open—type *net view /network:nw* to see a list of available NetWare servers; *net view \ \server /network:nw* for a list of shares on a particular server). You can optionally add a comment, which will appear in lists of shares (this might be a good way to alert users that the share name in question is redirected), and designate a drive letter for local use. You can also designate a maximum number of users for the reshared drive (you may want to restrict this in order to minimize performance impact on the server in question, or to meet the legal requirements of your NetWare license agreement).

6. Click OK. If everything worked properly, the share will be accepted. If you've designated an invalid pathname, user, or password, you'll get an error message—go back to step 4 or 5 (as appropriate) and try again.

Using GSNW

Once GSNW is set up and shares are configured, using it is simple. On the NT Server desktop, it provides identical function to CSNW on NT Workstations (see the preceding). To remote clients, reshared NetWare volumes appear to be local shares from the NT server. Aside from GSNW's lower performance, it is functionally indistinguishable from a local share.

NetWare Migration Tool

Having the ability to use NetWare volumes as a client, and to reshare them as a server, provides NT with useful capabilities in a NetWare environment; but from the administrator's perspective, it does nothing to offset the single greatest difficulty of running a mixed network: maintaining two (possibly more, depending on the network setup) sets of user accounts.

To deal with this situation (and, in all honesty, to make it as easy as possible for NetWare administrators to migrate their LANs to NT), Microsoft introduced the NetWare Migration Tool with NT Server 3.5. This tool has recently been upgraded in conjunction with the FPNW beta (see the following), and will no doubt continue to be enhanced as long as NetWare and NT compete with each other.

Windows NT Migration Tool for NetWare automatically migrates NetWare users and Groups, Directory structures (including permissions), Login scripts, and Print Queues. It's run in conjunction with NetWare Gateway Services, and requires that you be logged in as both administrator on the NT server to which you're migrating and supervisor on the NetWare server from which you're migrating.

Installing the migration tool is quite simple—it's copied to the SYSTEM32 directory of a Windows NT Server during normal installation. You may or may not find an icon for it preinstalled in the Administration Tools or Network Administration group; if not, add one—the file name is NWCONV.EXE. Once the icon is available, simply double-click to launch the migration tool.

The details of using the Migration Tool are far too involved to cover here. Fortunately, the Migration tool's online Help is excellent—written in a tutorial format that makes operation easy to understand. However, we do want to mention one feature that serves as a tremendous confidence builder: Trial Migration with Logging. This lets you carry out a complete dry run to see what happens, without actually creating user accounts, copying files, or translating login scripts. If you begin with the *Overview* section of the Migration Tool's Help file, and practice using it with Trial Migration, you'll quickly gain the confidence to try it for real.

There are two drawbacks to using the Migration tool: First, it requires two complete servers—at least temporarily. You must have enough disk space on the NT server to store the complete directory structure (and files) from the NetWare server—which can be a real problem on a large LAN (in such a case, it may pay to consider a *stepwise migration*, initially duplicating only the users and groups, then the login scripts, then parts of the directory structure, then more—in each case, giving users access to the remaining, unmigrated directories (and printers) through the NetWare gateway).

The second problem is that migrating directly to NT from NetWare requires adding an NT requester to all LAN clients. Once the migration is complete, you can unplug the NetWare server and eliminate all NetWare client requesters—but during the migration both are necessary. For alternative approaches that avoid this problem, see the following section on Server-side Emulation software.

NetWare Client for Windows NT

Novell's approach to NetWare connectivity is the NetWare Client for Windows NT—a redirector for Windows NT implemented as an installable file system and a collection of drivers. It's delivered and maintained by Novell. As of this writing it's in beta test—and has been for well over a year. We anticipate that it will *eventually* be delivered in much the same way that Novell has delivered redirector clients for OS/2, DOS, and Windows.

Like CSNW, NetWare Client for Windows NT provides full file-and-print sharing services to the Windows NT client machine. How this is done, however, is very different from CSNW.

The Protocol Problem

In early versions of the NetWare Client for Windows NT, Novell chose to break with the NDIS standard for network drivers used by Microsoft, and introduced its own Open Datalink Interface (ODI) system. There are many arguments one could make about the relative merits of NDIS and ODI. ODI is potentially faster than NDIS, because it passes a pointer between the kernel-level network card driver and the protocol stack, essentially allowing the two layers to share memory. Unfortunately, this appears to violate the basic principles of NT's multilayer system protection, in which data is *never* shared between the kernel (in this case, driver) and user (in this case, protocol stack) layers, and it can lead to severe system crashes if the shared memory address is corrupted by either component.

NDIS drivers, by contrast, do not share common memory between the driver and protocol layers—instead, data is copied between separate memory regions in the two layers. This is a slower process, but it's safer (in fact, *either* approach should be completely reliable once the drivers are fully debugged).

Against this, there's one major advantage to using ODI drivers over and above the possible performance enhancement—the 32-bit revision (F) drivers in question are *the very same drivers used by NetWare 4.0 servers*. This can be extremely convenient for administrators in a NetWare 4.0 environment, because if you have NetWare 4.0 server drivers for your standard network cards, then you can use these same drivers with Windows NT systems.

However, there are two problems with using Novell's ODI drivers in a Windows NT environment: First, while over 100 different revision (F) 32-bit Open Datalink Interface (ODI) network drivers are available at this writing, not all drivers are available for all Windows NT platforms (in particular, we have yet to see any drivers for the Power PC architecture)—so you'll need to make sure that both your network card and CPU architecture are supported. The second problem is that while the driver .LAN files work perfectly with Windows NT, they require a customized OEMSETUP.INF file in order for Windows NT setup to install them.[6] As of this writing, OEMSETUP.INF files are available for about one hundred network cards. Novell has said that it's working on a tool to create these files automatically, but it hasn't announced whether this will be made

---

6. Documented in the Windows NT Device Driver Development Kit.

available to the public. Effectively, this means that Novell's ODI drivers are useful in an NT environment *only* if the vendor also supplies the Windows NT .INF file for the driver in question.

One or Two Network Cards?

Another problem with the need to use ODI drivers is that the ODI/NDIS incompatibility causes problems if you want to run *both* the NetWare redirector *and* built-in Windows NT networking (if you want to run *only* NetWare networking on your Windows NT systems, see "Eliminating Windows NT's Built-In Networking," later in this chapter). This arises because both ODI and NDIS want to *own* the network card—something that doesn't work out very well if you have only one network card in your system.

One solution is to use two network cards in the same machine—one bound to ODI for NetWare, and the other bound to NDIS for NT. This approach works and provides better performance and higher reliability than a single-card approach, but it's expensive and it creates a configuration problem (you can't run both cards at the same interrupt level and I/O address, for instance).

A single network card solution has been made available by Novell. This uses a custom *shim* driver called ODINSUP, which acts as a translator layer between the ODI network card drivers and the Microsoft NDIS system. Therefore, it's possible to run one network card, ODINSUP and the proper ODI driver, and have it run with *both* the NetWare NT Client *and* Windows NT's built-in networking—a solution that potentially offers better performance than using a pure NDIS approach.

NetWare DOS Utility Support

Recent versions of Novell's requester include a *NetWare DOS box* that runs custom versions of Novell's VIPX and NETX components, giving you capabilities similar to those you'd have on a real DOS client. Unfortunately, the connections established within a NetWare DOS box are local to that box—they don't apply to the rest of the system. Moreover, the NetWare DOS box doesn't support all NetWare VLM system calls—so some NetWare applications (NWADMIN, for instance) won't run in it.

NetWare APIs for Windows NT

As we went to press, Novell sources told us that the NT 3.5 version of their redirector, due to be available by the time you read this, will include a 32-bit version of NWADMIN. In order to do this, Novell has evidently completed a port of their API set to run on Windows NT, which means that over time, other

Novell utilities should make an appearance in a 32-bit form. At some point, this will hopefully allow an NT-based client to execute a NetWare login script.

NetWare Client Limitations

To date, Novell's requester provides only a FAT-compatible DOS-style name space. That is, applications, whether 16-bit or 32-bit, are restricted to eight-character names and three-character extensions. This is unfortunate, because NetWare is capable of supporting multiple name spaces, and long file name support has long been available for Macintosh clients (indeed, Microsoft's FPNW, described in the following, provides NT-compatible long file name support).

Finally, while versions of the NetWare Client for Windows NT exist for some RISC systems (including MIPS R4x00 and DEC Alpha AxP systems), availability of ODI drivers for these platforms remains something of an issue.

How to Install and Use Novell's NetWare Client for Windows NT

Installing NetWare Client for Windows NT is relatively easy. In the present beta situation you simply download the NWNT.EXE file from the NOVFILES forum on CompuServe (check the "Client Kits" section), then expand it (typically it's shipped as a self-extracting .EXE file) to an NWNT directory or floppy diskette. After the client software ships you'll presumably be able to order it through your Novell representative.

NetWare Client for Windows NT is installed from the Control Panel/Network applet (you need to be logged in with administrative privileges to carry out this operation). While installation has varied from version to version during the beta program, it typically involves the following steps:

1. Run the Windows NT Control Panel/Networks applet, and click the Add Software button.

2. Select <Other> Requires Disk from Manufacturer from the pick list, and click the Continue button.

3. An Insert Diskette dialog will appear requesting the full path name for the updated software files. Enter the path name for the directory or disk where you stored the expanded NWNT files; for example: D:\NWNT or A:\, and click the OK button. When the list of software you can install appears, select Novell NetWare Client from the list (Figure 9.7).

4. The Novell NetWare Client for Windows NT will load, and you'll be presented with a NetWare Client Installation dialog, asking which IPX protocol stack you want to use. The default is Novell IPX/SPX II, which requires ODI drivers. Alternatively, you can select Microsoft NWLink, which will work with the NDIS drivers included with Windows NT (and

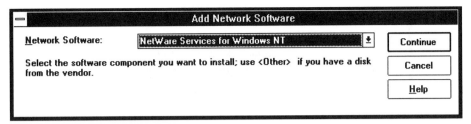

Figure 9.7 Control Panel/Netware Services.
Loading Novell NetWare Services for Windows NT is done using Control Panel/Network Settings Add Software button.

installed by default). You'll find more information on NWLink in the section on "Microsoft's NWLink Protocol Stack," later in this chapter.

5. If you selected Novell's IPX stack, a set of instructions will be presented for removing the NDIS driver already installed in your system (if present). Follow the instructions that appear on the screen.

6. If you're using ODI drivers, click the Add Adapter button. An Add Adapter dialog will appear asking you to select an ODI adapter driver. Select the ODI driver for your network card from the list (if it's not on the list, then your best move at this point is to abort the installation, find a revision (F) 32-bit ODI driver for your card, and then add it manually using the Control Panel/Networks Add Adapter button). Set the options (base address, IRQ, etc.) for the card and click the Continue button.

7. If you're using ODI drivers, an IPX Frame Type dialog appears. Select the proper Frame Type for your network from the list (the default, 802.3 EtherNet, is correct for most applications).

8. If you're using ODI drivers, at this point what happens depends on whether you need NDIS support for NT's built-in networking; and if so, whether it will be run on a separate network card or on the same network card as ODI. If you have two network cards, you will have been asked which card to bind the ODI driver to, and (provided you bound it to a card separate from NDIS—check with the Bindings button in Control Panel/Networks) you're done.

9. If you need to add NDIS support for NT's built-in networking on a machine that's got ODI installed (generally you will need this in any system with just one network card *unless* you want to completely disable NT's built-in networking, as mentioned previously), then click the Add Adapter button, and select Novell ODI support for NDIS drivers (ODINSUP) from the list, as illustrated in Figure 9.8. This will load the *software shim* described previously.

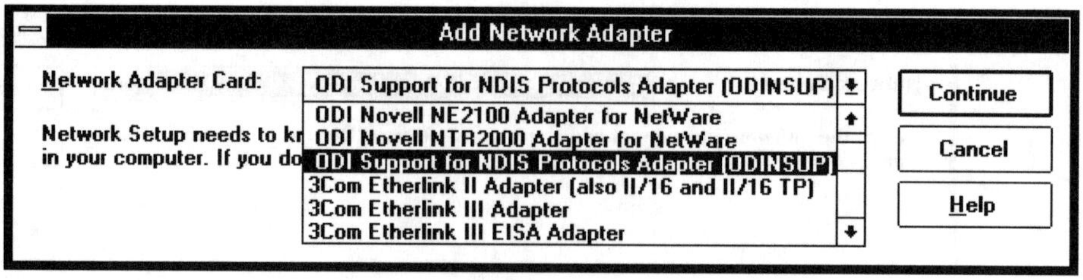

Figure 9.8 Control Panel/ODINSUP.

In environments where both Netware Services and Windows NT built-in peer network-
ing are to be used with a single network card, it's necessary to load Novell's ODI
Support for NDIS (ODINSUP) *shim* driver, using Control Panel/Network Settings Add
Driver button.

10. If you don't want *any* form of built-in networking, install the Microsoft
Loopback Driver, or disable the built-in network services, as described
in "Eliminating Windows NT's Built-In Networking" later in this chapter.

11. With NetWare Client and either Microsoft or Novell IPX protocol stack
and adapter drivers installed, click the Bindings button to bind the
adapters to the cards and review the order of the connections. Once
this is done, you can click OK to exit the Control Panel/Network
Settings applet. You will need to restart the computer before using
NetWare Client for NT.

If everything has gone right, the computer will restart normally. If the
computer does not restart normally, the odds are extremely high that some error
has been made in configuring the networking support for the network card.

The best solution in this case is ugly but fairly reliable. Turn off the
computer, physically remove the network card, and restart the computer. The
computer typically will start up and display an error message indicating that it
was unable to locate the network card and that one or more services are not
complete. From Control Panel/Network, select the network card driver, press
the configure button and check to verify that the interrupt and address of the
card are properly selected. Also, double-check to make sure you have in fact
installed the driver for the right network card.

Once these things have been verified and adjusted as necessary, turn the
computer off, put the network card back in, and reboot the computer. If it fails
again, the odds are high that one of two things has happened: Either you have
not successfully completed the preceding steps, or you have successfully completed the preceding steps but your particular network card and computer are
not compatible with the current generation of ODI drivers—in which case, your
only option is to turn off the computer, remove the network card, restart the

computer, use the Remove button in Control Panel/Network Settings to eliminate the Netware Client, reinstall the NDIS drivers for Windows NT, and proceed with one of the other options for NetWare compatibility described in this chapter.

Eliminating Windows NT's Built-In Networking

Many NetWare administrators wish to operate Windows NT clients in a NetWare-only environment without Microsoft's built-in peer networking. Unfortunately, this isn't possible with the current release of Windows NT (and for architectural reasons it's unlikely to be possible in future versions). Novell's NetWare Client for Windows NT is built on a number of the built-in subsystems, so attempting to eliminate it makes the NetWare Client unworkable. However, Microsoft and Novell jointly recommend one work-around, and we've found another.

First, the official approach (recommended by Novell and Microsoft): Disable the built-in network services using the Control Panel/Services applet. Set a Startup Type of Disabled for the Alerter, Workstation, Computer Browser, Messenger, and Net Logon services. This will prevent any of Windows NT's built-in networking features from starting.

Our approach is to follow the instructions we've previously given to install Novell's NetWare Client and the requisite ODI or NDIS driver, but do not install the ODINSUP binder for the built-in (NetBEUI) networking. Instead, install the MS Loopback Adapter Driver as a second network card driver, and bind NetBEUI to it. This will give you a working system with the built-in networking reflected back to itself, and the NetWare networking bound to the proper ODI driver and network card—we've tried it and it works.

We recommend the latter approach because some Windows NT applications expect to see the built-in networking features, and completely disabling them (particularly the network browser) can cause problems.

Administrators may find that the built-in networking's not a bad thing. From our experience, there doesn't seem to be any great problem in running both NCP and SMB traffic over the same network card; and running both networks gives you the added flexibility of having the peer networking available for administrative purposes. Rather than eliminating it, you may want to simply make it unavailable to your end users. You can do so with the following procedure:

1. Run User Manager from the Administrative Tools group.

2. Select the user (or group) that you don't want to use built-in network services.

3. Select User Rights from the Policies menu. When the User Rights Policy dialog (Figure 9.9) appears, make sure the Show Advanced User Rights

box is checked, select Access this computer from network, and click the Remove button. Then select Create permanent shared objects, and click the Remove button.

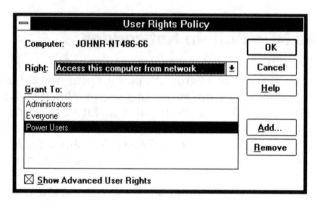

Figure 9.9 User Rights dialog.

Administrators who wish to effectively prevent users from employing Windows NT's built-in peer network services can make it impossible for anyone other than administrators to access Windows NT systems over the network. This is done using the User Manager Policies/User Rights dialog.

If you do this for all nonadministrative users on all of your Windows NT systems, you will render it impossible for any of them to use the peer-to-peer networking features. A user can create a temporary share in File Manager, but nobody else will be able to use it—and it will disappear when the user logs out. Administrators, however, retain the ability to create and use shared directories (and printers) for administrative purposes.

Configuring the NetWare Client for Windows NT

Once the NetWare Client is installed, it's a simple matter to use it, as we'll see shortly. There are a couple of configuration settings you may need to set, depending on your installation (these settings are available only if Novell IPX/SPX and ODI drivers are used; they are not available with NDIS drivers): They are the preferred server for NetWare login, and the frame type for IPX/SPX traffic. Of these, the preferred server most commonly needs attention—in a multiserver environment, NetWare tends to log in to the first one that responds when the client comes online; which may not be the server you want to access. Setting a preferred server eliminates this problem by forcing the redirector to log in to a specific server of your choice. You'll need to be logged in to the Windows NT system with administrative privilege to carry out the following steps.

To set a preferred server for NetWare login:

1. Start Control Panel/NetWare applet, and click the Configure button.
2. The Network Settings dialog appears. Select NetWare Workstation from the list, and click the Configure button.
3. The Netware Workstation Setup dialog appears. Select the appropriate server from the list, and click the OK button. You will have to restart the computer to make the preferred server selection take effect.

To change the frame type:

1. Start Control Panel/NetWare, and click the Configure button.
2. The Network Settings dialog appears. Select NetWare IPX/SPX II Transport from the list, and click the Configure button.
3. The Netware IPX Bind dialog appears. Click the OK button. The IPX Frame Type dialog appears. Select the appropriate frame type from the list, and click the OK button. You will have to restart the computer to make the frame type selection take effect.

Alternatively, it's possible to set the frame type using the Windows NT Registry Editor (REGEDT32.EXE). Edit the Frame Type entry in KEY_LOCAL_-MACHINE\SYSTEM\CurrentControlSet\Services\IpxSpxII\Parameters. Valid values are EtherNet_802.3, EtherNet_802.2, EtherNet_II, and EtherNet_SNAP. It's usually preferable to do this from the control panel, but the Registry approach can be used if you need to set a preferred server on a remote system, or if you want to create a batch file for changing preferred server settings.

Using NetWare Files and Directories

Fortunately, once the vagaries of the installation process have been navigated, using NetWare Client for Windows NT is generally quite pleasant. To access shared files and directories on NetWare servers:

1. Start File Manager, and select Disk/Connect Network Drive. You may also begin by clicking on the Connect Network Drive button in the toolbar if it's present.
2. The Connect Network Drive dialog box appears, which is shown in Figure 9.10. The Drive box contains the next available letter for your computer. To change this value, click on the down arrow key or press Alt+Down Arrow and select the drive letter you prefer.
3. If you have connected to this drive before, the path may be listed in the Path pull down list. The Path list shows the previous ten paths you have

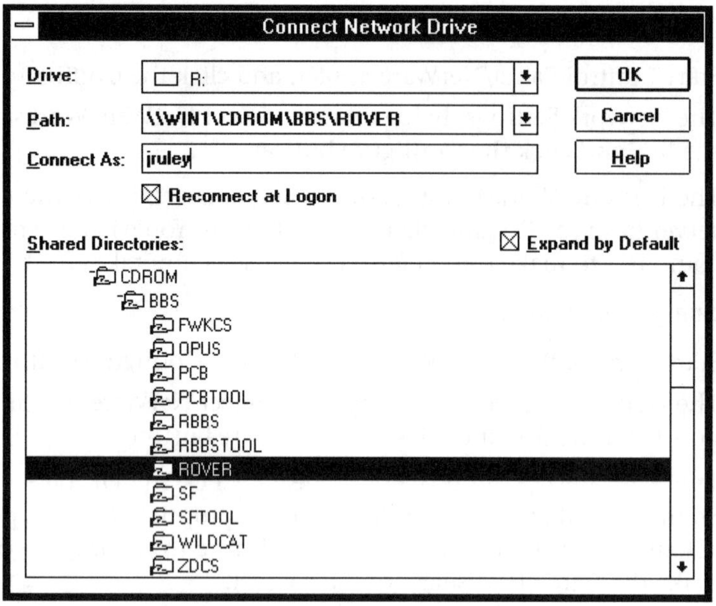

Figure 9.10 Connect Net Drive—Netware.

Windows NT users connect to NetWare shared directories just as they do to Windows NT shared directories—using the Connect Network Drive dialog in File Manager. Note that the need to use this dialog (and the associated browser service) makes it impossible to completely eliminate Windows NT built-in networking if NetWare Services are to be used. A work-around (binding the built-in networking to a *loopback* driver) is given in the text.

selected. If the path you want to connect to is displayed, select it and proceed to step 5.

4. There are two options for selecting the path:

   ❑ If you have not connected to this drive before, or your drive is not listed in the Path listbox, enter the path name directly—note that Windows NT uses UNC-format names, not NetWare NCP format; for example, \\WIN1\SYS\MSMAIL is correct, while WIN1/SYS\MS-MAIL is not correct.

   ❑ Alternatively, select the shared directory from the Shared Directories list. NetWare servers on the network will be listed under the NetWare Client list. Select the server you want to connect to by double-clicking on it. When you make your selection, File Manager displays the shared directories of your selection in the box at the bottom of the dialog box. Select the shared directory by single-clicking on it, or double-click to display subdirectories. File Manager displays the path in the Path box.

5. If your NetWare user ID and/or password differ from your Windows NT user ID and password, then type your NetWare ID into the Connect As: field. You will be prompted for your password when the connection is made.

6. If you want to reconnect to this directory automatically when you begin Windows NT, be sure to check the Reconnect at Logon box (which is checked by default). Caution: If the directory is on a computer that's not the server and is not certain to be running when you start Windows NT again, you will get a warning message asking if you want to proceed with connections. Therefore, we recommend that you check the Reconnect at Logon box only if you are connecting to a directory on the server for which there is a strong likelihood of availability when you log in. Note that if your NetWare user ID and/or password differs from your Windows NT user ID and password, you'll be asked for the NetWare password each and every time you log in.

7. Select OK.

Matters are greatly simplified, for obvious reasons, if the NetWare user name and the user name under Windows NT are the same. If so, connections proceed identically as if they were connections to the built-in networking. When you connect to a server in which a different user name and password are employed, it's necessary to type the appropriate user name into the Connect As: field.

Using NetWare Printers

It's just as straightforward to use NetWare printers as it is to use NetWare directories:

1. Select Printer/Connect to Printer, or select the Connect Printer button on the toolbar. The dialog box shown in Figure 9.11 appears.

2. Enter the name of the printer in the Printer text box. If you do not know the name of the printer, select one from the list in the Select Printers box. The printers are displayed in a hierarchical list, which can be expanded to show the printers, domains, and workgroups by double-clicking on an entry. Select a printer, and the name appears in the Printer text box. Select OK.

3. If the printer is shared by a Windows NT computer, you can now use the printer. The steps that follow should be followed if the printer is shared by a computer not running Windows NT.

4. Print Manager prompts you to install a driver. Select OK, then choose the driver from the Select Driver dialog box. Enter the location (drive and directory) of the Windows NT printer drivers, then select Continue.

5. Windows NT will install the driver for you.

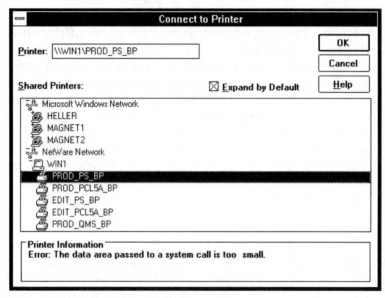

Figure 9.11 Connect Net Printer Netware.

NetWare printers are connected in exactly the same way as Windows NT network printers—using Print Manager's Connect Network Printer dialog. NetWare printers do require installation of local printer drivers on the client systems. It is also possible to *reshare* NetWare printers over the built-in networking for access by Windows NT (and other SMB) clients that do not have NetWare redirectors installed.

Resharing NetWare Printers

One surprising feature of NetWare client for NT is that it permits NetWare printers that have been connected using the Windows NT Print Manager to be reshared over the Windows NT (SMB) network, and accessed by Windows NT workstations that don't have the NetWare redirector installed. To reshare a NetWare printer (that's already been connected using the steps previously listed):

1. Open Print Manager and select the NetWare Printer you wish to reshare.

2. Select the Properties item from the Print Manager Printer menu.

3. Check the Share this Printer on the Network check box, type a name into the Share Name field, and click the OK button.

Other systems using Microsoft SMB networking (Windows NT, Windows for Workgroups, or LAN Manager systems) will now be able to access the printer as if it were installed locally. This approach is useful, among other things, for connecting NetWare printers to machines that don't have a NetWare requester for Windows NT installed. It can also be used to make NetWare printers available to Windows NT clients logged in using Remote Access Services (RAS). Whether this feature will be maintained in future versions of the requester we cannot say—but we hope so.

NetWare Messaging

Support for NetWare Messaging has varied in the beta versions of the NetWare Client for Windows NT that have been presented so far. While all versions of the requester can receive NetWare messages, early versions provided an interesting (and useful) Connections dialog in the NetWare applet of the Windows NT Control Panel that allowed for sending messages. Later versions eliminated this feature—and this leaves us somewhat confused, because the NetWare Messaging feature worked perfectly from the first. We presume that this feature will be reintroduced into the NetWare client at a later date. Consult the documentation that you receive with the NetWare Client for Windows NT for details.

Why Two NetWare Redirectors?

The availability of two competing approaches to connecting Windows NT to NetWare servers may appear confusing—but in our view it's an overall win for NT users. Both approaches work with Windows NT's native NDIS drivers, and Novell's Client gives you the option to use NetWare 4.0 server drivers if they're available. Microsoft's client, by supporting command-line access to NetWare servers, gives you the capability to write network-independant scripts. In general, the competition between both clients should assure Windows NT users of excellent NetWare connectivity in the future.

Server-Side NetWare Emulators

As mentioned earlier, the need to change network client software makes migrating from NetWare to NT a serious practical challenge. Administrators who might otherwise be happy to plug in an NT Server or two shrink from the prospect of changing the client software in dozens (or hundreds!) of desktop systems.

And thinking about it—Why should this be necessary? The historical accident of Microsoft selecting SMB as their key protocol, and Novell selecting NCP, shouldn't matter to administrators. After all, both protocols are functionally equivalent. That fact drove the development, first, of an NCP-SMB translator (GSNW, descibed earlier), and then of native 32-bit NCP implementations for Windows NT. Two are currently available: Beame and Whitside's BW-Multiconnect for Windows NT, and Microsoft's File and Print Services for NetWare (FPNW).

Beame and Whiteside's BW-Multiconnect

About six months after NT 3.1's release, Beame and Whiteside announced their NCP emulator.[7] BW-Multiconnect makes it possible for NetWare clients to access shared files and printers on Windows NT systems. It comes on just three diskettes, and installs as a standard Windows NT service. When you bring it up, be prepared for a shocked reaction from NetWare administrators, because they're going to see an additional NetWare server announce itself on the LAN.

BW-Multiconnect is implemented as a Windows NT service and a custom protocol stack. It uses NT's security system, but looks to the LAN (and to users on the LAN) exactly like a NetWare 3.11 server. For maximum performance, it provides its own BWS_ipx protocol stack, which may be operated alongside Microsoft's NWLink stack if desired. The server component of BW_Multiconnect (BWS_NW_Server) provides bindery services, queue management, printing to both local printers and print server devices connected to the LAN—and, of course, provides NetWare-compatible file sharing.

Specific instructions for installing and configuring BW-Multiconnect are beyond the scope of this book; suffice it to say that the product is easy to use. Moreover, Beame and Whiteside believe in the *try before you buy* concept—they're currently offering free evaluation copies of BW-Multiconnect that time out after 30 days of use. There is no better way to find out about the product than giving it a try!

FPNW

Microsoft's File and Print Services for NetWare (FPNW) is—like BW-Multiconnect—an add-on package that provides NCP-based file and printer sharing. Unlike BW-Multiconnect, FPNW runs only on Windows NT Servers. All types

---

7. Dunda, ONT, Canada—(416)765-0822.

of NetWare clients (DOS, Windows, OS/2, Windows NT, Macintosh, etc.) are supported. The NT Server appears to the clients as a NetWare 3.12 Server.

The NetWare emulation provided by FPNW is powerful enough to allow most NetWare applications to interact with NT in the same way they would with NetWare—for example, an NT Server running FPNW can be seen in the list of servers generated by the SLIST command-line utility (or equivalent Windows functionality). Similarly, users can set their passwords on FPNW servers, using the NetWare SETPASS utility. Indeed, FPNW's NetWare emulation is so complete that an FPNW-equipped NT Server can actually be administered using NetWare-standard supervisor utilities, such as SYSCON!

FPNW need not be managed using character-mode tools, however. It's installed through Control Panel/Networks Add Software.. button, in much the same way as other network services; and basic management of the server is done with an FPNW Control Panel item (see Figure 9.12). For administrators, FPNW ships with a set of extensions to NT Server's File Manager, User Manager, and Print Manager that allow complete control of NetWare user accounts. An

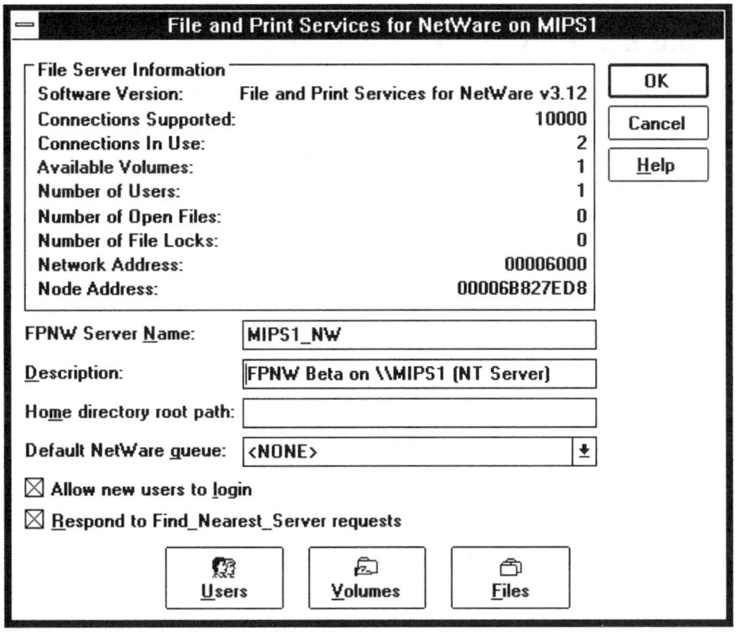

Figure 9.12 FPNW Control Panel.

For the ultimate in server-side NetWare compatibility, Microsoft's FPNW provides NetWare Corp Protocol (NCP) emulation that makes an NT Server functionally indistinguishable from a NetWare 3.12 server. It's managed from this Control Panel/FPNW dialog.

enhancement to NT Server's standard NetWare Migration Tool permits automatic cloning of an existing NetWare server's user account database.

Since FPNW is hosted on Windows NT, it provides significant advantages compared to NetWare 3.12: multiserver domain-wide single logon, and interdomain trust; NT Server's inherent Macintosh file and printer support; and built-in Remote Access Services. FPNW on NT Server also provides long-file-name support to Windows 95 and NT clients, and—since it's implemented as a portable, multithreaded, Windows NT service—full exploitation of NT's scalability on RISC and multiprocessor machines.

NetWare Client users see an FPNW-equipped server as an additional server on the LAN—with no obvious indication that it is running NT rather than NetWare.

As with BW-Multiconnect, the details of using FPNW are beyond the scope of this book (especially so, given that the product is currently still being beta tested). We have used FPNW and have found it to be easy to setup and trouble-free.

Comparing BW-Multiconnect and FPNW

BW-Multiconnect doesn't support login scripts, so if startup-script functionality is needed, you'll have to retain at least one real NetWare server for logins and then have users *attach* to NT systems running the product. It's also less well integrated with NT's administration and security tools (the volume setup in BW-Multiconnect is reminiscent of that in GSNW, and looks decidedly crude by comparison with FPNW's extensions to the Windows File Manager). BW-Multiconnect is also priced differently than FPNW—in particular, it requires a per-user fee that can make it quite expensive in a large installation.

However, BW-Multiconnect has one overwhelming advantage over FPNW: It can run on either NT Workstation or NT Server. This makes it an option that should be looked at quite seriously for small sites, such as branch offices, where the cost differential between NT Workstation and NT Server is spread out over a small number of people.

FPNW requires NT Server; but while final pricing has been announced as this is written, Microsoft *has* stated that FPNW will not require an additional per-client license fee over that required for NT Server—making FPNW a bargain in larger sites.[8]

Neither FPNW nor BW-Multiconnect supports server-side NetWare Loadable Modules (NLMs), ODI drivers, or NetWare 4.*x* features, such as NetWare Directory Service (NDS)—though NetWare 4.*x* client software can be used in

---

8. March 1995.

exactly the way it's used with NetWare 3.*x* servers, via bindery emulation. To put it simply, neither solution makes NT a true NetWare clone.

NetWare and RAS

As mentioned earlier, the original Gateway feature in NWCS/CSNW was a response to user complaints of difficulty accessing NetWare servers over RAS in NT 3.1. That happened because NT 3.1 RAS functioned purely as an SMB gateway. It used Microsoft's proprietary AsyBEUI protocol, which could not redirect NCPs. Curiously enough, even while Microsoft was perfecting the NetWare Gateway for NT servers, they were eliminating the original need for it from the clients—by extending RAS to be protocol-independant

Beginning with NT 3.5, RAS uses the industry-standard Point-to-Point Protocol (PPP) and handles all types of connections—SMBs, NCPs, and UNIX-style IP—transparently (it also retains AsyBEUI for compatibility with older versions, and supports SLIP as an alternative protocol for TCP/IP connections). As a result, dialing into an NT server (or PPP-compatible router) using RAS on an NT client gives you all the same connections you'd have on the LAN—including NetWare connections.

NetWare support built into the RAS client is consistent with Microsoft's view of RAS as a client-to-server connection tool, which makes a lot of sense in a central office environment with mobile users. But what about a true wide-area network (WAN) situation, where you need to connect offices? Combining RAS with the NetWare gateway in NT Server could be the answer—run one high-speed data link between the central office and an NT server at the remote office. Access the central office NetWare server(s) over that link using RAS. Then use the NetWare gateway to reshare the NetWare directories to users on the remote office LAN.

Finally—The FTP Back-Door Approach

With all the limitations we've described on both the Novell and Microsoft approaches to Windows NT/NetWare connectivity, you're probably wondering if there's an alternative. There is—although, to be honest, it's not one we think most users will take seriously. Basically, it exploits Windows NT's built-in UNIX-style TCP/IP networking (detailed in Chapter 6). Since Windows NT knows how to talk to TCP/IP, all you need to do is make NetWare talk TCP/IP, and you have them connected!

This sounds too simple to work—but it does. We've tested it (in fact, four of this book's authors together made up the first team to successfully connect a Windows NT client to a NetWare host, using exactly this approach, in late

1992). So, if all else fails, here's how to connect Windows NT to NetWare via TCP/IP:

1. Acquire and install the *Network File Service* (NFS) NetWare *Loadable Module* (NLM) on your NetWare Server.
2. Install TCP/IP networking on your Windows NT workstation(s), according to the instructions in the "Installing and Configuring TCP/IP" section of Chapter 6.
3. Assign IP address numbers to the NetWare server and the NT workstation(s).
4. Restart the NetWare Server with the NFS NLM installed and configured (including assigning the IP address).
5. Restart the workstation(s).
6. You can now access the NetWare Server via UNIX-style File Transfer Protocol (FTP), as described in the "FTP" section in Chapter 6.

Of course, you'll spot problem number 1 as soon as you look at step 1—the cost of the NFS NLM. Problem number 2 is that FTP isn't exactly an example of world-beating user interface design (it's actually a command-line interface similar to connecting with an old-fashioned text-mode bulletin board system). Problem number 3 with this approach is that while it does give you shared access to NetWare files, it doesn't give you any access to NetWare printers.

But in spite of everything, it *does* work!

Summary and Conclusions

In this chapter, we've reviewed the history of Novell NetWare, and discovered why Windows NT's built-in networking is incompatible with it. We've examined several approaches—from Novell (the NetWare Client for Windows NT); Microsoft (the NWLink protocol, Migration Tool for NetWare, and the alphabet soup of CSNW, GSNW, FPNW); and third parties (Beame and Whiteside Multiconnect IPX). Each has unique advantages and disadvantages. Finally, we've briefly described an alternative (using NT's built-in TCP/IP File Transfer Protocol service to access a Name File Service NLM) that isn't pretty but has been proved to work.

Overall, NT users (and administrators) now have a very broad range of options for using NT in a NetWare LAN environment: as a client, either locally on the LAN or remotely over RAS; as a gateway server, making NetWare directories available to clients without requiring NetWare client software. NT can even function as a *NetWare Clone* server, either by migrating the user accounts and directory structure (and ultimately the users themselves) from

NetWare to NT Server—or by running BW-Multiconnect or FPNW on the server, which makes NT look like NetWare to the clients.

This entire field is in a state of flux, and new developments happen daily. Indeed, as we go to press, FPNW and Novell's NT client are in beta, and there are rumors that Novell will soon deliver NetWare Directory Services (NDS) on Windows NT. Readers are urged to check our *Electronic Update* (available from the online locations specified in the Introduction), watch the trade magazines, and check both Novell and Microsoft's support forums on CompuServe (NDESKTOP and WINNT, respectively) for more information as this volatile subject develops.

For More Information

Clarke, D.J. (1993), *The Complete NetWare Construction Kit*. New York: John Wiley & Sons, ISBN: 1-471-58259-X. Clarke's information on NT is one-sided, but this book provides an invaluable practical overview of NetWare.

Custer, Helen (1993), *Inside Windows NT*. Redmond, WA: Microsoft Press, ISBN: 1-55615-481-X. Custer's description of the TDI-layer redirector is essential in understanding how the various kinds of NetWare connectivity fit into NT.

Microsoft Staff, *TechNet CDs*. Redmond, WA: Microsoft Product Support Services (PSS). TechNet is a monthly publication on CD-ROM containing a digest of topics from the Microsoft Knowledge Base, the *Net News* publication, Resource Kits and other information. This is the best place to find out about such new features as FPNW, and to benefit from the experience PSS has in supporting those features.

Various authors (1995), *Brainshare Presentation Books*. Provo UT: Novell Inc. Novell's annual Brainshare conference is comparable to Microsoft's TechEd. Brainshare presentations cover many aspects of the NetWare world—including NDS and the NetWare Client for Windows NT.

Other Connections

When you finish reading this chapter, you should have a better idea of where to go for further information on connecting Windows NT to other networks and vendor-specific platforms, including:

- ❏ **IBM LAN Server**
- ❏ **IBM SAA Networks**
- ❏ **DEC Pathworks**
- ❏ **Banyan VINES**
- ❏ **Advanced UNIX (X Windows and NFS) Networks**

Vendors are still struggling to deliver their connections to Windows NT as Microsoft adds and changes features nearly every six months. Although we were unable to fully test the products listed here, we present what information we were able to acquire about each. We *strongly* recommend that you contact the vendor directly for more information.

IBM LAN Server 3.0

Back when IBM and Microsoft were on civil terms, IBM licensed Microsoft's LAN Manager product, made a few changes, and sold the resulting product as the IBM LAN Server. Since then, the relationship between the two firms has become somewhat complex, but LAN Server networks still share a common core base with the SMB-based networking that's built into Windows NT and other Microsoft networking products. In fact, it's quite possible to use LAN Server

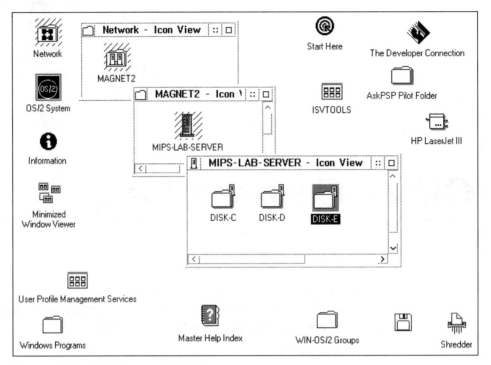

Figure 10.1 LAN Server (OS/2).

IBM LAN Server 3.0 for OS/2 provides a networking environment that's functionally equivalent to—and compatible with—Windows NT's built-in networking for file and printer sharing. Advanced management features of the two networks, however, are incompatible.

clients on Windows NT LANs (see Figure 10.1), and Windows NT clients on LAN Server networks.

Aside from the fact that it uses IBM's OS/2 2.1 as the base operating system instead of Windows NT, LAN Server is actually quite similar to NT (and other Microsoft networks) in operation.

Tuning LAN Server for Windows NT Interoperation

The most critical element in getting LAN Server and Windows NT networks to interoperate is protocol selection. As it happens, IBM's OS/2 NetBIOS protocol (the LAN Server default protocol) is functionally equivalent to NetBEUI (the Windows NT default protocol)—and since both systems use SMBs, they interoperate quite well at the resource-sharing level.

Beyond that level, however—especially when looking at the administration and management programs—LAN Server and Windows NT are quite different.

Windows NT workstations can operate in LAN Server environments as peers but cannot participate in LAN Server domain management; similarly, LAN Server systems can operate as members of Windows NT workgroups but not as members of Windows NT domains. The situation is similar to that described for Microsoft Windows for Workgroups in Chapter 8—LAN Server systems can function nicely as clients in the NT network, but cannot be effectively managed as servers, and vice versa.

LAN Server 3.0 is available from IBM Corporation. Call them at (800)342-6672 for more information.

IBM Systems Network Architecture (SNA) Environments

Although IBM mainframes and minicomputers have taken a beating lately as companies move applications to PC networks, there are still plenty of mainframes out there and they have lots of important data on them. High-end IBM systems use SNA to communicate with terminals and other computers, so there's a need for solutions to connect these SNA-based networks to NT.

Microsoft offers SNA Server for Windows NT as their solution to this problem. SNA Server installs on an NT system and provides a protocol gateway between the LAN and the SNA network (see Figure 10.2). It supports 3270/5250 terminal emulation, LU6.2 Advanced Peer-to-Peer connectivity, and LU0 protocols. It also supports IBM's NetView network management system. 3270/5250 terminal emulators are bundled with the product, although they offer only basic functionality; Microsoft expects third-party vendors to provide more extensive support.

Many vendors of terminal emulation and mainframe connectivity software have support for SNA Server for Windows NT and other vendors offer competing products as well. Contact and product names are listed in the following:

Company and Phone	*Product Name*	*Type*
Andrew Corp. *(800)328-2696* *(206)487-1065 fax*	5250 Elite for SNA Server	AS/400 terminal emulation
Attachmate *(800)426-6283* *(206)644-4010* *(206)747-9924 fax*	Extra! for Windows NT Automation Development Kit	3270 terminal emulation Mainframe application integration (HLLAPI)
Digital Communications Associates *(800)348-3211* *(404)442-4000* *(404)442-4366 fax*	IRMA Workstation	Terminal emulation

Company and Phone	Product Name	Type
Eicon Technology *(514)631-2592* *(514)631-3092 fax*	Access for Windows NT 3270 APPC Developer's Toolkit SNA Function Mgmt Developer's Toolkit	3270 terminal emulation SNA protocol stack
FutureSoft Engineering *(800)989-8908* *(713)496-1090 fax*	DynaComm/Elite for Windows NT	Terminal emulation and scripting
Intergraph *(800)345-4856* *(205)730-2700* *(205)730-2108 fax*	Graphics 3270 for Windows NT	3270 terminal emulation
McGill University Systems (514)398-3270 (514)398-6876 fax	TCP3270 for Windows NT	3270 terminal emulation through Windows Sockets
Microgate *(512)345-7791* *(512)343-9046 fax*	BSC3780 for Windows NT	3780 terminal emulation, BSC protocol
Microsoft *(800)426-9400* *(206)882-8080* *(206)936-7329 fax*	SNA Server for Windows NT	As described in text
Netsoft *(714)768-4013* *(714)768-5049 fax*	NS3270 for Windows NT	3270 terminal emulation
Network Software *Associates* *(714)768-4013* *(714)768-5049 fax*	Dynacomm/Elite NT; Elite/400 NT	Terminal emulation
Passport Communications *(512)328-9830* *(512)328-4773 fax*	Bisync 3780 for Windows NT	RJE 3780 emulation
Serengeti Systems *(800)634-3122* *(215)480-8729 fax*	3780Link	RJE 3780 emulation
ICL, TeamWARE Division *(408)982-9146* *(408)982-9946 fax*	TeamWARE HighWay for Windows NT	SNA server
Wall Data *(800)487-8622* *(206)883-4777* *(206)885-9250 fax*	RUMBA	Terminal emulation, mainframe application integration

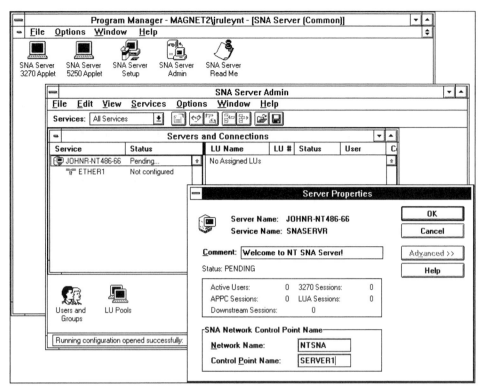

Figure 10.2 SNA Server (NT).

Microsoft SNA Server for Windows NT functions as a gateway between SNA networks and LANs. It's implemented as a Windows NT service, and takes full advantage of the Windows NT APIs to provide graphical administration, integrated security, and other advanced features. A large number of 3270 terminal emulator vendors have announced support for this product.

Digital Equipment Corp. (DEC) Pathworks

Like IBM's LAN Server, DEC's Pathworks is based on Microsoft's LAN Manager technology, which simplifies the problems of interoperability with Windows NT. Pathworks clients on any platform can access Windows NT Server systems, as well as Pathworks servers, based on the VMS, Ultrix, SCO UNIX, or OS/2 operating systems.

Pathworks for Windows NT is offered for Intel, MIPS, and DEC's own Alpha AxP processors, and interoperates with existing Pathworks clients (Windows 3.1, DOS, OS/2, and Macintosh).

One of the most significant interoperability items in Pathworks is the support for Digital's DECnet protocol at the network transport layer. This support can coexist with TCP/IP and NetBEUI protocols on the same server or workstation. DECnet events can be viewed through the standard Windows NT Event Viewer and Performance Monitor tools. Device drivers are provided for DEC's networking cards, including Digital's FDDI (Fiber Distributed Data Interface) EISA card.

In addition to support for NT's user- and administrator-level tools, there will be a Pathworks for Windows NT Developer Kit that provides API support for Pathworks Sockets and other DEC-specific networking protocols. The Windows NT APIs for WinSock, NetBIOS, and remote procedure calls are also supported when using DECnet as the network transport protocol.

The following vendors supply products intended for use in a Digital-oriented network environment:

Company and Phone	Product Name	Type
Attachmate (800)426-6283 (206)644-4010 (206)747-99243 fax	KEA! 340 for Windows NT	VT340 terminal emulation
	KEA! 420 for Windows NT	VT420 terminal emulation
Digital Equipment (508)635-8420 (508)635-8724 fax	PATHWORKS for Windows NT	Digital's network support
Digital Equipment (508)486-5735 (508)486-7417 fax	Digital DCE for Windows NT	OSF DCE software development kit
Meridian Software (714)727-0700 (714)727-3583 fax	Digital Network Printing Software for Windows NT	Client for Digital PrintServer
Meridian Technology (314)532-7708 (314)532-3242 fax	SuperLAT for Windows NT	DEC LAT protocol support
Persoft (800)368-5283 (608)273-6000 (608)273-8227 fax	SmarTerm for Windows, 32-Bit Edition	VT340 terminal emulation

Banyan VINES

The VINES (VIrtual NEtworking Software) network operating system from Banyan Systems has been a viable alternative to Novell and Microsoft networks, especially for large installations (see Figure 10.3). Its biggest strength is the StreetTalk network name service, which lets users use resources on the network without needing to know where the services are located.

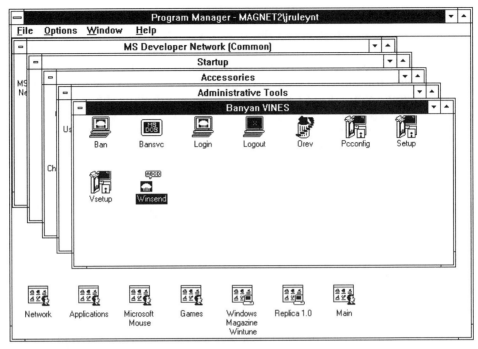

Figure 10.3 VINES (NT).

Banyan's VINES client for Windows NT is implemented as a Windows NT service and a set of Windows-based utility programs. The VINES client employs VINES/IP as the transport, and currently requires a separate login from the Windows NT security system. Banyan has announced plans for a more integrated version at a later date.

VINES server software is based on a version of AT&T UNIX, modified and supplemented by Banyan to provide a wide selection of network services. VINES can run on symmetric multiprocessor (SMP) systems with up to eight processors. Banyan sells VINES either preinstalled as part of a hardware/software bundle or as a software-only product.

Because VINES uses the standard Microsoft NDIS network driver model, it can coexist with NT's standard networking and use the same network card. VINES NT support includes the VINES IP transport protocol that is most commonly used by Banyan's networks. Most NT network operations are supported through VINES IP, including client/server applications, such as Microsoft's SQL Server.

The Banyan VINES Toolkit provides 32-bit versions of the VINES APIs. Existing Win-16 or DOS applications that use VINES APIs are also supported. The WinSock API is supported if you use Microsoft's TCP/IP transport on NT systems and then install FTP Software's PC/TCP on DOS or Windows systems that are running VINES. Although similar, the Microsoft TCP/IP and Banyan VINES IP protocols are not interoperable.

At the user and application level, Banyan takes advantage of Windows NT's Network Provider APIs to integrate VINES networking smoothly into the environment. For example, VINES StreetTalk names show up in the browse list when you connect a network drive, along with the system and share names from NT's built-in networking. However, the first version of VINES support will not support common login, so you will need to log in first to the NT system, then to the VINES network.

For more information, call Banyan at (800)222-6926 or (508)898-1000.

UNIX Connections (NFS, TCP/IP, X Windows)

Although Windows NT supports the TCP/IP protocol and offers a simple set of TCP tools (see Chapter 6 for more information), its UNIX connections could be better. Third-party companies long established in this field offer an expanded set of utilities that include Simple Mail Transfer Protocol (SMTP), NFS client software, and X Window server software:

Company and Phone	Product Name	Type
AGE Logic *(619)455-8600* *(619)597-6030 fax*	XoftWare /32 for Windows NT	X server
Beame & Whiteside *(416)765-0822*	BW-Connect NFS for Windows NT BW-Services	NFS client and TCP/IP software TCP/IP utilities
Consensys *(905)940-2900* *(905)940-2903 fax*	Portage Sockets Portage TTY	WinSock interface UNIX-style multiuser terminal interface
Dart Communications *(315)841-8106* *(315)841-8107 fax*	PowerTCP SDK Tools for Windows NT	C/C++ libraries
Digital Equipment *(800)344-4825* *(506)486-2311 fax*	eXcursion for Windows NT	X server
Distinct *(408)366-8933* *(408)366-0153 fax*	Distinct TCP/IP Tools/NFS	TCP/IP and NFS software
Frontier Technologies *(414)241-4555 x217* *(414)241-7084 fax*	Super-TCP for Windows NT	TCP/IP and NFS software

Company and Phone	Product Name	Type
Hummingbird Communications (905)470-1203 (905)470-1207 fax	eXceed/NT	X server
Intergraph (800)345-4856 (205)730-2700 (205)730-2108 fax	DiskShare-NFS for Windows NT PC-NFS Client for Windows NT	NFS server NFS client
NetManage (408)973-7171 (408)257-6405 fax	Chameleon32/NFS	NFS and TCP/IP utilities
Process Software (800)722-7770 (508)879-0042 fax	NFSware for Windows NT	NFS server
SunSelect (508)442-0000	Sun PC-NFS for NT	NFS client

LANtastic

Artisoft's LANtastic software and network protocols are not compatible with Windows NT's built-in networking, and the company has not (yet) announced any intent to support NT. However, the LANtastic EtherNet boards are supported by NT, since they are compatible with Novell's NE2000 board. If you are willing to abandon LANtastic, you can get a network running by installing Windows NT on your high-end systems, and Windows for Workgroups on the less capable ones. DOS workstations can use Microsoft's Workgroup Connection software, but cannot act as servers (i.e., share resources) on the network.

There may be an alternative by the time we go to press—we've recently been told that Artisoft is looking into providing some sort of LANtastic-to-Windows NT Bridging capability. No such capability has been shown, but we urge anyone who has a substantial investment in LANtastic to call Artisoft at (800)846-9726 and ask.

CHAPTER

Client/Server, Distributed Computing, and the Future of Windows NT

In this chapter, you will learn:

❑ **What characterizes client/server computing**

❑ **How Windows NT compares with other client/server platforms**

❑ **Why Windows NT is well suited for use in a client/server environment**

❑ **Why and how Microsoft plans to migrate Windows NT to a distributed computing model in the *Cairo* project**

Along the way, we'll provide examples of client/server applications for Windows NT from several different client/server categories.

Paradigm Shifts and the Rise of Client/Server Computing

It's often said that we're now in the *Fourth Generation* of computing.[1] While deciding just what constitutes a *generation* in data processing terms is difficult,

---

1. Thus 4GL for *Fourth Generation Language* when referring to client/server development tools.

483

it's certainly true that we're now into the fourth major paradigm for using computer resources. These paradigms have (so far) been as follows:

Batch Processing—The model for most computer use until the mid-1970s was that of the authors' experience—queues of users waiting in line to submit *jobs*—programs and data for the computer to run (typically, a punched card deck) for execution on the computer.[2] This model was a reflection of the sheer cost of computing—typical systems, such as IBM's 360/370 or Control Data's Cyber-700, cost upward of $1 million, required dedicated support staffs numbering in the dozens, and represented a major cost center at any organization. The only way such systems could be afforded by most corporations was to have many people use the computer during the course of a single day.

Host-Centric Remote Processing—Batch processing's major problem was that it required all users (or their assistants) to physically bring their jobs to the computer. In the mid-1960s, IBM developed a way around this called Remote Job Entry (RJE), which basically allowed an organization to have several card readers for batch processing in several locations—which at least made for shorter lines! However, as the cost of electronics dropped, a more sophisticated idea developed, called *time sharing*. In this approach, many users could share a computer that would execute each user's job in a round-robin manner. Unlike the batch (or RJE) approach, however, instead of running each job to completion, a certain amount of time would be spent on your job—then it would be *suspended* while the computer worked on someone else's.

Since the computers were far faster than the terminal users (who initially communicated through teletypewriters at a speedy 11 characters per second), many people could use a single computer *at the same time*. This model persisted for years (it still exists today in many UNIX environments), but the constantly falling cost of electronics caused the teletypewriter to speed up and evolve into a video display terminal (VDT) that could operate at much higher speeds. As more electronics became available inside the VDT, another paradigm shift occurred.

Shared Resource Servers—Eventually, several companies—notably IBM and Hewlett-Packard—added fairly sophisticated logic to their VDTs, making them into *smart terminals*; but it took someone outside the world of mainframe computing to envision the ultimate end result of this combination: Adding microprocessor-controlled logic *and* substantial local storage to the VDT made it into a completely separate unit—the *personal computer*, or PC. Initially, PCs were mainly used on a stand-alone basis, but the need to share expensive resources, such as hard disk drives and printers—not to

---

2. Well, *some* of us actually are that old!

mention sharing data—led to the idea of *resource sharing*. In this model, expensive resources are centralized on a *server*, and those resources are accessed by desktop computers (PCs) connected back to the servers over some sort of network hardware. This is the model that today is typified by Novell NetWare.

Client Server Computing-The Fourth Generation—Inevitably, the rise of shared-resource servers provoked a reaction from the makers of classical host (i.e., mainframe) systems. The first to react was IBM, which arrived at an idea called *Connectivity* (note that capital *C*). Connectivity, in IBM-speak, meant that the PC was to be treated as the terminal that would normally be connected to the host. Since IBM was, by this time, using quite sophisticated page-oriented VDTs in its host-centric systems, it wasn't all that much of a stretch to view the attached PC as a *client*, which would interact with a host-based *server* to accomplish the computing task at hand. The resulting *client/server* paradigm has gradually displaced the others as the mechanism of choice for high-value (especially *mission-critical*) computing tasks.

Why Is Client/Server Computing Important?

You may well ask why the client/server model has become so pervasive in high-end systems. The reason, in brief, is that it exploits the power available at *both* the client(s) *and* the server—and it does so *while keeping network traffic to a minimum.*

An example may make this clear: Let's consider a typical line-of-business application, say, travel agents querying an airline database for flight availability. If this application is host-based, then every keystroke issued at every agent's terminal must be transferred over the network and handled by the host.[3] The host then must react—even if the keystroke(s) it receives are incorrect (or simply irrelevant). Even if every user of such a system *always* enters data without introducing errors (a virtual impossibility), as the usage of the system rises, the amount of network traffic rises—until, at some point, the network (which is usually the slowest component in the system) saturates. At this point the *queuing effect* comes into play (see Appendix 6), with results familiar to everyone who has ever worked on such a system—response slows down (with the side effect that impatient users make more errors, that have to be processed and slow the system down still further).

Now consider the very same application implemented using client/server principles. Instead of a VDT, the agent has a personal computer that runs an

---

3. Eventually, some designers decided to offload the host by putting sufficient electronics to handle one full screen (or *page*) of information at a time *without* host interaction; giving us *page-oriented terminals* (sometimes called *smart terminals*), of which IBM's 3270 is the prime example.

appropriately designed client/server *front-end* application. The user never accesses the host computer directly—instead, the query on the host database is developed in an interaction between the agent and the front-end application, and only when this interaction is complete does the front end interact with the host. Network traffic is minimized, because *only* the bare minimum information needed to fulfill the query gets passed over the network (indeed, more sophisticated front-end applications have their own local data store, and fulfill some of the requests from that rather than passing all queries through to the host).

Types of Client/Server Computing

For historical reasons, the client/server model has been applied in three widely disparate environments. Windows NT can play in all of them (of course), but its unique features are fully exploited by only one, as we will see.

IBM SNA

Not surprisingly, as the company with the most to lose from the rise of microcomputers, it was IBM that invented a way to link them to larger systems. IBM's approach, part of their *Systems Network Architecture* (SNA) specification, basically replaced the page-oriented IBM 3270 or 5150 terminals used with mainframe-based applications with a PC. Initially, the PC just replaced the terminal (running appropriate emulation software), with little advantage gained; but the availability of computing power on the desktop gradually came to be used as a way to offload processing that didn't *have* to be done in the mainframe. This process of migrating computation to the desktop was eventually formalized in the *Advanced Program-to-Program Communications* (APPC) specification of SAA in 1984, and is still in use today.

The APPC networking approach basically amounts to using the old IBM 3270 page-oriented terminal protocol as a mechanism to transfer data between client and server. A front-end application, which may look totally unlike a 3270 terminal screen (in fact, it will often provide a Windows interface nowadays) will nonetheless send 3270 keystrokes to the host computer, which responds by sending information to the front-end application as if it were a 3270: one screen at a time. Windows NT brings to this environment all the features that make it a good platform for mission-critical applications, but there's little to differentiate it from other advanced operating systems for this sort of use—and in any case, the days of SNA/APPC networking are probably numbered.

Windows NT doesn't support SNA networks directly, but it's significant that one of the first applications Microsoft announced for Windows NT was SNA Server—and that it arrived with substantial third-party support from terminal emulation vendors. SNA Server for Windows NT is covered (briefly) in Chapter

Table 11.1 Windows NT Applications for SNA Environments

Product	*Company*	*Address*	*Phone*	*Comments*
APPC Developers Toolkit and SNA Function Mgt. Developers Kits for Windows NT	Eicon Technology	2196 - 32nd Avenue (Lachine) Montreal, Quebec H8T 3H7 Canada	514-631-2592	Advanced Peer-to-Peer Communications, via LU 0,1,2,3,6.2; C-language interface to SNA
Database Gateway for Windows NT	ShowCase	4131 Highway 52 North, Suite G111 Rochester, MN 55901	800-829-3555	Gateway environment coupling AS/400 to MS SQL Server
Matrix for Windows NT	Ampersand	331 West Arden Street, Suite 101 Glendale, CA 91203	818-548-9100	CICS transaction monitor, designed for OLTP; source-compatible with CICS COBOL apps
MOZART Composer	Mozart Systems	1350 Bayshore Highway, Suite 630 Burlingame, CA 94010	415-340-1588	IBM 3270/5250-compatible application extension tools
TranScend 400 for SNA Server	Andrew	10500 West 153rd Orland Park, IL 60462	206-487-1065	Windows NT-to-AS/400 file transfer; provides File Manager interface. Comaptible with SDLC, Twinpax, LANs; Twinpax, Token-Ring, EtherNet, and SDLC connections

10 of this book. Other products designed to leverage NT in an SNA environment are listed in Table 11.1.[4]

X Windows

Yet another approach to distributing computer power is provided by the X Windows system that's become popular in UNIX networks. X Windows was originally developed by the Massachusetts Institute of Technology, and is now controlled by the X/Consortium sponsored by MIT. The X.11 standard defines

---

4. *Note*: Tables in this (and other) chapters are based on Microsoft's *Win 32 Application Guide* and *NT Workstation Evaluation Guide* (both available from *ftp.microsoft.com*), along with other published sources. They are as up-to-date as possible as of this writing (May, 1995), but new applications for NT appear daily. We recommend that readers consult these sources and our own electronic update for up-to-date product information.

X Windows interfaces, which provide a client/server graphics interface for host-based applications (known as X/Clients). An X/Client is written using the X.11 APIs and protocols, and communicates through those protocols to X/Server software in the workstation computers. The workstations respond, in turn, by taking the action requested by the X/Server—drawing on the screen, in most cases. This is a powerful concept—it's as if you could execute a Windows application on someone else's computer, yet have the application draw on your screen and respond to your keyboard and mouse (more to the point, since one X/Client can access many X/Servers, X Windows provides unique *multiuser* capabilities for graphics software).

Much like IBM's SNA/APPC approach, while X Windows has its place, that place is primarily on the desktop—it's designed to maximize the effectiveness of host-based programs by making the workstations do all the work of drawing their own screen displays. Again, Windows NT is well suited to this kind of application in the general way that it's well suited to any high-end desktop use, but there's nothing special about it as a platform for X/Servers. While no X/Server is shipped in the Windows NT box, several are available from third parties—and we cover a representative selection in Chapter 10.

Aside from X/Server software that—in effect—turns Windows NT into an expensive X/Terminal, there are several products that offer a capability to access NT from a low-end client, as listed in Table 11.2.

Client/Server Databases

The preceding two sections could make one wonder what, if anything, justifies Microsoft's advertising of Windows NT as the operating system for client/server computing. Is it all just hype?

No!

You'll remember that IBM actually started the client/server movement by employing PCs to replace page-oriented terminals in such applications as order-entry. At about the same time, a number of companies began looking at applying minicomputer technology on the other end of that connection—the host computer.

Minicomputers of the late 1970s and early 1980s approached mainframe hosts in both processing power and storage capacity. In effect, you could replace a mainframe host with a minicomputer directly (as many people did, especially using DEC's VAX series of minis). This made it possible for big corporations to *downsize*, putting applications that heretofore ran on mainframes onto minis—and *most* of these applications involved databases.

Think about virtually *any* major line-of-business application—insurance claim processing, payroll, accounts receivable, airline reservations, you name it—and a major part of the job is maintaining (and manipulating) a database. For reasons that we will get to shortly, most of these databases are described as

Table 11.2 X Windows-like Environments for Windows NT

Product	*Company*	*Address*	*Phone*	*Comments*
WinDD	Tektronix	2660 S.W. Parkway P.O. Box 1000 Wilsonville, OR 97070-1000	503-685-2500	Provides access to Windows NT from X/Terminals.
ClientCenter for Windows NT (preliminary name at press time)	SunRiver Data Systems	Echelon IV, Suite 200 9430 Research Blvd Austin, TX 78759-6543	512-346-2447	Provides access to Windows NT from low-cost *Pizza Box* clients using standard PC keyboard, mouse, and monitor.
WinView	Citrix Systems	210 University Dr. Suite 700, Coral Springs, FL 33071	305-755-0559	Provides access to Windows NT from low-end (286 or better) PCs.

(more or less) *relational*, and virtually all use some form of *structured query language* (SQL) as the mechanism to get data in and out (don't worry too much about the precise meaning of those buzzwords just yet—we'll get to that); so virtually all downsizing involves moving SQL databases from mainframes to minis—or at least it *used* to.

Some years ago, Novell got the idea of putting a database on its NetWare servers. That database was Btrieve, and it was neither relational nor SQL—but it grew into an SQL NetWare Loadable Module (NLM). At around the same time, several companies—a major one being Sybase systems–started moving mini-computer SQL onto PCs (386s and 486s turned out to be plenty powerful to run the same UNIX operating system that runs on most minis), and this turned the downsizing movement into a virtual avalanche.

You see, the same money that'll buy one mainframe—or ten minis—will buy *a whole lot of PCs.*

While all this was going on in *back room* data center operations (and making life sheer hell for MIS departments, minicomputer makers—and eventually even for IBM), another revolution was taking place on computer desktops, where Apple's Macintosh, Microsoft's Windows, and (to a lesser extent) IBM's OS/2 got users to expect a graphical interface to their applications, and forced them to buy really powerful systems in order to run the graphics.

Hey! Isn't a powerful desktop system *exactly* what you need for client/server? Why fiddle around with 3270 emulators or X Windows? *Why not write a Windows- (or Mac- or OS/2-) based front-end application that sends SQL commands— and has enough intelligence built in to format the database queries itself?*

Good idea—and a dozen or so companies have overturned most of the information systems doing exactly that. Now let's take a look at where Windows NT fits into all this.

Client/Server Databases and SQL

First off, we'd better explain what Structured Query Language (SQL) is and why it's important. SQL was invented—like so much else in the computer industry—by IBM as a *lingua franca* for *relational databases*. Without going too deep into the theory involved, relational databases basically seek to protect us from ourselves.[5] Nonrelational databases are usually organized as some form of sequential list—an approach that works well until the list becomes very large or very complicated (sometimes, parts of the list are *pointers* to other lists, which makes things get complicated in a hurry). Relational databases are organized in such a way that you can always be *certain* that a properly formatted query will have an answer—it may be a ridiculously huge answer but there will be one.

SQL is the mechanism that assures the queries are properly formatted—it's a special language for data access that makes it *impossible* to issue an illegal query.[6] Moreover, by convention, modern SQL implementations include transaction-locking mechanisms that assure database integrity even if a query fails—the query isn't *committed* until all aspects of the transaction are complete.

But enough of the details. The point you need to understand is that *most* serious, large-scale databases for business use are relational, and *all* use some form of SQL. A wide range of such databases are available for Windows NT, which are listed in Table 11.3.

Client/Server Development Tools

The client/server database products in Table 11.3 are, for the most part, simply *database engines*—they provide the underlying foundation on which an application may be built, but do not constitute by themselves a useful business application. To create such an application, it's necessary to couple the database engine to a *client application*, which is typically developed to meet the special needs of a particular business.

The range of tools available for such development is immense and growing. It's not possible to provide a complete list, but Table 11.4 gives a representative selection of the products available—with special attention given to those that support Windows NT with a native, 32-bit, implementation.

---

5. If you must know, it's set theory. There—aren't you glad you asked? See *SQL Self-Teaching Guide* by Stephenson and Hartwig (in "For More Information" at the end of this chapter) for a somewhat lengthier explanation.

6. Well—almost impossible; the ability of people to screw up knows few absolute limits!

Table 11.3 Windows NT Database Software

Product	*Company*	*Address*	*Phone*	*Comments*
ACCELER8	Amalgamated Software of North America	611 Spruce Road PO Box 1668 Big Bear Lake, CA 92315	800-321-2762	AS/400-compatible ISAM database for Windows NT
ADABAS/c Server	Software AG	11190 Sunrise Valley Drive Reston, VA 22091	800-423-2227	Multiplatform DBMS; NIST validated (on MVS and UNIX)
CereBase	MicroQuill Software	4900 25th Avenue NE, Suite 206 Seattle, WA 98105	206-525-8218	Extensible database engine
INFORMIX-SE	Informix Software	4100 Bohannon Drive Menlo Park, CA 94025	800-331-1763 415-926-6300	Fully relational database server; does not require a database administrator
INGRES Intelligent Database 6.4	Computer Associates (ASK/Ingres)	Two Executive Drive Fort Lee, NJ 07024	510-748-2642	RDBMS with intelligent query optimizerm, rule system, resouce controls
Object Store 3.0 for Windows NT	Object Design	25 Mall Road, Burlington, MA 01803	617-674-5000	Object Database Management System
Objectivity/DB	Objectivity	3018 East Evelyn Avenue Mountain View, CA 94041	415-254-7100	Multiplatform object database. Supports application development in C++, Smalltalk, SQL; provides ODBC interface
Oracle Workgroup Server for Windows NT	Oracle	500 Oracle Pkwy Redwood Shores, CA 94065	800-ORACLE-1 415-506-7000	Preconfigured workgroup database with network client; ODBC client, Help-based online documentation
SQL Server 1.0 for Windows NT	Sybase	6475 Christie Ave. Emeryville, CA 94608	800-879-2273	High-performance RDBMS suited to mission-critical OLTP
SQL Server 6.0 for Windows NT	Microsoft	One Microsoft Way Redmond, WA 98052	800-426-9400 206-882-8080	High-performance multithreaded NT-native RDBMS with replication, e-mail integration, and advanced administration

(continues)

Table 11.3 (*Continued*)

Product	Company	Address	Phone	Comments
SQL XB Server	Quadbase Systems	2855 Kifer Road, Suite 203 Santa Clara, CA 95051	408-982-0835	Scalable client/server DBMS
SQLBase Server for Windows NT	Gupta	1060 Marsh Road Menlo Park, CA 94025	800-444-8782	PC-based client/server database
Supra Server for Windows NT	Cincom Systems	2300 Montana Avenue Cincinnati, OH 45211-3899	513-662-2300	High-performance multiplatform SQL database.

Table 11.4 Windows NT C/S Development Tools

Product	Company	Address	Phone	Comments
CA-Realizer	Computer Associates International	Two Executive Drive Fort Lee, NJ 07024	201-592-0009	32-bit BASIC language for Windows NT
CASE:W VIP for Windows NT	CaseWare	108 Pacifica 2nd Floor Irvine, CA 92718-3332	714-453-2200	Design tool and C/C++ code generator based on CASEWORKS technology; supports DDE, OLE
Distributed Computing Environment for Windows NT	Digital Equipment	110 Spit Brook Road Nashua, NH 03062-2692	508-486-5735	Multiplatform RPC per OSF/DCE specification; provides foundation for COM/Objectbroker
EasyCASE	Evergreen CASE Tools	8522 154th Avenue NE Redmond, WA 98052	206-881-5149	CASE tool with schema generation, chart editing, entity views; reverse engineers Xbase databases; compatible with most database engines
Ellipse System	Bachman-Cooperative Solutions	2125 Hamilton Ave. Suite 100 San Jose, CA 95125	408-377-0300	Misson-critical development environment and production system with integrated versioning

Table 11.4 (*Continued*)

Product	Company	Address	Phone	Comments
herCules	APIS Software	Bolongarostr. AA3, D-65929 Frankfurt, GmbH, Germany	(international) 49-0-69-30-3906	Portable (shrouded source code), secure (cypher data/password) database with C++ interface, report generator
Ideo	Sapiens (United States)	4001 Weston Parkway P.O. Box 4349 Cary, NC 27513	800-392-7028	SQL-based object-oriented 4GL development environment
Informix ESQL/C	Informix Software	4100 Bohannon Drive Menlo Park, CA 94025	800-331-1763 415-926-6300	Embedded SQL for C language programmers
NATURAL	Software AG	11190 Sunrise Valley Drive Reston, VA 22091	800-423-2227	Multiplatform interactive 4GL with transparent LAN access
NEXPERT OBJECT	Neuron Data	156 University Avenue Palo Alto, CA 94301	800-876-4900 415-321-4488	Multiplatform rule-based, object-oriented development tool
PACBASE	CGI Systems	1180 West Swedesford Road, Suite 350 Berwyn, PA 19312	800-FONE-CGI	Integrated multiplatform CASE tool
PowerBuilder	PowerSoft	561 Virginia Road Concord, MA 01742	800-395-3525	Object-oriented 16- and 32-bit development environment
RhaPC-d RPC development toolkit	Intergraph	1 Madison Industrial Park Huntsville, AL 35894-0001	800-345-4856	*Rhapsody* network-independant cross-platform (NT, UNIX) socket-level C/S tools
SAS System for Windows NT	SAS Institute	100 SAS Campus Dr. Cary, NC 27512-8000	919-677-8000 x7000	Multiplatform, client/server application development and access environment
SQL Database Server	Faircom	4006 West Broadway Columbia, MO 65203	800-234-8180	Portable ISAM/SQL database server
Tivoli/ADE	Tivoli Systems	9442 Capitol of Texas Highway North Arboretum Place North Austin, TX 78759	512-794-9070	Platform-independent distributed application development

(continues)

Table 11.4 (*Continued*)

Product	Company	Address	Phone	Comments
Trusted Network Technology	Blue Ridge Software	Box 406 112 W. Washington Monticello, IL 61856-0406	217-762-2375	Tools for creating a Trusted Computer Security B1-level computer network. Features include DES encrytion of all data on the trusted LAN, centralized security management, and auditing
UNIFACE Six	Uniface	1320 Harbor Bay Parkway, Suite 100 Alameda, CA 94501-6556	800-365-3608	Model-driven enterprise C/S development with graphical *forms painter*
Visual Basic, Office Development Kit	Microsoft	One Microsoft Way Redmond, WA 98052	800-426-9400 206-882-8080	BASIC-language visual development environment, OLE-based development kit for exploitation of MS-Office applications
Visual SQL	Blue Sky Software	7486 La Jolla Blvd., Suite 3 La Jolla, CA 92037	800-677-4WIN	C-lanuage code generator that supports any SQL database with an ODBC driver
VisualWorks	ParcPlace Systems	999 East Argus Avenue Sunnyvale, CA 94086-4593	408-773-7438	SmallTalk-based GUI builder with Visual Sub-classing, database access
XoftHost	AGE Logic	9985 Pacific Heights Boulevard San Diego, CA 92121	619-455-8600	OSF/Motif and X Windows development libraries for porting apps to NT

Other Client/Server Applications

Aside from the general-purpose categories mentioned earlier, there are many line-of-business and special-purpose applications that exploit the client/server model to fill a business need. While detailed coverage of these products is far beyond this chapter's scope, Table 11.5 should serve to give some idea of the breadth of applications available.[7]

---

7. For more information, acquire Microsoft's *Windows NT Workstation Evaluation Guide* and *32-bit Applications Catalog*. Both are available from Microsoft's anonymous file transfer site (ftp.microsoft.com).

Table 11.5 Windows NT Client/Server Vertical/Special-Purpose/LOB Applications

Product	Company	Address	Phone	Comments
(Various Products)	Intergraph	1 Madison Industrial Park Huntsville, AL 35984-0001	800-345-4856 205-730-2000	High-end database- enabled CAD with vertical applications for use in architecture, engineering, mapping/GIS, electronic design and other applications
Argent Performance Sort (APS)	Argent Software	49 Main Street Torrington, CT 06790	203-489-5553	Mainframe-class high-performance batch sort for Windows NT; up to eight keys, various record formats, SMP support
AutoCAD for Windows NT	Autodesk	2320 Marinship Way Sausalito, CA 94965	800-964-6432	General-purpose design, drafting, and modelling software used in many applications
CaseWarder	Finally	4701 Kelly CoveGlen Allen, VA 23060	804- 222-6623	Legal case management, including automatic plan of response
CIM/21	Industrial Systems	19204 N. Creek Pkwy Suite 104 Bothell, WA 98011	206-481-6325	Industrial Process Control; supports NetDDE, OLE, and ODBC
Claim Analyzer I	CMA	1341 Ocean Ave. Suite 531 Santa Monica, CA 90401	310-393-2727	Claims and asset research automation
Dynamics	Great Plains Software	1701 Southwest 38th St. Fargo, ND 58103	701-281-9941	LAN-based graphical accounting and business management
EagleEye	EagleSoft	810 Third Avenue Suite 208 Seattle, WA 98104	206-682-4830	Real-time warehouse management application; works with bar code scanners; supports EDI
FIX MMI/FIX DMACS	Intellution	One Edgewater Drive Norwood, MA 02062	617-769-8878	Distributed client/server manufacturing process control software; supports SQL, ODBC
FloSystem	Edinburgh Petroleum Services	Research Park Riccarton Edinburgh, Scotland EH14 4AP	(UK) 0314494536	Production optimization and modelling for oil-field management

(continues)

Table 11.5   (Continued)

Product	Company	Address	Phone	Comments
Inventory Management/ Payroll Accounting Vision / 32	Intellisoft	2114 West Mayfield Road Arlington, TX 76015	800-933-4889 817-467-7243	Warehouse inventory management and automatic payroll processing
MECHANICA for Windows NT	Rasna	2590 N. First St. Suite 200 San Jose, CA 95131	800-937-4432	Software tools for mechanical design
OmniVox NT	APEX Voice Communi- cations	15250 Ventura Blvd. 3rd Floor Sherman Oaks, CA 91403	818-379-8400	Software/hardware combination for voicemail and FAX applications
PV-WAVE	Visual Numerics	9990 Richmond Ave. Suite 400 Houston, TX 77042-4548	303-530-9000	Data visualizaton software; supports 2D, 3D, and 4D viewing; used in applications ranging from database analysis to scientific research
R/3	SAP America	300 Stevens Dr. Intl. Ct. Three Philadelphia, PA 19113	601-521-4500 800-USA-ISAP	Very high-end modular business application aimed at Fortune-1000 companies
SQUIRREL Restaurant Management System	Squirrel Companies	1586 Rand Avenue Vancouver, BC V6P 3G2 Canada	604-266-1336	Touchscreen-based point-of-sale system for restaurant and bar market
Stratford Healthcare Management	Stratford Healthcare Systems	840 Mitten Road Burlingame, CA	415-692-7970	Medical/Dental account management with electronic claims processing

The Future of Windows NT

While the Windows NT core was developed by Dave Cutler and a mixed team of ex-Digital employees, ex-OS/2 developers, and other malcontents—a longer-range plan to exploit NT as a base for advanced capabilities has been under way, led by Microsoft Business Systems' Vice President Jim Allchin (formerly of Banyan systems). The code name for this advanced development work is *Cairo*. Currently, little infomation about Cairo has been made public—but it's possible to piece together some hints about it from public statements by Microsoft officials. At the same time, a contrary view has begun to emerge that sees NT as a more conventional server platform.

What follows is some speculation—hopefully, *informed* speculation—about how NT's future might pan out.

NT: Windows Beyond the Desktop

NT's future may not depend on the Cairo project at all. Clearly, Windows NT is more than a graphical Windows shell. Indeed, it's a full-blown operating system that can exploit systems far more powerful than ordinary desktop PCs.

Today's desktop PC remains as it began—a single-user computer used for personal productivity. That, despite the fact that a 120 MHz Pentium system has *several orders of magnitude higher performance than a first-generation PC!* Consider the following comparison:

Feature	*IBM PC-XT (1983)*	*High-End PC (1995)*	*Ratio*
RAM	640KB	16MB	Over 20:1
Hard Disk	10MB	1GB	100:1
CPU Speed	4 MHz	120 MHz	30:1
Video Memory	32KB (640x200, 1 bpp)	7MB (1024x768, 8 bpp)	Over 200:1

Clearly, such machines are capable of undertaking tasks *well beyond* those of earlier PCs—yet most common PC tasks today are essentially the same as they were in 1983: word processing, database management, spreadsheets, and communications.

Are there fundamentally new and different applications to which the power of today's PC may be applied, or are we just modernizing the look and feel of yesterdays software?

Workstations

When Microsoft changed the name of NT's entry-level version to include the term *Workstation*, many observers assumed this was a bit of marketing fluff designed to obscure the evident overlap between the low end of the NT marketplace and the high end of the Windows 3.x (and later, Windows 95) market. This was partly true, but it also represented a real effort by Microsoft to make NT viable as a platform for the applications traditionally run on UNIX workstations in (among other things) engineering environments.

Engineering workstations are mainly used on a desktop by one person for applications beyond personal productivity. In UNIX environments, it's not uncommon to see two machines on each engineer's desk—a workstation on which design applications are run, and a separate PC used to write reports. Intergraph Corporation (which produced the first commercially available RISC workstations in 1984, based on a proprietary UNIX derivitive and custom RISC hardware), among others, has exploited this opportunity by introducing true NT-based workstations for their high-end CAD applications. NT offers several advantages in such environments: support for *legacy* DOS, Windows, and (with the addition of suitable X/Terminal software) X-based applications; reasonably high performance (Intergraph does not currently use RISC processors in their NT-based systems, preferring an SMP approach using standard Intel hardware), a familiar Windows look and feel—and of course, NT's inherent security and reliability.

Intergraph's workstations are sold as high-end computer-aided design (CAD) platforms for use in architecture; highway design; naval architecture; mapping/GIS; civil structural and design engineering; plant design; map design; cartography; photogrammetry and map publishing; electronic design automation (EDA); integrated data publishing (catalogs, documentation, etc.); and utilities management, among other fields. Intergraph's customers include the governments of Hong Kong (Hong Kong airport desgin), Kuwait (they supplied the Defense Mapping Agency with detailed maps for Operation Desert Storm), 40 of the 50 state highway departments, the US Navy, Bechtel, several retail chains, numerous architects, many telephone and electric companies—and many others.

In 1992, Intergraph CEO Jim Meadlock decided to back NT as a platform, initially planning to support it on a RISC CPU, but eventually switching to Intel's Pentium, which Intergraph uses in single- dual- and quad-processor configurations. Their new hardware and applications began shipping in 1993, and by the end of 1994, the entire product line (some 400 applications—more than are available for NT from any other vendor, including Microsoft) were running on NT.

Intergraph's success in moving their UNIX customer base to NT Workstation (they report many customers' only complaint about NT is that Intergraph isn't moving to it fast enough!) speaks volumes about its viability as a technical workstaton platform.

NT has also gained a foothold in the video postproduction *ghetto* outside Los Angeles; and in specialized software, formerly found on platforms ranging from Commodore's late, lamented Amiga to Silicon Graphics range of proprietary UNIX workstations, is now appearing on NT. One example is Elastic Reality, the makers of image-editing software used in many movies, including *Jurassic Park*, *Forrest Gump*, *Babylon 5*, and *SeaQuest DSV*, among others.[8] This is full-blown, professional-grade image editing—not a *toy* morph application—

8. 925 Stewart St, Madison, WI 53713. Tel: 608-273-6585.

and it's available on all NT platforms. If you need to create a Hollywood monster, NT is now a perfectly viable alternative to UNIX.

Servers

Local area network (LAN) file and print servers have traditionally been viewed as merely PCs with oversized hard disks. The move to *enterprise networking* is causing this view to change—much to NT's benefit. Traditional server operating systems, such as Novell's 3.*x*, treat each server as a separate administrative unit—a nightmare when a corporate network grows to include, perhaps, *dozens* of LANs and *hundreds* of servers. Advanced operating systems, such as NT Server (and Novell's NetWare 4.x), provide domain-wide management, in which groups of servers are administered as a single unit—and any given user requires just one account for the entire domain.

We've spent all of Chapter 7 and much of Chapter 6 detailing how NT works in an enterprise environment. Suffice it to say here that while NT isn't perfect, it clearly is competitive with other imperfect solutions, such as UNIX.

Mainframes

In certain applications—especially database services—NT-based systems are beginning to compete with and replace mainframe computers. Sequent Computer Systems' WinServer line—computers with up to six Pentium processors running in parallel—can compete with (and in some cases *beat*) mainframe computers in database performance.[9] They're ideally suited for use in such applications as decision support (DSS) and online transaction processing (OLTP). This is leading some surprising customers to the NT camp—among them, Australian Commonwealth Bank, National Westminster Bank, CompuServe, Citicorp, and the Irish Post Office.

This movement is not going to stop with six-Pentium systems. Sequent's next generation of NT-based servers will use larger per-CPU cache memory, and faster processors—including Intel's next-generation P6—in exotic Distributed Symmetric MultiProcessing (DSMP) designs, to deliver performance measured in *tens of thousands of transactions per second*. Sequent believes such systems will be necessary to handle global electronic commerce (OLTP over the Internet) in the next century.

Candidly, NT isn't ready for use in such applications today. The problems mentioned in Chapter 7, including the lack of chargeback accounting features, disk (and other subsystem) quotas, cluster support, and so on, make NT less than a perfect mainframe platform—yet, NT has been on the market for just two years at this writing. One wonders how these limitations will fare as NT matures.

---

9. 15450 S.W. Koll Pkwy, Beaverton, OR 97006-6063. Tel: 503-626-5700.

RISC Desktops and Personal Mainframes

Moving further from today's off-the-shelf technology, we begin to encounter more exotic possibilities. One that's often predicted is the RISC-PC: using the CPU architecture of a UNIX engineering workstation on the desktop. It's an attractive idea—so attractive that three generations of vendors have attempted it to date: MIPS Technologies (and partners) Advanced RISC Consortium (ARC), Digital's Alphas, and now IBM, Motorola, and Apple's Power-PC.

It's interesting that Intergraph and Sequent are using Intel CPUs in applictions where many observers expected to see RISC processors. Nevertheless, it's *possible* that one of the RISC players will eventually fabricate an extremely high processer at a cost low enough to provide a real competitive advantage. Such a development could only rebound to NT's benefit—it's the only CPU-neutral system in the Windows family.

A more exotic (and silly-sounding) concept is an NT-based *personal main-frame*. As the cost of technology falls, mainframe power—and such mainframe applications as DSS and OLTP—may become available to individuals (or at least small companies). Such a development may be essential if widespread electronic commerce is ever to become a reality—ordering products, be they pizza slices or auto parts—over the Internet *is*, after all, an electronic transaction.

The Cairo Project

Finally, there's the future according to Jim Allchin: Windows NT everywhere, as a distributed object server. The code name for this effort is *Cairo*, and as this chapter is written, the project's in something of a state of flux.

Up to spring, 1995, Cairo was assumed to be a major new release of Windows NT with three major new features: an OLE-based user interface, an object-oriented file system, and distributed processing support. In March 1995, Microsoft announced that a version of Windows NT would enter beta with the new user interface within 90 days of Windows 95's release—and it became clear that Cairo actually referred only to the file system and distributed processing features. Before venturing into the vapor and speculating about how those features might work, we need to take a slight detour into the mind of Microsoft's maximum leader, Bill Gates.

Information At Your Fingertips

Two years ago at Comdex, Gates presented a concept he called *Information at Your Fingertips* (inevitably, given the unfortunate acronym IAYF). This was a general concept based on the following ideas:

- ❏ Ubiquity of computers

- ❏ *More personal* PCs

❑ Data made independent of location

❑ Greater use of nontraditional data types, like voice and live (or animated) video

He didn't just give a slide show and make a speech—the concept was illustrated with an impressively produced multimedia video presentation to drive home his points. This showed computers being used in a much wider range of situations than just traditional desktop use—truly mobile (including pen-based) computing was a big part of the presentation. So were multimedia elements, such as video conferencing and video memos sent by electronic mail. But at the heart of the presentation lay a very powerful concept: that end users should need to know (or care) where and how data is stored.

If we might mix our examples a bit, the first episode of *Star Trek, The Next Generation* had one character bring up a map of this ship's internal layout.[10] She did this by saying "Tell me the location of Commander Data," *not* by saying something like Display MAPFILE\PERSONNEL\LOCATION\DATA, as we'd have to do today—the *computer* does the locating, *not the human operator.*

In Gates's COMDEX presentation, this was handled a little differently—instead of employing a File Manager-style interface to find files, he (and the actors in his IAYF show) used a query-based interface that worked a lot more like our *Star Trek* example: Rather than remembering (and regurgitating) the directory path to a file, a combination of dates, subjects, media type, and creator-name fields was used to create a query; and the result of that query was the information in question—truly information at your fingertips!

But that was all staged—does IAYF have any bearing on reality? And if so, where does Windows NT fit in?

Distributed Computing

Earlier in this chapter we examined the classical host-based and shared-resource models of computing, and saw how client/server computing naturally grew out of a combination of those two approaches (and the need to minimize network traffic). Let's consider a *fifth* model of computing, which to a certain degree competes with client/server computing. This is the *distributed computing* model.

In distributed computing, computing resources are distributed throughout the machines on the network, and computation is done at whatever location happens to be convenient. In particular, most computational models for distributed processing attempt to *equalize* resource utilization across the network. For instance, if computation work needs to be done, the system finds an idle processor and does the work there.

---

10. A production of Paramount Pictures.

The beauty of distributed computing is that it can fully leverage *all* network resources in a way that is impossible for any of the other models to achieve. Even the client/server model—with all the advantages we discussed earlier in this chapter—can leverage the resources of only a *particular* client and a *particular* server to accomplish a *particular* task. It doesn't matter that there may be over 100 CPUs on your network sitting idle—if the server's bogged, no work will get done.

A limited degree of distributed processing is possible by operating multiple servers (for example, having database functions provided by a database server, file functions provided by a file server, etc.). The limitation of this scheme is that you're still locked into the client/server model for any *particular* process—if the database server becomes overloaded with requests, the system will slow down even though the other servers are idle.

There's no way in a multiple client/server model to distribute the database server functions among other servers on the system—a single bogged server can slow down the entire network. In a Windows NT environment with properly designed server software that exploits symmetric multiprocessing, we can try to throw a bigger server at the problem—but at some point, even the largest SMP will run out of steam.

What's needed is a way to distribute the functions of the database server among multiple servers on the network. *That's* the goal of distributed processing.

From a programmer's perspective, the key element in any distributed computing scheme is a Remote Procedure Call (RPC). Windows NT provides a powerful RPC implementation that's partly compatible with the Open Systems Federation's Distributed Computing Environment (DCE) RPC.[11] Using RPCs, a programmer can write a program that will call functions transparently—*without knowing whether the functions are executed on the local computer or on another computer on the network*. A good example is the distributed Mandelbrot sample program provided by Microsoft in the Win32 Software Development Kit. Figure 11.1 illustrates this program, with the graphical console running on a Gateway 486 machine, and the computational engine running on a MIPS R4000 server machine. The Performance Monitor, which is shown overlapping the Mandelbrot window, shows the actual system loads on the two systems—and you'll notice that the MIPS machine is actually undergoing a more severe CPU load than the local machine *even though the local machine is doing all the display work*.

This is a form of client/server computing—the MIPS machine is functioning as a *compute server* for the Mandelbrot demo application. However, a programmer *could* construct a variant of this program that would have an additional intermediate step: When making the remote procedure call that will carry out computations, the program could have a form of *indirection*, in which the remote procedure calls were issued to different machines based on a network

---

11. Documented in Appendix 1.

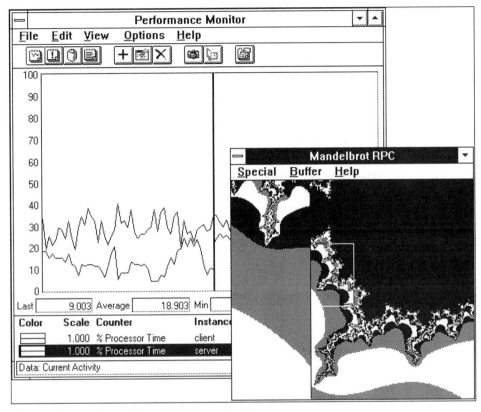

Figure 11.1 Mandelbrot RPC application.

Microsoft's 32-bit Windows System Development Kit (SDK) includes this example of a true client/server application. The client application, shown in the foreground, is responsible for all screen updates but does not perform the Mandelbrot fractal transform computations necessary to draw the figure. Instead, it uses Remote Procedure Calls (RPCs) to execute the computations in a separate server program that need not execute on the same system. The Performance Monitor screen shows % CPU Time for both processes.

task scheduler—on detection of idle time, for instance. The programmer would not know (or care) *where* the computation was being executed.

The present Windows NT implementation lacks any way of assigning the RPCs such that neither the programmer nor the computer user (nor ideally the system administrator) will need to know the specifics of which machine receives the assignment. Perhaps another example will help to clear up this issue. It's common in the publishing business to run out of disk space on the production file server (or servers) as an issue is produced. This used to happen at *WINDOWS*

Magazine constantly. As the production staff finished a particular issue, they created a large number of PostScript images—these take up a great deal of disk space. Several years ago one of us constantly found himself frustrated with the following situation.[12] The production server available at that time was an OS/2 LAN Manager computer (a lineal ancestor of Windows NT) with about one half a gigabyte of disk space. We would consistently overshoot that disk capacity by about 100MB, *yet we had over a dozen workstations on that same network, with a total excess disk capacity far in excess of 100MB.* Why couldn't we use the excess disk capacity on the other machines on the network?

With Windows NT (or Windows for Workgroups) this is possible in an *ad hoc* way. Each system can have a public shared directory, and by manually distributing files onto those public shared directories you could take advantage of the excess disk capacity. Yet this would create an administrative nightmare. If you're looking for a particular file, do you look for it on \\johnspc, \\davespc, or \\main_server? What's needed, again, is a mechanism for adding a *level of indirection.* That is, one needs the ability to refer to a disk storage location, say, \\DistributedDiskspace, *without being concerned about the physical location that's being referred to.*

Obviously, what's needed is some kind of mechanism for resolving those abstracted references into the precise physical references needed to locate the object in question. We say *object* because this concept need not apply only to disk files—it could as easily apply to named pipe addresses, for instance, or to compute services, as previously mentioned, The key to a fully effective form of distributed computing is *an object-oriented name space.* This sounds like a big buzzword; it's not. What it really means is quite simple: We need a *database—* and that's exactly what lies hidden at the heart of Microsoft's OLE 2.0 programming model.

OLE 2.0

Now that we've looked at the large-scale issue of distributed computing (and hopefully exposed some of the strategic considerations that involves), let's discuss *tactics.* In particular, let's consider what distributed computing might look like from an end-user perspective.

As we've discussed, the central issue of distributed computing is the creation of an object-oriented name space. That is, you stop referring to physical disk drives as locations for files—and you stop referring to servers as locations for computations such as database queries. Instead, you refer to *network objects,* which may span many storage volumes or many servers. Clearly the Program Manager/File Manager user interface of Windows 3.*x* (and Windows NT) is inadequate for this kind of situation.

---

12. John D. Ruley.

Microsoft realized this some time ago and began creating the foundation for an entirely new type of user interface. This foundation is the second generation of the Object Linking and Embedding (OLE) specification. OLE 1.0 is familiar to most Windows users as the mechanism by which one can, for instance, embed a Paintbrush picture in the middle of a word-processing document. Double-clicking on the picture then brings up the Paintbrush application with the picture loaded so that it can be edited by the recipient. It's a cute feature that is somewhat more convenient than simple cut and paste, but not greatly so.

OLE 2.0 is designed to go beyond this capability—and does so by providing an object-oriented name space (and thereby providing the all-important additional level of abstraction that we've determined is needed for the large-scale concept of distributed computing to become effective). In OLE 2.0, objects can either be *embedded in* or *linked to* a parent document. An object embedded in a parent document has its data embedded within the parent file. Among other things, this has the side effect that one can now receive relatively short word-processor documents that take up megabytes of disk space because of an embedded Paintbrush picture.

A more sophisticated alternative to embedding the data is to link it. In a linked object, the only thing embedded in the parent document is a *reference* to the file that is linked to the document. Unfortunately OLE 1.0 understood how to refer to only direct physical addresses. These could, in fact, be network addresses—it's possible (using the Object Packager, for instance) to provide a link to a network object—but you have to specify the precise address of the network object.

This gets away very nicely from the problem of multimegabyte word-processing documents, because of embedded pictures, but—since it requires a precise physical address, even if it's a network address, for the location of the parent file—it still doesn't provide that all-important additional level of abstraction that's needed. This has rather severe consequences—for instance, what happens if a linked file is moved? The link *breaks*. The next attempt to refer to the linked object within the parent document will result in an error, because OLE 1.0 does not provide the necessary level of abstraction.

OLE 2.0 *does* provide abstraction in the form of a *moniker*. An OLE 2 moniker is just a name that refers to an object without being specific as to its location. The name can be resolved either to a physical address or to a relative address. Monikers that expand to absolute addresses work exactly the same way that the absolute addresses do in OLE 1.0. Monikers that expand to *relative* addresses begin to show us some new capabilities. For example, if you use relative addressing on an embedded Paintbrush object that refers to the same directory in which the parent word-processing document is kept; then moving the contents of the directory will *not* break the link (because the new directory will still contain the Paintbrush picture). That may not sound like much of an improvement, but the fact that you now have a level of indirection through the moniker means that a number of extremely powerful capabilities can be provided.

OLE Automation

In addition to the capability of embedding foreign data types within a document, OLE 2.0 provides completely new features. Through OLE Automation it's possible for applications to expose their computational functions as OLE 2.0 objects. These objects can then be addressed by other OLE 2.0-compatible programs and documents in much the same manner as a Custom Control is accessed from Visual Basic. For example, it might be possible in future versions of Windows-compatible word-processing documents to expose the functionality of the Spell Checker. You can then use the spell checking functions in other programs—perhaps in a Mail client or some other type of application. For that matter, it may also be possible to build *compound* applications by combining features of these objects—replacing the Spell Checker included in a word processor with another one provided as a separate OLE 2.0 object, for example.

This capability is very new and has generally been discussed only in terms of leveraging the power already provided in applications on end-user desktops. That is a mistake. OLE 2 Automation is not something that an end user can easily do. The fact that an application exposes its spell checker as an object doesn't automatically mean that an end user can make use of that feature. An end user must find a way to access the features of that object (to adjust its properties, for instance) and determine whether it's case sensitive or not, which word or sentence or paragraph is being checked, whether the spell checking is interactive or batch mode, and so on.

This will most probably require the services of a programmer—at least a script programmer.[13] Properly using OLE 2.0 within an embedded application will require the use of some kind of application scripting capability. This is why Microsoft is now investing such heavy resources in their applications division developing Visual Basic for Applications (VBA) as a consistent scripting language for use between Microsoft applications. Doubtless other companies will follow suit in one way or another. But let's consider a more powerful possibility. After all, OLE Automation deals with objects. The fact that the object now contains code rather than data isn't relevant. That's the whole point of an object.

This feature of object-oriented models is called *polymorphism*. It means that you don't distinguish between code and data. Both are just objects. So it *should*

---

13. Possibly more—since this was written, Microsoft has gone to the extreme of releasing a full-blown development kit for use by those attempting to build custom applications by exploiting the OLE Automation features of Microsoft Office 4.x. As we said earlier, OLE Automation is *not* a panacea for end users!

be possible for the OLE Automation objects to be referred to, using monikers *in exactly the same way that the data objects can.*[14] Based on what we've discussed so far, this merely means that you can access the objects through link structures, and that the links won't break when you move them from directory to directory. That's because at this point we're looking at OLE 2 minus one important element. We're looking at it without an all-important *Object Server*—exactly what Allchin's Cairo project has been working on.

Cairo: Distributed OLE, OFS, and DFS

First of all, what will Cairo look like? Given Microsoft's March 1995 announcement that a version of NT will appear with the Windows 95 user interface by the end of the year, it's safe to assume that end users will see it as an enhanced Windows just as end users see NT as an enhanced Windows today. Microsoft has also publicly stated that Cairo will provide a new, object-oriented file system. This has been the subject of a great deal of speculation in the press, much of it very ill informed. You must be very careful when you hear the words *file system* used in respect to Windows NT. A Windows NT File System can refer to many things—it is, in effect, a *name space*. The UNC names used by Windows NT's built-in networking are in fact a file system—as is Novell's NetWare services. Therefore, we think that it may be more useful to back up a step and think about an object-oriented *name space* rather than an object-oriented *file system*.

An object-oriented name space has great advantages—particularly if we think about the OLE 2.0 *moniker* discussed earlier, and assume that these monikers can refer to object-oriented Cairo name space addresses as well as to conventional FAT or NTFS file names. We believe that the object-oriented name space provided by Windows NT will provide (through the OLE 2 moniker mechanism) a truly distributed environment with distributed object-oriented applications and documents.[15]

Consider embedding a Paintbrush picture within a word processing document. Up to now this has required *both* Microsoft Paintbrush *and* Microsoft Word (or another word processor) to be present on the client machine of any client that needed to edit the resulting compound document. We believe that Cairo will change this relationship. It will become possible (by exploiting the OLE Automation features across the object-oriented name space for applications and documents) to refer to components of objects located on other computers, particularly on Cairo-based Object Servers. Rather than having a local copy of

---

14. Be forewarned—we are speculating here. Just how far this capability works out in practice will depend on how good the distributed OLE design is—something we can only guess at now.

15. We've heard rumors that this will be based on Microsoft's Access database technology—which leads us to a matter of some concern: Is Access relational? If not, Microsoft would appear to be betting its future on a *weaker* technology than that available in its flagship database product! Perhaps we've been mislead. Or maybe Access really *is* relational, after all.

the word processor on every machine—or certainly *all* components of the word processor on every machine—when spell checking a document, there will be client/server communication over the network with a spell checking OLE 2 Automation *service* located on an Object Server.[16] The same logic applies to a wide variety of other applications.

As we said in Chapter 9, Windows NT services are the functional equivalent of NetWare Loadable Modules (NLMs) in NetWare 3.11 and NetWare 4.0. The combination of this with OLE 2 on the desktop provides the functional equivalent to Novell's *AppWare* approach to shrink wrapping client/server. In fact, this leads to one of our most tantalizing speculations—by fully applying the capability to use Windows NT Services over NWLink IPX/SPX, it *should* be possible for Windows Cairo servers to participate as AppWare servers in a NetWare network. If the server in question is running an appropriate Windows NT Cairo *service*, then that same server should be capable of providing similar services to the distributed OLE 2.0 equivalent to AppWare across the network. Thus, it may actually be possible for a single server to span *both* forms of distributed computing.

Microsoft has also said that it plans to replace NT's existing security object monitor subsystem with a system based on MIT's *Kerberos* distributed security system. Kerberos introduces the concept of a *security server* on a network that validates security requests against networked objects in much the same way that the Windows NT Security Object Monitor validates attempts to access internal objects in the system. The significance of this is that the physical location of an object becomes unimportant in determining its security context. The fact that a particular object exists in the local file system on your computer does not necessarily give you the right or the capability to access it.

This makes sense in the context of a truly distributed architecture like the one we've been describing. A compound document might wind up containing many linked objects from many directories, but the compounded document *as a unit* will have an owner—and will inherit the highest security certification level of any component (there may be embedded objects within it that are public, but as an embedded portion of the total document, they will be confidential if the overall container document is confidential).

Moreover, a confidential document *owned* by one person may not be read by another person—unless either the security administrator for the system or the owner has granted the right to read the document *even though that person might have confidential level access*. This would be appropriate (indeed essential) in upgrading Windows NT Cairo security to Department of Defense B-level

---

16. Again, note that this is sheer speculation. We know of no plans for such a spell-checker object at Microsoft or other vendors, but it certainly seems to make sense. A centralized spell checker could have a much larger dictionary than that available on a client, and it could provide more sophisticated services—context-sensitive grammar checking, for instance.

standards—which would permit it to handle information at the Secret classification level. It would also be useful in secure operations, such as banks or in the handling of financial information.

Of course, everything that we've said in talking about the brave, new Windows Cairo world has been concentrated on the new features. What we haven't pointed out is that in order for this to have any chance of actually happening, Microsoft *must* (and undoubtedly *will*) find a way to present these new capabilities while maintaining backward compatibility with the existing Windows NT system. Windows NT 3.*x* Services will almost certainly continue to work in the Cairo environment.

We can also reasonably anticipate that today's support for legacy applications will be maintained (perhaps even expanded) in the Cairo environment. In all probability, the resource requirements for Windows NT Cairo will be even higher than the resource requirements for the present version of Windows NT (Microsoft will direct those who cannot accept such high resource requirements to Windows 95). We can certainly hope that along the way some of the problems we've examined in this book may be resolved to the advantage of users and administrators.

Conclusion—The Operating System Designed to Connect

We began this book by defining Windows NT as the operating system designed to connect. We then examined a wide variety of the features and functions of Windows NT that indeed meet this specification. We've provided as much information as we think possible as of this writing on administration and maintenance features. We've provided as much information as was made available to us on connectivity to third-party products, such as NetWare, TCP/IP, Banyan VINES, and so forth; and we've now closed out with some speculative—but hopefully useful—information on where the Windows NT product is headed in the foreseeable future.

We hope you've found this book readable and interesting. Our greatest hope (of course) is that you'll find it useful. If you would like to write us about the book—perhaps with suggestions for future editions or just with comments on the current one—please do so in care of:

John Wiley & Sons, Inc.

605 Third Avenue

New York, NY 10158

The Windows NT world is an exciting (and *very* fast moving) one. It's difficult to keep up with—as we found out writing this book. Chapter 9 (on connecting NetWare and NT) was in its third and (we thought!) final revision the week that Microsoft announced its own NetWare Requester. Just two days later, Beame and Whiteside announced that they were going to provide network core protocol services for Windows NT—we were forced to rewrite Chapter 9 literally at the last minute (and in fact delayed putting the book to press) so that we could get the most recent information out to you. We hope we've provided something that you'll find useful, and we'd like to hear from you. Besides physical mail, you can reach us electronically at:

John Ruley   jruley@cmp.com

Dave Methvin   dmethvin@cmp.com

Arthur Germain   agermain@cmp.com

Eric Hall   ehall@tgv.com

Martin Heller   mheller@bix.com

For More Information

Renaud, Paul (1993), *Introduction to Client/Server Systems*. New York: John Wiley & Sons. ISBN: 0-471-57774-X. Excellent overview of client/server theory. A bit thick for the average reader, but worth working through if you really want to understand the topic.

Stephenson, Peter and Hartwig, G. (1992), *SQL Self-Teaching Guide*. New York: John Wiley & Sons. ISBN: 0-471-54544-9. Solid introduction to SQL, focussing on user (and programmer) issues rather than on theory. Invaluable in understanding the SQL Server manuals.

Sawyer, Tom (1993), *TPC Benchmark™ B Full Disclosure Report for Compaq ProLiant 2000 Model 5/66-4200A and Compaq ProLiant Model 486/50-4200A Systems using Microsoft SQL Server for Windows NT*. Houston, TX: Compaq Computer Corp. This report gives the gory details on a full TCP-B evaluation of Windows NT on Compaq hardware, as done by Tom Sawyer of Performance Metrics, Inc.

Voth, Gary (1993), *Microsoft SQL Server Business and Product Update*. Redmond WA: Microsoft Corp. This set of slides from the SQL Server for Windows NT press tour in September 1993 largely duplicates the information in Microsoft's published white paper—in particular, including the stunning TPC-B results that are covered by Sawyer in more detail.

Microsoft Staff (1991-1992), *Using Microsoft SQL Server on a NetWare Network*. Redmond WA: Microsoft Corp. A technical note (part number 098–32655) from the SQL Server for OS/2 days, but still useful in understanding SQL Server on NetWare issues.

Steele, Tammy (1993), *The Win32 story: Targeting Windows 3.1, Windows NT, Chicago and Cairo with the Win32 API*. Article on Page 1 of *Microsoft Developer Network News*, Volume 2, Number 5, Redmond WA: Microsoft Developer's Network. Good (if limited) overview of the relationship between Chicago, Cairo, and OLE 2.0 for developers.

APPENDIX

Programming NT Networks

In the rest of this book, we've concentrated on matters of concern to end users and system administrators—but there are network issues for programmers as well. While it's not possible to cover network programming in depth (that's a topic for another book entirely!), we endeavor here to give a solid general overview. First, we'll talk about the issues and APIs that apply to all server processes, and then we'll discuss network and interprocess programming.

One thing to note: NT's APIs have changed, with new functionality appearing in each release of the operating system. This overview will be as complete as possible—but given the rate at which new APIs appear, we recommend that you keep yourself informed with *Microsoft Developers Network News*, *Microsoft Systems Journal*, or another periodical source. With that out of the way, let's look at the server APIs.

Networks and Services

Many network-specific programs act as servers for multiple clients. On UNIX systems, they might be *daemons*; in Windows NT, they are typically *services*. Windows NT has considerable support for services: It allows them to start when the system boots, to continue when users log in and out, to have different privileges than the current user, to use a standard interface, to use a standard way to report errors, and it gives them a standard way to post runtime statistics.

The service control manager is the piece of the NT system that allows services to start at boot time and continue across logins and logouts. It also provides the services a standard user interface. The event logging subsystem gives services a standard way to report not only errors, but also warnings and benign system events. NT's event browser provides the interface for the user or administrator who needs to examine and act on system events.

Services can post runtime statistics by exposing blocks to the performance monitor. Performance counters are queried through the registry, and available both locally and across the NT network.

When writing servers, consider supporting internationalization by using the UNICODE character set. Unfortunately, not all clients support UNICODE, so it may be necessary to support multibyte character sets on some clients, using the character set translation APIs.

Server performance can be critical. Beginning with version 3.5, NTsupports an optimized mechanism for asynchronous file I/O, known as I/O completion ports, which is accessed through the CreateIoCompletionPort and GetQueued-CompletionStatus functions combined with ordinary Win32 file I/O. NT versions from 3.5 on also support the SetThreadAffinityMask function, which allows a given thread to run only on certain CPUs in a multiprocessor system; and the SetPriorityClass function.

Both SetThreadAffinityMask and SetPriorityClass need to be treated with great care: They are dangerous power tools with sharp edges and no safety shields, intended for use only by trained professionals. If you find yourself resorting to setting a high or real-time priority class to get the performance you need, for instance, consider the possibility that your service architecture may need to be redesigned to accomplish your goals in a way that allows the rest of the system to run, too.

Service Control Manager

A service is an executable object that is installed in a registry database maintained by the service control manager. The services database determines whether each installed service is started on demand or is started automatically when the system starts up; it can also contain logon and security information for a service so that a service can run even though no user is logged on.

Win32 services conform to the interface rules of the Service Control Manager. Driver services conform to the device driver protocols for Windows NT. The Service Control Manager functions are listed in Table A1.1. Device drivers are beyond the scope of this work.

The service control manager is actually an RPC server, so you can control services on remote machines. You can write three kinds of programs that would use service control functions: a Win32 service process, which provides executable code for services and provides status information to the service control

Table A1.1 Win32 Service Control Manager Functions

Function	*Action*
ChangeServiceConfig	Changes service configuration parameters.
CloseServiceHandle	Closes Service Control Manager object.
ControlService	Sends a control to a service.
CreateService	Creates a service object.
DeleteService	Removes service from SC Manager database.
EnumDependentServices	Enumerates services dependent on device.
EnumServicesStatus	Enumerates services in SC Manager database.
Handler	Controls handler function of a service.
LockServiceDatabase	Locks specified SC Manager database.
NotifyBootConfigStatus	Notifies/responds to acceptability of boot configuration.
OpenService	Opens an existing service.
OpenSCManager	Connects to Service Control Manager.
QueryServiceConfig	Gets service configuration parameters.
QueryServiceLockStatus	Gets service database lock status.
QueryServiceObjectSecurity	Gets service object security descriptor.
QueryServiceStatus	Gets service status.
RegisterServiceCtrlHandler	Registers service control request handler.
ServiceMain	Main function of a service.
SetServiceStatus	Updates service status to SC Manager.
SetServiceObjectSecurity	Modifies service object security descriptor.
StartService	Starts running a service.
StartServiceCtrlDispatcher	Connects thread as dispatch thread.
UnlockServiceDatabase	Unlocks specified database

manager; a service configuration program, which manipulates the service control database; and a service control program, which starts a service and controls a running service.

The SDK SERVICE sample demonstrates a simple service process, a client for it, and a program to install and remove service processes. SIMPLE.C is a service process that echoes and mangles input it receives on a named pipe.

CLIENT.C sends a string on the named pipe and displays the resulting echo. And INSTSRV.C demonstrates using CreateService and DeleteService.

A Win32 service process has to include a main function that immediately calls the StartServiceCtrlDispatcher function to connect the main thread of the process to the Service Control Manager. It also needs an entry point function, ServiceMain in Table A1.1, for each service that can run in the process, and a control handler function, Handler in Table A1.1, for each service that can run in the process. The actual names for the service entry points are determined by the dispatch table passed to StartServiceCtrlDispatcher:

```
VOID main() {
    SERVICE_TABLE_ENTRY dispatchTable[] = {
        { TEXT("SimpleService"), //first service in list
          (LPSERVICE_MAIN_FUNCTION)service_main },
        { NULL, NULL }//NULLs terminate list of services
    };

    if (!StartServiceCtrlDispatcher(dispatchTable)) {
        StopSimpleService("StartServiceCtrlDispatcher failed.");
    }
}
```

The actual name for the handler is determined by the main service entry point, and registered with the service control manager using the function called RegisterServiceCtrlHandler:

```
VOID service_main(DWORD dwArgc, LPTSTR *lpszArgv) {
    DWORD                  dwWait;
    PSECURITY_DESCRIPTOR   pSD;
    SECURITY_ATTRIBUTES    sa;

    // register our service control handler:
    //
    sshStatusHandle = RegisterServiceCtrlHandler(
                      TEXT("SimpleService"),
                      service_ctrl);
    if (!sshStatusHandle)
        goto cleanup;
```

A simple service process might include all the code it needed to do its job in its own executable. A more complicated service process might well spawn additional daemon processes. For instance, you could write a service process that accepted an SQL query on a named pipes, submitted the query to a separate database process through named shared memory, signaled the database that a query was pending using an event, and returned the query result to the originator via the named pipes.

It might also be possible to write a generic service process that did nothing but start and stop other processes. For instance, you might have a character-mode OS/2 server process that you want to run on your Windows NT system. You could make it look and act like a real NT server process, even though it runs in the OS/2 subsystem, by writing a small NT service process to start and control it. The OS/2 process would handle its own interprocess communications.

It's really fairly easy to turn a service application of any kind into a true Win32 service process. Consider doing this for any server application that should run independently of the current user—which applies to most network services. When it comes time to test your service, use the SC application supplied with the Windows NT SDK to communicate with the service control manager. You should also consider making your service configuration program a Control Panel applet. A Control Panel applet resides in a DLL, typically is given the CPL extension, and includes a standard callback entry-point function named CPlApplet, which must be exported. The application needs to include the CPL.H header file for the definition of the messages that Control Panel sends to the applet.

You can find all the information you need to write your own Control Panel applets in the Win32 SDK help by searching for *Control Panel Applications Overview*. From there, you can browse through the successive help topics, or investigate the cross-references. There is a fairly complete example included in one of the help topics as well, although it won't make much sense until you've read the preceding topics. In any case, doing a Control Panel applet isn't difficult—once you have the information.

Event Logging

One issue many server applications face is how to display error conditions. Often, the server process has no user interface, and can't even be sure it is running on a machine with an active screen: Even a standard message box might pop up on a screen that is powered down, or hidden in a closet. Event logging provides a standard, centralized way for applications (and Windows NT) to record important software and hardware events—not only error conditions, but also events that ought to leave an audit trail. The Windows NT Event Viewer offers a standard user interface for viewing the logs, and the event logging functions provide ways to examine and back up the logs as well as to report events. The Win32 event logging functions are listed in Table A1.2.

Table A1.2 Win32 Event Logging Functions

Function	*Action*
BackupEventLog	Saves an event log in a backup file.
ClearEventLog	Clears the event log.
CloseEventLog	Closes an event-log handle.
DeregisterEventSource	Closes a registered event handle.
GetNumberOfEventLogRecords	Gets number of records in event log.
GetOldestEventLogRecord	Retrieves number of oldest record.
OpenBackupEventLog	Opens a handle to a backup event log.
OpenEventLog	Opens an event-log handle.
ReadEventLog	Reads entries from an event log.
RegisterEventSource	Returns a registered event-log handle.
ReportEvent	Writes an event-log entry.

Events are classified as information, warnings, and errors. All event classifications have well-defined common data and can optionally include event-specific data. For example, information can assert that a service has started or is stopping, that a process connected or disconnected, or that some specific action was performed.

To give a moderately silly example, we might have a process that is controlling a soda machine. Information might record that the machine was filled, or that a column of cans was changed to a different kind of soda. Information might also record each transaction on the machine—what kind of soda was dispensed, what coins were tendered, and what coins were given in change. A viewing process for the soda machine's event log would be able to deduce the machine's exact status, plot historical usage, and predict future usage for ordering purposes.

Warnings are used for recoverable problems. For our soda machine, we might want to log a warning when any column drops below three cans, or when the machine gets low on change. Errors are used for nonrecoverable conditions that might cause an application to fail. For the soda machine, that might be running out of soda in any column, running out of change, or being unable to keep the soda cold.

Of course, you can use event logs for more serious purposes as well. Windows NT itself uses the event log for such conditions as drivers failing to load, disk drive time outs, and network errors. It also uses the event log to keep an audit trail (if the administrator enables it) of users logging in and out, security policy changes, system restarts, and so on.

Table A1.3 Win32 Performance Monitoring Functions

Function	*Action*
RegConnectRegistry	Connects to Registry on a remote system.
RegQueryValueEx	Retrieves the type and data for a specified value name associated with an open Registry key.
QueryPerformanceCounter	Obtains performance counter value.
QueryPerformanceFrequency	Returns performance counter frequency.

Performance Monitoring

Network administrators often need to monitor network and disk server performance in order to maintain and tune their facilities. Windows NT has a useful Performance Monitor program in the Administrative Tools group. True to the open spirit of Win32, the key functions used by the Performance Monitor are exposed in the API and available for anyone to use. They are listed in Table A1.3.

Why would anyone want to reinvent the Performance Monitor? You might, for instance, want to write a statistics-gathering program or an alarm panel. The statistics-gathering program might collect selected performance numbers from a list of machines on the network at predetermined intervals and save them in a database: A companion program would process the saved data on demand, computing means and standard deviations; displaying time series graphs, histograms, and scatter plots; and otherwise making sense of the network's behavior over time. The alarm panel would scan the network at intervals and send a message to the designated administrator when hard disks were full or performance figures fell outside their normal range.

NT's high-resolution performance counter functions allow you to access the system's high-speed timer. QueryPerformanceFrequency tells you the number of counts per second for the timer, and QueryPerformanceCounter tells you the current reading of the timer. These functions are similar to the C library function clock and the associated constant CLOCKS_PER_SEC, but might give you better time resolution.

NT's system performance numbers are accessed through the Registry, although they are not actually stored in the Registry. You can get system performance information by calling RegQueryValueEx with the key HKEY_PERFORMANCE_DATA. If you wish, use RegOpenKey to open the HKEY_PERFORMANCE_DATA handle, but remember to use RegCloseKey to close the handle when you're done with it.

Using RegQueryValueEx with HKEY_PERFORMANCE_DATA causes the system to collect the data from the appropriate system object managers.

To collect data from a remote system, use RegConnectRegistry with the name of the remote system, and the HKEY_PERFORMANCE_DATA key to retrieve a key usable with RegQueryValueEx to actually retrieve performance data from the remote system.

RegQueryValueEx returns a PERF_DATA_BLOCK structure followed by one PERF_OBJECT_TYPE structure and accompanying data for each type of object being monitored. The system being observed defines objects that can be monitored—typically processors, disks, and memory.

The performance data block describes the performance data returned by RegQueryValueEx:

```
typedef struct _PERF_DATA_BLOCK { /* pdb */
    WCHAR           Signature[4];
    DWORD           LittleEndian;
    DWORD           Version;
    DWORD           Revision;
    DWORD           TotalByteLength;
    DWORD           HeaderLength;
    DWORD           NumObjectTypes;
    DWORD           DefaultObject;
    SYSTEMTIME      SystemTime;        //time of measurement in UTC format
    LARGE_INTEGER   PerfTime;          //actual data value counts
    LARGE_INTEGER   PerfFreq;          //timer counts per second
    LARGE_INTEGER   PerfTime100nSec;   //data value in 100 ns units
    DWORD           SystemNameLength;
    DWORD           SystemNameOffset;
} PERF_DATA_BLOCK;
```

The PERF_OBJECT_TYPE structure describes the object-specific performance information:

```
typedef struct _PERF_OBJECT_TYPE {  /* pot */
    DWORD   TotalByteLength;
    DWORD   DefinitionLength;
    DWORD   HeaderLength;
    DWORD   ObjectNameTitleIndex;
    LPWSTR  ObjectNameTitle;
    DWORD   ObjectHelpTitleIndex;
    LPWSTR  ObjectHelpTitle;
    DWORD   DetailLevel;
    DWORD   NumCounters;
    DWORD   DefaultCounter;
```

```
    DWORD   NumInstances;
    DWORD   CodePage;
    LARGE_INTEGER PerfTime;
    LARGE_INTEGER PerfFreq;
} PERF_OBJECT_TYPE;
```

The PERF_OBJECT_TYPE structure for an object is followed by a list of PERF_COUNTER_DEFINITION structures:

```
typedef struct _PERF_COUNTER_DEFINITION { /* pcd */
    DWORD   ByteLength;
    DWORD   CounterNameTitleIndex;
    LPWSTR CounterNameTitle;
    DWORD   CounterHelpTitleIndex;
    LPWSTR CounterHelpTitle;
    DWORD   DefaultScale;
    DWORD   DetailLevel;
    DWORD   CounterType;
    DWORD   CounterSize;
    DWORD   CounterOffset;
} PERF_COUNTER_DEFINITION;
```

The PERF_INSTANCE_DEFINITION is used to define each instance of a block of object-specific performance data. Not all counters have instances. For instance, memory objects don't have instances, since the system has only one memory. Disk objects do have instances, because the system can have more than one disk:

```
typedef struct _PERF_INSTANCE_DEFINITION { /* pid */
    DWORD ByteLength;
    DWORD ParentObjectTitleIndex;
    DWORD ParentObjectInstance;
    DWORD UniqueID;
    DWORD NameOffset;
    DWORD NameLength;
} PERF_INSTANCE_DEFINITION;
```

Finally, the object-specific data is held in a PERF_COUNTER_BLOCK structure:

```
typedef struct _PERF_COUNTER_BLOCK { /* pcd */
    DWORD ByteLength;
} PERF_COUNTER_BLOCK;
```

The names of the objects and counters, as well as the text that explains their meaning, are kept in the Registry. To access them, open the registry node:

```
\SOFTWARE\Microsoft\Windows NT\CurrentVersion\Perflib\<langid>
```

The language node (*langid*) is the ASCII representation of the 3-digit hexadecimal language identifier. For example, the U.S. English node is *009*. This node, once opened, can be queried for values of either *Counters* or *Help*. The names of object types are included in the *Counters* data. The *Help* data supplies the Explain text. The *Counters* and *Help* data are stored in MULTI_SZ strings, listed in index-name pairs; for example:

```
2        System
4        Memory
6        % Processor Time
10       Read Operations/sec
12       Write Operations/sec
```

Navigating the Performance Registry tree is somewhat complicated. You can find some working code samples, however, in the Win32 help file: Search for Performance Monitoring Overview, then select the item Using Performance Monitoring. The two sections of the Help file that follow that one give examples that display counters and their titles.

Security

Windows NT has a centralized security facility in which all named objects, and some unnamed objects, have security descriptors (SDs), and all users and processes have access tokens and security identifiers (SIDs). Security descriptors include information about the owner of the object and an access-control list (ACL), which contain access-control entries (ACEs) that identify the users and groups allowed or denied access to the object.

When you program Windows NT, you access objects by getting handles to them, then using the handles. The security process applies when you try to get the handle: The system compares your access token with the object's access-control entries, and only grants you a handle if at least one ACE exists that allows your token access; additionally no ACE exists that denies your token access.

There can be two kinds of access control lists in a security descriptor. A system ACL is controlled by the system administrator. A discretionary ACL is controlled by the owner of the object.

With sufficient privilege, you can manipulate access programmatically, often by adding a discretionary ACL to an object's security descriptor. The functions to manipulate SDs, ACLs, ACEs, tokens, SIDs, and related objects, such as audit alarms, are listed in Table A1.4.

Table A1.4 Win32 Security Functions

Function	Action
AccessCheck	Validates a client's access rights.
AccessCheckAndAuditAlarm	Validates access; generates audit and alarm.
AddAccessAllowedAce	Adds ACCESS_ALLOWED_ACE to ACL.
AddAccessDeniedAce	Adds ACCESS_DENIED_ACE to ACL.
AddAce	Adds an ACE to an existing ACL.
AddAuditAccessAce	Adds SYSTEM_AUDIT_ACE to ACL.
AdjustTokenGroups	Enables/disables groups in a token.
AdjustTokenPrivileges	Enables/disables token privileges.
AllocateAndInitializeSid	Allocates and initiates SID with subauthorities.
AllocateLocallyUniqueId	Allocates an LUID.
AreAllAccessesGranted	Checks for all desired access.
AreAnyAccessesGranted	Checks for any desired access.
CopySid	Copies an SID to a buffer.
CreatePrivateObjectSecurity	Allocates and initializes a protected SD.
CreateProcessAsUser	Creates a new process and its primary thread as a specific user.
DdeImpersonateClient	DDE server impersonates client.
DeleteAce	Deletes an ACE from an existing ACL.
DestroyPrivateObjectSecurity	Deletes a protected server object's SD.
DuplicateToken	Duplicates an access token.
EqualPrefixSid	Tests two SID prefixes for equality.
EqualSid	Tests two SID security IDs for equality.
FindFirstFreeAce	Retrieves a pointer to first free ACL byte.
FreeSid	Frees an allocated SID.
GetAce	Retrieves a pointer to an ACE in an ACL.
GetAclInformation	Retrieves access-control list information.
GetFileSecurity	Gets file or directory security information.
GetKernelObjectSecurity	Retrieves kernel object SD.
GetLengthSid	Returns length of an SID.
GetPrivateObjectSecurity	Retrieves protected server object SD.

(continues)

Table A1.4 (*Continued*)

Function	Action
GetProcessWindowStation	Returns process window-station handle.
GetSecurityDescriptorControl	Retrieves SD revision and control info.
GetSecurityDescriptorDacl	Retrieves SD discretionary ACL.
GetSecurityDescriptorGroup	Retrieves SD primary group information.
GetSecurityDescriptorLength	Returns SD length.
GetSecurityDescriptorOwner	Retrieves SD owner.
GetSecurityDescriptorSacl	Retrieves SD system ACL.
GetSidIdentifierAuthority	Returns ID authority field address.
GetSidLengthRequired	Returns required length of SID.
GetSidSubAuthority	Returns subauthority array address.
GetSidSubAuthorityCount	Returns subauthority field address.
GetThreadDesktop	Returns thread desktop handle.
GetTokenInformation	Retrieves specified token information.
GetUserObjectSecurity	Retrieves server object SD information.
ImpersonateLoggedOnUser	Lets the calling thread impersonate a user.
ImpersonateNamedPipeClient	Pipe server acts as client.
ImpersonateSelf	Gets impersonation token for calling process.
InitializeAcl	Creates a new access-control list.
InitializeSecurityDescriptor	Initializes a security descriptor.
InitializeSid	Initializes an SID.
IsValidAcl	Validates an access-control list.
IsValidSecurityDescriptor	Validates security descriptor.
IsValidSid	Validates an SID.
LogonUser	Attempts to perform a user logon operation.
LookupAccountName	Translates account name to SID.
LookupAccountSid	Translates SID to account name.
LookupPrivilegeDisplayName	Retrieves a displayable privilege name.
LookupPrivilegeName	Retrieves a programmatic privilege name.
LookupPrivilegeValue	Retrieves LUID for privilege name.
MakeAbsoluteSD	Creates absolute SD from self-relative.

Table A1.4 (*Continued*)

Function	Action
MakeSelfRelativeSD	Creates self-relative SD from absolute.
MapGenericMask	Maps generic access to specific/standard.
ObjectCloseAuditAlarm	Generates audit/alarm when object is deleted.
ObjectOpenAuditAlarm	Generates audit/alarm when object is accessed.
ObjectPrivilegeAuditAlarm	Generates audit/alarm on privileged operation.
OpenProcessToken	Opens process token object.
OpenThreadToken	Opens thread token object.
PrivilegeCheck	Tests client security context for privileges.
PrivilegedServiceAuditAlarm	Audit/alarm on privileged system service.
RevertToSelf	Stops impersonation.
SetAclInformation	Sets information in an ACL.
SetFileSecurity	Sets file or directory security.
SetKernelObjectSecurity	Sets kernel object security.
SetPrivateObjectSecurity	Modifies existing SD.
SetSecurityDescriptorDacl	Sets DACL information.
SetSecurityDescriptorGroup	Sets SD primary group information.
SetSecurityDescriptorOwner	Sets SD owner.
SetSecurityDescriptorSacl	Sets SACL information.
SetTokenInformation	Sets various token information.
SetUserObjectSecurity	Sets security-descriptor values.

We won't give any security example programs here: You can find them readily in the Win32 SDK Help files and in the CHECK_SD, EXITWIN, REGISTRY, SIDCLN, and TAKEOWN samples. We will summarize the key points, though.

If you want to deny all access to an object, you can add an *empty* discretionary ACL to its security descriptor. If you want to allow all access to an object, you can give it a NULL discretionary ACL. Note the difference between empty and NULL here: Empty means there is an ACL, but it has no entries; NULL means there is no ACL.

Both File Manager and REGEDT32 include security editors that use the preceding functions extensively. These security editors follow certain conventions about combining ACEs: For instance, they don't allow you to mix access-denied ACEs and access-allowed ACEs in the same list. If you want the security editors to work on an object whose security you've set programmatically, follow the editors' conventions.

Using Threads and Processes

Network programs, and particularly server programs, often need to be designed using multiple threads of execution and/or multiple processes to work efficiently and scale well. It is important to understand the difference between threads and processes. An application can contain more than one process; a process can contain more than one thread.

A thread is the basic entity to which the NT operating system allocates CPU time. A thread can execute any part of the application's code, including a part currently being executed by another thread. All threads of a process share the virtual address space, global variables, and operating system resources of the process.

A process, in turn, is an executing application that consists of a private virtual address space, code, data, and other operating system resources, such as files, pipes, and synchronization objects that are visible to the process. To complete the circular definition, a process also contains one or more threads that run in the context of the process.

Designing multitasking applications is more of an art than a science, and not an easy art at that, but it can be approached using a few rules of thumb. First, anything that you think of as a background task is a good candidate to be in a *thread of its own*. Printing a document, for instance, can be done by a background thread, as can recalculating a spreadsheet or reformatting a document.

Anything that can usefully be spread over multiple CPUs—and that's often the case for network server tasks—should use *multiple threads*. For instance, some image-processing tasks use a lot of CPU time and operate on only a few pixels at a time. It would be relatively simple to spawn multiple threads and use all the CPUs in a multiprocessing system for such a task. Anything that needs to be independent and responsive might usefully be given its own thread. For instance, you might want to assign a thread to each character in an animation, a thread to each independent window in an application, or a thread to each client of a service—as long as you don't wind up with too many running threads. We'll explain what constitutes too many threads in just a moment.

Finally, you might want to consider using threads in situations where an application spends a lot of time waiting for something to happen. Without threads, the application has to chew up CPU time checking some state; with threads, you can simply have a thread waiting for one or more events to happen or for one or more resources to become available, and rely on the system to block the thread from running at all until it can usefully do so.

When Not to Use Threads

When *wouldn't* you want to use threads? Well, in some cases using threads just makes things slower, and in other cases threads can't help because a resource is serialized. And in yet other cases multiple threads make accessing global data unsafe, requiring synchronization delays that wipe out the original advantage of using a threaded model.

For instance, all input is serialized in Win32 systems by USER32, so there's no point in having multiple threads handling input: One input thread will suffice. A printer is inherently a serial-access device, so one thread for printing will suffice. But printing should be a background task, and handling input should be a high-priority foreground task so that printing and user input shouldn't really be handled by the same thread.

How can threads make things slower? What you need to understand is the overhead involved in using threads so that you can balance it off against the gains you make with threads. Each time you spawn a thread, you create a new stack, a new register set, and another contender for the current time slice. In addition, you create complications every place the threads can interact. At some point, the cost of adding another thread on a given configuration will exceed the benefit of having that thread: It's a difficult point to predict at design time, but it's not too hard to determine experimentally.

Spawning a Thread

Before you can experiment, however, you have to know how to spawn a thread. Using the Win32 API set, you'd call CreateThread. If you're using Visual C++ without MFC, Microsoft recommends that you call the runtime library functions _beginthread or _beginthreadex instead of CreateThread to avoid incurring memory leaks in C runtime functions. If you're using MFC, Microsoft recommends that you use AfxBeginThread, or else construct a CWinThread object and call its CreateThread member.

In the Win32 API, you'd call SetThreadPriority to designate the priority of a foreground or background thread. Using MFC, you can set the thread priority as part of the AfxBeginThread call; you can also distinguish between worker threads and user interface threads by the form of the AfxBeginThread call you choose. A worker thread is the sort of thread you'd use for background printing; a user interface thread handles user input and responds to user events.

You create a worker thread by passing AfxBeginThread the address of your thread procedure. You create an MFC user interface thread by first deriving a class from CWinThread, declaring it with DECLARE_DYNCREATE and implementing it with the IMPLEMENT_DYNCREATE macro. You then pass your derived class to AfxBeginThread, which creates and initializes an object of your class, then starts the thread by calling CWinThread::CreateThread. AfxBeginThread takes great care to properly release objects if any step of the process fails.

How Many Threads?

Now that we know how to create a thread, we can think about our thread model. The simplest is, of course, the default: one thread for the whole application. That's what we want to get beyond.

A second obvious model uses a thread per distinct function. In a program that does a dozen or so distinct functions, this can work well—as long as the synchronization issues can be addressed. A thread per function can help utilize multiple CPUs in SMP systems, but this thread per function model doesn't allow for highly CPU-bound tasks.

When you have a CPU-bound task that can be decomposed, you might want to invoke a third model: a thread per CPU. Find out how many CPUs are in the system using GetSystemInfo, then spawn that many low-priority threads for the CPU-bound task. You don't need to worry about counting your other threads—the CPU-bound threads will soak up all the background processing time and the other threads will get in when they need to.

For a server, you can consider spawning a thread per client. This is a natural thing to do when handling named pipes, sockets, and so on. A thread per client will scale until you have too many threads—that is, when the time the system spends switching from thread context to thread context becomes a significant part of the total CPU time. In general, you don't want to have more than 20 or 30 runnable threads in your process contending for the CPU. In other words, you aren't going to create a usable server for 1,000 clients using 1,000 threads.

Worker threads can be made to handle more than one client, at some cost in code complexity. For instance, each thread in an FTP server might be able to handle 10 to 20 sockets if it performed asynchronous or overlapped I/O on the sockets and disk files; a total of 30 threads handling 20 sockets each would serve 600 simultaneous FTP client sessions. Worker threads can also use *I/O completion ports*, a special form of overlapped I/O introduced in Windows NT 3.5, to achieve even higher file transfer performance both on disk file handles and on sockets.

Synchronizing Your Threads

Those of you with a course in concurrent programming under your belt must be wondering why I haven't talked about Dining Philosophers or Petri nets yet.

Well, I'm not going to. If you know about them, you know about them; if you don't, you don't—although you can certainly look them up.[1] I will say, however, that synchronizing multiple concurrent threads and/or processes is a nontrivial task, one that requires a good deal of knowledge and experience as well as care and patience.

The three worst problems people face in this area are data corruption, race conditions, and deadlock conditions. You typically get data corruption when two threads or processes are trying to change the same data at the same time. You get race conditions when one thread relies on another thread to complete some action without having any synchronization between the two threads. The process works if the second thread wins the race by completing its action before the first thread needs it; otherwise you're out of luck. You get a deadlock condition when two threads each need to obtain two resources to continue, and each thread obtains one resource and waits forever for the other.

You typically fix data corruption problems across threads by guarding the data with *critical section* objects. If you have data corruption problems across processes, you can fix the problem by guarding the global data or global resource with *mutex* objects. You can also use *interlocked increment* calls to change data atomically: Instead of using the C increment construct count++ in a thread, you'd use the system call InterlockedIncrement(LPLONG lplVal) to increase the value of a variable by 1 without any possibility of another thread interrupting the operation. Similarly, you'd use InterlockedDecrement and InterlockedExchange calls instead of the equivalent C language constructs.

Race conditions are often solved by synchronizing things among threads and processes using *events* or *semaphores*. If one thread or process needs another to get to a certain point, it can wait for an event to fire, which is set by the other thread or process. The waiting thread would use WaitForSingleObject on the event handle; the other thread would signal the event with SetEvent.

---

1. Some good references on concurrency are Ben-Ari, M., *Principles of Concurrent Programming.* Englewood Cliffs, N.J.: Prentice-Hall, Inc., 1982; and Bic, L. and A. Shaw, *The Logical Design of Operating Systems.* Englewood Cliffs, N.J.: Prentice-Hall, Inc., 1988. For Petri nets, look at Murata, Tadao. "Petri Nets: Properties, Analysis and Applications." Proceedings of the IEEE 77 (April 1989): 541-580; Peterson, James L. *Petri Nets and the Modeling of Systems.* Englewood Cliffs, N.J: Prentice-Hall, 1981; and Reisig, W. *A Primer in Petri Net Design.* Berlin: Springer-Verlag, 1992.

You can find additional material on concurrent programming and Petri nets applied to Windows NT in a series of articles by Ruediger Asche on Microsoft's Development Library CD-ROM. "Multithreading for Rookies" introduces the whole topic. "Using Multithreading and C++ to Generate Live Objects," and "Synchronization on the Fly" deal with concurrent programming. "Compound Win32 Synchronization Objects" expands on the theme and explains how to build useful synchronization structures such as reader/writer locks, from Win32 primitives. "Detecting Deadlocks in Multithreaded Win32 Applications," "The Implementation of DLDETECT.EXE," and "Putting DLDETECT to Work" cover Petri nets. Another article, "Multiple Threads in the User Interface" by Nancy Cluts, deals with the issues involved in using threads that run window procedures and process message queues.

Events tell you something happened; semaphores are used to allow *n* things to happen, and no more. For instance, a database might limit itself to 20 users; it could set a semaphore to an initial value of 20 and make each user claim the semaphore before giving access.

You usually fix deadlocks by standardizing the order in which objects are claimed, by using critical sections, by using mutex objects, by using the WaitForMultipleObjects system call, or by some combination of the these. For instance, you might need to write locks on two database tables in order to perform a proper debit and credit to an accounting system. You could assign a mutex to each table for a write lock. If two threads claimed the mutex objects in different orders, you could easily get a deadlock condition. But if the threads always claimed the two mutex objects simultaneously with a WaitForMultiple-Objects call, no deadlock would be possible.

Sorting Out NT Interprocess Communications

Windows NT, and specifically its 32-Windows subsystem, Win32, contains a plethora of interprocess and networking mechanisms of varying degrees of complexity. The fledgling Win32 network programmer often feels like a kid in a candy store. Let's start by briefly tasting each networking, interprocess communication, and related mechanism: NetBIOS, WNet, mailslots, MAPI, pipes, RAS, sockets, RPCs, DDE, NetDDE, OLE, memory-mapped files, security, service control, event logging, and performance monitoring.

The NetBIOS function supports raw IBM NetBIOS, a very low-level protocol controlled by network control blocks (NCBs). According to Microsoft, NetBIOS is included in Win32 primarily for compatibility with existing systems written to NetBIOS that need to be ported to Windows and Windows NT. On the other hand, NetBIOS will work whether your Windows NT system is communicating via NetBEUI, TCP/IP, or IPX/SPX. Various NetBIOS commands allow the use of communication sessions with individual partners, as well as datagram broadcasts to specific recipients or entire networks. The Win32 NetBIOS function works in Win32s as well as Windows NT; other implementations of NetBIOS are available for DOS, OS/2, and 16-bit Windows.

The WNet functions allow you to enumerate, connect, and disconnect from network resources (shares). One of the WNet functions also gives you access to the current network user name. The WNet functions work in Win32s as well as Windows NT.

A mailslot is a one-way interprocess communication (IPC) mechanism, amounting to a temporary pseudofile, which works over a network. Mailslot communications are not guaranteed to be reliable, as they use the datagram, but they are convenient for broadcasting messages throughout a domain. Mailslots do *not* work in Win32s.

MAPI is the Messaging Application Program Interface. MAPI gives an application a simple way to send messages and files to network users via the Microsoft Mail application included with every copy of Windows NT and Windows for Workgroups. Don't confuse MAPI with mailslots: MAPI is really the programmatic interface to Microsoft Mail, while mailslots are a system-level interprocess communication mechanism. MAPI is supported in 16-bit Windows and in Windows NT, but not in Win32s.

A pipe is a communication conduit with two ends: A process with a handle to one end can communicate with a process having a handle to the other end. Win32 supports both named pipes and anonymous pipes; only named pipes can work over a network. Named pipes were the preferred IPC mechanism in OS/2, so applications ported from OS/2 to Windows NT often use named pipes. Pipes are inherently reliable—they use a protocol that lets you know that each message has been received—and are therefore preferable to mailslots when reliability is important. Named pipes can be a two-way mechanism, whereas mailslots are strictly a one-way mechanism. However, pipes cannot broadcast messages to multiple clients: For broadcasting, mailslots are preferable to pipes. Named pipes are not supported in 16-bit Windows or in Win32s.

Remote Access Services (RAS) allow one Windows NT machine to connect to another over a serial line, modem, X.25 connection, or ISDN connection. While the Windows NT RAS applets probably will allow most people to use RAS well enough, it is possible to use the RAS API functions to control the process from within another program—which might make sense for applications involving remote reporting and wide-area networking. RAS services are not supported in Win32s.

Sockets are a standard networking mechanism that originated in Berkeley UNIX; more recently, the Windows Socket (WinSock) specification codified extensions to Berkeley Sockets for the Windows environment. Windows NT implements a 32-bit version of Windows Sockets. Sockets allow for a wide variety of network addressing schemes and protocols, although they were historically associated with TCP/IP. Sockets are supported in Win32s as well as in Windows NT and most UNIX implementations. Implementations of 16-bit Windows Sockets are available from several vendors.

The Windows NT Remote Procedure Call (RPC), a partial implementation of the OSF DCE (Open Software Foundation Distributed Computing Environment) specification, is conceptually a simple mechanism for distributed computing, but is by its nature complex to program and debug. The NT implementation of RPC includes a Microsoft implementation of the Interface Description Language (IDL) compiler used for specifying the interface to remote procedures and generating the required local stub functions; RPC runtime libraries, which let the local stubs call the remote procedures; and the actual network transport used by the client and server runtime libraries.

RPC can use a variety of transports, network address formats, and protocols. Windows NT RPC 1.0 supports TCP/IP, named pipe, NetBIOS, and Local Procedure Call transports. Network addresses can be in IP, DECNet, or OSI formats, as needed. The RPC protocol can be NCA connections or NCA datagrams. The exact combination of protocol, address format, and transport used by a given connection is specified by an ASCII *protocol sequence*, which is combined with the actual end points to form a *binding*. RPC *naming services* allow a client to find a server on the network.

NT RPCs are supposed to work with DOS and Windows clients and UNIX servers, as well as other NT RPC clients and servers. The DOS/Windows client software ships with the NT SDK, although it needs to be installed separately from the native Windows NT tools. It is not clear whether NT RPC servers will work with all UNIX clients, as the UNIX clients might rely on DCE services not present in the NT RPC implementation. RPC is not supported in Win32s.

Dynamic Data Exchange (DDE) is an old local Windows interprocess communication protocol that is supported in Windows NT in both 16-bit and 32-bit form. NetDDE is an enhancement to DDE that allows it to work over networks. DDE works in Win32s and 16-bit Windows as well as in Windows NT.

Object Linking and Embedding (OLE) is a different enhancement to DDE to support compound documents and application programmability. OLE is expected to be the basis for directory services in Cairo, just as OLE is already the basis for shell interaction in Windows 95. OLE automation can be considered a universal mechanism for remote control of applications, and the underpinning for common objects. OLE is not completely network-enabled as I write, but will be when Cairo ships.

OLE is such a large subject that we can't even outline it in an appendix like this one. Your best bet for including OLE in an application is to use your compiler's Wizard or Expert tools to generate the correct OLE options for your application framework, and add your code to that.

Memory-mapped files are Windows NT's answer to shared memory, which is not supported, since each process in Windows NT has its own address space. While not useful as a network connection, memory-mapped files are useful as a high-bandwidth interprocess communications method on a single machine, which might well provide a network service. For instance, memory-mapped files could be used to implement the high-bandwidth part of a database server involving several processes; one of these processes could then accept queries and send results over the network using named pipes or another network transport. Memory-mapped files are supported in Win32s as well as in Windows NT.

Windows NT has built-in security designed to be certifiable at the U.S. C2 level. While security functions are not specifically interprocess or networking functions, it is often in networking applications that the programmer must pay attention to security issues. Similarly, the Windows NT Service Control Manager, Event Logging, and Performance Monitoring services are not specifically for networks, but are often used when programming for networks. Windows NT also includes the full LAN Manager API, although this is not considered part of the Win32 API. Existing LAN Manager code can be ported to Windows NT with little more than some code tweaks and a recompile. More information on the LAN Manager API under Windows NT can be found in DOC\SDK\MISC\-LMAPI.HLP on the Windows NT SDK CD-ROM.

In the balance of this appendix, we will briefly examine the functions provided by each of the service groups previously mentioned. When appropriate, we will go over simple examples of their use.

There are a few other function groups that deserve mention, which are not generally important enough to merit their own sections. First, *telephony*: Microsoft will be providing a 32-bit development kit for TAPI, the telephony API, and TSPI, the telephony service provider interface, sometime in the future. There is a beta version of this kit, which implements 32-bit TAPI by thunking to 16-bit TAPI, in the MSTOOLS\TAPI directory on the Windows NT 3.51 SDK CD-ROM. You can also find out more about TAPI and TSPI now by looking at the 16-bit TAPI SDK available through MSDN, or by looking at the Windows 95 SDK.

If ICMP means anything to you, you might be interested in an implementation of the ICMP echo request API which exists on the Windows NT 3.51 SDK CD-ROM. Look in the MSTOOLS\ICMP directory tree for the .H and .LIB files you'll need to access IcmpCreateFile, IcmpCloseHandle, and IcmpSendEcho.

SNMP, the Simple Network Management Protocol, is supported in Windows NT as a layer on top of Windows Sockets. SNMP is good for making your application manageable in a heterogeneous environment, especially one where UNIX management station software is already present. On the Windows NT 3.51 SDK CD-ROM, you can find slides explaining SNMP extensions in the file PDC\SLIDES\ROSAT251.PPT, and code samples in the directory PDC\SNMP.

NetBIOS

There is one and only one function to support NetBIOS in Win32, NetBIOS. It takes one parameter: a pointer to a network-control block (NCB) structure, which holds all the semantic content for the service. The NCB contains a command, a return code, information about the network environment, and a pointer to a buffer that is used for messages or for further data about the network:[2]

2. This and succeeding reference materials in this appendix are based on information supplied by Microsoft in their Win32 documentation from the *Windows NT System Development Kit.*

```
typedef struct _NCB { /* ncb */
   UCHAR    ncb_command;  /* command code                   */
   UCHAR    ncb_retcode;  /* return code                    */
   UCHAR    ncb_lsn;      /* local session number           */
   UCHAR    ncb_num;      /* number of network name         */
   PUCHAR   ncb_buffer;   /* address of message buffer      */
   WORD     ncb_length;   /* size of message buffer         */
   UCHAR    ncb_callname[NCBNAMSZ];
                          /* blank-padded name of remote */
   UCHAR    ncb_name[NCBNAMSZ];
                             /* blank-padded name of local  */
   UCHAR    ncb_rto;      /* receive timeout/retry count */
   UCHAR    ncb_sto;      /* send timeout/system timeout */
   void (*ncb_post) (struct _NCB *);
                            /* POST routine address       */
   UCHAR    ncb_lana_num; /* lana (adapter) number          */
   UCHAR    ncb_cmd_cplt; /* 0xff => command pending     */
   UCHAR    ncb_reserve[10]; /* reserved, used by BIOS      */
   HANDLE   ncb_event;    /* signaled when ASYNCH completes */
} NCB, *PNCB;
```

The Win32 implementation of the NetBIOS function includes some enhancements that are not part of the IBM NetBIOS 3.0 specification, and a few differences in implementation from IBM NetBIOS 3.0. The enhancements allow POST routines to be called from C, and allow for completion notification using a Win32 event object. The differences are minor.

The *ncb_command* member of the NCB structure specifies the command code and a flag in the most significant bit (the ASYNCH constant) that indicates whether the NCB is processed asynchronously. The command codes have the actions given in Table A1.5. Note that the symbolic NCB command names used here, which match those in the NB30.H file supplied with the Win32 SDK, might be somewhat different from the symbolic names defined for DOS NetBIOS programming environments.

The ncb_retcode member of NCB specifies the return code. This value is set to NRC_PENDING while an asynchronous operation is in progress. Once the operation is completed, the return code is set to one of the values listed in Table A1.6.

The ncb_lsn member of NCB specifies the local session number, ncb_buffer points to the message buffer, and ncb_length specifies the size, in bytes, of the message buffer. ncb_callname specifies the string that contains the remote name, and ncb_name specifies the string that contains the local name. Trailing space characters should be supplied in both names to pad the length of the strings out to the length specified by the NCBNAMSZ command.

Table A1.5 NetBIOS Commands

NCB Command Code	Action
NCBACTION	Enables extensions to the transport interface. NCBACTION commands are mapped to TdiAction. When this value is specified, the ncb_buffer member points to a buffer to be filled with an ACTION_HEADER structure, which is optionally followed by data. NCBACTION commands cannot be canceled by using NCBCANCEL.
NCBADDGRNAME	Adds a group name to the local name table.
NCBADDNAME	Adds a unique name to the local name table.
NCBASTAT	Retrieves the status of the adapter. When this value is specified, the ncb_buffer member points to a buffer to be filled with an ADAPTER_STATUS structure, followed by an array of NAME_BUFFER structures.
NCBCALL	Opens a session with another name.
NCBCANCEL	Cancels a previous command.
NCBCHAINSEND	Sends the contents of two data buffers to the specified session partner. For Windows NT, this is equivalent to the NCBCHAINSENDNA command.
NCBCHAINSENDNA	Sends the contents of two data buffers to the specified session partner and does not wait for acknowledgment. For Windows NT, this is equivalent to the NCBCHAINSEND command.
NCBDELNAME	Deletes a name from the local name table.
NCBDGRECV	Receives a datagram from any name.
NCBDGRECVBC	Receives broadcast datagram from any host.
NCBDGSEND	Sends datagram to a specified name.
NCBDGSENDBC	Sends a broadcast datagram to every host on the local area network (LAN).
NCBENUM	Enumerates LAN adapter (LANA) numbers. When this value is specified, the ncb_buffer member points to a buffer to be filled with a LANA_ENUM structure.
NCBFINDNAME	Determines the location of a name on the network. When this value is specified, the ncb_buffer member points to a buffer to be filled with a FIND_NAME_HEADER structure, followed by one or more FIND_NAME_BUFFER structures.

(continues)

Table A1.5 (*Continued*)

NCB Command Code	Action
NCBHANGUP	Closes a specified session.
NCBLANSTALERT	Notifies the user of LAN failures that last for more than one minute.
NCBLISTEN	Enables a session to be opened with another name.
NCBRECV	Receives data from the specified session partner.
NCBRECVANY	Receives data from any session corresponding to a specified name.
NCBRESET	Resets a LAN adapter. An adapter must be reset before any other NCB command that specifies the same number in the ncb_lana_num member will be accepted. The IBM NetBIOS 3.0 specifications document several NCB_RESET NCBs. Win32 implements the NCB.RESET Using the Dynamic Link Routine Interface. Particular values can be passed in specific bytes of the NCB. More specifically: If ncb_lsn is not 0x00, all resources associated with ncb_lana_num are to be freed. If ncb_lsn is 0x00, all resources associated with ncb_lana_num are to be freed, and new resources are to be allocated. The byte ncb_callname[0] specifies the maximum number of sessions, and the byte ncb_callname[2] specifies the maximum number of names. A nonzero value for the byte ncb_callname[3] requests that the application use NAME_NUMBER_1.
NCBSEND	Sends data to the specified session partner. For Windows NT, this is equivalent to the NCBSENDNA command.
NCBSENDNA	Sends data to specified session partner and does not wait for an acknowledgment. For Windows NT, this is equivalent to the NCBSEND command.
NCBSSTAT	Retrieves the status of the session. When this value is specified, the ncb_buffer member points to a buffer to be filled with a SESSION_HEADER structure, followed by one or more SESSION_BUFFER structures.
NCBTRACE	Activates or deactivates NCB tracing. Support for this command in the system is optional and system-specific.
NCBUNLINK	Unlinks the adapter.

Table A1.6 NCB Return Codes

Return Code	Meaning
NRC_GOODRET	The operation succeeded.
NRC_BUFLEN	An illegal buffer length was supplied.
NRC_ILLCMD	An illegal command was supplied.
NRC_CMDTMO	The command was timed out.
NRC_INCOMP	The message was incomplete. The application is to issue another command.
NRC_BADDR	The buffer address was illegal.
NRC_SNUMOUT	The session number was out of range.
NRC_NORES	No resource was available.
NRC_SCLOSED	The session was closed.
NRC_CMDCAN	The command was canceled.
NRC_DUPNAME	A duplicate name existed in the local name table.
NRC_NAMTFUL	The name table was full.
NRC_ACTSES	The command finished; the name has active sessions and is no longer registered.
NRC_LOCTFUL	The local session table was full.
NRC_REMTFUL	The remote session table was full. The request to open a session was rejected.
NRC_ILLNN	An illegal name number was specified.
NRC_NOCALL	The system did not find the name that was called.
NRC_NOWILD	Wildcards are not permitted in the ncb_name member.
NRC_INUSE	The name was already in use on the remote adapter.
NRC_NAMERR	The name was deleted.
NRC_SABORT	The session ended abnormally.
NRC_NAMCONF	A name conflict was detected.
NRC_IFBUSY	The interface was busy.
NRC_TOOMANY	Too many commands were outstanding; the application can retry the command later.
NRC_BRIDGE	The ncb_lana_num member did not specify a valid network number.
NRC_CANOCCR	The command finished while a cancel operation was occurring.
NRC_CANCEL	The NCBCANCEL command was not valid; the command was not canceled.

(continues)

Table A1.6 (*Continued*)

Return Code	Meaning
NRC_DUPENV	The name was defined by another local process.
NRC_ENVNOTDEF	The environment was not defined. A reset command must be issued.
NRC_OSRESNOTAV	Operating system resources were exhausted. The application can retry the command later.
NRC_MAXAPPS	The maximum number of applications was exceeded.
NRC_NOSAPS	No SAPs available for NetBIOS.
NRC_NORESOURCES	The requested resources were not available.
NRC_INVADDRESS	The NCB address was not valid. This return code is not part of the IBM NetBIOS 3.0 specification. This return code is not returned in the NCB; instead, it is returned by the NetBIOS function.
NRC_INVDDID	The NCB DDID was invalid.
NRC_LOCKFAIL	The attempt to lock the user area failed.
NRC_OPENERR	An error occurred during an open operation being performed by the device driver. This return code is not part of the IBM NetBIOS 3.0 specification.
NRC_SYSTEM	A system error occurred.
NRC_PENDING	An asynchronous operation is not yet finished.

ncb_rto sets the receive time-out period, in 500-millisecond units, for the session, and is used only for NCBRECV commands. Likewise, ncb_sto sets the send time-out period, in 500-millisecond units, for the session, and is used only for NCBSEND and NCBCHAINSEND commands. A value of 0 implies no timeout.

ncb_post specifies the address of the routine to call when an asynchronous NCB finishes. The completion routine is passed a pointer to the completed network-control block.

ncb_lana_num specifies the LAN adapter number. This zero-based number corresponds to a particular transport provider using a particular LAN adapter board. ncb_cmd_cplt specifies the command-complete flag, which has the same as the ncb_retcode member. ncb_reserve is reserved and must be set to zero.

ncb_event specifies a handle to a Windows NT event to be set to the signaled state when an asynchronous network-control block finishes. The event is signaled if the NetBIOS function returns a nonzero value. The ncb_event member of NCB must be zero if the ncb_command member does not have the

ASYNCH value set or if ncb_post is nonzero. Otherwise, NRC_ILLCMD is returned. In other words, you can't ask for more than one notification that a NCB request has completed: It is either synchronous, signals an event, or calls a completion routine.

The event specified by ncb_event is set to the nonsignaled state by the system when an asynchronous NetBIOS command is accepted, and is set to the signaled state when the asynchronous NetBIOS command finishes. Using ncb_event to submit asynchronous requests requires fewer system resources than using ncb_post. Also, when ncb_event is nonzero, the pending request is canceled if the thread terminates before the request is processed. This is not true for requests sent by using ncb_post.

Only manual reset events should be used with NetBIOS. A given event should not be associated with more than one active asynchronous NetBIOS command.

How can we use NetBIOS? Let's go through a very simple example, one that doesn't actually do anything but does illustrate working successfully with NetBIOS from Win32. We'll start by initializing the session and adding a name. This is normally done from the server:

```c
#define WIN32
#include <windows.h>
#include <nb30.h>
#include <stdlib.h>
#include <stdio.h>
#include <memory.h>

#define NSESSIONS 1
#define NNAMES    1
//...
char chNameBuffer [ NCBNAMSZ ];
unsigned char ucRc;
int i;
NCB ncb;
//...
// Code to initialize chNameBuffer should come here (not shown)
//....

/* reset NetBIOS session */

memset(&ncb,0,sizeof(ncb));
ncb.ncb_command = NCBRESET;
ncb.ncb_callname[0] = NSESSIONS;
ncb.ncb_callname[1] = NNAMES;
```

```
ucRc = NetBIOS (&ncb);

/* Add a Name */

memset(&ncb,0,sizeof(ncb));
ncb.ncb_command = NCBADDNAME;
memcpy (ncb.ncb_name, chNameBuffer, NCBNAMSZ);
ucRc = NetBIOS (&ncb);
if (ucRc )
   return (1);
```

The server would normally start a session and post a receive at this point, assuming it uses connections and not datagrams. Basically the server now has to wait for the client. The client first has to find the server by name:

```
struct {
    FIND_NAME_HEADER fnh;
    FIND_NAME_BUFFER fnb;
    } fn;

/* Find the Name  */

memset(&ncb,0,sizeof(ncb));
memset(&fn.fnh,0,sizeof(fn.fnh));
memset(&fn.fnb,0,sizeof(fn.fnb));
fn.fnh.node_count = 1;
fn.fnb.length = sizeof(fn.fnb);
ncb.ncb_command = NCBFINDNAME;
memcpy (ncb.ncb_callname, chNameBuffer, NCBNAMSZ);
ncb.ncb_buffer = (PUCHAR)&fn.fnh;
ncb.ncb_length =  sizeof(fn);
ucRc = NetBIOS (&ncb);
```

Now we can send a datagram, or establish a session and send messages. When the server is all done, it needs to delete the name:

```
/* Delete the Name */

memset(&ncb,0,sizeof(ncb));
ncb.ncb_command = NCBDELNAME;
memcpy (ncb.ncb_name, chNameBuffer,  NCBNAMSZ);
ucRc = NetBIOS (&ncb);
```

If you're already familiar with NetBIOS programming from DOS, Windows, or OS/2, you probably now understand the Win32 NetBIOS function well enough to use it. If you aren't familiar with NetBIOS programming and need to use it from Windows NT, you'll want to consult a good NetBIOS programming book—but expect to have to mentally translate systems.

The Win32 NetBIOS function, unlike DOS, doesn't require you to issue interrupts. Unlike Windows, it doesn't require you to call it from assembly language, from a DLL, or with locked NCBs. Unlike OS/2, it doesn't require you to call additional functions. Like all of those, however, it requires NetBIOS names to be padded with blanks, so you'll want to use a function like CopyToBuffer to work with them:

```
void CopyToBuffer ( char *pchDest , char *pchSrc)
{
    register count;

    /* Check for null pointer */
    if ((!pchDest) || ( ! pchSrc))
        return ;

    /* set the name field with nulls */
    memset ( pchDest, 0x20, NCBNAMSZ);

    /* copy from source to destination */
    count =  NCBNAMSZ;
    while ((*pchSrc) && ( count))
    {
        *pchDest++ = *pchSrc++;
        count-;
    }
    return;
}
```

As you are probably aware, you can build entire client-server systems using only NetBIOS—although no one would call that a convenient way to develop new programs. Fortunately, Win32 supports a number of other network mechanisms.

WNet

The WNet group of functions allows you to explicitly manipulate network disk and printer connections and other network resources from your applications. As such, they allow you to add some of functionality of File Manager, Print

Table A1.7 WNet Functions

Function Name	*Action*
WNetAddConnection	Redirects a local device to a network resource.
WNetAddConnection2	Redirects a local device to a network resource.
WNetCancelConnection	Breaks an existing network connection.
WNetCancelConnection2	Breaks an existing network connection.
WNetCloseEnum	Ends a network resource list.
WNetConnectionDialog	Starts a network connection dialog box.
WNetDisconnectDialog	Starts a network disconnection dialog box.
WNetEnumResource	Continues listing network resources.
WNetGetConnection	Gets name of network resource.
WNetGetLastError	Returns last error for network functions.
WNetGetUser	Gets the current network user name.
WNetOpenEnum	Starts listing network resources.

Manager, *net use*, and *net view* to your own programs. The WNet functions are listed in Table A1.7. To use any of these functions, you need to link to MPR.LIB, the multiple provider router library.

Note that WNetAddConnection and WNetCancelConnection are already obsolete: They are present in Win32 for compatibility with Windows for Workgroups programs, and have been replaced with WNetAddConnection2 and WNetCancelConnection2, respectively, which are considerably more flexible. WNetAddConnection2 and the resource enumeration functions WNetOpenEnum, WNetEnumResource, and WNetCloseEnum use the NETRESOURCE structure to describe network resources:

```
typedef struct _NETRESOURCE {  /* nr */
    DWORD  dwScope;           //connected, global, or persistent
    DWORD  dwType;            //any, disk, or print
    DWORD  dwDisplayType;     //domain, generic, server, or share
    DWORD  dwUsage;           //connectable or container
    LPTSTR lpLocalName;       //i.e. H: or LPT3:
    LPTSTR lpRemoteName;      //remote network name
    LPTSTR lpComment;         //provider-supplied comment
    LPTSTR lpProvider;        //provider name
} NETRESOURCE;
```

If you want to give control of network connections to the user, use the WNetConnectionDialog function to put up a dialog box, enumerate the network resources and display them, and allow the user to connect to resources:

```
DWORD dwResult;
dwResult = WNetConnectionDialog(hWnd, RESOURCETYPE_DISK);
if(dwResult != NO_ERROR) {
    MyErrorHandler(hWnd, dwResult, (LPSTR)"WNetConnectionDialog");
    return FALSE;
  }
```

In general, the alternatives to RESOURCETYPE_DISK are RESOURCETYPE_PRINT and RESOURCETYPE_ANY. WNetConnectionDialog, however, works only with RESOURCETYPE_DISK—it brings up the standard Connect Network Drive dialog (Figure A1.1). One wonders whether some future version of the function will implement printer browsing as well.

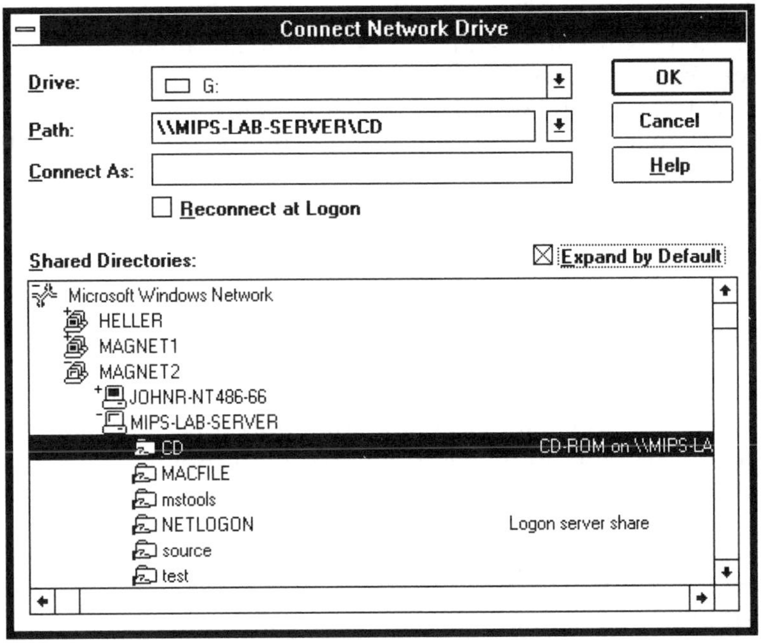

Figure A1.1 WNetConnectionDialog.

The WNetConnectionDialog Win32 API function generates the familiar Connect Network Drive dialog used to associate drive letters with network resources in Windows NT.

One more function in this group bears comment. WNetGetUser does more than meets the eye: It not only can find the current default user name, but it can also find the user name used to establish any given network connection:

```
DWORD WNetGetUser(lpszLocalName, lpszUserName, lpcchBuffer)

LPTSTR lpszLocalName; /* address of local name to get user name
                            for */
LPTSTR lpszUserName;  /* address of buffer for user name*/
LPDWORD lpcchBuffer;  /* address of buffer-size variable*/
```

If you use NULL for the local name, you get the current user name for the process. If you specify a share name, you will get the user name used to connect to the share. If there are multiple connections with multiple names, you'll get one of the user names—but there's no telling which one.

Closely related to the WNet and security APIs are some group and user control APIs with *Net* prefixes. These are not LanMan APIs, even though they appear to be from their naming.

The global group APIs—NetGroupAdd, NetGroupSetUsers, NetGroupAddUser, NetGroupSetInfo, and so on—control global groups of users in a way that can be used across domains.

The local group APIs—NetLocalGroupAdd, NetLocalGroupSetMembers, NetLocalGroupAddMember, and so on—control sets of users with common permissions in the security database.

User APIs—NetUserEnum, NetUserGetGroups, NetUserGetLocalGroups, NetUserAdd, NetUserDel, NetUserGetInfo, and NetUserSetInfo—control individual user accounts in the security database.

Mailslots

As we mentioned earlier, mailslots are convenient for broadcasting messages and other one-way communications tasks. Only three API functions are needed to support mailslots, as shown in Table A1.8; the rest of the mailslot functionality is performed with standard file functions, since mailslots act as pseudofiles.

Table A1.8 Mailslot API Server Functions

Function	Action
CreateMailslot	Creates a mailslot.
GetMailslotInfo	Retrieves mailslot information.
SetMailslotInfo	Sets mailslot read time out.

Note that, unlike real files, mailslots are temporary. When every handle of a mailslot is closed, or the process owning the last handle exits, the mailslot and all the data it contains are deleted. The data in a mailslot message can be in any form, within the length limit set when the mailslot was created.

A server process creates a mailslot with the CreateMailslot function, which returns a handle to the mailslot:

```
HANDLE CreateMailslot(lpszName, cbMaxMsg, dwReadTimeout, lpsa)

LPCTSTR lpszName;               /* address of string for mailslot name*/
DWORD cbMaxMsg;                  /* maximum message size*/
DWORD dwReadTimeout;           /* milliseconds before read timeout*/
LPSECURITY_ATTRIBUTES lpsa;   /* address of security structure*/
```

The lpszName parameter to CreateMailslot is required to be of the form \\.\mailslot\[path]name, and must be unique. The name may include multiple levels of pseudodirectories separated by backslashes. For example, both \\.\mailslot\example_mailslot_name and \\.\mailslot\abc\def\ghi are valid names. The cbMaxMsg parameter specifies the maximum message size that can be written to the mailslot, in bytes; zero means that the size is unlimited. dwReadTimeout specifies the amount of time, in milliseconds, a read operation can wait for a message to be written to the mailslot before a time out occurs. A value of zero means that reads return immediately if no message is present, a value of MAILSLOT_WAIT_FOREVER, defined as -1, means that reads to the mailslot never time out.

lpsa is a security descriptor for the mailbox; we'll discuss security descriptors a little later on. Most of the time you can safely use NULL for the security descriptor, which causes the object to get default security attributes. You'll need a real security descriptor if you want to pass the mailbox handle to child processes, or you actually want to restrict access to the mailbox to authorized processes.

To open a mailslot from a client process, use on the mailslot name, with FILE_SHARE_READ and OPEN_EXISTING specified as flags. If the mailslot is local to the client, its name is the same one used when it was created; for example, \\.\mailslot\name. If the mailslot is remote, you can specify \\computername\mailslot\name, \\domainname\mailslot\name, or *\mailslot\name. The last two forms are used for domain-wide broadcasts: The * form broadcasts in the local system's primary domain, and the \\domainname form broadcasts in the specified domain. If you use either domain-wide broadcast form, you cannot write more than 400 bytes at a time to the mailslot.

Note that opening a mailslot from the client side can return a valid handle even if the mailslot doesn't exist. And remember that mailslot communications use datagrams, which are not inherently reliable. Don't use a mailslot for a message that absolutely must get through.

Once you've opened the mailslot, you can write messages to it using WriteFile and the handle returned from CreateFile. The server reads messages with Read-File. When you are done with the mailslot, release it with CloseHandle.

The only other functions that can be used with mailslots are Get-MailSlotInfo, SetMailSlotInfo, GetFileTime, SetFileTime, and DuplicateHandle. Mailslot clients should restrict themselves to CreateFile, DuplicateHandle, WriteFile, and CloseHandle.

MAPI

While mailslots are good for sending transient one-way interprocess messages and message broadcasts, they are inappropriate for persistent messages, reliable messages, and applications that require two-way communication. For persistent, reliable one-way messages, it might be better to use MAPI, the Messaging Application Program Interface. For transient, reliable two-way interprocess communications, named pipes might be a better choice. Let's address MAPI first.

MAPI is a set of high-level functions that applications use to create, manipulate, transfer, and store messages. MAPI provides a common interface, which application developers use to create mail-enabled and mail-aware applications independently of the underlying messaging system. In addition to a message store interface used to create and manage collections of messages, MAPI also includes an address book interface for access to mail recipients and distribution lists.

MAPI comes in two flavors: Simple MAPI and Extended MAPI. Simple MAPI is built into Windows NT and Windows for Workgroups, as Microsoft Mail comes with both systems. You can add Simple MAPI capabilities to a Windows 3.1 system by adding Microsoft Mail to the system. Extended MAPI will require a *Windows Messaging Subsystem*, expected in a future release of Windows, probably both Chicago and Cairo.

Extended MAPI augments Simple MAPI with additional functions for advanced addressing, and folder and message management. Applications will be able to use Extended MAPI to create and deal with large and/or complex messages, to access portions of a directory service, and to organize and search a large store of messages.

The Simple MAPI functions are listed in Table A1.9. To use these functions, you will need to include MAPI.H and dynamically link to MAPI32.DLL (from a 32-bit application) or MAPI.DLL (from a 16-bit application).

The following code will allow you to dynamically link to the MAPI service DLL and get the address of the single function needed to mail-enable an application, MAPISendDocuments:

Table A1.9 Simple MAPI Functions

Function	Description
MAPIAddress	Addresses a Mail message.
MAPIDeleteMail	Deletes a Mail message.
MAPIDetails	Displays a Recipient Details dialog box.
MAPIFindNext	Returns the ID of the next (or first) Mail message of a specified type.
MAPIFreeBuffer	Frees memory allocated by the messaging system.
MAPILogoff	Ends a session with the messaging system.
MAPILogon	Begins a session with the messaging system.
MAPIReadMail	Reads a Mail message.
MAPIResolveName	Displays a dialog box to resolve an ambiguous recipient name.
MAPISaveMail	Saves a Mail message.
MAPISendDocuments	Sends a standard Mail message using a dialog box.
MAPISendMail	Sends a Mail message, allowing greater flexibility in message generation.

```
#ifdef WIN32
#define MAPIDLL "MAPI32.DLL"
#else
#define MAPIDLL "MAPI.DLL"
#define SZ_MAPISENDDOC "MAPISendDocuments"
extern ULONG (FAR PASCAL *lpfnMAPISendDocuments)(ULONG, LPSTR,
                                           LPSTR, LPSTR, ULONG);

extern HANDLE hLibrary;

int FAR PASCAL InitMAPI() {
  if ((hLibrary = LoadLibrary(MAPIDLL)) < 32)
    return(ERR_LOAD_LIB);
  if ((lpfnMAPISendDocuments= GetProcAddress(hLibrary,
          SZ_MAPISENDDOC)) == NULL)
    return(ERR_LOAD_FUNC);
  return(0);
}
```

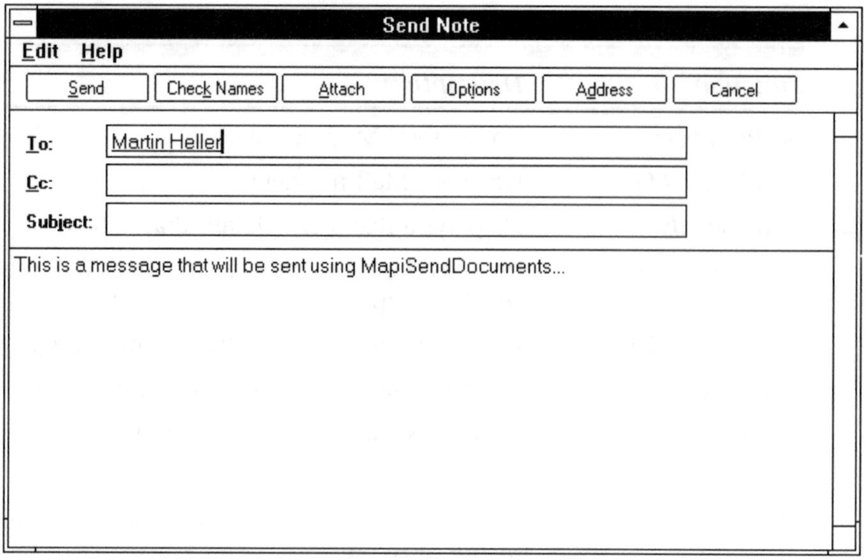

Figure A1.2 MAPISendDocuments.

The MAPISendDocuments Win32 API function generates the Send Mail dialog shown here. This allows applications to be mail-enabled with a minimum of programming.

Once you've successfully linked to MAPI32.DLL or MAPI.DLL and retrieved a pointer to MAPISendDocuments, you should add a Send menu item to the File menu of your application. Enable the menu item when there is a current document in the application, and disable it when there is no current document. When the menu item is picked, you'll need to process it. If yours is an MDI application, you might want to offer a choice between "Send current document" or "Send all documents." Whether you are sending a single document or multiple documents, the logic for each document is the same: Save the current file as a temporary, call MAPISendDocuments for the temporary file, and finally delete the temporary file. The following code snippet calls MAPISendDocuments:

```
ulResult = (*lpfnMAPISendDocuments)(hWnd, ";",
 lpszFullPathToTemporaryFile, lpszTemporaryFileName, OL);
```

Amazingly, that's all there is to mail-enabling an application. The user will see a Login dialog if not already logged into Mail, and then will see a Mail dialog with the file already listed, like the one shown in Figure A1.2. Where in the world did all *that* user interface come from? From MS-Mail. You're actually using MAPI to tap into MS-Mail, which is acting as the mail service provider.

That's quite a bit of application to get from one function call. If you want to send documents or mail messages without involving the user—or you simply want more control over the message—you can use an alternate function, MAPISendMail:

```
ULONG MAPISendMail(lhSession, ulUIParam,  lpMessage, flFlags,



                 ulReserved)
LHANDLE  lhSession;    //session handle, 0 or as returned by MAPILogon
ULONG  ulUIParam; //parent window handle, or 0
lpMapiMessage  lpMessage; //pointer to MapiMessage structure
ULONG  flFlags;    //specify whether or not to display login and send
                   //message dialogs, and whether to use a default
                   //MAPI session if it exists
ULONG  ulReserved; //must be 0
```

You can use MAPISendMail to accomplish much the same end as MAPI-SendDocuments, if you wish:

```
long err;
MapiFileDesc file = {0, 0, "c:\tmp\tmp.wk3", "budget17.wk3", NULL};
MapiMessage note = {0,NULL,NULL,NULL,NULL,NULL,0,NULL,0,NULL,1,&file};

err = MAPISendMail (0L,0L,&note,MAPI_DIALOG,0L);
if (err != SUCCESS_SUCCESS )
   printf("Unable to send the message.\n");
```

Or, you can use MAPISendMail to send a completely automated message:

```
MapiRecipDesc recip[2];
MapiFileDesc file = {0, 0, "c:\budget17.wk3", "budget17.wk3",
                     NULL};
MapiMessage note = {0,NULL,
   "Attached is the budget proposal.\r\nSee you Monday.\r\n",
   NULL,NULL,NULL,0,NULL,2,NULL,1,&file};

recip[0].ulReserved = 0;
recip[0].nRecipClass = MAPI_TO;
recip[0].lpszName = "Sally Jones";
recip[0].lpszAddress = NULL;
recip[0].ulEIDSize = 0;
```

```
recip[0].lpEntryID = NULL;

recip[1].ulReserved = 0;
recip[1].nRecipClass = MAPI_CC;
recip[1].lpszName = "Marketing";
recip[1].lpszAddress = NULL;
recip[1].ulEIDSize = 0;
recip[1].lpEntryID = NULL;

note.lpRecips = &recip;

err = MAPISendMail (0L,0L,&note,0L,0L);
if (err != SUCCESS_SUCCESS )
    printf("Unable to send the message.\n");
```

None of the other Simple MAPI functions are any trickier than this. You would use MAPILogon and MAPILogoff to control sessions; MAPIFindNext, MAPIReadMail, MAPISaveMail, and MAPIDeleteMail to read and dispose incoming mail; and MAPIAddress, MAPIDetails, and MAPIResolveName to assist the user in addressing outgoing mail. MAPIFreeBuffer is needed to release memory allocated by MAPIAddress, MAPIReadMail, and MAPIResolveName.

Pipes

A pipe is a communication conduit with two ends: a process with a handle to one end can communicate with a process having a handle to the other end. Pipes can be one-way—where one end is read-only and the other end is write-only, or two-way—where both ends of the pipe can read or write. Pipes are similar to mailslots in that they are written to and read from like files. Win32 supports both anonymous (unnamed) pipes and named pipes. The pipe functions are listed in Table A1.10.

Anonymous Pipes

Anonymous pipes are unnamed, one-way pipes intended to transfer data between a parent process and a child process, or between two child processes of the same parent process. Anonymous pipes are always local: They cannot be used over a network. The CreatePipe function creates an anonymous pipe and returns two handles: one to the read end and one to the write end of the pipe. The read handle has only read access to the pipe, and the write handle has only write access to the pipe. To communicate through the pipe, a handle to one of the ends must be passed to another process. Usually, this is done through inheritance, where a child process inherits a handle from its parent process.

Table A1.10 Pipe Functions

Function	Action
CallNamedPipe	Multiple pipe operations.
ConnectNamedPipe	Waits for a client to connect.
CreateNamedPipe	Creates an instance of a named pipe.
CreatePipe	Creates an anonymous pipe.
DisconnectNamedPipe	Disconnects server end of a named pipe.
GetNamedPipeHandleState	Returns named-pipe handle information.
GetNamedPipeInfo	Returns named-pipe handle information.
PeekNamedPipe	Previews pipe-queue data.
SetNamedPipeHandleState	Sets pipe read and blocking mode and controls local buffering.
TransactNamedPipe	Reads and writes a named pipe.
WaitNamedPipe	Waits for a named pipe.

To read from the pipe, a process uses the read handle in a call to the ReadFile function. To write to the pipe, a process uses the write handle in a call to the WriteFile function. Neither ReadFile nor WriteFile returns until the specified number of bytes has been read or written or an error occurs. Asynchronous I/O is not supported for pipes. An anonymous pipe exists until all handles to both read and write ends of the pipe are closed by the CloseHandle function.

Named Pipes

Named pipes are considerably more flexible than anonymous pipes. Named pipes can be one-way or two-way, they can work over a network, and a server process can use a named pipe to communicate with one or more client processes.

The server process uses CreateNamedPipe to create one or more instances of a named pipe. All instances of a named pipe share the same pipe name, but each instance has its own buffers and handles and provides a separate conduit for client-server communication. When a client process specifies a pipe name in the CreateFile or CallNamedPipe functions, it connects to an instance of the pipe. This enables multiple client processes to use the same named pipe simultaneously. It is entirely possible for a single process to act as both a named pipe client and server.

The CreateNamedPipe function offers a number of options:

```
HANDLE CreateNamedPipe(lpName, dwOpenMode, dwPipeMode,
    nMaxInstances, nOutBufferSize, nInBufferSize, nDefaultTimeout,
    lpSecurityAttributes)

LPCTSTR lpName;                         /* address of pipe name*/
DWORD dwOpenMode;                       /* pipe open mode*/
DWORD dwPipeMode;                       /* pipe-specific modes*/
DWORD nMaxInstances;                    /* maximum number of instances*/
DWORD nOutBufferSize;                   /* out buffer size in bytes*/
DWORD nInBufferSize;                    /* in buffer size in bytes*/
DWORD nDefaultTimeout;                  /* timeout time in milliseconds*/
LPSECURITY_ATTRIBUTES lpSecurityAttributes;/* security attributes*/
```

The pipe name at creation has the form:\\.\pipe\pipename. The pipe name part of the name can include any character other than a backslash, including numbers and special characters. The entire pipe name string can be up to 256 characters long. Pipe names are not case sensitive. When a client connects to a named pipe over a network, it uses the name form \\servername\pipe\pipename. If the pipe is local, the \\.\pipe\pipename can be used by the client.

The pipe's open mode can be PIPE_ACCESS_DUPLEX, PIPE_ACCESS_INBOUND, or PIPE_ACCESS_OUTBOUND, corresponding to bidirectional data flow, flow from client to server, and flow from server to client, respectively. A pipe can optionally use write-through and/or overlapped mode, which can vary for different instances of the same pipe.

FILE_FLAG_WRITE_THROUGH, which enables write-through mode, affects only write operations on byte-type pipes, which we'll explain shortly. Write-through mode keeps the system from buffering data written into the pipe: In write-through mode, any function that writes to the pipe returns only when the data is actually transmitted across the network to the remote computer. Write-through mode improves reliability at the expense of efficiency.

FILE_FLAG_OVERLAPPED, which enables overlapped mode, allows functions that perform read, write, and connect operations to return immediately. Overlapped mode allows one thread to service multiple instances of a pipe, or perform simultaneous read and write operations on the same pipe handle. The alternative to overlapped mode, assuming that you want your named pipe server to handle multiple clients, is to spawn a thread per client.

In addition to directionality, write-through, and overlap, a named pipe's open mode can include any combination of security access flags, which can be different for different instances of the same pipe. The three possible security access flags are WRITE_DAC, which gives the caller write access to the named pipe's discretionary ACL; WRITE_OWNER, which gives the caller write access to the named pipe's owner; and ACCESS_SYSTEM_SECURITY, which gives the caller write access to the named pipe's system ACL.

An ACL is an access control list, the basic security control structure in Windows NT. A discretionary ACL is controlled by the owner of the object; a system ACL is controlled by the system administrator.

All of the preceding options apply to the named pipe's open mode, specified in the second parameter to CreateNamedPipe. A named pipe's *pipe* mode, specified in the third parameter to CreateNamedPipe, determines the pipe's type, read mode, and wait mode.

We mentioned earlier that a pipe must be in byte mode for write-through mode to be effective. PIPE_TYPE_BYTE means that data is written to the pipe as a stream of bytes. The alternative, PIPE_TYPE_MESSAGE, means that data is written to the pipe as a stream of messages. A pipe's write mode has to be the same for all instances.

In addition to a type or write mode, a named pipe has a read mode and a wait mode, which can differ among instances. PIPE_READMODE_BYTE is valid no matter what write mode was specified for the pipe.

PIPE_READMODE_MESSAGE works only for a message type pipe: The pipe data has to be written as messages to be read as messages, but messages can always be broken down into bytes.

PIPE_WAIT enables blocking mode, which means that transactions do not complete until there is data to read, all data is written, or a client is connected. Blocking pipes can in fact wait indefinitely. For nonblocking pipes, enabled by PIPE_NOWAIT, ReadFile, WriteFile, and ConnectNamedPipe always return immediately. Nonblocking mode is basically there for compatibility with LAN Manager: If you want to enable asynchronous pipe I/O, use FILE_FLAG_OVER-LAPPED in the open mode.

The fourth parameter to CreateNamedPipe specifies the maximum number of instances that can be created for the pipe, in the range of 1 through PIPE_UNLIMITED_INSTANCES. The fifth and sixth parameter size the pipe's output and input buffers, in bytes: The system will actually round the suggested sizes to allocation boundaries and limit them to some range. The sixth parameter assigns the pipe a default time-out value, in milliseconds. The final parameter points to a SECURITY_ATTRIBUTES structure; it can be NULL if you want the pipe to have a default security descriptor. The server calls CreateNamedPipe the first time, specifying the pipe's maximum number of simultaneous instances. To create additional instances, the server calls CreateNamedPipe again.

Once a pipe instance is created, a client process can connect to it by calling either CreateFile or CallNamedPipe. If a pipe instance is available, either returns a handle to the client end of the pipe instance. If no instances of the pipe are available, a client process can use WaitNamedPipe to wait for one to become available, then try CreateFile again.

CallNamedPipe is a client function that combines connecting to a pipe instance (and waiting for one to be available if necessary), writing a message, reading a message, and closing the pipe handle. CallNamedPipe can be used only with a message-type pipe.

The server process uses ConnectNamedPipe to determine when a client process is connected to a pipe handle. If the pipe handle is in blocking mode, ConnectNamedPipe does not return until a client is connected.

Both clients and servers can use ReadFile and WriteFile with pipes. Alternatively, ReadFileEx and WriteFileEx functions can be used if the pipe handle was opened for overlapped operations.

PeekNamedPipe performs a nondestructive read on a pipe, and also reports information about the pipe instance. TransactNamedPipe, which works only with message-type pipes in message-read mode, writes a request message and reads a reply message in a single operation.

DisconnectNamedPipe is a server function to close the connection to the client process: It makes the client's handle invalid (if it has not already been closed), and discards any unread data in the pipe. The server can avoid closing the connection before the client has read all the data by calling FlushFileBuffers prior to calling DisconnectNamedPipe. Once the client is disconnected, the server can either call CloseHandle to destroy the pipe instance, or call Connect-NamedPipe to let a new client connect to this instance.

GetNamedPipeInfo returns the type of the pipe, the size of the input and output buffers, and the maximum number of pipe instances that can be created. GetNamedPipeHandleState reports on the read and wait modes of a pipe handle, the current number of pipe instances, and so on. SetNamedPipeHandleState function sets the read mode and wait modes of a pipe handle, maximum number of bytes to collect (for a client), and/or the maximum time to wait before transmitting a message.

Let's recap the high points of named pipes. Named pipes are reliable network pseudofiles of the form \\servername\pipe\pipename. They can be unidirectional or bidirectional, buffered or unbuffered, overlapped or synchronous; and can contain byte or message streams. For compatibility with LAN Manager, pipes can be nonblocking, but normally you should use blocking pipes and enable overlapping if you want asynchronous I/O. Servers can create multiple instances of a pipe, and vary some of the pipe's parameters on an instance-by-instance basis; they can spawn a thread per synchronous pipe instance, or use a single thread to service multiple asynchronous pipe instances. Clients connect to a single instance of a pipe at a time.

Named pipes are reliable and have good performance for communications across a network. Because a single named pipe server can optionally connect to multiple clients, named pipes can be the basis of any client/server application requiring 1 to 1 or 1 to n connections in which it is reasonable for each client to establish its own connection. Named pipes would be a reasonable choice of transport for a database server, a transaction-processing system, a multiuser chat application, or a multiplayer game. Named pipes would not be a reasonable way to implement a message broadcast facility—that would be better implemented with mailslots, which don't require each receiver to explictly connect to the sender.

Microsoft supplies code for a multithreaded server service (and associated client) in the MSTOOLS\SAMPLES\SERVICE directory of the SDK. You might also want to examine the SDK example programs NPSERVER and NPCLIENT, which together implement a primitive multiuser chat system. In the Windows NT SDK, you'll find them under the \MSTOOLS\SAMPLES\NAMEPIPE directory; in Visual C++ for NT, you'll find them under \MSVCNT\SAMPLES.

Remote Access

The Remote Access Services (RAS) functions offer the opportunity to develop applications that log into physically distant networks over modems and phone lines, or over better connections, like X.25, ISDN, or T1 links. The RAS functions are listed in table A1.11. RAS is an attractive alternative to developing your own remote access protocols or setting up bulletin board systems for remote reporting.

As you can see, the RAS API exposes the high-level functions used by the Windows NT RAS applets: functions to dial to and hang up from remote networks, functions to list the active connections and the entries in a RAS phone book, and a function to report the status of a connection. This set of functions is simple, so we won't show you a code sample: You won't have any trouble figuring out how to use them yourself. Once you have a connection established, you can use the WNet services to connect to remote hard disks, and then use ordinary file services to transfer information to the remote server.

Sockets

Aside from being the standard network programming mechanism in Berkeley UNIX, sockets are quite flexible and fairly simple to use. The Windows and

Table A1.11 Remote Access Functions

Function	Action
RasDial	Establishes a RAS connection.
RasDialFunc	Callback function called by RasDial on state changes.
RasEnumConnections	Lists active RAS connections.
RasEnumEntries	Lists entries in a RAS phone book.
RasGetConnectStatus	Reports current status of a RAS connection.
RasGetErrorString	Converts RAS error code to error string.
RasHangUp	Terminates a RAS connection.

Windows NT implementation of sockets includes some extensions to make sockets more efficient, but you really have to use only the initialization and termination routines (WSAStartup and WSACleanup) from the Windows extensions.

The basic Berkeley-style socket routines included in Windows Sockets are listed in Table A1.12; the so-called *database* or *getXbyY* functions are listed in Table A1.13; and the Windows extensions are listed in Table A1.14.

You initialize Windows Sockets by calling WSAStartup. You'll find the appropriate logic in the WM_CREATE section of MainWndProc in the WSOCK.C sample application Microsoft supplies with the Windows NT System Development Kit (SDK). A client can connect to a server by calling *socket* with the required socket type and the desired protocol, as shown in the WM_COMMAND / IDM_CONNECT case of MainWndProc; identifying the server, which is done in FillAddr in the example; and calling *connect*, shown in the IDM_CONNECT case.

A server waits for a connection with *socket*, *bind*, and *listen*, as shown in the IDM_LISTEN case. When a client connects, the server calls *accept*. The WSA-AsyncSelect function causes window messages to be sent when socket events, such as incoming data, need to be handled. Alternatively—most appropriately in a threaded application—the server can use *select* to determine when a socket needs to be read, or simply use *recv* or *recvfrom* to read the next data packet. This is demonstrated in AcceptThreadProc. To send data, use *send* or *sendto*, as shown in case IDM_SENDTCP.

The functions *recv* and *send* work only with connected stream sockets—the rough equivalent of NetBIOS sessions or named pipes. The functions *recvfrom* and *sendto* can also work with datagrams—the unreliable protocol that also allows broadcasting. You can use datagram sockets in the same sort of applications as you would use NetBIOS datagrams or mailslots.

If you are using connected sockets in Windows NT 3.51 or later, you can optimize file transfers by using the new TransmitFile function, which reads the file data directly from the system's cache manager and avoids the buffer-copying overhead incurred by calling ReadFile and Send. Sockets provide no inherent security mechanism, but Windows NT sockets support SSPI, the Security Support Provider Interface, which returns security *blobs* for the client and server to exchange. An SSPI server is provided in Windows NT 3.5 and above, and SSPI clients are included in Windows NT and Windows 95, and available for Windows 3.1.

Many socket programs falter on the issue of protocol-dependence. The "RNR" APIs in NT (beginning with version 3.5) and Windows 95 allow for service registration and name resolution, and are particularly useful when establishing sockets. EnumProtocols obtains information about network protocols active on a local server; GetAddressByName returns the local address

Table A1.12 Berkeley-Style Socket Routines

Function	*Action*
accept()	An incoming connection is acknowledged and associated with an immediately created socket. The original socket is returned to the listening state.
bind()	Assigns a local name to an unnamed socket.
closesocket()	Removes a socket descriptor from the per-process object reference table. Only blocks if SO_LINGER is set.
connect()	Initiates a connection on the specified socket.
getpeername()	Retrieves the name of the peer connected to the specified socket descriptor.
getsockname()	Retrieves the current name for the specified socket.
getsockopt()	Retrieves options associated with the specified socket descriptor.
htonl()	Converts a 32-bit quantity from host byte order to network byte order.
htons()	Converts a 16-bit quantity from host byte order to network byte order.
inet_addr()	Converts a character string representing a number in the Internet standard "." notation to an Internet address value.
inet_ntoa()	Converts an Internet address value to an ASCII string in "." notation; for example, a.b.c.d.
ioctlsocket()	Provides control for descriptors.
listen()	Listens for incoming connections on a specified socket.
ntohl()	Converts a 32-bit quantity from network byte order to host byte order.
ntohs()	Converts a 16-bit quantity from network byte order to host byte order.
recv()[*]	Receives data from a connected socket.
recvfrom()[*]	Receives data from either a connected or unconnected socket.
select()[*]	Performs synchronous I/O multiplexing.
send()[*]	Sends data to a connected socket.
sendto()[*]	Sends data to either a connected or unconnected socket.
setsockopt()	Stores options associated with the specified socket descriptor.
shutdown()	Shuts down part of a full-duplex connection.
socket()	Creates an end point for communication and returns a socket descriptor.

[*] The routine can block if acting on a blocking socket.

Table A1.13 Socket *Database* Functions

Function	Action
*gethostbyaddr()**	Retrieves the name(s) and address corresponding to a network address.
gethostname()	Retrieves the name of the local host.
*gethostbyname()**	Retrieves the name(s) and address corresponding to a host name.
*getprotobyname()**	Retrieves the protocol name and number corresponding to a protocol name.
*getprotobynumber()**	Retrieves the protocol name and number corresponding to a protocol number.
*getservbyname()**	Retrieves the service name and port corresponding to a service name.
*getservbyport()**	Retrieves the service name and port corresponding to a port.

* The routine can block under some circumstances.

information needed to bind the protocol to a socket, and is more powerful than the socket function gethostbyname.

For further information on socket programming, read through WSOCK.C, browse the WinSock help, and have a look at PDC\SLIDES\TREAD251.PPT for tips on making your socket-based application perform as well as it can.

Remote Procedure Calls

Remote Procedure Calls (RPCs) are simultaneously the simplest and most complicated network programming mechanism supported by Windows NT. They are the simplest in concept: A program on one machine asks another program possibly running on another machine to perform some function on its behalf in a way that looks a lot like an ordinary function call. But they are the most complicated in practice: Defining the interface to a remote procedure requires a whole separate specification language, IDL, and implementing the call requires several layers of services.

The *RPC Programmer's Guide and Reference* is completely separate from the five-volume *Win32 Programmer's Reference*. The RPC manual and the MIDL compiler come with the Windows NT SDK; they do not come with Visual C++ for Windows NT. Obviously, I'm not going to give you the contents of a 650-page

Table A1.14 Windows Asynchronous Socket Functions

Function	*Action*
WSAAsyncGetHostByAddr() *WSAAsyncGetHostByName()* *WSAAsyncGetProtoByName()* *WSAAsyncGetProtoByNumber()* *WSAAsyncGetServByName()* *WSAAsyncGetServByPort()*	A set of functions that provide asynchronous versions of the standard Berkeley getXbyY() functions. For example, the WSAAsyncGetHostByName() function provides an asynchronous message-based implementation of the standard Berkeley gethostbyname() function.
WSAAsyncSelect()	Performs asynchronous version of select().
WSACancelAsyncRequest()	Cancels an outstanding instance of a WSAAsyncGetXByY() function.
WSACancelBlockingCall()	Cancels an outstanding *blocking* API call.
WSACleanup()	Signs off from the underlying Windows Sockets DLL.
WSAGetLastError()	Obtains details of last Windows Sockets API error.
WSAIsBlocking()	Determines if the underlying Windows Sockets DLL is already blocking an existing call for this thread.
WSASetBlockingHook()	*Hooks* the blocking method used by the underlying Windows Sockets implementation.
WSASetLastError()	Sets the error to be returned by a subsequent WSAGetLastError().
WSAStartup()	Initializes the underlying Windows Sockets DLL.
WSAUnhookBlockingHook()	Restores the original blocking function.

manual here: All I want to do is give you a good feel for what RPCs can do and how to go about learning more. Table A1.15 lists the RPC API functions, but the API functions don't give you the whole picture.

In addition the the RPC API functions, you need to understand the Interface Definition Language (IDL), bindings, attributes, and transports. You can get all of this from the Microsoft RPC documentation, but you'll find it hard going unless you're already familiar with another implementation of RPCs, such as the Open System Foundation's Distributed Computing Environment (OSF DCE)

Table A1.15 RPC API Functions

RpcAbnormalTermination	RpcNetworkInqProtseqs	RpcNsProfileEltInqDone
RpcBindingCopy	RpcNetworkIsProtseqValid	RpcNsProfileEltInqNext
RpcBindingFree	RpcNsBindingExport	RpcNsProfileEltRemove
RpcBindingFromStringBinding	RpcNsBindingImportBegin	RpcObjectInqType
RpcBindingInqAuthClient	RpcNsBindingImportDone	RpcObjectSetInqFn
RpcBindingInqAuthInfo	RpcNsBindingImportNext	RpcObjectSetType
RpcBindingInqObject	RpcNsBindingInqEntryName	RpcProtseqVectorFree
RpcBindingReset	RpcNsBindingLookupBegin	RpcRaiseException
RpcBindingSetAuthInfo	RpcNsBindingLookupDone	RpcRevertToSelf
RpcBindingSetObject	RpcNsBindingLookupNext	RpcServerInqBindings
RpcBindingToStringBinding	RpcNsBindingSelect	RpcServerInqIf
RpcBindingVectorFree	RpcNsBindingUnexport	RpcServerListen
RpcEndExcept	RpcNsEntryExpandName	RpcServerRegisterAuthInfo
RpcEndFinally	RpcNsEntryObjectInqBegin	RpcServerRegisterIf
RpcEpRegister	RpcNsEntryObjectInqDone	RpcServerUnregisterIf
RpcEpRegisterNoReplace	RpcNsEntryObjectInqNext	RpcServerUseAllProtseqs
RpcEpResolveBinding	RpcNsGroupDelete	RpcServerUseAllProtseqsIf
RpcEpUnregister	RpcNsGroupMbrAdd	RpcServerUseProtseq
RpcExcept	RpcNsGroupMbrInqBegin	RpcServerUseProtseqEp
RpcExceptionCode	RpcNsGroupMbrInqDone	RpcServerUseProtseqIf
RpcFinally	RpcNsGroupMbrInqNext	RpcStringBindingCompose
RpcIfIdVectorFree	RpcNsGroupMbrRemove	RpcStringBindingParse
RpcIfInqId	RpcNsMgmtBindingUnexport	RpcStringFree
RpcImpersonateClient	RpcNsMgmtEntryCreate	RpcTryExcept
RpcMgmtEnableIdleCleanup	RpcNsMgmtEntryDelete	RpcTryFinally
RpcMgmtInqStats	RpcNsMgmtEntryInqIfIds	RpcWinSetYieldInfo
RpcMgmtIsServerListening	RpcNsMgmtHandleSetExpAge	UuidCreate
RpcMgmtSetComTimeout	RpcNsMgmtInqExpAge	UuidFromString
RpcMgmtSetServerStackSize	RpcNsMgmtSetExpAge	UuidToString
RpcMgmtStatsVectorFree	RpcNsProfileDelete	YieldFunctionName
RpcMgmtStopServerListening	RpcNsProfileEltAdd	
RpcMgmtWaitServerListen	RpcNsProfileEltInqBegin	

standard for UNIX. I'd like to walk you through "Hello World," done with RPCs at the most basic level (as basic as Chapter 2 of the RPC manual, but more concise) so that you'll be ready to attack the Microsoft RPC materials on your own.

I won't bore you with the standard code for "Hello World." The example we'll use first takes the small step of using a HelloProc function to write the string (I won't bore you with that, either); then it makes HelloProc a remote procedure.

The first step in setting up a remote procedure is to define the interface in IDL. An IDL file also needs a unique identification string, which you generate by running UUIDGEN, a tool that comes with the NT SDK. A minimal IDL file for HELLO might look like this:

```
[ uuid (6B29FC40-CA47-1067-B31D-00DD010662DA),  version(1.0) ]
interface hello
{
void HelloProc([in, string] unsigned char * pszString);
}
```

The top line of the file, the IDL header, contains the unique ID and the version number in square brackets. The last three lines of the file—the curly brackets and the declaration—constitute the IDL body. The non-C stuff in square brackets in the declaration gives additional information about the interface—in this case, pszString is an input string variable.

In addition to an IDL file, you need an ACF (Application Configuration File). A minimal ACF file for HELLO might look like the following:

```
[implicit_handle(handle_t hello_IfHandle)]
interface hello
{
}
```

While the IDL file contains the interface definition, the ACF contains RPC data and attributes that don't relate to the transmitted data. In this case, a binding handle is defined, which the RPC client uses to connect to the server. The interface name has to match the interface name given in the ACF file; the interface body is empty.

Compiling the IDL and ACF files with MIDL generates client and server C stub files and an include file. The stub files generated are actually pretty complicated—they're C programs to handle the client/server interaction over the network with RPC function calls. For instance, the client and server stubs for HelloProc look like this:

Hello_C.C (HelloProc client stub generated by MIDL)

```
#include <string.h>
#include "hello.h"
handle_t hello_IfHandle;
extern RPC_DISPATCH_TABLE hello_DispatchTable;
static RPC_CLIENT_INTERFACE ___RpcClientInterface = {
```

```
      sizeof(RPC_CLIENT_INTERFACE),
      {{0x906B0CE0,0xC70B,0x1067,{0xB3,0x17,0x00,0xDD,0x01,0x06,0x62,
        0xDA}},  {1,0}},
      {{0x8A885D04L,0x1CEB,0x11C9,{0x9F,0xE8,0x08,0x00,0x2B,0x10,0x48,
        0x60}},  {2,0}}, 0,0,0,0 };
RPC_IF_HANDLE hello_ClientIfHandle =
      (RPC_IF_HANDLE) &___RpcClientInterface;
void HelloProc(unsigned char *pszString)
  {
  unsigned char * _packet;
  unsigned int    _length;
  RPC_STATUS _status;
  RPC_MESSAGE _message;
  PRPC_MESSAGE _prpcmsg = & _message;

  ((void)( _packet ));
  ((void)( _length ));
  _message.Handle = hello_IfHandle;
  _message.RpcInterfaceInformation =
        (void __RPC_FAR *) &___RpcClientInterface;
  _prpcmsg->BufferLength = 0;
  if (pszString == (void *)0)
   RpcRaiseException(RPC_X_NULL_REF_POINTER);
  tree_size_ndr(&(pszString), _prpcmsg, "s1", 1);
  _message.ProcNum = 0;
  _status = I_RpcGetBuffer(&_message);
  if (_status) RpcRaiseException(_status);
  _packet = _message.Buffer;
  _length = _message.BufferLength;
  _message.BufferLength = 0;
  tree_into_ndr(&(pszString), _prpcmsg, "s1", 1);
  _message.Buffer = _packet;
  _message.BufferLength = _length;
  _status = I_RpcSendReceive(&_message);
  if (_status) RpcRaiseException(_status);
  _status = I_RpcFreeBuffer(&_message);
  if (_status) RpcRaiseException(_status);
  }
```

Hello_S.C (HelloProc server stub generated by MIDL)

```
#include <string.h>
#include "hello.h"
```

```
extern RPC_DISPATCH_TABLE hello_DispatchTable;
static RPC_SERVER_INTERFACE ___RpcServerInterface = {
 sizeof(RPC_SERVER_INTERFACE),
 {{0x906B0CE0,0xC70B,0x1067,{0xB3,0x17,0x00,0xDD,0x01,0x06,
  0x62,0xDA}}, {1,0}},
 {{0x8A885D04L,0x1CEB,0x11C9,{0x9F,0xE8,0x08,0x00,0x2B,0x10,
  0x48,0x60}}, {2,0}}, &hello_DispatchTable,0,0,0 };
RPC_IF_HANDLE hello_ServerIfHandle =
  (RPC_IF_HANDLE) &___RpcServerInterface;
void __RPC_STUB hello_HelloProc(PRPC_MESSAGE _prpcmsg)
 {
 unsigned char *pszString = (void *)0;
 unsigned long _alloc_total;
 unsigned long _valid_lower;
 unsigned long _valid_total;
 unsigned char * _packet;
 unsigned char * _tempbuf;
 unsigned char * _savebuf;
 RPC_STATUS _status;
 _packet = _prpcmsg->Buffer;
 ((void)( _alloc_total ));
 ((void)( _valid_total ));
 ((void)( _valid_lower ));
 ((void)( _packet ));
 ((void)( _tempbuf ));
 ((void)( _savebuf ));
 RpcTryExcept
   {
   _tempbuf = _prpcmsg->Buffer;
   // recv total number of elements
   long_from_ndr(_prpcmsg, &_alloc_total);
   if (pszString == (void *)0)
     {
     pszString = MIDL_user_allocate ((size_t)
      (_alloc_total * sizeof(char)));
     }
   data_from_ndr(_prpcmsg, (void __RPC_FAR *) (pszString),
     "s1", 1);
   }
 RpcExcept(1)
   {
       RpcRaiseException(RpcExceptionCode());
   }
```

```
RpcEndExcept
if ((((unsigned int)(((unsigned char *)_prpcmsg->Buffer)
  - _packet)) > _prpcmsg->BufferLength)
    RpcRaiseException(RPC_X_BAD_STUB_DATA);
RpcTryFinally
  {
  if (_prpcmsg->ManagerEpv)
    {
    ((hello_SERVER_EPV *)(_prpcmsg->ManagerEpv))
        ->HelloProc(pszString);
    }
  else
    {
    HelloProc(pszString);
    }
  _prpcmsg->BufferLength = 0;
  _prpcmsg->Buffer = _packet;
  _status = I_RpcGetBuffer(_prpcmsg);
  if (_status) RpcRaiseException(_status);
  }
RpcFinally
  {
  MIDL_user_free ((void __RPC_FAR *)pszString);
  }
RpcEndFinally
}
```

You aren't, however, saved from writing all the RPC code. In this application, the client is responsible for connecting to the server. You notice that the default protocol sequence used is for a named pipe, \pipe\hello:

From HELLOC.C *(hand-written client code)*

```
RPC_STATUS status;
unsigned char * pszUuid              = NULL;
unsigned char * pszProtocolSequence = "ncacn_np";
unsigned char * pszNetworkAddress   = NULL;
unsigned char * pszEndpoint          = "\\pipe\\hello";
unsigned char * pszOptions           = NULL;
unsigned char * pszStringBinding    = NULL;
unsigned char * pszString            = "hello, world";
unsigned long ulCode;
int i;
```

```
//...
status = RpcStringBindingCompose(pszUuid,
                                 pszProtocolSequence,
                                 pszNetworkAddress,
                                 pszEndpoint,
                                 pszOptions,
                                 &pszStringBinding);
printf("RpcStringBindingCompose returned 0x%x\n", status);
printf("pszStringBinding = %s\n", pszStringBinding);
if (status) {
    exit(status);
  }
status = RpcBindingFromStringBinding(pszStringBinding,
                                 &hello_IfHandle);
printf("RpcBindingFromStringBinding returned 0x%x\n", status);
if (status) {
    exit(status);
  }
printf("Calling the remote procedure 'HelloProc'\n");
printf("Print the string '%s' on the server\n", pszString);

RpcTryExcept {
    HelloProc(pszString);  // make call with user message
  }
RpcExcept(1) {
    ulCode = RpcExceptionCode();
    printf("Runtime reported exception 0x%1x = %ld\n", ulCode,
           ulCode);
  }
RpcEndExcept

status = RpcStringFree(&pszStringBinding);
printf("RpcStringFree returned 0x%x\n", status);
if (status) {
    exit(status);
  }

status = RpcBindingFree(&hello_IfHandle);
printf("RpcBindingFree returned 0x%x\n", status);
if (status) {
    exit(status);
  }
```

Boiled down to its essentials, the above code amounts to composing the binding string, establishing the binding, calling the remote procedure through its stub, freeing the binding string, and freeing the binding.

In addition to establishing its own binding prior to calling the remote procedure, the client has to provide callback routines so that the RPC libraries can allocate and free memory. In this case, they are trivial:

```
void    __RPC_FAR * __RPC_API midl_user_allocate(size_t len)
{
    return(malloc(len));
}

void __RPC_API midl_user_free(void __RPC_FAR * ptr)
{
    free(ptr);
}
```

On the server side, you need to write code to set the protocol sequence, register the interface, and listen for a client. The protocol used has to match on client and server:

```
RPC_STATUS status;
unsigned char * pszProtocolSequence = "ncacn_np";
unsigned char * pszSecurity          = NULL;
unsigned char * pszEndpoint           = "\\pipe\\hello";
unsigned int    cMinCalls            = 1;
unsigned int    cMaxCalls            = 20;
unsigned int    fDontWait            = FALSE;
int i;
//...

  status = RpcServerUseProtseqEp(pszProtocolSequence,
                                 cMaxCalls,
                                 pszEndpoint,
                                 pszSecurity);  // Security descriptor
printf("RpcServerUseProtseqEp returned 0x%x\n", status);
if (status) {
    exit(status);
    }


  status = RpcServerRegisterIf(hello_ServerIfHandle, //interface
                               NULL,    // MgrTypeUuid
```

```
                                  NULL);  // MgrEpv
printf("RpcServerRegisterIf returned 0x%x\n", status);
if (status) {
    exit(status);
    }


printf("Calling RpcServerListen\n");
status = RpcServerListen(cMinCalls,
                         cMaxCalls,
                         fDontWait);
printf("RpcServerListen returned: 0x%x\n", status);
if (status) {
    exit(status);
    }


if (fDontWait) {
    printf("Calling RpcMgmtWaitServerListen\n");
    status = RpcMgmtWaitServerListen(); // wait operation
    printf("RpcMgmtWaitServerListen returned: 0x%x\n", status);
    if (status) {
        exit(status);
        }
    }
```

You'll need to provide midl_user_allocate and midl_user_free callbacks on the server side: They're the same as on the client side. And finally, you'll need a way to tell the server to shut down, which we've omitted here for brevity. (You'll find it in the Microsoft MSTOOLS\SAMPLES\RPC\HELLO sample.) If we build the client and server, and run the server we'll see:

```
RpcServerUseProtseqEp returned 0x0
RpcServerRegisterIf returned 0x0
Calling RpcServerListen
```

Then the server will stop. If we run the client on another machine or in another CMD session on the same machine, the server will continue and display:

```
hello, world

Calling RpcMgmtStopServerListening
RpcMgmtStopServerListening returned: 0x0
```

```
Calling RpcServerUnregisterIf
RpcServerUnregisterIf returned 0x0
RpcServerListen returned: 0x0
```

What the client will display in its CMD session is:

```
RpcStringBindingCompose returned 0x0
pszStringBinding = ncacn_np:[\\pipe\\hello]
RpcBindingFromStringBinding returned 0x0
Calling the remote procedure 'HelloProc'
Print the string 'hello, world' on the server
Calling the remote procedure 'Shutdown'
RpcStringFree returned 0x0
RpcBindingFree returned 0x0
```

Obviously, that was an awful lot of work to make "Hello World" display. On the other hand, a great deal of the work was done with a few lines of IDL and ACF code, and the resulting client/server application works not only on a single Windows NT machine, but between two NT machines linked by a network, and between a DOS or Windows client and a Windows NT server. In addition, it works on a variety of network transports: In addition to named pipes, the NT implementation of RPC supports NetBIOS and TCP/IP transports. The Windows implementation supports all three of these plus DECnet, and the DOS implementation supports all the aforementioned plus SPX. There is no Win32s implementation of RPCs, however, at least in version 1.1 of Win32s.

We don't have space to cover many of the refinements you'll need to know about to write good distributed systems with RPCs, but there are a few tips you might want to consider to get decent runtime performance:

❑ Don't block threads in your RPC server.

❑ Keep the number of round trips to a minimum: Combine functions to the highest level that makes sense.

❑ Shut down your idle connections.

❑ Don't adjust your thread priorities.

❑ Disable thread library calls in your DLLs.

❑ Avoid allocations in your server.

Despite substantial propaganda to the effect that RPCs are the best network mechanism since sliced bread, the high development cost and mediocre runtime performance of RPCs prompts us to recommend caution in selecting this mechanism. If you already are using RPCs, or if RPCs are clearly the most appropriate fit to your architecture, by all means use them. But if you are looking for high bandwidth communications, other mechanisms may turn out to be better choices.

DDE and NetDDE

DDE is the principal mechanism for interprocess communication in 16-bit Windows. The Microsoft Windows Dynamic Data Exchange (DDE) protocol defines a method for communicating among applications, which takes place as applications send messages to each other to initiate conversations, to request and share data, and to terminate conversations.

In the *hot link* form of DDE transfer, the *server* application sends data to the *client* application whenever the data changes; this guarantees that the derived form of the data (perhaps a table in a word processing document) will always reflect the current state of the original data (perhaps a spreadsheet). A variation of this, the *warm link*, notifies the client when the data has changed, but sends the data only if the client wants it; this enables the client to control the rate at which it receives data. A simpler mechanism, the *request*, is equivalent to a single copy operation from the server and a single paste operation to the client, without the need for the intermediate step of putting the data on the clipboard.

DDE also supports a back-channel transfer, the *poke*. And *execute*, perhaps the most intriguing DDE mechanism of all, allows one application to control another.

DDE supports a *client/server* architecture in which both client and server programs carry on multiple *conversations* with other applications. Each conversation has a *topic* and may include multiple *advisories*, each of which refers to an *item*. The application is responsible for keeping track of ongoing conversations and advisories; conversations are uniquely identified by the window handles of the client and server.

Windows NT and Windows for Workgroups continue to support DDE as an interprocess communication protocol, and additionally support NetDDE, a special form of DDE that allows it to work across the network. Because of NT's security requirements and change from 16-bit handles to 32-bit handles, a few new DDE functions have been added in Win32. They are listed in Table A1.16.

The functions PackDDElParam and UnpackDDElParam allow the 32-bit program to pack and unpack parameters in the DDE message's lParam: Use them instead of MAKELONG, LOWORD, and HIWORD. ReuseDDElParam and FreeD-DElParam allow you to manage the dynamic memory used for packing parameters. The two impersonation functions allow a DDE server to take on the security attributes of its client: This is useful when a server has more privilege than the client and needs to maintain security. While you can still program DDE by sending messages, the preferred method for programming DDE is to use the Dynamic Data Exchange Management Library (DDEML). Both methods are

Table A1.16 New DDE Functions in Win32

Function	Action
DdeImpersonateClient	Impersonates a DDE client window.
DdeSetQualityOfService	Specifies DDE quality of service.
FreeDDElParam	Frees a DDE message lParam.
ImpersonateDdeClientWindow	Impersonates a DDE client window.
PackDDElParam	Packs data into a DDE message lParam.
ReuseDDElParam	Reuses a DDE message lParam.
UnpackDDElParam	Unpacks data from a DDE message lParam.

explained in Chapter 5 of my book Advanced Windows Programming. For your convenience, the DDEML functions are listed in Table A1-17.

NetDDE is a minor variation on DDE that can be used by all DDE-aware applications. Normally, you establish a DDE conversation with an application on a topic, and specify items within the topic. With NetDDE, the true application and topic are maintained in a DDE share, which is kept in a database. You establish a DDE conversation indirectly, by connecting to the special application NDDE$ on the remote machine, using the share name as the topic. This is the way the ClipBook applet works: It establishes a DDE share for each ClipBook page on each machine.

NetDDE acts as a redirector for DDE, and communicates over the network using NetBIOS. In Windows NT, NetBIOS can work on any transport protocol. When NetDDE establishes the conversation, it retrieves the DDE share and connects to the real application and topic locally. Then the applications can exchange data on the actual items, and neither application needs to explicitly be aware of NetDDE.

On the other hand, a network application that is aware of NetDDE can browse for shares, establish its own shares, and delete its own shares. The Network DDE Functions are listed in Table A1.18.

With the exception of the functions that deal with trusted shares and security, the Win32 NetDDE functions are also supported in Windows for Workgroups. They are not, however, included in Win32s. Accessing them in Windows for Workgroups programs requires you to have a copy of NDDEAPI.H and NDDEAPI.LIB, or dynamically link to the functions in NDDEAPI.DLL.

Should you build networked applications with NetDDE? If you want them to work on Windows for Workgroups and Windows NT machines, or they already support DDE, certainly. If you need to access other environments, no. And if you have a high-volume communications application and care about transfer rate, consider another mechanism.

Table A1.17 DDEML Functions

Function	Action
DdeAbandonTransaction	Abandons an asynchronous transaction.
DdeAccessData	Accesses a DDE data object.
DdeAddData	Adds data to a DDE data object.
DdeCallback	Processes DDEML transactions.
DdeClientTransaction	Begins a DDE data transaction.
DdeCmpStringHandles	Compares two DDE string handles.
DdeConnect	Establishes a conversation with a server.
DdeConnectList	Establishes multiple DDE conversations.
DdeCreateDataHandle	Creates a DDE data handle.
DdeCreateStringHandle	Creates a DDE string handle.
DdeDisconnect	Terminates a DDE conversation.
DdeDisconnectList	Destroys a DDE conversation list.
DdeEnableCallback	Enables or disables one or more DDE conversations.
DdeFreeDataHandle	Frees a DDE data object.
DdeFreeStringHandle	Frees a DDE string handle.
DdeGetData	Copies data from a DDE data object to a buffer.
DdeGetLastError	Returns an error code set by a DDEML function.
DdeInitialize	Registers an application with the DDEML.
DdeKeepStringHandle	Increments the usage count for a string handle.
DdeNameService	Registers or unregisters a service name.
DdePostAdvise	Prompts a server to send advice data to a client.
DdeQueryConvInfo	Retrieves information about a DDE conversation.
DdeQueryNextServer	Obtains the next handle in a conversation list.
DdeQueryString	Copies string-handle text to a buffer.
DdeReconnect	Reestablishes a DDE conversation.
DdeSetUserHandle	Associates a user-defined handle with a transaction.
DdeUnaccessData	Frees a DDE data object.
DdeUninitialize	Frees an application's DDEML resources.

If you're interested only in networked communications, you can skip the rest of this appendix. On the other hand, there's more to network programming than the core communications functions, so you might want to read on.

Table A1.18 Win32 Network DDE Functions

Function	Action
NDdeGetErrorString	Converts net DDE error code to error string.
NDdeGetShareSecurity	Obtains net DDE share's security descriptor.
NDdeGetTrustedShare	Retrieves net DDE trusted share options.
NDdeIsValidAppTopicList	Validates net DDE app and topic string syntax.
NDdeIsValidShareName	Validates net DDE share name syntax.
NDdeSetShareSecurity	Sets a net DDE share's security information.
NDdeSetTrustedShare	Applies trust options to a net DDE share.
NDdeShareAdd	Adds a net DDE share.
NDdeShareDel	Deletes a net DDE share.
NDdeShareEnum	Lists net DDE shares.
NDdeShareGetInfo	Obtains information about a net DDE sharer.
NDdeShareSetInfo	Modifies an existing net DDE share's info.
NDdeTrustedShareEnum	Lists trusted shares in calling process's context.

File Mapping (Memory-Mapped Files)

File mapping does not work over a network, but it is often used for interprocess communications—partly because it allows high-rate local communications, and partly because it is very similar to a UNIX mechanism often used to implement databases. 16-bit Windows allows you to pass pieces of global shared memory among processes: File mapping is as close as Windows NT comes. The Win32 file mapping functions are listed in Table A1.19.

Table A1.19 Win32 File Mapping Functions

Function	Action
CreateFileMapping	Returns handle to a new file mapping object.
FlushViewOfFile	Flushes a byte range within a mapped view.
MapViewOfFile	Maps a view into an address space.
MapViewOfFileEx	Maps a view into an address space.
OpenFileMapping	Opens a named-file mapping object.
UnmapViewOfFile	Unmaps a file view.

File mapping actually has two uses. The first is to let you treat a file like memory: Mapping is the copying of a file's contents to a process's virtual address space. The copy of the file's contents is called the *file view*, and the internal structure the operating system uses to maintain the copy is called the *file-mapping object*.

The second use is data sharing. Another process can create an identical file view in its own virtual address space by using the first process's file-mapping object to create the view. Any process that has the name or a handle of a file-mapping object can create a file view. Note that you can map named files, or simply ask for shared memory backed by the system paging file. The signal that you want shared memory backed by the page file is a file handle of (HANDLE)FFFFFFFF.

The following example demonstrates data sharing using file mapping. As you can see, the process creating the shared memory uses CreateFileMapping and MapViewOfFile, while the process sharing the memory uses OpenFileMapping and MapViewOfFile.

```
//—————————————————————--
// In creating process
//—————————————————————--
hFileMapping = CreateFileMapping(
        hFile,              //file handle to map
        NULL,               //security
        PAGE_READWRITE, //protection
        dwSizeHigh,     //high 32 bits of size
        dwSizeLow,      //low 32 bits of size
        "NameOfFileMappingObject");
assert(hFileMapping);
base = MapViewOfFile(
        hFileMapping,
        FILE_MAP_WRITE, //access mode
        dwOffsetHigh,   //high 32 bits of file offset
        dwOffsetLow,    //low 32 bits of file offset
        dwSizeToMap);   //size to map, 0 means whole file
// base points to mapped view of file
assert(base);
//...


//—————————————————————--
// In sharing process
//—————————————————————--
hFileMapping = OpenFileMapping(
        FILE_MAP_READ,  //access mode
```

```
        FALSE,          //inherit handle?
        "NameOfFileMappingObject");
assert(hFileMapping);
base = MapViewOfFile(
        hFileMapping,
        FILE_MAP_READ,  //access mode
        dwOffsetHigh,     //high 32 bits of file offset
        dwOffsetLow,    //low 32 bits of file offset
        dwSizeToMap);     //size to map, 0 means whole file
//
// base points to mapped view of file.
// Note that the value of base
// is not necessarily the same in both
// processes sharing the file
// mapping object.
//
assert(base);
```

When the processes are done with the mapped file, they should call UnmapViewofFile to remove the map from their address space and flush any dirty pages to the disk image of the file. Processes that need to commit portions of the shared file map to disk without unmapping the file can use FlushView-OfFile as needed.

Summary

We've introduced a lot of material here. We looked briefly at Windows NT security, services, event logging, and performance monitoring. We examined a road map to the different NT interprocess communication mechanisms, then went over the details of programming the individual mechanisms.

In a few cases, we've given enough information for you to actually write programs. In the rest of the cases, we only got you started. You'll find more information in the Win32 SDK Help files and in the references listed in the following section.

For More Information

Arick, M. (1993), *The TCP/IP Companion*. Wellesley, MA: QED Publishing Group, ISBN: 0-89435-466-3. Good end-user-oriented discussion of TCP/IP and utilities.

Chan, Chuck, Margaret Johnson, Keith Moore, and David Treadwell (1994), "Write an NT WinSock Service," *Byte*, December.

Heller, Martin (1993), *Advanced Win32 Programming*, New York NY, John Wiley & Sons, Inc., ISBN:0-471-59245-5.

Heller, Martin (1992), *Advanced Windows Programming*, New York NY, John Wiley & Sons, Inc., ISBN: 0-471-54711-5.

Microsoft Windows NT Software Development Kit (1993), *Remote Procedure Call Programmer's Guide and Reference*, Redmond, WA, Microsoft Corporation.

Microsoft Windows NT Software Development Kit (1993), *Programmer's Reference Vols 1–5*, Redmond, WA, Microsoft Corporation.

Nance, Barry (1990), *Network Programming in C*, Carmel, IN, Que Corporation., ISBN: 0-88022-569-6.

Sinha, Alok, and Raymond Patch (1992), "An Introduction to Network Programming Using the NetBIOS Interface," *Microsoft Systems Journal*, March–April.

Sinha, Alok, and Raymond Patch (1992), "Developing Network-Aware Programs Using Windows 3.1 and NetBIOS," *Microsoft Systems Journal*, July–August.

The OSI Seven-Layer Model, Windows NT's Network Architecture, and Networking Protocols

Operating systems don't normally know much about networks. They understand I/O, but may not care exactly how the data got in or where it's going. Windows NT is different in this regard, as it *does* know about and understand issues pertinent to networking.

When a product such as Windows NT comes to the marketplace, potential buyers want to be assured that the product will be compatible with the hardware and software they already have. One way to ensure compatibility is to develop the product in accordance with industry standards. This appendix explains, in basic terms, such industry standards as the OSI Refernce Model and some common protocols, and shows you how Windows NT fits into the basic scheme followed by other computer industry vendors.

The Need for Standards

The basic function of networking software is to move information between one device and another. This process usually consists of transmitting requests from one device to another, carrying out the request, and then returning the results to the original device. Sometimes these devices are on the same local-area network; sometimes they are located on different segments of a wide-area network (one that connects separate network sites, such as buildings or even cities). These devices are usually computers, but they can also be printers or any other type of networked machine.

To handle these requests, the network software has to determine how to reach the destination device. Then it has to put the request into a form that can travel across the network and be understood by the destination device. Once the request has arrived safely, it must be checked for errors, put into a form the device can use, and be properly executed. Then the return information (if there is any) must be put back into proper transmission form and returned to the original sending device.

The networking industry is constantly searching for viable standards that the various members of the industry can use as they design new hardware, new operating systems, new protocols, or other new concepts. Once certain standards have been accepted within the industry, it becomes easier for manufacturers to create products that work well together. In this way, information can eventually be transmitted anywhere in the world, no matter whose equipment is being used to send, carry, or receive it. This ideal scenario has yet to be achieved, but such vendors as Microsoft are working with other vendors, including competitors, to make this kind of transparent communication possible.

The OSI Reference Model

The OSI Reference Model is a communications model defined by the International Organization for Standardization, or ISO (the real name is French, and reversed). The ISO is a voluntary, international standards organization whose communications protocols are widely accepted. (A protocol is a set of rules that make it possible for all computers that know these rules to communicate with each other.) Founded in 1946, the ISO is comprised of standards bodies from more than 75 countries. Similar organizations include ANSI (American National Standards Institute), which represents the United States in the ISO; CCITT (Comite Consulatif International de Telegraphie et Telephonie), an international committee that sets communications standards; and IEEE (Institute of Electrical and Electronic Engineers), who have set many standards used in LANs.

In 1978, the ISO published the Open Systems Interconnection (OSI) Reference Model. This model, sometimes referred to as the *seven-layer model*, has become the basis for designing and evaluating methods of communication between devices. The OSI Reference Model has been helpful to the networking industry, as manufacturers of networking products strive for compatibility between their products and those of other vendors. It gives independent vendors a common set of criteria to discuss implementation techniques.

As a set of protocols, however, the official implementation of each layer as a standard has been under development for many years, with very few actual implementations commerically available. Top-down standards, burdened by bureaucracy, achieve popularity much more slowly than grassroots *de facto* standards, usually created by vendors in leadership positions in their industry niches.

The seven layers of the OSI Reference Model are numbered consecutively from the actual physical hardware connections (layer 1) up to the layer that services the applications, or programs, that run on the network (layer 7). Each layer communicates only with adjacent layers. The model looks like this:

Layer	*Client*		*Server*
7	Application	<—- virtual communication —->	Application
6	Presentation	<—- virtual communication —->	Presentation
5	Session	<—- virtual communication —->	Session
4	Transport	<—- virtual communication —->	Transport
3	Network	<—- virtual communication —->	Network
2	Data Link	<—- virtual communication —->	Data Link
1	Physical	<—- virtual communication —->	Physical

The Seven Layers

❑ *Level 1 (the physical layer)* is concerned with the actual transmission of data over the local-area network. This layer is comprised of the physical media used in interconnecting different network components. Examples of such media are fiber optics, twisted-pair cable, or coax cable. The RS-232 interface is a Level-1 standard for microcomputers.

❑ *Level 2 (the data link layer)* is concerned with the transmission techniques used to place the data on these different media. This layer is responsible for gaining access to the network and transmitting data packets from one device to another. Examples of transmission techniques include tokens and error-detection codes. This layer retransmits data packets that fail to reach their destination.

❑ *Level 3 (the network layer)* is responsible for finding the workstation the data is addressed to. If there are several possible routes on the LAN the data could travel across, the network layer must choose the best one. Level 3 is the highest layer that understands the physical configuration of the network.

❑ *Level 4 (the transport layer)* provides reliable transportation of data. This layer is responsible for converting messages into the required formats for transmission over the network. If the transmission isn't successful, the transport layer may request a retransmission.

❑ *Level 5 (the session layer)* establishes a connection so that one application (or user) can communicate with another application on another device. This layer also queues incoming messages and terminates connections. It also recovers from an abnormal termination.

❑ *Level 6 (the presentation layer)* must make certain that the commands and the data of an application can be understood by other computers on the network. In other words, it converts one format to another. It also provides data encryption and compression mechanisms.

❑ *Level 7 (the application layer)* refers to direct interaction with application processes. This layer consists of the messages that applications use to request data and services from one another. This layer provides distributed processing services, including file transfer, database management, and network control.

OSI and Windows NT

Because of the multivendor environment in which many users must work, the standards laid down in the OSI Model have influenced Windows NT development. Windows NT offers what Microsoft calls *built-in networking*. This means that Windows NT users can communicate with other personal computer users without the need for a separate network operating system. (The term *operating system*, or OS, refers to the software that controls a personal computer. The term *network operating system*, or NOS, refers to the software that manages a network or server.) You can share data with other users, send and receive messages, and use a remote printer without any of these machines having to become a server. In other words, Windows NT can function as a peer-to-peer network. In addition to communicating with other computer users in your own workgroup, you can communicate with servers on other types of networks, such as Novell's NetWare or Banyan's VINES.

When your Windows NT workstation communicates with another workstation, both machines use a seven-layer system based on the OSI Model. When you send a transmission over the network, it passes down each layer on your machine, travels across the network, then passes up each layer on the receiving machine until it reaches the layer that can properly handle your request.

There are three distinct layers of activity within Windows NT's network subsystem. At the bottom, a set of device drivers provides hooks into network adapters. Above that, protocols bind to the network adapters to provide well-defined means to communicate with other systems. Finally, network redirectors provide user- and application-level interfaces to other systems using those protocols.

Any of these layers can act in a many-to-many relationship with the neighboring layer. That is, multiple adapters can service a single protocol, or multiple protocols can run over a single adapter. Likewise, multiple redirectors can run over a single protocol, or a single redirector can run over multiple protocols. However, redirectors and adapters can't speak to each other directly. They must use a common protocol in between them, and communicate directly with it. In effect, the protocol layer becomes a traffic cop, saying who can send data where and over what media.

Above each of the layers are *interfaces* that provide virtual portholes for layers to communicate through. The NDIS Interface maps network adapters to protocols for example, while the TDI Interface maps redirectors to protocols. If multiple redirectors are in use, a Provider Interface maps incoming network requests to the appropriate redirector.

Windows NT Network Architecture

Just like a computer needs a video adapter to display output, it also needs a network adapter to communicate over a network. The network media may be coaxial cable, modems and phone lines, or even radio waves broadcast over the air. Regardless of the media, the operating system and the computer must have a way to communicate with the hardware that provides the network signalling.

This is handled through device drivers loaded at boot time. These drivers tell Windows NT what type of communications media is in use, the speed of the link, and so on. Parameters stored in Windows NT's Registry tell Windows NT how to communicate directly with the adapter so that it knows when the network needs servicing. A NIC (Network Interface Card) may use hardware interrupts (the same as a keyboard) to grab the CPUs attention. It may also use shared memory (like most SCSI cards) for the exchange of data between the system memory and the NICs memory. It may also use port addresses (like serial ports) for data I/O. Information stored in the Registry tells Windows NT how the adapter is configured and how to communicate with it.

To the user, this information is represented and configured in the *Network* control object within Control Panels. Network adapters are installed, adjusted, and removed here. For more information, refer to the chapter on installing Windows NT. Multiple adapters can be installed. As long as the adapters don't conflict with each other or any other peripherals within the computer, they can all be used. However, they are completely useless without protocols to take advantage of them.

Network Device Interface Specification (NDIS)

The NDIS Interface provides a way for protocols to bind to the underlying network adapters. Without this layer, each protocol would have to implicitly know about each adapter and the network media it used. By providing an interface between the NICs and protocols, the latter has to send data to only the interface for processing. It in turn has already registered information about the specific adapters and can make changes to the data, as needed.

Another benefit of using the NDIS Interface is that multiple adapters can be bound to a single protocol, or conversely, multiple protocols can use a single adapter. In the earlier days of networking, using multiple protocols meant you *had* to use multiple adapters, as each one would be locked to the other. The NDIS Interface provides a virtual network layer that protocols can address. The virtual layer then passes the data to the appropriate adapter.

Transport Protocols

Webster defines a protocol as "the code of ceremonial forms and courtesies ... accepted as proper and correct in official dealings." That about defines network protocols as well. A protocol is simply a well-defined method for computer systems to use when communicating with other devices. Two computers must use the same protocol in order to communicate.

Different protocols are well suited to different kinds of network environments. For example, NetBEUI uses *names* for computers as the primary method of distinction between systems. Although this makes the network easy to use and diagnose, other problems are introduced that limit the protocol's effectiveness on large networks. In contrast, TCP/IP uses a 32-bit binary addressing scheme, which makes it quite effective but a nightmare for users to interact with (without help, anyway).

A protocol is generally implemented as a background process, such as a TSR under DOS, or as a daemon under UNIX. With Windows NT, protocols run as threads within the privileged subsystem, as a part of the kernel.

The TDI (Transport Driver Interface)

Some network software—like Windows NT's native LAN Manager stuff—let users run multiple protocols. This makes it more effective in complex environments. Just as the NDIS Interface provides a single point of communication between NICs and protocols, the TDI Interface provides a link between redirectors and protocols. Without this interface, the redirector software would need to explicitly understand each of the protocols and their capabilities. Whenever a new protocol was introduced, the redirector would have to be rewritten.

For example, Windows NT's native network software can run over NetBEUI, TCP/IP, or even IPX. It doesn't have to know anything specifically about all of these protocols however. It simply needs to communicate with the TDI, which handles the necessary conversion and spoofing needed to make the network software work over the appropriate protocol.

The biggest problem with this design is that there must be a virtual protocol for the redirectors to address. In Windows NT's case, that protocol happens to be based on NetBEUI, which isn't very robust. In order for TCP/IP or IPX to act like NetBEUI, lots of trickery has to occur. You lose a lot of the features that came with the underlying protocols by using a lowest-common-denominator approach such as this.

Redirectors

Although the protocol does the majority of the grunt work in terms of finding and communicating with other systems, the network redirector is what handles the presentation of resources on the network, and also acts as the component that communicates directly with the Windows NT kernel.

Under Windows NT, network redirectors run as file system drivers, the same as FAT, NTFS, and CD-ROM file system drivers. This allows the network resources to appear exactly the same as any device that is physically attached to the system. When an application makes a call for a file or device, the application doesn't need to know anything about the device, since the underlying file system management subsystem handles all the communications.

For example, File Manager doesn't understand network concepts explicitly, but instead relies on the redirector to handle requests for it. Since all filesystem requests are passed to the Windows NT kernel, when you open a folder, the kernel looks to see if the resource is local or remote. If remote, it passes the request to the redirector, which passes it to the remote system. That system processes the request and returns some sort of data. The redirector then passes the data back to the kernel for presentation to the application that requested it. A redirector can communicate with remote systems using any protocol that both systems understand and have configured.

Provider Interface

Just as you can bind multiple protocols to multiple adapters, you can also bind multiple redirectors to multiple protocols. In order for Windows NT to present and understand these different networks cleanly, a method for making them all look the same had to be devised. The result is the Provider Interface.

This interface is really made up of several smaller modules, each of which provide specialized services. The Multiple Provider Router (MPR) tracks what network a request is for, and coordinates communication between the application and network.

Another module is the WNet API, which provides a consistent *look and feel* to different vendors' networks (see Appendix 1 for details). NetWare resources typically look like server/resource, while NFS resources are represented by /server/resource, and LAN Manager resources look like \\server\resource. Part of the WNet subsystem maps all network resources into the Microsoft favored and built \\server\resource format, called the Universal Naming Convention (UNC).

The WNet subsystem, in conjunction with the MPR and several other modules, combine to form the Provider Interface. This allows you to use Microsoft's LAN Manager software as well as Novell's NetWare, Banyan's Vines, or any other redirector, with almost any Windows NT application and without the developers having to code in support for all these networks directly. If you're using only one redirector, you won't need the Provider Interface layer, although portions of it may be in use, anyway.

Popular Network Protocols

Different network protocols exist for a reason. Each provides a different level of functionality in different areas. While one protocol may work well for a certain kind of network, that protocol may be completely unsuitable for a different network that seems to be similar on the surface. There are a few key areas of concern that span across all protocols, however. Memory consumption, bandwidth utilization, level of functionality (simple data transport versus applications), and scalability are all very important.

For example, your network may need to read and write files off only a relatively small file server, meaning you want fast transport performance and little else. To get that performance, you may pick a protocol that uses little memory and carries no application overhead. Another network may need to allow users to log in to interactive hosts and transfer large amounts of data. For these users, a protocol rich in functionality and features is more important than size or performance.

On a Windows NT network, the most likely protocols to be encountered are Microsoft's NetBEUI, Novell's IPX, and the worldwide standard TCP/IP. NetBEUI is the smallest, fastest, and easiest to use of the three, but it's also the least feature-rich, and the most limiting in large environments. Novell's IPX, while also small and fast, has the capability to run in complex networks that would break NetBEUI. Finally, TCP/IP is the most complex and scalable of the lot but isn't very small, and most implementations of it aren't very fast.

NetBIOS and NetBEUI

NetBEUI, in it's simplest terms, is Microsoft's favorite protocol. As such, it is a moving target, as it has been redefined, rebuilt, and repackaged many times in many products, including LAN Manager, Windows for Workgroups, and now Windows NT. NetBEUI means different things to different people, depending on when they bought it. In its earlier releases, NetBEUI was a large monolithic protocol, hardly distinguishable from IBM's NetBIOS, on which it was based.

When IBM started work on NetBIOS, the goal was to develop a network protocol that would work on small networks of PCs. The keyword in that sentence is *small*. At the time, the practical limit for an EtherNet segment was 30 nodes, while IBM's own vaunted and undelivered Token Ring was limited to 255 nodes. There was no need to build in capabilities for moving data between multiple network segments, since nobody was doing it, and the use of gateways to link networks was assumed. When IBM reworked NetBIOS into NetBEUI, they did include some capabilities for moving data across multiple network segments, but only on Token Ring networks that used IBM's Source Level Routing.

Thus, the design goal was to build a very small and fast protocol. The protocol would provide APIs for the development of network-specific applications that could communicate on a machine-to-machine or application-to-application basis. Also, the network naming system would allow for human-assigned names of devices, such as *MyServer*, which is easier to remember and work with than a complex numbering scheme. This is actually pretty insightful, considering that this is the same company that gave us SNA. Unfortunately, like the PC itself, this simple yet limited design would prove to haunt users even through today.

NetBIOS was (and continues to be) a broadcast-intensive protocol. Since the assumption was that there were only a few nodes on the network, and that devices would be appearing and disappearing at random (as PCs are apt to do), then it was best to be able to locate a device with a broadcast rather than with any sort of centralized registry. Unfortunately, broadcast packets don't work in today's router-based networks, since the routers don't pass packets that aren't specifically destined for another network segment. And since the NetBIOS naming structure is nonhierarchical, devices can't specify remote network segments. Thus, the only way to make NetBIOS work in large networks is to bridge the various segments into a large virtual network. Unfortunately, NetBIOS's reliance on broadcasting limits its use to relatively small networks, so large bridged networks don't work very well, either.

When Microsoft chose NetBIOS as the basis for its MS-Net software, they added another component specific to their software, called Server Message Blocks (SMBs). Although SMBs are covered in more detail further in this appendix, suffice it to say for now that SMBs provide network-specific functionality to the mix, beyond what NetBIOS provides by itself.

Today's NetBEUI doesn't look much like the original NetBEUI. While the old version was a single, monolithic protocol, the new one is segmented into its three unique components: the NetBIOS API, SMBs, and the NetBIOS Frame (NBF) transport protocol. Figure A2.1 below shows the various modules and how they interrelate.

A lot of people confuse NetBEUI with NetBIOS. It's important to remember that the term NetBIOS generally refers to an API for network applications, and does not specify how data is moved between systems, but only how data is

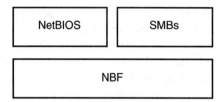

Figure A2.1 NetBEUI Stack.

Microsoft's NetBEUI protocol stack has three layers—the NetBIOS API, Server Message Blocks (SMBs) and the NetBIOS Frame (NBF) transport.

packaged and acquired by applications. NetBEUI is generally recognized as a transport protocol, an API, and an SMB processor.

NetBIOS the API

NetBIOS-based applications, such as the Chat applet bundled with Windows NT, work with the NetBIOS APIs. These high-level applications are not generally concerned with users, but interact with workstation names instead. When a NetBIOS-based application needs to communicate with a counterpart application, it locates the partner device and initiates the dialog. When the applications are finished, they disconnect—sometimes gracefully, sometimes not.

NetBIOS applications range from the simple Chat-like applets to mainframe gateways and multiuser databases. Any application that needs to communicate with another can use the NetBIOS APIs to do so. Lotus's Notes server for Windows is a NetBIOS application, for example. Also, Microsoft Mail for Windows NT can support NetBIOS. This allows one NT mail client to notify another client that new mail has been sent, using a NetBIOS message. The normal method requires that the recipient workstation check the inbox on a file server's shared drive for any unread messages.

Server Message Blocks (SMBs)

When two Windows NT (or LAN Manager, or Windows for Workgroups) nodes communicate, they use the X/Open standard Server Message Blocks (SMBs) protocol. SMBs provide a well-defined method for servers and nodes (called *consumers* in the SMB definition) to communicate with each other, similar to the way that NetBIOS-based applications do.

The SMB specification contains a dictionary, more or less, of commands specific to network I/O. For example, if a user wants to open a file that resides on a server, then the SMB command *SMBopen* is passed between the two systems. This occurs at the redirector level, of course, since all the user did was simply double-click on the file.

SMB commands exist for a wide range of functions, and provide a quick and cost-effective way to do the most common network functions. Commands exist for such things as login security, printing, and working directly with files and directories. In other words, the SMB protocol is the heart of the network, providing a common language for all the clients and servers to use.

The commands that make up the SMB specification can be thought of as lowest-common-denominator commands. Since the SMB spec assumes that there will be different types of machines on the network, the use of *extension protocols* is allowed to streamline operations significantly. For example, two DOS PCs would both use the DOS extension when speaking with each other, while two NT systems would use the NT extension, and so on. This allows nodes to communicate in the most efficient manner possible, while also guaranteeing compatibility between dissimilar devices.

NetBIOS Frames (NBF)

The lowest level of the NetBEUI protocol block is the NBF protocol. NBF provides both the transport- and network-layer functions, and provides the raw connectivity services between devices. When network I/O occurs, the upper layers (either NetBIOS applications or SMB transactions) pass data directly to NBF for processing. NBF then encapsulates the data into frames, locates the device(s) it needs to communicate with, and hands the data to the NIC for delivery.

NBF also handles the error correction services if needed, although through different mechanisms. Some services are established as connection-oriented, meaning a detailed and highly monitored conversation is held through a virtual circuit between two systems. Other services are established as connectionless using datagrams. In this situation, packets are sent and then forgotten about. This is generally used in situations where repetetive broadcasts get sent frequently, such as status updates and the like.

NBF is another weak link in the NetBEUI stack. Like NetBIOS, NBF is a nonroutable protocol, meaning that it can communicate only with devices that it sees on the immediate subnet, or one that is bridged into a virtual subnet. However, since none of the overhead is required for maintaining routing tables or the like, NBF is extremely small and fast, and is the ideal protocol for small networks of less than 100 devices. Also, since NetBEUI was designed by IBM with Token Ring in mind, the default frame size of the packets is 4,096 bytes, which allows for great throughput on networks that can handle it.

IPX and Complementary Protocols

Novell's protocol set is considerably different from NetBEUI, mostly in that it is somewhat larger and much more usable in complex environments. Indeed, its design called for multiple network segments from the start, and the usage of numbers instead of names for both networks and resources. Devices still have names, but this is seen at the higher-level redirector, and not by the lower-level protocols themselves.

The heart of the NetWare protocol suite is based largely on Xerox's XNS (Xerox Network System). In fact, the two are almost identical, with the exception of some slight differences in some of the subprotocols. For example, Novell's IPX (or Internetwork Packet Exchange) is based on Xerox's IDP (or Internetwork Datagram Packet). Novell did not copy the entire stack, however, since XNS includes subprotocols for such things as mail handling and the like. A lot of the secondary protocols were not needed in the PC environment, and others were not even published until after Novell did their initial developments. Many other networking products are based on XNS, including VINES, Ungermann-Bass, and older 3Com software. Indeed, Microsoft's own internal network has used XNS for years, only recently starting to shift toward the use of TCP/IP.

The NetWare protocol suite looks something like figure A2.2 below.

IPX

IPX, the protocol most generally associated with NetWare, resides at the bottom-most layer of the stack, and provides the *network* functions for the rest of the suite. In this instance, the term *network* refers to the network layer of the OSI model.

IPX tracks the various network segments that are available, and directs the delivery of data accordingly. If a recipient node is local, the data is handed directly to it; and if remote, the data is handed to a router for delivery. IPX provides other network-layer functions, such as encapsulation of higher-level protocols, and is the single data-moving protocol for the NetWare environment. IPX does not guarantee delivery, or provide error-correction services, however. These functions are left to the transport protocols, SPX and PEP.

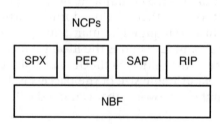

Figure A2.2 IPX/SPX stack.

Novell's IPX/SPX stack has Netware Core Procol (NCP) APIs at the top layer; Sequenced Packed Exchange (SPX), Packet Exchange Protocol (PEP), Service Advertisment Protocol (SAP), and Routing Information Protocol (RIP) in the second layer; and the Internetwork Packet Exchange (IPX) transport.

Another aspect of IPX is that it determines packet sizes based on the *strength* of the media that it is attached to. Although the minimum (and theoretical maximum) size of an IPX packet is 512 bytes, if two nodes are directly attached to an EtherNet segment, they will use 1,024-byte packets. If they are both on Token Ring, they will use 4,096-byte packets. IPX routers, however, always convert the packets back to 512 bytes.

SPX, PEP, and NCPs

SPX (or Sequenced Packet Exchange) is an API similar to NetBIOS. Applications can use SPX to pass data directly between systems or applications. This is assisted by SPX's virtual circuit capabilities, which provide guaranteed delivery of data over IPX. SPX does not acknowledge all packets but instead uses a *window* method, acknowledges all the packets it has received within the window, and conducts error-recovery based on that information.

Another higher-level transport protocol is PEP (Packet Exchange Protocol), used exclusively for the delivery of NCP (NetWare Core Protocol) commands. NCPs are similar to SMBs in that they provide a dictionary of I/O-related network commands. NCPs are the heart of the NetWare server system, and are guarded by Novell as if they were the crown jewels. PEP is considered a part of the NCP subsystem, and is just as undocumented.

PEP provides error-correction services with the use of *timers*. When a packet is sent from PEP, an internal timer is started within NCP, and no other NCP packets are generated until a response is received. If the timer expires, PEP rebuilds the packet, and NCP restarts the timer. This handshaking and waiting consumes lots of NCP utilization bandwidth, but guarantees that the packets get delivered. On small LANs, this goes unnoticed; but in large or exceedingly complex networks, performance can suffer tremendously.

SAP

The advertisement of network devices and resources is managed by the Service Advertisement Protocol (SAP), naturally enough. SAP provides information about servers, routers, intelligent printers, and the like. Although SAP is really an application-level protocol, it uses IPX directly. Other subprotocols, such as NCP and SPX, rely on SAP for information as well.

Since NetWare is a number-based network, there must be a way to translate human-defined device names into the device's *real* numerical address. SAP provides this Registry service. When a program or service becomes available, SAP picks up on it and creates an entry in its tables. Although this dynamic name-keeping registry makes life easy for users, the constant updating of information can consume network bandwidth very quickly, since every device has its own SAP tables. For users in a WAN environment, filtering SAP entries at your routers is a good way to get back your bandwidth.

RIP

Remember that IPX is a network-layer protocol. It doesn't know anything about other networks other than the fact that they exist. When IPX has a packet for a remote subnet, it passes it to the closest router and forgets about it. RIP (or Routing Information Protocol) provides the routing services for IPX packets. When a node first comes onto the network, it issues a RIP request to find out what network number it is on.

If it is on multiple networks and configured as a router, then it will send out a RIP update to all the nodes on the network, advertising the routes it can offer. Routers send out RIP updates every sixty seconds, telling other devices what networks it knows about. If a router doesn't send out an update within an allotted time, the router is assumed to be down and the entry is removed.

IPX networks are nonhierarchial, meaning all routers must know how to get to every other network segment. As networks grow, this becomes an unmanageable and extremely overhead-expensive way to track remote net-works. Novell has developed a link-state routing protocol, called NLSP (for NetWare Link State Protocol), which works much better in extremely complex networks. Rather than routers continuously broadcasting information about every other network and router they know of, they send out only information that has changed, which greatly reduces the amount of bandwidth required. As of this writing, NT doesn't support NLSP, so you'll still have to use RIP on your NT segments.

The TCP/IP Protocol Suite

First and foremost, TCP/IP is not a single protocol but a term used to define a variety of protocols that act in union to provide a variety of connectivity functions. These protocols are all very specific in function, ranging from the mundane task of providing transport services to more esoteric ones that provide extended management functions.

Most network operating systems use a very small set of proprietary proto-cols. For example, Microsoft's Windows NT uses NetBEUI and SMBs for almost all of its network services, and Novell uses IPX, SPX, and NCP for its connec-tions. These very small and very functional protocols allow the network operating system to streamline their operation, resulting in very fast file and print sharing.

However, these protocols by themselves don't allow for much of anything else. Neither the LAN Manager nor NetWare environments allow a user to log in to the server and run an interactive application within the remote server's memory. You must run the applications from a client PC, perhaps running the program from the server's shared file system, but that's as far as it goes. Thus the LAN Manager and NetWare server platforms are very contained, and are highly optimized for the specific function of file and print sharing.

TCP/IP, on the other hand, offers an incredible breadth of services. Users can share files and printers just like they can with LAN Manager or NetWare. They can also use terminal emulation services to execute applications on remote machines, allowing them to harness large system horsepower for specific applications. TCP/IP is a highly scalable set of protocols, and users can choose to implement any subset they wish, as either client or server services.

Another important aspect of TCP/IP is the issue of *openness*. While Microsoft's LAN Manager uses the publicly available SMB specification for communicating, it incorporates proprietary network services into other aspects of the product. You can't just put any SMB-based client into a LAN Manager- or Windows NT-based domain, and expect it to work. Novell is even worse, since they guard their proprietary NCPs as if they were the crown jewels.

Sure, both Microsoft and Novell license their server products to run on a variety of platforms, including minicomputers and mainframes. But you as a user must run that network service on each host and client in your organization, an exceedingly expensive and ungainly prospect at best. By comparison, TCP/IP is a fully public-domain specification. Addenda to the specifications can be offered by anybody (even you), and the process is witnessed in full sight. Thus, many companies already offer integrated TCP/IP protocols and services into their platforms. This makes it easy for an end user to connect resources together without relying on any one vendor.

TCP/IP's third great advantage is that it is a very robust set of protocols that are highly efficient in wide-area networks. NetBEUI and IPX were both designed for small LANs of 30 users or less. LAN Manager's NetBEUI is a *nonroutable* one, meaning that users on one network wire can't see servers on another unless the two segments are *bridged* into a single logical network wire. This doesn't work well in WAN environments by any measure. NetWare's NCP runs over IPX, which is a completely routable protocol. However, NCP relies on acknowledgments for all network packets sent, which is ungainly over slow WAN links. TCP/IP was originally written for connecting hosts over WANs, and as such it is both routable and efficient. These benefits apply to LANs just as well, making them a good choice for both small and large environments.

These three elements (scalability, openness, and robustness) make TCP/IP an attractive choice for users in mixed environments. They can run the same protocols and services on almost all of their host and client systems. For this reason, many customers have made TCP/IP a check-off item for network purchases. No wonder Microsoft put TCP/IP into the basic Windows NT package! Of course, all is not rosy with TCP/IP, and we'll explore these limitations alongside its advantages.

A Very Brief History of TCP/IP

Back in the very early days of commercial computing (the late 1960s), most users bought a single large computer for their data processing needs. As the user needs expanded, they rarely bought a different system from a different vendor. Instead, they added on to their existing platforms, or they replaced them with newer, larger models. Cross-platform connectivity was essentially unheard of, and was not expected by customers. They were generally too busy just trying to keep these newfangled computers running.

These systems used proprietary networking architectures and protocols. For the most part, networking in those days consisted of plugging *dumb* line printers or terminals into a *smart* multiplexer or communications controller. And just as the networking protocols were proprietary, the network nodes were proprietary as well. To this day you still can't plug an IBM terminal into a DEC computer and expect it to work. The architectures and protocols are completely incompatible.

In an effort to help major research sites share resources, the Advanced Research Projects Agency (ARPA) of the Department of Defense (DOD) began coordinating the development of a vendor-independent network to tie together the sites. The logic behind this is clear: The cost and time to develop an application on one system was too much for each site to reengineer the application on other incompatible systems. Since each facility used different computers with proprietary networking technology, the need for a vendor-independent network was the first priority. In 1968, work began on a private packet-switched network, using Honeywell-based communications hardware.

In the early 1970s, authority of the project was transferred to the Defense Advanced Research Projects Agency (DARPA), which began developing and implementing protocols that would allow for the connection and use of the various systems. Although the original protocols were written for use with the ARPA network, they were designed to be usable on other systems as well. In 1981, DARPA placed the TCP/IP protocol suite into the public domain. Shortly thereafter, it was adopted by the University of California at Berkely, who began bundling it with their freely distributed version of UNIX. In 1983, DARPA mandated that all new systems connecting to the ARPA network had to use TCP/IP, thus guaranteeing its long-term success.

During the same time period, other government agencies, such as the National Science Foundation (NSF), were building their own networks, as were private regional network service providers. These other networks also used TCP/IP as the native connection mechanism, since it was both a completely *open* protocol, as well as readily available on a number of different platforms.

When these various regional and government networks began connecting to each other, the term *Internet* came into play. To *internet* (with a lowercase *i*) means to interconnect networks. You can create an internet of Macintosh networks using AppleTalk and some routers, for example. The term *Internet* (with a capital *I*) refers to the global network of TCP/IP-based systems, originally consisting of the ARPA and regional networks. Any organization (or any*one* for that matter) can join the Internet, and information on where to look is provided at the end of this appendix.

TCP/IP's Architecture

This anarchic peer-to-peer structure is purposefully designed directly into TCP/IP's architecture. Consider the distributed nature of TCP/IP in contrast with the classic security model of other host-based architectures of the time. Most systems had a hierarchial structure that permeated throughout the entire computing architecture. Everything was managed by the central host, including the network services themselves. Two nodes couldn't communicate without sending data through the host.

With TCP/IP, there is no central authority. Nodes communicate directly among themselves, and each maintains complete knowledge about the available network services. If any host fails, none of the others know or care. (Unless they need data from the down machine!) This is fairly similar to Windows NT's basic server design, where servers are relatively independent of each other (the Windows NT Server unifies servers into a single logical entity, however, which eases management but also breaks the independence of each system).

Addressing

In order to identify themselves in this peer-to-peer environent, nodes are given explicit addresses that identify not only the computer, but also the network segment that it is on. For example, the address 192.123.004.010 specifies node number 10 on network 192.123.004. Another node on the same network segment might be numbered 20, and so on. Networks and the nodes on them are separate entities with separate numbers.

Host 10 from the preceding example might also be connected to network 192.123.005 on a different network adapter. This host could then act as a router between networks 192.123.004 and 192.123.005. Routers perform the task of moving traffic betwen networks. A node that needs to send data to another node on another network will send the data to the router, and the router will send the data to the destination node. If the destination isn't on an immediately connected network, the router will send the data to another router for delivery. This network-based routing scheme allows devices to keep their local overhead low. Otherwise, they'd have to remember how to get to each node, which would require a tremendous amount of processing and memory. Network-based routing requires much less in terms of end-node resources.

Each node's address is actually a 32-bit binary number (such as 11000000 01111011 00000100 00001010). For convenience, this is broken into four 8-bit fields, called *octets*. TCP/IP represents these binary octets with their decimal equivalents (192.123.004.010 in this case). This makes life much easier for us humans. Although computers have no trouble dealing with 32-bit binary strings, I know I sure do!

The four octets signify different things in different networks. Some sites have only a single large network but millions of nodes. They would use the first octet of the address to identify the network, and the remaining three octets would be used to identify the individual workstations. This is known as a *Class A* address. The most common users of Class A addresses are network service providers, who maintain extremely large and flat networks with thousands of end points.

Another site may have thousands of nodes split across many networks. They would use a *Class B* addresses, where the first two octets (or 16 bits) are used to identify the network, and the remaining two octets are used to identify the individual nodes. Universities and large organizations are the most common users of Class B addresses.

Finally, the most common address is the *Class C* address, where the first three octets (or 24 bits) are used to identify the segment, and the last octet is used to identify the workstations. These are good for users with only a few dozen nodes on many separate networks. This is most often found in LAN environments, which average around 40 nodes per network segment.

When connecting a Class A network to a Class B network, there must be some way for the router to recognize the difference between the two. Otherwise, it would think that traffic originating from the Class C network and destined for a Class A node would be identifiable by the last octet. In truth, the Class A node is identified by the last three octets, a significant difference. Without this knowledge, the router would attempt to locate the three-octet network that the one-octet host is on. In actuality, it should be trying to send the data to the one-octet network that the three-octet host is on.

TCP/IP uses the first three bits of the first octet to identify the class of network, allowing devices to automatically recognize the appropriate address types. Class A addresses are identified by the first bit being set to 0. This leaves only 7 other bits for identifying the network portion of the address (remember that Class A addresses use the first octet to identify the network, and the remaining three octets to identify the nodes). Since there are only 7 available bits, there can be only 128 possible networks. Network numbers 000 and 127 are reserved for use by software, so there are really only 126 possible networks (001 through 126). However, there are 24 bits available for identifying nodes, for a maximum of 16,777,124 possible node addresses for each of these networks.

Class B addresses are identified by having the first two bits set to 0. Since they use the first two octects to identify the network, this leaves 14 bits to identify each network segment. Thus, there are a possible 16,384 Class B addresses, ranging from 128.001 to 191.254 (numbers 000 and 255 are reserved).

Class C addresses are identified by having the first three bits in the first octet set to 0. Class C addresses use the first three octets to identy the network, so there are 21 bits available. The possible network numbers range from 192.001.001 through 254.254.254, a whopping 2,097,152 possible segments. However, since there is only one octet left to identify the nodes, there can be only 254 possible devices on each segment.

Out of Addresses

All told, there are over 4.7 *billion* possible host addresses. Now most of you are probably thinking that almost 5 billion possible addresses is plenty, but unfortunately, the four-octet structure causes some major restrictions. Every time a Class A address is assigned to an organization, almost 17 million host addresses go with it. If all 126 of the Class A addresses are assigned, then over 3 billion of the 4.7 billion possible addresses are gone. If all of the 16,000 Class B addresses are assigned, then another billion host addresses are gone as well. Whether or not all the workstation addresses are actually put to use is irrelevant; they have been assigned to a specific network and cannot be used again.

Class C addresses represent the biggest problem, however, for two reasons. First, there are less of them than with the other nodes (only about 500 million possible node addresses are available). Second, they are the most popular, since they reflect the size of the majority of the LANs. However, every time you assign a Class C address to a network segment, you take 254 possible node addresses with you. Remember that you need a new network number for every separate network. People who have three segments and only 60 nodes are therefore wasting over 700 possible workstation addresses (3 segments x 254 node addresses = 762 addresses - 60 active nodes = 702 inactive addresses). Clearly, at this rate, the available workstation numbers will run out soon.

To some readers, the logic for having different *classes* of addresses may seem vague at best. With the current design, there are only 2,113,662 possible networks. If all networks used the first 24 bits (without using *class bits*) to identify the segment, there would be a possible 16,777,124 networks, with 254 nodes on each of them.

Remember, however, that TCP/IP networks are inherently router-based. It requires much less overhead on the part of nodes and routers to remember a few networks than many. Having to process 16 million networks would quickly overwhelm the router databases, and network traffic would slow down tremendously. Having network classes allows routers to deal with large networks easily, and performance is maintained.

Remember also that the original architecture of the Internet consisted mostly of large networks connecting to each other. It was easy to give one address to Milnet (a network of unclassified military hosts) and another to NSFnet (the National Science Foundation's network). By doing this, routers only have to remember another router's address in order to pass data to literally millions of hosts.

For you and me, however, the potential side effects of address depletion are frightening. No new organizations could connect to the Internet, and the existing networks couldn't expand. A new version of IP has been developed that will overcome most of these limitations. However, it will be several years before IPng (next generation, or IP v6) will be implemented on enough commercially available equipment for you to take advantage of it on an enterprise-wide basis.

Subnet Masks

There are ways to get more mileage from a single network number, however. Remember that the 32-bit binary address is divided into four logical 8-bit octets? Well, there's nothing to prevent you from changing this structure. Although you can't change the binary values of the address itself, you can change the way that your software interprets it. The interpretation of the address is called the *Subnet Mask*.

For clarification, let's look at the host address 192.123.004.010 from before. This is a Class C address. The first 24 bits identify the network number (3 bits for the Class C identifier, and 21 bits for addressing). The remaining 8 bits identify the host. You could just as easily set the subnet mask so that the first 30 bits identify the network, and the remaining 2 bits identify the host.

Since the first 24 bits in a Class C address identify an organization, the remaining 8 bits can be used any way that organization sees fit. If they wish to use the bits for identifying hosts, they certainly can. However, another option would be to assign some of the remaining 8 bits to *sub*networks. In essence, the network portion of the address gains another field, while the range of host numbers possible shrinks.

Let's show an example here to help clarify the discussion. Our imaginary company, Windows, Inc., has both an EtherNet and Token Ring network. However, they have only a single Class C network address of 192.123.004. Rather than use the last octet to identify 254 hosts on a single network, they decide to add a subnet mask to their address by *borrowing* the first bit of the last octet. This creates two subnets with 128 possible hosts in each of them.

Now when they look at the network numbers, they see the following:

Segment	Network Address	Node Addresses*
Ethernet	192.123.004	001 - 127
Token Ring	192.123.004	128 - 254

* Numbers 000 and 255 are reserved.

Remember, however, that devices on the network don't see this logical breakdown automatically. Based on the Class C identifier in the head of the address, they still think that the last 8 bits of the address represent a host. All of the devices on a network segment have to be told about the mask.

The subnet mask uses a very simple algorithm. If a bit mask is set to 1, it is part of the network number. If the bit mask is set to 0, it is part of the host number. Therefore, the subnet mask for our preceding example looks like 11111111 11111111 11111111 10000000. The default subnet masks for the different network classes are:

Class	Subnet Mask
A	11111111 00000000 00000000 00000000
B	11111111 11111111 00000000 00000000
C	11111111 11111111 11111111 00000000

The subnet mask for a node is appended to its binary address when processed by routers. Just as the router would look to see if network 192.123.004 were locally attached before forwarding the packet, it would now look to see if the subnet mask of the destination network matched as well. If the subnet mask doesn't match the local network, then the data is forwarded to another router that does match.

In order for subnet masking to work, all of the devices on a subnet must support it. Some older TCP/IP client programs don't support subnet masking, so make sure that they do before you try this at home. By the way, some software packages convert the binary subnet mask values into their decimal equivalents for ease of use. For example, Windows NT doesn't show the default Class C subnet mask, but rather shows it as 255.255.255.0, the decimal equivalent of the binary octets. Again, this is to make life easier for us humans.

Sub Protocols

Again, TCP/IP is a collection of protocols that span the OSI reference model from top to bottom. There are application-specific protocols, such as Telnet and FTP, a collection of maintenance protocols, at least two major transport protocols, and one network-layer protocol. Figure A2.3 shows the major subprotocols in the TCP/IP suite.

IP and ARP

IP, or the Internet Protocol, is the basic building block for all TCP/IP traffic, and works at the network-layer of the OSI reference model. It is where the internet address assignment is realized, and the layer of software responsible for determining how packets are passed to other networks. Other than that, IP is a pretty

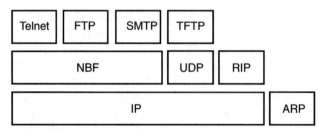

Figure A2.3 TCP/IP stack.

The TCP/IP protocol suite includes Telnet, File Transfer Protocol (FTP), and Simple Mail Transfer Protocol (SMTP) at the user-interface layer; Tranmission Control Protocol (TCP), User Datagram Protocol (UDP), and Routing Information Protocol (RIP) in the middle; and two transport protocols: Internet Protocol (IP) and Address Resolution Protocol (ARP).

boring little protocol. All it does is get internet packets from one node to another, across the best route possible.

IP converts Internet addresses into *real* network addresses, such as EtherNet addresses, through the use of ARP (Address Resolution Protocol) and RARP (Reverse Address Resolution Protocol). An ARP packet will be sent with the destination IP address in the header, and if the receiving node is online, it will send back a response packet containing its real network address. RARP is used when a node needs to find out the IP address corresponding to a node's real address. Either way, when an ARP or RARP reply comes back, the node stores the address in a cache buffer for reuse.

TCP and UDP

The protocols that provide the transport-layer services are TCP (Transmission Control Protocol) and UDP (User Datagram Protocol). Since IP provides no error-recovery or control services, applications that need it go through TCP, and those that don't go through UDP. Almost all applications use TCP or UDP for the delivery of data, both of which pass packets to IP for delivery. Very few applications speak directly with IP.

TCP provides error-correction through the use of a connection-oriented transaction. A *start* packet is built and sent to the destination node (via IP), and when an "Okay, I'm ready" packet comes back, a monitored conversation between the hosts and/or applications begins. If a packet is lost or corrupted, TCP resends the data. The size, time-out interval, and other critical factors are determined by TCP, judging from the strength of the media to which the node is connected.

UDP, on the other hand, simply sends the damned data. If no error-correction or monitoring services are needed, then an application is best off using

UDP, since it's much faster and requires less overhead than TCP. Like TCP, UDP makes decisions about packet sizes based on the strength of the underlying media, and passes the fully contained parcel to IP for delivery. This is what makes IP so boring; it just delivers the data, since all the big decisions have already been made for it.

RIP

If RIP looks familiar to you, it should. It is the same RIP (Routing Information Protocol) that NetWare uses with IPX, and is derived from the XNS source code. It was not originally a part of the TCP/IP suite, but Berkeley included it with their distribution, and it has since become one of the most popular routing protocols around. It also carries many of the same limitations that Novell's version has, and there are many, many alternatives available. If you use a non-RIP routing protocol on a router, however, you need to make sure that you use it on *all* of them, since that's how they communicate with each other.

HOSTS Files and DNS

Once your system knows how to connect to the outside world, you are ready to start communicating with other systems. Although you can use IP addresses for communicating with other TCP/IP resources, this is undesirable for several reasons. First and foremost, IP addresses change quite often. Second, working with machine *names* is much easier than trying to remember 32-bit sequences of numbers.

The most common mechanism in use today for assigning names to IP resources is the use of a text file called HOSTS (on NT systems, this file is located in the \winnt35\system32\etc directory). Another mechanism that is much more flexible and easier to manage in large environments in the Domain Name System (DNS). DNS servers manage hierarchical databases of IP addresses, host names, and networks. IP nodes use a DNS resolver to query the DNS server for IP addresses whenever a host name is used. If a resource moves to another network, or if the IP address changes for any other reason, then the network administrator has to update only the DNS server's database, and all subsequent client queries are correctly resolved. This is much easier than manually editing HOSTS files on every client system in the enterprise.

Getting Connected to the Internet

Connecting to the Internet requires you to follow some very specific procedures. First of all, you must decide whether you will connect your network directly to a service provider's network, or connect on a per-user basis using SLIP or PPP dial-up systems. You can also connect directly to the Internet backbone if you're sponsored by a government agency.

If you use a service provider for a full-time link, you will likely be given everything you need for the connection. This will include a block of registered IP addresses, a domain name, and a router. You will pay for the onetime setup fees, and a monthly service charge. You may also pay the telephone line charges, unless they are part of the monthly service fees. Each service provider does business a little differently, so shop around for the deal that works best for you and your budget.

Once your setup with this connection, however, managing your Internet resources is entirely up to you. You must take care of your DNS servers, allocate IP addresses to your clients, and make sure that mail is being routed correctly. Having to hire somebody to manage all of this can cost you much more than the line charges.

If you choose to buy individual dial-up accounts, then you will be faced with less management work, but more choices. Most dial-up service providers give you an interactive account on a UNIX system, where you read mail and newsgroups, and run your Gopher and WWW browser clients. Some providers give you a SLIP or PPP connection, however, which allows you to run Windows-based applications on your local PC, acting as an extension of their network. Either way, you will be under the service provider's domain, and your resources will be managed for you.

An excellent starting point for getting yourself or your organization connected to the Internet is the book *Connecting to the Internet*, by Susan Estrada (publisher information is listed at the end of this appendix).

For More Information

Malamud, C. (1990), *Analyzing Novell Networks*. New York, NY: Van Nostrand Reinhold, ISBN: 0-442-00364-1. Great low-level peeks at what goes on in NetWare LANs.

Miller, M. (1991), *Internetworking*. Redwood City, CA: M&T Books, ISBN: 1-55851-143-1. Solid reference material on XNS, IPX, and TCP/IP protocols.

Arick, M. (1993), *The TCP/IP Companion*. Wellesley, MA: QED Publishing Group, ISBN: 0-89435-466-3. Good end-user-oriented discussion of TCP/IP and utilities.

Black, U. (1992) *TCP/IP and Related Protocols*. New York: McGraw-Hill, ISBN: 0-07-005553-X. Mandatory desktop reference for the TCP/IP administrator.

Albitz, P. and Liu, C. (1992) *DNS and BIND*. Sebastopol, CA: O'Reilly & Associates, ISBN: 1-56592-010-4. Great book for learning about the Domain Name System (DNS).

Estrada, S. (1993) *Connecting to the Internet*. Sebastopol, CA: O'Reilly & Associates, ISBN: 1-56592-061-9. Essential guide for getting yourself or your organization connected to the Internet.

Legacy Applications

With some exceptions, Windows NT generally will run applications compiled to run in DOS, Windows 3.1, and character-based OS/2 1.3. In addition, it supports the POSIX API (a generic subset of the UNIX API) so that application source code written to POSIX can be recompiled and run under Windows NT. This appendix details the operation and limits of compatibility for legacy applications.

Chapter 11 of the *Microsoft Windows NT System Guide* details the settings and operation of many aspects of legacy applications. Information is also available in the *Windows NT Resource Kit, Volume 1*, Chapters 13 and 15. This appendix supplements the information in those sources.

Non-x86 Limitations

If you plan to make heavy use of legacy applications, you should be aware of important limitations with Windows NT on non-x86 (e.g., MIPS R4000/4400, Intergraph Clipper, DEC Alpha, or other RISC-based) systems. (In this appendix, x86 refers to the Intel 386, 486, and Pentium; plus Intel-compatible chips produced by Cyrix, AMD, NexGen, and others.) Non-x86 systems use emulation software to interpretively execute the x86 instruction set. Two problems exist with this approach: performance and emulation level. Because the emulator must execute multiple non-x86 instructions to interpret one x86 instruction, it is slower by about a factor of 10 than a native application. So although the MIPS R4400 is about the equal of the Pentium for native Windows NT applications, it's only about as fast as a 386/25 when running a Windows 3.1 application.

What may be a more important limitation for many people is that the emulation software on the non-x86 versions of NT does not emulate 386 instructions. That means it runs Windows 3.1 in standard mode, not 386 enhanced mode. Similarly, the emulator cannot run 386 DOS extended applications. Native OS/2 1.3 applications are not supported at all on non-x86 platforms, despite the fact they generally do not use 386 instructions. If you have an EXE file compiled as an OS/2 family mode (bound) application (which combines both DOS and OS/2 executables in a single file), it will run on a non-x86 platform but execute the DOS code in the EXE file, not the OS/2 code.

Finally, although DOS applications run on non-x86 systems, they can do so only in a window. The full-screen operation provided by x86 systems assumes VGA hardware compatibility that isn't present on non-x86 systems. (Conceivably, some x86 systems might not offer VGA compatibility either, but that's not true at present.)

DOS Support

NT uses the virtual-86 feature of the 386 and 486 chip to provide a separate virtual machine for each DOS application you run. Most DOS applications will run under NT with no problem, but device drivers and low-level utilities may not. This was a conscious design decision by the NT designers to trade compatibility for security and system stability. If NT let DOS software access hardware directly, it could put hardware into an unstable state or corrupt the hard disk. So some poorly behaved DOS apps will not run under NT.

However, if the definition of a poorly behaved DOS app means that it accesses the hardware directly, then nearly all DOS apps are poorly behaved. Most of them write directly to VGA video buffers, reprogram the timer chip, or access the serial port hardware. Therefore, NT makes this most basic PC hardware available through Virtual Device Drivers (VDDs). A VDD virtualizes hardware so that each DOS application believes it is using the actual hardware, when it really is not. This lets NT arbitrate access to the real hardware device when multiple DOS applications (or DOS and NT) try to access it.

There are two major trouble areas in DOS support under NT:

1. *Specialized hardware that requires custom device drivers or TSRs.* This includes high-resolution DOS video drivers, the fax section of the Intel SatisFAXtion 400, video capture boards, and many scanners. Vendors need to write VDDs for any hardware they want to be supported under NT, using the Windows NT Device Driver Kit.

   You cannot install DOS-based drivers for network cards, tape drives, or CD-ROMs in NT, since these typically interface to custom hardware. These devices should be installed under NT and accessed in DOS through the NT support. The SYSTEM32 directory includes special versions of the network redirector and MS CD-ROM extensions that are used with DOS and loaded in the AUTOEXEC.NT file (see the following).

2. *Utilities that require low-level access to disk drives.* This includes disk-compression software, including Stacker and DoubleSpace, and the disk doctor tools in Norton Utilities or PC Tools. These utilities present security and integrity risks, and assume things about the structure and layout of the disk that aren't necessarily true under NT. If you require these types of utilities, you will need to find NT equivalents. To perform an operation, such as disk defragmenting on a FAT disk volume, you should reboot into DOS and run the application from there.

The DOS compatibility built into NT is basically at the level of DOS 5.0, although the Get DOS Version API call actually returns 5.32 as the version number. Since most applications aren't sensitive to DOS versions, this shouldn't be a problem. However, if you have your system set up to dual-boot between a DOS 6.0 and NT, you will find that many DOS 6.0 utilities fail with an "Incompatible DOS version" error if you try to run them in NT. Most of those utilities (such as MORE or FIND) have equivalents in NT. You can overcome these version incompatibilities by using the SETVER.EXE utility that comes with DOS (version 5 and later). Load SETVER in the CONFIG.NT file, as described in the following.

When you log on, NT reads the AUTOEXEC.BAT file from the boot drive, and sets any environment variables it finds for later use by DOS or NT applications. It also adds directories from any PATH statement onto the end of the path that NT uses. NT sets the path so that its SYSTEM32 directory is searched before any other directory, so 32-bit equivalents to DOS commands will be found first.

Each time you start a command prompt window or launch a DOS application from ProgMan or FileMan, NT reads the CONFIG.NT and AUTOEXEC.NT files in the SYSTEM32 directory to configure the environment for the new application. These files are similar to their DOS analogs, and let you configure each DOS session for maximum memory, or load a particular set of TSRs or device drivers. Chapter 11 of the *NT System Guide* details the commands available in these two files. Each DOS session has its own environment, complete with high memory area. As with DOS, you can specify commands to load TSRs or device drivers into high memory. Since hardware devices aren't mapped into the high memory of these virtual DOS environments, you may be able to put much more into high memory than in true DOS.

Like Windows 3.1, NT also supports Program Information Files (PIFs) for DOS applications (see Figure A3.1). In fact, you can use the same PIFs you have been using under Windows 3.1, although NT ignores most of the DOS and Windows parameters. It does use the startup directory, EMS/XMS memory

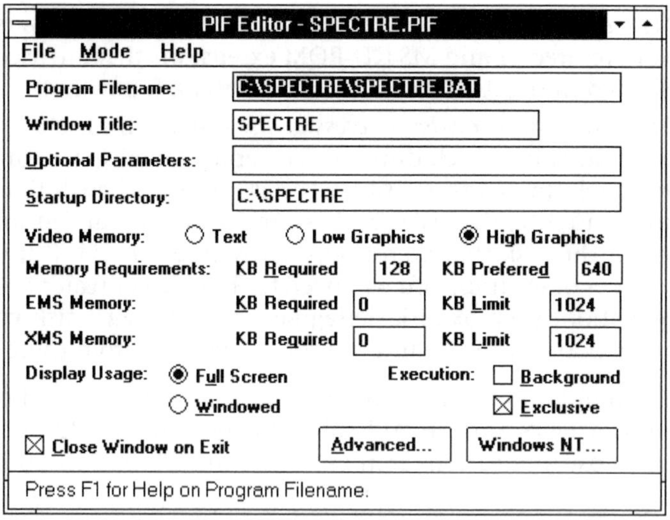

Figure A3.1 PIF Editor.

The Windows NT Program Information File (PIF) Editor allows you to customize settings for legacy applications, including 16-bit DOS, Windows, and OS/2 applications.

usage, priority, shortcut keys, and display usage; details are in chapter 11 of the *NT System Guide*. You can also specify different AUTOEXEC and CONFIG files that can be used to initialize DOS before running this particular application, rather than the ones in SYSTEM32. For example, if you have a particularly memory-hungry DOS application, you could create a custom CONFIG.NT file to remove CD-ROM and/or network support to save memory.

If you are using an NTFS volume, NT creates DOS-compatible names for any files that violate the DOS 8.3 naming convention. When DOS applications are using files on NTFS, they see only the DOS-compatible names. The following rules are used:

- ❑ Lowercase letters are converted to uppercase.
- ❑ Characters that aren't legal in DOS files are converted to underscores (_). (NTFS uses the 16-bit Unicode character set, whereas DOS uses 7-bit ASCII.)
- ❑ Spaces are removed.
- ❑ If the name has more than one period, all but the last (rightmost) are removed.
- ❑ The name is truncated to its first (leftmost) six characters before the period.
- ❑ The extension (after the period) is truncated to three characters.

❏ A tilde and sequence number (e.g., ~1) are added to the name to create a unique file name. If a single digit doesn't produce a unique name, the name is truncated to five characters and a two-digit sequence number is used.

Here are some examples, assuming that the files here are created in order (which affects the sequence numbering):

NTFS Name	*DOS Name*
This.Is.A.Very.Long.Name	THISIS~1.NAM
This Is A Very Long.Too	THISIS~1.TOO
This is a very_big.name	THISIS~2.NAM
Monthly Budget.DOC	MONTHL~1.DOC
Monthly Report.DOC	MONTHL~2.DOC

If you are not sure what DOS file name will be produced from the long name, you can select View/All File Details in File Manager or type *DIR /X* from the command prompt, to see both the long and short names (see Figure A3.2).

In truth, though, much confusion will be saved in mixed (DOS and NT) environments if you stick to using DOS-style 8.3 names. This eliminates the

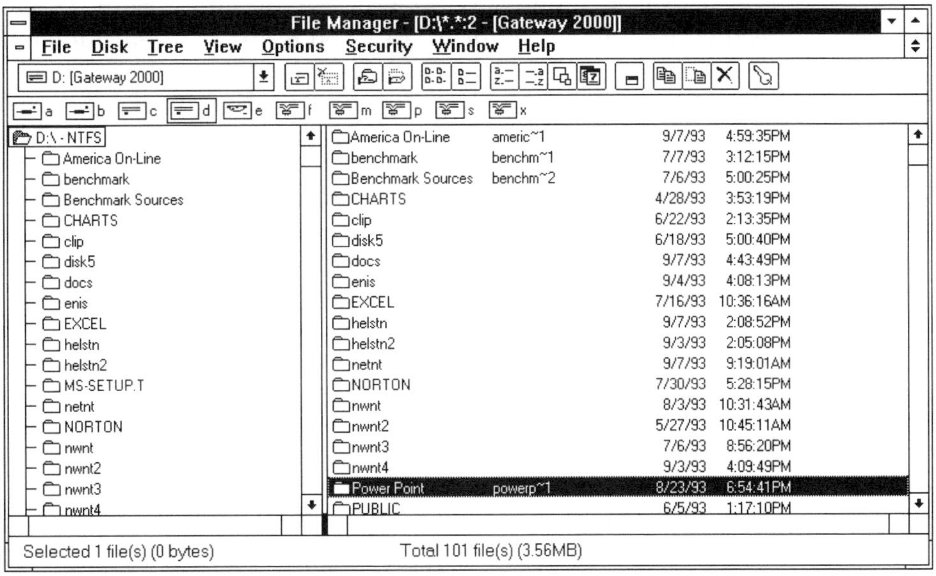

Figure A3.2 File Manager.

Windows NT supports legacy applications by automatically generating DOS-style 8.3 file name equivalents to long file names in the New Technology File System. You can see both versions of the file's name using the View/All File Details option in File Manager.

need to remember that Monthly Report.DOC on the NT system is the same as MONTHL~2.DOC in DOS!

Windows 3.x Support

NT's support for Windows 3.x is similar to Windows enhanced mode on x86 systems, but adds several significant improvements. (See the section at the beginning of this appendix for a discussion of non-x86 system limitations.) Like Windows 3.x enhanced mode, virtual memory is supported.

One major advantage with running 3.1 applications under NT is that they are not limited to a tiny pool of 128KB system resources, as they are in Windows 3.x. This means that a Windows NT system can have more Windows 3.x apps running simultaneously than Windows 3.x. It also means that a resource-hungry program, such as Microsoft Excel 5.0, can have *many* more worksheets open at once. For example, under Windows 3.x you can open only about 30 empty Excel worksheets before running out of system resources; under NT we've opened more than 470 (yes, that's four hundred and seventy) before running out of paging file space. By increasing the paging file space (or adding more physical memory) we could go even higher.

As with DOS support, Windows 3.x applications cannot access hardware directly. The primary problem area you're likely to encounter here is with applications that add their own drivers to the [386enh] section of SYSTEM.INI. Like the DOS emulation, if these drivers control custom hardware, you will need to contact the vendor to see if there is an NT driver. However, some vendors include drivers that simply work around problems with the standard Windows drivers, the most common one being COMM.DRV. You may find that you can run such applications successfully under NT without the driver (NT's built-in comm support is superior to that in Windows 3.x).

When you install Windows NT, it looks to see if you already have Windows 3.x (or Windows for Workgroups) installed on your system; for example, in C:\WINDOWS. If so, it suggests you install NT in the same directory. There's little danger that installing NT will cause your Windows 3.x setup to misbehave; nearly all of the NT files actually go into a new \WINDOWS\SYSTEM32 directory, and NT uses its own Registry database (rather than WIN.INI or SYSTEM.INI) to save system settings.

The advantage of installing Windows NT and Windows 3.x in the same directory is that NT will set up your Windows 3.x applications for you. The first time you log onto NT after doing a same-directory install, NT will create program groups that are equivalent to your custom groups in Windows 3.x. Each time NT is booted, the system updates its Windows 3.x configuration based on the WIN.INI, SYSTEM.INI, and REG.DAT (Object Linking and Embedding) information. When NT is running Windows 3.x apps, they will be able to use the information in your existing Windows setup, including private INI files in the \WINDOWS directory and application-specific settings in WIN.INI. Whether you install an application in Windows 3.*x* or NT, you will be able to run it in either environment.

If you choose to install NT in a location other than your Windows 3.*x* directory (for example, \WINNT), running 3.1 applications under NT can be a bit more complicated but still quite possible. One simple approach is to reinstall the application under NT but specify the same destination for the application files. This will usually recreate any changes required to INI files in the \WINNT directory without actually having a second copy of the application on disk. Remember that if you don't install NT and 3.1 in the same directory, the INI files can get out of sync. That is, if you boot into 3.1, change some settings in an application, and later run that application in NT, you may find those settings are not changed.

From version 3.5 on, NT also has the ability to run each 16-bit Windows application in a separate memory space. Although each DOS application always runs in its own memory space, by default 16-bit Windows applications run in a single memory space for compatibility reasons. However, there are two definite advantages to separate memory spaces for 16-bit applications. First, a 16-bit application that crashes or locks up its own message queue will not affect other 16-bit applications. Second, each separate memory space also has a separate thread of execution, so they can be preemptively multitasked. The two biggest drawbacks of separate memory spaces is that they confuse some applications (utilities mostly) that expect a single address space, and they consume more system memory.

You can choose from four options to launch a Win16 program in a separate memory space:

1. From a command window, run the program using a command line of the form *CMD /C START /SEPARATE programname.*

2. Run the program using Program Manager's File/Run dialog, and check the "Run in separate memory space" option. Note that this option can be changed only if Program Manager determines the executable file you specify is a Win16 application; otherwise it will be disabled (see Figure A3.3).

3. Create a program item in Program Manager. In the Program Item Properties dialog, check the "Run in separate memory space" option (see Figure A3.3).

4. To change a file association so that it always launches the application in a separate memory space, use File Manager's File/Associate dialog. Enter the file type extension, then click the Change Type button. For the command entry, type *CMD /C START /SEPARATE programname %1*, where *programname* is the full path and file name for the Win16 application (see Figure A3.3).

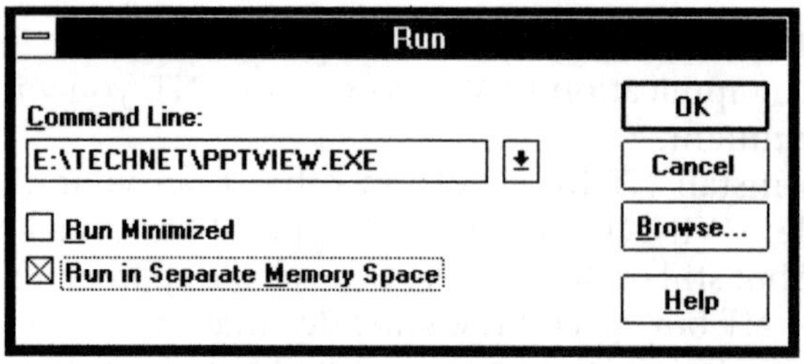

```
┌──────────────────────────────────────────────────────┐
│ ─                         Run                          │
├──────────────────────────────────────────────────────┤
│  Command Line:                        ┌──────────┐     │
│  ┌──────────────────────────┐ ┌─┐     │    OK    │     │
│  │ E:\TECHNET\PPTVIEW.EXE   │ │±│     └──────────┘     │
│  └──────────────────────────┘ └─┘     ┌──────────┐     │
│  ☐ Run Minimized                      │  Cancel  │     │
│  ☒ Run in Separate Memory Space       └──────────┘     │
│                                       ┌──────────┐     │
│                                       │ Browse...│     │
│                                       └──────────┘     │
│                                       ┌──────────┐     │
│                                       │   Help   │     │
│                                       └──────────┘     │
└──────────────────────────────────────────────────────┘
```

Figure A3.3 Program Manager File/Run Dialog.

Beginning with version 3.5, NT supports running 16-bit Windows applications in separate sessions. This allows such applications to be preemptively multitasked, and prevents them from blocking one another. Designating an application to be run in a separate session is done using the Separate Session check box shown here, or using the /separate switch with the *start* command-line function.

Windows 95 Support

At the time this book went to press, Microsoft had just made their preview beta of Windows 95 available. Since Windows 95 isn't quite done yet, the question of compatibility can't be definitively answered. However, based on this beta version we can already point out potential problem areas for users who want to migrate from, dual-boot NT with, or run Win32 applications targeted for Windows 95.

Although it isn't a problem yet, *migrating* from a Windows 95 installation to a Windows NT one would seem to be quite a challenge. NT 3.5 doesn't know anything about the Win95 directory organization. NT cannot automatically migrate Program Manager groups; since Program Manager has been replaced in Win95 by the Explorer, there are no longer any .GRP files. Also, NT's existing FAT file system does not handle the shortcut (LNK) file capabilities that are essential to Win95 (this will undoubtedly be changed when NT is updated with a Win95-style user interface).

Even with the Win95 beta, it is quite simple to install both operating systems on one PC and dual-boot between them. However, if you are doing so, we recommend that you stick to the FAT file system—Win95's lack of support for NTFS could create a migration nightmare if you try to use it.

In theory, the arrival of Win95 could actually be a good thing for NT, because it increases the pool of users who can run 32-bit applications. Another theoretical boost comes from Microsoft's Windows 95 logo program that, as part of its requirements, says that any Win95-logo application must also run on NT. However, there is an escape clause: Microsoft seems willing to make exceptions for utilities that it judges to be too Win95-specific to work under NT without significant changes. Thus, an undelete utility or disk formatter might be able to gain a Win95 logo but be completely unable to run on NT.

To some extent, Microsoft's inconsistent implementation of the Win32 API on the two platforms may encourage vendors to exercise that escape clause. For example, although Win32 and its NT implementation has API calls to format a floppy disk or to get hard disk geometry (sectors, tracks, cylinders, and the like), the Win32 implementation on Win95 uses a different and incompatible method based on the legacy DOS/BIOS APIs. How significant these differences are and whether they impact NT won't be clear until the first wave of Win95 applications and utilities hit the market after Win95 ships.

OS/2 1.3 Support

On x86-compatible systems, NT runs 16-bit OS/2 character-based applications out of the box. It won't run OS/2 applications that depend on Presentation Manager (even some character-based apps do), and it won't run 32-bit OS/2 applications. NT doesn't run OS/2 applications at all on non-x86 systems (see the first section in this appendix). However, Microsoft has an add-on package available that provides Presentation Manager support (see the next section).[1]

When you start NT the first time, it looks at the CONFIG.SYS file on the boot disk; if it detects OS/2 commands, NT will add entries for PROTSHELL, COMSPEC, and OS2LIBPATH to the Registry based on the entries in this file. These go into the NT environment along with the NT and DOS environment settings; you can examine them all using the System applet in Control Panel. Nearly all other commands in the CONFIG.SYS file are ignored by NT; chapter 11 of the *NT System Guide* details how they are handled.

Most likely, you will need to deal with CONFIG.SYS changes when an OS/2 application installs itself and changes this file. To handle this situation, Microsoft created an unusual approach: An OS/2 application (it *must* be an OS/2 application) can edit the file named C:\CONFIG.SYS. In response, NT retrieves the OS/2 configuration data from the Registry and puts it into a temporary text file. When the file is closed, NT parses the file and updates the Registry. If you don't have an OS/2 text editor, you can't get NT to perform this magic. However, you can examine the OS/2 CONFIG.SYS by using REGEDT32 to edit the key HKEY_LOCAL_MACHINE\SOFTWARE\Microsoft\OS/2 Subsystem for NT\1.0\config.sys (see Figure A3.4). Be aware, however, that Microsoft does not recommend changing the file in this way.

Like NT, OS/2 generally insulates applications from the hardware through device drivers. However, OS/2 has a *trapdoor* that allows applications to perform I/O directly to devices, called *IO Privilege Level* (IOPL). OS/2 applications that require IOPL will not run under NT. Although OS/2 device drivers are not supported under NT, you can map an NT device so that it appears as an OS/2

---

1. Windows NT Add-on Subsystem for Presentation Manager (PM).

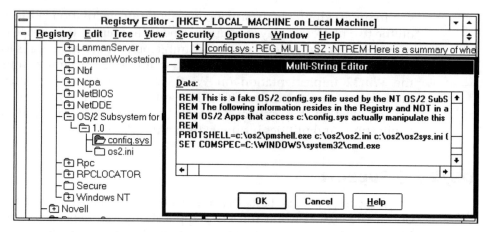

Figure A3.4 Registry Editor.

The Windows NT Registry includes a complete OS/2 CONFIG.SYS file, which can be edited either using an OS/2 text editor (the preferred method), or by opening the appropriate subkey in the Registry Editor.

device, using the DEVICENAME command in CONFIG.SYS. This approach should allow most 16-bit OS/2 application software to run correctly.

OS/2 Presentation Manager (PM) Support

Users needing a greater degree of OS/2 application support should investigate Microsoft's Presentation Manager subsystem add-on kit. The kit replaces and enhances NT's OS/2 subsystem, allowing OS/2 1.2/1.3 Presentation Manager (PM) applications to execute under Windows NT. PM applications do *not* share the Windows NT desktop with other (Win32, DOS, OS/2 character mode, POSIX, Win16) applications—instead, there is a single OS/2 full-screen desktop managed by the Presentation Manager Shell (PMSHELL.EXE) application. All PM applications share that desktop (see Figure A3.5).

In addition to requiring a separate desktop, the PM subsystem enforces some other limitations on PM applications, including:

❑ All PM applications share a single event queue—thus, if an application *hangs*, it will probably hang the entire subsystem.

❑ Applications are not permitted to perform direct hardware access—such access will hang the application (see Figure A3.6) and in all probability require that the PM subsystem be restarted.

❑ Only VGA-compatible video drivers and display resolutions are supported by default (the PM subsystem documentation includes a special

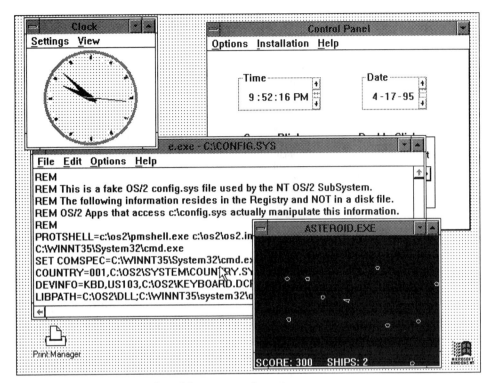

Figure A3.5 Presentation Manager subsystem.

Microsoft's Presentation Manager add-on for Windows NT supports running graphical OS/2 1.2 and 1.3 applications in a separate screen group from NT applications.

procedure—launching PMSHELL.EXE with a /w command-line switch—to reconfigure the subsystem for other display resolutions).

□ Printing requires an OS/2 print driver (half a dozen are supplied with the subsystem), and only the PMPRINT queue manager is supported. Printing to shared network printers is possible by redirecting the relevant print queue to a network printer from the NT command line; for example, *net use LPT1: \\win1\edit_pcl* redirects the queue associated with LPT1: to \\win1\edit_pcl. PM-based printer-sharing applications are not supported.

□ Interprocess communication between PM applications is supported using all the methods supported by OS/2, including shared memory. Communication between PM applications and Windows (16- and 32-bit) applications, however, is limited to the clipboard (text and bitmap formats only), named pipes, mailslots, and NetBIOS. DDE between PM applications and other applications is not currently supported.

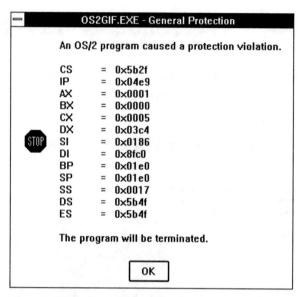

Figure A3.6 Protection Fault in Presentation Manager application.
Attempting to execute a PM application that directly accesses hardware may result in the following dialog. Unfortunately, this usually hangs not just the application, but also the entire subsystem—requiring you to shut it down and restart it.

❑ PM applications do not recognize many of the standard NT control panel settings, including those for screen appearance, mouse settings, and communication ports. These must be set from the PM Control Panel included with the subsystem. Time and Date settings are global and may be made from either the PM or NT Control Panel. Other NT Control Panel settings are unlikely to be recognized by the PM subsystem.

Note that these restrictions are *in addition* to those imposed by the normal, character-mode OS/2 support provided in Windows NT (OS/2 applications are supported only on Intel processors; ring-2 IOPL code is executed at ring-3; interrupt suspend/resume applies only to the OS/2 subsystem, *not* to the entire system). The subsystem is also provided without the OS/2 file manager, desktop manager, and command prompt—instead PM applications are launched from a PM group in Windows NT Program Manager (see Figure A3.7). The PM subsystem maps OS/2 groups to Presentation Manager groups, but does not support drag-and-drop between PM applications and the NT desktop.

On the whole, the level of integration provided by the PM subsystem is quite a bit less sophisticated than that provided for other types (Win16, OS/2 character mode, or POSIX) of legacy application in NT. However, the subsystem *does* work—and that may be all that matters if you depend on a particular

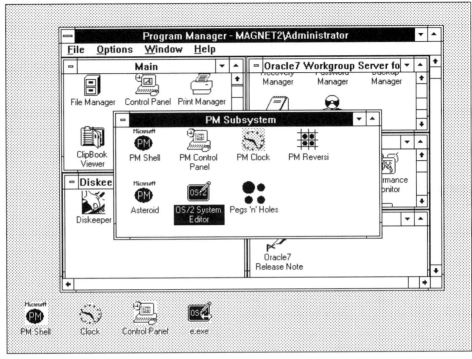

Figure A3.7 PM group in NT Program Manager.

The Presentation Manager add-on for NT does not support using an OS/2 desktop or file manager. Instead, a special Program Manager group is provided for PM applications, which are then launched by double-clicking their icons in much the same way as other applications. Note the icons on the bottom of the screen—they represent running PM applications. Clicking on these icons will bring up the PM subsystem screen group shown in Figure A3.5.

PM-based application. A few final notes about the PM subsystem: You may need to reinstall it after updating NT with a service pack; you will probably need a new version if you upgrade from one version of NT to another (release of PM subsystem updates has lagged new NT versions by a few months). Non-U.S. users should check with Microsoft before purchasing the subsystem for use with a national-language version of NT (at this writing only English and French system messages are supported, though it's possible to support several foreign keyboard layouts using a procedure in the PM subsystem documentation).[2]

Finally—a note about installation: The PM subsystem is installed using a batch file (INSTALL.CMD) that creates an OS/2 directory in the root of drive C

---

2. April, 1995.

and copies files into it. This can have highly undesirable side effects if executed on a system that's been set up to dual-boot between OS/2 and NT—it may render the OS/2 installation unusable. Back up any such OS/2 files before installing the PM subsystem. Another point of note: PM applications (including the subsystem itself) are best closed from within the subsystem—while it's possible to shut down applications from the NT desktop, the procedure is time-consuming and (at this writing) somewhat unreliable. The best way to close down the subsystem is to invoke the PM task manager (by clicking the right mouse button from within the PM desktop), and select the Shutdown PM button.

POSIX Support

Windows NT has already begun to make inroads into areas where the UNIX operating system is currently used. To increase the attractiveness of Windows NT to the UNIX community, Microsoft has added a large degree of UNIX compatibility to the operating system. Another impetus for Microsoft is that the U.S. government favors the use of UNIX-compatible systems in many projects. Windows NT could not compete for many government projects without UNIX compatibility.

For an example of the encroachment of NT into UNIX territory, you don't need to look any further than the NT Resource Kit. On the CD that comes with the kit, there's a set of the basic UNIX utilities, such as *grep* (see Appendix 4 for further details). Third-party providers, such as MKS Systems and Hamilton Labs, offer even larger sets of UNIX-compatible utilities

There are actually many different versions of UNIX in addition to operating systems that are UNIX-like but not licensed to use the UNIX name. In the mid-1980s the Institute for Electrical and Electronics Engineers (IEEE) sponsored a committee to define the UNIX environment in a vendor-neutral way that would promote standardization. By 1990, that work progressed into International Standards Organization (ISO) standard IS-9945, but commonly called POSIX. There are actually a family of POSIX standards that define the system API, graphical interface, command shell language, tools (such as *grep* and *awk*), security, and networking. However, most of these are still being defined. One of the few parts of POSIX that is fully standardized is POSIX.1, the C-language API to system services. This is the part of POSIX that Windows NT currently addresses.

The POSIX support in Windows NT is different from other legacy application support because it is not at the binary (EXE-file) level, but at the source-code level. Source code must be recompiled on Windows NT using the POSIX compatibility libraries. For an end user with shrink-wrapped applications this is not feasible, but it's standard procedure for the UNIX developers that Microsoft is targeting with POSIX compatibility.

UNIX developers are also familiar with another trade-off created by POSIX: portability versus functionality. The POSIX.1 API standard is bare-bones, mostly providing access to the file system and the ability to start and communicate with other processes. There is simple TTY-style I/O, but nothing like the event-driven graphical interface that is the basis of both Windows 3.*x* and Windows NT. (UNIX systems often provide a graphical user interface called X Windows, but this is outside the scope of POSIX.1 and covered instead by the unfinished POSIX.12 standard).

Generally, the POSIX libraries are just thin wrapper functions that translate POSIX API calls into their Windows NT equivalents. The operating systems use models that are similar enough that there are not major problems in most translating operations. Since POSIX applications are compiled using a Windows NT 32-bit compiler, their performance can be quite good compared to 16-bit DOS or Windows 3.*x* applications.

POSIX applications generally expect a file system that behaves like a UNIX file system. NTFS has some features specifically designed for maximum compatibility with POSIX. For example, NTFS is normally case preserving when creating files, but not case sensitive when opening files. Thus, you can save a file to an NTFS partition as DaveM.DOC, but open it later using the string davem.doc. However, when using the POSIX subsystem you must specify the capitalization exactly, because a POSIX application expects the file system to be both case sensitive and case preserving. Using POSIX you can, in fact, create a file named DAVEM and a different one called DaveM in the same directory.

You can start POSIX applications like any other application, either by typing the application name from a command line, or through File Manager or Program Manager.

For More Information

Microsoft Staff (1995), *Windows NT Resource Kit (Volume 1)*. Redmond, WA: Microsoft Press. Part V (Chapters 15 through 17) gives details on NT's built-in Win16, OS/2 character-mode, and POSIX support.

Microsoft Staff (1994), *Microsoft Windows NT Add-On Subsystem Release for Presentation Manager (PM)*. Redmond, WA: Microsoft Press. The combined documentation (overview and release notes) for the PM subsystem amounts to just 26 pages. It's available *only* by purchasing the subsystem.

APPENDIX

The Windows NT Resource Kit

Throughout the chapters in this book, we've referred to utility software, documentation, and tools that Microsoft packages in the *Windows NT Resource Kit*. The kit was first made available a few months after the release of NT 3.1, and has since been updated for NT 3.5 (in its second edition). We expect that future editions will appear more or less annually.

The kit is so extensive that we cannot hope to cover it in detail here—instead, we present a brief overview of its contents, with some notes on items we find particularly interesting.

In brief, the NT resource kit is a positive gold mine of tricks, tips, and utility software. It currently includes a four-volume set of books (*Windows NT Resource Guide, Windows NT Networking Guide, Optimizing Windows NT,* and *Windows NT Messages*), one CD, and several diskettes; at an *estimated retail price* (Microsoft no longer quotes list prices) under $150. The programs and other information on the CD alone are easily worth that price. They include Help files that completely document all variables set using the Configuration Registry Editor (REGENTRY.HLP); give technical specifications (including settings and a visual diagram) of all NT-compatible network cards (NTCARD35.HLP); list all Windows NT-compatible hardware(HCL*mmmyy*.HLP); and document the tools on the CD (RKTOOLS.HLP). Tools include a graphical interface for the the AT command-line function that lists all scheduled batch jobs (WINAT.EXE); a graphical monitor for domain servers (DOMMON.EXE); a graphical monitor of domain browser activity (BROWMON.EXE); The Server Manager for Domains, User Manager for Domains, and User Profile Editor tools from Windows NT

Advanced Server—along with administrative tools for use with Services for Macintosh in NT Server environments.

The resource kit also includes a reasonably complete suite of POSIX 1.0-compatible command-line utilities, including *ar, cat, cc, chmod, chown, cp, devsrv, find, grep, ld, ln, ls, make, mkdir, mv, rm, rmdir, sh, touch, vi,* and *wc*—although, to be honest we cannot recommend them due to the POSIX subsystem's many limitations (we suggest that users with a need for UNIX-style utilities investigate the *Hamilton C-Shell* and *MKS Utilities* packages discussed in Chapter 3, Table 3.3).

End-user-oriented utilities include an editor for creating your animated cursors (ANIEDIT.EXE), a multiple *virtual* desktop tool (TOPDESK.EXE), a graphical UNIX Uuencode/decode tool (NTUUCODE.EXE), and a Windows-based interface to the Compuserve Information Service (WINCIM.EXE), among others.

Network and administrative tools include a mechanism for getting user input in batch files (CHOICE.EXE), a tool for dumping the event logs as a text file (DUMPEL.EXE), a tool for disabling floppy disks in high-security environments (FLOPLOCK.EXE), a Simple Network Management Protocol (SNMP) Management Information Block (MIB) compiler, crude tools for operating a network-based modem pool (WINVTP.EXE), a command-line interface to services (NETSVC.EXE), a per-user file permissions command-line utility (PERMS.-EXE), and a secure (relatively speaking) remote command-line for Windows NT—in the second edition, available as both a command-line program (RE-MOTE.EXE) and an NT *service* background application (RCMD.EXE).

In the first edition of *Networking Windows NT*, we speculated that it should be possible to. write a *universal* service application that would allow any compatible program to be treated as a network service (started and stopped remotely, etc.). Evidently Microsoft was listening (or the old platitute about *great minds think alike* applied)—in the Resource Kit's second edition, SRVANY.EXE appeared. It does exactly what we'd suggested, and provides a simple but powerful way for administrators to convert batch jobs, DOS (or OS/2) executables, and even Windows (16- or 32-bit) applications into manageable network services.

Other tools include Microsoft's Computer Profile Setup (CPS), which is theoretically useful when installing a standard Windows NT configuration throughout an organization (we've never used it, nor have we spoken with anyone else who has—in all candor, the command-line and .INF file options available with WINNT.EXE and WINNT32.EXE really make the CPS redundant); a uniprocessor-to-multiprocessor kernel converter (necessary if you add processors to an upgradable system); and a graphical Transmission Control Program/Internet Protocol (TCP/IP) configuration utility that can greatly simplify the management of NT systems in an IP environment.

Beginning with the Resource Kit's second edition, Microsoft added a complete set of Internet services (many developed at EMWAC—the European

Microsoft Windows Academic Centre, operated by Edinburgh University), including World-Wide Web (WWW), WAIS, Gopher, and DNS Services—as described in Chapter 6. These services augment the FTP service provided in the box with all NT systems, making it not only possible but relatively simple to make an NT server available as an Internet *node*.

Other tools in the kit include a command-line utility to create new user accounts, Dynamic Host Configuration Protocol (DHCP) management tools, tools to compact and manage the *Jet* database used by (among other things) the message database, and a screen saver for use in secure environments, which logs off the current user automatically after a fixed period of inactivity.

The four books included in the kit are essential for NT administrators, and highly recommended for advanced end users. The *Resource Guide* contains up-to-date infromation on NT setup, printing, configuration (Registry) management, and migrating Windows, OS/2, and POSIX applications to NT. *Windows NT Messages* documents all error and warning messages generated by Windows NT and its subsystems. *Optimizing Windows NT* provides vital information on Performance Monitor objects, disk cache tuning, high performance graphics programming—and documents the NT Registry. (It's also the best written of the books—where else can you find an author suggesting that "there are many ways to make a computer go faster, such as dropping it from a fourth-floor window.")

Windows NT Networking Guide, which first appeared in the Resource Kit's second edition, collects supporting information formerly found in various supplemental NT documents—adding some details not available elsewhere. Among other things, it covers NT 3.5's revised PPP-based RAS architecture—with extensive information on writing and debugging RAS scripts; how to write logon scripts, including use of environment variables and considerations for the various client operating systems Windows NT supports; implementation details of NT's NetBios Frame (NBF) core network protocol—and other supported protocols, including TCP/IP, Data Link Control (DLC), NetWare-compatible IPX/SPX, IBM host-compatible System Network Architecture (SNA); and the net-library and DB-Library protocols used by NT databases.

Support professionals will find information on NT's NetLogon service—including user authentication and domain discovery for both local and networked systems—and a much needed chapter on NT's network browser *invaluable* for solving problems when NT, WFWG, and DOS/Lan Manager users cannot *see* each other on an otherwise functional LAN.

The *Networking Guide's* Chapters 10 through 22 provide some 270 pages of detail on NT's TCP/IP implementation—beginning with an overview and ending with NT on the Internet. This information is *essential* for anyone attempting to implement an NT-based Internet server. It completely documents NT's TCP/IP implementation, how it relates to standard IP models, how it's used with NBF, and the Internet-related services discussed earlier.

Coverage includes exotic topics: WINS Hub Replication Frequency in Multinational WANs, DNS to WINS Name Translation, Setup and Maintenance of NT's LMHOSTS Name Resolution File, Hidden Registry Settings for the FTP Service, TCP/IP-Related Performance Monitor Counters, Using NT as an IP Router and Setting Up an Internet *Firewall* to Minmize Security Risks—among other topics.

The Resource Kit does have some weaknesses, including limited information on Internet security and third-party routers, poor e-mail coverage (chapters 8 and 9 of volume 1 cover the workgroup postoffice included with NT, but don't discuss upgrades), and limited troubleshooting information.

In Extremis

Aside from the utilities and documentation mentioned earlier, the Resource Kit includes some troubleshooting tools (formerly supplied in the \SUPPORT directory of NT 3.1 distrubution CDs) that can be extremely valuable when used in conjunction with the tools and techniques discussed in the troubleshooting sections of Chapters 2 and 5. These include:

- ❑ BROWSESTAT.EXE—This is a utility that displays, sets, and resets browser status (covered in Chapter 8), which can help enormously in a situation where you find that the system is taking an appalling length of time to respond to *net view* commands, or to react when you issue a Connect Net Drive command from the File Manager.

- ❑ DRIVERS.EXE—This is a program that displays information on device drivers and may help in debugging problems with access to low-level hardware devices.

- ❑ EXETYPE.EXE—This is a very simple command-line program that displays details of the type and subsystem of an executable file. If you find that you're having problems running a particular EXE file on a particular system, try typing *exetype filename.exe*, where *filename* is the name of the EXE file you're having trouble with. This will give you details on whether this in a Windows NT, OS/2, or 16-bit Windows program; what instruction set it is designed for, and so on—and may help identify what's causing the problem.

- ❑ FIFO.CMD—This is actually a batch command file that turns on support for first in/first out (FIFO) buffering for modems that require it. There is an equivalent set of steps available that will perform the same functions through the Registry Editor. Note that the FIFO.CMD file requires the use of the REGINI.EXE program described later.

- ❑ PMON.EXE—This is the Process Resource Monitor that provides detailed information about the execution of processes, including the thread count, working set size, and so forth. In general, the very same functions can be achieved using the Windows NT Performance Monitor, but PMON.EXE provides an alternative user interface and may provide more detailed information. Also, as it's a character-based tool it can be executed from script files if necessary.

❑ PSTAT.EXE—This is a character-based program that displays a list of all programs running in the system, along with status information; this can again be used in conjunction with the script program.

❑ PVIEWER.EXE—This is a graphical program that provides detailed information about processes comparable to that provided by the PMON.EXE program. Again, in general, the functions here are duplicated by the Windows NT Performance Monitor, but it provides an alternative user interface.

❑ REGINI.EXE—This is a command-line program that allows a Registry command to be changed using a script. This is (like the Registry Editor itself) one of the most powerful and also one of the most dangerous utilities included in the Support Tools directory. The obvious usefulness of it to a system administrator is that having once decided that a certain set of changes needs to be made to the Registries of a variety of systems, you can do it using a Registry script and the REGINI.EXE command executed from the command line. This means, of course, that you can execute Registry changes *simultaneously* on many systems at once by meddling with their login script file—but *beware*.

If you mess up that script file (and therefore mess up the Registry), you can not only produce the machine-gun effect we described earlier in describing the Registry, but you can also machine-gun *all* of your servers (and /or workstations, as the case may be); so this needs to be used with care.

Microsoft provides no documentation whatsoever on the Registry Script Format. However, you will find examples of the Registry Script Format in question in the FIFO_OFF and FIFO_ON INI files located in the SUPPORT/SUPTOOLS/I386 directory of the CD, which are associated with the FIFO.CMD file. This is a very much *use at your own risk* situation. We *strongly* recommend that if you are for any reason considering use of the REGINI.EXE function, experiment with it on an isolated Windows NT workstation first and then make sure the system will survive a reboot after the Registry has been modified. Only after you have done that and you're satisfied that the script is safe should you attempt to do it on other systems, particularly servers.

❑ SMBTRACE—The SMBTRACE utility is potentially of great use for network professionals attempting to that network problems. This is a server message block trace program that functionally amounts to a network sniffer implemented in software. It allows capture of SMBs from the server or redirector, and allows a wide range of options for determining just how much data is captured and to what degree it impacts system performance. Like PMON, NBSTAT, and so forth, it is a character-based utility.

Conclusion

It's impossible to overestimate the value of the NT Resource Kit. It is a tremendously valuable set of tools and documentation, and is by far the least expensive investment that an NT site can make in support (it costs about as much as one support call to Microsoft). We give this kit our highest recommendation.

CPU Architectures and NT Performance

The architecture of Windows NT makes it possible to use a variety of different types of computers with this advanced operating system. Selecting the right type of computer for a particular Windows NT application is a matter of cost versus performance, and could dramatically affect the cost effectiveness of a Windows NT installation. Alternatives supported by the current release of Windows NT, over and above the single processor PC-compatible system, include Symmetric Multiprocessor (SMP) and Reduced Instruction Set Computer (RISC) systems.

Why Not a Conventional PC System?

Before we examine the more exotic alternatives, it's worth considering just what might drive you to a decision to purchase a more exotic design. After all, the conventional PC architecture systems are well understood, and technically mature—and let's not ignore the most important feature: They are cheap. The basic reason to consider an unconventional architecture is performance. In the classic conventional PC-compatible performance is limited, because only a single central processor (CPU) can be used in each machine, and the performance of that CPU is limited to the highest performance of the highest available Intel microprocessor, currently the 120MHz Pentium chip. In order to understand why we might wish to consider moving to an SMP or RISC architecture, we need to consider just what the performance limitations of the Intel chips are.

Integer Performance

The most commonly used measure of a CPU's performance is the figure of Millions of Instructions per Second (MIPS). This is a direct measure of the computational performance of any microprocessor chip. It refers to the number of individual instructions or steps that can be executed in a single second. Such steps might include fetching a data word from memory, performing an addition or subtraction, comparing one data word to another, and so on. Computer programs are nothing more than a collection of such steps, so any given program will execute twice as fast on a machine that performs at twice as many MIPS.

Intel microprocessors capable of running Windows NT span a considerable range of MIPS in their current configurations. The *minimum* system for running Windows NT currently is a 25MHz Intel 386 processor capable of somewhere in the vicinity of 15 MIPS. The highest performance processor currently available is a 120 MHz Pentium processor that employs an exotic dual unit of issue designed to achieve over 200 MIPS.

A particular characteristic of the Intel architectural design that affects its integer performance is the fact that Intel processors have, up to now, been designed according to a Complex Instruction Set Computer (CISC) architecture rather than a RISC design. In a CISC microprocessor the instruction set is very rich, and single instructions can carry out quite complex tasks. For instance, it's possible to copy an entire character string from one location to another in an Intel 486 or 586 system with a single instruction. However, the availability of such a rich set of instructions enforces some limitations on the design, which are such that individual instructions may take many clock cycles to execute. This is particularly apparent in the 386 design, where it quite commonly takes two to four clock cycles to execute an instruction.

Thus, although one is running a 25MHz 386 chip, one cannot reasonably expect to achieve 25 MIPS performance. The 486 chip is much more nearly RISC-like in its performance. The Pentium chip actually exceeds this by a design that involves two parallel instruction pipelines and that can under certain circumstances execute two instructions at the same time, a process called *superscalar execution*. However, again the point is that all RISC designs can achieve throughputs as high as the clock rate—and some can use multiple instruction units to achieve superscalar results, just as the Pentium can. A 50MHz MIPS R4000 processor, for instance, by definition will achieve at least 50 MIPS—and if multiple units of issue are employed, it may reach 100 or 150 MIPS.

Floating-Point Performance

There is a second important figure of merit for CPU performance—Millions of Floating-Point Operations per Second (MFLOP). Like the MIPS figure, MFLOPS refers to the number of simple floating-point instructions (such as fetching a floating-point operand into memory, performing a floating-point multiplication or division, comparing two floating-point operands, and so on, that can be performed per second). The significance of this figure by comparison with the MIPS figure of merit is that for certain operations, especially in technical applications, the floating-point figure becomes overwhelmingly important. This is also significant because a major weakness of Intel microprocessors prior to the Pentium chip has been a substantially lower floating-point performance than integer performance.

For example, a 50MHz Intel 486DX chip will achieve somewhere in the vicinity of 40 to 45 MIPS throughput executing 32-bit code, such as Windows NT. It's capable, however, of only less than 20 MFLOPS because of the limitations of its floating-point unit design. Typically, RISC processors have been designed with significantly more efficient, better optimized floating-point units, and can achieve floating-point execution speeds approaching those of their integer execution speeds. For applications that are floating-point intensive, such as Computer Aided Design/Computer Aided Engineering (CAD/CAE), scientific applications, and the like, this could be a significant advantage. With an understanding of these figures of merit, we can now look at the alternatives available for Windows NT.

Figures A5.1 and A5.2 summarize the performance range covered by Windows NT systems, based on bench tests conducted at WINDOWS Magazine on a variety of systems using Intel and RISC processors in both single- and dual-processor configurations. Figure A5.1 presents performance parameters of special importance for file servers, namely: integer performance and disk I/O throughput.

Several points about this figure are worth noting. First, an *Ideal* system, with both high compute (integer or floating-point) and I/O (disk or video) performance should appear in the upper right corner of either chart. No systems do this—clearly, to a greater or lesser extent, performance in practice involves a trade-off between high compute speed and high I/O bandwidth. Taking this into account, it's interesting to note that the tremendously high compute performance of the dual Pentium-90 and dual Mips R4400-150 symmetric multiprocessor (SMP) systems are not matched by equally high I/O bandwidth. Why? I/O design in SMPs is an art form—Sequent Computer, which puts up to six Pentiums in its WinServer line, makes use of multiple disk controller, multiple network cards—and multiple data busses—to achieve high performance. The systems illustrated here were optimized for use as engineering and sofware development workstations, rather than as servers.

Speaking of workstations, Figure A5.2 presents data on the same systems as Figure A5.1, but with more of a classic *workstation* orientation—in this case floating-point performance is plotted against video display speed.

As in Figure A5.1, the trade-off between compute power and I/O is apparent—although in this case, it's a little clearer that the SMP architecture in the dual-processor machines is paying for itself by delivering superior compute

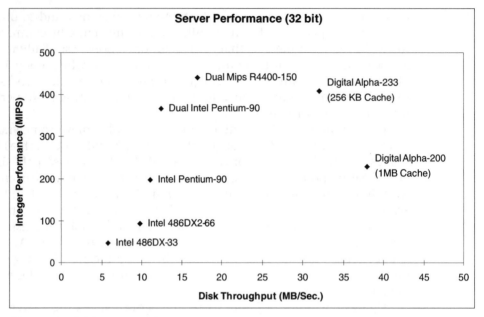

Figure A5.1 Server performance.

Plotting integer compute performance vs. disk I/O gives a useful measure of performance for systems to be used as file servers. Note that the dual-processor machines offer about twice the compute performance of the others—but the RISC-based systems offer better disk I/O.

performance (though this may not pay off as well in real-world applications as in synthetic benchmark tests—as we'll discuss later in this appendix).

Note also that of the two Digital Alpha RISC-based systems, the 200MHz server consistently outperformed the 233MHz workstation, in terms of I/O bandwidth (indeed, in this figure you can clearly see that the server has a 2:1 advantage in I/O, while the workstation is only about 20 percent faster in raw compute performance). We also saw this effect in real-world application performance.

Why would a 200MHz system outperform a 233MHz one? To understand this, we need to examine the effect of CPU caching, which is illustrated in Figure A5.3 (it's based on testing of an old Intel 486-33 processor, but the same point applies to later Intel processors and RISC processors as well).

The important things to note here are: First, the horizontal scale in the figure is exponential rather than linear—the big *hump* at the left end of the chart (due to the 486 CPUs level-1 cache) covers only 8KB of RAM, while the region covered by the level-2 cache (when used) extends to 256KB. Second, using 32-bit instructions really *does* double throughput, at least for this test (which makes

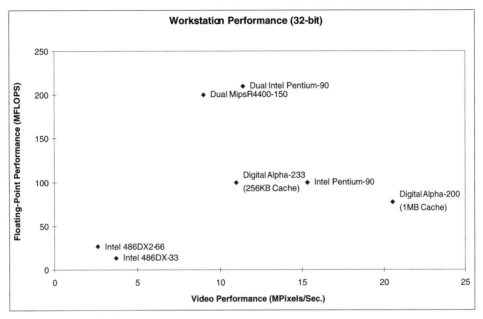

Figure A5.2 Workstation performance.

Traditional graphics workstations are rated by their floating-point compute performance and graphics speed, as illustrated here. Note that, as with the preceding figure, dual-processor machines have the edge in compute performance (provided the applications used are multithreaded—otherwise they cannot utilize the full power of both CPUs), but video performance is dominated by CPU cache effects. (The video testing on which this figure was based did not employ NT 3.5 OpenGL graphics—had it done so, the dual-processor Intel system, which supports OpenGL in hardware, would undoubtedly have done better.)

intuitive sense, given that 16-bit instructions, by definition, make use of only half the memory bandwidth available in the 32-bit processor). Third, level-2 CPU cache memory has a tremendous effect on performance. This effect carries through to applications, where we've seen performance improvements of 20 percent or more by upgrading the inadequate 8KB on-chip cache in 486 systems with 256Kb of level-2 cache on the motherboard.

With this information available, the higher I/O bandwidth of the 200MHz Alpha server in Figures A5.1 and A5.2 is easy to understand—that machine had *four times as much cache (1MB)* as the 233MHz workstation. Since overall disk subsystem throughput in windows NT is actually dominated by memory performance, making the memory system more efficient has a disproportionate impact on overall performance. The high-performance cache also enabled the video system in the server to achieve full performance, outperforming the workstation.

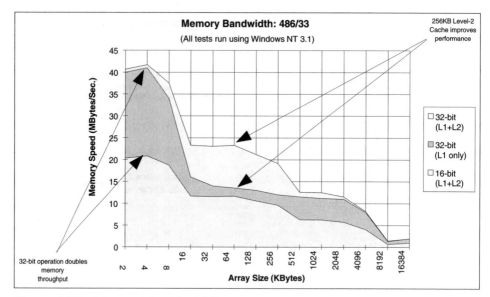

Figure A5.3 Memory bandwidth.

Even older hardware, such as the 486/33 system illustrated, gains a significant benefit from 32-bit applications. The test shown here (timed execution of a large number of memory moves) doubles in performance when executed in 32 rather than 16 bits. Note also the gain in midrange (16KB to 256KB) performance when a 256KB level-2 CPU cache is enabled. This gain actually has a greater effect on overall application performance than one might think from the figure shown here.

This brings us to our final point: The preceding set of charts should have made clear that high-performance RISC processors, such as Digital's Alpha, really do offer a significant performance advantage when used with 32-bit software. Indeed they do—as we'll see later. Unfortunately, this performance comes at the expense of several practical problems, the most serious of which is the *emulation penalty* illustrated in Figure A5.4.

At first glance this result seems absurd—how is it possible that *all* our RISC machines, including the heretofore unbeatable (at least in raw compute power) dual MIPS R4400 deliver performance *below* that of an ancient 486DX-33? The answer is simple: When RISC processors execute 16-bit DOS or Windows code, they must *emulate* the Intel instruction set. This emulation comes at a cost—it typically takes 5 to 10 RISC instructions, on average, to perform the work of one Intel instruction, which largely nullifies the RISC machine's performance advantages. This is offset to some degree by the higher I/O bandwidth the RISC machines have—but not enough to compensate for the RISC machine's other disadvantages when running legacy code (about which, more in the following).

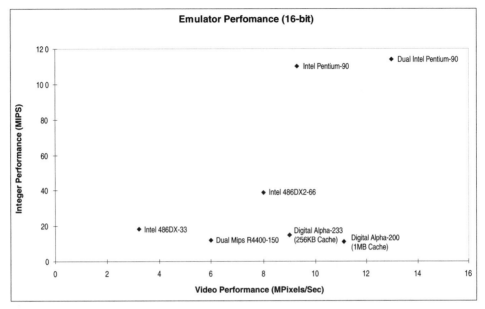

Figure A5.4 Emulator performance.

When executing 16-bit Intel binaries, RISC machines are at a significant disadvantage, as shown here. The performance advantages of a RISC architecture illustrated in Figures A5.1 and A5.2 simply cannot compensate for the penalty imposed by emulation software. *Before writing off RISC systems, however, see Figure A5.6.*

Note also that while our dual Pentium-90 system remains faster than its single-processor sibling, the speed advantage is hardly 2:1. Considering the relative prices of the two systems (the former costs around five times as much as the latter), the results don't justify the cost.

The lesson? Exotic architectures *may* offer a performance advantage in *some* applications—but not in all, and especially not when running legacy DOS and Win16 code. With that thought firmly in mind, let's look at the architectures Windows NT supports.

The First Alternative: Classic Intel PC-Compatible Single Processor Systems

Let's begin by looking at what is possible with the conventional architecture. Currently available Intel CPUs span performance ranges to over 200 MIPS and 100 MFLOPS in the 120MHz Intel Pentium chip. This performance compares very favorably with individual RISC processors, and competes quite effectively against the lower end of the symmetric multiprocessor machines. Single processor PC compatibles have a number of significant advantages as Windows NT platforms.

The first of these, of course, is *price*. The Intel PC compatible market is very much a commodity market—a variety of manufacturers and assemblers provide machines in any given performance class. This competition tends to drive the price down. There is also a tremendous infrastructure of peripheral devices, service, and support available for these machines—and it should not be overlooked that these are the *only* machines that will run Windows NT *and* other operating systems, such as DOS, OS/2, or NetWare. an investment in such a machine is safe. If Windows NT for any reason fails to live up to your expectations, you can replace it with another operating system. And, as we've noted previously, neither SMP nor RISC will give you substantially better legacy application support.

Symmetric Multiprocessors (SMP)

No feature of Windows NT has received more attention than its SMP support. Press reports treat this, for all intents and purposes, like science fiction—referring to machines that can deliver mainframe class performance. And indeed the raw specifications can be quite impressive. Sequent Computer Systems has demonstrated Windows NT on a 30-processor SMP machine theoretically capable of somewhere in the vicinity of 1,500 MIPS—far beyond the performance of any single CPU system. Yet, one should beware when reading mind-boggling benchmark numbers for SMP systems—raw integer performance does not provide an adequate guide to overall system capabilities.

The Problem of Contention

The basic idea of a symmetric multiprocessing system is quite simple. A number of identical CPUs share the computer's memory and data busses. Each executes a copy of Windows NT's microkernel, and each can execute either kernel or application code at any given time. Under ideal conditions, this will provide n times the performance of a single processor (where n is the number of processors). Unfortunately, this *linear scaling* assumption breaks down whenever any two or more processes *contend* for a single resource.

Contention can occur when any two or more processors attempt to access a shared resource. A shared resource can be an I/O device, such as the video display; or a network card; or it can be a memory location in the system; or it can be a component of the operating system. For instance, while Windows NT can execute multiple copies of its microkernel, there are certain shared resources within the kernel. The most critical of these is the task switcher database that determines when each task in the system may be scheduled for execution. It should be obvious that only a single copy of that database can be maintained, so each processor will at various times have to access that database. When any one processor is accessing it, the other processors cannot. In the event that they attempt to, they will have to spin lock, waiting on that database until the other processor or processors release it.

Designing an SMP architecture to minimize contention is something of an art form. It demands careful attention to the memory architecture of the system. Consider a four-way Pentium SMP. Such a system is theoretically capable of four times the performance of a single Pentium—on the order of 800 MIPS. Since all four processors can attempt to access memory simultaneously, in order to achieve full throughput it would be necessary for this system to have a memory architecture capable of supporting up to 800 million memory fetches per second.

Don't hold your breath!

The problem can be mitigated to some extent by providing large secondary cache memory for each central processor. In most existing SMP designs it's typical to see each processor buffered with 256KB of level-2 cache—and we expect to see even large caches become the norm in future systems. Such a design is based on the assumption that most memory fetches can be satisfied by the cache. Contention can occur only when a cache is reloaded from (or flushed to) the main system memory.

Unfortunately, that assumption doesn't hold. No matter how much cache memory is provided for each CPU, at some point cache data has to be written to main memory—and from there, to disk or a network. At that point, contention appears. An example: During test procedures at *WINDOWS Magazine* in May of 1993, we experimented with an early two-processor machine based on the Intel Pentium CPU, and we saw very impressive performance from it. However, in an effort to determine the real-world performance of this system, we experimented with running multiple graphical applications simultaneously on it and got something of a shock—as additional graphical applications were added we found that with both processors operating, beyond a certain number of instances of graphics applications running, the system would actually run more slowly with two processors than with one.

The reason for this turned out to be contention for the display as a shared resource. Consider two applications attempting to access the screen at the same time. Each issues operating system calls to its own copy of the Windows NT microkernel. One copy of the Windows NT microkernel then accesses the screen. The other spin locks, waiting on the screen. The data rate is now limited to the performance of the video subsystem—and a multiprocessor actually pays a penalty in additional overhead (all those spin locks!) waiting on the video board (in this case, a slow Super VGA display).

It's highly unlikely that this particular kind of situation will occur in practice. Systems designed for graphics-intensive use have highly optimized graphic display subsystems that are unlikely to be fully loaded by their processors. But the point still holds: SMP is not a panacea. It will produce very fast results on computationally intensive tasks, where the maximum advantage can be taken of multiple simultaneous computations exploiting local cache memory. However, if a large percentage of the work requires fetching data from outside the processor caches, or contention for external I/O, system performance can be expected to slow down dramatically.

Moreover, deriving maximum benefit from an SMP depends on having applications that are designed to exploit it. Consider the example illustrated in Figure A5.5.

In this case, a large software company was porting a popular client/server application to NT from another operating system. The other system supported threads (the basic programming construct used in SMP programming), but not MP hardware. A first, direct port yielded an application that ran—slowly—on

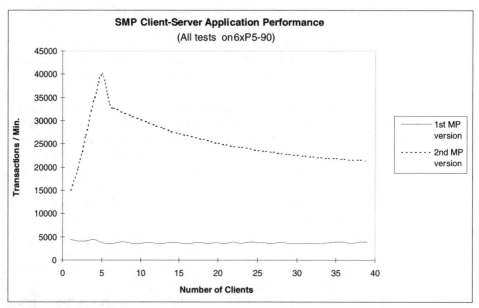

Figure A5.5 Multiprocessor contention.

The benefit gained from a multiprocessor system is highly dependent on the application's design. This chart illustrates the effect of internal changes to an early NT port of a popular network messaging server. The first version, bottlenecked on a shared resource, did not scale with additional users—regardless of the number of CPUs available. The second version did scale—but in a highly nonlinear manner. This is a direct result of using one thread per client. An ideal design would use a thread pool containing only as many threads as there are processors (in this case six)— theoretically, such a design would scale nearly linearly up to six clients and remain flat thereafter. (Chart based on presentation at Windows NT Server Professional Developers Conference, Seattle, 1995.)

single-CPU NT systems, but crashed on SMP hardware (insufficient attention had been paid to shared resource synchronization issues). When those problems were addressed, the lower curve on Figure A5.5 resulted—which did not scale as additional users (and thus, additional threads) accessed the service.

At this point, the programmers took a hard look at the design and discovered that they had a major contention problem. When that problem was relieved (by redesigning the service's I/O interface), the upper curve in the figure resulted.

As you should now understand, the assumption that you will achieve five times the performance of any given application with a five-processor SMP machine is naive. You *may* achieve five times the performance (more likely a bit less) *if* the application has been fully optimized for SMP use. The moral of this story: Check out your applications thoroughly before buying an SMP to run them on!

Finally, consider cost. Which is more expensive—a single CPU RISC-based machine operating at 300 MIPS, or a three-processor Intel machine with three 100 MIPS processors? Thinking about this, naively one can assume that the three-processor machine will give some advantage because, after all, one can indeed have three tasks executing at the same time. This logic is incorrect.

Regardless of a system's architecture, it has an upper limit—the total number of MIPS it can execute. If you have three 100 MIPS processors, the most computational work you can get done is 300 MIPS. That identical figure can be achieved by a single-processor machine operating at 300 MIPS. But the single-processor machine needs to have only a single cache. It will not require the additional system board complexity of a multiprocessor memory controller. It will almost certainly be cheaper. It will also be more reliable because—in general—the reliability of a system is inversely proportional to its parts count.

Therefore, use of an SMP system should never even be considered unless all possible single-CPU alternatives have been exhausted. There can be one exception to this rule. Some of the SMP designs offered for Windows NT are *scalable*. That is, you may purchase them with a single processor and then add more processors as your needs grow. This can be a very attractive approach, especially if you are uncertain of your ultimate needs but expect them to grow over time. In such a case, a scalable SMP may be worth considering. However, you should carry out a cost analysis, as you may find that the cost of upgrading your SMP system to add more processors exceeds the cost of replacing a single processor system with a more powerful single-processor system when the time comes. If the cost is higher, then there is no reason to use the SMP.

You should also very carefully examine the contention issue discussed earlier. Is the system supplied with enough network bandwidth to support the kind of loads you will see as you add multiple processor cards? There's no sense providing a system with an additional processor card, when that processor will spend most of its time waiting for access to the network! In a desktop application, is the application principally bound by graphic speed? If a graphic card is in use in a system that is capable of only 100 million graphical operations per second, adding processors to push performance above 100 MIPS may not produce a significant performance improvement in graphic-intensive applications.

Evaluate these facts very carefully. For large scale client/server use—particularly for mainframe replacement in downsizing applications—the SMP may very well offer the best alternative, but be sure you understand the issues before you buy!

Alternative Three: RISC

It's an odd coincidence that the acronym for Reduced Instruction Set Computing should sound *risky* to so many people. But RISC solutions do represent a risky alternative. The promise of the RISC approach is significantly higher performance from a given set of components. Intel processors in the 386 and 486 series generally offer about half the number of MIPS as the number of MHz. In general, it takes two clock cycles for them to complete an average instruction. Thus a 50MHz Intel 486 generally delivers about 25 MIPS. Floating-point performance of these systems tends to be even less—on the order of four clock cycles per instruction. This can be compensated to a certain extent by *clock doubling,* in which the CPU runs internally at twice the external clock rate. For instance, in Intel's 486DX2-66 chip, a 33MHz external clock is doubled internally to 66MHz. Since the 486 on the average requires two clock cycles to accomplish an instruction, the 66MHz internal clock is well matched to an effective throughput of 33 MIPS.[1]

The problem with this approach is that access to external devices and memory has to be mediated at the external clock rate of 33MHz. Thus the chip cannot be serviced at any more than a 33-million-memory-fetch-per-second rate. Since the chip generally accomplishes 33 million instructions per second, this tends to work out reasonably well and the 486's 8KB on-chip cache provides sufficient buffer capacity to make up the difference. But it can become a problem at higher rates—as users of the 486DX4-100 (actually a 99MHz clock-tripled 486 chip) are well aware.

As discussed earlier, RISC processors, by limiting the number of instructions and optimizing these instructions for speed, attempt to achieve an overall throughput of *at least one instruction per clock.* Thus a 50MHz RISC processor should, theoretically, achieve 50 MIPS or more. They also attempt to do the same thing for floating-point instructions, although they are generally less successful with this. But the overall result is approximately twice the perform-

---

1. There are individual instructions on the 486, which can be executed in just one clock. Other instructions may take much longer. On the average, taking into account the limits of the 486 8KB on-chip primary cache, we believe two instructions per clock is approximately correct.

ance that is provided by an equivalent x86 chip at a given clock rate. That is, at a given clock rate in MHz, you will see twice the performance from a RISC processor as from an otherwise equivalent 386/486 (the Pentium is something of an exception—as we will see later on). Since the cost of a computer tends to be governed by the number of components and the clock rate—particularly the clock rate at which memory is accessed—a computer that can accomplish twice as much as a given clock rate has an obvious advantage.

All things being equal, the world would long since have converted from CISC processors (such as the Intel 386/486) to one of the various RISC processors. Of course, this has not happened—and the reasons why it hasn't have a lot to do with the *risky* nature of the alternatives.

No Single Standard

While Intel is not viewed with love by vendors in the computer industry, the fact that a single company has dominated the microprocessor market for the last ten years has had a number of notable advantages. It's now possible to order a computer from hundreds of vendors—even by mail—and be reasonably certain it will execute the hundreds of PC-compatible applications on the market without being seriously concerned about the possibility that some applications will prove to be incompatible. The reason for this is that all of these computers use the Intel family of microprocessors and are thus inherently compatible. No such compatibility exists in the RISC market. Indeed, Intel itself has made several different varieties of RISC chips, the *i*860 chip among them.[2] Other major players in the RISC business have at various times included SUN Microsystems, Data General Corporation, IBM, Hewlett-Packard, Fairchild, and virtually every maker of silicon in the United States (among other places).

This situation has produced what might be called a RISC anarchy. There are *dozens* of different RISC processors available today—all more or less incompatible—each running their own operating system. The operating systems have this in common—they are all called UNIX. The resemblance begins and ends right there. Microsoft, of course, hopes to change this. As we noted in Chapter 1, Windows NT was designed to be portable. Providing Windows NT for a new architecture requires only that the portable C-based NT source code be recompiled for that architecture and that a new Hardware Abstraction Layer be written for the architecture. However, it's worth noting that when one moves to RISC, one leaves behind all that vast legacy of compatibility—you cannot expect to run DOS, OS/2, SCO UNIX, or any other Intel-based operating system on a RISC machine. When you buy into RISC, you effectively lock yourself into Windows NT.

---

2. This was, in fact, the first CPU upon which NT was implemented.

The 16-Bit Legacy Application Issue

Windows NT endeavors to overcome the problem of RISC anarchy in a second way. Beyond the portability of Windows NT itself to the new architecture, a high degree of legacy application support is provided for DOS and Windows applications.[3] Windows NT accomplishes this by providing a special version of Insignia Systems SoftPC emulator optimized for each version of Windows NT. On RISC processors, Soft PC provides a software environment that appears to legacy programs as though it were in fact a PC—specifically a very fast 286 (AT-compatible) PC. The effectiveness of SoftPC is actually generally quite good. We routinely run Visual Basic, Word for Windows, Microsoft Project, Microsoft Excel, and various other applications on a MIPS R4000 machine. All of these are 16-bit Intel programs (just as you'd buy in a local software store) and all, for the most part, perform on the MIPS machine as happily as if they were running on the 486 machine on the other side of the office.

Unfortunately, they do not perform as well—that is, as *fast*—as they do on the 486. The way SoftPC works is to examine each Intel instruction in the legacy application that is executing. This instruction, for instance, the single 486 instruction that copies strings, is then emulated by a number of RISC instructions. Ideally, in the string copy this might be no more than one instruction per byte. But that is *eight times* less efficient than the 486 implementation. In general, our experience is that the Soft PC emulation on NT RISC machines tends to require approximately five to ten RISC instructions per Intel instruction. Thus it has the effect of slowing down the machine by a factor of five, and our clock-doubled 100MHz R4000 machine thus runs no faster than a 20MHz 386SX.

You might wonder at this point why we bother running 16-bit applications, such as Visual Basic 3.0 and PowerPoint, on a RISC machine when it gives only 20MHz performance. The reason is that we have been oversimplifying a bit. The raw integer performance is equivalent to a 20MHz machine. The other performance parameters, however, are somewhat improved. We get an average of about 1.5 megabytes per second of disk access speed out of the machine. That is three to five times what you would get on a 386SX. Similarly we get significantly better video performance and somewhat better floating-point performance than on a slow machine. The overall result has a throughput that *feels* like a 486SX—quite acceptable for most tasks. You would not wish to use it for a performance-intensive application—it's irritating to wait while Excel recalculates large spreadsheets, but for most purposes it is fine.

---

3. Of course, NT also provides source-level support for POSIX 1.0 applications—and OS/2 1.3 support. The former requires that applications be recompiled for a particular processor, and thus avoids the aforementioned emulation penalty. The latter is available only on Intel x86-based systems.

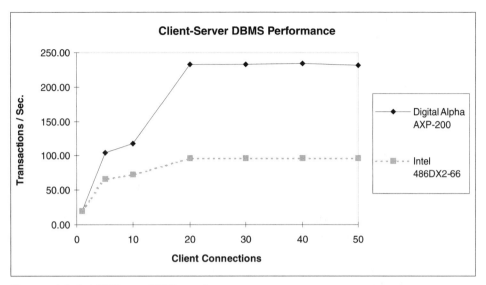

Figure A5.6 RISC vs. CISC performance.

With all other factors being equal (and assuming, of course, that the RISC architecture in question is supported by the desired application), RISC CPUs outperform CISC CPUs and client/server application platforms. The reason for this can be traced to the single-processor performance illustrated in Figures A5.1 and A5.2, which shows significantly higher compute and (perhaps more importantly) I/O performance from RISC-based systems. Performance equal to that of the RISC system illustrated here could probably be achieved using a dual-processor CISC system—but at the expense of higher hardware cost, and depending sensitively on the application design, per Figure A5.5.

32-Bit Windows Applications—The Holy Grail

Of course, running largely 16-bit applications on a 32-bit RISC machine is slightly ridiculous. This effectively cuts the clock rate of the machine by a factor of five, so you've bought 386 performance at a 586 price. However, as soon as 32-bit applications compiled for the machine become available the situation changes. Consider Figure A5.6.

This chart compares the client/server database performance of CISC-based (486DX2-66) and RISC-based (AXP-200) servers. As you can see, the RISC machine delivered well over double the throughput of the 486-based system. A Pentium-based system would likely have done better than the 486, but in view of the I/O bandwidth limit illustrated in Figure A5.1 earlier, it's unlikely that it would have equalled the RISC system. Getting this kind of performance from Intel CPUs would have required an SMP configuration, with all the complexity that implies.

This illustrates the principal problem with the 32-bit Windows applications: They have to be compiled separately for each version of Windows NT. That's a great burden for software developers. It means that the developer of a Windows NT utility, for instance, cannot simply compile one Windows NT executable file and ship this, blindly assuming that it will work on every machine in sight. If the application is properly designed, it will run on all *Intel* machines, including symmetric multiprocessor (SMP) machines, without modification. But to provide a version for a RISC platform, the developer must compile it for that specific platform. To support another platform, the developer must compile it again.

Currently announced platforms for Windows NT include Intel 386/486/ Pentium (and soon, P-6), MIPS R4000/4200/4400/4600 (and soon, T-5), Digital's Alpha AXP processors, and Motorola's Power-PC 601/603/604 (and soon, 620). There are a variety of other platforms that are widely rumored but have not been announced (including advanced versions of Sun Microsystems's SPARC processors). An application developer wishing to cover the entire market then must, as of today, supply at least four separate executable versions of each application—one for each family (we've seen several examples where multiple versions are supplied for a given family, as for example, providing a standard Intel build and a special version optimized for the Pentium).

Moreover, the developer must keep a close eye on the news and plan to provide versions for new architectures as they become available. This problem is accentuated by the fact that as of this writing the development tools for newer platforms are different (Microsoft currently ships Visual C++ for Intel, MIPS and Alpha; the Power-PC requires a separate SDK). It is therefore necessary to have access to each of these machines in order to compile an application for it. There is as of yet no cross-compiler that would allow you to compile, say, a MIPS version on an Intel machine (though Symantec has been working on such a technology). That, to coin a phrase, is bad.

Pentium: RISC in a CISC Box?

As if things were not already confusing enough, in 1993 Intel introduced its long-awaited Pentium chip. The Pentium combines most of the generally accepted advanced features of RISC architectures with full x86 compatibility. In effect, the Pentium is a RISC chip that happens to be x86 compatible. This would appear to offer the best of all things. At 120MHz external clock rate the Pentium with a dual pipeline architecture is capable of internal throughputs well over 200 MIPS. It has an eight-stage floating-point pipeline that can achieve floating-point execution rates of over 100 megaflops. It compares very favorably with the various RISC processors (as illustrated in Figures A5.1 and A5.2). As a member of Intel's x86 processor familiy, the Pentium doesn't suffer from the 16-bit emulation penalty. Thus it would appear that those who are interested in RISC performance have an easy solution. Buy a Pentium—get the RISC performance without taking any risks.

Again, matters are not so simple. First-generation Pentium chips suffered from high cost, high power consumption—and in rare cases heating problems severe enough to cause system crashes. Intel solved these problems by 1994, only to have a floating-point math error surface that caused a major public-relations flap. That problem has been dealt with, too—but as Figure A5.1 shows, a single-processor Pentium system is simply not competitive in overall performance with the latest RISC processors.

With that said, properly configured Pentium systems can approach the performance of RISC systems—generally at a lower cost. In high-performance applications, SMP systems based on Pentium processors can equal or beat equivalent RISC configurations (if necessary, by adding additional processors), albeit with all the SMP caveats previously mentioned and the Pentium has one tremendous advantage by comparison with true RISC processors: It is *safe*. The widest possible range of software and peripherals are available for it—unlike a RISC processor, you *can* run DOS, Windows 3.*x,* or even OS/2 on a Pentium.

Given All That, How Do You Choose?

Selecting a CPU architecture for Windows NT is a bottom-line decision that needs to be subject to a rigorous cost justification. There are some rules of thumb that can prove useful. We will examine them. We will build a simple decision tree to take you through the process of elimination that makes it possible to make a rough decision as to the types of systems you should examine.

Step 1—Determine and *write down* your requirements.

Step 2—Decide whether these requirements can be met by a conventional 386/486/Pentium-based PC-compatible system. (No cheating—this is not the place to worry about whether you have adequate growing room or whether this system will scale!) If you answered Yes—stop here. The cost advantages of a PC compatible, along with their known reliability and the huge supply of PC-compatible software, outweigh any other consideration. If you spend $2,000 or $3,000 today on a PC compatible and you outgrow it, then simply recycle that system to another application and upgrade to the next larger system.

Step 3—Is 16-bit legacy application performance is a major issue—then don't bother with the RISC machines. The thing to bear in mind here is that the RISC machines are always going to be a bad deal for 16-bit application support. It is true that higher-performance RISC machines will show higher 16-bit performance, as shown in Figure A5.4. Compare the $15,000 to $20,000 one pays for a RISC machine today to the few thousand dollars one pays for a PC compatible.

One balancing thought: 16-bit applications are almost *never* run on servers. That being the case, it's worth noting that there is nothing to prevent you from running classic x86 machines in connection with a RISC-based server. And indeed, this combination can be cost effective. If 16-bit legacy application performance is a nonissue, take a close look at RISC. Why? Because dollar per MIPS, RISC is always a better deal than SMP: The cost of any computer system is largely a function of the number of components in the system. Take the lid off the system and count the chips. You'll find you can get a very close correlation between the number of chips on the motherboard and the cost of the system. Indeed, the decreasing cost per performance of systems over the years is attributable to the fact that the density with which electronic components can be incorporated into a chip doubles approximately every 18 months.

If you've ever wondered why you never quite seem to get two years of use out of your system before it becomes obsolete, that's your answer. A single-processor RISC machine at any given performance level has approximately the same number of components as a single-processor classic x86 machine. The SMP machine, on the other hand, has to have a second processor, support chips to support that processor (mostly custom AISC chips), cache RAM to support the second processor, and a more sophisticated memory controller architecture. Therefore, at a given performance level, the number of chips, and therefore the cost, increases. So the minute classic performance becomes an issue, if the 16-bit problem doesn't bother you, then you need to look at RISC.

The only situation where you should have any concern about RISC in a server environment is if you are concerned about application services rather than file and print services. If you are dependent upon applications services or particularly interested in these services, it would be wise to check which platforms are supported before selecting a platform for your server. But again, for basic file and print services, any RISC architecture is a good bet.

Step 4—If there is no other way to achieve acceptable performance, look at SMP. Because it is complex, SMP is expensive. But as mentioned earlier, SMP machines can deliver *thousands* of MIPS—performance that boggles the mind. There is no way (today) to achieve this performance with single processors.

For More Information

Custer, Helen (1993), *Inside Windows NT.* Redmond WA: Microsoft Press, ISBN: 1-55615-481-X. Good detail on how SMP and RISC systems are supported.

Patterson, David (1988), and John Hennessy, *Computer Architecture—A Quantitative Approach.* San Mateo CA: Morgan Kaufmann Publishers, Inc., ISBN: 1-55880-069-8. Covers Amdahl's Law, which governs system performance in both single-processor and multiprocessor cases.

Van Zandt, John (1992), *Parallel Processing in Information Systems.* New York NY: John Wiley & Sons, ISBN: 0-471-54822-7. Good general work on multiprocessor systems.

Kane, Gerry and Joe Heinrich (1992), *MIPS RISC Architecture*. Englewood Cliffs NJ: Prentice-Hall, Inc., ISBN: 0-13-590472-2. Aside from details of the R4000/4400 architecture, Chapter 1 gives an outstanding overview of basic RISC theory, and was extremely helpful in formulating this chapter.

Sites, Richard (1992), *Alpha Architecture Reference Manual*. Burlington MA: Digital Press, ISBN: 1-55558-098-X. Not for the faint of heart, this is an engineering text on the Alpha CPU design. Interesting, but far too technical for general readers.

6

Principles of Preventive Maintenance

Chapter 5 gives all the details available to us on the specific steps you can take to tune Windows NT system performance and correct faults when they happen—but a larger question is how to prevent the faults from happening in the first place. As we said in the opening to Chapter 5, the main approach to this is called *Preventative Maintenance (or PM)*, and in this appendix we explore PM concepts in some detail.

In principle, computer *software* does not wear out (indeed, it tends to become more reliable with age)—but hardware does. People refuse to realize this, but it's a fact. But computer software, in the main, doesn't wear out and it should not normally require adjustment. Examination of one simple fact should show you that this nice theory breaks down when it's applied to a Windows NT network or any other network.

Why Does Software (and Hardware) Fail?

First of all, the probability of a piece of software malfunctioning is roughly proportional to the number of lines of code that make up that software—simply because the more code that a programmer writes, the more likely he is to make a mistake. There's been a good deal written about Windows NT, much of it misinformation, but many writers seem to agree on one point: Windows NT, as of this writing (it's just reaching production), contains some *two million* lines of code. Would anyone care to place a bet with me on the odds that all two million lines of code are bug free?[1]

---

1. It's amusing to note that between the time this sentence was written and the time it was sent to

Beyond this we have to bear in mind that even though the probability of failure of any single component, software or hardware, in a modern PC system may be infinitesimally small, that infinitesimal smallness has to be multiplied by the number of connections in a network. The basic microcomputer we know today can be described as a *state machine*—a very large table that says that when the input state is X, the output state is Y. At the time I went to technical school, state machines were the basic mechanism used to describe all sorts of interesting things ranging from simple switches to microprocessors. The state machine for a modern microprocessor is slightly large—the size of one's office perhaps. But the state machine that you'd need to describe a modern microprocessor, disk controller, video controller, several dozen megabytes of RAM, and the rest of a Windows NT PC would be *appallingly* large.[2]

It gets worse—connect two of those machines together on a network and I defy anyone to write a state table that completely describes the resulting (very simple) network. No one can write that state table—*the state of one machine may depend on the state of another*. In a Windows NT network, the size of each state machine is multiplied by the number of machines connected on the local segment, perhaps also by the state of the gateway that connects one segment to another, perhaps by the state of the server.

Such a system can't be described by the use of a state table. If you'll forgive me for dragging in some modern mathematics, such a system is, by definition, *chaotic*. It is describable only in probabilistic terms. Take heart, this doesn't mean that the operational status of your network is a crap shoot! *You can load the dice.*

The way you can load the dice is to employ a technique that people in the insurance business have been using since time immemorial. It's called *actuarial statistics*, and we're now going to examine it in detail. Let's begin with one of the most overused terms in computing today, *mean time between failure* (MTBF). MTBF is the statistical number that's used to describe hardware reliability, and the MTBF numbers that are quoted are typically pretty huge. It's not uncommon, for instance, to find a hard disk with an MTBF quoted at 30,000 hours. Since there are just 8,760 hours in a calendar year, it is not surprising that most people look at a 30,000-hour MTBF disk drive and assume that they don't have to worry about it for three years or so.

Such an attitude is naive. The MTBF refers to the *mean* time to failure—that is, the *average*. While a disk drive may have a mean time to failure of 30,000 hours, it in fact may fail at 15,000 hours or it may run perfectly up to 45,000 hours. You can't make a precise prediction of exactly how long a disk drive will

---

production of our first edition, Microsoft released the first bug-fix disks for Windows NT—so it really wasn't bug-free after all (and I win the bet!)—JDR.

2. Maybe, if you write very small, the size of the state of New York... then again, given the permutations introduced by the state of the RAM, a Windows NT state table *might* be larger than the size of the known universe!

operate—but on average it will operate for 30,000 hours. This becomes significant if you have an installation with a large number of disk drives. Let's say, for instance, that your organization bought ten drives with a mean time to failure of 30,000 hours. Since each disk drive has a mean time to failure of over three years, the naive approach would be to assume you could run them all for three years and then buy ten new disk drives. But let's look at the statistics.

With ten drives operating, the probability of failure is multiplied. It is now *ten* chances in 30,000, or *one chance in 3,000 hours*. Guess what? 3,000 is a good bit less than one year! So the probability that one of the ten drives will fail within the first year is very high. The way you approach this problem is to buy insurance—in the form of buying spare disk drives. If you have ten of these drives, you can be reasonably certain that one is going to fail the first year. So don't buy ten, buy 11. Then you have the hardware in position and can respond as quickly as possible once the failure occurs.

The second thing you can do is monitor the performance of all ten disk drives—because disk drives, being electromechanical devices, very often will give some indication of failure before they fail completely. You may begin to notice a high error rate, low data transfer rate, continuing detection of soft errors, or any of a variety of things that will give you early warning of an impending failure *if you take the time to look for the warning*.

Therefore, by maintaining a maintenance history of all ten disk drives and comparing them, you *may* be able to determine a drive is going to fail before it does—but you can never be certain of predicting that—so you can't wait and buy a spare disk drive when the maintenance history begins to indicate that a drive failure is likely.[3] You may get no warning at all.

You also can't wait and assume that you're going to be able to transfer data from a drive after it has given indications that it's going to fail onto a new disk drive. For this reason it's essential to run backups of mission critical information so that you're in a safe position, in the worst case. If the drive has failed without giving any prior indication, you're in a position to pop in a new disk drive, restore the backup data, and lose no more than the last 24 hours or so of work. This consideration should be looked at very carefully in establishing the backup procedures for your organization. If you can't afford to lose 24 hours of work, then you had better do backups more frequently than once every 24 hours!

The Mathematics of Fault Prediction

As we've seen in the preceding section, probably the most critical number one deals with in setting up a maintenance system for Windows NT (or any other hardware/software environment) is the *mean time between failures* (MTBF). This number is generally part of the specifications for any hardware device—when

---

3. Depending on the nature of the failure—some failures give no warnings at all.

you're quoted a price on a system, if you look closely at the specifications, you will see an MTBF listing. You will also see MTBF listings for disk drives, memory components, and so on.

For software, of course, MTBFs are never stated—because the software industry persists in a naive belief, first of all, that they can produce things that never fail (hah!); and also, one suspects, that the software industry would be unwilling to publish its MTBF numbers because they are likely to be so poor. However, it is possible to achieve a statistically valid set of MTBF information over time simply by recording how frequently errors occur and building your own database. In any case, with MTBF information available to you, it becomes possible to get quite elaborate in predicting the availability of a system, and making statistical predictions that you can use to predict when problems are going to occur—and then fix them before they occur.

Availability and Reliability

Of course, the goal of any system maintenance project should be to maintain the highest possible availability of the overall end-to-end system. Achieving a 100 percent availability is impossible, frankly, but you can get quite close to it if one pays sufficiently close attention to the reliability of individual components (see Figure A6.1).

We'll have to begin with some definitions and a little mathematics (trust me, the mathematics aren't that difficult—and if you pay attention you will achieve some considerable insight into what's going on). Let's begin with the reliability of a system: Assuming a constant failure rate (that is, that on average failures occur at a fairly constant interval), it can be shown that the reliability over time will follow the equation:

$$r(t) = e^{-at4}$$

where:

    r is the reliability at any given time.

    t is time the component has been in operation.

    a is a constant characteristic of the component in question.

Given that one knows these figures for the reliability, you can then predict the mean time between failure (MTBF) which is equal to $1/a$ (and obviously, this means you can get a if you have the MTBF—it's just $a = 1/MTBF$).

This model is generally accurate for hardware components. Software, however, tends to be very different. The reason for this should be obvious. Hardware tends to wear out. After an initial burn-in period (which isn't covered by this equation), hardware will be at its most reliable when it is new and then it wears

---

4. This and other equations in this appendix are taken from *Introduction to Client/Server Systems* by Paul Renaud (details in "For More Information" at the end of this appendix). While the author disagrees with Mr. Renaud's centralized approach to systems management, his book is very good!

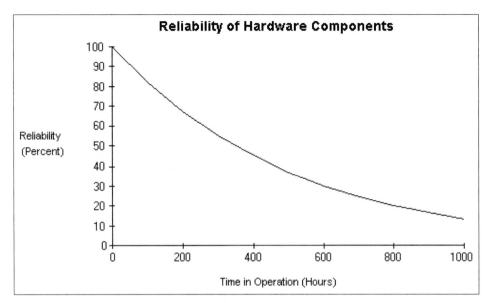

Figure A6.1 MTBF for hardware.

Reliability of hardware components falls off over time after an initial burn-in period, thus as components become old they are certain to fail.

out over a period of time at a generally constant rate. So reliability falls off with time—as shown by the equation.

The equation for software tends to be exactly the opposite. A new piece of software is apt to be buggy, but it will tend to become less buggy over time as bugs are found and fixed. There is no simple equation that can describe this adequately for all cases. One that is widely used will have the unavailability over time go as:

$$u(t)=a(1-e^{-bt/a})$$

Where *a* is the total number of defects, and *b* is a system-dependent constant.

The mean time between defects then is:

$$MTBD = (1/b)e^{at/b}$$

Since a failure is by definition a defect, this equation also covers MTBF. The best way to find the *a* and *b* constants is by collecting data on a software system over time and then fitting the equation to the data—the fit will tend to improve with time as the amount of data increases. For instance, if you're running a piece of database software, the appropriate thing to do is to maintain a log of the bugs that are discovered in the software, the frequency with which they are discovered, and how long it takes to get a repair or a bug-fix in place. It's then possible over time to fit the equation to the statistics. Please note that this equation will essentially start again when you upgrade to a new piece of software. New versions, while they will never be as unreliable as the first version (have you ever wondered where the hackneyed old expression *never buy version 1 of anything* came from?) will represent a new start to the equation, so the curve will not be a simple downward slope as one might expect (see figure A6.2).

Similarly, the MTBF equation given earlier does not cover the burn-in period for hardware—and for this reason it is highly desirable. For instance, in our *buy 11 disk drives* example, you might burn in all 11 disk drives for some time before they're actually used. A general rule of thumb is that the burn-in period should be on the order of one tenth of 1 percent of the total life of the drive—for a 30,000 hour MTBF disk drive, the burn in period should be on the order of 30 hours. This can be conveniently accomplished by having a laboratory or maintenance shop set up with a test stand so that individual pieces of equipment can be subjected to continuous testing. A relatively simple program written in BASIC that will cycle the disk drive, continuously writing data and reading it back, is sufficient. One can then run it for a 30 hour burn-in period and once this is complete (assuming that the disk hasn't had any problems), format the disk and store it. A disk can then be taken out and applied as necessary. The odds are quite high that any burn-in defects will be detected during the burn-in period. That is, the drive will fail—at which point you can

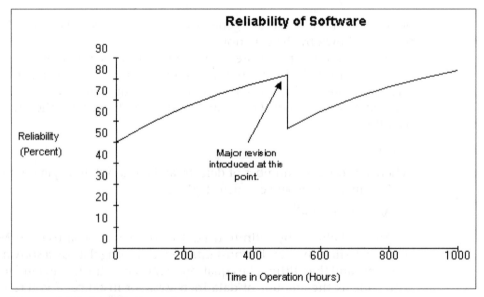

Figure A6.2 MTBD For software.

In contrast to hardware, the reliability of software improves over time—except for temporary unreliabity introduced by new versions.

conveniently send it back to the manufacturer for replacement, since this will happen within the warranty period.

Given that the MTBF (or MTBD) is known, the one remaining factor that affects availability is the *mean time to repair*, or MTTR. This will be the time that it takes to correct the defect—the time to replace a failed disk drive, or to find and fix a bug in the software (or provide a workaround —such as reindexing a corrupted database, for instance). Given this number, the availability of any component is then given by:

$$A = MTBF/(MTBF + MTTR)$$

Components in Series

The availability of a system that depends on a number of components connected together in series can be computed by multiplying the availability of the individual components. As an example, suppose that you have a network backup system that's used to back up data on three file servers. If we ignore the issue of software reliability, the availability of the total backup will be equal to:

$$a_{Total} = a_1 \times a_2 \times a_3 \times a_{BS} \times a_{Net}$$

where:

a_1, a_2, a_3	Availability for file servers 1 to 3, respectively
a_{BS}	Availability of the backup system
a_{Net}	Availability of the network

If the backup system and file servers each have an availability of 99 percent, and the network has an availability of 90 percent, the total availability will be a total of:

$$a_{Total} = .99 \times .99 \times .99 \times .99 \times .90 = .87$$

That is, the total reliability is just 87 percent. Notice that the governing factor is always the least reliable component—which will tend to reduce the reliability of the entire system, something that should be obvious from common sense in any case.

Redundancy

If you have a system with a certain number n of redundant components in which the operation of the system depends only on the correct functioning of one, then the overall availability will be:

$$a_{Overall} = 1-((1-a_1) \times (1-a_2) \ldots (1-a_n))$$

where n is the number of components in parallel.

Suppose, for example, that you have a server that contains two mirrored disk drives, each of which has an MTBF of 10,000 hours and a mean time to repair of 2 hours. Availability of each drive will be over 99.98 percent, but the availability of the mirrored pair will be:

$$a_{Overall} = 1-((1-.9998) \times (1-.9998)) = .9999999$$

or 99.99999 percent.

The overall availability in this case is actually *higher* than the availability of any single component—exactly the opposite of the series case previously discussed. This is the reason that the highest reliability systems are achieved by the maximum use of redundant components. Indeed, in the ultimate case, where one has to deal with systems that cannot be permitted to crash, one will typically run actual backup servers and employ mechanisms, such as the Windows NT Server's *directory replication* feature to see that the data on one server is always duplicated on the second server.[5]

All These Numbers Are Great—So What Do We Do with Them?

As was covered in Chapter 4, Windows NT includes some extremely sophisticated built-in system performance monitoring and event logging features. We suggest that you maintain a continuous maintenance history on your system based on the information from the event log and the performance monitor. If you maintain this information over the life of your system, you can apply to it the mathematics we have just described—and you will find that you then know a great deal more about the system behavior than you would otherwise.

For example, you can on a regular basis conduct some simple performance tests on a system. First, examine event logs to note whether there have been any disk errors. If there have been any disk errors, these should be entered into a statistical log and the cause of the errors should be investigated. If you graph these disk errors over time, you are likely to find that they will fit the hardware reliability equation given earlier. As these errors begin to arise, you'll see that the reliability is decreasing with time—and at some point it's going to become apparent to you that if this trend continues, the component will fail. This is the time to replace the disk drive—*before* it fails.

Similarly you can maintain a record of overall system performance for a variety of components: the CPU, disks, network, and so on, and so on. This can be particularly valuable in two ways. First, just as with maintaining a record of information on the disk drive, it'll let you predict failures before they occur. But it also has another important advantage—the record can help you detect system bottlenecks and maximize throughput.

---

5. See Chapter 7 for details on replication.

This is particularly important as networks grow. Initially, you may be able to simply stick network cards in PCs, link them together into an EtherNet, and assume that everything's going to work. But as the network becomes larger and larger, some inherent limitations of the hardware are going to start to show up. EtherNet has a maximum throughput (on conventional 10-base-2 or 10-base-T cabling) of 10 million bits per second. It should be obvious, for instance, that if one continues to add machines to an Ethernet segment, you are eventually going to find that you are trying to push more than 10 million bits down the wire each second. You can't do that. And you are going to find that your overall system performance will degrade. This is because of something called a *queuing effect*.

Queuing Effect and Performance Tuning

Queuing refers to the fact that in any kind of a shared service environment (such as a network), multiple simultaneous requests for access to the service will have to be *queued*—that is, suspended while they await a response. There will then be some average response time each request will experience before it can be responded to. The relationship between these factors is covered by the equation:

$$r = n_s/t$$

Where *r* is the response time, n_s is the average number of requests competing for service, and *t* is the overall throughput (responses per second) of the service. Obviously the response time increases as the number of requests increases.

This equation, for instance, governs the response time of a server with multiple clients competing for a response, say, from a database server with multiple clients attempting to access it simultaneously. Response time will increase as the load on the server increases. If simple queuing effects apply (actual queuing models can become quite complex and while the mathematics involved are fascinating, they are far beyond the realm of this book), one can estimate the utilization of the system and the delay due to queuing, according to a very simple model.

Utilization of the system will be governed by the equation:

$$U = r/x$$

where *r* is the rate of requests per second, and *x* is the maximum throughput in transactions per second. Thus, if the number of requests per second is equal to the transactions per second, you have a utilization of 1.0, or 100 percent. The delay due to queuing will then be:

$$d = (U/x)/(1-U)$$

Total response time for the system will be the sum of the delay due to queuing ,plus the amount of time needed to process the request:

$$R = d + 1/x$$

The *perceived* throughput at any workstation will then be equal to *1/R* (that is, the user will see the system as slow because he sees a slow response), although the actual system throughput is always going to be equal to the arrival rate (*r*). If you think about it this should be obvious. The system becomes fully loaded, then each workstation will experience a slowdown and will perceive the system as being slow, when in fact the system is working at full capacity. That by itself is the single most important implication of the overall queuing equation for our purposes.

The other thing that's important to understand is that queuing effects occur for networks just as they do for servers. In effect, you can treat the LAN or WAN in a system as being a sort of server from the point of view of queuing delays. And, again, bear in mind that the maximum throughput of an EtherNet is 10 million bits per second. It should be obvious that the perceived response degrades as the number of requests on the system begins to approach 10 million bits per second.

An example: If clients on a system generate 50 packets per second over a million bit-per-second network, and the packets have a mean size of 8,192 bits (1KB, standard for NetBEUI), the throughput will be:

$$x = 1,000,000 / 8192$$

or 122.1 packets per second. Utilization will be:

$$U = 50 / 122.1 = .41 \text{ or } 41\%$$

Then *d* will be equal to 6 milliseconds, and perceived throughput will be 71 packets per second. The significance of this is that although the total throughput that the network experiences is 122.1 packets per second, *perceived* throughput at any station is only 71 packets per second. This is key to understanding how low data rate lines in a WAN environment can become a bottleneck.

The Throughput Chain

Any network is inherently an end-to-end system. There is a *chain* of throughputs involved that extends from the client to the server. Consider a system in which each client CPU can process 1,000 transactions per second, the network interface cards can handle 1,000 packets per second, the LAN can carry 10,000 packets per second before saturating, routers can forward 5,000 packets per second, the WAN can handle 500 packets per second, and the server CPU can handle 5,000 transactions per second—but the server's only disk can perform just 50 I/O accesses per second. Then you have a chain extending from the client through the network interface to the LAN to the router to the WAN to the server to the disk—but the fastest that this overall system can work is only 50 transactions per second, assuming that a transaction requires one disk operation.

The server's disk drive is now the bottleneck for this system. If we upgrade the server's disk drive to something that can handle 3,000 I/O operations per second, then the governing factor will be the next slowest link in the chain—the WAN that can handle only 500 packets per second. You get the point? It's important in examining the operation of an end-to-end system to examine the throughput of each component, looking for the slowest one, which is called a *bottleneck*.

The issue of Performance Tuning then is simply to find and eliminate all bottlenecks—a subject covered in detail in the "Performance Tuning" section of Chapter 5.

For More Information

Renaud, Paul. (1993), *Introduction to Client/Server Systems*. New York: John Wiley & Sons. ISBN: 0-471-57774-X. This is an *outstanding* text on maintenance and performance, as well as general LAN issues—in addition to providing good client/server coverage.

Jain, Raj. (1991), *The Art of Computer Systems Performance Analysis*. New York: John Wiley & Sons. ISBN: 0-471-50336-3. A much deeper treatment of performance issues than Renaud; Jain gets deep into queing theory, simulation, and modelling.

Fortier, Paul. (1992), *Handbook of LAN Technology (2nd Ed.)*. New York: McGraw-Hill, Inc. ISBN: 0-07-021625-8. Good modelling and simulation coverage, along with excellent general coverage of LANs from an engineering perspective.

Index

O

P